CONTEXT AND THE LEXICON
IN THE DEVELOPMENT
OF RUSSIAN ASPECT

Context and the Lexicon in the Development of Russian Aspect

Neil Bermel

UNIVERSITY OF CALIFORNIA PRESS
Berkeley • Los Angeles • London

UNIVERSITY OF CALIFORNIA PUBLICATIONS IN LINGUISTICS

Editorial Board: Leanne Hinton, Larry Hyman, Pamela Munro,
William Shipley, Sandra Thompson

Volume 129

UNIVERSITY OF CALIFORNIA PRESS
BERKELEY AND LOS ANGELES, CALIFORNIA

UNIVERSITY OF CALIFORNIA PRESS, LTD.
LONDON, ENGLAND

© 1997 BY THE REGENTS OF THE UNIVERSITY OF CALIFORNIA
PRINTED IN THE UNITED STATES OF AMERICA

Library of Congress Cataloging-in-Publication Data

Bermel, Neil.
   Context and the lexicon in the development of Russian aspect / Neil Bermel.
      p.   cm. — (University of California publications in linguistics ; v. 129)
   Includes bibliographical references.
   ISBN 0-520-09812-9 (pbk. : alk. paper)
   1. Russian language—Verb. 2. Russian language—Aspect. 3. Russian language—1300–1700—Verb. 4. Russian language—1300–1700—Aspect. I. Title. II. Series.
PG2306.B47   1997
491.75—dc21   97-18525
                                                                            CIP

The paper used in this publication meets the minimum requirements of American National Standard for Information Sciences—Permanence of Paper for Printed Library Materials, ANSI Z39.48-1984.

*For my parents
and for Andy*

Contents

Preface, xv

Abstract, xvii

1. Scope and definitions	1
1.0. On studying the history of Russian aspect	1
1.0.1. Scope of the investigation	1
1.0.2. Structure of the study	2
1.0.3. Methods and texts	3
1.1. Definitions of aspect	5
1.1.1. When tenses show aspect	7
1.2. Terms referring to grammatical aspect	7
1.3. Terms referring to lexical aspect	9
1.3.1. Atelic acts	9
1.3.2. Telic acts	10
1.3.3. Punctualizable (or punctual) acts	10
1.3.4. Other factors involving agents and experiencers	11
1.4. Syntactic and morphological definitions	12
1.4.1. Syntactic definitions	12
1.4.2. Prefixes	12
1.4.3. Suffixes	13
1.4.4. Morphological categories of verbs	14
1.5. Definitions of contexts	14
1.6. Meaning, function, sense and usage	16
1.7. Languages cited	16
1.8. Conventions and methods of citation	17
1.8.1. Transliteration and normalization	18
1.8.2. Translations into English	18
1.8.3. Textual sources	19
1.8.4. Alphabets and punctuation	20
1.8.5. Format of examples	21
1.8.6. Proper names	21
1.9. A tour of Old Russian verbal morphology	22

2. Describing Modern Russian aspect 25
  2.0. The nature of the debate 25
  2.1. Aspect as a grammatical opposition 27
    2.1.1. Forsyth 1970 28
  2.2. Aspect as a lexical category 30
    2.2.1. Maslov 1948 30
    2.2.2. Vendler 1967 33
    2.2.3. Kučera 1983 34
  2.3. Aspect and Aktionsart 36
    2.3.1. Townsend 1980 36
    2.3.2. Isačenko 1960 37
  2.4. Action contours and theories of verbal aspect 39
    2.4.1. Timberlake 1982, 1984a 39
    2.4.2. Durst-Andersen 1992 41
  2.5. Aspect as a discourse function 43
    2.5.1. Gasparov 1990 43
    2.5.2. Chvany 1984, 1990 44
    2.5.3. Chaput 1984 46
  2.6. Summary of analyses of aspect 47
  2.7. Synchronic models in historical analyses 49
    2.7.1. Discourse models in historical analysis 49
    2.7.2. Grammatical models in historical analysis 50
    2.7.3. Lexical models in historical analysis 51

3. The history of Russian and Slavic aspect 57
  3.0. Directions of historical research 57
    3.0.1. Periodicization and organization 58
  3.1. Aspect according to the handbooks 59
    3.1.1. Borkovskij and Kuznecov 1965 59
    3.1.2. Vlasto 1986 61
    3.1.3. Summary of handbooks 63
  3.2. Work on Prehistoric Slavic aspect 64
    3.2.1. van Wijk 1929 64
    3.2.2. Kuryłowicz 1929 66
    3.2.3. Borodič 1953 67
    3.2.4. Kuznecov 1953 71
    3.2.5. Kölln 1957 72
    3.2.6. Němec 1956 74
    3.2.7. Maslov 1961 76
    3.2.8. Forsyth 1972 80
    3.2.9. Galton 1976 82
    3.2.10. Holden 1990 83
    3.2.11. Conclusions 84

3.3. Work on Old Church Slavic aspect	86
3.3.1. Structure of Dostál 1954	86
3.3.2. The definition and provenance of aspect	87
3.3.3. Difficulties in Dostál's lexical analysis	89
3.3.4. Past tense definitions and aspect	90
3.3.5. Summary of Dostál's monograph	91
3.4. The morphological history of Russian aspect	91
3.4.1. Silina 1982	91
3.4.2. A history of aspect and aspectualizers	92
3.4.3. Aspect and tense	94
3.4.4. Chronology of aspectualization	95
3.4.5. Summary of Silina 1982	96
3.5. The semantic history of Russian aspect	97
3.5.1. Aspect in the Primary Chronicle	97
3.5.2. Difficulties with Ruzicka's methodology	98
3.5.3. Summary of Ruzicka	102
3.5.4. Budich's view of aspectual genesis	103
3.6. Conclusions and directions for research	105
3.6.1. Biaspectuality or anaspectuality?	105
3.6.2. Using tense to study aspect	106
3.6.3. A chronology of aspectual development	107
3.6.4. Place of this study in the debate	108
4. Case studies of the Chronicles	110
4.0. The Chronicles and Russian aspect	110
4.1. Methodology and methodological pitfalls	111
4.1.1. The corpus	111
4.1.2. Aspect in a chronologically heterogeneous text	112
4.1.3. Treading carefully with aspect and tense	116
4.1.4. Aspectual assignment, terminology, and circularity	118
4.2. Useful terms for lexical groups	119
4.3. Introduction to atelic acts	120
4.4. Punctual atelics *(viděti)*	120
4.4.1. Infinitives of *viděti*	121
4.4.2. Non-past forms of *viděti*	122
4.4.3. Past tense forms of *viděti*	123
4.4.4. Participles of *viděti*	125
4.4.5. The verb *uviděti*	127
4.5. Punctual atelics of emotion *(diviti sja)*	128
4.6. Stative acts *(stojati)*	132
4.6.1. Non-past forms of *stojati*	132
4.6.2. The past tense forms of *stojati*	133
4.6.3. Prefixed forms of *stojati*	134
4.7. States or atelic actions? *(knjažiti)*	136

4.8. Atelic actions *(bljusti)*	137
4.8.1. Forms of *bljusti*	138
4.8.2. Prefixed forms of *bljusti*	140
4.9. Degrees of telicity	141
4.10. Accretive telicity *(staviti)*	143
4.10.1. The simplex verb *staviti*	143
4.10.2. The derived form *stavljati*	144
4.10.3. The prefixed verb *postaviti*	145
4.10.4. The derived verb *postavljati*	148
4.10.5. Other prefixed forms from *staviti*	149
4.10.6. The verb *ostaviti*	153
4.11. Problems in assigning telicity *(voevati)*	155
4.12. Natural conatives *(iskati)*	160
4.12.1. Prefixed forms of *iskati*	161
4.13. High telicity *(pasti–padati)*	165
4.13.1. The derived form *padati*	166
4.13.2. Prefixed forms of *pasti*	168
4.14. Telic acts with no simplexes *(umereti)*	171
4.14.1. The verb *umirati*	172
4.15. Punctual telic acts *(suditi)*	175
4.15.1. Prefixed verbs from *suditi*	178
4.16. Communicative acts *(prositi)*	181
4.16.1. Participles of *prositi*	181
4.16.2. Non-past forms of *prositi*	182
4.16.3. Infinitives of *prositi*	183
4.16.4. Past tense forms of *prositi*	184
4.16.5. Prefixed forms of *prositi*	185
4.17. Degrees of punctuality *(kazati)*	188
4.17.1. *Nakazati* and related forms	191
4.17.2. *Pokazati* and related forms	193
4.17.3. *Skazati* and related forms	197
4.18. Hypertelic acts	201
4.19. Semelfactives *(strěliti)*	201
4.20. Preliminary conclusions about aspect	204
4.20.1. Contextual factors and the genesis of aspect	204
4.20.2. The place of lexical aspect	205
4.20.3. The expansion of both Old Russian aspects	206

5. More issues from the Chronicles ... 208
    5.0. Introduction ... 208
    5.1. Overview of chapter structure ... 208
    5.2. Aspectuality in non-past forms ... 209
        5.2.1. Nonpunctual telic acts with non-past forms ... 209
        5.2.2. Atelic acts with non-past forms ... 213
        5.2.3. Punctual telic acts with non-past forms ... 216
        5.2.4. Conditional sentences ... 217
        5.2.5. Summary of findings on the non-past ... 220
    5.3. Aspectuality in the infinitive mood ... 221
        5.3.1. Nonpunctual telic acts in the infinitive mood ... 221
        5.3.2. Atelic acts in the infinitive mood ... 225
        5.3.3. Punctual telic predicates in the infinitive mood ... 227
    5.4. Aspectuality in preterite forms ... 229
        5.4.1. Nonpunctual telic acts in the preterite ... 230
        5.4.2. Atelic acts in the preterite ... 234
        5.4.3. Punctual telic acts in the preterite ... 236
    5.5. Aspect and lexical class summarized ... 239
    5.6. Special uses of the imperfect tense ... 240
    5.7. Chronology and prefixation ... 249
        5.7.1. Spatial prefixation ... 251
        5.7.2. Telicizing prefixation ... 252
        5.7.3. Prefixation and motion verbs ... 257
        5.7.4. Pure perfectivizing prefixation in Old Russian ... 265
    5.8. Late appearance of simplexes ... 269
    5.9. Development of suffixed forms ... 270
        5.9.1. The verbs *množiti sja, umnožati (sja)* ... 271
        5.9.2. The verbs *koriti (sja), ukarjati* ... 272
        5.9.3. The verbs *krěpiti (sja), ukrěpljati* ... 273
        5.9.4. The verbs *mysliti, pomyšljati* ... 275
        5.9.5. The verbs *slati (sja), posylati (sja)* ... 276
        5.9.6. Conclusions about simplexes and derived verbs ... 279
    5.10. Conclusions ... 279

6. The Journey Across Three Seas ... 281
    6.0. Introduction ... 281
        6.0.1. Explanation of contexts ... 282
    6.1. Old Russian simplexes ... 283
    6.2. Unprefixed derived forms in Old Russian ... 286
    6.3. Prefixed derived forms in Old Russian ... 290
    6.4. Other strategies for conveying iterativity ... 298
    6.5. Summary of contextual factors ... 302
    6.6. Remnants of lexical aspect ... 305
    6.7. Conclusions ... 311

7. The Taking of Tsargrad — 313

- 7.0. Introduction to the text — 313
- 7.1. Tsargrad and the history of aspect — 314
- 7.2. Lexical aspect — 315
- 7.3. Atelic predicate classes — 315
  - 7.3.1. Punctual atelic predicates — 316
    - 7.3.1.1. Past tense forms — 316
    - 7.3.1.2. Infinitives — 318
    - 7.3.1.3. Prefixed derivatives — 319
    - 7.3.1.4. Participles — 320
  - 7.3.2. Stative acts — 322
    - 7.3.2.1. Non-past forms — 322
    - 7.3.2.2. Past tense forms — 323
    - 7.3.2.3. Infinitives — 326
    - 7.3.2.4. Prefixed and suffixed forms — 327
  - 7.3.3. Atelic actions — 333
    - 7.3.3.1. Non-past tense forms — 333
    - 7.3.3.2. Past tense forms — 335
    - 7.3.3.3. Infinitives — 337
    - 7.3.3.4. Prefixed and suffixed derivatives — 338
- 7.4. Telic predicate classes — 342
  - 7.4.1. Overview of nonpunctual telic predicates — 342
    - 7.4.1.1. Telicity and aspectual singularities — 343
    - 7.4.1.2. Telicity and meaning — 343
    - 7.4.1.3. Iteration in nonpunctual telic predicates — 349
  - 7.4.2. An overview of punctual telic acts — 349
    - 7.4.2.1. Non-past forms — 349
    - 7.4.2.2. Past tense forms — 351
    - 7.4.2.3. Infinitives — 358
    - 7.4.2.4. Conclusions — 361
  - 7.4.3. Semelfactive acts — 361
    - 7.4.3.1. Unanalyzable semelfactives — 361
    - 7.4.3.2. Prefixed semelfactive roots — 364
    - 7.4.3.3. Conclusions about semelfactive acts — 365
  - 7.4.4. Conclusions about telic predicates — 365
- 7.5. Contextual aspect: cautionary tales — 366
  - 7.5.1. Difficulties in comparing aspectual data — 366
- 7.6. Perfectivity and imperfectivity in context — 367
  - 7.6.1. Old protoperfectives map to modern imperfectives — 368
    - 7.6.1.1. Inceptive acts — 368
    - 7.6.1.2. Negation — 371
    - 7.6.1.3. Iterative acts. — 372
    - 7.6.1.4. Contexts with duration — 376
    - 7.6.1.5. Speech functions — 378
    - 7.6.1.6. Background noise — 381

	7.6.2. Old protoimperfectives map to modern perfectives	381
	7.6.2.1. Historical present tense forms	381
	7.6.2.2. Imperfect tense forms	382
	7.6.2.3. A grab bag of other forms.	387
7.7.	The role of secondary imperfectivization	391
	7.7.1. Derived form found only in Modern Russian	391
	7.7.2. Derived form found only in Old Russian	396
	7.7.3. Old and modern derivational suffixes are different	400
7.8.	Conclusions	402

8. The Grand Prince of Muscovy — 405

- 8.0. The text — 405
- 8.1. The state of the verbal system — 406
- 8.2. Frozen anaspectual forms — 409
- 8.3. Tests for aspectuality — 416
  - 8.3.1. The compound future with *budu* + infinitive — 416
  - 8.3.2. The historical present — 418
  - 8.3.3. Monoaspectuality, biaspectuality, and anaspectuality — 422
- 8.4. The range of the Old Russian simplex — 425
  - 8.4.1. The greater specificity of prefixes — 426
  - 8.4.2. Concrete vs. abstract meaning — 431
  - 8.4.3. Contextual distinctions in usage — 436
- 8.5. Resultativity, conativity and aspect — 442
  - 8.5.1. Problems with resultativity — 442
  - 8.5.2. Aspect and conativity in Old Russian — 445
- 8.6. Result and duration under negation — 449
- 8.7. Conclusions — 456

9. Russian aspect and language change — 459

- 9.0. Structure of the chapter — 459
- 9.1. Grammaticalization and language change — 459
- 9.2. The path(s) of grammaticalization — 460
- 9.3. Metaphors, metonyms, and aspect — 464
  - 9.3.1. Metaphoric and anti-metaphoric processes — 467
- 9.4. Aspectualization and abstractness — 469
- 9.5. Telicity, aspect and futurity — 470
- 9.6. Conclusions — 474
- 9.7. Epilogue, from the final page of the Laurentian ms. — 476

Bibliography
    Scientific literature and dictionaries, 477
    Texts, translations and commentary, 483

Preface

This work originated as a doctoral dissertation at the University of California, Berkeley, under the direction of Professor Alan Timberlake. In preparing it for publication by UCPL, I added, deleted and revised numerous sections and analyses to address issues raised by colleagues after I had finished the dissertation. To make the work more readable and accessible, I completely revised my organization of examples and added English translations of all Old Russian material. In the process, I revisited and revised many of my analyses of these examples as well.

I would like to thank Alan Timberlake, Johanna Nichols, Gary Holland, and Francis J. Whitfield of the University of California, Berkeley, for their helpful suggestions, revisions, and support in the course of this project. Their efforts are visible on every page, and in many cases their substantial contributions have no doubt gone unacknowledged in the text.

I am grateful to Bernard Comrie, who reviewed the manuscript for UC Publications in Linguistics and provided detailed and useful commentary, and to the second, anonymous reviewer of the manuscript. I also owe a debt of gratitude to Rose Anne White at the University of California Press, and to the copy editor, Kathleen MacDougall, for their help. Andrew Swartz expertly designed the document templates when I began this work, and helped revise them to meet press standards for preparing camera-ready copy.

Grace Fielder, Michael Flier, Herbert Galton, Emily Klenin, Christina Kramer, Susan Kresin, David Matthews and Mary Rees read portions of this book and related work, and contributed helpful insights and commentary. Boris and Ida Yermash, Olga Kagan and others commented on many of my Modern Russian examples. Francis and Celina Whitfield offered constant moral, intellectual and alimentary support as I wrote and wrestled with this work in its dissertation phase. And among my family, Andrew Swartz and my parents often lent a patient ear and a kind word and learned more than they ever cared to know about Slavic aspect. Responsibility for any errors appearing in this work is assigned on page 477.

Financial support for the research and writing of this work was provided by the Department of Slavic Languages and Literatures of the University of California, Berkeley, in the form of lectureships and instructorships, and by a Chancellor's Dissertation Fellowship in 1993–1994 from the University of California, Berkeley. The revisions and camera-ready copy were prepared during my time at the University of California, Los Angeles and here at the University of Sheffield, and I thank my colleagues at both schools for their support and guidance.

Sheffield, England
February 1997

Abstract

Modern Russian is said to encode an aspectual opposition of imperfective versus perfective in its verbal system, with every verb reflecting a single invariant aspectual meaning each time it is used. The provenance of this opposition, however, is the subject of debate; it does not appear to originate in Indo-European and is often said to arise in Prehistoric Slavic times, although the morphology of aspect has changed substantially since the earliest Russian texts.

This work examines data from five Old Russian texts to assess the nature of the aspectual opposition at each point in history and how it developed. In doing so, it proposes replacing traditional grammar-based and determinacy-based approaches to aspect in the oldest Russian texts with a lexical- and context-based model of aspect supported in the data. It also tracks the nascent imperfective–perfective opposition as it develops up through the sixteenth century and evaluates its status at each point. Furthermore, it examines the semantic effects of prefixation and suffixation, which play pivotal secondary roles in creating aspectual distinctions and regular aspectual pairings.

Its conclusions challenge traditional aspectual scholarship in two respects. First, they indicate that, from the beginning of the historical era (e.g., after the eighth century A.D.), aspect was in a transitional state from lexical to grammatical system. Second, they indicate that the semantics of the aspectual opposition, and the functions of prefixed and suffixed forms, continued to develop in step with morphological changes, rather than an early change in function being reflected later as a change in form.

This study fills a gap in the history of Russian by using detailed studies of aspectual usage in older texts to show an overall reduction in the prominence of the lexicon and context in Russian aspect and an increase in grammatically defined usage and discourse features. In doing so, it lends support to lexical, contextual, and discourse-based approaches to Modern Russian aspect. Furthermore, it provides copious evidence for some basic tenets of grammaticalization theory, as well as striking counterexamples that advance our understanding of the development of aspectual systems.

1. Scope and Definitions

1.0. ON STUDYING THE HISTORY OF RUSSIAN ASPECT

The history of aspect in Russian has intrigued and confounded scholars for over a hundred years, and the reasons for this prolonged interest are rooted in some of the more troublesome and pressing problems confronting historical and synchronic linguistics. First, of the Indo-European languages, only Slavic languages have such a fully developed realization of aspect in the grammar and—in the case of some languages, such as Russian—a correspondingly small range of expression in the area of tense. For historical linguists, then, Slavic can provide crucial support for theories that Indo-European had an aspect-based, a tense-based, or a mood-based verbal system—depending on how the history of Slavic aspect is reconstructed. Second, the Slavic aspectual opposition is unusually extensive. It encompasses not only the preterite realm but also the non-past, and this makes it a typological oddity whose development could be quite different from those of aspect-based verbal systems that reflect aspectual distinctions only for preterite verb forms.

Russian is a promising choice for detailed historical studies of Slavic aspect for several reasons. It has a well-attested literary tradition unbroken since the tenth century, with texts in a wide variety of styles and genres. The history of aspect's morphological features—the appearance and disappearance of various methods of prefixation and suffixation—has been thoroughly researched and reconstructed. However, little is known about the functions of these forms in the premodern era, and especially about the semantic relationships between various morphologically related forms.

In many respects, scholarship on the history of Russian past tenses provides an instructive analogy for the study of Russian aspect. Scholars have found it quite easy in Old Russian to trace the occurrence of various tenses and catalog them. However, it has proven more difficult to discern what the scope of function and usage was for any of the three basic past tenses—aorist, imperfect, and perfect—or what the relationship was between all three of them. With aspect, the latter question is even more difficult, because, unlike with tense, there are no morphemes that are unequivocal markers of aspect. A new dimension to the problem thus appears: the multiplicity of markers we group together as "aspectual" may not necessarily have had uniform functions, and the distinctions we see expressed may not be strictly aspectual ones.

1.0.1. Scope of the investigation

The purpose of this study is threefold. First, it analyzes the place of aspect in the verbal system at several distinct points in Old Russian. Second, it assesses the contributions of other factors, both lexical and contextual, that fall outside the realm of "aspect" as it is usually understood in Modern Russian. Third, it places these aspectual and quasi-aspectual systems in a historical context, both in relation to the history of aspect as it develops from Prehistoric Slavic into Modern Russian and in relation to the numerous scholarly works on the history and current state of Slavic aspect.

In the course of this work, I will show that aspect in the earlier recorded stages of Old Russian was not primarily grammatical in any meaningful way; in other words, assigning verbs to "perfective" and "imperfective" aspects, which each have an invariant perspective on all acts, does not yield substantial or reliable information about the usage and behavior of those verbs. Instead, the best predictor of a verb's behavior in Old Russian is the inherent shape of its sublexemes, as determined by a few easily recognized features; in other words, features which mark the "lexical," "natural," or "objective aspect" of a verbal act.

At this stage, a partial invariant aspectual opposition did play a role in certain lexical classes of predicates but was not generalizable to the verbal system at large. Certain predicates occurred only in a predictable subset of available aspectual meanings; the remaining set of aspectual meanings were expressed by another form, usually one related to it in a moderately predictable morphological fashion. This is a definition for a protoaspectual pair.

In later Old Russian, the lexically based system slowly disappears, and the patterning mentioned above is extended even to the most marginal cases (i.e., those predicates where no clear aspectual pairing is possible). However, many of the lexical features mentioned continued to play an indirect role in influencing aspectual choice and assignment. As the influence of the lexicon retreated, however, contextual and discourse-related features enjoyed a burst of prosperity; it is likely that many of the temporal features associated earlier with the lexical meaning of the predicate came to be borne by surrounding features in the sentence, and these contextual and discourse features then came to play a larger role in influencing the choice of aspect.

This study should serve both as material for further research and as an analysis of an important problem in the history of aspect. As a collection of linguistic material, it fills a gap by examining aspect as a category in Old Russian. In doing so it provides a firm basis for the study of Prehistoric Slavic aspect, which should properly follow from, not precede, detailed analyses of existing Slavic languages in their earliest recorded forms. Furthermore, this study provides sufficient ancillary evidence to support the claim for lexical aspect as a major determiner of so-called "aspectual" behavior in Modern Russian and offers a model of how a lexically based aspectual system can develop into a system in which aspect appears to be a grammatical category.

1.0.2. Structure of the study

The study is divided into nine chapters. Two—the first chapter and the final one—address general concerns; two—the second and third chapters—cover the scientific literature on Russian and Slavic aspect. The remaining five chapters are devoted to analyses of data from Old Russian texts. The Old Russian texts are discussed in what is generally acknowledged to be the order of their composition.

Chapter 1 addresses general concerns about the subject of study, the texts involved and the collection of data and contains definitions of terms in the study.

Chapter 2 discusses how to define aspect in Modern Russian and examines several different approaches that have been used in recent years. A final section of the chapter looks at the relevance of these approaches for research on Old Russian aspect and explains the methods used in this work and the reasoning behind them.

Chapter 3 covers literature on the history of Slavic aspect. A large portion of the chapter is given over to the nature of aspect in Prehistoric Slavic, because this has been the focus of work on the history of aspect. Four longer works outside this field—Dostál's *Studie o vidovém systému v staroslověnštině*, Ruzicka's monograph on the Primary Chronicle, Budich's study of the First Novgorod Chronicle, and Silina's history of aspectual morphology—are covered in subsequent sections.

The next five chapters analyze data from individual texts.

Chapter 4 is the first of two chapters on the Primary Chronicle and the Suzdal' Chronicle. Using data from both texts, it takes an in-depth look at aspectual usage in a small number of verbs and proposes a lexical or sub-lexical interpretation of aspect in this period.

Chapter 5 considers other features of aspectual usage in the two chronicles. It looks at prefixation, motion verbs, and at aspectual usage in selected contexts, including conditional sentences and iterative sentences.

Chapter 6 examines aspect in a more colloquial fifteenth-century text, the *Journey Across Three Seas*. It focuses on the development and spread of secondary imperfectives in various contexts, as well as other features that have an impact on the development of aspect.

Chapter 7 covers a more literary text of the same period, the *Tale of the Taking of Tsargrad*. It analyzes the differences between the predominantly lexical aspectual system found in the earlier texts and the predominantly grammatical one seen in this text, while tracking features of the aspectual system that clearly recall these lexical divisions.

Chapter 8 discusses data from the latest text, the sixteenth-century *History of the Grand Prince of Muscovy*. It examines the aspectual system of this text, which bears a strong resemblance to that of Modern Russian, and finds numerous subtle but pervasive differences—primarily in the realms of context and discourse features—that testify to the evolving character of aspect in Russian.

Chapter 9, the concluding chapter, draws general connections between the aspectual systems of these texts and relates the analysis to existing studies of grammaticalization and semantic change in languages.

1.0.3. Methods and texts

I will discuss the approach I used in detail in section 2.7, but a few fundamental principles I followed will be mentioned here. This study is based on data collected from five Old Russian texts of varying time periods and styles. In each instance, the goal was to create a corpus of forms that was comprehensive for any given verb. I relied on a variety of methods to achieve this comprehensiveness, depending on the exigencies of the particular text. The databases for shorter texts, like the *Tale of the Taking of Tsargrad* and the *Journey Across Three Seas,* include all verb forms—except *byti* 'be'—that are found in the text. The database that includes the Primary Chronicle and the Suzdal' Chronicle includes all forms derived from a set of 250-odd verb roots, excluding motion verbs. This method allowed a comprehensive survey of an extensive text without collecting information about verbs I did not need. The database for the *History of the Grand Prince of Muscovy* includes all verb forms except *byti* 'be' but is limited to the first fifty pages of the ninety-one-page text. It was my judgment that fifty pages of text yields a large enough sample of forms to make determinations about usage, meaning, and relationships between forms.

The texts represent a range of styles and genres but have similar thematic content. All the texts prominently feature descriptions of battles and wars; this similar content ensured that they would have similar vocabularies, making it easier to track developments with particular verbs from one text to the next. The works were also chosen to represent various time depths. The Primary Chronicle covers events from the beginning of the world to the year 1110, with individual year entries starting in 852; the first redaction to put the text in its current form is usually dated to the early twelfth century, several years after the date of the final entry. The Suzdal' Chronicle covers the years from 1111 to 1305. The earliest copy of both the Suzdal' Chronicle and the Primary Chronicle is the Laurentian manuscript of 1377, and therefore both contain a strong late-fourteenth-century overlay.[1] The next two texts, the *Journey across Three Seas* and the *Tale of the Taking of Tsargrad,* belong reliably to the end of the fifteenth century, although they have survived only in later copies. The final text, the *History of the Grand Prince of Muscovy,* was written in the second half of the sixteenth century, probably in the 1570s.

One of the most difficult tasks in such an endeavor is the inevitable comparisons between Old Russian aspect and Modern Russian aspect. Lacking the intuitive feeling of a native speaker that a form is "right" or "wrong," I made such distinctions on three bases. First, there are some objective criteria that can be established for aspectual usage in Modern Russian, and I relied on those when possible and appropriate. (These criteria are explained in some depth in chapter 2 and in various places in the analysis.)

Second, where appropriate I made use of translations of the texts into Modern Russian. Translations—and I emphasize this at numerous points throughout the work—are only helpful when the differences between the Old Russian and the Modern Russian are minimal, and this is not always the case. Often a translator restructures a sentence or an entire paragraph to avoid a particularly troublesome set of problems posed by the Old Russian text, and this restructuring in most cases

---

[1] A more detailed examination of the provenance of these texts is found in chapter 4.

renders the translation less useful. There are certain places, however, where a major change in sentence structure from the Old Russian to the Modern Russian is evidently the result of problems in relaying the aspectual content of the Old Russian into Modern Russian, and such examples are quite relevant.

To serve as a check on my own interpretations of the Modern Russian texts, I gave some of the translated passages—containing twenty-nine of the verb forms under investigation—to two Russians for evaluation. The citations were somewhat longer than the examples given in this work; they typically included one or two sentences before and after the sentence in which the verb in question appeared. In their text, I removed the verb form under evaluation, and in its place substituted two forms, one perfective and one imperfective. Twice, they substituted a third form because they did not like either of the ones that appeared, but this happened elsewhere in the examples, not with forms I was interested in. I observed them as they completed the survey and their comments and choices are noted where appropriate in the text.

Clearly, then, not all examples of mismatches between Old Russian and Modern Russian aspect are significant in and of themselves; in addition, some of them involve deliberate changes in function or perspective on the part of the translator. Furthermore, aspectual mismatches cannot simply be counted and averaged to find out which language, Old Russian or Modern Russian, contains "more" perfectives or imperfectives. Translations are only useful in analyzing individual examples, and then only as a supplementary tool to an independent analysis of the Old Russian forms in their own text. Chapter 7, where translations are used as an adjunct to contextual analysis, has a more detailed description of some of the problems involved.

One further problem is the intended purpose of a translation. To illustrate one general issue: in this study I used facing-page translations, which are meant to be used in conjunction with the Old Russian text, and independent translations, which are more likely to be read straight through, like a normal narrative. In some ways, independent translations make the best comparisons; being constructed as independent texts, they would seem to have more in common with the original Old Russian sources. However, as modern representations of ancient texts, they are more likely than facing-page translations to contain archaisms. These archaisms convey the feel of the Old Russian original to the reader but may be linguistically misleading. Facing-page translations need not imitate Old Russian style, since the original text is at hand; they can be more precise and prosaic in their rendering of the Old Russian text and are thus more reliable linguistic indicators of Modern Russian usage.

1.1. DEFINITIONS OF ASPECT

In sections 1.1 through 1.7, the items defined are boldfaced. Secondary terms or definitions mentioned along the way are italicized. Later references to a defined word as a term are in quotation marks, if appropriate. Readers familiar with the terms conventional in Slavic aspectology can read sections 1.3.1 through 1.3.3 and the beginning of 1.5 and return to the other sections later if the need arises.

Aspect refers to the manner in which an act is presented. In Slavic languages, which are said to have a grammatical category by this name, understanding such a definition is particularly problematic. An analogy may help point out why "aspect" is such a confusing term. English recognizes two words, *time* and *tense,* which refer to the temporal position of the act relative to the speaker. But there is a clear difference between them: the former refers to temporal position without reference to the language, whereas the latter refers to a grammatical phenomenon, a set of forms that represents "time" distinctions in language. The terminology allows us to explain a phenomenon like the historical present reasonably economically: it represents an action in past time, but it uses the present tense to do so. There are no equivalent and universally accepted terms that easily and automatically separate the grammatical manifestations of aspect from features that are inherent to the act.

We can examine the lexicon of any language by classifying verbs according to the shape of their acts; in other words, by looking at how the act begins, progresses, and runs its course in time. This sort of aspect goes by numerous names. Among them are *natural aspect, objective aspect,* and *Aktionsart,* although the latter term is commonly used in a more limited sense. In this study, I will use the term **lexical aspect** for this type of classification—the innate limitations on meaning and usage that derive from a predicate's semantic features and the organization of these predicates into groups based on shared semantic features. My classification of these features is in section 1.2.

Because I have in mind a specific classification into predicate types, I will avoid use of the term *Aktionsart* in this sense. Instead, I will reserve the term *Aktionsart* for specific types of modifications to acts that influence their endpoints (creating *inceptives, resultatives, exhaustives,* etc.).[2] This is a much more specific set of classifications than those I will use under the heading "lexical aspect."

By **grammatical aspect** I mean the positing of a basic feature for a binary aspectual opposition, which is reflected in every form of every verb, and implies a partitioning of the verbal lexicon into verbs expressing and verbs failing to express this basic feature.[3] Unlike lexical aspect, grammatical aspect cannot be detected in all languages; it is found in Slavic but not in Romance, for instance. (Another name for this phenomenon is *invariant aspect,* which emphasizes the supposed semantic immutability of the basic definition of the aspects.) As used here, the term "grammatical aspect" bears no connection to issues of grammaticalization discussed in later chapters; for that discussion the adjective *grammaticalized* will be used.

One set of terms that I have not mentioned is *derivational* versus *inflectional* aspect. General linguists have been interested in whether the aspectual opposition

---

[2] This usage is at variance with the German usage, which subsumes a much larger class of lexical shapes under Aktionsart, but is in conformity with standard English usage and with Russian use of the translated term *sposob dejstvija.*

[3] Because this work deals primarily with Russian, I chose a definition of "grammatical aspect" that would encapsulate the Russian system neatly in two words. It is easy to imagine a broader, more universal definition in which English also has "grammatical" aspect thanks to its progressive vs. non-progressive tenses.

in Slavic is a derivational feature marked in the lexicon or whether it is an inflectional feature generated in the language's syntax. This study does not aim to address or resolve the issue of derivation versus inflection (although it presents evidence for the derivational side), so I will not make use of these terms. The arguments presented here may, however, provide further fuel for the debate.

Of course, not all Slavicists accept the view that only the lexicon and the grammar determine aspect. A number of recent studies refer to the influence of **contextual features** on aspect. The word "contextual" can be narrowly interpreted, as some scholars have done, to include only certain adverbial phrases such as *often, every day, for a month,* but many definitions take in all elements in the sentence and the surrounding material that give information about an act's duration, repetition, and progress with respect to other acts. Context also yields information about subjective interpretations of the act, and much of the recent research on aspect focuses on the role of **discourse factors** such as knowledge sets and presuppositions in determining how speakers select aspectual forms. This approach, which makes use of the field of pragmatics, is often used independently but can also be coupled with both lexical and grammatical approaches to aspect.

1.1.1. When tenses show aspect

An additional terminological issue that arises in Old Russian is how to classify the **imperfect–aorist–perfect** distinction as tense or aspect? In traditional terminology, these three forms are called tenses, but as Vlasto points out, the semantic differences between these so-called "tenses" are actually aspectual, reflecting perspectives on the action or alterations in its shape rather than assignment to one or another realm of time. However, it is convenient for me to use the term "tense" in its traditional sense, since it allows me to distinguish between aspect within a single verb, shown by desinential alternations ("tense"), and aspect defined as a property of one verb or a set of verbs, where all forms of one verb or predicate carry the same aspectual assignment ("aspect"). Under this set of definitions, participles are also treated as "tenses."[4] A more detailed discussion of these problems is found in section 4.1.3.

1.2. TERMS REFERRING TO GRAMMATICAL ASPECT

This study deals primarily with how Russian develops its quasi-grammatical system of aspect. Because of this focus, then, it has been convenient to use the term **aspectual** in reference to grammatical aspect (in other words, as a substitute for the cumbersome "grammatically aspectual"). By "aspectual," then, I will mean that a form or verb conforms to an overall tendency in the verbal system to lock a verb

---

[4] This traditional use of the word "tense" is also found in many of the major works on aspectual genesis, making it convenient to retain in this work as well.

into a particular subset of functions and usages, while assigning functions and usages falling outside the attested subset to (an)other verb(s).[5]

Traditional analysis[6] says that Modern Russian has two aspects, or perspectives on action. The first, the **perfective aspect**, contains verbs marked for some feature indicating that the act is viewed as a whole. This feature has been described as [+completion], [+summation], or other equivalent terms. A somewhat more old-fashioned but equally accurate point of view is that the perfective expresses an external perspective on the act; that is, it is concerned with the endpoints of the act and their results, not on the character of the act itself.[7]

The **imperfective aspect**, on the other hand, is said to be unmarked for the features listed above but lacking any positive feature for itself. The older approach says that the imperfective expresses an internal perspective on the act, being concerned with how an act runs its course through time and not with how it begins or ends.

There is some question as to whether these terms can be accurately applied to Old Russian. Problems arise on two levels. First, it is unclear whether an aspectual opposition in Old Russian would have had exactly the same division by features; if it did not, then I would be glossing over the differences if I simply used the terms "perfective" and "imperfective" as is done in the modern language.[8] Second, the thrust of this study is that, while many of the morphological conditions for aspect may have existed in Old Russian, it is premature to speak of an aspectual opposition for the Old Russian verbal system in its earliest recorded stages. For these reasons, I have chosen to use two somewhat cumbersome terms that allow me to describe morphological and semantic features that resemble the modern features but are not an exact match for them, either because they have slightly different functions, or because they do not participate in a system as strictly defined as that of Modern Russian. A **protoperfective** verb or verb form has features associated with the perfective aspect in Modern Russian, but it need not actually be considered "perfective" in the way we define it for Modern Russian. Instead, the term "protoperfective" simply means 'roughly equivalent to a later feature or paradigm member labelled perfective for the modern language'. Likewise, a **protoimperfective** verb or verb form expresses features characteristic of the

---

[5] Holden 1990 uses the capitalized forms Aspect and Aspectual as shorthand for "grammatical aspect" and "grammatically aspectual," while reserving the lower-case forms for lexical aspect; this is certainly an acceptable solution but is not helpful when the word "Aspect" appears at the beginning of a sentence.

[6] The explanation as laid out here follows Jakobson 1927 but has its roots in work done much earlier.

[7] This definition, which relies on separate definitions for perfective and imperfective aspects, is characteristic of historically oriented scholars like Dostál (1954).

[8] For instance, we use the term "perfect participle" to describe the l-participle form in Old Russian, while for the exact same form in Modern Russian we use the term "past tense." The form is the same, but the functions and relations between different forms are clearly different, meriting different names at different points in history.

modern imperfective aspect (a set of imperfective functions and usages) but need not be taken as being imperfective itself; rather, it is a predecessor of what will be an imperfective verb, form, or function.

It is also possible for a set of forms to be classified as **anaspectual**, meaning they lack evidence of restriction to a particular set of aspectual functions and usages. The term "anaspectual," like the term "aspectual," refers to the absence or presence of grammatical aspect, not of lexical aspect (which cannot be absent); other terms for it are *nonaspectual* and *aspectually indifferent,* and these are cited in discussion of work done by other scholars. Anaspectuality is generally characterized by plasticity of application, i.e., an ability to apply across a range of tenses and functions normally associated with opposing aspects. It is easiest to posit anaspectuality for a verbal system that has a high number of such items in its core lexicon; true indifference to aspect is most likely if the category of aspect is more restricted in the number of verbs and/or situations it covers.

Verbs or predicates may also be **biaspectual**, and the distinction between biaspectuality and anaspectuality is a subtle but important one. Biaspectuality means that, while not restricted to a certain subset of functions and usages, the same verb or predicate functions in some places clearly like a perfective and in other places clearly like an imperfective. It is easiest to posit biaspectuality for marginal lexical items in a highly aspectual verbal system, such as that of Modern Russian.

1.3. TERMS REFERRING TO LEXICAL ASPECT

The basic term I use for the referent of a verbal form is an **act**. Acts are all forms of states and actions expressed by verbs. I divide acts according to two features: telicity and punctualizability (or punctuality), whose definitions are discussed below. These features are privative; in other words, the absence of a feature does not imply its negation. They are also gradated, meaning that different "strengths" of telicity, for instance, are possible. The lexicon is thus partitioned into telic and atelic, and into punctual and nonpunctual. In addition, there are a number of other features found in the lexicon that will be defined here. This roster of types serves primarily to classify acts that in Modern Russian are considered imperfective. This orientation is natural, since the telic–atelic distinction centers around the internal structure of the event, and as remarked above, perfective acts focus on result, not character, of the event.[9]

1.3.1. Atelic acts

Atelic means making no reference toward attainment of a goal. I classify atelic acts into three groups. (1) **Punctual atelics** are atelic acts that can transpire

---

[9] For the most part I use the term "event" as a synonym for "act." In some of the literature on aspect, such as Mourelatos (1981), the term "event" is used for a specific type of act: those which unfold toward an endpoint. In my terminology, these acts are called "telic acts."

instantaneously, without the need for passage of time, but do not indicate progress toward a goal. An example is *viděti* 'see'. (2) **Statives** are atelic acts expressing an unchanging state, with no action on the part of the participants. An example is *stojati* 'stand'. (3) **Atelic actions** are acts that imply effort or action on the part of the participant, but do not refer to attainment of a goal. An example is *strěšči* 'guard'. (Note that I draw a distinction between "action" and "act": the former is a subset of the latter. Action implies activity or movement, voluntary or otherwise; a state, for instance, is not an action, but is an act.[10])

(4) The placement of semelfactive acts is a problematic one. A semelfactive act is naturally instantaneous and indivisible; semelfactives can typically also be represented by a derived verb that expresses an unbroken series of individual acts as a process. Examples are *strěljati* 'shoot continuously', *mavati* 'wave'. This type can be called **iterative semelfactives** and they probably belong to the atelic actions, although there is some reason to place them among the punctual telic acts as well.

1.3.2. Telic acts

Telic means that an act makes reference to the attainment of a goal. I distinguish several subsets within this group. The most important are the first three. (1) With **accretive telics**, movement toward the goal inevitably accrues results, regardless of whether the goal is attained. An example is *pisati knigu* 'write a book'. This class corresponds roughly to Kučera's (as adapted from Vendler's) accomplishment class. (2) **Highly telic** means the act strongly implies attaining the goal. An example is *umirati* 'die'. This class corresponds to Kučera's (and Vendler's) achievement class.[11]

(3) We can also distinguish a class of **punctual telic** acts. In this class, the act can reach its goal without any perceptible passage of time, but need not necessarily do so. Examples are the *verba dicendi* and many abstract acts (*grěšiti* 'sin').

(4) A small number of acts are **naturally conative**. In naturally conative acts, although a goal is present, frustrating the attainment of the goal is built into the lexical properties of the verb. An example is *iskati* 'search for', or Modern Russian *prilagat' usilija* 'expend effort'.

1.3.3. Punctualizable (or punctual) acts

As opposed to telicity, which is a measure of the direction of the act in time, **punctualizability** (or, for short, **punctuality**) is a measure of the potential tempo of

---

[10] I am thus using the word "action" in the limited sense found in Kučera (1983), but many scholars use "action" more generally, to indicate any sort of verbal act.

[11] Since an informal poll has revealed that few Slavic linguists, this one included, can remember which class is for "accomplishments" and which for "achievements," I have chosen more mnemonic terms. Mourelatos 1981 uses the terms "developments" for the accretive telics and "punctual occurrences" for the highly telic class; this classification is not as handy for our analysis, since it lumps together classes (2) and (3).

the act. **Punctual** acts always have the possibility of being realized instantaneously, although they need not be. Consequently, punctual acts invariably involve perception and abstraction; they are acts that either occur in the brain or depend on a human interpretation of an event. Examples are *viděti* 'see', *diviti sja* 'be surprised', *rešiti* 'solve', *voprošati* 'ask', *velěti* 'order'. Note that they can be either telic (*rešiti, voprošati, velěti*) or atelic (*viděti, diviti sja*).

In one sense, the term "punctual" is unfortunate, since it implies that an act must be of instantaneous duration. The term *punctualizable* would undoubtedly be more accurate, but decisively fails to roll trippingly off the tongue.

For **nonpunctual** acts, reaching the goal inevitably entails the passage of time. Consequently, a large number of these acts are physically observable or produce some result in the physical world independent of human perception. Examples are *žiti* 'live', *tvoriti kumiry* 'make idols', *ubivati* 'kill'.

Since there is such a close connection between punctuality and abstraction, the question naturally arises: why not simply use the abstract–concrete opposition instead of the punctual–nonpunctual one? The answer is that "abstract" and "concrete" are not lexical aspectual distinctions. They do not structure or manipulate the time frame of acts in any way; instead, they are semantic distinctions. The terms "punctual" and "nonpunctual," while less immediately comprehensible, show the relationship between the category and the manipulation of the event's time frame, and are thus preferable.

1.3.4. Other factors involving agents and experiencers

There are a number of other lexical features—features inherent to the meaning of an act—that are mentioned in this work. None are temporal in nature, i.e., none of them affect lexical aspect directly, although they often affect it in an indirect manner. These definitions are of secondary importance (cf. the definitions in 1.3.1 through 1.3.3).

(1) **Volition**, or intention, can be marked in the lexicon and often constitutes a key component in distinguishing meaning and sometimes in distinguishing lexical class. A volitional act implies effort or conscious action on the part of the subject. For instance, it is the presence of volition that distinguishes *zrěti* 'look' from *viděti* 'see'. For our purposes, this same distinction contributes to rendering the former nonpunctual and the latter punctual.

(2) **Reaction** implies the presence of a stimulus. Acts involving emotion can be classified as nonreactive (Modern Russian *bojat'sja* 'fear') or reactive (Modern Russian *ispugat'sja* 'be frightened by'). Nonreactive emotions are closer in character to states; reactive emotions are punctual atelics.

(3) Among these factors are statements about the observable nature of the act. **Concrete** acts can be observed or take place physically; they have an independent physical reality. **Abstract** acts are more likely to take place in the mind or to derive their significance from their implications for thought or perception.

1.4. SYNTACTIC AND MORPHOLOGICAL DEFINITIONS

A few definitions concern syntactic categories, and a larger number address morphological structures. In attempting to avoid imposing aspectual judgments where they would be inappropriate or lead to confusion in the exposition, I often refer to morphological features rather than aspectual ones (for instance, I give preference to the term *derived form* over the term *secondary imperfective*).

1.4.1. Syntactic definitions

It is important to distinguish verbs (V) from predicates (VP). A **verb** is a collection of related lexical entries expressed by the same set of forms. It forms a single unit in Russian and may include the reflexive particle *sja*. A **predicate** is a verb form with its direct object and other relevant complements. Syntactically speaking, the VP is a higher level of organization, but semantically speaking, it is much narrower; the predicate expresses only one of the potential meanings and usages of the verb. This usage of the word "predicate" is parallel to (although slightly narrower in scope than) Kučera's use of the term *situation*.[12]

Each verb has a virtually infinite number of predicates, and I am not suggesting ascribing a separate meaning to each one. Instead, we can constitute groups of predicates whose temporal contours are nearly identical. The predicates in the Modern Russian sentences *Ivan pišet knigu* 'Ivan is writing a book', *Ivan pišet dve knigi* 'Ivan is writing two books', and *Ivan pišet stat'ju* 'Ivan is writing an article' are for our purpose lexically equivalent; all indicate an accretive telic act. However, the predicate *pišet učebniki* 'writes textbooks' in the sentence *Ivan pišet učebniki* 'Ivan writes textbooks' has a markedly different lexical shape; it expresses the writing of textbooks not as a process, but as an occupation, a state, or atelic action that simply serves to describe the person. Here it is lexically equivalent to the act in sentences like *Ivan pisatel': on pišet romany* 'Ivan is a writer; he writes novels'.

Looking at a verb's possible predicates is substantially different from looking at its possible **valences**. While valence (whether a verb can or must have complements, and what syntactic and morphological form those complements take) is a related notion, and overlaps with the exegesis of specific predicates, analysis that relies on particular valence patterns is a separate matter and will come into play mostly in the discussion of suffixed forms and their distribution.

1.4.2. Prefixes

A **prefix** is a unit preceding, and forming a single word with, a **root**, and has an influence on the meaning or usage of words formed from that root.[13] This study deals exclusively with *verbal* prefixes.

---

[12] See chapter 2 for discussion of the scope of "situations" in Kučera (1983).
[13] For the purposes of this work, I have used the word *root* to indicate a root and any more or less indivisible derivational suffixes. For a verb such as *pisati* 'write', then, I will

It is by and large the same set of prefixes that are applied to all verb roots and stems; of course, certain prefixes may be applied to one and not to another, but the distribution and lexical meaning of these prefixes is quite fluid. I will argue that each prefix has a range of functions, from spatial to temporal, and that these functions are determined at least partially by the meanings of the root or stem they are attached to. (1) A prefix with **spatial function** modifies the meaning of the simplex by limiting or directing its application in physical space. When I use the term "spatial" alone, I mean that in the given sentence, the prefix adds only a spatial component and no temporal one. (2) A prefix with **telicizing function** modifies the meaning of the simplex by adding a goal for the act, thereby limiting its trajectory through time and space. A subgroup of telicizing function is **Aktionsart** or **temporal function**, which adds a goal that is specifically temporal, limiting or directing the act's application over time. (3) Another subgroup of (2) are prefixes that add an **abstract function**, modifying the simplex's meaning in a more substantial way. This sort of prefixation increases the abstractness inherent in the meaning of the compound. (4) Finally, there are prefixes with a **pure perfectivizing function**, in which the prefix does not modify the simplex's meaning at all, but causes perfectivization. It is debatable whether this type even existed for Old Russian (or exists for Modern Russian).

1.4.3. Suffixes

A **suffix** is a morphological (or lexical!) unit following, and forming a single word with, a verb root or stem. It has an influence on the meaning or usage of words formed from that root or stem. In this work, I will pay attention almost exclusively to **derivational suffixes**. By "derivational" I mean a suffix added to a verb stem that induces a change in the usage of an existing verb without inducing a change in meaning. It will be immediately evident that this is a very narrow reading of the word "derivational," since it excludes other suffixes, like the semelfactive suffix {-nu-} and denominal suffixes like {-ovaj-}, which also have a deriving function. In the case of the semelfactive suffix, our definition excludes it because it effects a substantial change in meaning in the verb; in the case of the denominal suffix, our definition excludes it because it is a category-changing suffix that converts nouns to verbs. This definition also ignores all word-forming suffixes such as the {-a-}/{-j-} suffix of *pisati* 'write', a verb which does not exist in an unsuffixed form.

---

make reference to the "roots" {pisa-}, {piš-}, although from a morphological perspective this is clearly a root {pis-} with two suffixes {-a-} and {-i-}, forming a morphological stem. I will reserve the term "stem" for the entire form minus the desinential ending, so that in the verb *opisyvati* 'describe' the "stem" would be {opisyvaj-}, composed as it is of a root, a secondary derivational suffix {-ivɛ-}/{-ivaj-}, and a prefix {o-}.

I will often use the word "suffix" as a shorthand for the term *derivational suffix*. Outside the review of literature in chapter 3, I do not discuss the ordinary theme-vowel suffixes that are an integral part of most Slavic verbs, so this will not cause any problems.

1.4.4. Morphological categories of verbs

One important task of this study is defining the relationship between the morphological processes that create aspectual relationships in Modern Russian and the functions of the forms these processes create in Old Russian. Because aspectual terms like "perfective" and "imperfective" often prove anachronistic or induce a circular reading of the data, it is helpful to have terms that refer strictly to the morphological structure of a verb.

(1) A **simplex** verb is one that has no prefixes or derivational suffixes. Some verbs I treat under this rubric are truly simplexes, while others are *unanalyzable* verbs, meaning any prefixes or suffixes are so closely attached that the form with the prefix or suffix appears to be treated as a simplex. While this may seem like a semantic distinction, it must have some morphological reflection as well, such as the absence of a simplex form or an unusual derivational pattern. (Examples of unanalyzable verbs from this study are *odolěti* 'vanquish', *sovokupiti* 'gather'.)

(2) The opposite of "simplex" is "compound." A **compound** verb has either a derivational suffix or a prefix, or both. This is similar, but not identical, to the Czech term *komplexní* 'complex', which is stated as a semantic distinction but is overwhelmingly realized as a morphological one. The term "compound" is purely morphological in reference; categories (3) and (4) are subsets of it.

(3) A verb is **suffixed** or **derived** if it has a derivational suffix; this means it will probably become imperfective but will not necessarily do so. Note the restriction to derivational suffixes still stands. Suffixed verbs can have a prefix if so stated, yielding two subclasses: *prefixed suffixed* verbs, also called *prefixed derived* verbs, and *unprefixed suffixed* verbs, also called *unprefixed derived* verbs.

(4) A verb is **prefixed** if the root is preceded by a prefix. Such verbs can become either perfective or imperfective. Prefixed verbs can have a suffix if explicitly stated, as in (3). Sometimes it will be necessary to distinguish prefixed verbs with suffixes from those without suffixes; the latter group will then be called *simple prefixed* verbs.

1.5. DEFINITIONS OF CONTEXTS

A **context** is the environment in which an act takes place; it generally includes certain characteristics of the subject and direct object, such as abstractness and number, as well as adverbial phrases in the sentence that have an impact on the course of the event. Although the boundary between predicates and contexts is at times fluid, the concept of "context" is broader than that of "predicate" and can include pragmatic factors not enumerated below.

In Modern Russian, it is common to talk about imperfective and perfective contexts. An **imperfective** context is one that in Modern Russian conditions use of the imperfective aspect. There are four such clearly recognized contexts. (1) An **iterative** context is one in which the act is repeated. (2) A **progressive** context emphasizes the way an act unfolds in time, with the boundaries of this development unmarked either explicitly or implicitly. (3) A **durative** context also emphasizes how an act unfolds in time, but here the boundaries of its development are clearly marked by a phrase or by the context at large. (4) A **generalized** context marks an act as unarticulated, one where the verb simply affirms an act's occurrence or state of being. It is worth noting that while the overall heading of an "imperfective context" implies a *subjective judgment* about the quality of the act (if we accept a traditional definition of the Russian aspects), the four context types following can all be *objectively determined* to varying degrees of clarity (depending, of course, on the utterance), making them a reasonable subject of study in a dead language. See section 6.0.1 for a more detailed description of these four contexts.

There are also perfective contexts in Modern Russian—contexts that condition use of the perfective aspect. However, these are fewer in number and more idiosyncratic in their usage, and do not play a large role in this discussion.

The contexts listed above have certain general features in common. (5) **Articulation** is a feature common to progressive, durative, and iterative contexts. It focuses on constituent sub-acts, i.e. it describes an act composed of multiple, ongoing component acts that are observed as the act progresses. When termination of the act lies outside the narrative time frame, articulation increases; when termination of the act lies inside the narrative time frame or is absent from the reading of the act, articulation decreases. Iterative and progressive contexts have an external termination, because they refer respectively to multiple completions—some of which may lie inside the narrative time frame and others of which may lie outside it (iterativity)—or to a single completion, anticipated but still outside the narrative time frame (progressivity). Durative contexts, where the act's termination is inside the narrative time frame, increase focus on the endpoints and decrease focus on the internal workings of the act; generalized contexts, which mandate seeing the act as a single entity, are least likely to be seen as articulated. (6) The opposite of articulation is **summation**, in which the unity or wholeness of an event is marked. (7) **Duration,** or **processuality**, encompasses the feature common to progressivity and durativity, i.e. the act is given a temporal value, whether that value is bounded or unbounded.[14]

(8) Contexts can also be **conative**; that is, they can express the frustration of an act's completion or attainment of goal. This is an additional feature not necessarily related to any of the above contexts; a context might be both conative and iterative, or both conative and progressive, for instance. All contexts, of course, may be

---

14   For the sake of clarity, the noun "duration" will be used in this, its usual sense. Since the form "durative" has already been assigned a specialized meaning, the adjectival form meaning 'having duration' will be *processual*. The nominal form of "durative" in its specialized sense—a particular context—will be *durativity*.

defined by extra-sentential criteria: we may know that an act is durative, for instance, by the fact that it is surrounded by other acts in other utterances that bound it. However, conativity is the most clearly discourse-oriented of the contexts discussed here.

(9) Another discourse-oriented context is one indicating **volition,** i.e., one that presupposes a desire, predisposition, or conscious effort on the part of the subject to perform an act. (This differs from *lexical volition* as described above.)

1.6. MEANING, FUNCTION, SENSE AND USAGE

The terminology surrounding lexical and grammatical meaning is murky, not least of all because it differs from language to language. I have tried to limit my use of the word **meaning** to features I believe are connected with lexical semantics or clearly identifiable characteristics of categories. I have given preference to the terms **function, sense** and **usage** when the mapping relationship between lexical meaning and the operation performed is less straightforward. For instance, we often assign *meanings* to the two aspects, but the instantiation of present vs. future in the non-past is probably best described as a *function* of one or another aspect; a form should have present or future *sense* or we may examine its *usage* in different contexts, but strictly speaking these are not *meanings*. However, Russian aspectual scholarship has traditionally identified different *meanings (značenija)* of aspect and talks similarly about the *meanings* of tenses, the *meanings* of contexts, and so forth. I have thus stretched my self-imposed distinctions quite liberally, especially when reviewing the literature.

1.7. LANGUAGES CITED

A number of languages are referred to repeatedly in this work, and brief definitions for them will be helpful.

(1) **Proto-Indo-European** is the language or dialect group from which Slavic languages (as well as most other European languages) are descended. The term *Indo-European* is a genetic marker; it refers to the group of languages descended from Proto-Indo-European.

(2) **Prehistoric Slavic** is the group of Slavic dialects and/or languages in use prior to the advent of written Slavic languages. These dialects were not unified in appearance, and, by most accounts, at least five centuries separate the first differentiation of an ur-Slavic language into dialects from the first written Slavic texts. Following Slavistic convention, forms reconstructed for Prehistoric Slavic are given in the Latin alphabet and marked with an asterisk. The earliest phase of this period—when all Slavs spoke one mutually intelligible language or group of dialects—can be called **Proto-Slavic** or **Common Slavic**.

(3) **Old Church Slavic** is an early South Slavic written language that is believed to be the first systematic example of writing in a Slavic tongue. The earliest extant Old Church Slavic texts, translations of parts of the Bible, date from the ninth century A.D. Old Church Slavic is often taken as the closest recorded

relative of Prehistoric Slavic, for reasons of chronology, and in the scientific literature, Old Church Slavic material is often tacitly used to exemplify Prehistoric Slavic features that cannot otherwise be reconstructed.

(4) **Old Russian** is the written language used on East Slavic soil from the appearance of the first texts up to the seventeenth century. In its early stages it could justifiably be called Old East Slavic (and often is) instead of Old Russian. Without addressing the questions of diglossia and dialect differentiation within East Slavic—which is considerable—Old Russian can be said at the very least to encompass a range of styles and forms that depend on the text's genre and its audience. Since this study covers (at least) six centuries of Old Russian, the linguistic and aspectual differences between texts are substantial, and references to "Old Russian" may seem ambiguous: do they refer to the language of the eleventh or the sixteenth century? One could adopt terminology like "Early Old Russian," "Middle Old Russian," and "Late Old Russian," but these terms are neither concise nor informative; the "Middle Old Russian" of the *Tale of the Taking of Tsargrad* may have less in common with the contemporaneous *Journey Across Three Seas* than with the "Late Old Russian" of Prince Kurbskij. In this work, then, I have used the term "Old Russian," when discussing a single text, as a shorthand for 'the Old Russian of this text', but not necessarily for any Old Russian text of any period. When differentiation is necessary, I have been as specific as possible, referring to, for instance, "the (Old) Russian of the Chronicles" or "Kurbskij's (Old) Russian."

(5) **Modern Russian** technically begins in the eighteenth century, but I usually use this term in reference to contemporary standard Russian.

(6) **Church Slavic** is a stratum of Old Russian with a distinctive vocabulary, phonology and grammar borrowed from Old Church Slavic or other South Slavic languages masquerading as such, or derived using Old Church Slavic phonological or grammatical rules. Church Slavic features need not be universally applied for a text to be regarded as being primarily in Church Slavic. In the modern language, "Church Slavic" refers only to isolated phonological, morphological and lexical features inherited from this stratum.

(7) **Old Czech** is the written language of Bohemia and Moravia prior to the widespread Germanization of the Czech lands that took place in the seventeenth and eighteenth centuries.

(8) **Modern Czech** is the literary language of Bohemia and Moravia from the late eighteenth century onwards. In this work I refer only to contemporary standard Czech *(spisovná čeština)*, not to the Czech interdialect *(obecná čeština)*

(9) **Old Polish** encompasses the written language of Poland up to the seventeenth century.

(10) **Modern Polish** is the contemporary written language of Poland.

1.8. CONVENTIONS AND METHODS OF CITATION

This section covers the formats I have used to cite Old Russian examples and modern scientific literature, as well as methods of transliteration (which correspond to existing Slavistic standards).

1.8.1. Transliteration and normalization

Russian text is normally cited in Latin transliteration in the body of the text, and in Cyrillic in numbered examples. When transliterating, I use the standard Slavic transliteration with diacritics (ч is rendered by *č*, й by *j*, and so forth). Prehistoric Slavic forms are cited in the Latin alphabet, as is traditional, and are distinguished by the use of an asterisk. (By convention, the asterisk is also used for ungrammatical or hypothetical forms in both Old and Modern Russian.) As is customary when citing Old Church Slavic and Prehistoric Slavic forms, I have treated the jers (ъ, ь) as vowels and let them stand in the text instead of following the convention for Russian, which is to replace jers with single or double quotation marks when transliterating.[15]

When discussing a dictionary or grammatical entry for an Old Russian form, I have used a variant that conforms to Old Russian "norms." Thus, I write *stojati* 'stand' for the Old Russian infinitive, *stojat'* for the 3. pl. non-past form, and *stojaxu* for the 3. pl. imperfect form in a discussion of the forms in general, regardless of whether the particular example I am discussing happens to have, for instance, 3. pl. non-past *stojat"* or 3. pl. imperfect *stojaxut'*. These forms will vary further depending on the period under discussion. I have not used back jers/hard signs (ъ or ") in final position for these grammatical-entry forms, since the Old Russian texts do not respect them regularly.

Readers unfamiliar with the grammar of these languages can refer to Vlasto 1986 for comparative paradigms of Old Russian and Old Church Slavic verbs or to the brief guide in section 1.9.

1.8.2. Translations into English

I have rendered material in foreign languages into English by one of three means. In the case of quotes from the scientific literature, short quotations may be given in English with important terms cited in the original language in parentheses. Longer quotations from the scientific literature are given first in the foreign language and are translated in a footnote. Words and phrases from modern languages are consistently glossed following the original text.

All examples of Old Russian are followed by an English translation. (In a few places, the translation is incorporated instead into the body of the analysis.) I have not provided interlinear translations, although I provide transliterated forms of the relevant Old Russian verbs in the English translations.

The English translations serve two purposes: to make the context of each verb form clear to the reader and to provide an overall picture of the structure of the phrase, sentence, or paragraph. My translations strike a sometimes awkward compromise between style and function. In most instances I opt for a translation

---

[15] In Modern Russian these two letters indicate the hardness (ъ or ") or softness (ь or ') of the preceding consonant and have no phonetic value in and of themselves; this situation can also be presumed to exist for much of the Old Russian period.

that hews closely to the Old Russian grammatical structure over one that treats the text as literature. (For this reason, although I consulted the two published English translations of these texts—Cross and Sherbowitz-Wetzor's translation of the *Primary Chronicle* and Fennell's translation of the *History of the Grand Prince of Muscovy*—I did not take my translations from them.) My hope is that presenting English translations will make the analysis accessible to scholars who have some acquaintance with Modern Russian or Old Church Slavic but only minimal knowledge of Old Russian.

1.8.3. Textual sources

The Old Russian texts come from three sources, one of which is considerably more faithful to the original manuscripts than are the other two.

The source for the Chronicles was a reprint of the *Polnoe sobranie russkix" letopisej (Complete Collection of Russian Manuscripts)*, which reproduces most of the archaic characters and uses Old Russian punctuation. The provenance of the text reproduced in this edition is clearly marked in all places, as are variant readings and suggested corrections for obvious errors in the manuscript.

My other sources were more heavily edited, with somewhat modernized spelling and modern punctuation. Since punctuation is crucial for explicating the syntax of the text, and the provenance of alternate readings is sometimes important, I compared these texts with other editions.

The text of the *Journey across Three Seas* is taken from the 1986 edition by Lur'e and Semenov. This edition reproduces several versions of the work; I followed the Ètterov manuscript version, which Lur'e describes as the oldest and most faithful to the proposed protograph. I made some emendations from the Troickij manuscript that are suggested in the commentary. Most of the emendations are sections missing from the Ètterov manuscript., while others clarify obscure points in it.

I compared Lur'e and Semenov's edition with that of the *Pamjatniki literatury drevnej Rusi (Monuments of Old Russian Literature)*, and found the texts very similar, with differences being mainly in the degree of fidelity to the primary manuscript. As far as spelling and morphology, the only differences I noticed were occasional hard signs and other such details—nothing that would affect readings of aspect.

My analyses of the *Taking of Tsargrad* and the *History* are based on the texts in the *Pamjatniki literatury drevnej Rusi (Monuments of Old Russian Literature)* series. This series has two main defects: the editors modernized spelling and punctuation, and incorporated corrections from other manuscripts directly into the text. Their edition of the *History of the Grand Prince of Muscovy* is based on the Pogodinskoe Sobranie manuscript.[16] There are some corrections from G. Z. Kuncevič's 1914 edition of Kurbskij's work, which is based on a different manu-

---

[16] From the Gosudarstvennaja publičnaja biblioteka, rukopisnyj otdel, Pogodinskoe sobranie, No. 1494. This full citation is found in Fennell 1965: xi.

script.[17] I compared the *Monuments* version with the one found in Fennell's 1965 edition and translation, which reproduces the text of the 1914 edition (although it gives only those variant readings that Fennell considered significant). Fennell's edition bears the marks of an overzealous editor's hand but is useful for its textual commentary, copious notes, and the very fact that it is drawn from a different edition of the work.[18]

Here as well, I did not notice differences between these editions that would affect verbal aspect. In the occasional cases where the editing obscured a point in the text, I have mentioned it in my analysis.

1.8.4. Alphabets and punctuation

The *Complete Collection* retains most Old Russian spelling and punctuation faithfully, and I have rendered those as closely as possible in this study. The other three editions I consulted have considerably modernized spelling conventions and have replaced Old Russian punctuation with modern punctuation.

In the case of the *Complete Collection,* more far-reaching changes were necessary in order to reproduce the text using available Cyrillic fonts. Ligatured *e* and *a* are rendered by *e* and я, respectively. Front nasal is printed as ѧ, back nasal as ю. Both *e* and є are given as *e*. Modern Russian ы stands in for the similar Old Russian character beginning with ъ. All single characters representing the phoneme /u/ are given as *y*. The digraph *oy* remains in the text, as does the character ѣ. Transliterated words are rendered from these "normalized" forms.

For abbreviated words, two rules apply. Letters appearing above the line or above other letters are brought down to the baseline; those omitted in the source are inserted but enclosed in parentheses to mark the insertion. Ligatures over words are not given.

The most common Old Russian punctuation mark—a dot at mid-character height, following a word—is rendered with a period. Capitalization is respected for proper names and ethnonyms and is marked when it appears (which it does only sporadically) at the beginning of an Old Russian clause or sentence. Numbers are written out using Arabic numerals instead of the conventional old Cyrillic letters. Insertions or changes from other manuscripts indicated by the editors are given, where necessary to make sense of the passage, in parentheses. More substantial or controversial alternate readings (especially those concerning verb forms) are given in footnotes. These conventions will, I hope, make the Old Russian text easy to read without compromising material important to this study.

---

[17] From the Central'nyj gosudarstvennyj arxiv drevnix aktov v Moskve, fond 181, delo 60 (Fennell 1965: xi).

[18] Fennell modernizes orthography to an extraordinary extent, removing even such common Old Russian letters as ѣ and final ъ. Textologically, the *Monuments* edition is thus preferable, since it is drawn primarily from one ms., not from an edition of a compilation of mss., and modernizes orthography to a much lesser degree.

1.8.5. Format of examples

Examples are numbered sequentially, beginning anew each chapter. The typical format for examples is to give the Old Russian text followed by a translation into English. The relevant verb forms are set in bold type in the Russian text and in italics in the English translation, with a transliteration of the Russian form in question. In certain instances, translations into Modern Russian play a role in the discussion. Where it would be of use to the reader, I inserted the Modern Russian translation of a verb or predicate into the Old Russian translation following the phrase in question. Such insertions are set in italics and enclosed in parentheses. In sections where I regularly and explicitly made reference to the Modern Russian translation, I included a complete translation following the Old Russian text, with the corresponding verb form(s) set in bold. The translation is given the same number as the Old Russian example, with a letter "a" following. Thus, an Old Russian example might have the number (5), while its Modern Russian translation would follow immediately and be numbered (5a). For further ease of identifying such translations, they appear with the notation *tr:* at the beginning of the quotation.

In the case of Soviet editions, I did no editing whatsoever of the text, letting stand even obvious Soviet-era alterations of the type *bog"* 'god' for *Bog"* 'God' found in the *Monuments*. I also left intact certain changes, such as the occasional emendation of и to й, that the editors evidently made for ease of reading. Texts from the *Monuments* are typically based on the most authoritative version of that manuscript, with insertions and interpolations from other manuscripts made to correct obvious corruptions or to add missing material. The editors noted these changes by placing them in italics; because I use italics in quotations for other purposes (see above), I did not mark these editing changes.

Two changes were made when quoting passages from heavily edited texts. First, direct speech in these texts is marked with Russian quotation marks (although they most likely were not used in Old Russian); when I excerpted portions of direct speech from these texts, I added quotation marks where necessary. Second, although I maintained the sentence structure and capitalization suggested by the editors, I did not always feel obliged to use ellipses when beginning an example in "mid-sentence," since in many cases the sentences were obviously composed of numerous independent Old Russian clauses. Ellipses appear at the beginning of a citation when it clearly picks up in the middle of a thought.

I use ellipses in quotations from the Chronicles when the quotation begins or ends in the middle of a clause, as marked by the Old Russian punctuation. In all texts, ellipses in the middle of a quotation indicate words or passages that I omitted (or, in rare instances, gaps in the manuscript where words or passages are apparently missing from the original text).

1.8.6. Proper names

In translating Russian proper names, I have in most cases left them as they are found in the text; therefore, readers will find references to *Gjurgij* (or sometimes

Georgij) and *Volodimer* instead of the Modern Russian normalized *Jurij* and *Vladimir* or the English *George*. Names of religious figures and foreigners are, where appropriate, given in a form recognizable to a Western eye; thus I write *Constantine* instead of *Kostjatin* and *Theodosius* instead of *Feodosij*. In translating geographic names I have tried to give equivalents comprehensible to the modern reader; for example, I have called the *Varangian Sea* the *Baltic* and the *Xvalisian Sea* the *Caspian*. Because it is riskier to do the same with tribal names, I have by and large left the tribal designations as the Old Russians saw them (thus *Varangians,* not *Vikings)* but have often modified them to give them a shape English speakers will recognize as an ethnonym (hence *Polovtsians* instead of a direct transliteration *Polovci)*. More controversially, I have rendered the ethnonyms *Rus'*, *rus'kie* as *Russia* or *the Russians*. This decision has more to do with the familiarity and readability of these terms (as opposed to *Rus', the Rusians,* or *the East Slavs)* than it does with an ideological belief about the provenance of these texts and the literary tradition to which they ultimately belong, and I urge readers not to take umbrage at this essentially capricious choice. This study concerns itself with the history of a written language and that the the works I refer to in it are clearly part of the direct written heritage of Russia, whoever the speakers and writers themselves might have been and whatever other nations may also rightfully claim them as their literary and cultural heritage.

1.9. A TOUR OF OLD RUSSIAN VERBAL MORPHOLOGY

This section provides a brief introduction to Old Russian verbal morphology in Latin transcription. It is designed to help non-Russianists cope with the bewildering array of forms and variants found in the citations.

The Old Russian verb has at minimum **non-past, imperfect, perfect,** and **aorist tenses** and, in addition to the **indicative**, has **conditional** and **imperative moods**. There is no regular future tense; instead, futurity is indicated by compound forms using the infinitive or perfect participle after an auxiliary or phasal verb, or by simple non-past forms. There are also **pluperfects** and **past conditionals**. These tenses employ the perfect participle with various auxiliaries.

A verb form must have a **root**, and can in addition have **prefixes** and **suffixes**. The prefixes in Old Russian have a number of functions; their primary one is that of changing the meaning of the verb, although they may change its aspectual character as well. In order of closeness to the root, suffixes can show verb class, aspect, tense, and person/number (a single marker in Russian). The stem may change from tense to tense; suffixal tense markers appear for only some tenses, while for others the choice of stem and the set of personal endings tell us which tense is being used.

Russian has a **reflexive marker**, which frequently indicates the performance of an action on the subject or in its domain (a middle or passive voice function). In many instances it is lexicalized and cannot be said to have a discrete meaning or function. In Old Russian, the reflexive marker *sja* is often found word-finally. It is usually written together with the verb, although it can also precede the verb form (sometimes with a word in between them) or follow the word after the verb, in which cases it is written separately. My citation forms treat it as a separate particle following the verb form. Other reflexive forms found in these texts are: *si sa, s', s.*

Like most medieval languages, Old Russian was not standardized. It existed in a written tradition that included non-Russian texts such as the monuments of Old Church Slavic, and it was used in a range of environments, from Ukraine to the far Russian north, and by a range of scribes, from monks to merchants. Written Old Russian thus of necessity reflects a wide variety of literary, linguistic and cultural influences, and its forms vary commensurately from text to text and even within texts. Some of the most important variables are given below.

The **jers** (ъ, ь, transliterated as ", ') are respectively back and front lax mid vowels. Phonetically the jers are gradually being either lost or merged with the vowels *o, e* in Old Russian. For any "correct" jer listed in the paradigms or the citation form, texts may have either jer, *o, e,* or nothing. Conversely, jers may appear in the texts in places where none appear in the paradigm or citation form.

In the texts, the **low front vowel** ѣ (transliterated *ě)* is sometimes confused with its higher neighbor *e* (transliterated *e).*

The final-position morph *-t* (also *-t', -t")* is found regularly on some third person forms and is regularly absent on others. However, it is not infrequently missing where expected, and present where unexpected.

Competition between forms adopted from **Old Church Slavic** and native Russian forms means that multiple variants of a word exist. Russian Church Slavic *a* alternates with native Russian *o;* Russian Church Slavic *šč* can stand in for native Russian *č;* Russian Church Slavic *žd* sometimes appears for native Russian *ž*.

Under the influence of Greek, the **rounded back vowel** written у and transliterated as *u* often appears as оу, transliterated as *ou.* There is no difference in pronunciation, structure or meaning between *oustaviti* and *ustaviti* 'decree'.

There is variation in what vowels are written after the **hushing consonants** *(*ш, ч, щ, ж, ц, transliterated *š, č, šč, ž, c)* and after **velars** *(*г, к, х, transliterated *g, k, x).* Sometimes palatalizing vowels *(*я, и, ю, transliterated *ja, i, ju)* will be written; other times the nonpalatalizing vowels *(*а, ы, у, transliterated *a, y, u)* appear.

Chart 1.9.1 gives sample verb conjugations, with stem separated from desinence; while far from exhaustive, it should acquaint the reader sufficiently with the range of forms met in this work. I have omitted the much rarer dual forms from all the paradigms, and the analytic forms of the imperative (1. sg., 3. sg. and pl.) to avoid clutter and confusion. This information is loosely based on Vlasto 1986.

In addition to finite verb forms, numerous types of active and passive **participles** exist (see chart 1.9.2). Like Modern Russian, Old Russian differentiates between participles expressing a present or concurrent act and those expressing a past or anterior act. Some forms situate an act with respect to other acts performed by the subject; these approach to the Modern Russian concept of the verbal adverb. Their form and syntax, however, is variable; often they resemble short adjectival participles, and sometimes do so in cases that do not match the subject of the sentence. I have labelled these forms 'participial' to emphasize similarities in their functions, although studies exploring their differences find much to say as well.

Chart 1.9.1. Old Russian finite verb forms

non-past					
1. sg.	2. sg.	3. sg.	1. pl.	2. pl.	3. pl.
nes-u	nes-eši	nes-et'	nes-em"	nes-ete	nes-ut'
proš-u	pros-iši	pros-it'	pros-im"	pros-ite	pros-jat'
imperfect					
nes-jax"	nes-jaše	nes-jaše	nes-jaxom"	nes-jašete	nes-jaxu
zna-x"	zna-še	zna-še	zna-xom"	zna-šete	zna-xu
aorist					
nes-ox"	nes-e	nes-e	nes-oxom"	nes-oste	nes-oša
xodi-x"	xodi	xodi	xodi-xom"	xodi-ste	xodi-ša
perfect					
esm' da-l(a)	esi da-l(a)	(est') da-l(a)	esm" da-li	este da-li	(sut') da-li
conditional					
byx da-l(a)	bys da-l(a)	by da-l(a)	byxom" da-li	byste da-li	by da-li
imperative					
--	nes-i!	--	nes-ěm"! or nes-em"!	nes-ěte! or nes-ite!	--
--	pros-i!	--	pros-im"!	pros-ite!	--

Chart 1.9.2. Old Russian participles from čitati *'read' and* nesti *'carry'*

present active participle (short forms later become adverbial)	present active participle (long forms remain adjectival)	past active participle (short forms later become adverbial)	past active participle (long forms remain adjectival)
čitaj-a, čitaj-u(š)č-e, čitaj-u(š)č-i	čitaj-u(š)č-ij, etc.	čita-v-", čita-vš-e, čita-vš-i	čita-vš-ij, etc.
nes-a, nes-u(š)če, nes-u(š)či	nes-u(š)č-ij, etc.	nes-", nes-š-e, nes-š-i	nes-š-ij, etc.
present passive participle (short form)	present passive participle (long form)	past passive participle (short form)	past passive participle (long form)
čita-em-", etc.	čita-em-yj, etc.	čita-n-", etc.	čita-nn-yj, etc.
nes-om-", etc.	nes-om-yj, etc.	nes-en-", etc.	nes-enn-yj, etc.

The paradigms in Chart 1.9.2 are greatly simplified; for example, where the notation *etc.* appears, a variety of standard short and long adjectival endings can occur. For a more complete set of paradigms consult Vlasto (1986: 169-178).

2. Describing Modern Russian Aspect

2.0. THE NATURE OF THE DEBATE

Aspect can be defined as a presumption about the way an act proceeds in time. Languages express aspect in at least three ways that will be considered in this chapter. First, they express it through lexical features, elements of a predicate that prescribe how the act unfolds. The existence of lexical aspectual features is a linguistic universal; an act like *stand* takes place differently from an act like *explode*.

Second, languages can express aspectual distinctions through contextual features, adding adverbial phrases *(immediately, gradually, slowly, for three hours)* and other elements that describe the temporal contour of the act more precisely than does the verb form itself; this type of aspect is also universal to some degree.

Third, aspectual distinctions may appear in the grammar. When scholars speak of a *grammatical feature,* like tense or mood, they usually have in mind a morphological alternation of some regularity that imposes a particular meaning on all lexemes that undergo this alternation. To take tense as an example, using the past tense form of the verb indicates that the action has already taken place, and this past tense form tends to have a predictable and recognizable shape. Some languages clearly make aspectual distinctions in the grammar. English, for instance, distinguishes a progressive view from a non-progressive view (*I go* vs. *I am going,* with similar examples for other tenses) for most acts, while French expresses this aspect only partially in the grammar, distinguishing habit and duration from summation in the past (*imparfait* vs. *passé composé* and *passé simple),* but not in the present.

The picture in Russian is quite different. Most sorts of acts in Russian are expressed by two verbs, one taking an external perspective on the act (perfectivity) and one that fails to take this external perspective, or alternately, expresses an internal perspective on the act (imperfectivity). These two verbs are usually related by one of a variety of morphological means, and, it is claimed, have consistent, complementary restrictions—both semantic and morphological—that mark the aspectual distinction as being part of the grammar.

In Russian, therefore, aspect is usually acknowledged to be a grammatical category of the verb, like tense or mood; this becomes evident through simple formal tests that are widely (although not always universally) applicable throughout the Russian verbal system. The best example of such a test is the formation of a compound future tense, which is possible for imperfective verbs but not for perfective verbs; thus forms like *budu čitat'*[I] 'I will read[I]' and even *budu pročityvat'*[I] 'I will read through[I]' are acceptable, but forms like **budu pročitat'*[P] 'I will read through[P]' are not acceptable. Similarly, past passive participles can only be formed productively from perfective verbs in contemporary Russian (although this was not the case as recently as a hundred years ago, and frozen imperfective participial forms (*čitannyj, pisannyj* 'read, written') are still occasionally found).

25

Certain contexts prescribe the use of only one aspect, such as phasal verbs followed by an infinitive (*načinat'*[I]*–načat'*[P] 'begin', *končat'*[I]*– končit'*[P] 'end', *prodolžat'*[I]*–prodolžit'*[P] 'continue' are followed only by imperfective verbs), as in (1) below. Durative contexts govern only one aspect; an accusative time expression (*dve nedeli* 'two weeks', *mesjac* 'a month') indicates duration and requires an imperfective verb[1], as in (2), while a construction with the preposition *za* and the accusative case (*za nedelju* 'in a week', *za mesjac* 'in a month') indicates completion and almost always modifies a perfective verb, as seen in (3).

(1)   On načal čitat'[I].
       'He began to read[I].' (phasal)

(2)   Ona dve nedeli čitala[I] ètu knigu.
       'She was reading[I] that book for two weeks.' (durative)

(3)   Ona pročitala[P] ètu knigu za dve nedeli.
       'She read[P] that book in two weeks.' (summative pf. *pročitala*)

Such tests support the conclusion that an abstract distinction at a deeper level underlies the imperfective–perfective opposition, encoding it in the grammar.

To a large extent, the history of research on Russian aspect represents the unfolding of this view. Two of the best-known volumes on the subject, O.P. Rassudova's 1982 work *Upotreblenie vidov glagola v sovremennom russkom jazyke (Aspectual Usage in Contemporary Russian)* and James Forsyth's 1970 *Grammar of Aspect: Usage and Meaning in the Russian Verb,* presuppose a grammatical category of aspect with one invariant meaning assigned to the perfective aspect and a series of secondary meanings assigned to the imperfective, whose "invariant meaning" is the lack of expression of perfectivity. Both Forsyth and Rassudova are thorough treatments that have served as a standard against which to measure other descriptions of Russian aspect. Herbert Galton's 1976 monograph extends this view beyond Russian, treating all of Slavic aspect as minor variations on this single invariant opposition.

From the earliest descriptions of Russian aspect, however, scholars have been aware that not all verbs respect aspectual distinctions in identical fashion, and that for this purpose verbs can be grouped into semantic or lexical categories that behave in a more or less similar way. Some scholars, like Maslov (1948), have argued that these lexical groupings are in fact more important and tell us more about aspectual usage than descriptions of invariant meanings assigned to the perfective and imperfective aspects. Others, like Isačenko (1960), have subsumed these lexical groupings under the heading *Aktionsarten* (*sposoby dejstvija* or, to use Isačenko's

---

[1] A special dispensation is usually made for Aktionsart perfectives of specified duration with *po-* and *pro-*, where accusative durations are possible, e.g., *on prožil*[P] *tam dva goda* 'He lived[P] there for a full two years'. See section 2.3 for an assessment of how central these Aktionsart prefixes are to our understanding of aspect.

term, *soveršaemosti dejstvija*)² and assigned primacy over aspectual categories to these Aktionsart categories. Neither of these approaches is very popular among Slavic linguists; Maslov later turned to more grammatical and contextual approaches to aspect, and Isačenko's view is not widely accepted, to judge from the treatment it receives in the literature. Both, however, stand as important critiques of grammar-based models of aspect.

A third approach to aspect, which has gained popularity in recent years, is to treat aspect as a subset of discourse considerations. This approach is broader in scope than the contextual approach, because it takes into consideration not only the immediate context of the verb, but pragmatic factors as well. In this view, aspectual choice is governed by external considerations, and its main purpose is to influence the flow of the narrative. Any "meanings" of an aspect are derived from the verb's function in the text; for instance, instead of "bounded" and "unbounded" actions, the textual terms "connected" and "isolated" actions could be used to describe respectively the perfective and imperfective aspects.³

For the sake of convenience, I will consider these three basic viewpoints about the nature of Russian aspect: first, that it encodes a basic grammatical opposition; second, that its usage is largely governed by lexical factors; and third, that it is a discourse category. I will refer to these in shorthand as the **grammatical**, **lexical**, and **discourse** approaches to aspect. It is important, however, to note that these viewpoints are not mutually exclusive, and it is possible (and quite popular) to combine two or more viewpoints in a single model. With the large number of models and theories on the market, however, the task of researchers has become correspondingly more difficult: one must not only propose a workable solution but also demonstrate its superiority to other models of differing (or similar) approaches.

In the concluding section of this chapter, I will discuss the appropriateness and applicability of these models to studying a dead language and propose a method for studying Old Russian aspect that combines features of the three approaches.

2.1. ASPECT AS A GRAMMATICAL OPPOSITION

This understanding of aspect is the most widely known and accepted. The two principal monographs on Russian aspect take a grammatical approach, as do a great majority of Russian textbooks and grammars. The modern grammatical approach to aspect owes its beginnings to Jakobson's 1927 article "Zur Struktur des russischen Verbums," which applied the structuralist concept of privative opposition to the

---

2   The German term is usually used in the plural when making reference to the members of the category, and the Russian term is consequently also cited in the plural. I will use the singular *Aktionsart* to refer to this class of occurrences, and the plural *Aktionsarten* only when I specifically want to emphasize the existence of different members of the set. This makes the usage parallel to *aspect* vs. *aspects*. For the adjective, I will use the singular form *Aktionsart*.
3   These particular terms were suggested by Dr. A.E. Matveeva in a course on aspect and grammar I took in 1987 at the Pushkin Institute.

Russian verb. Jakobson opposed marked features to unmarked features and noted that being unmarked was not equivalent to negating the marked feature. In Jakobson's terms, if a member of a category (such as aspect) expresses feature A, then another member of that category may fail to express feature A—which does not mean that the second member expresses the opposite of A or some complementary feature. Paired members of categories, then, according to Jakobson, are not equally weighted, with each having a certain feature present. Instead, one member is marked by the presence of that feature, and the other is unmarked by the presence of that feature. This approach explained linguists' failure to find a meaning for the imperfective aspect that would complement the definition proposed for the perfective aspect: in fact, under Jakobson's system, the imperfective cannot be assigned a single meaning but must encompass all meanings not subsumed under the more uniform and easily defined perfective aspect.

In later versions of the Jakobsonian system, the marked aspect (perfective) has as its feature summation, demarcation (*dostiženie predela*), completeness (*celostnost'*) or some other term close in meaning. The unmarked aspect (imperfective) lacks this feature.[4] The various meanings and uses of aspect are seen as reflections of this essential opposition, not as primary grammatical oppositions in and of themselves. The task of the investigator is to document these manifold circumstances and to show how they represent the basic opposition.

2.1.1. Forsyth 1970

This approach to aspect is best exemplified in Forsyth 1970, which begins by establishing the central privative opposition of perfective (marked) versus imperfective (unmarked) and then considers the usage of these aspects in various tenses, moods, and sentence types as reflections or outgrowths of this central distinction.

The morphology of aspect is one of the major stumbling blocks for considering aspect a regular category; its irregularity of form makes it unlike number, person, tense, and other categories that have more or less regular reflections in the morphology, and Forsyth acknowledges this problem while trying to mitigate it, saying that "although the form of a verb and its aspect are inter-connected, the relationship is not simple, and it is impossible to recognise the aspect of a verb simply from its form" (Forsyth 1970: 17).

However, this problem may have further-reaching implications than he admits. After all, in Russian a number of perfective verbs have an "imperfectivizing" suffix: note perfectives like *porassuždat'* 'spend some time judging something', and lest it be suspected that this is the result of the double prefix, we can add the imperfective *porazgovarivat'* 'spend some time in conversation' for comparison. Furthermore, imperfectives frequently have prefixes, which are the only morphemes identifiable as markers of perfectivity. It follows that there are no clear markers of perfectivity, and that markers of imperfectivity are unreliable. The closest we can come to

---

[4] This view is laid out in Rassudova (1982/84), among others.

establishing perfective and imperfective "morphemes" is to decree that certain combinations of prefixes and suffixes are likely—but not sure—to produce verbs of one or another aspect.

From this a further problem arises: as Timberlake (1982) notes, it is disturbing that if the perfective is the marked member of a privative opposition, that it is the imperfective which comes closer to having clear morphological markers; this, after all, violates Jakobson's dictum that forms will follow function.

Forsyth more successfully addresses problems raised by, among others, Maslov and Isačenko, who questioned the importance of aspectual verb pairs (e.g. *čitat'^{I}–pročitat'^{P}*) to Russian grammar. The existence of aspectual verb pairs is decisive for Forsyth, since positing one verb in each aspect gives the system a regular and predictable shape and makes it more analogous to tense, person, or number in its "one meaning, one form" correspondence. Maslov and Isačenko have contended that verbs are grouped in a variety of configurations—pairs, triplets, and singularities are the most common types—and that these groupings more closely reflect lexical categories of verbs than any grammatical system. In defense of the regularity of pairs in a grammatical system of aspect, Forsyth offers a solution—suggested by Maslov himself in his 1948 article—that by transposing a sentence from the past to the present tense (as in (4) and (5)), imperfective counterparts to the perfective verbs become evident.

(4) On vstal^P, podošel^P k oknu i otkryl^P ego.
     'He got up^P, went over^P to the window, and opened^P it.'

(5) On vstaet^I, podxodit^I k oknu, i otkryvaet^I ego.
     'He gets up^I, goes over^I to the window, and opens^I it.'

This test becomes Forsyth's chief defense of pairedness; the fact that in different situations different pairings may result (for instance, *ubit'^{P}* 'kill' might sometimes be paired with *ubivat'^{I}* 'be killing, kill repeatedly' and sometimes with *bit'^{I}* 'beat') is not then a function of the verb itself, but merely of context (Forsyth 1970: 34-46).

It is possible, however, to read this test in a different way (which, I believe, was Maslov's point): the "historical present" test does not prove the necessity of pairedness, but rather the fluid, morphologically random character of pairedness. It is this character that argues against aspect as a grammatical phenomenon (Maslov 1948: 306-307).

An analogy may be helpful here. In an imaginary language, a verb has one form that is used for the present tense and anywhere from one to six future tense forms, only one of which is appropriate in any given situation and which may in fact be identical to the present tense form. One might question the wisdom of saying that the language had a single "future tense" or, come to think of it, a "present tense." Instead, the linguist might decide that "tense" as such was not a particularly relevant category for the present–future distinction and focus instead on the individual uses of the forms, figuring there might be more information about the system in the lexemes than in the present vs. future distinction.

2.2. ASPECT AS A LEXICAL CATEGORY

The lexical approach has an equally long tradition and has received attention from such well-respected academics as Maslov and Isačenko, but in recent years has found more favor in the West than in the former Soviet bloc. Many Western scholars have used Vendler's categories of verbal action to study how basic verbal meaning shapes the possibilities for its morphological expression. Maslov has since shifted his views to a more discourse-oriented approach to aspect, and in recent years Henry Kučera has come to the fore as an advocate of a lexical understanding of aspect. Other work in this field has been done by Timberlake, Chvany and Eckert. (The first two scholars have combined lexically-oriented and discourse- or context-oriented analyses.)

2.2.1. Maslov 1948

Maslov's 1948 article "Vid i leksičeskoe značenie glagola v sovremennom russkom literaturnom jazyke" ("Aspect and the Lexical Meaning of the Verb in Contemporary Standard Russian") combines a well-reasoned critique of the grammatical approach to aspect with a meticulously divided and described map of the verbal lexicon. Maslov argues that grouping verbs by the types of actions they represent provides a better understanding of their aspectual behavior than starting from one basic opposition in the meanings of the imperfective and perfective aspects. Such lexical groupings allow us to predict a verb's paired status (unpaired imperfective, unpaired perfective, paired imperfective, paired perfective) as well as its performance according to formal criteria (for example, in test sentences of the sort *Umiral^I, no ne umer^P* 'He was dying^I, but didn't die^P' or with certain adverbs and expressions). His conclusion is that aspect does not reflect one basic opposition in meaning; instead, aspectual oppositions derive from a more fundamental set of lexical criteria, and the nature of the aspectual opposition is determined first and foremost by the type of action involved.

Maslov's argument against the grammatical view of aspect starts from five basic imperfective–perfective oppositions (which are outlined in Chart 2.2.1.1). Noting that most verbs exclude one or more of these five contexts and cannot form grammatical sentences with all of these models, Maslov hypothesizes that semantic features encoded in each verb—not a single invariant global feature—lie at the basis of aspectual oppositions. On the basis of the five oppositions in Chart 2.2.1.1, he defines three superclasses (*razrjady*) of verbs: unpaired imperfectives, unpaired perfectives, and paired verbs. Within each (aspectually delimited) superclass, verbs are assigned to lexical classes and subclasses. These groupings show the numerous and significant convergences between aspectual behavior and lexical features.

Chart 2.2.1.1. Five aspectual oppositions according to Maslov 1948

Type A: Action in the process of fulfillment or development (I) vs. action as accomplished fact, leap, completion of action (P)
Kogda ja vyxodil^I iz domu ja vstretil znakomogo. / Ja vyše!^{P} iz domu.
'As I was leaving^I home I met a friend. / I left^P the house.'

Type B. Tendency toward a particular fact, attempts or intention to attain a result (I) vs. the actual accomplishment of the fact, attainment of the result, success of the action (P)
Umiral^I, no ne umer^P; lovil^I, no ne pojmal^P; vstrečal^I, da ne vstretil^P.
'He was dying^I, but didn't die^P; he fished^I, but didn't catch^P anything; he went to meet^I (them) but didn't meet^P them.' (Ostrovskij, *A Girl with No Dowry*)

Type C. Indefinite duration of an action in progress, action with no set limits (I) vs. fleeting quality or fixed temporal limits (P)
On čuvstvoval^I sil'nuju bol'. / On počuvstvoval^P sil'nuju bol'.
'He was^I in great pain. / He felt^P a sharp pain.'

Type D. Ordinary, undefined number of repetitions of an action (I) vs. singular action or an action repeated a finite number of times (P)
On čital^I lekcii. / On pročital^P lekciju desjat' raz.
'He gave^I lectures. / He gave^P the lecture ten times.'

Type E. Action "in general terms" or generally undefined with relation to the concrete terms of its realization (I) vs. a concrete occurrence (P)
Ty pisal^I emu? / Ty napisal^P emu?
'Have you (ever) written^I him? / Did you write^P him?'

For instance, the verb *carstvovat'* 'reign' belongs to the first superclass (unpaired imperfective verbs), and within that to the group "verbs of staying and perspectiveless duration." Its subclass is "verbs marking the subject's membership in a specific social group," into which fall verbs of occupation, as well as specific instances of other verbs that usually indicate action, such as *šit'* 'sew' in *ona š'et mužskie vešči* 'she sews men's clothing' or *pisat'* 'write' in *ona pišet v raznyx gazetax* 'she writes for various newspapers'. If put through the aspectual tests in chart 2.2.1.1, *carstvovat'* would participate in a Type C opposition, with a corresponding perfective *pocarstvovat'* 'rule for a while' or *procarstvovat'* 'rule all the way through a set period of time'.

To determine exactly how the imperfective–perfective opposition worked for any given pair of verbs, Maslov proposed basic classes for imperfective verbs that include: atelic verbs, endeavors, processual non-endeavors, and nonprocessuals, which are further split into subclasses.[5] *Atelic verbs* include the "natural" imperfectives, predicates that by their nature do not express completion or result; they divide into states, processes and natural conatives. *Endeavors* encompass telic predicates that oppose an attempt or a tendency in the imperfective to success or realization of an action in the perfective; they divide according to the conversability of process and result, since verbs' imperfectives can imply different degrees of progress toward completion of the action, depending on the type of action. *Processual non-endeavors* lack the semantic component of attempt or tendency; every performance of an act includes its implied attainment of telos. Verbs of reactive emotion, perception and communication form semantic subgroups in this class. *Nonprocessuals* include predicates that altogether lack a processual component in the imperfective, which has only iterative meaning; this class is divided into simple nonprocessuals, like *prixodit'* 'come' and iterative semelfactives like *stučat'* 'knock' that allow a "process" to be visualized from numerous quasi-independent instantaneous actions. (There is a further class of predicates which are *perfectiva tantum* and limit acts in ways that preclude imperfectivization.)

Imperfective predicates in the endeavors, processual non-endeavors, and nonprocessuals all have perfective counterparts. Perfective endeavors contain a component of success or realization of an action; perfective processual non-endeavors and perfective nonprocessual predicates lack this. Maslov does not directly compare the perfectives of processual non-endeavors and nonprocessual predicates the way he does with imperfectives of those classes; the classes seem to be formulated around the ranges of possible imperfective meanings, or more specifically around the functions and meanings a pair acquires, usually as a result of the specific imperfective meanings available.

How does Maslov's analysis measure up to grammatical analyses of aspect? Superficially, the system is not appealing: with its confusing welter of some twenty classes and subclasses of verbs, it lacks a single, easily graspable rationale; and it depends on maddeningly precise definitions, to the point where the names of certain categories run to two or three lines of text in length. However, in other respects it has notable advantages. Once a verb is placed into its correct semantic group, its entire behavior pattern is predictable, including pairedness, aspectual usage, and the range of any given aspectual form within the full spectrum of meanings. A further benefit of Maslov's analysis is that one perceives how central a role grammatical explanations of aspect allot to canonical aspectual pairs like *brat'–vzjat'* 'take' and *smotret'–posmotret'* 'watch', while the disturbing number of monoaspectual verbs in the system are pushed to the side or forced into pairs and the heterogeneous

---

[5] The names that follow are mine. Maslov avoids naming his classes with single-word tags and instead uses names like "Verbs of attempt vs. attainment or tendency vs. realization." These names are ultimately more accurate but inconvenient to use, so I have developed shorthands for them. He uses the word *verb* somewhat loosely; given his reliance on verbal complements to distinguish meaning, he could have more accurately used the terms *predicate* or *situation*.

nature of aspectual usage is minimized. Maslov's system, working from usage (based on a number of possible test sentences) to theory, is structured to avoid these pitfalls.

2.2.2. Vendler 1967

Vendler's article "Verbs and Times" has served as a starting point for much of the later Western work on aspect. Although his analysis rests entirely on the basis of English examples and does not specifically address a category of aspect, it suggests the powerful influence of lexical groupings on the formal structure of the verbal system. In English, this approach concerns itself with the ability of verbs to appear in certain tenses such as the imperfect—making it implicitly an examination of several facets of the English aspectual system.

Vendler (following other language philosophers like Reichenbach) noted that each predicate contains intuitive and implicit limitations on its meaning that are expressed in limitations on its usage: one can say *Yesterday he was mowing the lawn for five hours* or *Yesterday he was drawing circles for five hours* but one has more trouble saying *Yesterday he was drawing a circle for five hours* or *Yesterday he was reaching the top of the mountain all day*.[6] He classifies predicates into four types: state, activity, accomplishment and achievement, and demonstrates through the use of different tenses that our perceptions of these predicates' meanings prevent or condition the use of certain inflectional forms.

This approach is immediately appealing on three counts. First, predicates, if accurately translated, should retain about the same range of permissible and impermissible formulations from one language to the next; the Russian sentence **Včera on ves' den' dostigal^I veršiny* is as unacceptable as the English alternative presented above. Aspect, like tense, is seen as a phenomenon regulated by lexical categories of verbs, which should be similar cross-linguistically. Second, it considers the variety of meanings presented by a whole predicate, instead of focusing on the verb as the bearer of consistent aspectual meaning. This highlights the multiple "contours" that a single verb can have, depending on its complements. Third, and most important, it focuses on groups of predicates that actually do behave alike in their distribution of aspectual forms, instead of working with two large and unwieldy groups (imperfective and perfective) that exhibit widely varying usages. This approach can be used to explain certain apparent discrepancies in aspectual behavior. For instance, a sentence like *Včera ja čital^I kogda on smotrel^I televizor* 'Yesterday I read^I while he watched^I television' is perfectly acceptable, while **Včera ja čital^I kogda on prixodil^I sjuda* '*Yesterday I read^I while he was arriving^I here' is unacceptable. Using lexical groupings, we can see that *prixodit'* 'arrive' is an achievement predicate, meaning it cannot indicate an ongoing action,

---

[6] Vendler actually states that the latter two sentences are impossible, which clearly is not true; the error of his ways was pointed out in numerous subsequent articles, but the distinction between achievement and accomplishment, which rests at least partially on this erroneous conclusion, has stayed with us.

while *smotret'* 'watch' is an activity and thus usually indicates an ongoing action. A similar approach can be used to sort out the regular discrepancies that occur between simplex and secondary imperfectives.

Vendler's analysis differs from Maslov's mainly in depth; Vendler defines only four types of action contours versus Maslov's twenty. Vendler's system is thus more correctly seen as an outline or draft for a system, which it is up to other scholars to fill in and describe for individual languages. Interestingly, neither approach draws much of a distinction between the verb and the predicate as a whole, acknowledging the nonverbal components of the predicate only sporadically. Vendler notes only in passing that nonverbal components (draw *a circle,* reach *the top,* etc.) must somehow be accounted for in filling out his system.

2.2.3. Kučera 1983

A synthesis of the theories of Maslov and Vendler can be found in the work of Henry Kučera. Taking Vendler's action types as a basis for his explanation, Kučera constructs a branching diagram of lexical classes that predict elements of the grammar and usage patterns for Russian, Czech and English. Kučera divides "situations" (roughly equivalent to predicates, although fuzzier in scope) into three superclasses: processes, events, and states. (See chart 2.2.3.1.) Processes, which are imperfective verbs, are divided into telic (possible accomplishments), atelic (action with no accomplishment possible), or incipient achievement. Events, which are all perfective, are atelic (marked for duration but not for progress toward a goal), accomplishments (segmentable processes), or achievements (nonsegmental processes that presuppose the fact of completion). States can be of either aspect, and can be nondynamic or habits/attributes. This last class is further broken down into open series of processes, open series of events, and quantified states.

One area in which Kučera's and Maslov's analyses diverge is in their assignment of the broadest categories of verbal action. This has an impact on what grammatical categories and usage patterns the two systems can predict. Maslov uses aspectual pairing or grouping as his highest-level marker; verbs fall into unpaired imperfective, unpaired perfective, and paired categories. The actual meaning of the aspects, however, is reduced to a series of distinctions at the lowest level of the system; lexical categories can be defined by an aspectual opposition if verbs of both aspects occur in the category.

For Kučera, on the other hand, although aspectual distinctions also appear at the broadest level of analysis, this fact is supposed to be an accident; he defines his lexical categories to exclude verbs of differing aspect from occupying the same category. In order to separate perfective from imperfective at the most detailed level of analysis, however, category definitions contain a mixture of lexical aspectual features and grammatical aspectual ones. His process–state distinction is clearly lexical; the classification of "events" vs. "non-events," however, recalls a grammatical definition of aspect, and in fact separates imperfective from perfective verbs on all levels (processes vs. events in superclasses, and open series of processes vs. open series of events in subclasses).

Chart 2.2.3.1. Summary of Kučera's verb classification charts (1983: 176-178)

Processes (I)
- atelic (no accomp.): hraje tenis/он играет в теннис 'he plays tennis'
  pršelo/шел дождь 'it rained'
  Pavel studoval ruštinu/Павел изучал русский язык 'Pavel studied Russian'
- telic (possible accomp.): Petr píše knihu/Петр пишет книгу 'Peter is writing a book'
  otec stavěl dům/отец строил дом 'Father was building a house'
- incipient achievement: dostihuje vrcholu/он достигает вершины 'he is reaching the summit'
  strýc umíral/дядя умирал 'Uncle was dying'
  ?Nataša nachází klíč/?Наташа находит ключ '?Natasha was finding the key'

Events (P)
- atelic: posedět/посидеть 'sit a while' and other po- and pro- verbs
  vydržet/выдержать 'last through'
- accomplishments: Petr napsal knihu/Петр написал книгу 'Peter wrote a book'
  otec postavil dům/отец построил дом 'Father built a house'
- achievements: dostihl vrcholu/он достиг вершины 'he reached the summit'
  strýc umřel/дядя умер 'Uncle died'
  Nataša našla klíč/Наташа нашла ключ 'Natasha found the key'

States (I or P):
- non-dynamic (I) znát/знать 'know'
  milovat/любить 'love'
- habits/attributes:
  - open series of processes (I): Pavel mluví rusky/Павел говорит по-русски 'Pavel speaks Russian'
    Jan píše knihy/Иван пишет книги 'John writes books'
  - open series of events (P): Jednou za rok řekne pravdu/Раз в год он правду скажет 'Once a year he'll tell the truth'
  - quantified states (I_2): psávat, býbat, mívat 'write, be, have (often)'
    хаживать, бывать 'go, be (often)'

(© 1983 by Henry Kučera. Reprinted with permission of the author.)

Kučera's subclasses do accurately predict the aspectual assignment of a verb in any given situation, but they do not tell as much about the relationship between a verb and its supposed pair as Maslov's system does. Of course, Maslov's system itself refutes the primacy and necessity of the "aspectual pair," so this may not be a flaw at all but rather a reflection of the insignificance of pairedness in such an approach. Where Kučera succeeds is in showing the interrelatability of the English tense system and Slavic aspectual systems; a system like Maslov's, which is highly specific to and based only on Russian, requires more substantial modification to be relevant for other languages.

Lexical definitions of aspect therefore differ from grammatical ones, in that they affirm the primacy of the *lexical contour,* or the innate shape of the verbal act, as the governing feature in aspectual choice. The special status of Russian, as a language with morphologized aspect, is relegated to a secondary feature. This rejection of the primacy of grammatical aspect in Russian is troublesome, if only because grammatical structures are usually presumed to exist on a deeper level of the language than the lexicon, and here the reverse situation is proposed specifically for verbal morphology. None of the authors discussed here have proposed or refer to an analogous development for nominal morphology or any other portion of the grammar.[7]

2.3. ASPECT AND AKTIONSART

The lexical approach to aspect—considering the contour of verbal action before the presence of an opposition between perfective and imperfective—is an extension of the uncontroversial idea that predicates express different sorts of action (termed in German *Aktionsarten*, in Russian *sposoby dejstvija*, and in Czech *způsoby slovesného děje*). The German term *Aktionsart* has been adopted into English in studies of aspect, but since the phenomenon has different ramifications in different theories, the meaning scholars assign to the terms varies widely. Here I will generally use the term in its narrower sense.

2.3.1. Townsend 1980

As presented in a structuralist work like Townsend's *Russian Word-Formation,* the domain of Aktionsart in Russian consists of modifications to verbs that enact a change in the temporal contour of an action, typically limiting it in some way that leaves the meaning of the base verb substantially intact. This change is accompanied by an aspectual shift (imperfective to perfective) and is performed mainly through prefixation. An important effect of prefixation of this type is that it leaves a verb whose contour is not susceptible to interruption and incompleteness,

---

[7] Work by Timberlake on thematicity suggests a profitable way of resolving this problem by classing predicate complements and relating these classes to lexical or aspectual classes. "Predicates as Text(ual) Histories)," delivered at the AATSEEL conference, December 1991.

making it an unlikely (but not impossible) candidate for secondary imperfectivization. In a structuralist view, Aktionsart prefixation (and suffixation) is a limited device that accounts for a small, vaguely troublesome area of aspect: the fact that not all verbs are aspectually paired and that a large number of these verbs are prefixed perfectives.[8]

In his approach to Aktionsart, Townsend offers a list of prefixes that he calls *sublexical,* which he distinguishes from prefixes that are *lexical,* i.e., that change the meaning from the stem more substantially. Sublexical prefixes modify only the scope of an action and could equally well be called Aktionsart prefixes. Townsend is careful to note that including a prefix in his sublexical list does not mean that all uses of that prefix are sublexical; for instance, there is a lexical prefix {vy-} and a sublexical prefix {vy-}. This caveat is important, but it is often difficult to distinguish the shades of difference in meaning he describes. At points, prefixed verbs seem to be assigned to lexical or sublexical categories based simply on their ability (or lack thereof) to imperfectivize, not on any independent semantic criteria. For instance, the use of the prefix {na-} in the sense of 'do a lot of something with some unpleasant result' as in *nagovorit'* 'say a lot of nasty things,' *nadelat'* 'cause a lot of trouble' Townsend classifies as sublexical, while use of the prefix {vy-} in the meaning of 'do or finish successfully' is classified as lexical (as in *vyučit'* 'learn', *vydumat'* 'think up', *vyigrat'* 'win')—although the same prefix used simply to indicate completion he calls sublexical (*vypit'* 'drink up', *vyspat'sja* 'get enough sleep', *vykurit'* 'smoke up'). I found myself wondering why ordinary completion and negative completion should be sublexical, while positive completion remains lexical.

For Townsend, Aktionsart is a limited phenomenon that he accepts as a piece of counterevidence against the regularity and primacy of a grammatical aspectual system. Since verbal prefixes can be assigned to different grammatical classes (lexical and sublexical), thereby classifying their behavior, and since according to Townsend these grammatical classes explain the semantics of the prefixes, the damage to the overall system can be limited to this small corner of morphology.

2.3.2. Isačenko 1960

Isačenko's approach to Aktionsart in his *Grammatičeskij stroj russkogo jazyka v sopostavlenii so slovackim (The Grammatical Structure of Russian Contrasted with Slovak)* starts from the viewpoint that pure aspectual opposition is in covariance with another form of opposition, which in his view is represented by the modification of an action's course or shape. In Isačenko's system, both systems have regular morphological reflections: aspectual oppositions are represented by suffixation (so-called "secondary" imperfectivization), and action contour oppositions (*soveršaemosti dejstvija*) by prefixation (formation of prefixed

---

[8] Against this one could pose Maslov's superclass of unpaired imperfectives, which is more heterogeneous and more important from an aspectological standpoint than the superclass of unpaired perfectives.

perfectives) or suffixation (represented in Russian by the suffix {-nu-}). An example of action contour oppositions is the set of verbs related to *kričat'* 'shout, scream' (adapted from Isačenko 1960):

kričat'^{I}–*zakričat'*^{P} 'shout: begin to shout' shows [±inception]
kričat'^{I}–*pokričat'*^{P} 'shout: shout a bit' shows [±limitation]
kričat'^{I}–*kriknut'*^{P} 'shout: shout once' shows [±singularity]

According to Isačenko, there is no aspectual opposition for these verbs; each verb constitutes an aspectually unpaired singularity. Likewise, the verb pairs *pisat'*^{I}–*napisat'*^{P} 'write' and *delat'*^{I}–*sdelat'*^{P} 'do' are related by the semantic opposition [± resultativity *(rezul'tativnost')*], which he claims is more akin to lexical oppositions like *iskat'*^{I}–*najti*^{P} 'search–find' or *est'*^{I}–*naest'sja*^{P} 'eat–eat one's fill' than it is to clearly aspectual oppositions like *sprašivat'*^{I}–*sprosit'*^{P} 'ask'. Isačenko does not allow prefixes to have a grammatical function but no semantic function, as he does not believe abstractness of prefixal meaning warrants labelling a prefix grammatical in nature (1960: 155-159)[9]. As proof of this he presents two oft-cited perfective "partners" of the verb *učit'*^{I} 'teach, learn, study.' Since *naučit'*^{P} and *vyučit'*^{P} are not used in the same contexts, Isačenko concludes that they cannot be synonymous, and yet it is not possible to say that one or the other is the "true" perfective pair of *učit'*^{I}. This is for him definitive proof that *učit'* is an unpaired verb, as are the vast majority of simplex verbs.

While Isačenko, unlike Forsyth and Rassudova, exploits the contradictions presented by predicate complements, he uses them mainly as a tool for knocking down the pairedness hypothesis. For him, apparently, the lexical core of *učit'* remains untouched, whether in the expression *učit' slova* 'learn words' (perfective *vyučit' slova*) or *učit' detej azbuke* 'teach children the alphabet' (perfective *naučit' detej azbuke*). The choice of perfective prefix here, he says, depends on the lexical nuance of the verb (*leksičeskij ottenok glagola*, 1960: 168-172). He does not explore the notion of homonymous verbs such as *učit'*$_1$ (*učit' slova* 'learn words'), *učit'*$_2$ (*učit' detej* 'teach children'), or *rezat'*$_1$ (*rezat' xleb* 'cut bread'), *rezat'*$_2$ (*rezat' kuricu* 'slaughter a chicken'), each with different meanings and thus different perfectives; this approach becomes the refuge of grammatical aspectologists like Forsyth to deal with the issue of apparent multiple perfectives.

Isačenko also does not deal directly with the fact that every operation on an action contour also creates a switch in aspectual assignment; thus, for instance, *pisat'*^{I}–*napisat'*^{P} 'write' may be differentiated by the feature [±resultativity], but they are also differentiated by the aspectual feature [±perfectivity]. In similar fashion, *stojat'*^{I}–*postojat'*^{P} 'stand–stand a while' may be differentiated by both the feature [±limitation] and the aspectual feature [±perfectivity]. It may be that the two

---

[9] But further along he relents and admits that in isolated instances a prefix may become so devoid of meaning that the prefixed verb effectively becomes a perfective partner of the simplex imperfective. What the difference is between allowing this and setting up a homonymous empty prefix is not clear (Isačenko 1960: 175).

systems overlap: "aspect" may simply be a feature parallel to the verb's action contour, or aspect may be subordinated to or conditioned by the action contour. Since Isačenko posits a more discourse-oriented meaning for aspect in its narrow sense—the perspective of the speaker "from inside" or "from outside" the event in question—it could be argued that an aspectual change, i.e., a switch from inside to outside (discourse level) occurs when an action contour (lexical/grammatical level) changes, but that still begs the question of why that should be so (1960: 133).

Isačenko's claim about the morphological distribution of aspect and action contour is less appealing than it seems at first, not only for this reason, but also because it again requires separating prefixes that modify action contour from those that modify semantics of the verb. In Isačenko's system, prefixed perfective verbs are either related to the original simplex imperfective by an action contour relationship or are lexically unrelated due to a major shift in root meaning (1960: 218-219). Distinguishing these uses is not easy, since these prefixes are homonymous, and it is often a tossup as to which is a better interpretation. Has the predicate *vyučit' (slova)* 'learn (words)' strayed far enough in meaning from *učit' (slova)* 'learn (words)' to be treated separately (maybe as a new aspectual pair *vyučivat'–vyučit'*), or is it opposed to the verb *učit'* by the feature [± successful completion]? Often these decisions seem to be determined by the pairedness of the verb, rather than the other way around.

Although objections to Isačenko's theory can be raised, it is a cogently reasoned alternative approach to the relation between aspect and the contour of predicate action. One of the more alluring parts of the theory—the tantalizing offer of a neat morphological reflection of these two categories—is not entirely supportable, however, and might have been better off stated as a tendency instead of a rule. As Townsend points out, Isačenko's claim about morphological regularity forces us to look at *pisat'^{I}–napisat'^{P}* 'write', *delat'^{I}–sdelat'^{P}* 'do' as differing in action contour by virtue of their relation by prefixation, and these two examples make it hard to accept the full extent of Isačenko's propositions (Townsend 1980: 116-117).

2.4. ACTION CONTOURS AND THEORIES OF VERBAL ASPECT

Two scholars have used lexical verb categories to develop more all-encompassing theories of aspect and verbal action. Alan Timberlake proposes a way of distinguishing types of acts based on "sighting" of the act at different points in time and shows the relevance of such groupings to aspectual usage. Per Durst-Andersen has developed a general theory of aspect and action based on Russian data; using a "mental model" of aspect, he proposes that aspectual perceptions of action are more basic than other sorts of perceptions (tense or mood, for instance), thus explaining the relative popularity of aspect in the languages of the world.

2.4.1. Timberlake 1982, 1984a

Timberlake has further developed Vendler's and Isačenko's concept of action contour for use as a guiding force in aspectual determination ("Invariance and the

Syntax of Russian Aspect," "The Temporal Schemata of Russian Predicates," "Reichenbach and Russian Aspect."). The first two articles can be read as a series; in the first one, Timberlake argues that a system that insists on the primacy of aspect as a grammatical category without reference to the lexical content of predicates is inadequate, and he shows that certain formal morphological criteria (namely nominative-instrumental predicate nominals and sequencing of tenses) are better predicted by scales of semantic metafeatures for the predicate (i.e., lexical aspect) than by the grammatical aspect of the verb. In the case of predicate nominals, a feature showing limitation of the action (such as one with temporal boundaries) promotes use of the instrumental; unlimited action promotes use of the nominative. As a series of discrete events, iteratives are most strongly limited, followed by perfectives; simple imperfectives are unlimited (see chart 2.4.1.1)

Chart 2.4.1.1. Timberlake 1982: 326 on case assignment and aspect

metafeature	unlimited	<———>	limited
semantic features of predicate	permanent actual		temporary counterfactual
aspect	impf $_{simple}$	pf.	impf $_{iterative}$
morphology	nom ?instr	nom †instr[10]	†nom instr

(In Hopper, Paul J., ed., *Tense-aspect: Between semantics and pragmatics,* © John Benjamins Co., 1982. Reprinted with permission of the publisher)

For tense sequencing, Timberlake argues that semantic classes of stative vs. process verbs can be predicted using the feature "synchronized vs. nonsynchronized" but not by using the opposition "perfective vs. imperfective aspect". He defines "synchronization" as the matching of two actions in time; here it relates tense in a subordinate clause (the embedded verb) to the action in the main or governing clause (the matrix verb) that come into play when the matrix verb is in the past tense. Nonsynchronized verbs (simple imperfectives or perfectives) govern relative tense (present tense) in embedded clauses, whereas synchronized verbs (iterative imperfectives) govern absolute tense more often (see chart 2.4.1.2).

Much of the structuralist argument for the grammatical invariance of aspect revolves around the regular correspondence of aspect with formal elements.

---

[10] The dagger (†) in this chart and in chart 2.4.1.2 indicates that the form is acceptable but not preferable; the question mark (?) indicates that the form is marginally acceptable.

Chart 2.4.1.2. After Timberlake 1982: 322 on aspect and tense sequencing

metafeature	nonsynchronized	<———>	synchronized
semantic features of predicate	stative		process
aspect	impf $_{simple}$	pf.	impf $_{iterative}$
morphology	present ?past	present ?past	†present past

(In Hopper, Paul J., ed., *Tense-Aspect: Between semantics and pragmatics,* © John Benjamins Co., 1982. Reprinted with permission of the publisher.)

Timberlake damages the structuralist model by using formal criteria that are clearly related to aspect and yet are met not by aspectual oppositions but by verbal characteristics outside the grammatical aspectual distinction (in this case, lexical-semantic groupings). Moreover, since both of these morphological categories—relative tense and nominativity vs. instrumentality—are intuitively connected with verbal features like temporality, the logical conclusion is that nonaspectual predicate groupings are more basic than aspectual ones in the categorization of verbal action.

In "The Temporal Schemata of Russian Predicates" Timberlake sets up an aspectual system that derives from a more basic notion of action contour. He bases his analysis on a type of "sighting" of an act using three points in time to evaluate the nature of the action as stative, active, or result-oriented (which includes achievement and accomplishment). By grounding lexical classes in a synthesis of contour and perspective, he avoids the fragmentation common to the lexical approach, whereby one is left with seemingly arbitrary groupings of predicates into classes that act alike, without any clear idea of why these particular divisions should be crucial ones in the verbal system. The system also brings together the lexical approach (action contour) and discourse (presupposition about the point of view of the action and the way it will be perceived) in a fairly simple package. However, as Timberlake notes in "Temporal Schemata," his analysis has not dealt with some of the less appetizing problems in aspect, such as the general factual usage of imperfective verbs. Further elaboration of this idea will be the test of it as a system.

2.4.2. Durst-Andersen 1992

In his monograph *Mental Grammar: Russian Aspect and Related Issues,* Durst-Andersen applies cognitive linguistic and child language development theory to the question of Russian aspect in specific and to the larger question of aspect's place in verbal systems.

Durst-Andersen begins from the premise that humans perceive two basic types of situations: *processes* and *states*. The latter are inherently *stable* pictures, where all parties are static; the former are *instable* pictures, where some motion takes place against a static background. Our ability to compare and link situations yields a third possibility: we may link a process (MOTHER CARRIES CHILD) and a state (CHILD LIES IN BED) to produce a complex portrait of an *event:* MOTHER PUT CHILD TO BED. The situations are linked by invoking *telicity:* MOTHER CARRIED CHILD FOR THE PURPOSE OF PUTTING CHILD TO BED. Thus, telicity is not an inherent component of either the process or the state; it comes from the linkage of the two into an event, a linkage that we are prompted to make by comparing divergent situations (Durst-Andersen 1992: 51-66).

Such linkages are also, Durst-Andersen proposes, of use in constructing models of how we assimilate and organize states, processes and events into longer stories that reflect our perception of reality. In his account, our brain stores memories of past situations as either *films* or *photographs,* corresponding to whether we witnessed the situations as processes or states. We also compact these memories using a sort of "event notation": if a thief steals a watch, the presence of a watch is a state. The notion of an event (I STOLE THE WATCH) is a shorthand for a comparison the thief makes between earlier nonpossession and current possession of the watch; what is currently relevant is the presence of the watch, although the thief still has available a film of the process of stealing. However, for the moment he can put this film into deep storage, as it is not particularly relevant to the present (Durst-Andersen 1992: 93-95).

Durst-Andersen proposes that humans link states to other states by positing intermediate situations or anterior states to provide, respectively, methods and motives. These linkages he likens to inscriptions on a film cannister or on the back of a photograph, whose purpose is to reconcile differing views of reality. This process of reconciliation and reevaluation must be ongoing, so as to reflect the constant new input we receive. A complex flow chart shows how situations are linked and then evaluated so that they end up stored in our memory either as states (the final product of a state or an event), which are part of our present world picture, or processes (the final product of a process), which are part of our past world picture but need not have relevance for the present (Durst-Andersen 1992: 95-96).

The view of aspect proposed in Durst-Andersen's book, then, is both lexical and contextual in its approach. While his model rests on the shape and form of situations, it also must account for the necessity and sufficiency of actions to produce situations, and this leads Durst-Andersen into territory more reminiscent of traditional aspectology. In the second half of his monograph, Durst-Andersen explains how traditional problems of aspectology can be explained by reference to his lexical models when considered against some of the presuppositions and implications encoded in various situations.

Both Timberlake and Durst-Andersen, then, take lexical "pictures" of verbal action as the basis for aspect but acknowledge the influence of context and discourse on aspectual choice. For Timberlake, context and discourse are integrated into his original model; for Durst-Andersen, they represent a separate set of concerns which he appends to his basic cognitive model. Durst-Andersen's approach, based as it is on mental "pictures" of acts and on how the brain itself understands verbal acts and processes them into language, is initially more appealing than the more abstract system presented by Timberlake, but this appeal comes at a price. In the end, Durst-Andersen's analysis, while more complete and possibly more accurate in the way it maps the brain's perception of action, depends on a baroque array of terms, formulae and multistep processes; some simplified form of this analysis, which gave the same results, would be desirable. In this respect, Timberlake's analysis can serve as a "shorthand" for much of Durst-Andersen's theory; it yields much the same results with less work, mainly because it does not attempt to model the brain's response to verbal action in as comprehensive a fashion.

2.5. ASPECT AS A DISCOURSE FUNCTION

A growing area of aspectology is the investigation of aspect as a discourse function; its proponents see aspect primarily as a means of expressing notions of presupposition, focus, and connectedness that are shaped at the level of the utterance and find reflection in one of a number of categories. Three such recent approaches—Gasparov's, Chvany's, and Chaput's—are representative of the ways aspect can be reinterpreted as a function of discourse instead of grammar. Whereas Gasparov relies on a system that strongly recalls a reworking of structuralist binary oppositions, Chvany integrates discrete discourse and lexical functions into a complex hierarchy, and Chaput relies on an understanding of the speaker's presuppositions and the respondent's reaction to them to predict aspectual usage.

2.5.1. Gasparov 1990

The attaching of overarching, all-encompassing meanings to each aspect has been portrayed as inherent and unique to grammatical approaches to aspect, but need not be so. Boris Gasparov has promulgated a theory that begins with a binary opposition but that avoids the central marked–unmarked distinction of Jakobson and Forsyth and rejects a meaning-based approach to aspect. Instead, Gasparov posits "two different world outlooks constituting two opposite modi of presentation of reality in language" (Gasparov 1990: 194). He defines two different perspectives: external-segmenting (perfective) and internal-continuous (imperfective), where the point of departure for the narrator predicates a particular view of action as discrete and bounded or process- and experience-oriented. This is a more fully explicated version of arguments presented by Isačenko (1960: 131-134) and others such as Dostál (1954: 17-18).

By referring aspect to the speaker's "state of mind," Gasparov accomplishes two important goals with a single stroke. First, the need for precise definitions of aspectual meaning are rendered superfluous; second, the question of the primacy of aspect becomes irrelevant, since aspect is here merely a reflection of a deeper-level distinction. Gasparov's theory is intuitively satisfying, because it captures in a readily comprehensible form the discourse-oriented rationalizations of aspectual usage often promulgated by native speakers. For this reason, it deserves careful examination from a critical perspective.

The morphological form Gasparov's discourse opposition takes is clear (perfective vs. imperfective aspect), but its relation to other phenomena is not always discernable. Gasparov presents both a subjective–objective axis, which presumably refers to the deeper-level distinction, and a process–result axis, which presumably refers to the surface (aspectual meaning) distinction. However, the two axes are often used interchangeably, as if the secondary process–result explanation were equal to the subjective–objective one. Second, the nature of these modi of presentation remains elusive. It is never clear to what extent these positions are voluntarily adopted by the speaker or determined by previous or expected context. Gasparov acknowledges this with his choice of deliberately neutral terminology and elocution; when he refers to "modi" or to the speaker who "assumes an external (objective) perspective" (Gasparov 1990: 194-195), the language is carefully chosen so as not to touch the issue of volition.

More troubling is the fact that in several areas, Gasparov's analysis relies on an implicit privative opposition, which he has already rejected. In his treatment of the general factual imperfective *(—Vy čitali^I ètu knigu? —Da, čital^I.* ' "Have you read^I this book?" "Yes, I've read^I it." '), Gasparov's argument for the aspectual assignment of this class rests first on the fact that it does not fit the perfective "mold" and is thus assigned to the imperfective fold of meanings, even though it does not fit there particularly well either. This treatment is reminiscent of the marked–unmarked opposition of perfective and imperfective in structuralist work (Gasparov 1990: 198).

In order for this theory to compete successfully with the grammatical theories of aspect, a more detailed mapping of this discourse opposition onto particular sentence types and situations is needed. In the this version of the model, Gasparov does not differentiate formal verbal categories in their treatment; it is not clear whether this is a matter for further study or whether this is unnecessary. Questions are not treated as a form of discourse, even in the section discussing the general factual meaning of the imperfective. Further explanation of the varied meanings and functions of the imperfective and perfective could account for the full range of usages found.

2.5.2. Chvany 1984, 1990

The system proposed in Chvany 1984 makes use of two sliding scales that have numerical values assigned to their components. On the predicate level, Chvany uses a Vendleresque verb classification (see chart 2.5.2.1). On the discourse level, the relation between the predicate and the utterance as a whole is assigned four different values based on a series of 0-4 scales, collectively referred to as the "discourse saliency" of the predicate (see chart 2.5.2.2). Predicates thus receive a value that determines their aspect based not only on factors encoded in the verb, but also those grounded in other, sentence-wide factors.

Chart 2.5.2.1. Chvany's classification of predicates (1990:219)

4	he reached the summit/drew a circle	accomplishment/culmination
3	she arrived/fainted	event/accomplishment
2	I was working	activity
1	they worked at MIT	habit/uncounted iteration
0	Boris knew Ivan	state

(In Thelin, Nils B. ed., *Verbal aspect in discourse,* © John Benjamins Co., 1990. Reprinted with permission of the publisher.)

Chart 2.5.2.2. Chvany's saliency hierarchy (simplified presentation)

Foreground (4 >)	Background (< 0)
And related indexes	And related indexes
action affecting individual	action affecting object
main clause	subordinate clause/verbal adverb
direct speech/dialogue	introduction thereof
nominative case	oblique case
indicative mood	hypotheticals, 'irrealis'
(others)	(others)

Chvany uses this interaction of hierarchies to advance the claim that perfectivity can be induced by a number of different factors and that there is therefore no inherent "perfectivity of result" encoded in the predicate, as under the grammatical understanding of aspect. This claim is dealt with more directly in Chvany 1990, which makes the relationships between context (narrative and non-narrative) and lexical features more explicit.

Although they both begin from an attempt to integrate lexical and discourse-based analysis, Chvany's system is in many respects the inverse of Timberlake's. Timberlake's strives for synthesis; Chvany's is deliberately heterogeneous, involving many different hierarchies in determining a verb's aspect. Her analysis exposes the complexity of the factors in aspectual choice and explains the multitude of potential factors that give rise to the often seemingly odd and arbitrary aspectual usages attested in Russian. One unstated but obvious point that increases this theory's palatability is that in many instances aspectual choices are more or less automatic; not every speech event requires a hierarchy of this complexity to determine aspect. If we add this disclaimer to Chvany's saliency hierarchy, the number of factors involved can in many instances be reduced to a more manageable number.

2.5.3. Chaput 1984

Chaput has examined one of the more troublesome areas for aspectology—the problem of aspect in commands, questions, and responses—from the perspective of pragmatics. She uses not only the speaker's perspective, but the speaker's response to the perceived perspective of the listener in formulating her analysis. In this way her approach resembles Yokoyama's dialogic approach to the study of word order; in both, the listener's perceived state of mind and the speaker's attempt to respond to it become crucial factors in the analysis.

Central to Chaput's argument is the speakers' manipulation of volition, obligation, and closure. The latter operates both on a lexical level (telic vs. atelic acts) and on a propositional level. (Chaput's "real time limit" (RTL) is defined as a moment past which the action referred to ceases to be associated with real times and expectations; she cites an example where someone is asked if they have been to the post office yet, with different aspects favored depending on whether the post office is still open or not and what the chances are of still getting there.) She states that volition plays a role in determining aspectual choice less often than other factors, but she nonetheless notes exchanges like (6) and by extension (7), where the presence (I) or absence (P) of volition determines the aspect.

(6)   Model: Ne lomaj^I karandaš! 'Don't break^I the pencil (intentionally)!' vs.
       Ne slomaj^P karandaš! 'Don't break^P the pencil (accidentally)!'

(7)   Target: —Možet byt' ja smogu prostudit'sja^P. Togda ja ne dolžen budu pojti.
       —Ne prostuživajsja^I, ne stoit. ' "Maybe I can catch^P a cold. Then I won't have to go." "Don't catch^I a cold (intentionally), it's not worth it." ' (Chaput 1984: 225)

Obligation is a subjective concept, and Chaput claims that speakers can use aspect to impose and accept obligation (perfective aspect) or to shy away from and deny it (imperfective aspect). While it is difficult to deny closure of events in the lexical sphere (contexts where lexical closure can be manipulated will be limited), it is not difficult to see where notions of propositional closure can become a field for contention, using aspect to deny closure (imperfective aspect) or admit it (perfective aspect).

Chaput finds that only where speaker and addressee are presumed to agree on obligation and the closure of RTL is the perfective used; in other cases (disagreement in either or both components, or agreement that neither obligation nor closure is present), the imperfective is used. Action type, however, has no effect on the conclusion that a shared presupposition of obligation and RTL is necessary to invoke the perfective.

Chaput's model draws attention to a little-understood part of aspectology and to the consideration of volition as a possible component of aspectual usage—something ignored in other discourse-oriented models, where it should be an important issue. However, given that it was devised as an answer to a single problem, this theory requires further testing and elaboration The question remains open as to whether one needs a pragmatic analysis of aspect or whether a nonpragmatic, context-based division—in which perfectives emphasize connectedness, continuation, linkage of events to each other, while imperfectives emphasize isolatedness, lack of continuity, the action itself as opposed to its consequences—would serve as well.

2.6. SUMMARY OF ANALYSES OF ASPECT

Each of the three major categories discussed above has made a substantial contribution to the debate on aspect's nature and place in the Russian language. The categories are far from homogeneous, as is obvious from the variety of approaches found in each one, but general strengths and shortcomings can be found for each group (see chart 2.6.1.)

The grammatical approach is best appreciated for its predictive value in numerous simple formal tests. It addresses the heterogeneity of the imperfective by use of the markedness hypothesis, which also accounts for the relatively limited scope of the perfective. However, it does not cover all usages adequately for both aspects and does not account for places where the binary privative opposition seems not to function or to become less important than other factors.

The lexical approach's best claim to primacy is its ability to tie together aspect and action contour, which are intuitively similar phenomena that scholars have often separated sharply for the sake of theoretical concerns. In integrating these two concepts, it writes basic differences due to lexical meaning into the rules governing aspect. Furthermore, the lexical approach proves a better predictor of aspectual choice in certain other formal tests and copes with sentence-level issues like nominative vs. instrumental and the tense of embedded clauses. On the negative side, lexical analyses can leave a sense of fragmentation or lack of overall rationale in defining multitudinous categories, and none of them have yet provided adequate explanations for phenomena like the general factual imperfective.

Discourse approaches to aspect are the only ones to provide mechanisms for sorting out contextual variation of aspect where multiple possibilities exist. Furthermore, they allow natural metaissues such as prominence, knowledge sets, and presuppositions to have a role in determining aspect, whereas these issues are systematically excluded from other approaches. Thanks to this attention to context, examples can be drawn from actual speech situations and larger written contexts.

Chart 2.6.1. Pluses and minuses of approaches to aspect

GRAMMATICAL

+
- accounts for simple tests, such as compound future, infinitives after modal verbs, aspect with expressions such as *tri mesjaca* 'for three months', *za nedelju* 'in a week', etc.
- successfully links many meanings of the imperfective
- fits in well with structuralist theories of language
- addresses the general limitedness of the scope of the perfective

−
- does not cover all meanings of perfective and imperfective adequately
- does not account for places where the inherent "primacy" of the imperfective–perfective opposition seems not to function or to be less basic than other features

LEXICAL

+
- ties together related areas of aspect and action contour, which intuitively should be related
- writes basic differences due to lexical meaning into the rules governing aspect
- copes with sentence-level issues like nominative vs. instrumental, tense of embedded clauses
- accounts for a different series of results in other formal tests of aspect

−
- can leave a sense of fragmentation, lack of overall rationale in some analyses
- does not handle general factual meaning

DISCOURSE

+
- provides mechanism(s) for sorting out contextual variation of aspect where multiple possibilities exist
- allows natural meta-issues (prominence, knowledge sets, presuppositions) to have a role in determining aspect
- is drawn from actual speech situations and written contexts

−
- can ignore larger coherence in aspectual system
- can introduce an unmanageable number of variables into the picture, all for the sake of producing a two-way choice

Discourse approaches can, however, ignore a larger coherence in the aspectual system and can introduce an unwieldy number of variables into the picture all for the sake of producing a two-way choice.

2.7. SYNCHRONIC MODELS IN HISTORICAL ANALYSES

The researcher who tries to lift any one of the above approaches for use with the historical language immediately runs into a number of obstacles. Some methods turn out to be inappropriate for studying a dead language; others can be used but are of questionable worth when applied specifically to Old Russian.

2.7.1. Discourse models in historical analysis

Discourse methods are difficult to apply to historical texts. They often rely on a "feeling" a native speaker has about a particular form, particularly what degree of urgency or connectedness it conveys. Without native speakers, the researcher has to apply Modern Russian standards to the older text—a shaky proposition at best.

To make matters more complicated, Old Russian texts give the reader fewer extra clues as to their emotional content. This is perhaps the reason why, when recommending an approach to aspect that takes more account of context, studies like Silina 1982 recommend only studying certain narrow and easily definable contextual situations, such as the aspectual complements of Old Russian phasal verbs (*načinati–načati* 'begin', *končati–končiti* 'finish') and the use of aspect with certain adverbs *(mnogo* 'a lot', *často* 'often', *rědko* 'rarely').

Contextual study can give us more information than this, however, without getting hopelessly mired in discourse considerations. Fairly basic contextual categories such as iterative, durative, and progressive, as described by Timberlake, can be determined with a reasonable degree of surety for many occurrences. Knowing the contexts in which a verb is used, we have a much clearer picture of its range of meanings and functions, both lexical and aspectual. In addition, context can often (but not always) give us discourse information about features such as conativity (the failure of an act to reach its stated goal), volition, and expectation that are central to understanding the development of the Russian aspectual system.

However, focusing on these more straightforward types of contextual analysis has its problems as well. Context and lexical content overlap, and it is often difficult to sort out whether a particular reading comes from the nature of the predicate (i.e., from "inside" the predicate) or from the surrounding context (i.e., from "outside" the predicate). One symptom of this difficulty is that I have named a type of predicate that usually indicates a static condition ("stative"), yet I have also named a context that does this ("generalized"). In a similar vein, I have labelled contexts "progressive" when they describe a situation that is ongoing (possibly while some other act is applied); yet I have also named a lexical type that expresses action continuing for some period of time ("processes"). At a certain point it becomes difficult to tell what parts of the sentence are included in the predicate and what is part of the background surrounding it. Kučera's approach can be said to subsume context entirely in the predicate (witness his use of the term "situations", i.e., metapredicates, such as *raz v god on pravdu skažet* 'he'll tell the truth once a year'). I have decided not to take this position, but this means taking care to define what is meant by the "predicate" and what is meant by "context," and simply accepting the overlap between context and the lexicon as a hazard—albeit one that in a sense proves the necessity of considering both in formulating an approach to aspect. As for the strict definitions, I will consider objects of the verb as part of the predicate and hence part of the lexical meaning of the predicate.[11] Adverbs, other predicates in the sentence, and narrative considerations, to the extent they are helpful, will be considered part of the context. Areas like singularity vs. plurality of objects and subjects are, however, ill-defined, since a plural subject and/or object can induce a completely different reading of a sentence and can rightly be considered areas of overlap between the lexicon and context.

2.7.2. Grammatical models in historical analysis

Grammatical approaches have been applied to Old Russian aspect, but the results, in my opinion, have been uneven. Many grammatical approaches to Old Russian have started from the assumption that an aspectual distinction roughly paralleling Modern Russian's already exists for the vast majority of verbs. (The class of motion verbs is usually cited as an exception and is said to adhere to an older determinate–indeterminate axis.) Verbs that show fluctuation in usage are classed as biaspectual; the different contexts in which they are found are sorted out respectively as showing perfective or imperfective meaning. Aspect in Russian is thus an *a priori* structure; the history of aspect is the history of historical forms coming gradually more and more closely into line with a Modern Russian aspectual system. This approach assumes a grammatical aspectual system for Old Russian simply because many forms in Old Russian look similar to the Modern Russian ones, despite the fact that one cannot subject the Old Russian data to the kind of rigorous testing for grammatical regularity that Modern Russian has undergone.

This proposal would be acceptable if the deviations in Old Russian aspect from the modern plan were minimal; I could then invoke Occam's razor to claim insufficient evidence for a major reanalysis. Given the number of differences in Old Russian from the Modern Russian plan, however, it does not seem productive to start off by asserting the existence of a grammatical system.

However, it will be useful to check for grammaticality at various periods in the history of Old Russian to see when a grammatical system comes into play. This can be done by applying some of the classic tests for grammatical aspect, with appropriate modifications for use with historical texts.

The most important of these modifications concerns the regularity of aspectual distinctions across tenses. In a Modern Russian model of grammatical aspect, regular distinctions in past tense usage are paralleled in the non-past system by the

---

[11] This is consonant with work done on equating multiple meanings with differing valence patterns, such as that of Jurij Apresjan.

existence of a compound future assigned exclusively to the imperfective aspect, and a rigid separation of functions in the non-past tense between future (perfective) and present (imperfective). A few well-established sets of exceptions (the use of the imperfective non-past for an immediate future and the use of the perfective non-past for the so-called "exemplary" function) are allowed.

In Old Russian, we will forego the most clear-cut of these tests—the existence of the analytic future with the auxiliary verb *budu* 'will be'—because it is not well-attested until later on. While Old Russian does have analytic future forms with *xotěti* 'want', they are not found exclusively with one aspect, and thus cannot serve as a test of aspectuality. However, the tests for future and present function of simple non-past forms will still be valid, and my analysis will touch on this point quite often.[12]

2.7.3. Lexical models in historical analysis

As long as the meanings of most Old Russian words can be readily established, lexical factors will be useful in tracking aspectual development in Old Russian. Maslov and others have suggested that aspect in Russian develops from the interaction of the determinate–indeterminate opposition with the terminative–aterminative opposition characteristic of verbs with Aktionsart prefixes (Maslov 1961: 190). If Maslov is correct, then a verb's position in these oppositions depends in large measure on its lexical meaning, and we would expect to find verbs participating in the aspectual system to different degrees and in different ways depending on the lexical groups they belong to. It will be important to test this hypothesis by paying close attention to how closely verbal behavior correlates with lexical class.

I have decided, however, not to use the lexical categories proposed in Maslov 1961 for Prehistoric Russian and Old Russian. In attempting to justify the lexical nature of Old Russian aspect, Maslov linked his lexical categories to morphological features (specifically, to basic verbal suffixes like {-a-} in *čitati*, {-ě-} in *smotrěti*). While this method provides a powerful argument for his hypothesis, it ultimately springs from the article's focus on Prehistoric Slavic and is less useful for attested languages than purely semantic groupings of lexical items because it draws distinctions where they may not be necessary or useful and ignores other distinctions that may prove crucial. I have chosen instead to work from a combination of the systems presented in Maslov 1948 and Kučera 1983, which treat the aspectual properties of Modern Russian lexical groupings. The resulting system follows Kučera's broader groupings of telicity, while adding a second type of distinction inspired by Maslov's classification.

---

[12] Using the time reference of non-past forms as a marker of Old Russian aspect is not particularly controversial, although Galton (1976: 297-298) is one of a few scholars who dismiss this sort of evidence as "worthless." See chapter 3 for a fuller discussion of Galton's views.

Neither Maslov 1948 nor Kučera 1983 is wholly transferrable to Old Russian. First, several of Maslov's classes depend on the ability to distinguish precisely whether a verb can have a conative function *(sdaval^I èkzamen, no ne sdal^P ego* 'he took^I the exam, but didn't pass^P it'*)*. Lacking native speakers of Old Russian, I would have to undertake one of two dubious practices: either depend on finding conative examples in texts to reliably assign a verb to a particular class, assigning them elsewhere if the examples couldn't be found; or use Modern Russian equivalents to categorize Old Russian verbs. In such instances it will be advantageous to have broader categories, as proposed by Kučera. Second, the welter of distinctions Maslov proposes may not be necessary for Old Russian, as its diversity may obscure the overall tendencies. Third, in his analysis of telic acts Maslov relies on an inherent comparison between the perfective and imperfective verbs, which makes analyzing any single verb without its counterpart quite difficult. A system that relies on easily observable distinctions in each component will serve us better for Old Russian, where pairs are not always as bountifully attested. Furthermore, it makes the analyses of telic predicates conform to the analyses of atelic and post-telic (perfective) predicates that he proposes.

What is most valuable in Maslov's analysis—and lacking in Kučera's—are four fine distinctions. First, telic predicates that categorically prohibit fulfillment of telos (like *iskat'* 'search for') may behave differently from other telic predicates. Maslov thus groups them with statives and other atelics; while we may not want to go this far, it will be useful to hold them apart from other telic predicates.

Second, Maslov's system has a clear place for predicates that have absolutely no progressive component, such as *prixodit'* 'arrive', and for predicates where progression only appears as a type of iteration (the semelfactives, like *streljat'* 'shoot'). Kučera has no clear place for predicates like this in his system; presumably they would fall into the category of "End-in-sight Processes (Achievements in Process)," but as he correctly points out, the verbs he uses to found this category, like *dostigat'* 'reach', often appear in progressive contexts when achievement of telos is imminent.[13]

Third, and on a more general level, in lumping both members of an aspectual pair together in the same class Maslov acknowledges the interplay between imperfectives and perfectives to a much greater extent than does Kučera. Kučera suggests aspectual connections through similarity of naming conventions between processes and their corresponding events, but the effect is to equate pairs like *dostigat'–dostič'* 'reach' or *pisat'–napisat'* 'write' with pairs like *sidet'–posidet'* 'sit–sit for a while' or *žit'–prožit'* 'live—live through', when one of the main points of lexical analysis is to separate "true" aspectual pairs from those separated by a much wider gulf in meaning. I will therefore treat some of Kučera's imperfective categories along with their perfective counterparts, while leaving others distinct.

Fourth, Kučera does not tackle the problem of verbs like *videt'* 'see', which seem to be stative but behave aspectually quite differently from statives. These are

---

[13] As it turns out, this distinction will not be important for simplex verbs.

handled in Maslov's analysis by analyzing telos as a point that moves from infinity to ground zero in the scope of the predicate's meaning. The gradations are roughly: impossibly distant (*iskat'* 'search for'), notably distant (*umirat'* 'die'), partially attained with each performance (*pisat' stat'ju* 'write an article'), and attained as soon as the act is said to have begun (*videt'* 'see'). Maslov includes in this last category verbs like *sudit'* 'judge', *prosit'* 'ask' and asserts that for such predicates, sentences of the type *umiral^I, no ne umer^P* 'he was dying^I, but did not die^P' are impossible (1948: 314); we cannot say **govoril^I, čto pridet, no ne skazal^P, čto pridet* '*he was saying^I he would come, but did not say^P he would come' or **videl^I ego, no ne uvidel^P ego* '*he was seeing^I him, but did not see^P him'.

However, the issue here is not a single continuity of telicity, since calling acts like *videt'* 'see' telic is a far stretch for the definition of telicity. Furthermore, the idea that all of them reach telos instantly is not consistent with fact; one could hardly argue that *prosit'* actually contains a request before the request is finished. If we accept Maslov's formulation, why not also say that statives like *stojat'* 'stand' have reached their "telos" of "being in a standing position" as soon as the act commences? Some better definition needs to be found.

One possibility is to take into account the minimum duration of an act required to say that the act takes place. Some acts require that an act continue for some perceptible period of time; in this group are all acts describing physical processes (*stojat'* 'stand', *spat'* 'sleep', *pisat'* 'write', *padat'* 'fall, be falling', *umirat'* 'die, be dying'). Others can be said to exist without any minimum duration at all; in a sense, then, these acts can always be reduced down to a single point in time and are *punctualizable*. As compared to the *nonpunctualizable* acts, they tend to represent acts that do not objectively exist or that require an act of human perception to exist; they are abstract deeds.

This notion of minimum duration can also be said to have an effect on the aspectual pair, just as Maslov's notion of instantaneous telicity does. If we accept that these predicates differ by virtue of their innate ability to represent a punctual act, then the basic shape of each such predicate encompasses a range of acts, from instantaneous to drawn out, all with the same lexical meaning (*ja videl^I* 'I saw^I' and *ja uvidel^P* 'I glimpsed^P' do not differ in their ability to express an instantaneous act). By contrast, other telic predicates do not express punctuality unless telos is attained (thus *on umiral^I* 'he was dying^I' and *on umer^P* 'he died^P' differ in their ability to express a punctual act, and that ability is conferred with the other restrictions that perfectivity places on the act). These predicates can resemble on the one hand the *prixodit'*-type predicate, with the insistence on completion being attained from the outset, and on the other hand the *stojat'*-type predicate, where telos is respectively irrelevant.

It remains to explain what communicative acts like *govorit'–skazat'* 'say' are doing in this group. After all, an utterance certainly takes some minimal amount of time, so this grouping may seem unorthodox. I argue that such predicates are punctualizable not because the action of *speaking* is uninterruptable, or cannot be broken off uncompleted, but rather because the idea of *saying* implies that the listener perceives or at least assumes *from the very first moment of speaking* that the speaker is offering a whole or coherent text. In this way, these predicates depend on a type of perception similar to the other abstract acts and verbs of perception in this class. In Russian, then, predicates like the one in *On govoril^I časami* 'He talked^I for hours' are atelic and nonpunctual, whose perfective analogues are created with Aktionsart prefixes, whereas predicates like the one in *On govoril^I nam ob ètom* 'He told^I/was telling^I us about it' are punctualizable and telic and have a perfective analogue in *On skazal^P nam ob ètom* 'He told^P us about it'.

A caveat to using lexical systems, which can be seen in this explanation of *govorit'* 'talk/say' and was mentioned earlier in the discussion of Vendler 1967, is that a single verb can occur in various lexical groups. For instance, the Modern Russian verb *pisat'* 'write' is an atelic action in (8), but is telic with incremental progress toward completion in (9).

(8) Ivan—pisatel': on pišet rasskazy i romany.
     'John is a writer: he writes stories and novels.'

(9) Ivan uže dva dnja pišet ètu stat'ju.
     'John has been writing that article for two days already.'

In (8), the verb *pišet* 'writes' describes a profession or habit. Whether or not John is physically writing at any given time is immaterial. In (9), however, *pišet* describes the creation of a particular work in progress. Unlike (8), this action is telic, but it is also realized incrementally, with each episode of writing theoretically bringing John closer to the completion of his article. The verb *pisat'* 'write', then, will fall into at least two categories, depending on the meaning invoked. These categories have an impact on the verb's aspectual behavior: for instance, whether it perfectivizes and whether a secondary imperfective is possible as a substitute.

Maslov and Kučera both address this concern, but for Maslov it is more of a sidelight to his system, whereas for Kučera the lexical plasticity of verbs and the importance of their complements is central to his concept of verbal aspect. Needless to say, this plasticity complicates the analysis of verbs immeasurably, but it is clearly a necessary component to the analysis. It is therefore important to keep a consistent distinction between the **verb**, which is the sum of all available usages of a set of forms, and the **predicate**, which is a narrower classification encompassing only specific usage patterns. According to the traditional model, aspect is assigned to an entire verb, and we may safely speak of a Russian verb as being "perfective" or "imperfective." Lexical classes, as seen above in (8) and (9), refer more properly to predicates; although there are verbs whose usages fall entirely within the scope of a single lexical class, there are many verbs that fall into multiple lexical classes.

With all of the above in mind, it is possible to create a system (outlined in chart 2.7.3.1) that incorporates the features of Maslov's and Kučera's systems most suited to an analysis of Old Russian.

Chart 2.7.3.1. An axis model of lexical groups (using Old Russian verbs)

| *Punctual, atelic* | – TELIC | *Non-punctual, atelic* |

stative:
стояти 'stand'

punctual atelic:
видѣти 'see'
дивити ся 'be amazed'

atelic action:
блюсти 'guard'

+PUNCTUAL ─────────────────────── –PUNCTUAL

accretive telic:
ставити 'build'
писати 'write'

telic :   conative:
воевати   искати
'war'   'search'

punctual telic: highly telic:
судити 'judge'   умирати 'die'
просити 'ask'

indivisible:
достигати 'attain'

semelfactive:
стрѣляти 'shoot'

| *Punctual, telic* | + TELIC | *Non-punctual, telic* |
| *(obligatory punctuality)* | *(possible punctuality)* | *(punctuality impossible)* |

First, I will use the types of telicity proposed by Kučera; this yields a typology of imperfectivity that does not depend on an interplay between perfective (event) and imperfective (process) verbs. Predicates are classified as telic or atelic, and telic predicates are then labeled achievement-telic or accomplishment-telic. Kučera's categories are strung along the y-axis of the diagram, which runs from atelic at the top to telic at the bottom. We will then need to add a number of extra groups to account for some verbal behavior in Modern Russian and Old Russian that does not fit Kučera's typology. First, the group of accomplishment telics deserves further articulation; we can distinguish subgroups that express gradually accruing action, like *pisat'* 'write', and those that express a stronger sense of telos, like *umirat'* 'die'. The remaining predicates in this class will lie somewhere in the middle. Second, we need to account for the usage patterns of verbs like *iskat'* 'search for', which are highly telic but noncompletable; we can either add these into the telic group or keep them aside.

Special categories are set aside for verbs that constitutionally cannot express process, either because they are naturally instantaneous or because they represent a summation of the sort that does not even allow an achievement reading.

The last classification problem is what to do with punctualizable predicates like those from *videt'* 'see', *sudit'* 'judge', *prosit'* 'ask'? The distinction of punctual and nonpunctual is the x-axis of the graph, with obligatory punctuality lying to the left, punctualizability to the left of the axis, and nonpunctualizability to the right of it. Adding a second axis to the system neatly sidesteps the problems that result when all the predicates are lined up in a single row by telicity only, which inevitably gives a misleading picture of their relationships to one another and to additional factors that contribute to their semantic makeup.

This resolution of the issue has several advantages. It retains the simplicity of Kučera's approach while tackling some problems raised by Maslov's categorizations. By relying on a definition inherent in the lexical meaning of the predicate, it eliminates the subtle pairedness bias of Maslov's system, where no predicate can be evaluated without respect to its aspectual partner (or on the basis of its lack of one). Its categories can be ranked on a scale of telicity, from absent to weak to strong, which interacts with a scale of acceptability of punctuality. The system is thus well supported by other factors and combined with the overlapping contextual categories mentioned above, will serve as a basis for analyzing data in later chapters.

3. The History of Russian and Slavic Aspect

3.0. DIRECTIONS OF HISTORICAL RESEARCH

Research into the history of Russian aspect falls into two distinct lines of inquiry, which I will call the "aspectual provenance" line and the "aspectual development" line. The former line looks mainly backward, from the historical period into the prehistoric; its goal is to seek out the origins of the current quasi-grammatical system of aspect, and it has concentrated on determining how much of the modern system is a legacy from Proto-Indo-European and how much is a Slavic or Balto-Slavic innovation. The latter line is forward-looking, since it accepts the modern language as having a grammatical aspectual system, and evaluates the older stages of the language against it.

The existence of these two lines of inquiry has meant that older texts have often been the object of study, but rarely has this research aimed to describe the texts' own aspectual systems. In the aspectual provenance line of research, Old Russian texts are only a starting point for research on the genesis of aspect in the protolanguage; in the aspectual development line, scholars have (with a few exceptions) concentrated on a few trends which make the sweep of aspectual history look more convincingly uniform in direction, while largely ignoring some of the thornier problems. The result is that the history of Russian aspect has remained tantalizingly incomplete, with a wealth of works devoted to prehistoric aspect and a relative paucity of research that does not impose a Modern Russian imprint on Old Russian aspect.

In aspectual provenance research, morphological clues and isolated individual examples from the Slavic daughter languages are collected and examined to yield up clues about the state of aspect in the prehistoric period. Much of the debate originally focused on the possible connections between Slavic aspect and the aspectual system reconstructed for Proto-Indo-European; those who thought such connections minimal concentrated on finding other features of the verbal system that could have given rise to aspect. One such feature that has figured prominently in the debate is a category of determinacy–indeterminacy, which in Modern Russian is restricted to motion verbs. Most of the Slavic data used in these studies came from Old Church Slavic, with some drawn from Old Russian.

With some exceptions,[1] the examples cited in these studies do not refer to any comprehensive analysis of data from a single text or series of texts; systematic analysis is eschewed in favor of reliance on isolated clues and exceptions, a standard and perfectly acceptable procedure for this sort of research. A number of studies are based entirely on secondary sources (Dostál's monograph is a frequent source).

---

[1] Notably studies by Borodič, Dostál, Budich, and Ruzicka.

The aspectual development line has concentrated on explicating the morphology of Old Russian aspect. Numerous studies and doctoral dissertations, most of which appeared in the former Soviet Union, have traced the appearance, spread, and variation of different suffixes and prefixes. This concentration on morphology reflects the difficulty of doing semantic or syntactic research into a dead language and the prevailing belief that the Old Russian aspectual system was overall so semantically similar to the Modern Russian one that such research would be redundant and unlikely to yield interesting results. Only a few studies, such as Ruzicka 1957 and Budich 1969, break this mold.

3.0.1. Periodicization and organization

This chapter reviews the contributions to the debate on the origins and development of Slavic and Russian aspect. It does not purport to be exhaustive; instead, I have selected some of the most influential and interesting works of the past fifty or sixty years. If a disproportionate number of the studies date from the 1950s, this bias merely reflects the extraordinary productivity and interest of scholars at the time.

Rather than group the studies by their viewpoint—which would be nigh impossible, since the field looks more like a continuum than like two opposing camps—I have chosen to separate them by subject matter and date. Strangely enough, scholars have rarely sought to make such a distinction, often treating studies of Old Church Slavic or Old Russian and the data from them as immediately applicable to Prehistoric Slavic. I hope that separating these types of studies will allow us to judge the authors' conclusions in the realm in which they meant their work to be judged and to decide whether or not they rate wider application.[2]

I will begin with the treatment of aspect in two historical grammars, one Russian (Borkovskij and Kuznecov 1965) and one Western (Vlasto 1986). Section 3.2 will treat the plethora of views on the origins of Slavic aspect. Section 3.3 examines the most comprehensive work on Old Church Slavic aspect, Dostál's *Studie o vidovém systému v staroslověnštině (Studies on the Aspectual System of Old Church Slavic)*. Section 3.4 discusses Silina's work as a representative of the morphological studies forming the core of work on Old Russian. Section 3.5 treats Ruzicka's *Der Verbalaspekt in der altrussischen Nestorchronik* and Budich's *Aspekt und verbale Zeitlichkeit in der I. Novgoroder Chronik*, which are among the few works to take a detailed look at the semantics of Old Russian aspect. A summary of major approaches and stumbling blocks appears in section 3.6.

---

[2] Although most of the scholars discussed below contributed more than one published article on the subject of aspect, in the interests of brevity I have taken only one publication from each author to analyze. The remaining works figure in my summaries and comments, but I do not address them directly. (One scholar does appear here twice—Kuznecov—but the reason for this is evident: a college-level textbook and a scholarly article are clearly different genres.)

3.1. ASPECT ACCORDING TO THE HANDBOOKS

Handbooks and textbooks are a useful starting point because their formulations usually reflect a conservative or prudently neutral view, and they tend to present matters in a more simplified, less ambiguous light than scholarly articles. With these necessary evils in mind, it will be interesting to see what the strengths and weaknesses are of the versions of aspectual history meant for public consumption at colleges and universities.

3.1.1. Borkovskij and Kuznecov 1965

The widely used handbook *Istoričeskaja grammatika russkogo jazyka (A Historical Grammar of the Russian Language)* takes a practical, cautious approach to the history of aspect. The section on aspect begins as follows:

> В древнерусской глагольной системе, помимо времени, был и вид, но значения видовых форм, а также отношения вида и времени во многом были иными, чем теперь. Основное видовое различие современного языка — различие совершенного и несовершенного видов, — начавшее складываться еще на праславянской почве, достаточно ясно выступало уже в древнерусском языке, хотя и с некоторыми отличиями от современного. (1965: 279) [3]

Borkovskij and Kuznecov say that in Old Russian the already extant bipolar aspectual system encompasses a wide variety of action types, which they call by Potebnja's term *stepeni dlitel'nosti* 'degrees of duration'. Under this heading they group Aktionsarten as well as other morphologically identifiable groupings in Old Russian, like certain evolutive verbs and directionality and nondirectionality of actions.[4] They then proceed through the derivational verb classes in Old Russian, showing how portions of each group express similar sorts of actions (1965: 280-284).[5] Finally, the problematic nature of assigning all prefixed verbs to the

---

[3] "In the Old Russian verbal system, beside tense, there was aspect, but the meaning of aspectual forms, and also the relations between aspect and tense, were different in many ways than they are now. The basic aspectual distinction of the modern language—the distinction between perfective and imperfective aspects—having started to form already on Proto-Slavic soil, was already clearly enough in evidence in Old Russian, although with several differences from the modern language." (This and all subsequent English quotations from this text are in my translation.) It is not clear whether their use of the term "Proto-Slavic" *(praslavjanskij)* refers to the period of Slavic linguistic unity or merely to the prehistoric era.

[4] Presumably the term *sposoby dejstvija* 'Aktionsart' is too closely bound to the Modern Russian class of verbs and prefixes it usually describes, and thus for this slightly wider concept they have chosen Potebnja's somewhat misleading term.

[5] Their work by and large attempts to treat Old Russian as a single, coherent system; with tenses, for example, paradigms are given which may be too conservative for one period and too innovative for another. While aspect has no "paradigms" to complain about,

perfective aspect is touched on, and the standard example from the Primary Chronicle is given in which geographical descriptions use apparently "perfective" verbs. The imperfect of perfective verbs is treated briefly in an added section on "aspect and tense." Two final paragraphs in the analysis present some of the problems I will touch on frequently again:

> По мнению некоторых исследователей, к сравнительно позднему времени относятся четкие разграничения значений совершенного и несовершенного видов в бесприставочных глаголах. Некоторые из них сохраняют значение обоих видов, определяемое контекстом, и до настоящего времени. Таковы в современном языке глаголы старого IV класса *женить(ся), казнить, велеть*. В древности таких глаголов было больше.
>
> Многие различия, передаваемые у нас теперь разными видами, в древности передавались различием времен, которых, как известно, было больше. Однако тот факт, что времена были небезразличны к виду, но одни в большей степени образовывались от основы таких глаголов, которые в дальнейшем, несомненно, принадлежат к совершенному виду, а другие от основы таких, которые в дальнейшем относились заведомо к несовершенному виду, говорит о том, что противопоставление совершенного и несовершенного видов в древнерусском языке уже наметилось. (1965: 284)[6]

Both statements are at the least controversial and alert the reader to ongoing debates in the field that have not yet satisfactorily been resolved.

---

this atemporal view of Old Russian causes other difficulties for their explanation of aspect. I assume that their statements refer mainly to early Old Russian, but this is never directly stated, only hinted at through the use of vague terms like "later." Typeface, often a convention for distinguishing Prehistoric Slavic (Latin type) from Old Church Slavic (old Cyrillic type) and Old Russian (new Cyrillic type), is not a helpful indicator here.

6   "According to some researchers, the sharp delimitation of meaning for the perfective and imperfective aspects of unprefixed verbs belongs to a relatively late period. Some of them retain the meanings of both aspects as determined by context down to the present day. Among them are the verbs in the modern language of Class IV: *ženit' sja* 'marry', *kaznit'* 'punish', *velet'* 'order'. There were more such verbs in olden days."

"Many differences we now convey by means of aspectual differences were formerly conveyed by temporal differences, which, as is well known, were more numerous. However, tenses were not indifferent to aspect, but rather some to a large degree were formed from roots of verbs which at least in the future would undoubtedly belong to the perfective aspect, and others were formed from roots which would belong to the imperfective aspect, and this fact testifies that the opposition of perfective and imperfective aspects was already evident in Old Russian."

Borkovskij and Kuznecov take a stand on aspect that is conservative but not close-mindedly so. Their statement that Old Russian aspect subsumes all "degrees of duration" is debatable, but at least it admits them as complicating factors. Usage questions are limited to a few well-known examples from the Primary Chronicle. This treatment is in conformity with the prevailing attitude toward aspect in Old Russian: that the aspects were well-established, dominant and pervasive from the earliest days and that, with allowances for usage differences and complicating factors, the system can be assumed to look much like that of Modern Russian.

3.1.2. Vlasto 1986

A.P. Vlasto's *A Linguistic History of Russia to the End of the Eighteenth Century* has a different emphasis in its treatment of aspect. Where Borkovskij and Kuznecov stress the continuity between Old Russian and Modern Russian aspect as grammatical categories, Vlasto stresses that this continuity exists only when aspect is treated as a broad semantic category, not a grammatical one. Vlasto's broad conception of aspect is both the most controversial point in his analysis and the foundation on which his entire hypothesis rests:

> There are only three *temporal* relations—present, past, future. Any finer distinctions which a verbal system may show, within a single voice or mood, are aspectual.... Aspect defines the mode or scope of the action (Ger. *Aktionsart*)....
>
> Early ESl. shows much the same point of development as OCS. *Aspect* is a quality of the verbal stem... A single verbal idea was usually compounded of two aspectual stems: a present and an aor./inf. .... Other aspectual differences (*Aktionsarten*) were evolved in Prehistoric Slavic by more recent processes of derivation, either suffixation, or as cpd. (analytical) formations. (1986: 238-239) [7]

Vlasto subsumes a number of discrete concepts under the heading "aspect": "grammatical" aspect as we understand it to apply to Modern Russian; various temporal limitations on the act, which we normally call Aktionsarten; lexical distinctions, such as state vs. action; and certain distinctions expressed by Old Russian tenses. His limited definition of what constitutes tense, for instance, leads him to posit extra aspects alongside the traditional perfective and imperfective. For instance, he finds a "habitual aspect" formed with the {-va-} suffix, which creates verbs like *byvati* 'be regularly'; still, he says, this verb is "essentially durative (imperfective) and therefore lacking an aorist," calling into question exactly what these categories are if "habitual," "durative," and "imperfective" all overlap to this degree. He also designates a "perfect aspect" with present, future, and past tenses (*esm' dal"* 'I have given', *budu dal"* 'I will have given', *bjax" dal"* 'I had given').

---

[7] Vlasto's "early East Slavic" overlaps with what I have been calling Old Russian; according to his periodization (1986: 33), early East Slavic covers the period up to 1250. Italics and abbreviations in the text are original.

The replacement of aorist and imperfect by the perfect, he says, sacrifices the unique meaning of this category.

Grammatical aspect, according to Vlasto, was a natural later development from this earlier system:

> It is untrue to assert that aspectual differences were only in the process of definition in early ESl.: they are inescapably present in all verbal forms. It is their grammatical expression which has changed.

> Given that the expression of aspect (mode of action) remained in Russian (as in most Slav languages) as more fundamental than that of temporal relations with respect to some fixed point (the main verb), it follows that the *aspectual indicators* became more strictly organized so that in all appropriate cases a perfective and an imperfective verb, complementing one another... provided all the required forms. (1986: 243)

Vlasto has seized on an important point here, but the economy of handbook presentation works to his disadvantage. Lexical aspect and grammatical aspect are, as he says, quite similar, in that both determine the shape and scope of the action, and I fully agree with him that Modern Russian aspect has its roots in the lexical aspectual distinctions of early Slavic. However, Vlasto implies that the crystallization of aspect into a grammaticalized system entails no semantic repercussions, only a reorganization of existing meanings under the rubric of two overarching aspects.[8] The possibility that meanings and oppositions present in Modern Russian were in fact absent in many Old Russian verbs—or, for that matter, vice versa—goes largely unmentioned.

Vlasto's assumption that the two Modern Russian aspects are no more than the sum of earlier lexical- and tense-based aspects will no doubt seem heretical to some and is undoubtedly a deliberate oversimplification. His discussion, as opposed to that of Borkovskij and Kuznecov, presents a more radical theory of aspectual development, relying on a broad lexical and temporal interpretation of aspect in the earliest period of Russian history; he then submits this lexical aspectual system to a major structural reorganization that changes it into a grammatical category. If the semantic concerns expressed above were incorporated into his analysis, it would have a substantial conceptual advantage over the view advanced by Borkovskij and Kuznecov.

---

[8] Still, Vlasto, puzzlingly enough, retains the labels "perfective" and "imperfective" for even the oldest forms, calling into question exactly what his view of aspect in Old Russian is. It seems most likely that he simply wishes to view the overarching criteria as relatively weak in Old Russian and somewhat stronger in Modern Russian. The evidence for this is the ability of morphological factors to determine semantics in Modern Russian, i.e., that prefixed simplexes are to be perfective, that their non-past tense expresses a future act, etc.

3.1.3. Summary of handbooks

Portions of the scholarly debate on aspect appear in microcosm in the handbooks we have examined. Lexical factors clearly play a large role in determining the meaning and usage of the Old Russian verb, and yet scholars are reluctant to abandon the grammatical system of aspect as it appears in Modern Russian, for the obvious reason that its predictive power holds in many, although far from all, cases in Old Russian. One way around the problem is to assume, like Borkovskij and Kuznecov, that grammatical aspect subsumes all other lexical distinctions in Old Russian; lexical aspect is implicitly relegated to the prehistoric era. A footnote can then be added to the effect that Old Russian aspectual distinctions were in some ways different from those of Modern Russian. Another way around the problem is to posit a weaker perfective–imperfective distinction for Old Russian, as Vlasto does, and ascribe the differences between Modern Russian and Old Russian to the weakening of lexical factors as a primary, grammatical aspectual opposition comes to dominate.

One feature of both handbooks mirrors a problem in the aspectual debate at large. There are several passages appearing in these handbooks that are cited in nearly every article on the subject: a geographical description and a description of pagan practices from the Primary Chronicle, and a law from the *Russkaja Pravda:*

бѣ путь изъ Варягъ въ Греки. и изъ Грекъ по Днѣпру. и верхъ Днѣпра волокъ до Ловоти. (и) по Ловоти внити в-Ылмерь озеро великое. из негоже озера потечеть Волховъ и вътечеть в озеро великое Ново...а от Ц(а)рягорода. прити в Понотъ моря. в неже втечет Днѣпръ рѣка. Днѣпръ бо потече из Оковьскаго лѣса и потечеть на польдне. а Двина ис тогоже лѣса потечет. а идетъ на полуночье и внидеть в море Варяжское. ис того же лѣса потече Волга на въстокъ. и вътечеть семьюдесять жерелъ в море Хвалисьское... (*Повесть временных лет:* 7)[9]

аще кто оумряше творяху трызно надъ нимъ. и по семь творяху кладу велику и възложахуть и на кладу м(е)ртвца. сожьжаху. и посемь собравше кости. вложаху в судину малу. и поставяху на столпѣ... (*Повесть временных лет:* 14)[10]

---

[9] 'There was a route from the Varangian lands to Greece. And from Greece (it went) along the Dniepr (river), and (there was) a portage from the head of the Dniepr to the Lovot'; via the Lovot' one enters the great Lake Ilmer (Il'men'), from which lake the Volxov (River) rises and flows into the great Lake Novo.... And from Constantinople one can enter the Hellespont Sea, into which the Dniepr flows. For the Dnepr rises in the Okovskij Forest and flows south, while the Dvina rises in the same forest and flows north and enters the Baltic Sea. From the same forest the Volga rises and runs east and empties through seventy mouths into the Caspian Sea...' (*Primary Chronicle:* 7)

[10] 'when someone died, they would have a ceremony in his honor, and then they would make a large block and would place the dead man on the block, burn him up and then,

которая ли вьрвь начнеть платити дикую виру колико лѣт(ъ) заплатять ту виру занеже безъ головника имъ платити. (*Русская правда.* 4)[11]

One expects handbooks to cite only a few crucial examples, but it is surprising to find that many scholarly articles offer no greater depth of coverage. It is easy to get the impression that numerous theories have been built around the existence of these three examples without a detailed look at the remaining data from those texts.

3.2. WORK ON PREHISTORIC SLAVIC ASPECT

Research into the history of aspect in Prehistoric Slavic came in three waves, starting in the late nineteenth century with the works of scholars such as Ul'janov and Potebnja. The second round of works, led by van Wijk, Koschmeider, Meillet, and others, appeared in the 1920s and 1930s and by and large were concerned with the problem of whether Slavic aspect was inherited from Proto-Indo-European aspect or whether it represented an innovation. The case for a direct transmission of aspect was in the end seen as too tenuous and was compounded by further questions about exactly what status aspect held in Proto-Indo-European. In the early postwar period, a new generation of scholars tackled the question: if the category of aspect is not inherited from Proto-Indo-European, where does it come from? Scholars like Borodič, Maslov, Vaillant, Kölln, and Němec came to sharply divergent conclusions about the usefulness of categories like determinacy for the development of aspect.

Since Maslov's 1961 article on the provenance of aspect, the literature on the history of aspect has concentrated overwhelmingly on the morphological sources of aspect. There are, of course, a few exceptions. The noted aspectologist James Forsyth made a contribution to the debate; his 1972 article reevaluates the facts and conclusions presented in the discussions of the 1950s. The most recent contribution in this survey is that of Kyril Holden (1990), which integrates newer work on lexical aspect into a theory of aspectual genesis.

The works appear here in rough chronological order. I chose not to discuss the earliest works here (except inasmuch as other scholars have referred to them in their own studies), since the notion of a direct Proto-Indo-European provenance for Slavic aspect is no longer widely accepted.

3.2.1. van Wijk 1929

Until the end of the 1920s, many scholars labelled Slavic aspect a direct descendant of Proto-Indo-European aspect. Van Wijk's work in the late 1920s was

---

having collected the bones, would put them in a small vessel and place it on a pillar' (*Primary Chronicle:* 14)

[11] 'If a village shall begin to pay a collective murder-fine, then they shall pay off the fine over as many years as it takes, for in their case there is no murderer paying.' (*Russian Law,* article 4)

the first to convincingly suggest that Slavic aspect might in fact have arisen on Slavic soil from the category of determinacy. He poses two questions: did Proto-Indo-European aspect have the same form and function as Slavic aspect; and if so, was the grammatical aspectual opposition transmitted directly from Proto-Indo-European to Slavic with no break in the continuity of the system?

The first portion of his article is devoted to showing how little relationship there really is between Proto-Indo-European aspect and Slavic aspect. Van Wijk starts from the hypothesis of Ul'janov, who claimed on the basis of the Greek aorist that the Proto-Indo-European aorist had the same syntactic value as the Slavic perfective aspect. While van Wijk does not dispute the Greek facts, he questions whether this aorist aspect can be shown in any other Indo-European language, casting doubt on its provenance. Furthermore, he reminds the reader that Greek is also said to have a perfect aspect, whose functions also correspond to that of the Slavic perfective, but which has come down to Slavic as a separate verb class (statives in {-i-}).

Having discredited the Proto-Indo-European aspectual system as a source for aspect, van Wijk turns to the Proto-Indo-European lexical category of determinacy, which he supposes to have been a much larger and more meaningful opposition than that found in the small group of Slavic verbs bearing that name today (van Wijk 1929: 239-240).[12] He labels this category an "objective" one, meaning that it is grounded in the meaning of the verb, and not in a perspective on the action. (Perspectives he calls a "subjective" category, which therefore subsumes modern Slavic grammatical aspect.) Expanding his definitions, van Wijk proposes that all "objective" categories, including Aktionsart distinctions, must therefore fit into the determinate–indeterminate scheme. During the late prehistoric period, objective categories in Slavic give way to subjective categories as organizers of the verbal system, while the latter assimilate some differences and oppositions found in the former.

Much of van Wijk 1929 is devoted to introducing and reintroducing concepts into the debate on aspect, rather than to supporting his hypothesis with detailed examples. However, its innovativeness spurred a debate around the question of aspect that lasted into the 1960s. In defining the terms of the debate, van Wijk also set its parameters. Aspect had been previously said to descend directly from a similar Proto-Indo-European category; van Wijk set out to establish that this was not so. He went about this task first by examining the deficiencies of the old hypothesis and second by suggesting another category that could serve as its replacement. In doing so, van Wijk assumed that the ultimate goal of the debate must be to find another source category, preferably one bearing a close resemblance to aspect. This predilection for finding the source category had a decisive influence on research in the years that followed.

---

[12] The fact that virtually all the evidence van Wijk cites is once again on the basis of Ancient Greek seems not to trouble him this time around, since "traces" of these categories have been found in other languages.

3.2.2. Kuryłowicz 1929

In his 1929 article "La genèse d'aspects verbaux slaves," Kuryłowicz takes up the question of how verbal aspect appeared in Slavic. In his view, aspectualization moved through the lexicon as certain pairs of verbal acts aspectualized before others. Kuryłowicz posits that pairs of the type *dvignǫti–dvigati* 'move–be moving' came at some point to represent a grammatical (aspectual) opposition. This aspectual opposition was later extended to verb pairs previously characterized by a lexical opposition only, such as *ubiti–biti* 'kill–beat'. The opposition was now both lexical and grammatical. Forms like *ubivati* 'be killing' arose to rebuild this complex opposition on the model of *dvignǫti–dvigati*. Because *ubivati* was opposed to *ubiti* purely grammatically, it replaced the more complex opposition *ubiti–biti* in the Slavic aspectual system (1929: 647).

Some pairs, such as *zagrati–grati* 'begin to play–be playing', continued to express a lexical opposition even as they acquired the new grammatical opposition from the *dvignǫti–dvigati* and *ubiti–ubivati* types. According to Kuryłowicz, adding these pairs to the grammatical opposition both expanded it and made it less uniform, changing it back again from a pure grammatical opposition into one tolerating lexical oppositions as well.

As to where the original aspectual opposition *(dvignǫti–dvigati)* came from, Kuryłowicz traces the nasal suffix {-nǫ-} and the nasal infix {-n-} to Proto-Indo-European, where the former had a terminative function and the latter a terminative or inchoative function, depending on whether it was opposed respectively to an action or a state.[13] This double opposition of infixed verbs, he says, is crucial to understanding why the Slavic perfective expresses futurity in the non-past tense. Used inchoatively, the verb implies that the act has not yet begun; if it has, then the meaning is identical with that of the state. The future-oriented function is thus a natural outgrowth of the opposition "inchoative–state," and is then extended to verbs in the opposition "terminative–action." In order for this extension to take place, Kuryłowicz proposes uniting terminatives and inchoatives under the label "determinate." All other present tenses (states and iteratives) he calls "indeterminate." Further extension and refinement of this system brings us to the one seen in modern Slavic languages.

In seeing the nasal suffix and infix as the grammatical source of aspect, and in deriving the aspectual opposition from a bifurcation of function in the non-past tense, Kuryłowicz strikes out in a different direction from van Wijk . Although he advances no chronology, his use of quasi-Prehistoric Slavic forms suggests that he believes the formative period of aspect to have occurred before the advent of written language. This belief is hard to reconcile with the generally accepted observations that the non-past tense showed considerable variation in its usage well into the Old

---

[13] The example given is from Modern Polish: *zasnąć* 'fall asleep' is terminative when opposed to *zasypiać* 'be falling asleep' but inceptive when opposed to *spać* 'sleep'. He exempts {-nǫ-} verbs that are not opposed to verbs without this suffix, since it is the opposition, he claims, which gives them their unique role.

Russian period, and that this variation was especially common with motion verbs, which are among the prototypical determinate and indeterminate pairs.[14]

The nasal infixes are a further problem. Although Kuryłowicz leads the reader to think he is proposing the entire class of nasal suffixed verbs as the source for aspect, in reality he proposes a two-stage process in which the nasal infix verbs are the first stage. Since there are only a few of these verbs attested in Slavic, this approaches making an overwhelming and universal change to the verbal system based on a handful of verbs.[15]

3.2.3. Borodič 1953

A seminal article in the 1950s debate on aspect is Borodič's "K voprosu o formirovanii soveršennogo i nesoveršennogo vida v slavjanskix jazykax" ("On the Question of the Formation of the Perfective and Imperfective Aspects in the Slavic Languages"), which makes a forceful case for determinacy as the basis for the Modern Russian aspectual system. Borodič's aspectualization process is based on actual historical Slavic examples, and she sees the past tense system as the main arena for the development of grammatical aspect.

One source of the appeal of Borodič's explanation—and also its greatest weakness—comes from her broad interpretation of the category of determinacy (*opredelennost'*). Instead of limiting it to oppositions of the type *nositi–nesti* 'carry regularly–be carrying', she includes within it a component of terminus (*terminativnost'*). Her definition, drawing on an earlier one by Delbrück, calls determinacy a terminative lexical aspect focusing on a concrete act. Indeterminacy is a nonterminative lexical aspect focusing on the static quality of an act (Borodič 1953: 74-5).[16] This opposition, then, is not binary; each member has its own independent criteria, and it encompasses oppositions like stative vs. mutative (*stojati–stati* 'be standing–stand up'), stative vs. factitive (*b"děti–buditi* 'be alert–waken') and stative vs. semelfactive (*kasati–kosnuti* 'concern–touch on'). This stance allows Borodič to claim a Proto-Indo-European heritage for this category, since the lexicon Prehistoric Slavic inherits from Proto-Indo-European has ample reflections of these oppositions.

Borodič claims that in Old Church Slavic, aorist forms are found with "nonstative" verbs and imperfect forms with "stative" verbs. This pattern extends to participles, where stative verbs have only present participles, and determinate verbs

---

[14] A partial explanation is offered in Kuznecov 1953. See my discussion of this article in the relevant section.

[15] Not that this is impossible, only improbable. After all, most of the Modern Czech 1.sg. non-past verbs have an ending borrowed from the athematic verbs, despite how few athematic verbs there originally were. Janda 1994 discusses this phenomenon of "exaption"—the adoption of a marginal form as the central form of a system—in Slavic languages.

[16] My use of the word "aspect" here follows her own usage on p. 75 (*opredelennyj vid*), although "lexical class" might be less confusing.

have only past participles (1953: 75-77).[17] Determinate non-past forms describe either a present or future act, while indeterminate non-past forms describe a timeless act (1953: 78). From these oppositions Borodič concludes that a codified determinate–indeterminate opposition existed in Prehistoric Slavic.

Eventually determinate verbs obtain imperfect tense forms, which gradually become disassociated from the original verb and acquire new infinitives. The process is schematized in chart 3.2.3.1.

Chart 3.2.3.1. Borodič's view of the birth of derived verbs

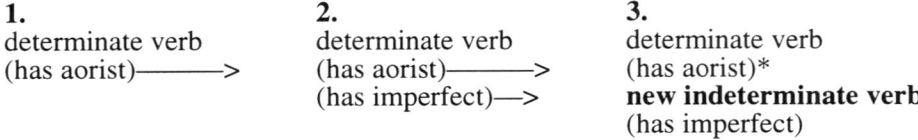

1.	2.	3.
determinate verb	determinate verb	determinate verb
(has aorist)———>	(has aorist)———>	(has aorist)*
	(has imperfect)—>	**new indeterminate verb**
		(has imperfect)

Author's query: does the original determinate verb still have an imperfect?

Newly minted determinate verbs, meaning those with prefixes, originally expressed a change in state. They too acquire an imperfect tense, and then can form new infinitives from that imperfect. The new imperfects from determinate verbs express a concrete process, as opposed to the old iterative meaning found in indeterminate imperfectives; this new imperfect usage becomes the basis for the imperfective aspect. Aorists then start to be formed from indeterminate verbs, in an opposing process where the tense limits the state; in this group are aorists like *vidě* 'saw', *slyša* 'heard' (1953: 79-81).

Eventually, Borodič argues, the imperfective aspect arises as a broadening of the concepts originally embodied in the indeterminate verbal group. The perfective aspect arises as a subset of the usages originally expressed in the determinate group (1953: 84).

Once aspect is already established in the past tense domain, it spreads to the non-past domain. Non-past tenses of determinate verbs describe a present or future act; non-past tenses of indeterminate verbs describe a generalized timeless act. (1953: 82)[18] Gradually the indeterminate present tense takes on a concrete meaning; eventually the determinate verbs lose the possibility of present tense reference, reinforcing the aspectual system by giving rise to aspectual distinctions in

---

[17] It is hard to confirm or refute this statement, since the data she presents are incomplete, and there are no references to more complete studies. Copious examples—but little analysis of them—can be found in Borodič 1954, which reads more like a list of Old Church Slavic examples partially supplementing her 1953 claims. See the quite different distribution in the Primary Chronicle discussed later in this study.

[18] Borodič curiously uses examples with the verb *viděti* 'see' to establish this for determinate verbs, having earlier (correctly) classed it as an indeterminate verb.

the non-past tense. Because imperfectivity has its roots in both original indeterminate usage (multidirectional, habitual) and in the imperfect tense (repeated or ongoing action), it is broader in scope than the indeterminacy it replaces. Because perfectivity encompasses only a subset of the functions of determinacy, it is narrower and more homogeneous as a category (1953: 84).

The advantages to Borodič's approach are its striking simplicity and the broad base on which it builds the modern aspectual opposition. It starts with a quasi-lexical semantic distinction and transforms it into a grammatical one. It brings tense and aspect together in a coherent fashion, explaining both the rise of aspect and the growing extraneousness of tense after an initial period of prosperity. The motley nature of imperfective function and usage and the more uniform outline of perfective function and usage are implicit in her explanation.

The disadvantage to this approach is the motivation and process by which the original category develops into a more grammatical opposition. First, the reader is essentially asked to accept on faith that the formation of the imperfect and aorist tenses is the immediate reason for the division of verbs into perfective and imperfective aspects; the only motivation cited is that the tenses create an inner conflict in the verbal system.

The most frequently voiced objections to Borodič's theory concern her discussion of the imperfect tense and its role in aspectualization. She insists on a relative chronology that gives a rather mechanical primacy to the imperfect tense's role in aspectual history, as indicated in chart 3.2.3.2.

Chart 3.2.3.2. Borodič's chronology of aspectual derivation

1. Formation of the imperfect tense
2. Formation of secondary imperfectives in {-ja-}
3. Formation of secondary imperfectives with stem vowel lengthening, etc.

Borodič claims that this chronology holds not only as a general principle (i.e., that the imperfect tense developed before derived forms as a class), but also as a developmental principle for every verb (i.e., every verb later classified as imperfective must have developed from a determinate imperfect tense form prefiguring its later shape). This gives us a development as outlined in chart 3.2.3.3 for the three verbs *vratiti* 'return', *roditi* 'give birth', and *s"brati* 'collect'.[19] Of course, a verb like *roditi* would normally be expected to have an imperfect like **rož(d)a(a)x"*, while the attested derived verb is in fact *raždati*. Borodič skirts this issue by positing an unattested imperfect **raždaax"* from *roditi*.

---

[19] Borodič does not regularly use asterisks to indicate whether forms are attested or not, so in reporting her conclusions I have not added them unless Borodič clearly states that a form is hypothetical, or unless I am myself positing an unattested (hypothetical or prehistoric) form in my own response.

Chart 3.2.3.3. Development of three Old Russian verbs from Borodič 1953

Original verb	vratiti 'return'	roditi 'give birth'	s"b'rati 'collect'
Lengthened imperfect	vrati-a-x"	radi-a-x"	s"bir-a-x"
Consonant mutation	vrašč-a-x"	ražd-a-x"	s"bir-a-x"
New derived verb	vrašč-a-ti	ražd-a-ti	s"bir-a-ti

This theoretical imperfect "in all likelihood" arose by analogy to the few acknowledged prehistoric forms with /o/~/a/ alternations. The imperfect form then serves as a base for forming a new verb *raždati*.[20] She applies the same rationale to the development of new roots in {-va-} and with root vowel lengthening.

> Но самый процесс образования производных глаголов от этого не изменяется, т.е. удлинение гласной и вставка -в- происходит в форме имперфекта, образующейся от простой глагольной основы. (1953: 80)[21]

Since Borodič does not posit the existence of an aspectual system until sometime in the Old Russian period, this statement is not just a matter of a theoretical relative chronology in Prehistoric Slavic.[22] It is crucial to her contention that aspect does not develop out of determinacy until the historical period. By insisting that ontogeny (the development of any given verb pair) must recapitulate phylogeny (the development of grammatical aspect as a whole) she can call verbs like *roditi* preaspectual even if forms like *raždaax"* exist, because the imperfect alone does not show the existence of a derived verb, even if its stem differs from that of the simplex verb.

This explanation also turns commonly established ideas about the relative chronology of certain verb forms on their head. Because Borodič sees the formation of the imperfect tense as the basis for aspect, she wants verbs resembling regular imperfect tense forms—in other words, the most regular class of verbs—to be the oldest class of derived verbs. This leaves three problematic groups of verbs whose imperfects, if formed regularly, would have different stems from the attested derived verbs. A few forms, such as *ložiti–lagati* 'lay', Borodič permits to be of ancient provenance, but all vowel-length alternations of the type *s"b'rati–s"birati* 'collect' and consonantal insertions of the type *v"stati–v"stavati* 'get up', and most forms with /o/~/a/ she assigns to a later date. The latter two groups, she claims, are

---

20 Němec 1956, among others, objects strongly to this chain of events.
21 "But the process of formation of productive verbs in and of itself does not change; that is, the lengthening of the vowel and the insertion of {-v-} takes place in the imperfect tense form, which is formed from the simplex verb root."
22 Her claim is that "the process of developing aspect (perfective and imperfective) occurred on the soil of individual Slavic languages; in Common Slavic only the preconditions for their development were laid down" (1953: 81).

neologisms that arise because homonymy in the infinitive prompts vowel lengthening or the insertion of a {-v-}.[23] No textual evidence for this is advanced.

A few modifications could make Borodič's theory more palatable.[24] Most importantly, eliminating the need for each verb to proceed through certain formal stages would give a more gradual picture of the development of aspect, suggesting a partially formed system in Old Church Slavic and Old Russian to which verbs are added directly either by lexical category or by other means.

3.2.4. Kuznecov 1953

The eminent Soviet linguist Kuznecov made an early contribution to this debate with his 1953 article "K voprosu o genezise vido-vremennyx otnošenij drevnerusskogo jazyka" ("On the Problem of the Genesis of Aspectual-Temporal Relations in Old Russian").

The first portion of the article is devoted to a lengthy discussion of terminology (aspect, tense, category, Aktionsart). It puts Kuznecov firmly in the camp of those who view aspect as a grammatical category "expressing the relationship of an action to its passage in time," as opposed to what he calls the "outmoded" view of aspect as an opposition "of differences in the relation of an act to its limit (*predel*), up until which it [the act] is in effect and after which it does not take place" (Kuznecov 1953: 225).[25]

Kuznecov spends the bulk of the article discussing the nature of aspect and tense in Proto-Indo-European and what sort of impact the Proto-Indo-European situation had on Slavic. His conclusions can be summarized as follows: both Proto-Indo-European and Prehistoric Slavic had means of codifying tense and aspect distinctions in their morphology. Slavic aspect as we know it, however, is an innovation arising at the tail end of the Prehistoric Slavic period. The old aspectual system inherited from Proto-Indo-European, he asserts, explains some of the apparently archaic features of Slavic aspect and is partially co-opted into the new system once it has already taken root. His reasoning is that aspect in the early historical period is a new and developing system that only partially resembles modern Slavic aspect. Yet he is able to hedge this statement by claiming that

---

23 Both types are clearly Prehistoric Slavic formations, because the vowel alternations they present make sense only in an older vowel system characterized by four vowels paired for length: short and long /a/, /e/, /o/, /u/. Later developments in Prehistoric Slavic turn long /a/ into /o/, long /e/ into /ě/, long /i/ into the front jer, and long /u/ into the back jer. Of course, we need not assume that all these verbs developed in early Prehistoric Slavic, but enough of them must have to create a productive pattern.

24 According to Maslov, a number of suggestions along this line were made at the 1958 International Congress of Slavists' session on the history of verbal aspect, but Borodič rejected these emendations to her theory (Maslov 1959: 155-157).

25 Kuznecov is essentially opposing grammatical to lexical aspect in this passage. The latter view, however, is no longer entirely outmoded, due to recent reevaluation and refinement of its weaker points (cf. Maslov, Vendler, Kučera and others choosing the lexicon as a basis for aspectual oppositions).

despite the recent origins of aspect in the modern sense, the place and role of aspect is deeply entrenched in Slavic thanks to its Proto-Indo-European heritage.

Kuznecov believes, along with Kuryłowicz, that aspect arises on the basis of oppositions in the non-past tense. Prefixed verbs, where the non-past obtains a definite future slant, are grouped into a perfective aspect, as of yet opposed only to a general aspect. When a large enough number of verbs are so classified, the unprefixed general aspect verbs begin to be classified as imperfective, opposed in function to the perfective. Unprefixed verbs may, under certain circumstances, become perfective, thanks to the waning but persistent influence of Proto-Indo-European (lexical) aspectual groups. Kuznecov sees suffixation entering the picture only considerably later, which strengthens but does not initiate the rise of aspect as a category.

Since Kuznecov stresses prefixation over suffixation as the source for Old Russian aspect and since he emphasizes the future reference of the prefixed verbs' non-past tense, he needs to explain the large number of prefixed verbs in Old Russian with present tense reference. According to Kuznecov, prefixes have three roles in Old Russian: spatial *(prostranstvennye)*, temporal *(vremennýe)*, and purely grammatical *(čisto grammatičeskie)*. Prefixes are not restricted to a single role; they can be place markers in one verb, for instance, and time markers in another. As an example Kuznecov produces the familiar passage from the Primary Chronicle cited in 3.1.3 above. In contrast to numerous examples of {po-} as an inceptive prefix, Kuznecov's example shows it in a spatial sense, opposed to the prefix {v-}, and verbs with these and other spatial prefixes belong to the imperfective aspect. Kuznecov is also the only scholar to claim, contrary to convention, that prefixation can form grammatical aspectual pairs in early historical Slavic. He cites examples with *sъdělati* 'make, do' from Old Church Slavic to support his contention.

In the early stages of aspect, Kuznecov speaks of a "propensity" *(tjagotenie)* for imperfective verbs to appear in certain tenses and perfective verbs in others, but does not establish a causative relationship between tense and aspect. Instead, he sees the spread of aspect in the past tenses as reflecting the changing state of the past tense system, where the imperfect is clearly on the wane from the earliest texts. According to Kuznecov, the above propensities are eventually replaced by a more mechanical mapping of relationships (imperfective verb = imperfect tense; perfective verb = aorist tense) when the imperfect dies out in the vernacular and its use is correlated with that of the imperfective aspect, which takes over its functions.

With respect to the early Slavic historical era, Kuznecov raises a number of excellent points ignored by other scholars. By basing his conclusions on the state of aspect in Old Russian and Old Church Slavic, he provides a welcome counterweight to some of the more abstractly driven theories.

3.2.5. Kölln 1957

Borodič and Kölln share some common assumptions about aspectual genesis in Slavic. Both start from the belief that Indo-European aspect and Slavic aspect represent parallel evolution from a basic similarity in the lexicon, not a direct inheritance. Both take a determinate–indeterminate opposition as the basis for the rise of aspect. And both rely heavily on Old Church Slavic data to deduce the state of Prehistoric Slavic aspect.

However, where Borodič sees an aspectual system in gradual development through the beginning of the historical period, Kölln claims that aspect enters the historical era in fully developed form. As for determinacy, Borodič expands it to include a heterogeneous lexical and grammatical group of factors, while Kölln construes the determinate–indeterminate opposition even more narrowly than in modern Slavic, and only later in the process includes the aorist–imperfect opposition among the factors expanding the scope of Slavic aspect. Along with Dostál and Němec, he contends that grammatical aspect is firmly established in Slavic by the prehistoric era and that its usage resembles that of Modern Czech.[26]

Kölln 1957 follows van Wijk in seeking a Prehistoric Slavic protocategory that would be an appropriate forerunner of grammatical aspect; he, too, is convinced that determinacy, and not Indo-European aspect, is the source of Slavic aspect. However, Kölln warns against equating the sort of determinacy found in Prehistoric Slavic with the modern Slavic category of that name.

Kölln's criteria for determinacy in Prehistoric Slavic are threefold: the verb must have goal or directionality inherent in its lexical meaning; show a tendency to perfectivize in modern Slavic; and form derivatives with an {-aj-} suffix, not an {-i-} suffix. While some verbs in the modern determinate group, like *běžati* 'run', do reflect an "innate" determinacy, Kölln outlines a primary group of Prehistoric Slavic determinate verbs that fall outside the modern category, i.e., **pasti* 'fall', **stǫpiti* 'step', **pustiti* 'allow', **dvignǫti* 'move', **lešti* 'lie down', **sěsti* 'sit down', **stati* 'stand up', **skočiti* 'jump', **minǫti* 'pass by', **vratiti sę* 'return', **dati* 'give', etc.[27]

If determinacy provides the argument for splitting the lexicon into perfective and imperfective verbs, then Kölln proposes that many functions we call "aspectual" today originally resided in the Prehistoric Slavic tense system. He declares the aorist/past participle vs. imperfect/present participle opposition to be the indicators of a binary Prehistoric Slavic aspectual system encoded at first in tense distinctions and transplanted to a system of aspectually opposed verbs at a later date. As a mechanism for this change, Kölln suggests that functions originally ascribed to tense morphemes become attached to opposed verbal stems.

This can happen, Kölln claims, because the coincidence of determinacy and tense assignment was quite high. For instance, he states that prefixed derived verbs were originally found only in the present and imperfect tenses of the indicative

---

[26] Although there are numerous small differences between Modern Russian and Modern Czech aspect, one global statement is possible: Modern Czech aspect seems to be more sensitive to context and lexical shape than Modern Russian aspect.

[27] This solution has an interesting parallel in the Czech grammatical tradition, where no distinction is drawn between the prefixation of motion verbs and that of non-motion verbs. Compare this to Modern Russian, where traditionally prefixation in non-motion verbs is strictly separated from prefixation occurring with motion verbs.

mood, the infinitive and imperative moods, and the present participle, meaning that imperfectivity was incompatible with the aorist and past active participle. Further proof is in the fact that 90 percent of all aorist forms in Old Church Slavic are with perfective verbs, and only 10 percent are with imperfective verbs.

Kölln then cites statistics from Dostál 1954 to prove that imperfectivity is nothing more than a revision of features found in the imperfect tense and the present participle, while perfectivity is a revision of features found in the aorist and past participle.[28] He pushes lexical aspect to the side as marginally present but no longer relevant. By the historical period, Kölln states, grammatical aspect competes with tense-based aspect in Old Church Slavic, Old Russian, and other languages (1957: 97-98).[29]

Kölln's chronology captures an important shift in Slavic aspect from a lexical- and tense-based system to one based on pairs and groups of verbs, and does it without the mechanical transformation Borodič depends on. Yet his contention that by the late Prehistoric Slavic period, aspect in what is more or less its modern shape is expressed primarily through tense, without recourse to lexical factors, strikes a false note. There is a bias in Kölln's arguments that is subtle but pervasive: he often construes tendencies as sharp prohibitions or commands and thus imposes a one-to-one correspondence on tenses and aspects that, in reality, do not match as closely as he wants. If tenses in Prehistoric Slavic or Old Russian represent aspectual distinctions, then it is clearly an expression of aspect that has different oppositions and different boundaries than that found in the modern Slavic languages. Saying that tense-based aspect simply transfers its functions to its successor category is no more than papering over problems in the development of paradigm-based aspect.

3.2.6. Němec 1956

With the work of Igor Němec, the field of aspectual history moved into a phase of reexamination and reconciliation between theories. In his 1956 article "Kategorie determinovanosti a indeterminovanosti jako základ slovanské kategorie vidu" ("The Category of Determinacy and Indeterminacy as the Basis for the Slavic Category of Aspect"), and his *Genese slovanského systému vidového (The Genesis of the Slavic Aspectual System),* a 1958 monograph expanding on his earlier thesis, Němec critiques and revises the hypothesis that aspect is not a proto-Slavic category but arises later on from a determinate–indeterminate category. His view steers a course between the radical version of this theory propounded by Borodič and the earlier, more circumspect version by van Wijk, and also tries to reconcile these theories with the traditional view of aspectual history exemplified in Dostál 1954.

Němec 1956 agrees with Borodič 1953 that the category of determinacy must be expanded to include stative vs. inchoative oppositions and imperfect vs. aorist

---

[28] In my opinion, Dostál's convergent definitions of tense and aspect leave these particular statistics open to criticism. See my discussion in section 3.3.

[29] This can be seen as a more categorical version of Vlasto's claim that "aspect" is reflected in both tense and grammatical aspectual distinctions.

oppositions if it is to account for the rise of grammatical aspect. He also agrees with her general thesis that imperfectivity arises from the mixing of these two oppositions (the rise of determinate imperfects). However, Němec is suspicious of Borodič's general insistence that aspect developed only in the historical period and that the earliest written texts show only a highly developed system of determinate–indeterminate oppositions. The difficulties in her explanation, according to Němec, result from placing of the brunt of aspectual genesis on developments in the preterite, instead of the non-past (Němec 1956: 499-501).

Němec's analysis is based on a survey of Prehistoric Slavic roots, their reflexes in the daughter Slavic languages, and analogous forms found in other Indo-European languages (foremost Greek, Baltic, and Germanic). He categorizes these early Slavic roots and their reflexes as either *complex* or *noncomplex (komplexní, nekomplexní)*. A complex act is one that includes information about how the act takes place and also about a change from one state into another. A noncomplex act includes only information about how the act takes place. These distinctions suggest lexical information that can be encoded in the grammar of a language as well. In early Prehistoric Slavic, as in Proto-Indo-European, this opposition was a lexicalized determinate–indeterminate opposition, whose members express respectively an act in process (with a goal) and a state (or act conceived as state). As Prehistoric Slavic developed tenses, however, the tenses took over some of the functions of this formerly lexical aspectual distinction. The complex–noncomplex opposition was then expressed by tense, while the determinate–indeterminate opposition remained a characteristic of the verb stem. The two categories overlapped in some instances. (See chart 3.2.6.1; examples are cited in Old Church Slavic.)

Chart 3.2.6.1. Němec 1956 on the overlap of tense and complexness.

present stem:	present stem:	preterite stem:
indeterminate noncomplex aspect	determinate noncomplex aspect	determinate complex aspect
bljudetъ 'guards'	buditъ 'wakes'	vъzbъde 'woke up'

Němec's complex–noncomplex opposition therefore describes a semantic (but not yet grammatical) opposition in a Prehistoric Slavic aspectual system that springs from the same lexical source as determinacy but develops differently. Complex or noncomplex aspect in the protolanguage is assigned by a combination of lexical and tense-related factors, whereas in the historical epoch a verb (considered as a set of potential forms) is assigned to the perfective or imperfective aspect. Němec's use of the term "aspect" (Czech *vid*) for both complexness and determinacy suggests a similarity between lexically determined constraints on verbal action and grammatically determined constraints, much as suggested by Vlasto above.

The next task is to account for the gradual growth of the category of complexness into a grammatical aspectual category. Němec proposes that it is the decoupling of complexness from determinacy that allows the former category to expand and grammaticalize. The growth of complexness is seen in the growing restriction of non-past forms to future meaning, especially among prefixed verbs, the new bearers of complexness. This shift creates a grammatical aspectual opposition between prefixed and non-prefixed forms.

As this aspectual opposition spreads, old simplex determinate forms, which had both complex and noncomplex meaning, continue to give way to prefixed forms in the historical period (early Old Church Slavic aorists *xotě* 'he wanted', *slyšaša* 'they heard', *divi sja* 'he was surprised' become prefixed forms in later Old Church Slavic: *vъzxotě* 'he began to want/he wanted', *uslyšaša* 'they heard (once)', *podivi sja* 'he was surprised/he was taken by surprise').

Němec's explanation reconstructs two sides to the creation of an aspectual system. Old indeterminate stems developed in one way, spinning off their noncomplex meaning to give birth to the imperfect tense and the imperfective aspect, whereas old determinate stems developed in another fashion, developing a specific future usage in the non-past of {-n-}-suffix verbs and prefixed verbs.

The wealth of well-chosen non-Slavic data gives Němec's argument added weight, although it remains baroque in the amount of terminology used and the number of stages required to effect a single change (this may be a byproduct of trying to reconcile too many theories at once). His use of the complexness opposition to relate lexical, tense-based and grammatical aspect has a great deal of merit. In the end, however, the transition Němec proposes from complex–noncomplex to perfective–imperfective is not thoroughly convincing because he attributes it to the Prehistoric Slavic era and presents the historical aspectual systems as immutable, established fact. All facts that argue for leaving some parts of aspectual development until later—discrepancies in the imperfect tense, odd usage patterns of certain verbs—he dismisses as relics of an older system, despite their systematic character in Old Russian texts.

3.2.7. Maslov 1961

In 1961 Jurij Maslov summarized his view of the genesis of aspect in the article "Rol' tak nazyvaemoj perfektivacii i imperfektivacii v processe vozniknovenija slavjanskogo glagol'nogo vida" ("The Role of So-called Perfectivization and Imperfectivization in the Formational Process of Slavic Verbal Aspect"). Maslov had long been part of the debate over the genesis of aspect, and this article represents his attempt to reconcile previous theories with his own observations.[30]

---

[30] Maslov had contributed a lengthy article in 1954 to *Voprosy slavjanskogo jazykoznanija* entitled "Imperfekt glagolov soveršennogo vida v slavjanskix jazykax" ("The Imperfect of Perfective Verbs in Slavic Languages"), which, while not directly concerned with

In Maslov's eyes, efforts to derive modern aspect solely from the prehistoric category of determinacy were fatally flawed for two reasons. First, scholars were forced to employ a three-way determinate opposition, because it is nigh-impossible to force all verbs into a determinate or indeterminate mold. The resulting system of determinate (*pluti* 'swim', *dvignǫti* 'move', *ubivati* 'kill', *sъdělati* 'do, accomplish'), indeterminate (*plavati* 'swim [regularly]', *dvigati* 'move about', *bivati* 'hit [regularly]') and a middle nondeterminate category (*biti* 'hit', *dělati* 'do, work') Maslov finds disturbingly vague and imprecise.[31] Second, he notes that indeterminacy is supposed to give rise to imperfectivity, but disputes the assertion that determinacy must consequently give rise to perfectivity. In every modern Slavic language, he states, determinate verbs are imperfective; how then can they give rise to the perfective aspect? (1961: 173-176.)[32]

Maslov therefore looks to a more easily definable category for the genesis of aspect. He notes that the category of determinacy as defined in the literature is often an admixture of two different categories: the determinate–indeterminate opposition as understood in modern Slavic—that is, the presence or absence of actual motion directed toward a goal—and the terminative–aterminative (*predel'nyj–nepredel'nyj*) opposition, defined as the presence or absence of a limit or boundary (*predel*) on the action. The terminative member of the opposition is composed largely of prefixed verbs and those with the nasal suffix. He diagrams the relationship between determinacy and terminativity using Modern Russian examples in chart 3.2.7.1 (1961: 177).

---

aspectual genesis, tackles a crucial point in this debate and is discussed in chapter 5. That he had already considered the problem directly and was deeply involved in it is apparent in his 1959 note for *Voprosy jazykoznanija*, entitled "Voprosy proisxoždenija glagol'nogo vida na IV. Meždunarodnom s"ezde slavistov" ("Issues in the Origin of Verbal Aspect at the Fourth International Congress of Slavists").

[31] Maslov invokes Němec's observation that determinate verbs can sometimes behave indeterminately—such as Czech *hodiny jdou* 'the clock runs/is working'(lit. 'goes') and *do nádoby vejdou 3 litry* 'the container will hold three liters' (lit. 'three liters will go into the container')—as proof that the categories of determinate and indeterminate are impossible to establish firmly (Maslov 1961: 173-174).

[32] This argument is a venerable one—Kölln invoked it as well—but there are two problems with the way Maslov formulates it. First, it ignores the expanded definitions of determinacy proposed by Němec, Borodič et al.; instead, it assumes determinacy is the same in Prehistoric Slavic as in Modern Slavic. Second, it neglects the potentially important fact that in Modern Czech, the determinate form frequently stands in for the deponent prefixed perfective. Thus there is *půjdu* 'I will go' and *pojď!* 'come!' (cf. Modern Russian *pojdu* 'I will go', *pojdi!* 'go away!'), but in the past tense and infinitive only *šel jsem domů* 'I went/was going home' and *chtěl jsem jít* 'I wanted to go' (cf. Modern Russian *ja pošel/šel domoj* 'I went/was going home' and *ja xotel pojti* 'I wanted to go'). These perfective uses of *jít, jet* 'go', *nést* 'carry', etc. are arguably as common as the imperfective uses, muddying the aspectual status of these Czech verbs (which in some Czech linguistic traditions are described as perfective anyway).

Chart 3.2.7.1. Interaction of terminativity and determinacy in Maslov 1961

terminative	aterminative	aterminative
vojti 'enter'	idti 'go'	xodit' 'go (regularly)'
vxodit' 'enter'		
determinate	determinate	**indeterminate**

A terminative–aterminative system is lexical in nature,[33] and Maslov argues that Prehistoric Slavic shows ample morphological support for a lexical aspectual system where suffixation and prefixation distinguish types of action and Aktionsart.[34] He finds a decided trend toward common suffixes within each of these categories: stative verbs, mutative verbs, semelfactives, evolutives, and aterminative-iterative verbs. Prefixed verbs, of course, also divide into lexical categories by prefix; Maslov lists resultatives, inceptives, and, later in history, limited duratives.

The terminative verb class consists of all prefixed and {-nǫ-} verbs, plus a few other mutative and evolutive verbs like *sěsti* 'sit down', *stati* 'stand up', *pasti/padǫ* 'fall', *jati* 'seize, take'. They are opposed to aterminative verbs (exclusively statives); outside the opposition lies a group of neutral verbs, the core of which is the evolutive class (*pьsati* 'write', *mlěti* 'mill, grind', *dělati* 'do, make'). Certain verbs in this class are predisposed toward terminativity (*dati* 'give', *pustiti* 'let, release', *staviti* 'set, build') while others are predisposed toward aterminativity (*rasti* 'grow', *pasti/pasǫ* 'pasture').

Terminative verbs had a much wider range of functions in Maslov's Prehistoric Slavic system than they do today. Resultative (prefixed) verbs could, like all other verbs, express completed action, ongoing action, or repeated action. Maslov gives the following examples: *velitь sъbьrati* 'he orders to collect', *sъbьra* 'he collected' but *načęšę sъbьrati* 'they began to collect' *se sъbьretь* 'hark, he is collecting', *sъbьraaše* 'he was collecting/used to collect' and *sъbьret čęsto* 'he often collects' (1961: 188).[35]

---

[33] The similarities between terminativity and complexness (see Němec 1956) are obvious; the difference is that Maslov's terminativity is strictly lexical, whereas Němec defines complexness more broadly so that it can take in tense distinctions as well.

[34] This classification looks far different from the systems proposed by Němec and others because Maslov confines himself to Slavic data, whereas Němec drew heavily on other Indo-European (especially Greek and Baltic) sources, thus implicitly reconstructing a much earlier stage of Slavic. Maslov's approach is consistent with his belief that it is not possible to make a meaningful reconstruction of the ties between Slavic and Indo-European on the basis of available evidence (Maslov 1961: 165-167).

[35] Since he marks all of these examples with an asterisk, they are presumably his own hypothetical creations for Prehistoric Slavic. (The Prehistoric Slavic verb forms above

In one subset of this class—prefixed motion verbs with suffixes—verbs had exclusively iterative meaning; Maslov cites Prehistoric Slavic *vynositi~iznositi* 'carry out (regularly)'. The corresponding nonsuffixed verbs with prefixes—he cites *vynesti~iznesti* 'carry out'—had both iterative and non-iterative meaning, as above. This relationship was similar to the relationship between *nesti* 'carry' and *nositi* 'carry (regularly)', with the exception that it contained a reference to limits or boundaries not implied in the unprefixed verbs.

Maslov then describes a system in which the perfective aspect traces its roots to terminativity, while the imperfective aspect arises from indeterminacy.[36] He proposes the following stages in the creation of an aspectual system. Verbs like *sъbьrati* (which unlike *vynesti* had no iterative forms) were in the position of expressing two different sorts of meaning: processual directionality toward attaining a result *(processnaja napravlennost' na dostiženie rezul'tata)* and the attainment of the result itself. On the model of *vynesti–*vynositi,* these verbs obtained a secondary form, *sъbirati,* which then developed a processual meaning alongside the indeterminate-iterative one. Thus the form *sъbirajetь,* which originally meant 'usually or regularly collects' came also to mean 'is collecting'. This processual usage then spread back to the *vynositi* type.

This development signals the formation of a highly marked imperfective aspect, which was opposed to a general aspect *(obščij vid)*. The perfective aspect did not yet exist. General aspect verbs still retained all their former functions (i.e., *se sъbъretь* still meant 'hark, he is collecting'), so that use of the imperfective aspect was optional for the time being.

In time, the use of the imperfective aspect broadened to monopolize the sphere of processual action. Verbs of general aspect that had an imperfective counterpart lost the ability to express process. This marked the creation of a perfective aspect. Aspect was still a partial system; all neutral and aterminative verbs remained outside it. The next stage of aspectual development was the gradual encompassing of other verbs in the language.

The neutral verbs were the first to be absorbed into one or the other category. Those with a natural lexical predilection for terminativity (*dati* 'give', *lišiti* 'deprive', *pustiti* 'release, let') followed the path of terminative verbs, utilizing either already existing indeterminate-iterative forms or creating them. Those with a natural lexical predilection for aterminativity (*dělati* 'make', *pьsati* 'write') formed aspectual pairings with lexically similar prefixed verbs.

Later, verbs in the aterminative category, like statives, were absorbed into the imperfective category as *imperfectiva tantum* verbs, and the remaining terminative

---

he does not mark with an asterisk, possibly because their existence is more certain; I have marked them with an asterisk as well to keep my conventions consistent.)

36 Part of the attraction of this hypothesis, according to Maslov, is that it explains an internal contradiction in the modern aspectual system: if in a true aspectual pair the imperfective is the unmarked aspect semantically, why then is it the marked aspect morphologically? (Maslov 1961: 170, 189-190.)

forms—inceptives, limited-duration, and semelfactive verbs—were absorbed into the perfective category as *perfectiva tantum* verbs.

Maslov's explanation falls short on only two counts, both connected with the instant of aspectualization. In the first place, he states that "the need arises for a formal, grammatical differentiation of the two semantic possibilities" of resultative verbs like **sъbbrati,* and that this is the impulse behind the rise of new forms like **sъbirati*. This motivation seems unclear at best and ignores the fact that, if Maslov is correct, the dual function of **sъbbrati* had long existed in Prehistoric Slavic; he offers no other developments in the verbal system that would have prompted such a need to arise. Furthermore, he fails to explain why and how iterative forms acquire processual meaning; his "examples" simply restate the premise that a form like **sъbirajetь* acquires the meaning 'is collecting' in addition to the expected meaning 'often or usually collects'.

If Maslov set out to explain the why and how of aspectual genesis, he has provided a convincing explanation of the "how." He has not fully succeeded, however, at the "why" part of the task; the reasons for the appearance of aspect remain just as unclear and unsupported by fact.

3.2.8. Forsyth 1972

James Forsyth, the author of *A Grammar of Aspect: Usage and Meaning in the Russian Verb* (1970), contributed a brief study in 1972 to the debate on the history of aspect. Much of it is a response to Maslov's and Ruzicka's works on the subject. As a strong proponent of the invariant meaning of aspect, Forsyth is not eager to see aspect grounded in a lexical perspective, as proposed in Maslov 1961, or to acknowledge the numerous ways in which the Old Russian aspectual system deviates from the Modern Russian system, as laid out in Ruzicka 1957.[37] Forsyth's study is noteworthy as a structuralist response to a debate conducted mainly on nonstructuralist turf.

While Forsyth admits that Ruzicka is correct in saying some simplex verbs are aspectually indifferent, he still finds no reason to doubt aspectuality as a grammatical category in Old Russian, especially given Ruzicka's rather mechanical and somewhat circular methods of assigning aspect to Old Russian verbs.[38] The

---

[37] Forsyth states at the outset that his purpose is "to examine current views [of aspectual history] in the light of what seems to the author to be the most satisfactory definition of the perfective: imperfective correlation, namely that which was first presented as a theoretical basis by R. Jakobson [in 'Zur Struktur des russischen Verbums']" (Forsyth 1972: 493).

[38] Forsyth makes good use of the weaknesses in Ruzicka's method of argument and presentation. Ruzicka classes all forms as having perfective or imperfective function, and then classes the verb as a whole as to aspect, allowing Forsyth to compare Ruzicka's aspectually indifferent verbs to Modern Russian biaspectual verbs. Forsyth does Ruzicka an injustice, however, in invalidating his argument wholesale. See the discussion of Ruzicka's work in section 3.5.

elegance of Forsyth's binary aspectual opposition, after all, is that once a single aspect is firmly established, the other aspect exists at least by default, even if its characteristics do not match those of the modern imperfective aspect.[39] He concludes his discussion of Ruzicka's work with this dismissal:

> In opposition to Ruzicka's view I would therefore say that these verbs in Old Russian (including even дати) are indeed unmarked as to aspect, and that it is precisely in this status that they in fact do participate in the category of aspect as it was defined above. (1972: 496)

In reference to Maslov 1961, Forsyth is troubled by Maslov's assignment of the main formative role to secondary imperfectives. By his own count, secondary imperfectives in Modern Russian and Old Russian constitute a small percentage of all verb forms in the language when actual word counts are done (1972: 500). He also points out another awkwardness of Maslov's theory: Maslov assumes that aspectuality develops simultaneously in all tenses and forms of the verb, a view Forsyth charitably labels "rather abstract" (1972: 501).

Forsyth's view of aspectual genesis is that in the initial stage, an opposition of tense systems exists between non-past and past. Within the preterite system, the aorist is the semantically unmarked member and the imperfect is the marked member. The perfect lies outside this system.

In the second stage, the semantic load of the perfect shifts. Formerly it gave a description of a state arrived at through prior action, and the semantic load lay at least partially on the copula. With the shift, the participle now bears the full semantic weight of the form, and the copula begins to lose ground, setting the stage for its eventual disappearance. This brings it into semantic competition with the aorist and imperfect tenses. Verbal prefixes strengthen this tendency by underlining the completeness of the action. This development shows that around the same time, prefixes were becoming restricted to expressing result, aim, sequence, or condition of the action. Forsyth calls this restriction membership in a perfective aspect, which is opposed to the general aspect (or lack of aspect, but at least in some respects an imperfective aspect) of all other verbs.

In the third stage, a need arises for forms that convey the same functions as the restricted perfectives, but without the syntactic limitations they are subject to. The already existing iterative verbs become morphological models for these new forms. By this time, the perfectivizing content of the prefixes has been diffused to the verb root as well, meaning that a secondary verb need not be subject to the syntactic restrictions of the perfective solely because of the presence of a prefix. A class of secondary imperfectives thus comes into being.

---

[39] Here it is worth remembering a caveat from Timberlake 1982: it is often possible to lump together unlike elements because they lack a particular feature—i.e. calling a varied group of verbs "imperfective" simply because they lack a certain feature that defines "perfectivity"—but this sort of analysis yields little information about the behavior of these verbs, bringing its usefulness into question.

In the fourth stage, the ascendance of the perfect tense in the preterite system allows an opposition to develop as well between simplex verbs and prefixed perfectives of the sort *tvoril"–s"tvoril"* 'did (impf.)–did (pf.)'. The simplex verbs are thus included under the imperfective rubric by analogy. Other simplex verbs become imperfective simply by virtue of not being marked for perfectivity (1972: 502-506).

Forsyth's hypothesis is the only one to link the ascendance of the perfect in the preterite system with aspectual genesis in a comprehensible and plausible fashion. Like Maslov's hypothesis, it derives a limited category (perfectivity) from another limited category (Maslov's lexical category of terminativity or Forsyth's morphological category of prefixation). Unfortunately, it does not seem as successful in other ways. It once again relies on an ambiguous "arising of need" for a change that he fails to ground in any other manner. Furthermore, while it deals adequately with prefixed verbs, Forsyth's method for including the rest of the verbal system seems suspect. Its main purpose, one suspects, is to equate nonperfectivity with imperfectivity from the very beginning, thus erasing the notion of non-aspectuality at any point in the later development of aspect.

3.2.9. Galton 1976

While Herbert Galton's *The Main Functions of the Slavic Verbal Aspect* is not primarily historical in its orientation, Galton treats aspect as a more or less unified pan-Slavic feature springing from a common source, and this treatment has necessitated some explanation of his views on the genesis of aspect. Galton sees aspect as a Slavic innovation, one that arose in Prehistoric Slavic independent of the categories of tense and determinacy. His most significant contribution to the debate on aspectual genesis is undoubtedly his analysis of how non-past usage and aspect interact.

In a cogently reasoned section on the perfective non-past, Galton argues that the future function so often cited as basic for this form is in fact a later, rather haphazard graft postdating the appearance of grammatical aspect. In Galton's view, "succession" is adequate to explain all uses of the non-past perfective across all Slavic languages, whereas making futurity a basic function of the perfective (opposed to presentness as a basic function of the imperfective) requires severe limitations on both the sort of examples considered and the languages referred to (South Slavic, for instance, is ruled out because of its specific future markers). All questions of tense and the non-past, in this interpretation, are questions of developments within preexisting individual aspectual systems; they cannot be used to show aspectual genesis.

Although Galton gives a convincing account of the "perfective present," I am less satisfied with his conclusion that grammatical aspect is therefore extant in even the oldest Slavic texts. His explanation, in fact, calls into question the whole notion of a "grammatical category": if a category is said to express a particular function, but that function has no regular reflection in or effect on the language's other categories, how can we define it as grammatical? I would argue that this aspectual system is therefore, in the oldest stages, lexical in nature, as it differs sharply from verb to verb and has only sporadic reflection in the grammar of Old Russian. The addition of the present–future distinction is in fact, as Galton points out, a relatively late one, but as such is precisely one of the features that indicate grammaticalization of the category of aspect in Old Russian and probably in other Slavic languages as well.[40]

3.2.10. Holden 1990

A recent article by Kyril Holden (1990) re-examines the history of Russian aspect and the scholarship devoted to it in the light of recent work on historical change and cognitive linguistics. Although he offers an outline for aspectual history throughout the history of Russian, Holden's main interest is in the Prehistoric Slavic era, hence the article's inclusion in this section.

Holden's views in many respects coincide with Vlasto's, in that he sees small-a aspect (i.e., all variations in the temporal shape of an act) as the motivation for the development of big-a Aspect (i.e., the specific reflection of aspect in the grammar) in Russian. The lexical categories inherited from Indo-European thus have a role to play in the formation of grammatical aspect, as do the aspectual components of the preterite tenses that develop in Prehistoric Slavic. In Old Russian, he traces the extension of aspectual meaning from the preterite to the non-past domain, completing the tendency to encapsulate aspectual distinctions in paired verbs. By the fourteenth century, when the perfect tense replaces the aorist and imperfect tenses, he says, we can now speak of grammatical aspect as existing in Russian. From that point on, "only a relatively minor development—an attempt from the XV to XVIII centuries to extend the productivity of the iterative -yva- suffix in the past tense...—distinguished the aspectual system of Russian of that period from CSR [Contemporary Standard Russian]" (Holden 1990: 149).

Holden gives a well-reasoned, convincing synthesis of existing literature on Slavic aspect and historical change, and his reconstruction of the Prehistoric Slavic situation nicely blends the influence of lexical categories and the existing tense categories. Furthermore, his description separates the initial appearance of certain meanings and functions from their full encoding in the grammar, a distinction that is too rarely made in earlier studies. I found only two points to disagree with in Holden's analysis, both of them relatively minor.

First, much is imputed to the textual properties of the aorist and imperfect, which Holden sees respectively as causing foregrounding and backgrounding in

---

[40] The history of South Slavic languages such as Bulgarian also seems to support this view. The appearance of a periphrastic future particle used with both aspects is an even more recent development overlaid on a system similar to that of Old Church Slavic, which has a nascent present vs. future opposition in the non-past. Furthermore, while the primary method of forming the future in Bulgarian is a periphrastic construction with the particle šte, traces of an older present vs. future opposition can be found in the modal meanings assigned to the two aspects (G. Fielder, personal communication).

Prehistoric Slavic, early Old Russian, and Old Church Slavic. The implication of this view is that these discourse functions eventually transferred to the perfective and imperfective aspects, which were developing out of lexical categories. The evidence Holden presents does have several convincing examples of foregrounding and backgrounding, but on the basis of other evidence from the Primary Chronicle I see these properties as secondary functions of the aorist and imperfect which are not consistently reflected in the data (whereas less textually oriented functions of the aorist and imperfect are more consistent at this early date).

Second, the statement that aspect had attained its current character by the fourteenth century is somewhat misleading; the present study indicates that numerous subtle but important discourse-oriented changes continued to take place at least through the sixteenth century. I thus agree with Holden that "as the pairing of new semantic classes of verbs increased, the prototypical 'center' of the aspectual opposition continually shifted, not only along the original dimension of telicity, but, by logical extension, into the "new pragmatic dimension of discourse sequencing, foregrounding and backgrounding, a semantic level associated with information shared by the speaker/hearer" (1990: 152). However, I do not agree that these discourse categories played a large role in the Prehistoric Slavic era; based on my data, they seem to make a distinctly later appearance.

3.2.11. Conclusions

The hypotheses presented here revolve around a finite number of issues presented to us by the oldest attested Slavic verbal systems and the verbal systems of Baltic and other Indo-European languages.

Historical depth. Is Slavic aspect a direct descendant of Proto-Indo-European aspect or not? Most scholars agree that it is not, although there is an revival of the view underway that sees in Slavic aspect the hand of an older, possibly inherited aspectual system (see Holden 1990). The modern twist on this century-old view is that this older system is construed not as a grammatical aspectual system but as a lexical aspectual system, reflecting a universal linguistic tendency to give semantically similar verbs similar morphological structures. Kuznecov in essence makes this argument, although he does not phrase it in this manner.

Role of determinacy. From the 1920s until the late 1950s, the category of determinacy was seen to play a crucial role in aspectual genesis. Now it appears to be more of a sidelight; its indeterminate category is no longer seen as a semantic source of the imperfective, merely as a convenient morphological source for suffixes. Only Borodič, who proposes a fairly extreme view of aspectual development, asserts that determinacy is the only important factor in aspectual genesis, and to do so she is required to greatly expand and dilute the definition of determinacy. Other scholars prefer to subordinate determinacy to some other quality, such as complexness (Němec), terminativity (Maslov), telicity (Holden), or prefixation (Forsyth). All four of these "new" categories have the laudable result of largely separating off prefixed verbs from other verbs, thus isolating the group of verbs that provided the most favorable conditions for the development of a separate category of aspect.

Role of prefixation. First proposed by Kuryłowicz, the use of prefixation to drive aspectual genesis has been invoked more and more frequently in recent articles, although Galton, for instance, rejects the importance of prefixation and insists that suffixation is the only true marker of a grammatical aspectual system. Proponents of prefixation argue over whether prefixed verbs generate perfectivity directly, or first generate derived verbs that spawn imperfectivity, in opposition to which the perfective aspect comes into being. As Holden's analysis makes evident, this concern is superceded to a certain extent by invoking telicity, terminativity, and other concepts that embrace prefixation but are more comprehensive.

Role of tense systems. Scholars have often been of the mind that aspect came into existence first in only one tense system—past or non-past—and then spread to the other. Convincing arguments exist on both sides. Borodič, Kölln, Holden, and Forsyth, for example, make use of the existing oppositions in the preterite system to generate an aspectual system from it. On the other hand, Kuryłowicz, Němec and Kuznecov link the existence of aspect with the loss of ability to express presentness in the non-past tense. Galton, in a third approach, studies tense systems carefully but nonetheless refuses to give one tense system primacy in the formation of aspect.

Morphologically (and typologically), the evidence seems to favor the preterite as the source for aspect, since the first imperfectivizing suffixes are identical to the suffixes of the imperfect tense. Semantically, the edge goes to the non-past; Kuryłowicz's argument on this count is particularly well thought out. One can also ignore tense systems altogether, as Maslov does, but this approach entails a certain conceptual fuzziness.

Tense and the order of aspectual genesis. As noted above, many scholars believe aspect arose first in one tense system (either present or past) before spreading to the other. Committing to either view also entails making a choice about which aspect arose first. Scholars who believe that aspectual differentiation first takes place in the non-past tense tend to believe the perfective aspect arose first; those who favor the preterite tenses as the foundation for the aspectual opposition assume that the imperfective aspect is the earlier of the two.[41]

Scholars who choose the non-past as the birthplace of aspect focus their attention on the directionality and terminative nature of prefixed forms, which leads to the gradual abandonment of presentness. Once a group of verbs has restricted itself in function, this means a perfective aspect has been created, which is opposed at first to an undifferentiated general aspect (later the imperfective aspect). On the other hand, using the past system as a basis for aspect leads naturally to the early rise of an imperfective aspect: given the relatively early demise of the imperfect tense, its imperfective-like character in many instances, and the identity of imperfect and imperfective suffixes, one is led to establish the imperfective aspect first as a limited, marked domain and later plot its expansion.

---

[41] Forsyth is an exception to this trend; he believes that the perfective aspect arose first, but in the preterite tense system.

Preterite tenses as a source for aspect. Direct statements to the effect that preterite tense distinctions determine aspect, like Kölln's, have obvious flaws.[42] Several scholars, however, have tried to integrate semantic distinctions made through the use of various tenses into a list of oppositions that eventually coalesce into aspect. This approach, found in the work of Vlasto, Galton, Holden, and Němec, is more convincing, since it counts features of the various tenses as contributors to the grammaticalization of aspect, instead of assuming a direct mapping of tense onto aspect.

3.3. WORK ON OLD CHURCH SLAVIC ASPECT

There is good reason for including a study of Old Church Slavic aspect in a study of Old Russian aspect. First, as the oldest Slavic written language, Old Church Slavic is chronologically the closest language to Prehistoric Slavic. Second, the ties between Old Church Slavic and Old Russian are strong enough to warrant consideration and examination without claiming that the latter is descended from the former. Third—in and of itself—is the existence of Dostál's study of aspect in Old Church Slavic, which in every respect remains a groundbreaking work in the field of historical aspectology thanks to its scope and thoroughness; many of Dostál's conclusions, data and methods had a profound impact on the debate over aspect's origins in the 1950s.

3.3.1. Structure of Dostál 1954

Dostál's seven-hundred page tome is divided into seven sections. In the introductory chapters he lays out his definition of aspect and how it relates to other verbal categories, such as tense and determinacy, and to the morphology and lexicon of the language. He then discusses how to determine aspect in Old Church Slavic.

A verb inventory and analysis constitutes the bulk of the work. Dostál's classification takes into account two main factors: aspectual behavior and morphology. Morphology is used to provide the broadest division: into simplex and prefixed verbs. Within these divisions, gradations of aspectuality occur; for

---

[42] I agree here with Galton, who writes: "If the genesis of the Slavic verbal aspect had merely followed the lead provided by the presumably inherited opposition of Aor. and Ipf., we would, as has been pointed out by Vaillant, expect the inherited aoristic stem to be regularly pv. in Slavic, but this is far from being the case.... No more did it grow out of the (lexico-semantic) category of determinacy, though this surely accounts for something in the constitution of the fully fledged aspectual system. The category of determinacy (oppposing *nesti–nositi* etc.) has either subsisted as such, affecting a maximum of 15 verbs expressing motion, as in the individual Slavic tongues, or it has not, and where it has not, as in the South-East, this has had no effect on the development of the aspect. Formal means are indispensable for the constitution of a grammatical category, but they do not bring it about while assuring its functioning and stability." (1976: 301)

instance, Dostál recognizes perfective simplexes, biaspectual simplexes that are more often perfective, biaspectual simplexes that are more often imperfective, and imperfective simplexes. The verbs in each gradation are analyzed according to their conjugation class. By relegating conjugational morphology to this level, Dostál is implicitly minimizing the connection between Prehistoric Slavic lexical-morphological categories and aspect.[43]

A number of verb groups, of course, fail to fit into these categories. These derivational or semantic sports are treated at the end of the aspectual analysis; they include double-prefixed verbs, compounds, denominals, and finally iteratives, which are treated separately. The final section contains comments on usage of other verbal categories (tenses, participles, nonfinite forms).

3.3.2. The definition and provenance of aspect

For our purposes, Dostál's conclusions about individual Old Church Slavic verbs will be less important than his overall methods, principles, and handling of particularly thorny questions, like the relationship between aspect and determinacy or iterativity. We will likewise leave aside his analyses of aspect and tense in language overall.

One point, however, is worth touching on briefly: Dostál's definition of aspect. In the canonical structuralist model examined earlier, the perfective aspect is marked for a particular feature, such as closure, while the imperfect is the unmarked member of the opposition. As such, the imperfective is impossible to define or pin down to a single meaning. Dostál appears not to believe this:

> D a ND vyjadřují postoj mluvícího k ději (k vnější události nebo popudu). Slovanské jazyky si vytvořily vedle prostředků lexikálních k vyjádření tohoto postoje v gramatickém systému jazyka ještě zvláštní kategorii vidu. Při D jde o celkové (ucelené) pojetí, plynoucí z postoje mluvícího k vnější události, při ND naopak o necelkové (neucelené) pojetí děje. D je v korelaci perfektivnosti podstatným členem, kdežto ND členem vedlejším.[44]

A structuralist would say that the imperfective is *not* concerned with the *complete (achieved)* view of the act. Dostál's definition is in this sense questionable (at least for Modern Russian, where the imperfective can be used to express the so-called "constatation of fact," which can certainly be complete or achieved); in the

---

[43] He states this belief explicitly later in his exposition (1954: 145).

[44] "P[erfective] and I[mperfective] express the attitude of the speaker to the act (an exterior event or failure). The Slavic languages have created, in addition to the lexical means of expressing this attitude in the grammatical system of the language. a further special category of aspect. P is concerned with the completed (achieved) view, proceeding from the attitude of the speaker to an external act; I is concerned, on the other hand, with an incomplete (unachieved) view of the act. In the correlation of perfectivity, P is the basic member, while I is the secondary member" (Dostál 1954: 15-16).

context of his analysis, however, it allows him to use a single criterion for imperfectivity that he would not otherwise have.⁴⁵

Having a definition for both aspects, then, Dostál is able to state that "the category of the aspects appears to us to be *completely self-contained and independent from the category of tense.*"⁴⁶ Analyses in which temporal oppositions somehow generate aspectual ones are categorically ruled out. Dostál is equally adamant in denying that lexical factors or any definition—extended or otherwise—of determinacy and indeterminacy underlie Old Church Slavic aspect. He limits lexical influences on aspect to the following categories: verbs of motion, verbs of speaking and understanding, verbs expressing sensual perception, and a few other minor groupings (1954: 33). Although he does concede that lexical semantics have more of an influence on aspect than the other two categories mentioned, Dostál feels compelled to state emphatically (and circularly) that, "of course, to base the study of aspects only on the lexical meanings of the verb would be incorrect, since the aspects *are not a lexical matter, but rather a grammatical one*" (1954: 34; italics in original).

Dostál reserves his harshest criticism for the use of "determinacy" to explain the provenance of aspect in Old Church Slavic. He takes pains to show that the definition of this term is quite slippery, and that even once defined with reasonable precision, the definitions of perfectivity and imperfectivity differ so greatly from determinacy and indeterminacy as to make a genetic relationship between them improbable. Dostál admits some similarity between indeterminacy and imperfectivity in that both reflect the "interrupted or dispersed quality" *(roztříštěnost)* of the act, but resolutely denies any similarity between determinacy, which expresses an act "flowing in a single uninterrupted stream *(neroztříštěným proudem)* to the goal" and perfectivity as earlier defined (1954: 36).

Dostál then turns to the question of how to determine aspect in a dead language, noting that the vast discrepancies between scholars in their aspectual assignment for many verbs show the difficulties of establishing such criteria. He concludes quite correctly that no single criterion gives accurate results in every case and recommends a judicious use of a range of features.

Expression of future modality is, in Dostál's view, an important criterion in determining aspect, although not the sole one. He accepts the premise that regular usage of the non-past form to express futurity indicates perfectivity, although he cautions that further research on the distribution of non-past forms with future function is important. He rejects other criteria, such as the verb's ability to form

---

⁴⁵ Of course, having a single criterion for imperfectivity actually makes the analysis more difficult in some ways. Forsyth, for instance, simply established a perfective aspect in Old Russian and then stated that everything which was not perfective must therefore have been imperfective. Dostál has in effect disallowed this route for himself by requiring positive proof of imperfectivity.

⁴⁶ "Po těchto výkladech jeví se nám kategorie aspektů *zcela samostatnou a na kategorii temporis nezávislou*" (Dostál 1954: 29; italics are original).

compound future tenses; this ability applies across aspects in Old Church Slavic (1954: 44).[47]

Somewhat more promising are methods of defining aspect by looking at the situation of the act *(situace děje)*—in other words, at context. This method can be understood broadly, as an evaluation of all factors in the surrounding sentences, or narrowly, as confined to specific formal features. Dostál notes that although formal features have the advantage of removing subjectivity from the process, they are also occasionally deceptive and should be used with care.

3.3.3. Difficulties in Dostál's lexical analysis

Although Dostál belittles the influence of lexical categories on aspect, part of the reason for this is evidently his choice of rather narrow interpretations of the lexicon, which is understandable given the state of research on lexical aspect when he was writing in the mid-1940s.[48] For instance, his lexical-semantic categories for perfective verbs consist of: change of place (*pasti* 'fall', *vratiti sę* 'return', *dvignǫti* 'move'); bodily functions (*dъchnǫti* 'breathe', *roditi* 'give birth'); spiritual acts (*mьstiti* 'avenge', *sramiti* 'shame'); verbs of speaking; causatives (*jazviti* 'wound', *kupiti* 'buy'); religious terminology (*vlasvimisati* 'blaspheme', *krьstiti* 'christen, cross'). Dostál sees in some of these groupings a common element of "a quick, short action." In others, like the verbs of speaking and causatives, he can find no unifying element (1954: 100-101). For biaspectual verbs, he finds much the same sort of groupings, except he sees in them a lexical content that is "much more concrete and closely limited" than for the previous group (1954: 143-144). Imperfectives are assigned to the following categories: change of place (*nesti* 'carry', *vlěšti* 'drag'); motionlessness, states and qualities (*bljusti* 'guard', *pasti/pasǫ* 'pasture'), verbs of speaking; bodily functions (*sъsati* 'suck', *doti* 'blow'). He finds the imperfectives to be more prone to express an act that is slow, repeated, composite, or incomplete (1954: 240-242).[49] It can also express the regularity of an act or the potential for it to occur.

Dostál's groupings are indeed lexical ones, but they represent a very narrow concept of what constitutes lexical similarity. He does not consider the notion of goal or progress toward it as a way of separating verbs. Furthermore, his categories

---

[47] Dostál's rejection of negative criteria seems wise; explicitly equating a construction's lack of *presence* in a manuscript with a lack of *ability* to exist seems rash.

[48] In his introduction, dated 1951, Dostál says that the work was completed in 1947 and alludes to political considerations that precluded its publication. He says that subsequently only minor alterations were made. The work was finally published in 1954.

[49] The term "composite" here translates the Czech *složitý* and refers to an act that is composed of numerous parts. A better term is "complex," but I have already used it to translate Němec's term *komplexní*, by which he means, of course, the opposite: a perfective-type act that encompasses both action and completion. To confuse matters further, Dostál uses the word *kompositum* to refer to acts Němec calls *komplexní*. We will thus translate Dostál's *kompositum* via English "complex act."

are by no means exclusive to one or another aspect, and when he tries to define the difference between verbs in the same lexical grouping that have different aspectual behavior, he often transgresses the boundaries of lexicality into the realm of contextual information. For instance, if an act could be said to be naturally "slow" or "quick and short," as he claims, that could indeed be a lexical trait, as might exclusive iterativity. Elements like regularity, potentiality, compositeness, and incompletion are not likely to be expressed in the lexicon; they are features of the context at large. What Dostál inadvertantly shows in his analysis is that a more systematic division of lexical groups is needed, and that contextual features interact closely with the lexicon to attach specific lexical-aspectual meanings to verb forms.

3.3.4. Past tense definitions and aspect

A second problem arises with Dostál's evaluation of Old Church Slavic tenses. While Dostál forbids us from equating the old tense system with aspect, his definitions of the aorist and imperfect tenses are close enough to his aspectual definitions to cause problems.

> Aor vyjadřuje pravidelně, že děj, o kterém se mluví, je v okamžiku mluvení hotov, Impf takového významu nemá. Tak je tomu ve většině dokladů na Aor. Proto se Aor užívá zvláště tehdy, když ve vyprávění následuje několik dějů po sobě, takže vyslovením takového tvaru, jenž postupný děj jazykově hodnotí, nastává postup ve vyprávění.... Impf. se užívalo naopak o dějích, které pravidelně netvoří pokrok ve vyprávění, nýbrž jen popisují, vysvětlují a také vyjadřují děje, které se konají současně s dějem jiným, na př. s takovým, který znamená postup v ději (1954: 601).[50]

This definition of past tense usage shows marked similarities to the definition of aspect presented in section 3.3.2. In Modern Russian aspectology, these two perspectives (marked for completion vs. unmarked for completion, external perspective on the act vs. internal perspective on the act) are often considered two sides of the same coin; an act is said to be perceived externally if its realization presents us with the picture of a completed act. Dostál's definition of tense is simply a more concrete, usage-based version of his definition of aspect. The only substantial difference between them is the number of features. Dostál's aspectual definition is nonbinary, with marked features for each member of the opposition, while his temporal definition is binary, with only one feature: completion.

---

[50] "The aorist as a rule expresses that the action under consideration is complete at the moment of speech; the imperfect does not have this meaning. Thus it is in the majority of examples of the aorist. Therefore, the aorist is used especially in narration where several actions follow one another, so that through the use of a form which linguistically evaluates a sequential act, progress in the narration is introduced.... The imperfect is used, on the contrary, for actions which as a rule do not create progress in the narration, but rather merely describe, explain and also express actions that take place concurrently with another action, for example with an action marking position in an action."

The net effect of letting temporal definitions converge with aspectual definitions in the past tense is that Dostál can assign aspect directly from tense forms while insisting that aspect and tense are not directly linked, because the definitions are not identical; they simply yield the same result.

3.3.5. Summary of Dostál's monograph

The main achievement of Dostál's work is his careful historical analyses of different epochs in the Old Church Slavic canon, which provide ammunition for his conclusions. Furthermore, Dostál's formulation for determining the aspect of Old Church Slavic forms provides a counterbalance to some of the less rigorous methods discussed in other sections of this chapter. However, the tack he takes does at times limit the effectiveness of his analysis. By insisting on the strict bipolar aspectuality of Old Church Slavic—and then explaining numerous examples of deviation from this norm as differing degrees of "biaspectuality"—Dostál goes against the most obvious conclusion inherent in the data. There are also certain problems in his discussions of lexical aspect and iterativity. Furthermore, his nonbinary definition of aspect is inadequate in the prevailing grammatical theory of aspect, which demands a strict marked–unmarked definition.

3.4. THE MORPHOLOGICAL HISTORY OF RUSSIAN ASPECT

Much of the work on the morphology of Old Russian aspect consists of unpublished doctoral dissertations from the former Soviet Union. One comprehensive published study is V. B. Silina's chapter on aspect in the multivolume study *Ističeskaja grammatika russkogo jazyka (A Historical Grammar of Russian)*, which is based on material from the Institute for the Russian Language's extensive card files for a dictionary of Old Russian.[51]

Morphological studies of aspect are in many senses tangential to this study; they examine the mechanism of aspectual development without the motive. But a brief appreciation of the morphological history of aspect offers clues to its semantic development as well. However, this tradition has tended to regard the Russian aspectual system as being fully established by the beginning of written history; in this view, only the morphological details remain to be worked out in the historical period, and this bias informs many of the conclusions adduced from the data.

3.4.1. Silina 1982

Silina's "Istorija kategorii glagol'nogo vida" ("A History of the Category of Verbal Aspect") takes a conservative approach to aspect, albeit with nods to the more radical theories outlined in Maslov 1961. Using a comprehensive analysis of

---

[51] Peter J. Mayo's monograph *The Morphology of Aspect in Seventeenth-Century Russian* also contains material germane to this discussion, but since the time frame of his research falls outside the scope of this work, the book will not be treated here.

Old Russian forms, Silina proposes time frames for the initial occurrence and heyday of different features. She starts by asserting that "the main driving force behind the morphological aspectual system is suffixal imperfectivization, that is, the formation of productive imperfective verbs with the help of various suffixes." The use of prefixes solely to mark aspect—changing their function "from lexical elements to aspectualizing elements"—is placed tentatively at a later date and labeled a secondary phenomenon (Silina 1982: 159-160).

3.4.2. A history of aspect and aspectualizers

Silina adopts some of the basic arguments from Maslov 1961—such as the existence of a "general aspect" in early Old Russian—but stresses the indeterminate–determinate opposition as the basis for the imperfective–general opposition of aspects in the prehistoric period.[52] She takes indeterminate verbs as the core of the category, saying that unprefixed derived verbs like *metati 'cast repeatedly', *skakati 'jump repeatedly', *dajati 'give repeatedly', *lijati 'pour repeatedly', *padati 'fall repeatedly' were the first to function as imperfectives. Pairedness of imperfective and perfective verbs, on the other hand, first develops in the determinate class out of old iteratives. Examples of pairs are *vyletěti–*vylětati 'fly out', *naliti–*nalijati 'pour', *podati–*podajati 'give, serve', etc. (1982: 164).

Silina then lays out a chronology of suffixal appearance and usage. She calculates the age of a suffix by looking at its earliest attested forms. Since simplexes are attested early and gradually give way to prefixed forms, the proportion of simplex vs. prefixed forms is important. A lack of unprefixed forms with a particular suffix indicates a later date of application to that verb. A large number of unprefixed forms with a suffix points to a long history of usage.

The first suffixes to be used as imperfectivizers were those seen in the Old Russian verbs *dvigati (dvižut')* 'move', *dajati (dajut')* 'give', *běgati (běgajut')* 'run', *nositi (nosjat')* 'carry'. Silina names suffixes by references to the allomorphs found respectively in the infinitive and present tense; the suffixes appearing in the above verbs are thus, in order, {-a-~-j-, -ja-~-j-, -a-~-aj-, -i-~-Ø-} (1982: 164-169).[53] None of these older suffixes gained wide productivity; Silina's interpretation is that their multifunctionality by and large hindered them from developing a strong identity as imperfectivizers. The first two, {-a-~-j-, -ja-~-j-}, also served as thematicizers, making old athematic verbs into thematic ones. They thus formed perfective as well as imperfective verbs and are thus less than ideal markers of imperfectivity. The last suffix, {-i-~-Ø-}, became associated with other types of verbal formation, such as causatives (*moriti 'cause to die', *saditi 'plant',

---

[52] Maslov's contention was that the imperfective aspect arises within the terminative category, but on the model of indeterminate verbs outside it.

[53] Silina discusses this notation on pp. 161-162. Although more precise than mine, it is cumbersome for work in the historical period, where few of these older suffixes overlap with the newer, morphologically transparent ones. Silina does not use this notation for the suffixes {-ova-} and {-iva-}.

učiti 'teach') and denominal derivation; it retains a link to imperfectivity only in the realm of motion verbs. The third suffix, {-a-~-aj-}, is also associated with denominals, but is the best represented of the oldest layer of suffixes.

In the next stage, which Silina calls "the development of specialized means of imperfectivization," Prehistoric Slavic began to use two suffixes, {-va-~-vaj-} and {-ja-~-jaj-}, which have no discernable nonaspectual uses. As a result, these suffixes obtained a greater degree of productivity in Slavic than the older suffixes had. The highest degree of productivity for the {-va-~-vaj-} suffix came in the fourteenth to seventeenth centuries, Silina suggests. The {-ja-~-jaj-} suffix retains the consonant-mutating properties of earlier, multipurpose suffixes but had the advantage, Silina says, of remaining visible in both present and past allomorphs of the verb root, increasing its productivity. It was especially productive in verbs with the thematic suffix {-i-~-Ø-}, such as Old Russian *v"zvysiti–v"zvyšati* 'elevate, glorify', *zaščititi–zaščiščati* 'defend' (1982: 169-172).

The Old Russian suffix {-ova-} (including its variant {-eva-}) was used as both an imperfectivizer and a denominalizer. Silina records numerous examples of derived forms in {-ova-} built on verbs with thematic {-a-} suffixes, which she claims is the most suitable environment for it. (She also finds many i-stem verbs that could take the {-ova-~-eva-} suffix.) In Silina's view, although this suffix enjoyed high productivity as an imperfectivizer in the eleventh through fourteenth centuries, it gave way in succeeding centuries to the competing suffix {-yva-~-iva-}, which was monofunctional and thus more suited to be a widescale imperfectivizer.

In the section on "the development of a uniquely Old Russian model of imperfectivization," Silina suggests (following Nikiforov and Kuznecov) that this suffix came into being as a reanalysis of older verbs formed with the {-va-~-vaj-} suffix; in essence **by-va-ti* is reanalyzed as **b-yva-ti,* and **bi-va-ti* as **b-iva-ti*. Two factors made this suffix especially useful: first, the initial vowel allowed it to stand after roots ending in a consonant; and second, the convergence of [i], [y] in Russian as allophones of a single phoneme /i/, depending on the palatalization status of the previous consonant, meant that these two suffixes could be considered allophonic variants of a single suffix. Their application would be conditioned by the nature of the preceding consonant (1982: 172-175).

The suffix {-yva-~-iva-} is attested as early as the eleventh century, but its frequency in Old Russian documents exploded in the fourteenth century. The sixteenth and seventeenth centuries were the "phase of maximal productivity" for this suffix. It appeared, according to Silina, as a regular formation from practically every verb and began to replace forms with older suffixes, creating imperfective doublets such as: *vstupati sja~vstuplivati sja* 'enter^I', *ispravljati~ispravlivati* 'correct^I', *otstavati~otstavyvati* 'fall behind^I'. The emergence of a new literary norm in Russian, however, halted this process by favoring the older, less productive forms. In this way, Silina says, the use of {-yva-~-iva-} as a universal imperfectivizer was derailed, and the morphological regularization of aspect was halted. Without a universal imperfectivizer, Modern Russian was forced to realize the choice of aspectualizers at the level of the lexicon, not the grammar. Still, {-yva- ≈ -iva-} remained productive for new forms, and in Modern Russian dialects approaches the status of a regular aspectualizer.

3.4.3. Aspect and tense

Silina hypothesizes that the processual meaning that is the basis for the imperfective aspect was created first in the non-past. Her rationale is that the greatest urgency of distinguishing processuality is at the moment of speech, not at some future point. Further, the multifunctionality of the non-past was overly dependent on context to clarify temporal reference; the creation of a specifically present-tense form would ease this dependency. As support for this idea, Silina points to particularly ancient imperfectivization models, which distinguish forms only in the non-past. A clear example is the alternation of {-a-~-j-} with {-a-~-aj-} in the conjugation of verbs like Old Russian *pomazati* 'to spread': *pomažu, pomazaju* 'I (will) spread, I spread'.

Since a distinction between processual and non-processual already existed in the past tense, Silina proposes that the aorist–imperfect opposition be identified with the initial perfective–imperfective aspectual opposition as schematized in chart 3.4.3.1.

Chart 3.4.3.1. Silina's proto-Russian aspect paradigm

infinitive	non-past		past	
	bare	suffixed	aorist	imperfect
*pomazati	*pomažut'	*pomazajut'	*pomazaša	*pomazaxu
pf.? impf.?	pf.	impf.	pf.	impf.

In some cases (she mentions *sъbьrati—*sъbirati 'collect') the new formation generated a different infinitive as well. In this case, the aspectual opposition was not contained within a single verb, as laid out above, but would be divided between two separate verbs, each with a partial paradigm in the past tense (see chart 3.4.3.2).

Chart 3.4.3.2. Silina's aspectual paradigm for derived forms.

infinitive		non-past		past	
		bare	suffixed	aorist	imperfect
*sъbьrati	*sъbirati	*sъbьrut'	*sъbirajut'	*sъbьraša	*sъbiraxu
pf.	impf.	pf.	impf.	pf.	impf.

The complementary paradigm in the past tense developed gradually. Imperfectives were always limited to the imperfect tense, while other verbs could have both aorist and imperfect forms. Gradually the verbs marked as perfectives became restricted to the aorist form.

Only when the suffix {-yva-~-iva-} gains wide currency as an imperfectivizer does the instability of the non-past's temporal reference disappear, since unambiguous present tense forms were now available. The crystallization of analytical imperfective future forms in the fifteenth through seventeenth centuries strengthens the aspectual paradigm and gives it its contemporary shape. The analytical future, Silina says, has one narrowly defined function and permits no derived or figurative usages (1982: 198).[54] She draws an analogy between this restrictedness and the narrow range of derived imperfectives in the proto-Russian phases of aspectual development.

3.4.4. Chronology of aspectualization

At the end of her article, Silina proposes a chronology for the development of aspect, which is encapsulated in chart 3.4.4.1. (1982: 277-279).

Chart 3.4.4.1. Summary of Silina's chronology

1. *Tenth or eleventh centuries to beginning of twelfth century*:
   Prehistoric Slavic aspectual forms are still in effect. Grammatical aspect is found mainly in prefixed verbs. Imperfective verbs are clearly defined as against general-aspect verbs, which show some signs of becoming perfective. Prefixes play primarily a lexical, not a grammatical, role.

2. *Middle of twelfth century to end of fourteenth century:*
   An increase in aspectual pairs parallels the productivity of the {-iva-~-yva-} suffix . Perfectivity is standardized. Relics of general aspect are lost altogether: remaining simplexes are gathered into the aspectual opposition.

3. *Fifteenth to seventeenth centuries:*
   {-iva-~-yva-} becomes maximally productive as an imperfectivizer, and expands into the area of iterative verbs. Prefixes become a possible method of aspectualization. The aspectualization of simplexes is complete.

4. *Eighteenth century to beginning of nineteenth century:*
   Normativizing trends strengthen. Many new {-iva-~-yva-} formations are rejected, putting an end to the use of this suffix for iteratives in mainstream speech and writing.

---

[54] Silina does not mention common usages of the analytical future such as *Vy budete čaj pit'?* 'Would you like tea?' (lit. 'Will you be drinking[I] tea?') and *Vy budete vyxodit'?* 'Please let me by' (lit. 'Will you be getting[I] off [the train/bus]?'), both of which display modal (i.e., derived or figurative) functions.

3.4.5. Summary of Silina 1982

While Silina's analysis of the appearances of various suffixes and prefixes is highly useful, too much weight is given in her analysis to the value of monofunctionality. Silina hangs her theory of the inevitable triumph of {-yva-~-iva-} as imperfectivizer on the assumption that because other suffixes served multiple functions, they were unfit for the task. This line of logic might hold true for Russian, but in formulating it as a general linguistic rule, Silina overplays its significance. To take a contrasting example, Czech has {-ova-} as its primary imperfectivizing suffix. A researcher looking at Czech aspect would note that use of the {-ova-} suffix as a denominalizer added to its frequency and thus to its functionality as an aspectualizer. The conclusion would be the opposite of Silina's: that multifunctionality adds to the imperfectivizing abilities of a suffix. This hypothesis is equally unfounded; a single language's data do not allow us to generalize about the advantages and disadvantages of multifunctionality in morphemes. A language-specific formulation of this conclusion—that Russian has throughout its history resolved suffix competition by choosing the one with the lowest functional load in other contexts—would, if true, be more appropriate.

Silina's conclusions about the interaction of tense and aspect suffer from a lack of supporting textual and theoretical material. In particular, she sees aspectual assignment among verb pairs as a simple continuation of the old aorist–imperfect distinction, and this view demands more support than she provides. It would be convenient if we could assume that Old Russian tenses expressed the same opposition found between later perfective and imperfective verbs—it would make aspectual assignment in Old Russian a matter of rote—but the presence of imperfects from perfective-type verbs and aorists from imperfective-type verbs in early Old Russian argues strongly against this position. Silina sees the need for a filter to correct the obvious deficiencies in these assignments, but ends up appealing to native-speaker intuition to create this filter. She begins by assigning all aorists to the perfective aspect and all imperfects to the imperfective aspect, but when the result is contrary to expectations (which are based on Modern Russian aspectual assignment), she simply labels the verb "general aspect" instead. The results may in fact be reasonably accurate, but the method is circular and thus suspect.

This problem is endemic to the purely morphological approach to aspect. Without reference to contextual and lexical factors, the researcher is left with an interplay of various verbal morphemes and forms—suffixes, prefixes, tenses—which are inadequate to the task of fully explaining the reasons behind aspectual change and the movement of change through the verbal system. One can fall back on various hypotheses about language universals, hence the discussions of monofunctional vs. polyfunctional suffixes. Or one can appeal to structuralist principles of "filling holes" in "incomplete" systems, a concept often encountered in the course of this article.[55]

---

[55] An example: "Although this area of aspectual formation was served by two models of imperfectivization—the formation of parallel non-past forms in {-a-//-aj-}... and the

3.5. THE SEMANTIC HISTORY OF RUSSIAN ASPECT

Virtually alone among the works on aspect in Old Russian, Rudolf Ruzicka's *Der Verbalaspekt in der altrussischen Nestorchronik* (1957) and Wulf Budich's *Aspekt und verbale Zeitlichkeit in der I. Novgoroder Chronik* (1969) take the semantics of aspect as their primary subject. Ruzicka contends quite correctly that Old Russian aspect is far less regularized and developed than is ordinarily thought, and while I question many of the specifics of Ruzicka's arguments and have reservations about his methodology, his work stands out as a bold attempt to challenge prevailing beliefs about early Russian aspect.[56] Budich's methods are far more dependable, and his conclusions about the role of duration in aspectual formation are largely compatible with the ones in this study.

3.5.1. Aspect in the Primary Chronicle

While Ruzicka claims to approach aspect from a semantic perspective, the morphological character of aspectual research that prevailed at the time has a discernable influence on his work. He analyzes the Old Russian verbal system according to stem and suffix type, with the exception of motion verbs, which he treats separately. This perspective has a tradition in semantic analyses of Prehistoric Slavic aspect: it attempts to link aspectual assignment with a quasi-lexical protosystem reflected in the stem and suffixal morphology of the verb. For each verb listed, Ruzicka determines on the basis of examples from the Primary Chronicle (and occasionally from other sources) which aspect the verb belonged to. He labels his examples according to their corresponding modern aspectual assignment, so that, for example, one finds examples of *dati* 'give' that he calls "imperfective" by modern standards and others he calls "perfective."

Ruzicka concludes that while aspect clearly exists as a system in Old Russian, there are so many verbs that do not fit into a single aspect that it is problematic to simply label them all biaspectual along the lines of Modern Russian *ženit'sja* 'get married (pf. and impf.)'. Instead, he proposes that simplex verbs in Old Russian are often nonaspectual, and that aspect itself has a less regular character in Old Russian than in Modern Russian. He claims that much of the surrounding context—which we ordinarily assume derives from or is determined by the aspect of the verb—is in

---

formation of imperfectives with {-ova-}—neither had much chance to increase its productivity.... For this reason the Old Russian language was in need of a new means of imperfectivization, simple and precise in its formulation, universal and regular in its application and specialized in its function. The search for it continued throughout the early Old Russian period. Toward the end it became clear that the imperfectivizing suffix {-iva-, -yva-} had stepped into this role" (Silina 1982: 174-175).

56 The material I present in chapters 4 and 5 was analyzed before Ruzicka's work was brought to my attention, making it all the more significant that our conclusions show some similarities in outline.

fact wholly independent of aspect in the early Old Russian period. Instead of assuming, for instance, that sequences of events normally require the perfective, we can say that sequencing is a separate phenomenon that is unaffected by the aspectual assignment of the verbs involved. Far more contexts—and subsequently far more verbs—are therefore classified as neutral with respect to aspect.

Ruzicka posits that aspectuality in Old Russian is at least partially a function of morphology. He generally acknowledges that simplex verbs are more likely to be nonaspectual than prefixed verbs or derivationally suffixed verbs. Furthermore, in treating verbs by stem and (nonderivational, nondesinential) suffix class, he observes that verbs of certain classes are more likely to be nonaspectual than those in other classes. In particular, verbs with an {-i-} suffix are highly likely to be nonaspectual, whereas verbs with an {-a-} or {-ě-} suffix are likely to be imperfective, and those with a bare stem are likely to be perfective. Of course, there are numerous exceptions within each group, and Ruzicka admits that much of a verb's apparent aspectuality may derive from its lexical tendencies.

In acknowledging the influence of context and lexical groupings on aspect, Ruzicka excepts three contexts and one lexical group from his overall conclusions. He treats geographic descriptions, chains of events, and participles apart from other contexts, and proposes that motion verbs as a group be considered nonaspectual, regardless of their morphological status. (He admits the existence of a determinacy opposition at this point in history but says it does not play a role in assigning motion verbs to one or another aspect.)

Ruzicka correctly notes that in Old Russian one cannot predict or determine perfectivity simply by situating events in a temporal chain, as is often posited for Modern Russian. Furthermore, he notes a tendency in geographical descriptions to prefer verbs with a determinate base; this could erroneously lead us to describe the context as "perfective" in Old Russian, but he assures us this is more a feature of determinacy than of aspect. Ruzicka also cautions against an interpretation of Old Russian participial forms in a manner identical to that of Modern Russian. He claims that Old Russian participles are not dependent temporally or causally on the sentence's main verb in the way Modern Russian participles are. This, he theorizes, explains the differences in participial usage between Old Russian and Modern Russian.

3.5.2. Difficulties with Ruzicka's methodology

Precisely because Ruzicka's conclusions agree with my own, I will subject his methodology and examples to close scrutiny. As noted earlier, Ruzicka's arguments and conclusions were sharply criticized in Forsyth 1972; these objections will serve as a useful starting point. Forsyth says:

> Ruzicka rightly criticises Dostál's categorisations [ex. "usually imperfective, but in exceptional cases perfective"] as improbable, and concludes that these verbs, both in Old Church Slavic and early Old Russian, did not yet participate in the category of aspect, and that they must be considered still unmarked in respect of

aspect. Unfortunately Ruzicka means by 'unmarked' that these specific verbs are somewhat exceptional within the predominantly aspectual system of Old Russian because they are neither perfective *nor imperfective*. The reason for considering them to be not imperfective appears to be that in such sentences as: И убиша Асколда и Дира, и несоша на гору, и погребоша и на горѣ (Пов. 6390, Likh. p. 34) and Се слышавъ царь посла к Игорю лучиѣ боляре (Пов. 6452, Likh. p. 34) the imperfective verbs, corresponding to modern понесли and услышав, do not express processuality. This is indeed true (and parallels occur even in modern Russian) but as we have seen processuality is not the criterion of imperfective aspect. (Italics are original.)

Forsyth then hedges his bets by saying that even if some of the verbs are truly nonaspectual, then nonaspectuality is a form of aspectuality (Forsyth 1972: 496).

This objection strikes at a critical weakness in Ruzicka's methods: Ruzicka has tried to prove nonaspectuality by referring and comparing Old Russian exclusively to modern Slavic aspect. He classes every usage as "perfective" or "imperfective," stating that these labels of course refer to the modern assignments. But having done so and having obtained a list of verbs that appear in both perfective and imperfective usages, he reaches a stalemate: imperfectivity plus perfectivity could easily equal biaspectuality, or some other division of aspectual relations in Old Russian; it need not necessarily indicate nonaspectuality. All that his examples can prove is that aspect in Old Russian is not exactly identical to aspect in Modern Russian. Although he does not formulate it this precisely, Forsyth picks up on this terminological and conceptual gap in Ruzicka's argument—notice his disparaging use of the phrase "appears to be" in the quote above—and uses it to discredit the entire hypothesis.

There is, of course, a way to make the argument for nonaspectuality more foolproof, but it requires more information than Ruzicka provides. Instead of categorizing each form as appropriate to one or the other modern aspect, the researcher must develop one set of semantic and syntactic criteria that establishes aspectuality, and another set that establishes nonaspectuality. Only verbs that fail the first test and pass the second should be seen as nonaspectual.[57]

A second problem is less methodological than it is organizational: Ruzicka classifies verbs morphologically, and this method is less fruitful than he believes to be the case. His rationale is presumably that morphologically similar verbs were assumed to be semantically similar as well in some stage of Prehistoric Slavic, making it probable that aspect (or the lack thereof) and morphology would be linked. Also, since Ruzicka notes that simplex verbs are more often nonaspectual than prefixed or derivationally suffixed ones, it was reasonable to assume that subclasses of simplex verbs would yield further refinements. In my opinion, Ruzicka fails to show substantial correlation between aspect and morphological verb

---

57 My criteria for aspectuality and nonaspectuality are laid out and employed in subsequent chapters.

class; in his attempts to salvage an aspectual morphology-semantics connection he turns to problematic linguistic techniques.

The difficulties Ruzicka experiences become apparent early in his analysis, in the examination of the {-iti~-jat'} verb class:

> Der gleiche "Aspekt" dieser Verben, d.h. die alte relative Einheitlichkeit ihrer Neutralität, die potentiell beide Aspekte implizierte, wurde zerrissen und Verben gleichartiger Struktur auf die zwei Seiten verteilt: ipf. судить, мстить — pf. пленить, явить, молвить, лишить (vgl. auch die Liste bei Mazon, Morph. 23). Einer Reihe von Verben zeichnet allerdings die zuständliche Aktionsart den Aspekt vor: z.B. aruss. любити, княжити, служити, мыслити u.a. Das Gesagte gilt nur für die Simplicia. (1957: 24)[58]

If these verbs had such similar aspect in the Primary Chronicle, one wonders what later forces them into different aspects, and whether the fault is not in grouping them together in the first place. After all, a classification that yields no predictions is not particularly useful. Furthermore, an odd distinction is drawn: certain verbs are said to behave indifferently with respect to aspect (the first list above) while others are said to behave like imperfectives—but thanks only to their Aktionsart (the second list).[59] Ruzicka combines true statives with atelic actions, claiming for both an underlying aspectual indifference that is covered up by semantic factors. One wonders how this underlying indifference to aspect can be assumed if these verbs truly show all signs of being imperfective.[60] This appeal to a notion of underlying indifference serves another function as well: it swells the ranks of the "naturally nonaspectual" verbs, further supporting Ruzicka's hypothesis.

As it turns out, not all verbs are judged on the basis of their behavior in the Primary Chronicle, and the boundaries of Ruzicka's corpus and of applicable material from Old Russian overall are thus hazy and ill-defined. For instance, with the verb *m'stiti* 'avenge', Ruzicka lists three examples with a perfective function and one with a potentially imperfective function (I am not as fully convinced of its imperfectivity as he is). He then adds an example from outside his corpus (Sreznevskij's dictionary), which he designates as imperfective. Ruzicka can now

---

[58] "The similar 'aspect' of these verbs [in early Old Russian]—that is, the old relative uniformity of their neutrality, which potentially implied both aspects—was torn asunder and verbs of similar structure divided on either side: impf. *sudit'* 'judge', *mstit'* 'avenge' — pf. *plenit'* 'capture', *javit'* 'appear', *molvit'* 'pray, say', *lišit'* 'deprive' (see also the list in Mazon, Morph. 23). For a series of verbs, however, the stative Aktionsart indicates the aspect: ex. Old Russian *ljubiti* 'love', *knjažiti* 'reign', *služiti* 'serve', *mysliti* 'think', etc. The aforesaid holds only for simplexes." (I retain Ruzicka's use of the word *Aktionsart* here, even though he uses it in a much wider sense than is currently fashionable.)

[59] This list, furthermore, is only acceptable if true states like *ljubit'* 'love' are equated with atelic acts like *myslit'* 'think'.

[60] Actually, despite Ruzicka's claim, it is not at all clear that these verbs behave exactly like imperfectives. I discuss this matter in some detail in chapters 4 and 5.

claim nonaspectuality for *m'stiti*, since he has two imperfective and three perfective usages. Later on in his discussion, several more examples of *m'stiti* are brought to light. All function as perfectives.

The addition of material from a dictionary is troubling; after all, Sreznevskij's corpus is quite large, possibly not exhaustive for the sources it uses, and presumably not all examples from it show up in the dictionary. Picking single examples out of it to add to one's corpus would seem to upset whatever picture of the system a single text can give. Yet Ruzicka adds to his data isolated examples and quotations from Sreznevskij, Dostál, and other sources quite often and then gives them a weight equal to the examples from his own text in deciding the status of the verb. (For example, he does so with the verbs *tvoriti* 'do', *staviti* 'place, build', *krěsiti* 'raise', *svjatiti* 'consecrate', *živiti* 'give life'.)

The addition of dictionary examples might be of less concern if the reader had a more complete picture of the state of Ruzicka's corpus. Unfortunately, Ruzicka only exceptionally indicates whether he is presenting all examples of a verb found in the text or only a small portion of them. Even in the cases where he must have selected only a fraction of the available examples (for verbs like *stojati* 'stand', *viděti* 'see', *slyšati* 'hear', which are attested numerous times in the text), he does not present the reader with any statistics that would reveal the state of the data on those verbs as a whole. A classic example of this murkiness is his discussion of *praviti* 'direct, act' (1957: 28), where Ruzicka admits "numerous" examples with imperfective functions but warns also of evidence for perfective functions. One such example is presented, and the verb is declared to be nonaspectual. In consulting my own data on the Chronicles, I found this to be the only example that could possibly be construed as perfective out of a total of eight examples. While its "perfectivity" may be notable, one has the feeling that Ruzicka has overstated the case.

The main problems of Ruzicka's classificatory system, then, are that the morphological classes he proposes are of dubious benefit, and his examples do not reflect a clear and consistent set of data. The other sections on morphology suffer from the same defects: they concentrate too hard on fitting verbs from a single morphological class into similar patterns of behavior, with at best moderately convincing results.

The sections that follow Ruzicka's morphological scheme treat context in Old Russian, covering the realization of events in a chain, geographical descriptions, and use of participles. They are more convincing, if less interesting and innovative, than his arguments for aspectual indifference. Writ large, his point is that certain contexts that require one or another aspect in Modern Russian do not condition the appearance of any particular aspect in Old Russian. In some instances, however, his explanations cause more problems than they explain. If Old Russian participles lack the temporal and causal dependence on the head verb that they have in Modern Russian, how are they then to be used in evaluating aspect? If chains of events need not be perfective, what impact does this fact have on his earlier analysis that sentences like the aforementioned *I ubiša Askolda i Dira, i nesoša na goru, i pogreboša i na gorě* ('And they killed Askold and Dir, and carried them to the mountain, and buried them on the mountain') have *nesoša* 'carried' in a nonimperfective, nondurational meaning?

The two semantic divisions Ruzicka makes—excepting motion verbs from his morphology classification and geographical descriptions from his contextual analysis—also hint at a broader problem in his analysis. Why should Old Russian distinguish only two content-based groups from the great mass of verbs and contexts? It seems likely from the analysis of motion verbs (which is far more solid than his morphological analysis) that semantics play a role in determining aspectual behavior: why then could this not be true for the rest of the verbal system?

One final problem I have already alluded to: there is no explanation in Ruzicka's monograph as to where his classifications of perfective and imperfective function come from for any given example. There are three different possibilities, which are mentioned occasionally but never given directly as a source for his judgments. First, later manuscripts of the Primary Chronicle may give a variant reading that Ruzicka accepts as closer to the Modern Russian. Second, earlier researchers may have given a gloss or left a discussion that hints at their evaluation. (This includes definitions found in Sreznevskij.) Third, Ruzicka may be using his own intuition based on modern Slavic languages. In a few cases Ruzicka directly refers to one of the first two points to support his contention; in numerous instances, however, the reader must grasp at straws to figure out where Ruzicka's interpretation comes from, and often it is open to question.

3.5.3. Summary of Ruzicka

Ruzicka advances an innovative theory in his monograph on the Primary Chronicle but, as other researchers have noted, he falls short of adequately justifying it. Most cogent are his criticisms of earlier work: he effectively takes Dostál to task, for instance, for first insisting on the absolute rigidity of the Old Church Slavic aspectual system and then developing a baroque classification including all different degrees of aspectuality to cover up a large nonaspectual class. His ideas deserve consideration in further research.

His shortfalls are instructive for the student of Old Russian aspect. Classifying forms as "perfective" or "imperfective" by Modern Russian standards was an insufficient proof of nonaspectuality as a phenomenon distinct from perfectivity or imperfectivity and opened Ruzicka to dismissal by a structuralist critic. His attempt to link morphology and aspect is equally interesting but ultimately unsuccessful, leading him to stretch his conclusions farther than they would go.

Still, the core assertion of Ruzicka's work—that large portions of the Old Russian verbal system are indifferent to aspect—represents a step forward for the understanding of aspectual history. It is the goal of further research to find a more convincing proof of what was so evident to Ruzicka, and to define its parameters in a more logical, coherent fashion.

3.5.4. Budich's view of aspectual genesis

In his 1969 monograph *Aspekt und verbale Zeitlichkeit in der I. Novgoroder Chronik,* Budich examines the role that *Zeitlichkeit* (roughly 'temporal shape', equivalent to what I have been calling 'lexical aspect') played in giving birth to the aspectual system. He disparages Ruzicka's earlier efforts in this vein, saying:

> "Der Verbalaspekt in der altrussischen Nestorchronik"...von R. Ruzicka bleibt trotz seiner Einleitung "Zur Methode der historischen Aspektforschung" eine unbefriedigende "unhistorische" Untersuchung, die sich vergeblich bemüht, mit neurussischen Maßstäben das so andersgeartete altrussische Verbalsystem zu messen. Ruzicka konnte zwar feststellen, daß die "Aspektverhältnisse" im Altrussischen anders waren als im Neurussischen, doch nach dem aliud fragte er nicht; und an dieser Stelle allein kann eine historische Untersuchung ansetzen. Außerdem leidet die Untersuchung Ruzickas an dem methodologischen Mangel, daß das Material unvollständig und ohne Übersetzung der angeführten Beispiele vorgelegt ist. Dadurch bekommt der Leser ein vollkommen vom Verfasser gelektes Bild, ohne sich an semantischen Gegebenheiten orientieren zu können.[61] (Budich 1969: 5)

Budich's assessment of Ruzicka's conceptual limitations are more valuable than his comments about the presentation of Ruzicka's work.[62] He avoids many of the errors committed by Ruzicka: he outlines a history of the protoaspectual system and takes a fluid view of the Old Russian aspectual system, which he sees as neither clearly aspectual nor clearly lexical, but rather an aspectual system with lexical "subcurrents" that belie its lexical origin in the not-too-distant past.

According to Budich, aspect and tense are systems of subjective time-ordering that replace an older system of objective time-ordering, by which he means the

---

[61] *"Verbal Aspect in the Old Russian Nestor Chronicle ...*by R. Ruzicka remains, despite its introduction 'On the Methods of Historical Aspect Research' a disappointing and 'unhistorical' piece of research, which wastes considerable time trying to measure the differently-structured Old Russian verbal system with Modern Russian criteria. Ruzicka can hardly conceive that the 'substance of aspect' might be different in Old Russian than it is in Modern Russian, for he does not even ask about it; and it is on this basis alone that a historical piece of research can be launched. Besides, Ruzicka's research suffers from a methodological deficiency: the material is presented incompletely and without translations of the examples given. In this way, the reader receives a picture which is completely guided by the author, without being able to orient himself with respect to the semantic data."

[62] Budich, like Ruzicka (and, I would argue, like all scholars), is trapped between the need for explicitness and the need for conciseness. His text—while it does provide translations of many examples into German—contains very little analysis; most conclusions are simply stated after the examples are given, and the reasoning behind them must be deduced from the translations. Translations do not necessarily make the reader any less "guided by the author"; in fact, they can do the reverse by implying an exact, one-to-one equivalence between source and target language lexemes.

temporal shape of the action.[63] He limits this lexical distinction in large measure to the opposition durative–nondurative, which he believes was the basic opposition of the Balto-Slavic verb. In his view, then, the addition of tenses to this system of objective duration unbalanced it by creating a multitude of subcategories and eventually giving nondurative actions special durative forms and creating forms which curtail the durative element of naturally durative verbs. The former forms he called "displexives" (*Displexivbildungen*); the latter, "complexives" (*Komplexivbildungen*). For instance, aorists of durative verbs could be complexives; suffixed forms of nondurative verbs could be displexives. According to Budich, it is the creation of displexive forms which signals the formation of an aspectual system, not the creation of complexives; the latter alter the temporal shape of an action, while the former only create a difference in perspective on the action—this being the classic definition of a subjective difference (Budich 1969: 11-14).

The Old Russian aspectual system has, in his opinion, gone quite far toward creating an aspectual system, but numerous anaspectual remnants of the old system remain. The new system tends toward a morphological rationale for classification, so that nondurative like *žrǫ* 'I will swallow' undergo a change in meaning (*Bedeutungsänderung*) and become duratives like Modern Russian *žru* 'I eat (like an animal)', or undergo a purely formal transformation into a complexive (*formale Komplexivbildung*), as in the case of Old Church Slavic *požrǫ* 'I will swallow'. Natural duratives like *nazьrěti* 'watch, observe' are reanalyzed as nondurative and then undergo displexivization (*Displexivbildung*) to form a corresponding suffixed imperfective *nazirati* (Budich 1969: 17-18). Traces of these older meanings are still quite strong in Old Russian.

Budich's analysis is convincing and is largely congruent with my own observations about other Old Russian texts. His durative–nondurative opposition corresponds roughly to the distinction I draw between punctualizable and nonpunctualizable acts (although he sees the durative as the marked form and the nondurative as unmarked, whereas my classification suggests the reverse). However, I do not think the durative–nondurative opposition by itself adequately describes the lexical divisions in the Old Russian verbal system. As will be shown later in this study, gradations of telicity play an important role in determining aspectual behavior in Old Russian, and unfortunately these differences are masked in Budich's study by the fact that he treats only unsuffixed verbs ("e/o-stem verbs"). Because suffixed verbs are not discussed, there is no analysis of such common problematic verbs as *dělati* 'build/make', *pisati* 'write', *viděti* 'see', *stojati* 'stand' that point to including telicity as a necessary feature for describing the verbal system, on an equal footing with duration.[64]

---

[63] For concurrent opinions on the objective-to-subjective evolution of verbal forms, see Holden 1990 and van Wijk 1929.

[64] In invoking complexity as the bounding of an action, Budich establishes the importance of the notion of boundaries, but does not then acknowledge that telicity in general might play an important role in aspectual genesis. His explanation of displexivization

Budich carefully sidesteps the question of what it means to say that a "verb" is "durative" or "nondurative" when he clearly identifies numerous verbs which sometimes behave duratively and sometimes not. He frequently mentions the different "meanings" of a verb, evidently preferring to assume that, for example, *write a letter* and *write novels* simply exemplify two different "meanings" of *write*, which we could label *write₁* and *write₂*. This is an acceptable solution but sidesteps the problem of the extent to which such differences in meaning are a function of predicate arguments as opposed to a true change in meaning.

All in all, however, Budich's treatment of Old Russian aspect is a solid model that is both well-grounded in textual evidence and fits the historical development of the language as well, avoiding the confusion and lack of systematicity that plagues Ruzicka's study.

3.6. CONCLUSIONS AND DIRECTIONS FOR RESEARCH

There are three topics of concern to all the works in this chapter.

First, there exists a group of verbs (varying in size from analysis to analysis) that is acknowledged not to belong to a single aspect even in the early historical era. Scholars have come to different conclusions about how to treat these verbs: should they be considered biaspectual or nonaspectual, and should this group be considered systematic or exceptional?

Second, the interaction of tense and aspect has posed problems for studies of Old Church Slavic, Prehistoric Slavic, and Old Russian, especially with regard to the three-way aorist–imperfect–perfect preterite tense system. It remains unclear what aspectual features were inherent in these preterite tenses and what role tense itself or those particular features played in creating the modern quasi-grammatical aspectual system. A fundamental question overlooked in most studies is the following: even if we assume that tense begets grammatical aspect in a diachronic sense (i.e., that the aorist–imperfect distinction is in some ways the forerunner of the perfective–imperfective opposition), does that allow us to assume as well that tense indicates aspect in a synchronic analysis of Old Russian (i.e. that a given tense form marks a verb as perfective or imperfective)?

Finally, the question of chronology arises: what evidence does the body of scientific literature present us with for determining the timing of aspect's appearance and development?

3.6.1. Biaspectuality or anaspectuality?

There is a strong bias in the existing literature to regard the Russian aspectual system as essentially fully formed by the time of the oldest literary monuments. Certainly there is ample evidence to support the presence of regular aspectual

---

also implies the interruption of progress toward a goal, but fails to explicitly connect this goal with the goal implied in complexivization.

distinctions in Old Russian. In practical terms, this means that scholars analyze the verbal system as already consisting of a binary opposition of perfective–imperfective, in which all verbs participate. The definitions ascribed to the two aspects are presumed to be largely congruent with those in Modern Russian. Verbs whose usage patterns proscribe the assignment of a single aspect are held to be biaspectual; that is, expressing at some times perfective aspect and at other times imperfective aspect. The fact that this category is much larger in Old Russian than it is in Modern Russian is dismissed by pointing out that it still constitutes a small percentage of all verbs.[65] A broad understanding of biaspectuality thus implies viewing aspectually confused verbs as exceptions rather than as a class. Both definitions—that of biaspectuality and that of the term "exception"—presuppose the systemic, regular character of aspect.

A few scholars, such as Maslov, Ruzicka, and Budich, have pointed out that such a viewpoint is anachronistic and biased by the more strictly grammatical nature of aspect in Modern Russian and other Slavic languages. In their view, verbs that refuse to obey aspectual rules constitute a regular class and may be excepted entirely from the aspectual system, hence the term "nonaspectual." The task that then confronts them is to propose an alternative aspectual system based on some other principles. This task is not addressed in the case of Ruzicka, and in the case of Maslov, is addressed with the same broad generalizations that characterize the opposing side's arguments. Only Budich provides a complete accounting for his system—but does so by leaving out crucial information about suffixed verbs.

3.6.2. Using tense to study aspect

Tense as an independent phenomenon has been given a great deal of attention, especially in several areas: the usage patterns of the three most common past tenses (aorist, perfect, imperfect), the periphrastic tenses (especially the pluperfect and other similar-looking forms) and the various participles and verbal adverbs, along with analytical "tenses" formed from them. (I am treating participles under the heading of tense here, since most studies have seen fit to examine participles and finite tenses as complementary parts of a grammatical system.)

One confusing factor is that tenses have often been proposed as the bearers of Prehistoric Slavic aspectual functionality and are assumed to have yielded this function to aspect at some crucial juncture. This hypothesis runs through a number of theories, in particular those of Borodič, Němec, Kölln, van Wijk, Holden, Forsyth and Budich. However, a problem arises when aspectual genesis (i.e, the provenance of the functions we attach to the aspects in Modern Russian) is confused with aspectual assignment (i.e., the synchronic labelling of forms in the older languages).

---

[65] Dostál reasons that the presence of *pluralia tantum* nouns such as Modern Czech *dveře, brýle* 'door, glasses' or of *singularia tantum* nouns like *láska, nenávist* 'love, hate' does not lead us to abolish the category of number just because some nouns do not participate in it; likewise, he says, we should not abandon aspect simply because some verbs in Old Church Slavic do not participate in its opposition. Forsyth 1972 echoes this claim.

As Galton (1976) points out, just because the imperfect historically fulfills certain functions that later are filled by the imperfective aspect does not mean that at any point in Old Russian we can assign a verb with imperfect forms to the imperfective aspect. Kölln and Borodič, most notably, get snared in this trap. Němec, Holden, and Budich escape it by applying this principle strictly to aspectual genesis and not extending it to the analysis of Old Church Slavic or Old Russian forms.

Using tense to determine aspect creates a few inconsistencies. First, many scholars—including Kölln—have accepted a fully grammatical system of aspect for Old Russian. But in Modern Russian, a grammatical aspectual system implies that the aspectual functions specific to one tense or another are subordinate to the overarching functions that proceed from the aspectual opposition. If the Old Russian verbal system subordinates aspect to tense, we are left with a major difference between it and the Modern Russian verbal system that needs to be explained.[66] Second, although the dates are subject to dispute, it is widely accepted that certain tenses, such as the imperfect and pluperfect, as well as most participles, fell out of use early in the history of the spoken Russian language and lived on only in the literary language. This approach makes the tense system seem much more likely to be the secondary system in Old Russian. Suddenly a tense-based study of aspect starts to seem like a much more difficult and less rewarding enterprise.

Old Russian tenses cannot be treated as the motivating factors behind aspectual usage and assignment, regardless of their original role in the formation of grammatical aspect during the Prehistoric Slavic era. An attempt to relate Old Russian tenses to the coalescing perfective and imperfective aspects will be more successful if instead it accounts for the underlying factors that motivate both tense and aspectual usage. I assume that the major way in which tense assists us in determining aspect is through its reflection of underlying contextual and lexical factors—the same factors that can influence aspectual assignment independently.

3.6.3. A chronology of aspectual development

Having examined data from three periods in the history of Slavic languages, I will draw together some of the arguments and conclusions to see what sort of picture the existing scientific literature has given us and where the main points of contention have arisen. An overall picture of Slavic aspect emerges as follows: on the basis of a set of lexical-semantic divisions (determinate–indeterminate, bounded–unbounded, or others) of unknown provenance (possibly from Proto-Indo-European, but most likely early Prehistoric Slavic developments), aspect comes into being in the Prehistoric Slavic era (probably on the late side, most scholars agree) or shortly thereafter (according to Borodič, Maslov, and Ruzicka). This is the first stage. Lexical and/or grammatical influences with multiple sources underscore the nonsystematic character of Prehistoric Slavic aspect.

---

66   Borodič avoids this problem by refusing to acknowledge a binary aspectual system until a much later date, which in and of itself creates further problems.

The second stage in the development of aspect is its consolidation in the daughter languages. As befits this stage, wide applicability of the aspectual opposition in all languages is a given. This consolidation engenders a greater morphological uniformity of aspectual forms. (Morphologists like Silina try to motivate this uniformity internally, from the natures of the suffixes themselves.) The morphological factors that drove earlier changes now become a motivating force in and of themselves. The history of Russian aspect is from this point on the history of this morphological extension and regularization.

This outline accounts for the striking similarities in Slavic languages' aspectual usage by grounding them in a common semantic development. Furthermore, it explains the existence in all Slavic languages of analogous but not identical morphological structures coinciding with aspectual distinctions. The development of these structures is held to be a result of later developments in the daughter languages; these developments nonetheless trace their original appearances to a common heritage.

Scholars have frequently used this sort of outline to separate the history of aspect neatly into two stages: one in which changes occur on a semantic level, and one in which changes occur on a morphological level. They assume that aspect as a semantic relationship is virtually immutable after the first stage; thus, there is no need to examine how the aspectual opposition is used and how it reveals itself, and modern aspectual norms can be applied across the board to the aspectual system of an older language. Scholars like Maslov and Budich go against this trend, but they are in a minority.

3.6.4. Place of this study in the debate

I will not attempt to prove in this study the correctness of any particular chronology or set of factors causing the rise of aspect as a force in Prehistoric Slavic. However, if semantic and lexical distinctions are held to play a major role in the formation of Prehistoric Slavic aspect, I propose that it is worthwhile to look at these same factors in Old Russian aspect. There is no preordained reason why this later stage of development in the individual Slavic languages need be exclusively consigned to the province of morphology. Indeed, as I will demonstrate, the lexicon and context continue to exert a strong influence on the development of aspect when the Prehistoric Slavic stage is long past. As the morphology continues to take shape, so do the semantics of aspect continue to shift and revise themselves.

My research on Old Russian was not designed to yield any direct observations about the provenance of aspect; it is a study of an attested language, not a protolanguage. However, it does suggest a likely pattern for development. Aspect in all probability developed out of lexical groupings of the sort proposed by Maslov, and it developed in two ways. Aspectual development consists of both the genesis of an aspectual opposition (i.e., the reassignment of the lexicon into paired verbs) and the expansion of the nature of that opposition (i.e., the increase in the amount of information an aspectual form can convey).

In early Old Russian, my data show that aspect was not as extensive in either respect; that is, the aspectual opposition involved fewer verbs and encoded less information about the verbs it did encompass. The main indicators of verbal behavior were lexical criteria: telicity and punctuality. A grammatical aspectual opposition as we understand it existed only within the nonpunctual telic class of predicates (actions that were goal-oriented but whose processes could not be summed up instantaneously). One possible explanation for why aspectual oppositions arose in this particular class is that the ability to include or exclude the telos from the act creates a dichotomy in meaning that is quite sharp, and this sharp differentiation is conducive to the establishment of separate verbs for situations where telos is not achieved. Since prefixation often increases telicity, it is not surprising that many of the verbs in which aspect arose were prefixed.

Once process and result can be expressed by different verbs, a partially grammatical distinction now exists for aspect: where a single verb once sufficed, two or more verbs in gradually more and more mutually exclusive spheres cover the same range of meanings and contexts. This situation exists already in the late prehistoric period, but only in the historical epoch does this aspectual opposition gradually come to extend to all verbs, not just certain telic acts, and to slowly take its modern semantic shape.

As to the second point: it has been amply demonstrated that even in cases where Old Russian verb forms are clearly aspectual, the Old Russian aspectual opposition does not always encode the same information as the Modern Russian opposition does. Changes from early to late Old Russian amply demonstrate that the functions and usage of the aspectual opposition evolved and grew throughout the Old Russian period, a fact neglected by many researchers. The goals of the next five chapters of this work are to establish the limited lexical and semantic base of the aspectual opposition in early Old Russian and to track the spread of both these facets through the sixteenth century.

4. Case Studies of the Chronicles

4.0. THE CHRONICLES AND RUSSIAN ASPECT

Chronicles differ from the other texts used in this study in that the materials they contain do not fit clearly into one or another genre. In some ways, however, the "chronicle" itself is a separate genre in Old Russian, at least inasmuch as it has a loosely defined, year-by-year structure that contains certain types of stories and marks certain kinds of events as important. Although they contain elements of both the travelogue and the war tale, in general, chronicles are closer to war tales than to travelogues in that they are often didactic and allegorical, presenting stylized accounts that conform to a certain historical perspective. The Old Russian tense system is more fully utilized than in travel texts, with the aorist and imperfect tenses and a wide variety of participial forms making regular appearances. The authors also make greater use of complex syntactic structures than in travel texts, where simple chaining of independent clauses is a more common method of narration. Both of these factors have an impact on aspectual usage and its perception by the reader; aspectual usage does vary based on the style of the passage. On the one hand, the meaning of any given form and its aspect—or lack thereof—is made clearer by the use of a greater range of tenses and by the presence of more complex constructions showing temporal relationships. On the other hand, the possibilities of meaning are severely restricted by these factors, and individual verb forms in these passages have a correspondingly smaller range of meanings thanks to the presence of morphological (tense) and syntactic factors. I have discussed ways to deal with these extra factors in section 4.1.

Dating chronicles—on the face of it an easy task, given the date at the beginning of each entry—is also complex. The dates of the various entries record the year the events supposedly took place and do not necessarily correspond to the dates when they were written; numerous errors in the dating of events indicate that the chronicles were not annotated year by year but rather composed at greater intervals, and then revised, expanded, and edited numerous times. However, it seems certain that no chronicle was composed as a single unit; we are therefore dealing with a text that could show variation in aspectual usage across the various periods in which it was written.[1] While it will be difficult to assign precise dates for

---

[1] Not only this, but, as Šaxmatov (1908/1967) has pointed out, there are significant interpolations in the text that make such a study even more difficult. He bases his conclusions much of the time on apparent inconsistencies in the narrative. If one accepts all of his arguments, it would seem impossible to reconstruct any chronology for the text or undertake any statistical work that is at all dependent on the dating given, since the probability of interpolations is quite high. Still, differences between the beginning and end of the Primary Chronicle, or between the Primary Chronicle and the Suzdal' Chronicle, seem worth noting if they occur often and consistently.

the writing of individual portions of the text, I will note significant or consistent variation in similar contexts from the beginning to the end of the texts.[2]

4.1. METHODOLOGY AND METHODOLOGICAL PITFALLS

The data for chapters 4 and 5 are drawn from the two texts in the Laurentian manuscript: the Russian Primary Chronicle and the Suzdal' Chronicle (in the interest of brevity I will call them "the Chronicles"). I selected 250 verb roots (a total of 968 prefixed, suffixed and simplex verbs) and catalogued their every occurrence in the texts. To the extent possible, I stuck to the Laurentian manuscript of the Primary Chronicle as reprinted in the *Polnoe sobranie russkix letopisej (Complete Collection of Russian Chronicles)*. Where lacunae existed in the Laurentian manuscript, the editors of the Collection substituted clearly marked passages from the Radzivil or Academy manuscripts, and I have included forms from these passages in my data. In this study, I did not regularly take account of variant readings found in these manuscripts when the Laurentian text was extant, even when the comparison yielded interesting results.

4.1.1. The corpus

I selected my 250 verb roots based on a range of factors. I picked some roots that had prefixed derived forms in order to trace the development of such forms into aspectual verbs. At the same time, for the sake of balance, I looked for other common verbs that did not produce major numbers of derived forms. I included verbs from a wide range of semantic categories and verbs with Aktionsart-type prefixation, aspectual prefixation, and purely directional prefixation. A number of verbs were selected purely on the grounds that the copious number of examples they afforded and their plasticity of meaning in combination with various nouns would make for a more detailed analysis than is possible with other verbs.

To expedite the analysis, I excluded some verb roots and noted only exceptionally interesting occurrences of others. Eliminated wholesale were motion verbs of the *xoditi–idti* 'go (on foot)' type and forms of the simplex verb *byti* 'be'. Although these verbs are quite frequent in the texts, their aspectual reflection in Modern Russian is quite different from that of other verbs and will be treated only briefly in chapter 5. I further noted only exceptional or interesting uses of the verbs *xotěti* 'want', *imati–jati* 'take' and their derivatives, and *iměti* 'have'.

---

[2] Not all variation will, of course, be significant or consistent. Sometimes forms will vary with the style of the text, as authors or scribes choose verbs or tenses that they feel to be more appropriate in different settings; in other instances, the variation in forms will simply reflect the idiolect of different authors or scribes (a preference, say, for forms of *v"zvratiti sja* over *vratiti sja* 'return' or variation in the usage of *činiti, dělati* and *tvoriti* 'do, make' could easily fall into this category). The presence of these nonlinear variations makes it more difficult, but not impossible, to establish true diachronic changes.

I used the data from these texts to evaluate the aspectual semantics of old Russian verbs. In addition to developing criteria for evaluating grammatical aspectual usage, I also checked for patterns based on the "natural aspect," or lexical proclivities, of a verb's predicates and based on certain closely defined environments, such as progressivity, durativity, iterativity, and generalized contexts (see chapter 1 for definitions of these terms). In texts like the Chronicles, which are distinctly earlier than other texts in this survey, Old Russian may not yet have a fully realized grammatical aspectual system, so it will be important to consider not only whether verbs participate in secondary suffixation but also whether in fact they participate in the aspectual system at all, and if so, in which situations.

4.1.2. Aspect in a chronologically heterogeneous text

Scholars disagree strongly about the relevance that the diachronic quality of the Chronicles may have for linguistic analysis. Few believe that the entry dates represent a precise indication of when the text following them was written; for instance, there is no evidence that an entry from the year 1070 actually represents the written Russian language of that year. The Chronicles have enough examples of mistaken dating—events reported years too early, obvious factual confusion, and so forth—to make it clear that entries were composed and revised at larger intervals, some spanning decades. However, equally few scholars would claim that the entire manuscript is a single text, uniform in linguistic and stylistic features. In this view, a year-by-year chronicle would have been composed wholesale at a much later date, or else later redactions and copyings would have to have systematically erased all archaic features from the original text. This speculation does not correspond to observed fact; even copies of manuscripts made centuries later preserve linguistic features that were undoubtedly anachronisms at the time of copying.

The remaining happy medium, however, covers a wide area. While most scholars would be skeptical about precise dating of entries, they would acknowledge that the text was composed at intervals and that this time frame should—ideally—be reflected in differing language use. The degree of skepticism implied in the word "ideally" depends mostly on how much weight one gives to the provenance of individual examples and how much to the evidence of aggregate statistics.

One obvious source of chronological and stylistic differentiation in the Laurentian manuscript are the "seams" that mark a direct change in the source of material for the manuscript. Some of them are clearly marked by the scribes, while others were proposed by Šaxmatov in his studies of the Russian chronicles. He posits these seams based on changes in style and content, which he says are the result of numerous copyings and redactions of the text, sometimes several layers deep. The layering is most evident for the more ancient Primary Chronicle; for the newer Suzdal' Chronicle, Šaxmatov's provenance for the text is far simpler.

Virtually all of the Primary Chronicle (as it appears in the Laurentian manuscript) and much of the Suzdal' Chronicle came directly from an older source Šaxmatov identifies as the Vladimir Compilation *(Vladimirskij svod),* which is in and of itself compiled from various earlier redactions. Šaxmatov defines a number of clear breaks within the Vladimir Compilation. The most obvious one is the break between the Primary Chronicle and the Suzdal' Chronicle, which occurs after the entry for 1110. He divides the Primary Chronicle material as it appears in the Vladimir Compilation into an Initial Compilation *(Načal'nyj svod)* finished in 1095, covering the years up to 1093, and an addition made by the monk Silvester in 1116, which covers the years up through 1110 (he suspects that there were further entries covering the intervening years, which do not appear in the Laurentian manuscript) (Šaxmatov 1908: 10-11).

But the Initial Compilation itself is not homogeneous; Šaxmatov sees in it a combination of a southern chronicle, which had a relatively expansive treatment of events in Kiev and South Russia, with a northern version, which summarized the southern events more concisely. In subsequent redactions, probably beginning with Silvester's, more historical material was added to the text of the Initial Compilation, fleshing out some of the more concise entries and elaborating on events that were later seen to have great historical significance. It is likely that these additions were not composed from scratch at this later date but were instead drawn from preexisting manuscripts (some or all of which are no longer extant) thought to be authoritative (Šaxmatov 1938: 9-11, 15-17).

In the Suzdal' Chronicle, Šaxmatov attributes the entries of 1111 through 1184 to the selfsame Vladimir Compilation. The following section of the Suzdal' Chronicle (1185 to 1205), comes largely from the Perejaslav Chronicle *(Perejaslavskaja letopis'),* a direct forerunner of the extant Radzivil Chronicle. The remaining material from that period (specifically parts of the entries for 1193 to 1195) Šaxmatov traces to the Vladimir Polychron, which also serves as a source for later parts of the Suzdal' Chronicle. He claims that virtually all the text from c. 1260 onward comes from the Vladimir Polychron, while the text from 1206 to 1260 combines material from the Polychron and a Rostov-centered chronicle that appears after the Primary Chronicle in the Vladimir Compilation (1938: 9, 12, 15-16). There are thus seven "seams" in the Chronicles that may affect usage patterns: 1093, 1110, 1185, 1193, 1195, 1206, c. 1260. This segmentation is summarized in chart 4.1.2.1, along with page numbers for entries in the *Polnoe sobranie russkix letopisej* (PSRL), the edition quoted in this study.

The source materials identified in this chart are direct sources for the Laurentian manuscript; Šaxmatov proposes, in other words, that the compiler of the Laurentian manuscript or its prototype worked with these documents at his side. However, he also proposes, as was mentioned above, that we can project back through three or four generations of manuscripts and redactions to retrieve the prototypes for the first section, the Primary Chronicle.

Reconstructing the Primary Chronicle involves retrieving both the interwoven northern and southern versions of the Initial Compilation, as well as later insertions *(vstavki)* and reworkings of the text. Šaxmatov's claims are based largely on the discontinuity and repetitiveness of the Primary Chronicle's narrative in its modern form, and his careful, detailed analysis is to a certain degree borne out by comparison with other extant manuscripts.

Chart 4.1.2.1. Šaxmatov's sources for the Laurentian manuscript.

Entry dates	Source	Notes	PSRL page
through 1093	Vladimir Compilation	from the Initial Compilation, a heterogeneous source compiled and elaborated on later	1-225
1094-1110	Vladimir Compilation	Silvester's addition to the Initial Compilation	226-286
1111-1184	Vladimir Compilation	beginning of Suzdal' Chronicle	289-388
1185-1192	Perejaslav Chronicle	forerunner of Radzivil Chronicle; later provenance than Vladimir Compilation	389-409
(1193-1195)	(Vladimir Polychron)	(mixed in with material from Perejaslav Chronicle)	(409-412)
1195-1205	Perejaslav Chronicle		412-421
1206-c.1260	Rostov Chronicle	followed the Primary Chronicle in the Vladimir Compilation	421-475
1260-1305	Vladimir Polychron		476-488
1377	contemporary?	endnote following empty pages in manuscript	487-488 (lower)

The Laurentian manuscript, then, while the most authoritative of those still extant, contains a version of the Primary Chronicle that differs greatly from Šaxmatov's proposed "original" version. In addition to the usual changes made by scribes, there were purposeful reworkings of older stories: passages from other stories or later texts were added, and events were tinkered with to conform to the political exigencies of the day. We can recover these alterations, according to Šaxmatov, because of the discontinuities in the narrative that resulted when newer matter was spliced into the older text.[3]

Šaxmatov's interpretation rests on the assumption that the original versions of the Primary Chronicle did constitute well-formed, tightly knit texts, written without many of the digressions and awkward connections found in the Laurentian manuscript. There is no practical way to incorporate this level of reconstruction into

---

[3] An example of Šaxmatov's reasoning: in the entry for 6454 (946 A.D.), we find the words *i pobědiša Derevljany* 'and they defeated the Derevlians, which is followed by a lengthy account of Ol'ga's fourth act of revenge. At the end of this passage are the words *i v"zložiša na nja dan' tjažku* 'and they levied a heavy tribute on them'. This sentence, meaningless otherwise, belongs thematically with the defeat of the Derevljane; Šaxmatov thus concludes that the excursus about Ol'ga is a later interpolation (1908: 3-4).

a linguistic analysis, so the usefulness of a diachronic study of the Chronicles is called into question.

Such a diachronic study, after all, relies on two methods. The first involves comparing copies of the same work made at different times. Portions of older manuscripts can be compared to the corresponding places in younger manuscripts. The differences are then chalked up to linguistic change, if such a designation is warranted. The second method—which is the problematic one—involves comparing material within a single manuscript. Doing this requires assuming that the dates show the order in which material was written (i.e., that the bulk of the material dated, for example, 1070 was written prior to material dated 1230, although not necessarily that either passage was composed in precisely the year stated). However, going one step further—i.e., accepting the proposition that not only was the text as a whole composed at varying intervals but that the composition of each entry has numerous time depths—invalidates the study altogether.

So far, I have accepted Šaxmatov's "microlinguistic" approach, which examines the validity of using individual examples from any one passage. A "macrolinguistic" approach, focusing on overall patterns of usage, puts the problem in perspective. Two scholars have recently tackled the issue of whether a chronological reading of the Primary Chronicle gives reliable linguistic results. The subject of research, in both cases, was the distribution of preterite tenses, a choice that is especially fortunate for my purposes. Unlike the history of aspect, the history of the tense system is well documented. First, both the starting points and the ending points are well known: from a system in which aorist and imperfect tenses dominated, it eventually became one in which the once-peripheral perfect tense was the only past tense form. Second, determining where and how often tense forms occur is rarely problematic, thanks to clear and consistent differences in morphology. Klenin (1993) and Matthews (1995) have independently examined different facets of perfect tense distribution in the Primary Chronicle, and while the issue of chronology is not the focus of their papers, it is reflected in their data and conclusions.

Klenin finds that the Primary Chronicle shows a gradual increase in a certain type of perfect usage. The increase is gradual enough, she suggests, that—without committing ourselves to the precise dates found in the Chronicles—we can assume that the entries were written more or less in chronological order, since the direction of change in the text mimics what we would expect to find in natural language change. Matthews, in studying the use of direct-discourse preterite tenses in three chronicles, concluded that, when the data are adjusted to reflect differing thematic content, the ascendance of the perfect tense vis-à-vis the imperfect and aorist coincides with the assumed path of historical development, with a few exceptions indicating major changes in redaction. Changes in source material can also be reflected in the text; Matthews's data show that the commonly accepted break in the narrative found at the entry for 1095 parallels a sharp decrease in the use of aorist forms (Matthews 1995).

Klenin's and Matthews's conclusions suggest that whatever dating problems may surface for individual examples, using entry dates to predict chronological ordering does yield valid results overall for verbal forms. It will be advisable, then, to proceed with aspectual analyses on both a "microlinguistic" and a "macrolinguistic" level. Individual examples may, however, occasionally present an overly modern picture of the aspectual system for the time in question. Since the premise of this study is that strict aspectual correlations arose *later* than is normally supposed, and not earlier, the significance of these wayward examples is low. The hypothesis I have put forth assumes a more archaic form for Old Russian aspect; the presence of later, more innovative forms in the text, which make aspect look like a more complete and regular system than it in fact was at the time, simply make the criteria for my proof more stringent.

In view of the macrolinguistic results cited above, I decided, when looking for chronologically influenced features in the Primary and Suzdal' Chronicles, to give the most weight to those that show marked difference in usage across the textual seams proposed by Šaxmatov.

The finer patterning of early insertions and reworkings to the Primary Chronicle I will by and large ignore. In Šaxmatov's analysis, even the latest major additions to the Primary Chronicle are made soon after the completion of the Initial Compilation. Furthermore, he also states that, in general, later chroniclers did not write large chunks of new material when recopying older entries but did often compile excerpts from several contemporaneous sources. This seems especially likely when treating history that was already several hundred years in the past.[4] If one does not have pretensions of foisting precise dates on the reader, then it is safe to say that the Russian of that text dates from the eleventh and early twelfth centuries. This level of accuracy is sufficient for my purposes.

Although diachronic analyses do not provide crucial information about these texts, a number of issues do arise (in chapter 5) that require a diachronic treatment. For the most part, then, I treat the Primary Chronicle and the Suzdal' Chronicle as a single text in my analysis.

Whether or not one accepts the premise that the text is a patchwork of passages of various time depths, there is no doubt that it is a patchwork of styles. In many cases, accounting for variations in style will also account for problems in the source material, and style will naturally vary across seams in the Laurentian manuscript.

4.1.3. Treading carefully with aspect and tense

There are a number of methodological pitfalls involved in analyzing the Chronicles. The first concerns the relations between aspect and tense, and how tense is used to determine aspect and meaning in context. (For a more thorough discussion of the approaches used in other studies, see chapter 3.) While the Old Russian past tenses do mark aspectual distinctions in the sense that they modify the

---

4   Šaxmatov suggests this in particular for later portions of the Primary Chronicle, which he says are a compendium of South Russian and North Russian sources (1938: 16).

temporal shape of the act in question, they cannot be used as markers of either the perfective or the imperfective aspect, and doing so inevitably oversimplifies and weakens the overall analysis. It is tempting, for instance, to regard the aorist tense as the bearer of completed action and thus call the perfective aspect a continuation (or more often a narrowing) of the function of the aorist. The imperfective aspect can likewise be said to come from an expansion of the function of the imperfect tense. Immediately problems and inconsistencies start to arise. Consider the boldfaced forms in (1)-(7) below, which show a range of aorist usages that aspectually have very little in common.

(1) он же **погыбе** тѣломь и душею предавъся дьяволу (181)
'he *perished (pogybe)* in body and soul, having given himself over to the devil'

(2) и **сгорѣ** церкы та вся от верха и до землѣ (436)
'and the whole church *burned down (sgorě)*, from the spire down to the ground'

(3) и много села **воеваша** (215)
'and they *captured (voevaša)* many villages'

Examples (1) through (3) have aorists that indeed have a completive sense; however, aorists (4) through (7) lack that sense entirely.

(4) а Ярополкъ **княжи** лет 8 а Володимеръ **княжи** лет 37 (18)
'and Jaropolk *reigned (knjaži)* eight years and Volodimer *reigned (knjaži)* thirty-seven years'

(5) азъ бо Ляхомъ много зла **творих** (266)
'for I *have done (tvorix)* much evil to the Poles'

(6) и **хотѣ** похватити брата своего и мало не оутопе самъ (220)
'and he *wanted (xotě)* to grab his brother and almost drowned himself'

(7) азъ **видѣхъ** яко вчера спехнуша с мосту (75)[5]
'I *saw (viděx")* them throw [him] off the bridge yesterday'

They represent finite amounts of time in (4) and an evaluation of a past action in (5), a desire existing at a point in time in (6) and a perception in (7). If we look more closely, we have to concede that the function of the aorist is highly malleable and depends on the lexical category of the predicate. This point is especially clear in (3), where the verb *voevati* appears in the aorist. It is noteworthy that aorists of this verb can appear with a direct object, leading us to translate it as 'conquer, take control'; when it often appears without a direct object, it means simply 'to do battle,

---

[5] References are to page numbers in *Lavrent'evskaja letopis': Polnoe sobranie russkix letopisej, tom 1,* Leningrad 1926.

to make war'. In the former meaning it is highly telic; in the latter, atelic. Two different lexical senses of the verb thus influence what tenses are likely to appear and what those tenses mean. In (4)-(7), the aorist is, if anything, closer to a Modern Russian "constatation of fact" past tense (which is expressed by the imperfective aspect) than to any perfective-type function.

My intent is not to argue that tenses have no intrinsic function at all or that there is absolutely no correlation between the use of tenses and the eventual uses of aspect. It is simply to point out that because the aorist is widely used in the category of imperfective-like verbs and has widely disparate functions, it is primarily a temporal marker, not an aspectual marker. Those aspectual functions it does have complement, rather than duplicate, those found in the groupings of prefixed and suffixed verbs that comprise the Old Russian aspectual system. When we do see tenses reflecting aspectual meanings,[6] it is better to see these tense forms as a different reflection and organization of the same set of semantic factors as govern aspect, rather than to set up a causal link between tense usage and aspectual assignment or to simply equate the two. I will therefore use tense assignment to get at other factors that will be useful in my analysis, but only indirectly.

Since the thrust of this analysis will be to highlight the significance of lexical aspect in Old Russian, tense plays another important role in this discussion: the fact that tense usage varies along with predicate lexical class supports similar conclusions about the role of lexical aspect with respect to grammatical aspect.

4.1.4. Aspectual assignment, terminology, and circularity

Since the Chronicles are the earliest texts in this study, the first question that needs to be answered is: does grammatical aspect exist or not as a system at this stage in the history of Russian? Many verbs in the Old Russian of the Chronicles show behavior that parallels that of Modern Russian. This means that a Modern-Russian-like system of aspect does operate at least partially; however, it does not necessarily mean that we can automatically reconstruct an aspectual system for the language as a whole. Slavists have tended to overuse terms like *perfective, imperfective, determinate,* and *indeterminate* when talking about Old Russian, as if in order to treat a group of verbs together, the verbs necessarily had to have some single synchronic shared trait or group of traits throughout their development.[7] In fact, it may be the very heterogeneousness of the earlier lexical groupings—not their

---

[6] As I mentioned earlier, tenses do express aspect (in its most general sense, meaning that they modify way an action proceeds through time), but do not express the same opposition of perfective and imperfective found in the modern language or the version of this opposition found in Old Russian.

[7] From this point of view, Borodič's definition of determinacy is especially troubling, since it subsumes a number of disparate oppositions like stative–inchoative, determinate–indeterminate, and telic–atelic, largely on the basis of the fact that these categories can by and large be placed into either the perfective or the imperfective camp at a later date.

similarity—which gives Modern Russian aspect its distinctive mixture of usages and meanings.

The plasticity of the terms "determinate" and "indeterminate" is of special concern, since for different scholars they mean different things. The nebulousness of these terms often covers up a circular definition: determinate verbs are those verbs that become perfective verbs, and perfectivity therefore develops from determinacy. When terms like *perfective* and *imperfective* are used anachronistically, a similar problem results: if a majority of verbs in a system respond to the labels "perfective" and "imperfective" more or less as we use them today, it is tempting to apply these labels to verbs that do not fit these categories quite as well for the period in question but that we expect will do so eventually. This practice allows us to keep all verbs of a single future genus together. A side effect is the conclusion that, under one name or another, grammatical aspect has always existed in the historical period for all verbs; this deduction arises more as a result of these terminological shortcuts than as a result of concrete observations.

Since this study makes reference to both Old and Modern Russian, however, it will occasionally be useful to refer to verbs by the aspectual category they either belong to or will belong to; i.e., to group together all the verbs that will be imperfective or all the verbs that will be perfective, and have convenient terms to refer to them by. I use the self-explanatory terms *perfective-like* and *imperfective-like* where I want to suggest an affinity without commiting to a strict partition of the lexicon into these categories. Where I wish to group Old Russian verbs into groups of aspectual affinity that resemble but do not exactly match those found in Modern Russian, I will use the terms *protoperfective* and *protoimperfective*. In other instances I will use the more objective terms *simplex, prefixed,* and *derived* or *suffixed* to describe, respectively, verbs without derivational suffixes, verbs with prefixes, and verbs with derivational suffixes.[8]

4.2. USEFUL TERMS FOR LEXICAL GROUPS

In classifying verbal usage according to lexical type, I have adopted a mixture of Maslov's, Timberlake's, and Kučera's classifications of aspect in contemporary Russian. A summary of it is given in section 2.7.3. With any two-dimensional system like the one proposed in chart 2.7.3.1, the question arises of how to group and treat the categories in a linear text. I have chosen to start with the upper left corner of the chart, proceed through the upper right and lower right quadrants, and finish in the lower left quadrant. This has the desirable effect of aligning acts in a more or less telic order; the deformations that it causes will be corrected later.

For each of these categories distilled from Maslov and Kučera I have selected sample verbs that I will investigate in depth. Examples from other verbs will follow under the same heading in the next chapter. As noted before, the predicates of a single verb may belong to a number of different lexical categories. Maslov, for instance, notes that the Modern Russian verb pair *delat'–sdelat'* 'do, make' has a

---

[8] More detailed descriptions of these terms are given in chapter 1.

different contour depending on its complement. In the case of *delat'–sdelat' rabotu* 'do one's work', the difference between process and result is clear on a lexical as well as an aspectual level; every partial performance of the action still leaves a result. In the case of *delat'–sdelat' zamečanie* 'make a comment', it is impossible to separate the performance of the action from its result; the difference is purely aspectual. Certain verbs are thus assigned to multiple lexical groups, and their lexical plasticity is an important instrument in diffusing change and spreading aspectuality through the verbal system. In this initial analysis, however, I have largely depended on verbs that are easily identified with a single lexical class. Only after exploring at least one such well-defined verb for each class have I expanded the analysis to include verbs whose predicates fall into multiple lexical classes.

4.3. INTRODUCTION TO ATELIC ACTS

Atelic acts break down into three basic categories. One, represented by the Old Russian verb *stojati* 'stand', contains stative acts, which express a condition or state, but no change. Another, represented by the verb *bljusti* 'guard', contains atelic actions (actions that proceed without a clear goal or state-like qualities that are expressed by a habitual action). The boundaries within this group are permeable, with some verbs like *knjažiti* 'rule, reign' straddling the *stojati*-type and the *bljusti*-type, and other verbs with predicates in the atelic action class showing a variable inclination towards telicity.

Some predicates, however, can be atelic while referring to an act whose performance may be instantaneous (a characteristic normally associated with telic predicates, especially protoperfective ones). These acts constitute a third group, exemplified by *viděti*. On the one hand, acts like 'see', 'be frightened' are atelic, expressing a state rather than a goal-oriented process. On the other hand, they can easily be perceived as momentary, a reading that is virtually impossible for statives and atelic actions. In this group, we will expect to see simplex verbs that do not adhere closely to one or another aspect, and a relative richness of forms expressing similar functions. The bulk of this class is composed of acts of perception and reactive emotion.[9]

4.4. PUNCTUAL ATELICS *(VIDĚTI)*

Acts that are punctual and stative at the same time are found with *viděti* 'see'. Attested 198 times in the Chronicles, this verb offers ample evidence of the anaspectual character of simplex verbs in this class. The verb is found thirty-two

---

[9] The basic premise of this analysis is to use lexical contours as guidelines, not specific semantic groups; however, since certain larger groups of such specific verbs do fit into these classes, it seems appropriate to mention them. Classifications such as "communicative acts" and "acts of perception" are obviously on a different level than those such as "telic" and "atelic," and mentioning the former does not imply that they should be placed on a par with the latter in this analysis.

times (16 percent of total attestations) in the infinitive, eighteen times (9 percent) in the non-past, four times (2 percent) in the imperative, fourty-four times (22 percent) in the aorist, four times (2 percent) in the imperfect, seventy-eight times (39 percent) in the past participle, sixteen times (8 percent) in the present participle, and twice (1 percent) with perfect participles.[10]

4.4.1. Infinitives of *viděti*

The usage of infinitives demonstrates the appropriateness of the anaspectual label for *viděti*. We can distinguish several uses of the infinitive here; some, like the forms in (8)-(10), refer to the ability of an object to be perceived, either once as in (8) or over a period of time, as in (9). In Modern Russian, we would call this usage imperfective.

(8) быс(ть) **видѣти** страшно чюдо (44)
    'a terrible miracle was *seen (viděti)*'

(9) быс(ть) **видѣти** всѣм акы м(е)с(я)ць. четырь дни (460)
    'it was *visible (viděti)* to all like the moon for four days'

(10) знаменье явися на н(е)б(е)си. яко **видѣти** всеи земли (149)
    'a sign appeared in the heavens which was *visible (viděti)* all over the earth'

The expression of ability in (11) shows duration over a defined interval of time.

(11) одобьлѣша бо с(е)р(д)ца ихъ. оушюма тяжько слышати (а) очима **видѣти** (63)
    'it was difficult *to* hear with their ears (and) *see (viděti)* with their eyes'

The meaning in (12) covers all seeing over a set interval of time; it was frightening for all men, in general, to look upon.

(12) страшно бѣ **видѣти** ч(е)л(о)в(ѣ)комъ знаменье Б(о)жье (396)
    'it was frightening for men *to see (viděti)* the sign of God'

Infinitives following a negated verb, as in (13), have the same scope.

(13) оуслышав же Всеволодъ великыи князь Гюргевичь правовѣренъ сыи. бояся Б(ог)а и не хотя **видѣти** кровепролитья в них. посла к ним из Володимеря слы своя в Рязань (401)
    'when he heard this, Grand Prince Vsevolod Gjurgevič, being righteous, fearing God, and not wanting *to see (viděti)* bloodshed among them, sent his emissaries from Volodimer' to them in Rjazan' '

However, compare (14) and (15), where the infinitive follows the verb *xotěti*.

---

[10] Percentages are approximate, and therefore add to 99 percent.

(14) возведъ очи свои хотя **видѣти** игумена Никона. и видѣ осла
стояща. на игумени мѣстѣ (191)
'when he raised his eyes, expecting *to see (viděti)* the priest Nikon, he saw an ass standing in the priest's place'

(15) аще кто вылѣзяше ис хоромины. хотя **видѣти** (*желая увидеть*).
абье оуязвенъ будяше невидимо от бѣсовъ язвою (214-5)
'if anyone came out of the hut, wanting *to see*, he was immediately invisibly stricken by the devils with poison'

The Old Russian simplex verb expresses a one-time future act of quick duration adequately, while for both examples, the Old Russian simplex is replaced by a prefixed perfective in the Modern Russian translation. In (14), where the main intent of the Modern Russian perfective is to provide future modality, the translator turned to the volitional *posmotret'* 'look at^P' to avoid the connotation of punctuality often implied in the perfective *uvidet'*; in (15), the punctual *uvidet'* 'glimpse^P' is a possible reading, so it replaces Old Russian *viděti* 'see', adding future modality to the phrase. It is important to note, however, that the Old Russian form does not limit the action's occurrence in this way; present/future modality and varying duration are inherent in the simplex verb's functions.

4.4.2. Non-past forms of *viděti*

A similar reading can be found in the non-past verb forms. Present usage is found in (16)-(22); the action is taking place at the moment of speech. In (16)-(19) the verb indicates visual perception.

(16) **видите** ли горы сия (8)
'*do* you *see (vidite)* these mountains?'

(17) реч(е) ему Волга **видиши** мя болное сущю (67)
'Olga said to him: *do* you *see (vidiši)* that I am sick?'

(18) реч(е) Тукы братъ Чюдинь Изяславу. **видиши** княже людье възвыли. (171)
'Tuky, brother of Čudin, said to Izjaslav: *do* you *see (vidiši)*, o prince: the people have begun to clamor'

(19) **видимъ** нивы поростъше звѣремъ жилища быша (224)
'we *see (vidim)* the fields overgrown where animals made their homes'

These non-past forms often carry the secondary meaning 'understand, comprehend', as in (20)-(22). Here the "present" usage is easily interpreted as a general condition, as opposed to an ongoing act.

(20) **видиши** ли колько зла створиша Русь Грекомъ (110)
'*do you see (vidiši)* how much evil Russia has wreaked upon the Greeks?'

(21) понеже **видять** ч(е)л(о)в(ѣ)ка Б(о)г(о)мь почьщена (135)
'since *they see (vidjat')* man cleansed by God'

(22) **видиши** ли колико ся мнѣ склʼючи (200)
'*do you see (vidiši)* how much I have been through?'

However, (23)-(26) show future modality. This futurity is reflected in the Modern Russian translation's choice of forms. Examples (23)-(24) are from the parable about Prince Oleg, who hears from a fortuneteller that his horse will be the death of him; he decrees:

(23) николиже всяду на нь. ни **вижю** ег(о) боле тог(о) (38)
'neither will I sit upon him [i.e. my horse], nor *will I see (vižju)* him any more'

Once news reaches him that the horse has died, he decides to check the truth of the rumor:[11]

(24) и повелѣ оседлати конь. а то **вижю** кости ег(о) (39)
'and he ordered his horse saddled; "and so I *will see (vižju)* his bones"'

Future readings of the non-past are also obligatory in (25) and (26).

(25) **да видять** славу Б(ог)а нашего (107)
'*let them see (da vidjat')* the glory of our God'

(26) и егда **видить** месть. руцѣ свои оумыеть в крови грѣшника (242)
'and when *he sees (vidit')* his revenge, he will wash his hands in the blood of the sinner'

Of these four examples, (25) could be a periphrastic future, thanks to the modal particle *da* 'may, and', and (26) is a conditional sentence (the peculiarities of which I discuss in chapter 5), but (23) and (24) have no particles or structures that we can hold responsible for the future reading.

4.4.3. Past tense forms of *vidĕti*

The past tense examples show that the Old Russian simplex marks both short and long durations; neither aspect nor tense seems to play a significant role in marking the length of an event. The proportion of aorist forms to imperfect forms (fourty-four to four, or 92 percent to 8 percent) suggests that most basic narrative functions of this verb are served by the aorist. The imperfect tense examples in (27)-(30) show the tense's limited uses with the verb *vidĕti*.

---

[11] For those who want to know how the tale ends: Oleg goes personally to inspect the horse's bones, and the result is in example (248).

(27) в се время разболѣ Володимеръ очима и **не видяше** ничьтоже. тужаше велми (111)
'at the time Volodimer's eyes became sick, and *he could not see (ne vidjaše)* anything; and he was greatly sorrowed'

Generalized contexts have only aorists of *vidĕti;* the imperfect appears in durative contexts, such as (27), to describe Volodimer's loss of sight during an illness, and in iterative contexts (28) and (29) with the phrase 'if he *saw*...'.

(28) и аще кого **видяше** в помышленьи. обличаше и втаїнѣ и наказаше блюстися от дьявола (190)
'and if *he saw (vidjaše)* anyone lost in thought, he chastised him secretly and instructed him to beware of the devil'

(29) аще кого **видяше** ли шюмна. ли в коем зазорѣ не осудяше но вся на любовь прекладаше (264)
'if *he saw (vidjaše)* someone angry or shamed, he did not condemn him but reconciled them all'

In one instance, the imperfect shows the simultaneity of two events.

(30) бѣ Адамъ в раи. **видяше** Б(ог)а и славяше. егда анг(е)ли славях(у) (88)
'Adam was in heaven; he *saw (vidjaše)* God and praised Him when the angels praised [Him]'

The aorist forms cover a range of more general functions. They can indicate the failure of an act to occur within a specified period of time, as in (31)-(33). These contexts are durative in nature.

(31) и пребы нѣколко лѣт **не видѣ** ег(о) (38)
'and [having] remained there several years *he did not see (ne vidě)* him'

(32) въсприя бл(а)гая она. ихже око **не видѣ**. ни ухо слыша. ни на с(е)рдце ч(е)л(о)в(ѣ)ку не взиде (207)
'he received those blessings which the eye *did not see (ne vidě),* nor the ear hear, nor the heart of man foretell'

(33) оунъ бѣх и сстарѣхся. и **не видѣхъ** праведника оставлена. ни сѣмени его просяща хлѣба. (242)
'I was young, and I have become old, and *I have not seen (ne viděx″)* a righteous man abandoned, nor his offspring begging for bread'

The aorist also summarizes numerous, indefinite acts, as in (34).

(34) и приде в Римъ (и) исповѣда елико наоучи и елико **видѣ** (8)
'he came to Rome (and) told how much *he had* learned and *seen (vidě)*'

A third use of the aorist is for inception, as in (35) and (36), where duration is unimportant.

(35) **видѣхомъ** бо звѣзду его на въстоцѣ. и придохомъ поклонитися ему (102)
'for *we saw (vidĕxom")* his star in the east, and we have come to pay homage to him'

(36) приѣхавъше **видѣша** Игоря лежаща (318)
'when they arrived, *they saw (vidĕša)* Igor' lying down'

The inceptive form is significant, paralleling the inceptive use of statives *(stojati* 'stand'), which will be discussed in section 4.6. The aorist forms of the simplex cover a substantial amount of territory later given over to the perfective, as is clear from a comparison with the translation. Nearly a third (31 percent) of the aorists in the Primary Chronicle are translated with perfective forms *(uvidel, uvidev)* in the Modern Russian version.

4.4.4. Participles of *vidĕti* [12]

Participles show the ambiguous nature of Old Russian *vidĕti*. Although the verb is imperfective in Modern Russian, the Old Russian examples have a preponderance of past participles. Of the forms in the Primary Chronicle, for which modern translations exist, twenty-nine out of thirty-five past participles of the type *vidĕv* (or 83 percent of them) were translated with a Modern Russian perfective verb (typically *uvidev* or *uvidel);* only six (17 percent) were translated with an imperfective or other form denoting simultaneous, continuous action (*vidja* 'seeing', *pri vide* 'in the sight of', *znaja* 'knowing'). Used in conjunction with analysis of the Old Russian forms, the translations help provide a clearer picture of the variety of meanings found for Old Russian *vidĕti*. Its basic meaning, 'see', appears in (37)-(39).

(37) и **видѣвше** Греци и оубояшас(я) (30)
'and the Greeks *saw (vidĕvše)* and took fright'

(38) **видѣв** же первыи от анг(е)лъ. старѣишина чину анг(е)л(с)ку. помысли въ себе рекъ... (87)
'*having seen* [this] *(vidĕv)*, the first among the angels, the eldest of the angelic order, thought to himself, [and] said...'

(39) Володимеръ **видевъ** ц(е)рк(о)вь свершену. вшедъ в ню и помолися Б(ог)у (124)

---

[12] In this discussion and all subsequent discussions of participles, I will treat adjectival participles and verbal adverbs together under this heading.

'Volodimer, *having seen (viděv)* that the church was complete, went inside and prayed to God'

Occasionally the secondary meanings 'know, understand' are more prominent, as in (40) and (41).

(40) **не видѣвши** истлѣнья. на н(е)б(е)са взиде и сѣде одесную О(т)ца (113)
 '*not having known (ne viděvši)* corruption, he ascended into heaven and sat at the right hand of the Father'

(41) и **видѣвъ** Святополкъ яко люта брань. и побѣже (270)
 'and Svjatopolk *saw (viděv")* that the battle was fierce, and he fled'

Present participles of *viděti* are more likely to have the meaning 'understand', where the visual component is less important or absent altogether. Mixtures of meanings are found in (42)-(45).

(42) Авраму на лонѣ почивая. **видя** неиздреченьную радость. въспѣвая съ анг(е)лы (134)
 'Abraham, resting on the bosom [of the Lord], *seeing (vidja)* indescribable happiness, singing aloud with the angels...'

(43) и ту пакы стваряше праздник великъ. сзывая бещисленое множство народа. **видя** же лю(ди). х(ри)с(т)ьяны суща. радовашеся д(у)шею и тѣлом (125)
 'and here again he made a great festival, calling an innumerable number of people, *seeing/understanding (vidja)* that the people were Christians, he rejoiced in body and soul'

(44) Да аще быхом имѣли потщанье и мольбы приносили Б(ог)у за нь в д(е)нь преставленья его. и **видя** бы Б(ог)ъ тщанье наше к нему. прославилъ бы и (131)
 'For if we had persevered and had brought prayers to God for him on the day of his passing, God, *seeing (vidja)* our devotion toward him, would have glorified him'

(45) Георгии же **видя** его непокорьство к собѣ. сжалїси о погыбели людстѣи (347)
 'Georgij, *seeing (vidja)* his [Mstislav's] disobedience toward himself [Georgij], rued the people's death'

The translations change the sense of these examples notably. Replacing Old Russian *viděv"* 'having seen' with Modern Russian *uvidev* 'having glimpsed' limits the meaning of the form to that of a quickly perceived event, whereas this reading is clearly not intended in many of the Old Russian examples. This is the case, for instance, in (37), (38), (40), and (41). The Old Russian past participles and verbal adverbs are similar in content to the present participles in (42)-(45): they express an action of uncertain duration that may or may not have occurred simultaneously with other events in the narrative. They may express an instantaneous act, but this act is inceptive, not exhaustive as Modern Russian *uvidet'* 'see, glimpse' is in the past tense.

4.4.5. The verb *uvidĕti*

The prefixed verb *uvidĕti* 'see' is far less common than its simplex counterpart and to judge by translations is far less common in Old Russian than in Modern Russian. There are only eight examples of *uvidĕti* in the Chronicles, but they suggest a protoperfective predicate whose meaning and usage are quite different from those of its Modern Russian counterpart. Two examples, (46) and (47), show *uvidĕti* with a direct object, supporting the meaning 'see'.

(46) и шедше гражане и **оувидѣша** полкъ его и остася единъ (477)
  'and the citizens came and *saw (ouvidĕša)*[13] his troops and he was left alone'

(47) **оувидѣша** силу ратных иде противу кн(я)зя Олександра (479)
  'they *saw (ouvidĕša) the strength* of the troops [and] he went against Prince Alexandr'

However, all the examples of Old Russian *uvidĕti* in the Chronicles point to a meaning closer to Modern Russian *ponjat'* 'understand, grasp'. As mentioned earlier, the meaning 'understand, grasp' is possible with the simplex verb, but with *uvidĕti* it seems to be obligatory, and can overshadow the visual component of the meaning, as in (48).

(48) Оньдрѣю оучащю въ Синонии. и пришедшю ему в Корсунь. **оувидѣ** яко ис Корсуня близь оустье Днѣпрьское (7-8)
  'Ondrej was teaching in Sinonia, and having come to Korsun', he *saw/learned (ouvidĕ)* that from Korsun' it was not far to the mouth of the Dniepr'

Example (49) shows the interplay between these meanings. From his vantage point, Oleg's vision is unobscured, but more important is how he interprets what he sees; this interpretation prompts the use of the prefixed form *uvidĕ* here.

(49) придоста къ горамъ хъ Киевьскимъ. и **оувидѣ** Олегъ. яко Осколдъ. и Диръ. княжита (23)
  'they came to the mountains of Kiev, and Oleg *saw /found out (ouvidĕ)* that Askold and Dir were ruling [there]'

In (50)-(53) *uvidĕti* again indicates comprehension rather than visual perception.

---

13 The initial *o*- reflects the fact that in Old Russian the phoneme /u/ is often rendered as a digraph *ou*, possibly following the Greek diphthong ου.

(50) Болгаре же **оувидѣвше**. не могоша стати противу (19)
'The Bulgars, *having seen (ouvidĕvše)* [this], could not stand against [them]'

(51) Оугре же нашедше всю землю Болгарьскоу. пленовахоу. Семионъ же, **оувидѣвъ** на Оугры взратися (29)
'The Huns, having attacked the whole land of Bulgaria, were conquering [it]. Semion, *having seen/learned (ouvidĕv")* [this], returned to Hungary'

(52) и прослави Б(ог)а, рекъ. топерво **оувидѣхъ** Б(ог)а истиньнаго (111)
'and he praised God [and] said, for the first time *I have seen/known (ouvidĕx")* the true God'

(53) **оувидѣвъ** яко послани суть губитъ его (133)
'he *saw/understood (ouvidĕv")* that they were sent to kill him'

This obligatory second meaning for *uvidĕti* is not surprising, given the etymological relationship between *vidĕti* and *vĕdĕti* 'know' postulated for Prehistoric Slavic and Indo-European. If we accept that the Chronicles were not written all at once but gradually (although not necessarily in the years noted in the manuscript), it makes sense that in (46) and (47), which are separated from the other examples by 249 manuscript years, the meaning is far closer to that of the Modern Russian verb 'see, catch sight of, glimpse'. This verb is clearly a protoperfective.

There are a few more examples of verbs formed on this root *(providĕti* 'foresee', *zavidĕti* 'envy', *vzavidĕti* 'begin to envy'), but they are poorly attested. *Providĕti* and *zavidĕti*, which are stative verbs (like *stojati*), look much like protoimperfectives, further bolstering the ties between this group and the group of statives, whose prefixed forms can also be protoimperfectives.[14]

Conclusion. *Vidĕti* shows all signs of anaspectuality, including a variable range of durations from unbounded to punctual, a fluid boundary between present and future usage, a lack of derived forms, and a clear distinction in lexical content between it and its prefixed forms.

4.5. PUNCTUAL ATELICS OF EMOTION *(DIVITI SJA)*

In his analysis of lexical groups Maslov 1948 distinguishes between emotions that are independent of outside factors and those that occur as the result of an external stimulus. Modern Russian offers minimal pairs in *bojat'sja^I–pobojat'sja^P* 'fear^I–begin to fear^P' and *pugat'sja^I–ispugat'sja^P* 'be frightened^I–take fright^P'. The first, like *ljubit'^{I}* 'love^I', *želat'^{I}* 'desire^I', *nenavidet'^{I}* 'hate^I' is an emotion whose source is unclear; only the state of being afraid (or possibly some modification of the action contour by an Aktionsart prefix) is conveyed to the addressee. The second, like *udivljat'sja^I–udivit'sja^P* 'marvel, be amazed' implies an external cause of the emotion; one is prompted to amazement or wonder by some characteristic or action on the part of the object. It is no coincidence that many of these verbs are

---

14 *Zavidĕti* retains imperfective status in Modern Russian as well.

reflexives with nonreflexive counterparts *(pugat'¹* 'frighten¹', *udivljat'¹* 'surprise¹') that identify the source of these emotions.

The forms of Old Russian *diviti sja*[15] 'marvel, be surprised' fall into the punctual atelic category. Its simplex is attested twice in the Chronicles, and it has a number of derived and prefixed forms. The two examples of the unprefixed *diviti sja* are aspectually ambiguous; they describe acts of either aspect equally well.[16] In (54), for example, the metropolitan requests that after his death, his body is to be thrown to the dogs, not buried. After this is done, however, the prince apparently has second thoughts, takes the body and buries it; there is no hint for the reader as to where the public reaction to the metropolitan's manner of death fits in this scheme. A durative reading suggests that it was an isolated response, perhaps simultaneous with the bishop's actions. A punctual reading connects it more strongly to the bishop's deeds, suggesting that the prince's decision to bury the body may have been related to the public reaction.

(54) по оумертвии же его еп(и)с(ко)пъ то все створи повелѣная ему имь. народи же вси **дивишася** о см(е)рти его. на оутрии же д(е)нь С(вя)тославъ князь. здумавъ... (349)
'after his death, the bishop did everything he had commanded of him; the people all *marveled (divišasja)* at his death. The following day, Prince Svjatoslav, having thought it over...'

Example (55) is durative and iterative, reflecting the reactions of all those who came to the church during Cyril's tenure.

(55) и всѣм вѣрою приходящим въ с(вя)тую ц(е)рк(о)вь. Любовному оученью же и тщанью **дивлься**. сего ч(е)стнаго с(вя)т(ите)ля Кирила. с страхом и покореньем послушая. (458)
'and all those who came in faith to the holy church *marveled (divl'sja)* at the loving instruction and devotion of the honorable St. Cyril...'

The prefixed verb *udiviti sja* in (56)-(62), while showing evidence of protoperfectivity, overlaps in its usage with the simplex in (54) and (55). Compare (54), for instance, with (56), where the connection between the amazement and the acts that precede and follow it is more tenuous.

(56) и почаша ясти сами первое. потомь же Печенѣзи. и **оудивишася** и рекоша не имуть вѣры наши князи. аще не ядят сами (129)
'and they began themselves to eat first, and then the Pečenegs [began], and *they were amazed (oudivišasja)*, and said: our princes will not believe [this] if they do not eat it themselves'

---

[15] My citation form for reflexive verbs separates off the reflexive particle {sja}. In many cases, however, the editions of the texts I use do not reflect this convention.

[16] Note that the usage of the simplex in (55) is almost identical in context to the use of the prefixed form in (62), showing the simplex's plasticity.

In general, however, *udiviti sja* is used for acts that are perceived as a unified, completed whole and appears only in the aorist and past participle, as in (57)-(62).

(57) и видѣ ту люди сущая. како есть обычаи имъ. и како ся мыють (и) хвощются. и **удивися** имъ. иде въ Вариги (8)
    and he saw the people who were there, what their customs were and how they wash and drink, and *he marveled (udivisja)* at them; he went to the Varangians..'

(58) **удививъся** ц(а)рь разуму ея. бѣседова к неи и рекъ еи... (60)
    'the emperor, *having been struck (udiviv"sja)* by her knowledge, spoke with her and told her...'

(59) они же во изумѣньи бывше. **оудивившес(я)** похвалиша службу ихъ (108)
    'having been in awe, they *marveled (oudivivšesja)*, and praised the service'

(60) оукраси ю. иконами безъцѣньнами. и всякыми оузорочьями **оудиви** (367)
    'he adorned it with priceless icons and *surprised (oudivi)* [them] with all kinds of valuable baubles'

(61) тѣмь в памят оубьенья твоего **оудивишася** н(е)б(е)снии анг(е)ли (368)
    'so in memory of your murder the heavenly angels *marveled (oudivišasja)*'

(62) Тогож лѣт(а) родися Василку с(ы)нъ... И вся приходящая **оудивлес(я)**. (457)
    'that year a son was born to Vasil'ko...and everyone who came *marveled (oudivlesja)*'

While *udiviti sja* is protoperfective in virtually all its incarnations, then, *diviti sja* is not clearly protoimperfective, since it shares some of these protoperfective functions.

The derived form *divljati sja* appears in progressive (imperfective-like) contexts, as in (63); it appears in a Modern Russian translation with the verb *udivljat'sja*.

(63) и приде в Римъ (и) исповѣда елико наоучи. и елико видѣ...ты слышаще **дивляхус(я)** (9)
    'and he came to Rome and related how much he had learned and seen...those listening *marveled (divljaxusja)*'

The derived form *divovati sja* in (64) is not used in progressive contexts; it appears in a section of the *Testament of Vladimir Monomax* (a document in the *Primary Chronicle*) in which the ruler tells the Lord how awe-struck Christians are at the fact and manner of man's creation. It is thus closer to a general factual usage.

(64) Г(о)с(под)и твоимъ промысломъ. звѣрье розноличнии. и птица и
рыбы оукрашено твоимъ промысломъ Г(о)с(под)и. и сему чюду
дивуемъся. како от персти создавъ ч(е)л(о)в(е)ка. (244)
'o Lord by your work are the animals so varied, and the birds and fish are
decorated by your work, o Lord; and *we marvel (divuem"sja)* at this miracle,
how from dust you created man'

These two unprefixed derived forms, then, represent different facets of potential protoimperfectivity.

The form *podiviti sja* is close in meaning to *udiviti sja*, although it has more of an inceptive flavor.

(65) и варивше яша князи Печенѣзьстии. и **подивишася**. и поимше тали
своя. и онѣхъ пустивше. въсташа от града въ своя си идоша. (129)
'and when they had cooked it [the kissel], the Pečeneg princes ate and
marveled (podivišasja), and taking their hostages and releasing others, they
rose from the town and went back home'

(66) мы же **да подивимся** чюду новому и великому и преславному
м(а)т(е)ре Б(о)жья. како заступи град свои от великих бѣдъ. и
гражаны своя оукрѣпляеть (377)
'o *let us marvel (da podivimsja)* at the new, great and glorious miracle[17] of the
Mother of God, how she defended her city from great afflictions, and makes
her citizens strong'

(67) и паде нѣколико от руку его. и **подивишас(я)** силѣ и храбръству
его (480)
'and several fell by his hand[s], and they *marveled (podivišasja)* at his strength
and bravery'

For instance, (56) contrasts nicely with (65), since the two are found only a few sentences apart in the Primary Chronicle. In (56), a feeling of surprise is expressed, almost as if it were a verb of communication; in (65), the crucial point is that a state of surprise sets in, causing the Pečenegs to soften towards the Russians. Example (66) supports this interpretation, since the non-past *da podivimsja* 'let us marvel' has a future reading that implies inception. This is a likely reading in (67) as well. However, the context in (67) is ambiguous, so {po-} may behave as an Aktionsart prefix only part of the time.

Conclusions. *Diviti sja* shows signs of anaspectuality, although the small number of citations makes it difficult to judge. The verbs formed from it are more regularly aspectual than those of *vidĕti*. Its derived forms have imperfective-type funtions, while its prefixed forms exhibit the sort of regular inceptiveness and punctuality associated with protoperfective verbs. The morphology also argues for the anaspectual reading; the presence of both unprefixed derivations like *divovati*

---

17 Here I use a variant reading; for *čjudu novomu* the Laurentian ms. has *čjudnomu*.

sja, divljati sja and prefixed forms like *udiviti sja, podiviti sja* is typical of protoperfective simplexes like *pasti* 'fall'.

4.6. STATIVE ACTS (*STOJATI*)

The verb *stojati* 'stand' is attested in the Chronicles a total of 112 times. There are twenty-three non-past tense forms, thirty-two imperfect forms, twenty-one aorist forms, two infinitives, twenty-eight present participles, and six past participles.

4.6.1. Non-past forms of *stojati*

Most of the non-past tense forms represent a present state. This can be a state continuing from the past (eight examples, see (68)).

(68) и сани ее **стоять** в Плесковѣ и до сего дне (60)
      'and her sledge *stands (stojat')* in Pleskov unto this day'

However, it can also be a progressive state—that is, one in progress at the time another action took place. There are six examples in subordinate clauses, as in (69). Three examples occur in direct speech, as in (70). Three more concern a general statement of fact, as in (71).

(69) позрѣ по братьи. иже **стоять** поюще по обѣма странама (190)
      'he looked around the brethren who *were standing (stojat')* singing on both sides'

(70) Д(а)в(и)дъ реч(е) кде ес(ть) брат. они же рече ему **стоить** на сѣнех (259)
      'David said, "Where is my brother?", and they said to him, "*he is standing (stoit')* in the entrance" '

(71) имже приведенье обрѣтохом вѣрою. въ бл(а)г(о)д(а)ть сию. имже хвалимъся и **стоимъ** (120)
      'thanks to him we found through faith the way to this grace; thanks to him *we give praise and stand (stoim")* here'

One sentence, (72), contains a present act that continues into the future, and one, (73), can only be read as expressing futurity, which is reflected in the Modern Russian translation's choice of a future form *(budete stojat'* 'you will stand' for Old Russian *stoite).*

(72) дондеже сьяеть с(о)лнце и весь миръ **стоить** (47)
      'as long as the sun shall shine and the whole earth *shall stand (stoit')*'

(73) аще **стоите** за 10 лет. что можете створити нам (128)
      'if you *stand (stoite)* here even in ten years, what can you do to us?'

The non-past, then, is largely but not exclusively a present tense for this particular verb. It inclines away from direct limits on its duration, although acceptable readings may be further limited by context. Non-past tense forms may express an action in the past (in subordinate clauses), in the present, or in the future, and can connect those time frames, as in (68) and (72).

The presence of a future sense for non-past forms of this verb is significant. One of the hallmarks of a grammatical system of aspect is the reflection of a grammatical distinction in the morphology. In Modern Russian, the presence of a compound future tense serves as a grammatical marker of the imperfective aspect. Because this form is lacking in Old Russian, researchers have traditionally placed emphasis on the reflection of a grammatical distinction in the *semantics* of the forms: the general inability of imperfective verbs to express futurity in the non-past. If we find most verbs of this class express a future as well as a present sense with their non-past forms, we can posit that these verbs are less strongly connected to the aspectual system than has previously been supposed. A single future reading is, however, not conclusive; further evidence is in the system of past tense verbs and participles.

4.6.2. The past tense forms of *stojati*

To this end, the large proportion of aorists versus imperfects (aorists comprise 40 percent of all finite past tense forms for this verb) is especially notable. There is a contextual differentiation between aorist and imperfect usage; a great majority of aorists (seventeen out of twenty-one, or 81 percent) occur with an overt limitation on their duration, as in (74) and (75), and two out of the remaining four indicate occurrences on a particular day—as in (76)—which is also a kind of time limitation.

(74) и выступи противу ему из города. и **стоя** Глѣбъ до заоутрока и воротися опять. (319)
'and he rode out of the city against him, and Gleb *stood (stoja)* [firm] until morning, and then returned'

(75) и не смяху ни си онѣхъ. ни они сихь начати и **стояша** м(еся)цѣ 4 Противу собѣ. и воевода нача С(вя)тополчь ѣздя възлѣ берегъ оукаряти Ногородцѣ... (141)
'and the first [army] did not dare move against the second, nor the second against the first, and *they stood (stojaša)* facing each other for 4 months, and Svjatopolk's commander, riding along the bank, began to taunt the Novgorodians...'

(76) и **стоя** в монастыри у Взнесенья. на самыи праздник Възнесенья Г(оспод)ня (404)
'and *he stood (stoja)* in the Monastery of the Ascension on the very Feast of the Ascension of the Lord'

Two attestations do not fit this rule, permitting either a sequential reading (with an inchoative meaning, like a modern perfective) or a simultaneous one (like a modern imperfective).

(77) Всеволодъ же и Мстиславъ. **стояста** на Золотых воротѣх и познаста брата своего. Володимера. (461)

In (77), for example, there are two possible readings for *stojasta:* it can be progressive ('Vsevolod and Mstislav *happened to be standing* at the Golden Gate') but also inceptive ('Vsevolod and Mstislav *took up a position* at the Golden Gate'); such a reading would ordinarily be unusual, but the sentence structure and the form of the narrative, which is built around simple, sequential acts, argue for it. Earlier in the narrative, we were told that Vsevolod and Mstislav were inside the city; this is the first indication that they came out to face the Tatars, making this reading likely.

Imperfects of *stojati* express either background to an event in a subordinate clause (five out of thirty-two, or 16 percent), a state that holds while another event is occurring (four out of thirty-two, or 13 percent), a general statement of a past state (fifteen out of thirty-two, or 47 percent) or often a state limited by a time expression (eight out of thirty-two, or 25 percent). Notably, while the proportion of imperfects with time limitations is much lower than that of aorists, it does constitute a significant percentage of the sample, meaning that we cannot simply ascribe the limiting of time (durative function) entirely to the aorist and leave progressive functions to the imperfect. The aorist does play a marked role in that it is overwhelmingly used in contexts bounded by events or specific time periods. However, if the aorist–imperfect distinction is an aspectual one, it is not the same sort of aspectual distinction we see in Modern Russian, where all these forms are most neutrally translated by the imperfective verb *stojat'*.

4.6.3. Prefixed forms of *stojati*

Seven verbs in the Chronicles are formed from the verb *stojati* by prefixation. The prefixes are of two distinct sorts: they can add location to the basic verbal meaning or express a more abstract modification of the verb's meaning. In some cases, they fulfill both functions depending on context. In (78)-(81) the prefixes are of a spatial nature: to the meaning 'stand' they add an extra component showing the spatial relationship between subject and object (as in (78)).

(78) Ярославу же сущю Новѣгородѣ. вѣсть приде ему. яко Печенѣзи **остоять** Кыевъ (150-151)
      'When Jaroslav was in Novgorod, the news came to him that the Pečenegs *were surrounding (ostojat')* Kiev'

(79) оусты же чтуть мя а с(е)рдце ихъ далече **отстоить** мене (169)
      'with their lips they honor me but their heart *stands* far *from (otstoit')* me'[18]

---

[18] Matthew 15:8 and Mark 7:6. Also appears as example (146) in chapter 5.

(80) бѣ бо възложилъ на нь гривну злату велику. в неиже **предъстояше** пред нимь (134)
'for he had presented him with a large gold necklace, which *he wore when he served (pred"stojaše)* him'

(81) **пристояху** совѣту сему смыслении мужи (219)
'sensible men *adhered (pristojaxu)* to this advice'

In (78), 'stand' is used in its literal sense; in (79), there is a metaphorical reading of distance, while in (80) and (81) there is a more figurative interpretation.

In (82)-(86) the meaning of the prefixes is nonspatial. Some of them introduce into the predicate a limitation in time; these prefixes can be labelled Aktionsart prefixes, and are found in (82)-(84).

(82) по обычаю бо сему старцю. **отстоявшю** оутренюю пред зорями. идоша по кѣльямъ своимъ. се же старець послѣ исхожаше ис церкви. (190)
'as was this old man's habit, *when he had stood through (otstojavšju)* matins before dawn, they [the monks] would go to their cells; then the old man would leave the church'[19]

(83) отвѣщавши Ольга. и реч(е) къ сломъ. аще ты рьци такоже **постоиши** оу мене в Почаинѣ якоже азъ в Сюду то тогда ти дамь (63)
'in answering, Olga said to the emissaries: say *you'll spend (postoiši)* as long as my guest in Počain as I did in the Bosphorus, and then I will give it to you'

(84) и **постоявъ** мало. съступи на ц(е)рк(о)вь (284)
'and, *having stood (postojav")* for a short while, he went down to the church'

Other prefixes mandate a more abstract or figurative reading of the verb. The prefixes in (85) and (86), {pre-} in *prestojati* 'withstand' and {u-} in *ustojati* 'depend', fall into this category.

(85) почто губите себе. коли можете **престояти** нас (128)
'why are you destroying yourselves? Can you really *withstand (prestojati)* us?'

(86) аще ли вы будет(е) кр(е)сть цѣловати к братьи или г кому. а ли оуправивъше сердце свое. на немже можете **оустояти**. тоже цѣлуите. и цѣловавше блюдѣте (245)
'if you will swear oaths to your brothers or anyone else, then, having tested your heart as to whether you can *depend (oustojati)* on it, swear the oaths, and having done so, be on your guard'

---

19 Overlaps with material in example (147), chapter 5.

I have introduced these distinctions because they correlate with the aspectual usages indicated in the texts. Verbs with spatial prefixes tend to occur in progressive and durative contexts, just like the stem verb. Verbs with Aktionsart prefixes are preferred in sharply limited contexts characteristic in Modern Russian of the *perfectiva tantum* verbs. Verbs with figurative prefixes can be of both types.

One verb—*otstojati*—has the same prefix functioning lexically as an indicator of distance in (79) and as an indicator of Aktionsart in (82), where it expresses the exhaustion of an act. These prefixes can therefore take on multiple functions with any one verb in any given text, and it is important to avoid assigning them a single function for all occurrences. The other Aktionsart prefix, found in *postojati* 'stand for a while', does not have a corresponding lexical function attested for this verb. It behaves like a protoperfective verb, fitting into the category of verbs I will label "limited duration."

Conclusions. As a stative verb, *stojati* has a strong leaning toward progressive and durative contexts. Iterative contexts are not found. Evidence of grammatical aspect, however, is absent. There are no clear morphological markers in the texts that assign the verb to one category or another, since it is able to express both presentness and futurity with its non-past tense, and shows ample quantities of aorists, imperfects, and present and past active participles. Its prefixed derivatives are not necessarily protoperfectives. Instead, they are just as likely to express a more precise spatial relationship or a figurative relationship that has no bearing on aspect. Where protoperfectives are formed from this verb, they can fall into the category of Aktionsart-created verbs, which have a similar (although clearly not identical) meaning to the unprefixed form but a substantially different perspective on the action.

For the Russian of these chronicles, I would assign *stojati* the designation "likely to become imperfective" but would not grant it status as a protoimperfective verb. The characteristics of *stojati* were defined here by and large in lexical terms, so if this analysis is accurate, other predicates of its lexical type (i.e., statives) will show a similar (but not necessarily identical) spread of forms.

4.7. STATES OR ATELIC ACTIONS? *(KNJAŽITI)*

Verbs like *knjažiti* 'rule, reign' indicate profession and would seem to belong among the atelic action class. However, they do not in and of themselves imply any action; if we say someone "reigns in Kiev," it may mean only that this is his domain, while the translation 'rule' has a more active meaning. There is an overlap, then, between the stative and atelic action categories. The more concrete meaning 'rule' is found in (87), (89), (91), (92), and (94), while the more general, stative meaning 'reign' is found in (88), (90), and (93).

(87) аще бо бы (былъ) перевозникъ Кии. то не бы ходилъ Ц(а)рюгороду но се(и) Кии **княжаше** в родѣ своемь. (10)
'for if Kij had been a ferryman, he would not have gone to Constantinople; but this Kij *was ruler (knjažaše)* in his homeland'

(88)   а Ярополкъ **княжи** лѣт 8 а Володимеръ **(княжи)** лѣт 37 а Ярославъ **княжи** лѣт 40. (18)
'and Jaropolk *reigned (knjaži)* eight years, and Volodimer *(reigned) (knjaži)* thirty-seven years, and Jaropolk *reigned (knjaži)* forty years'

This verb has features common to both the stative and atelic action classes, including a variable time span that allows it to express both duration and summation—compare, for instance, (87) and (88). The infinitive and supine show a strong tendency to appear in unbounded progressive contexts, as in (89) and (90), as well as more generalized contexts, as in (91) and (92).

(89)   вся земля наша велика и обилна. а наряда в неи нѣтъ. да поидѣте **княжитъ** и володѣти нами. (20)
'our whole land is great and bountiful, but there is no order in it; come *reign (knjažit")* over and rule us'

(90)   в лѣт(о) 6421 поча **княжити** Игорь по Олзѣ. (42)
'in the year 913, Igor' began *to reign (knjažiti)* after Oleg'

(91)   аще ли сего не створишь а пустишь и. то ни тобѣ **княжи(ти)** ни мнѣ. (260)
'if you do not do this and you let him go, then it will be neither for you nor for me *to rule (knjaži[ti])*'

(92)   просимъ оу тобе с(ы)на **княжитъ** Новугороду. (415)
'we ask you for a son *to reign (knjažit")* in Novgorod'

Past and present participles and verbal adverbs allow us to view the act from either a summarized (aorist) perspective or a progressive perspective, as reflected respectively in (93) and (94).

(93)   **княживъ** лѣт 15. Кыевѣ. (217)
'*having reigned (knjaživ")* for fifteen years in Kiev'

(94)   и живяше Олегъ миръ имѣа ко всѣм странамъ. **кн(я)жа** в Киевѣ. и приспѣ осень. (38)
'and while he lived Oleg had peace with all nations, *ruling (knjaža)* in Kiev. And fall came...'

Conclusion: *knjažiti* is somewhat more aspectual than *stojati* but retains much of the same anaspectuality. It tends toward the protoimperfective aspect.

4.8. ATELIC ACTIONS *(BLJUSTI)*

The class of predicates expressing atelic action is far less clearly delimited than the class of stative predicates discussed above. At one end of the spectrum are verbs like *knjažiti* 'reign, rule' that, although they express a profession or a continuous act—a hallmark of this class—come very close to expressing a state. At the other end of the spectrum are verbs like *praviti* 'lead, direct' or *loviti* 'hunt' that normally express an atelic action but can be transformed into telic acts with the addition of a direct object under certain conditions. This fluidity makes it difficult to find verbs that express only atelic acts, but it will prove useful in understanding how aspectuality develops and spreads across the verbal system.

4.8.1. Forms of *bljusti*

The verb *bljusti* 'guard' comes closest to expressing a "purely" atelic act. It appears in the Chronicles a total of twenty-four times: ten times in the infinitive, three times in the non-past, four times in the imperative, and seven times as a present active participle. Examples (95)-(97) show the infinitive with a more general sense that does not represent a particular time span.

(95) и поучивъ ихъ како проводити постное время. в м(о)л(и)твахъ нощных и дневных. **блюстися** от помыслъ скверньных. от бѣсовьскаго насѣянья. (183)
 'and having taught them how to conduct the fasts in daily and nightly prayers, *to guard themselves (bljustisja)* against vile thoughts...'

(96) но аче добро есть **блюсти**. Б(о)жие блюденье лѣплѣѣ есть ч(е)л(о)в(ѣ)чскаго. (252)[20]
 'but if it is good *to be vigilant (bljusti)*, then divine vigilance is better than man's'

(97) Иоан княз с(ы)нъ Дмитриевъ ида в Ворду приказалъ Михаилу кн(я)зю **блюсти** очины своее и Переяславля. (484)
 'Prince Ioann, Dmitrij's son, upon going to Vorda, ordered Prince Mixail *to watch (bljusti)* over his domain and Perejaslavl' '

Only (97) can be interpreted as a durative context (i.e., to watch over these domains for a set period of time, while Ioann is in Vorda). A somewhat less clear example is the imperative in (98), which teeters between a general factual command and a progressive one emphasizing the present danger. (The reflexive form here indicates a greater degree of intensity and self-interest in the process of guarding; note also the ethical dative *ti*, found twice earlier in the sentence, which similarly point to the impact of events on the addressee.)

(98) о(те)ць ти оумерлъ. а С(вя)тополкъ сѣдитъ ти Кыевѣ оубивъ Бориса. а на Глѣба посла. а **блюдися** его повелику. (140-141)
 'your father has died, and Svjatopolk reigns in Kiev, having killed Boris; and he sent men to [kill] Gleb, so *guard yourself (bljudisja)* against him vigilantly'

---

20 The editor suggests *ače* (= *ašče* 'if') as a variant reading for the manuscript's *oče* (= *otče* 'o father'?), since the latter makes no sense here.

The non-past examples (99)-(101) are more aspectually ambiguous, especially when it comes to indicating a time frame.

(99) ты княже чюжея земли ищеши и **блюдеши**. а своея ся охабивъ. (67)[21]
'you, o prince, *are* searching for and *watching over (bljudeši)* another's land, while having abandoned your own'

(100) реч(е) Тукы братъ Чюдинь Изяславу. видиши княже людье възвыли. посли атъ Всеслава **блюдуть**. (171)
'Tuky, brother of Čudin, said to Izjaslav: do you see, o prince: the people have begun to clamor. Send that *they might keep watch over (bljudut')* Vseslav.'

Example (99) has a progressive or generalized present context. However, (100), with the modal word *at"* 'let' functions like a 3. pl. imperative, a reading that gives the sentence a hint of futurity. Example (101) is even clearer in this regard, especially when compared to the Modern Russian translation in (101a).

(101) да нонѣ отселѣ имемся въ едино с(е)рдце. и **блюдем** Рускыѣ земли. (256)
'and from now on we will join and be of one mind, and *we will guard (bljudem)* the Russian land'

(101a) *tr:* Да с этих пор объединимся чистосердечно и **будем охранять** Русскую землю. (372)

In (101) the form *bljudem* 'we (shall) guard' follows another simplex *imemsja* 'to join together', that indicates an imminent event. *Bljudem* thus unequivocally marks a future event, as reflected in the Modern Russian translation *budem oxranjat'* 'we will guard'.[22] Once again, the non-past tense has the ability to convey futurity.

The present verbal adverbs in (102) and (103) show that the watchfulness was simultaneous with other actions. No past participles or verbal adverbs are attested in the Chronicles.

---

21 Also example (197).
22 A quick perusal of the use of *da* in the Chronicles leaves the following impression: *da* inevitably appears directly preceding the verb form (although enclitic pronouns and the negative particle can come between them) when it is used as an exhortation or to indicate futurity. In this function, it can apply to more than one verb in the clause, but is often repeated before subsequent verbs when they themselves would not ordinarily convey futurity (e.g., the verb *iměti* 'have') or when more than one or two words separate the two verb forms. This leads to the conclusion that the form of *da* found in (101) is probably a conjunction, with only a weak hint of futurity in it. Otherwise, it would stand directly before the verb *imemsja* and would need to be repeated before the form *bljudem* as well in order to apply to it, given patterns typical of Old Russian usage.

(102) иже пасяше словесныя овця. нелицемѣрно с кротостью. и с
    расмотреньемь. **блюда** ихъ. и бдя за не... (212)
    '...he who pastured [his] spiritual sheep, straighforwardly, with humility and attention, *guarding over (bljuda)* them, and watching out for them...

(103) Изяслав же слышавъ то поиде по нем. **блюда** того дабы ся не
    снялъ с Володимерком. (333)
    'Izjaslav, having heard this, went after him, *being careful (bljuda)* not to meet up with Volodimerko'

4.8.2. Prefixed forms of *bljusti*

There are three prefixed verbs formed from *bljusti*: *pobljusti*, *sobljusti*, and *ubljusti*. Unlike prefixed forms from statives, these all show signs of perfectivity, although in different ways. All attestations of these verbs in the texts are reproduced below. Although it is hard to judge on the basis of one example, the verb *pobljusti* seems to have a purely Aktionsart prefix, indicating in (104) that Igor will be guarded for a finite amount of time.

(104) Игоря **поблюдут** сторожеве. а мы поидем к брату. (317)
    'the guards *will watch over (pobljudut)* Igor, and we will go to my brother'

In (104) the future reading is obvious. However, *sobljusti* is less clear; its prefix serves not to add its own meaning but to modify a meaning of the root, highlighting some inherent characteristics while neglecting others.

(105) **дабы** мя Б(ог)ъ **съблюлъ** от всякого зла. (61)
    '*may* God *protect (daby s"bljul")* me from all evil'

(106) **сблюди** мя твоими м(о)л(и)твами. (214)
    '*protect (sbljudi)* me with your prayers'

(107) и конь со мною поверже. и Б(ог)ъ неврежена мя **съблюде**. (251)
    'and my horse went down with me on it, and God *preserved (s"bljude)* me from harm'

(108) **сблюди** от всяко плѣненья вражья твои град (256)
    '*protect (sbljudi)* your city from all enemy captivity'

(109) поистинѣ о(т)ци наши и дѣди наши **зблюли** землю Русьскую. а мы
    хочем погубити. (264)
    'truly, our fathers and grandfathers *preserved (zbljuli)* the Russian land, and yet we would destroy it'

The meaning found in (105)-(109) is closer to 'protect, preserve, observe', which is a more active meaning and focuses more consistently on distinct occasions and regulations than does the simplex verb. This new predicate is not atelic and as such is better placed into the telic class (see sections following). It also has a derived protoimperfective form, as attested in (110) and (111).

(110) мы бо вѣмы м(и)л(о)с(е)рдье Ярополче. яко не радуется кровипролитью. но Б(ог)а ради всхощеть мира. то бо **сблюдаеть** землю Русскую. (306)
'for we know Jaropolk's mercy, that he does not rejoice in bloodshed, but for God's sake will want peace, for this *protects* the Russian land'

(111) заповѣди его во всем **сблюдающа**. (442)
'*keeping* his commandments in every way'

Both (110) and (111) have a progressive context. The non-past form in (110) has a present tense function. The verb *ubljusti* in (112) seems to be a variant of *sobljusti* or *pobljusti*; in manuscripts other than the Laurentian it is replaced by *sobljusti*.

(112) и едва Мстиславны товаръ **оублюдоша**. и то с нужею бьющеся. и тако възвратишася со многым полоном. (298)
'and *they* barely *saved (ubljudoša)* Mstislav's goods, and at that fighting desperately, and thus they returned with many prisoners'

Conclusions. In a few respects the data for this verb are similar to those for the predicates of the stative class, especially as concerns the function of the non-past tense. Overt signs of grammatical aspect are lacking, although this is partially because there are no past tense forms of the simplex in this text. At any rate, this verb tends toward the protoimperfective aspect. Verbs formed from *bljusti* can be assigned to grammatical protoaspects; the attested prefixes impose a different view of time, whether by a limitation of the original action or a modification thereof, and there are no prefixes with simple locative meaning. There is a prefixed derived verb in the group—*sobljudati*—that is a protoimperfective counterpart to the simple prefixed verb *sobljusti*. Overall, this verb is much closer to protoimperfectivity than is the stative *stojati*.

4.9. DEGREES OF TELICITY

A great number of acts have a telic component. They are actions that are seen as directed toward a goal; this goal can either be included in the expression of the act or left outside it, a distinction that in Modern Russian is partially reflected in the aspectual choice of the speaker.[23] (A small subclass, represented by the verb *iskati* 'search', contains natural conatives: acts where frustration or suppression of the goal is inherent in the lexical meaning.) It is my contention that predicates will show different aspectual behavior based on the type of telicity they exhibit.

---

[23] The specifics of aspectual assignment and its relation to context are discussed in more detail in chapter 2.

In discussing atelic predicates, there is a predictable pattern of development from Old Russian to Modern Russian: the simplex verb develops into an imperfective, while the prefixed verb is likely to develop into a perfective with inceptive or exhaustive meaning, or into an imperfective with spatial meaning. Anomalies thus existed mainly in the prefixed group: certain classes of predicates were less likely to have prefixed forms that showed a distinct tendency toward a single aspect. The development of telic predicates is quite different. The degree of telicity found in the predicates determines the likelihood of a simplex verb's development into perfective or imperfective, and has an impact on the aspectual development of its prefixed and suffixed forms.

For instance, accruing telic predicates (forms of *staviti* meaning 'build', appropriate forms of *pisati* 'write') indicate a process that heads toward a goal; even if the act stops short of the goal, however, there is still a measurable result. The distinction between perfective and imperfective in Modern Russian is one of reaching a specific goal vs. failing to reach that goal, not simply of effecting a change of state. We could posit that for these predicates, then, process is more basic than completion, and expect to see simplexes become imperfective.

Since the presence of an objective physical result plays a large role in uniting the predicates of this group, most of these predicates will describe an act that leaves physical traces. Prefixed and suffixed forms of this stem that retain the directional meaning of the prefix will remain within the subclass. Prefixed and derived forms that change the meaning of the stem will be likely to change groups. Most changes to the meaning of a stem introduce a more abstract meaning that is derived from a basic physical meaning, and abstractions are less concretely measurable and more prone to manipulation as concerns their full or partial attainment of a goal, so they will be more likely to belong to other subclasses of telic predicates.

Not all telic predicates describe an action that accrues measurably toward a goal. In many telic acts, the process that moves toward the goal is considerably less meaningful if the goal is not achieved, and this change of state once the goal is achieved is perceived as more basic. For instance, most predicates of verbs like *pasti* 'fall', *strětiti* 'meet', *poběditi* 'win' have a strong telic component; without the attainment of the goal, the action is seen as interrupted (in progressive or durative contexts) or deliberately focused elsewhere (in general factual, descriptive, and to an extent in iterative contexts). It is logical to expect the usages found in these contexts to be secondary and to derive them from a more basic usage, which includes the attainment of the telos.[24] Simplexes of this sort should become perfective, or alternately, disappear altogether in favor of a prefixed form.

---

[24] Of course, not all of the distinctions I have mentioned here are found in Old Russian aspect and are probably offshoots of other aspectual distinctions. The possibility of expressing failure, for instance, holds only for predicates of the telic class in Modern Russian and apparently does not apply in Old Russian (see chapters 7 and 8). Likewise, limitations on time—durative contexts—had a different realization in Old Russian, being protoperfective as often as protoimperfective The third distinction—that of focus of the event—seems most promising for evaluating Old Russian verbs.

Predicates describing an act that occurs mainly in the mind or as a result of perception usually have a possible instantaneous reading and can be classed as "punctual telic," a separate group discussed in section 4.15 and following.

If lexical classes do have a strong influence on aspectual assignment, there should be ample proof in the following sections.

4.10. ACCRETIVE TELICITY *(STAVITI)*

The verb *staviti*, 'build, set, assign, establish, settle' appears only rarely in its simplex form, a total of eight times in the Chronicles. Of the eight examples of the simplex, four, (113)-(116), are infinitives; three, (118)-(120), are aorists; and one, (117), is non-past.

4.10.1. The simplex verb *staviti*

The infinitives in (113)-(116) are all in progressive contexts following inceptive verbs (*načati*, *počati* 'start, begin').

(113)   се же Олегъ нача городы **ставити**. (23)
'thus Oleg began *to build (staviti)* towns'[25]

(114)   и нача **ставити** по градомъ ц(е)ркви. (118)
'and he began *to build (staviti)* churches in the towns'

(115)   и нача **ставити** городы по Деснѣ. и по Востри. и по Трубешеви... (121)
'and he began *to build (staviti)* towns along the Desna, and the Oster', and the Trubež...'

(116)   Ярославъ поча **ставити** городы по Рьси (150)
Jaroslav began *to build (staviti)* towns throughout Russia'

The single non-past form in (117) reflects the different meaning of the reflexive *staviti sja* 'stop'. The reflexive sense 'stop' is related to the nonreflexive meaning 'set, place' that appears in (118)-(120); it appears here in a generalized context.

(117)   ...птица н(е)б(е)сныя. изъ ирья идут. и первѣе наши руцѣ. и не **ставятся** на одинои земли. но и силныя и худыя идут. по всѣмъ землямъ. (244)
'the birds of the sky come from paradise and straightaway into our hands, and they *do not stop (stavjatsja)* in just one land, but both the strong and the weak go to all the lands'

---

[25] There is no indication as to whether this frequently found collocation *staviti gorody* means 'build towns' or 'build forts'. Lixačev and Romanov (1950) leans toward the former; Cross and Sherbowitz-Wetzor (1973) suggests the latter, since no towns are named, and their function could easily be military.

In contrast, the aorists all have a punctual, completed sense, giving this verb properties normally associated with both the protoperfective and protoimperfective aspect. The functions attested for the aorist, however, are quite different from those attested in the infinitive, as can be seen in (118) and (119).

(118)　а прокъ их **стави** платити дань (59)
'and the rest of them *she [Olga] set (stavi)* to pay the tax'[26]

(119)　Тое же зимы приехаша численици исщетоша всю землю Сужа-
льскую и Рязаньскую. и Мюромьскую и **ставиша** десятники и
сотники и тысящники и темникї. и идоша в Ворду. (475)
'that winter the tax officers arrived; they assessed the whole land of Suzdal'
and Rjazan' and Murom, and *assigned (staviša)* desjatniks and sotniks and
tysjačniks and temniks[27]; and they went on to the Orda'

Only (120) could possibly have the meaning 'build'. The aorist in (120) therefore recalls the durative-context aorists seen with *stojati* 'stand'.

(120)　в суб(о)ту. мясопущю. почаша наряжати лѣсы. и порокы **ставиша**
до вечера. а на ночь огородиша тыном около всего города
Володимеря. (462)
'on the Saturday of Great Lent, they began to prepare the wood, and *they built
(staviša)* battering rams until evening, and by night they had set fortifications
around the entire city of Volodimer''[28]

The aorist thus expresses the concrete, accretive meaning 'build' in (120) and the figurative meanings 'establish, assign, place' in (118) and (119). The infinitive expresses a narrower range, with the concrete meaning evident in all four examples, and a figurative reading possible for (114), in that churches can be either 'built' or 'established'. Imperfective-type contexts apparently fit best with the concrete, accretive meanings of *staviti*, whereas with the aorist, a wider range of meanings and contexts appears, both imperfective-like and perfective-like.

4.10.2. The derived form *stavljati*

An unprefixed derived form, *stavljati*, appears twice. It was mentioned earlier that the status of the verb's complements (its objects, direct, indirect, and otherwise)

---

[26] This usage of *staviti* is quite unusual, but not impossible, since similar readings are found with the prefixed form *postaviti*. A variant reading from the Radzivil and Academy mss. given in the *Polnoe sobranie* is *ostavi* 'left', and Lixačev and Romanov's translation adopts this reading.

[27] These are all commanders over regiments of various sizes.

[28] The meaning of *staviša* is not entirely clear here; Sreznevskij does not know what to make of this usage of *lěsy,* but if it does fall under the meaning *drova* 'wood', then the clear indication is that the defensive fortifications are in fact being built and finally placed around the city at the end of the sentence.

has an effect on our evaluation of an action's lexical meaning. Complements also have an effect on how we perceive the context of an action. Object distribution—the matching of members of one group of objects with members of another group of objects—has an impact on how we classify an action; it can influence our perception of whether the action is to be considered as an ongoing process or as a repeated action. This concept applies to two objects (*he gave the boys oranges* = 'to each boy he gave at least one orange' as opposed to 'he gave several oranges to a group of boys') or to subjects and objects (*the soldiers killed the townsfolk* = 'each soldier participated in killing at least one townsperson'). The unprefixed derived forms in (121) and (122) both have distributive objects in conjunction with the progressive contexts signalled by the imperfect tense and the verb *načati* 'begin'; they both involve an action repeated or continued several times with respect to different items.

(121) и ины ц(е)ркви **ставляше** по градомъ и по мѣстомъ. поставляя попы и дая имъ от именья своего урокъ. (153)
'and he built (*stavljaše*) other churches around the towns and in [other] places, appointing priests and giving them a salary from his own monies'[29]

(122) король же нача **ставляти** противу ему свои полкы на бродѣхъ же (337)
'the king began *to position (stavljati)* his troops against him at the fords'

In (121), several churches were constructed in each place or each town; in (122) the king began to position his regiments at different fords against his enemy. In each case one set of items (churches, regiments) is distributed among another set of items (cities/towns, fords). Object distribution in this instance, as well as in others, decreases the repetitive focus of an action and gives it more of a progressive feel.

4.10.3. The prefixed verb *postaviti*

The prefixed verb with the clearest semantic connection to the simplex *staviti* is *postaviti* 'build, establish, set'. It appears ninety-one times in the Chronicles. The non-past regularly expresses a single future act considered as a whole, as in (123) and (124).

(123) и **поставлю** пр(е)ст(о)лъ свои на облацѣх. сѣверьскихъ. (88)
'and *I will establish (postavlju)* my throne on the northern clouds'

(124) **поставлю** оуношю князя имъ. (140)
'*I will set (postavlju)* this youth as prince over them'

---

[29] One could adopt a more West Slavic reading of this passage: '...around the *forts* and *cities*...'

The imperative likewise requests that a single, complete act be performed, as in (125).

(125) и рѣша людье Самоилу. **постави** намъ ц(а)ря. (97)
'and the people said to Samuel: *appoint (postavi)* us a king!'

The infinitive forms in (126)-(128) are used in the same way. The meaning 'build' appears in (126) and (127); 'appoint' is found in (128).

(126) и тогда обѣщася Володимеръ **поставити** церковь Василевѣ. с(вя)таг(о) Преображенья. (125)
'and then Volodimer promised *to erect (postaviti)* a church of the Holy Transfiguration in Vasilev'

(127) и помыслиша **поставити** внѣ печеры манастырь. (158)
'and they decided *to build (postaviti)* a monastery outside the cave'

(128) и с(вя)тая Б(огороди)ца. изволи его **поставити** служителя своеи ц(е)ркви. (456)
'and the Holy Mother of God permitted him *to appoint (postaviti)* a clergyman for his church'

The distribution of forms of *postaviti* is heavily weighted toward the aorist, with sixty-seven examples (74 percent). Ten forms, representing 11 percent of the total, are infinitives. Eight examples (9 percent) have a perfect participle: of these, four are perfect tense forms (two with the copula *est'* 'is', two without), three are pluperfects (with the copula *bě* 'was'), and one is a conditional mood form (with the copula *byxom* 'we would'). There are two imperative forms and one imperfect tense form. As opposed to the simplex *staviti*, which shows signs of aspectual ambiguity, *postaviti* is unmistakably protoperfective.

An interesting distinction emerges between the use of the compound tenses with the perfect participle and the aorist tense forms. The perfect tense (and even other tenses and moods with the perfect participle) appears with singular objects, as in (129)-(134). Note both meanings of *postaviti* in (129)-(130) and (131), respectively with and without the copula.

(129) и **поставилъ ес(ть)** еп(и)с(ко)па (28)
'and *he appointed (postavil" es[t'])* a bishop'

(130) **поставилъ же есть** Б(ог)ъ единъ д(е)нь. в неже хощет судити пришедъ с н(е)б(е)се живымъ и м(е)ртв(ы)мъ. (105)
'for God *has established (postavil" est')* a single day, on which, when he comes down from heaven, he will judge the living and the dead'

(131) на тои могилѣ **поставилъ** ц(е)рк(о)вь св(я)т(а)го Николу (23)
'on this grave *he built (postavil")* the church of St. Nicholas'

Similar usages are found in the pluperfect and conditional in (132)-(134).

(132) кде ес(ть) конь мъи. егоже **бѣ поставил** кормити и блюсти ег(о). (38)
'where is my horse that I *had ordered (bě postavil)* [you] to feed and guard?'

(133) да бы Б(ог) повелѣлъ и твоя м(о)л(и)тва. да **быхомъ поставили** ц(е)рквьцю внѣ печеры. (158)
'let God and your prayer direct us *that we might build (da byxom postavili)* a small church outside the cave'

(134) митрополитъ же Никифоръ не хотяше поставити его. зане **бѣ** на мьздѣ **поставилъ** Николу Грьчина. (391)
'Metropolitan Nicephorus, however, did not want to appoint him, because, for a bribe, he *had appointed (bě postavil")* Nikola Grečin'

The aorist, however, retains the ability to encompass groups of like objects and represent them as a single attainment. Example (135) has a singular object.

(135) и малъ столпъ мраморен **постави** (на)д ним. (40)
'and *he set (postavi)* a small marble column over him'

Examples (136)-(140) have aorists of *postaviti* with multiple objects, summing up a series of actions in a single whole. Sometimes the action indicated is 'building' as in (136)-(139); elsewhere it is 'setting' or 'appointing', as in (140).

(136) (а) кельѣ **поставиша** многы. (159)
'(and) *they built (postaviša)* many cells'

(137) ц(е)ркви оукраси. и манастыря **постави**. (348)
'he adorned churches, and *built (postavi)* monasteries'

(138) и ц(е)ркви различны **постави** (367)
'and *he built (postavi)* various churches'

(139) и грады многы **постави** (468)
'and *he built (postavi)* many towns/forts'

(140) Мстислав же ему имъ вѣру **не постави** сторожовъ (239)
'Mstislav, however, decided to trust him, and *did not place (ne postavi)* guards [for him]'

Of interest is also the imperfect *postavjaxu* 'they placed, would place' in (141):

(141) аще кто оумряше творяху трызно надъ нимъ. и по семь творяху кладу велику и възложахуть и на кладу м(е)ртвца. сожьжаху. и посемь собравше кости. вложаху в судину малу. и **поставяху** на столпѣ... (14)

'when someone died, they would have a ceremony in his honor, and then they would make a large block and would place the dead man on the block, burn him up and then, having collected the bones, *would* put them in a small vessel and *place (postavjaxu)* it on a pillar'

Again, the imperfect of a prefixed verb indicates a repeated action performed in its entirety each time. Moreover, the event is set in the context of other events performed obligatorily as a series; each one must be finished before the next can be begun, lending weight to the perfectivity of the verb. The absence of a derived form makes it clear that iterativity as a context is treated differently from progressivity.

In the above examples, the prefixed verb is used in a wide variety of meanings: 'build' in (126), (127), (131), (133), (136)-(139); 'establish' in (123) and potentially (127); 'appoint' in (124), (125), (128), (129), (134), (140); 'set, put' in (135), (141); 'set down, decree' in (130), (132). This corresponds to the variety of senses found for the simplex, inasmuch as we can see them from the examples available. It is notable that only one of these meanings—'build, erect'—is realizable incrementally; the rest fall into the class of sharply telic predicates or punctual telic predicates. The semantic heterogeneity of the simplex verb leads here to heterogeneity within the prefixed verb; it will not do so in every case, as seen below.

4.10.4. The derived verb *postavljati*

A derived form, *postavljati* 'establish, set, appoint', appears eight times. The interaction between predicate class and meaning is seen in the development of this secondary prefixed form, which has a marked bent toward the more abstract, nonincremental meanings available from the simplex and primary prefixed form. Of the eight examples of this verb, only one could have the meaning 'build' (142); it represents the "object distribution" discussed in the previous section.

(142)   повелѣ рубити ц(е)ркви. и **поставляти** по мѣстом. идеже стояху кумири. (118)
'he ordered [them] to build the churches and *to set* them *up (postavljati)* in the places where idols had stood'

In (142), churches are built or set up in various places, one church to each place. The verb also appears in progressive contexts in (143) and (144); in the latter example, it coincides with the use of participial forms.

(143)   ...другия аки странь **поставляюще** и стрѣляху в ня. изимахуть опаки руцѣ съвязывахуть. гвозди желѣзныи посреди главы въбивахуть ихъ (44) [30]

---

[30] The Radzivil and Academy mss. have *im"* instead of *ix"*, and my translation reflects this alternate reading. This passage is discussed further as example (388) below and its structure is analyzed as example (124) in chapter 5.

'and, *setting (postavljajušče)* others to one side, they shot into them, seized them, tied their hands in back, [and] drove iron nails through their head[s]'

(144) и ины ц(е)ркви ставляше по градомъ и по мѣстомъ. **поставляя** попы и дая имъ от имѣнья своего урокъ. (153)
'and he built other churches in towns and other places, *appointing (postavljaja)* priests and giving them a salary from his own monies'

All five non-past forms express general truths like those in (145). In all non-past forms, *postavljati* is used in the meaning 'appoint'.

(145) яко Б(ог)ъ даеть власть емуже хощеть. **поставляетъ** бо ц(е)с(а)ря и князя Вышьнии. емуже хощеть дасть. (440)
'God gives power to whomever he desires; for the Highest *appoints (postavljaet")* [as] king and prince whomever he wishes to give it to'

4.10.5. Other prefixed forms from *staviti*

There are numerous other prefixed forms of *staviti* in this text, including *ostaviti, prestaviti, pristaviti, rasstavljati, sostaviti, sostavlivati, ustaviti, ustavljati, vosstavljati,* and *vstaviti*. The predicates are not all accretive, and do not all share the same derivational patterns. Several of them retain a directional sense from their prefixes *(pristaviti* 'attach, add onto', *rasstavljati* 'distribute, disperse', *sostaviti* 'bring together, compose', *vosstavljati* 'set up', *vstaviti* in the meaning 'set into, set upon') while having a meaning close to one or more of the simplex verb's; the remainder lack both a directional component and a clear relation to the sense of the simplex verb. Among the latter are *ostaviti* 'leave' and *ustaviti* 'levy, decree'.

Only isolated examples of these prefixed verbs will be cited here. Like *postaviti*, the other prefixed unsuffixed verbs are protoperfective, describing an act as an indivisible whole, as in (146) and (147).

(146) **преставлю** ц(а)рство дому Из(рае)л(е)ва. (98)
'*I will put an end (prestavlju)* to the kingdom of the house of Israel'

(147) послахом к тобѣ послы своя. ать **приставишь** к ним своя послы. (372)
'we sent our emissaries to you, so that you *would add (at" pristaviš')* your emissaries to them'

Non-past acts are consistently future, and aorist acts indicate completed actions, as in (148)-(150). Example (148) has a single act that applies to a number of participants, while (150) indicates either a single act or a number of acts grouped together.

(148) и **пристави** к ним моужи свои. показати им ц(е)рк(о)вную красотоу. и полаты златыа. и в них соущаа богатество... (38)

'and he *assigned (pristavi)* his men to them to show them the beauty of the church, and the golden chambers, where there was much wealth'

(149) а рукы вкладоша в судно. и **вставиша** на сани. Чернысѣ Русину. и поидоша отъ Ворогла. (481)
'and they put the [chopped-off] hands in a vessel, and *placed (vstaviša)* [it] on the sledge for Černysa Rusin, and they left Vorogol'

(150) Иде Вольга Новугороду. и **оустави** по Мьстѣ повосты и дани. (60)
'Olga went to Novgorod, and *established (oustavi)* along the Msta guest-houses and levies'

Aorists are heavily represented *(pristaviti* 'attach' has eight aorists out of eleven attestations; all examples of *ustaviti* 'decree' are aorist; the only example of *sostaviti* 'bring together' is aorist; four[31] out of seven examples of *vstaviti* 'put into' are aorist). None of the verbs mentioned above have an accretive meaning; all represent extensions of other meanings of *staviti*, some closely related, some more distantly.

Curiously, two of the derived prefixed verbs in this group with the {-ja(j)-} suffix—*rasstavljati* 'distribute, dispatch' and *vosstavljati* 'set up'—function more like protoperfectives than like protoimperfectives. While (151) could be read in two different ways, the aorist and the context of (152) make it clear that here *rasstavljati* is to be read as a protoperfective, followed by a listing of who was sent where.

(151) Володимерко же **роставлялъ бяше** дружину свою на бродѣхъ. индѣ пѣши. а индѣ конники. (337)
'Volodimerko *had dispatched/was dispatching (rostavljal" bjaše)* his forces at the fords, some on foot and some on horseback'

(152) повелѣ стрещи въ оружьи. д(е)нь и нощь около града. и **роставля** полкы по вратомъ. Костянтину с(ы)н(о)ви своему с Новгородци. и Бѣлозерци. одина врата на горѣ. а Ярославу с Переяславци 2-я врата. Д(а)в(и)ду с Муромци. третьяя врата... (432)
'he ordered [them] to guard with arms day and night around the town, and *he dispatched (rostavlja)* his troops to the gates: Konstantin, his son with the Novgorodians and the Belozerians to one gate on the hill, and Jaroslav with the Perejaslavians to the second gate, David and the Muromians to the third gate...'

Likewise in (153), *vosstavljati* is paired closely with a simple prefixed verb and is translated into Modern Russian by *postavit'*[P] 'set[P]', not by an imperfective.

(153) И повелѣ Олегъ воемъ своимъ. колеса издѣлати. и **воставляти** на колеса корабля. (30)

---

[31] Five, if one example with *v"staviti* is held to be a scribal error for aorist *v"stavi,* as the editors of the *Complete Collection* suggest.

'and Oleg ordered his soldiers to fashion wheels and *put* the ships *up* (*vostavljati*) on the wheels'

The operative clue is that both *rosstavljati* and *vosstavljati* perform object distribution—a type of iterativity described above, here construed as limited in scope. Considering this similarity of usage, and the fact that no simple prefixed forms are attested for these verbs, it appears that in certain instances the presence of a strong telic component (repeated attainment of telos over a finite number of objects) can make a derived verb behave like a protoperfective. In chart 4.10.5.1, then, instead of getting a clear division between protoimperfective and protoperfective marked by a vertical line between the prefixed and simplex verb, we obtain a diagonal line that takes highly telic verbs into the protoperfective aspect (and allows for some perfective-like uses of the simplex as well).

Chart 4.10.5.1. The interaction of progressivity, telos and aspect*

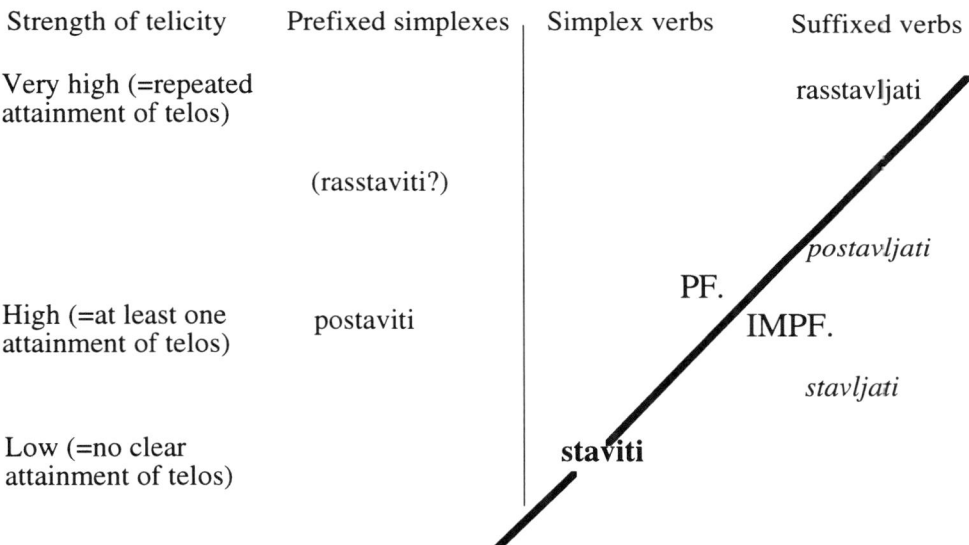

*Protoimperfective forms are in italics; protoperfective forms are in normal type; ambiguous forms are in boldface. The bold line marks the Old Russian protoaspectual division; the dotted line marks the Modern Russian aspectual division.

Further evidence for this is the fact that *ustaviti–ustavljati* 'decree', which does not have such a distributive property, behaves like an aspectual pair, with the context for *ustavljati* being progressive in (155).

(154) и нача оу него искати оустава. чернець Студиискыхъ. и обрѣтъ оу него и списа. и **оустави** въ манастыри своемь како пѣти пѣнья манастырьская. и поклонъ какъ держати... (160)
'and he began to examine the Rule of the Studion Monks with him [Mixail], and having obtained (it) from him, he copied (it) and *established (oustavi)* in his monastery how to sing monastic hymns, and how to show reverence...'

(155) иде Вольга по Дерьвьстѣи земли съ с(ы)н(о)мъ своимъ и съ дружиною **оуставляющи** оустави и оуроки. (60)
'Olga went across the Derevian land with her son and her company, *establishing (oustavljajušči)* laws and tributes'

The derived form from *sostaviti* 'bring together', which is found in a progressive context after *načati*, is not *sostavljati but *sostavlivati*, with the relatively rare {-iva(j)-} suffix seen in (157).

(156) и кадила вожьгоша. пѣнья и лики **съставиша**... (107)[32]
'and they lit incense; *they organized (s"staviša)* singing and choruses...

(157) начаста **съставливати** писмена азъбуковьная Словѣнски. (27)[33]
'the two of them began *to put together (s"stavlivati)* the letters of the alphabet in Slavic'

In some verbs, the prefixed form undergoes suffixation, and the result is a protoimperfective verb paired with a protoperfective; the simplex verb may also undergo suffixation, but does not necessarily do so. In others, suffixing a prefixed verbs apparently does not yield a protoimperfective verb; instead, it yields a protoperfective verb with object distribution.[34] Whether or not this happens seems to depend on the interaction between prefixal and root meaning.

---

[32] The Radzivil and Academy mss. have respectively *sostavleša, sostavleše*.
[33] The Academy ms. has *s"stavljati*.
[34] This may be similar to—although not identical to—the situation in Modern Czech, which has an extensive class of distributive verbs opposed to iteratives. Czech distributives are prefixed derived verbs that indicate an act was completed on a finite number of objects. They are considered perfective, not imperfective, and have a different morphological shape than the iteratives. Compare the following sentences:
Iterative: *Strýc chytával^{It} ryby už časně ráno* 'Uncle would fish^{It} bright and early'
Imperfective: *Strýc chytá^{I} ryby* 'Uncle catches^{I} fish'
Perfective: *Chytil^{P} do sítě najednou pět ryb* 'He caught^{P} five fish at once in his net'
or: *Chytil^{P} do sítě postupně pět ryb* 'He caught^{P} five fish one by one in his net'
Distributive: *Nachytal^{D} pět ryb* 'He caught^{D} five fish all told'
but **Postupně nachytal^{D} pět ryb* '*He caught^{D} five fish one by one all told'
Modern Russian creates distributive perfectives with the prefixes {po-}, {pere-} in the meaning 'do something a set number of times over a period of time'.

4.10.6. The verb *ostaviti*

The verb *ostaviti* 'leave' deserves mention on its own, thanks to its relatively frequent occurrence (thirty-four attestations) and its curious use of participial forms. It is highly telic (*pasti*-type) in all its occurrences; the prefix {o-} lacks any clear directional or Aktionsart meaning. Eleven occurrences (32 percent) are aorists, nine (28 percent) are past active participles or past verbal adverbs, eight (25 percent) are present active participles or present verbal adverbs, two (6 percent) are infinitives, three (9 percent) are non-past forms and one (3 percent) is an imperative.

The finite forms all represent a single action perceived as a unified whole, as seen in (158)-(161).

(158)   похорони вои въ лодьях. а другия назади **остави**. (23)
'he hid the soldiers in the boats and *left (ostavi)* the others behind'

(159)   а сам поиде на Супои. а брата своего Володимера **остави** Кыевѣ. (315)
'and he himself went to the Supoj, and *left (ostavi)* his brother Volodimer in Kiev'

(160)   много о том писати. но то **оставим**. (481)
'there is much to write about; but *let us leave (ostavim)* this'

A negated non-past has the force of an assurance, as in (161). While this assurance is meant to apply generally, the use of singular nouns here (a righteous man, a sinner) stresses its application to a particular situation.[35]

(161)   и по малых дн(е)хъ оускочи Игорь князь оу Половець. **не оставить** бо Г(о)с(под)ь праведнаго в руку грѣшничю. (399)
'and after a few days Prince Igor' escaped from the Polovtsians, for the Lord *will not leave (ne ostavit')* a righteous man in the hands of a sinner'

The examples with participles are more interesting. They constitute half of the attested examples of *ostaviti*, and are evenly split between past and present forms. The existence of both present and past forms is troubling, seeing as it occurs with a verb that otherwise shows all signs of being protoperfective.[36] The expected past

---

[35] Non-past perfectives with an exemplary function are discussed at greater length in chapter 5.

[36] If there were only or predominantly present participles and verbal adverbs, it would be easy to claim that this verb idiosyncratically takes present nonfinite forms despite its protoperfectivity. (Such occurrences are, after all, common enough in Modern Russian; witness the existence of perfective verbal adverbs like *vyjdja* 'having left', *prinesja* 'having brought' with imperfective verbal adverb endings.) Likewise, we might hope to see a logical distribution between adverbial and adjectival participles, but unfortunately, none of the seventeen examples has an adjectival participle; they are all adverbs (with

forms do indicate a single, completed act, as in (162)-(165). The act of leaving one's own city is clearly anterior to the act of arriving in a different city.

(162) он же **оставивъ** брата С(вя)тополка в Полотьскѣ. и приде в Переяславль на Г(о)с(по)жинъ д(е)нь. (302)
'*having left (ostaviv")* his brother Svjatopolk in Polotsk, he came to Perejaslavl' on the Lord's day'

(163) Ярополкъ же **оставивъ** м(а)т(е)рь свою и дружину Лучьскѣ. бѣжа в Ляхы. (205)
'Jaropolk, *having left (ostaviv")* his mother and his company in Lučesk, fled to Poland'

(164) **оставивше** Гюргя князя с Д(а)в(и)д(о)вичем. с Волдимером и с товары. противу Витечеву. а сами ѣхаша к Зарубу. (331)
'*Having left (ostavivše)* Prince Gjurgij with Volodimer Davidovič and the army against Vitečev, he himself went to Zarub'

(165) и **оставивъ** еп(и)с(ко)пью приде в Суждаль к с(вя)тому Дмитрию. в свою келью. (452)
'and *having left (ostaviv")* the bishopric, he came to Suzdal', to Saint Dmitrij's, to his own cell'

However, present participles are also quite numerous. One explanation is that forms in {-ja} suggest an action concurrent with the action in the main clause. In (166) and (167), for instance, a person leaves his domain by going somewhere else; he does not first leave his domain and then go somewhere else.

(166) Ярославъ княз Тфѣрьскыи... с своими бояры поѣха в Ладогу. **оставя** свою о(т)чину. (474)
'Jaroslav, prince of Tver', set out with his boyars to Ladoga, *leaving (ostavja)* his realm'

(167) Тогож лѣт(а). Митрополитъ Максимъ. не терпя Татарьско(го) насилья. **оставя** митрополью и збѣжа ис Киева. и весь Киевъ розбѣжалься. (485)
'That year Metropolitan Maksim, unable to bear the oppression of the Tatars, fled from Kiev, *leaving (ostavja)* his metropolitanate, and all Kiev scattered.'

There is some overlap between {-ja} and {-v-} forms when they describe leaving a person when departing on a trip, as in (162)-(164) and (168)-(171), but these are simply different interpretations of the same act: the former suggests concurrence, while the latter suggests anteriority.

---

greater or lesser degrees of certainty; it is unclear what to make of forms like *ostavl'*, which have adjectival form but are used adverbially here).

(168) он же **оставя** полкы свои с С(вя)тославомъ. а сам ѣха г Кыеву.
(342)
'*leaving (ostavja)* his troops with Svjatoslav, he himself went to Kiev'

(169) Гюрги же **оставя** с(ы)на своего Глѣба в Городци а сам иде Суждалю. (336)
'Gjurgij, *leaving (ostavja)* his son Gleb in Gorodec, went himself to Suzdal''

(170) Гюрги же **оставя** сына своего Василка. в Новѣгородѣ оу С(вя)тослава. а сам иде Суждалю (339)
'Gjurgij, *leaving (ostavja)* his son Vasilko in Novgorod with Svjatoslav, went himself to Suzdal''

(171) Мстислав же **оставя** брата Ярослава в Лучьскѣ. а сам иде в Ляхы. (345)
'Mstislav, *leaving (ostavja)* his brother Jaroslav in Lučesk, went himself to Poland'

These two different—aspectual—interpretations of an act are placed on it by, in this case, the form of the participle. *Ostaviti* clearly represents an act that can be completed and seen as a whole, but contextual implications, such as sequencing of acts, seem absent from the verb itself and are indicated instead by the participle form. The "perfectivity" of *ostaviti* is overridden by the synchronous interpretation of the present form, lending support to the notion that the aspect of a verb is at this stage more a lexical feature that can be overruled by context and grammar.

Conclusions. Although not frequent in its simplex form, the verb *staviti* is widely attested in prefixed and suffixed forms. It shows limited signs of anaspectuality, but its usage is generally consonant with that of protoimperfective verbs. While *staviti* itself can represent an action that is segmentable, its prefixed forms express non-segmentable actions, so much so that some of them fall clearly in the protoperfective camp where we would expect protoimperfectives. This testifies to the greater weight of telicity as a factor in lexical aspectual assignment of Old Russian verbs: those with very high telicity may take on functions associated in Modern Russian with the perfective category, despite their apparent morphological associations with imperfectivity. Data from prefixed forms support the contention that in some instances, tense factors can override any tendencies a verb may have toward one "aspect" or another. (This fact will surface again in the discussion of the imperfect tense in chapter 5.)

4.11. PROBLEMS IN ASSIGNING TELICITY *(VOEVATI)*

There is a large group of verbs that can express the same act as either a condition (Modern Russian *on pišet = on pisatel'* 'he writes = he is a writer') or as a process with a distinct telos (*on pišet = sejčas sidit za stolom i pišet* 'he is writing = right now he is sitting at the table and writing'). Into this group fall many verbs with telic predicates as well as Old Russian verbs like *dumati* 'think, take counsel', *tvoriti* 'do, make', that have a wider range of meanings depending on their complement.

The verb *voevati* 'make war, do battle' can be perceived in two ways, which influence the lexical group to which we assign it. We can say that the occupation of a warrior is to wage war, regardless of outcome or foe. In this case, the action is perceived as atelic (like *bljusti* 'guard'). If a particular battle is fought, there is the implication of beginning, end, and result; the action is then telic (like *staviti* 'build').[37]

An atelic use of *voevati* appears in (172); this usage is also seen in (179), (180), and (182)-(184). The imperfect tense indicates a progressive or durative context: war was waged that year, with its endpoints uncertain.

(172) поставленъ ц(а)рь Романъ въ Грекохъ. а Игоре **воеваше** на Печенѣги. (43)
'Roman was made king of the Greeks, and Igor *made war (voevaše)* on the Pečenegs'

A telic use of *voevati* is found in (173), which indicates an incomplete act; further examples of telic usage are in (177), (178), and (181).

(173) Въ си же времяна быша. и Обри (иже) ходиша на Арьклия ц(а)ря. и мало его не яша. си же добрѣ **воеваху** на Словѣнѣхъ. и примучиша Дулѣбы. сущая Словѣны. (11)[38]
'At this time there were giants as well, who went against Emperor Herculaeus, and nearly captured him; they *were making war (voevaxu)* on the Slavs successfully, and they subjugated the Dulěbians, who were Slavs'

In (174)-(175) and elsewhere, the exact placement of the act is obscure; it could be either telic or atelic, indicating that the two "meanings" I have proposed are really outgrowths of a single meaning.

(174) яко послаша Болгаре вѣсть ко ц(а)рю. яко идуть Русь на Ц(а)рьградъ... и почаша **воевати** Вифаньския страны и **воеваху** по Понту до Арьклѣя. и до Фафлогоньски земли. (44)
'for the Bulgars had sent tidings to the emperor that the Russians were marching on Constantinople...and they began *to make war (voevati)* in

---

[37] The inclusion of this verb in my list of simplex verbs may raise some eyebrows, since it is clearly suffixed (voj-eva-ti). However, the suffix in question is not an imperfectivizing one—although {-eva-/-ova-} is used in Old Russian verbal derivation—but a denominalizing one (from *voj* 'troop, battle'). I am therefore applying the term "simplex" verb or "unsuffixed" if the verb has no suffixes used in the process of verbal derivation. Otherwise I would have to eliminate from my analysis verbs with any sort of suffix, including those with {-ě-} and {-a-} suffixes, like *vladěti, uměti, dělati, kopati,* etc.

[38] The Radzivil and Academy mss. have *obri* 'giants' for *dobrě* 'well'.

Bythinia, and they *warred (voevaxu)* along Pontus as far as Heraclea and Paphlagonia'

(175) и начаша **воевати**. села и городы по Сулѣ. (303)
'and they began *to capture/fight over (voevati)* villages and forts on the Sula'

Like atelic acts, *voevati* has anaspectual characteristics, although it tends toward the protoimperfective. This is especially clear in the past tense examples, which make up the bulk of this verb's attestations. Both telic and atelic meanings are found in the aorist and imperfect tenses, but if we look at the aorist attestations we will notice an interesting divergence in the Modern Russian translations. The Old Russian telic aorists in (177) corresponds to the past perfective form *povoevali* 'subdued, conquered, captured' in Modern Russian; were a translation of (176) available, we would expect to find the same.

(176) идоша к Сереньску. град пожгоша. людем избѣгшим. ино же много **воеваша**. възвратишася въ своя си. (459)
'they went to Serensk [and] burned the town once the people fled; many others *they captured (voevaša)* [and] they returned to their own land'

(177) взяша 3 грады Пѣсочень. Переволоку. (Прилукъ). и многа села **воеваша** *(повоевали)*. по обѣма странома. (215)
'they took three towns: Pěsočen, Perevoloku, [Priluk], and *won (voevaša)* many villages on both sides'

The atelic aorists in (178)-(180) are translated by the Modern Russian imperfectives *voeval, voevali* 'he, they fought/battled'.

(178) **Воеваша** Половци оу Растовьця. и оу Ятина. (174)
'the Polovtsians *fought (voevaša)* near Rostovec and Nejatin'

(179) в се же лѣто **воеваша** *(воевали)* Половци. Ляхы. с Василькомь Ростиславичемь. (215)
'In this year the Polovtsians *fought (voevaša)* the Poles with Vasil'ko Rostislavič'

(180) В се же время **воева** *(воевал)* Куря с Половци оу Переяславля. и оустье пожже. (231)
'at this time Kurja *fought (voeva)* the Polovtsians near Perejaslavl' and set fire to Ust'e'

There is one apparently atelic aorist—in (181)—that is translated by a Modern Russian perfective *povoevali* 'fought'.

(181) нонѣ же плачь по всѣмъ улицам оупространися. избьеных ради. иже избиша безаконьнии Половци. (и) **воеваша** много и възвратишася к Торцьскому. (224)

'now the wailing spread through all the streets for those who had been killed, whom the lawless Polovtsians had murdered; and they *fought (voevaša)* a lot and returned to Torcskij'

This translation is probably due to the context of the previous sentence, which makes it clear that the Polovtsians not only did battle but specifically killed and captured a lot of people in one particular city, defeating them. The reading of (181) as telic is thus justified.

In these examples, then, Modern Russian prefers a perfective verb, especially in narrative mode where a string of events is being listed. Old Russian prefers an aorist form of the more neutral simplex verb, which shows a range of meanings from continuous (the imperfect tense examples and present participles) to summarizing. Context—including the presence and type of verb valence—determines the specific meaning of the verb.

The verb *voevati* is likewise ambiguous in the non-past tense. It can express a progressive present sense, as in (182), or a conditional future, as in (183) and (184). This conditional future usage occurs only periphrastically, with *da* 'let' or in a clearly defined future context.

(182)   ...приде вѣсть. оже Глѣбъ шелъ Володимерю инѣмъ путемъ. и **воюеть** около Володимеря. (383)
'news came that Gleb went to Volodimer' by a different route, and *was making war (vojujet')* near Volodimer' '

(183)   да аще твои мужь оударить моимь. **да не воюемъ** за три лѣта. аще ли нашь мужь оударить. **да воюемъ** за три лѣта. (122)
'and if your man strikes mine, then *we will not fight /let us not fight (da ne vojujem")* for three years; if our man strikes [yours], then *we will fight /let us fight (da vojujem")* for three years'

(184)   а о сихъ оже то приходять Чернии Болгаре. (и) **воюють** въ странѣ Корсуньстѣи. и велимъ князю Рускому да ихъ не пущаеть. (51)
'and on this matter: if the Black Bulgars come and *make war (vojujut')* in Korsun, we order the Russian prince not to let them through'[39]

The verb *povoevati* plays a different role in the Old Russian text than does the verb *povoevat'* in the Modern Russian translation. Old Russian *povoevati* is an Aktionsart verb; the prefix can limit the duration of the event, if atelic; this reading is rarer and is found in (185) and (186).

(185)   В се же время приде Бонякъ с Половци г Кыеву. В нед(е)лю от вечера. И **повоева** около Кыева. и пожже на Берестовѣмь дворъ княжь. (231)

---

[39] The alternate reading in this translation (*puščaet'* 'let through' for *počaet'* 'expect') comes from the Radzivil and Academy mss.

'at this time Bonjak came with the Polovtsians to Kiev on a Sunday evening, and he *made war (povoeva)* near Kiev, and set fire to the prince's palace at Berestovo'

(186)   и сам с Новгородци дошедъ Волгы. и **повоевавъ** ю и не оуспѣ ничтоже Гюргеви. (320)
'and having reached the Volga with the Novgorodians and having *done battle (povoevav")* for it but Gjurgij did not succeed'

More commonly, it indicates a highly telic end to the event: a victory, a bloodbath, or a conquest, as seen in (187)-(190).

(187)   и на ту зиму **повоеваша** Половци Стародубъ весь. (248)
'and that winter the Polovtsians *conquered (povoevaša)* all of Starodub'

(188)   и велику пакость створиша. села пожгоша. люди **повоеваша**. (349)
'and they did much harm: they burned villages, and *captured (povoevaša)* people'

(189)   Тое же зимы приде Изяславъ с Половци. и **повоева** волость Смолиньскую. и пославъ ко Андрѣеви... (350)
'that winter Izjaslav came with the Polovtsians, and *captured (povoeva)* the fief of Smolinsk, and having sent to Andrej...'

(190)   хотящю полонити Торкы проклятыя. и с тѣми **повоевати** Русску землю. (295)
'wanting to conquer the cursed Turks, and with them *to subjugate (povoevati)* the Russian land'

By contrast, Modern Russian *povoevat'*, while having these functions, has taken over far more of the functions occupied by the Old Russian simplex verb. It is more likely to simply summarize an event that took place, as shown above; it is a perfective that corresponds to all functions of the Modern Russian verb *voevat'*, whereas Old Russian *povoevati* corresponds only to certain limited functions of *voevati*.

What are the implications of these data for the verb *voevati*? The verb basically has atelic predicates; this fact explains its tendency not to have a regular protoperfective counterpart. It can also be treated as a natural conative (like *iskati* 'search'), where the success of an event (*povoevati*) is opposed to its non-completion (*voevati*).

Conclusions. The verb *voevati* shows signs of aspectual neutrality, although it tends toward imperfective-like functions. The range of meanings it has, moreover, extends from the telic to atelic, encompassing features considered in Modern Russian to belong to both aspects. The limited usage patterns of the verb *povoevati* in Old Russian support these conclusions.

4.12. NATURAL CONATIVES (*ISKATI*)

A small but distinct subclass of predicates shares many characteristics with telic predicates but deserves to be treated separately within the telic class because of the class's lexical prohibition on realizing telicity. These predicates are characterized lexically by their reference to lack of success in performing an action; as an example, the verb *iskati* 'search' describes the act only as long as the thing searched for remains unfound. If we cannot use *iskati* to describe a period of time that includes both the search and the finding, then all prefixed forms of the verb that include the idea of finding involve annulling part of the verb's lexical meaning.[40] We can call predicates like *iskati* natural conatives.

There are twenty-three examples of the simplex verb *iskati* attested in the Chronicles. Of these, three are non-past forms, four are imperfects, six are present participles, two are past participles, two are imperatives, and six are infinitives or supines. It is noticeable how often forms of *iskati* are contrasted to those of *obrěsti* 'find', as in (191)-(195), although this is obviously not a condition for its usage.

(191) аще ли есть неимовитъ (створивыи убииство) и оускочить же. **да ищють** его дондеже обрящется. (51)
'if a commoner (who has committed murder) escapes, *let* them *search (da iščut')* for him until they find him'

(192) ...азъ любящая мя люблю. и **ищющии** мене обрящють мя. (62)
'I love those who love me, and those *who seek (iščjuščii)* me shall find me'

(193) Ростислава же **искавше** обрѣтоша в рѣцѣ. (221)[41]
'*having searched (iskavše)* for Rostislav, they found [him] in the river'

A typical nonfinite form in a progressive context is (194):

(194) и вшедъ Ярополкъ въ градъ Ольговъ. перея власть его. и посла **искатъ** брата своего. и **искавъше** его не обрѣтоша. (75)
'and Jaroslav, having gone into Oleg's city, seized his land, and sent *to search (iskat")* for his brother, and *having searched (iskav"še)* for him, they did not find him'

---

[40] It is important to distinguish this lexical meaning from the function we can often ascribe to certain groups of Modern Russian imperfective verbs, most noticeably those of the *umirat'* class in sentences such as *umiral, no ne umer* 'he was dying, but didn't die' or *lovil, no ne pojmal* 'he fished, but didn't catch it'. In both of these sentences context creates the impression of unfulfilled or frustrated intent or expectation, but sentences, especially iterative or durative ones, can be imagined where this impression is entirely lacking, for example: *sobaka lovila kusočki mjasa* 'the dog caught pieces of meat'. Whether such a class of verbs exists also for Old Russian is a point to be taken up later.

[41] The Radzivil and Academy mss. have *iziskaša* 'they sought out (aorist 3 pl.)'.

(195) нача **искати** правила чернечьскаго. и обрѣтеся тогда Михаилъ
чернець. манастыря Студинскаго. (160)
'he began *to search (iskati)* for a monastic rule, and then Mixail turned up, a monk from the Studion monastery'

Example (196) shows an interesting use of the verb with an infinitive complement, in a progressive context indicating the mood or actions of the Jews.

(196) архиерѣи (и) книжници исполнишася зависти. **искаху** оубити и. и имѣше и ведоша къ гѣмону Пилату. (103)
'the archpriests and learned men were filled with envy, and they *sought (iskaxu)* to kill him, and seizing him they led him to the governor Pilate'

Present tense and imperfect forms indicate an act in progress or an act that is perceived as appearing sporadically but as part of the same general process (in other words, a generalized context), as in (197)-(198).

(197) ты княже чюжея земли **ищеши** и блюдеши. а своея ся охабивъ. (67)[42]
'you, o prince, *are searching (iščeši)* for and watching over another's land, while having abandoned your own [land]'

(198) си бо от възраста бл(а)ж(е)ная Ольга. **искаше** м(у)др(о)стью. все въ свѣтѣ семь. налѣзе бисеръ многоцѣньныхъ еже есть Х(ри)с(то)съ. (62)
'from a young age, the blessed Olga *sought (iskaše)* with wisdom all that which is [best] in this world; she found invaluable pearls, which is to say Christ'

There are no specifically iterative examples represented in my corpus, although (198) could be interpreted this way with a bit of stretching; this is not surprising, as the nature of the verb tends to restrict it to progressive contexts.

4.12.1. Prefixed forms of *iskati*

Prefixed verbs from *iskati* are numerous and include several derived forms. In this lexical class, prefixed verbs do not have the same range of prefix meanings and types found in the statives and atelic actions. The reason for this is clear: Aktionsart prefixation will be much rarer with this lexical class, since any view of the process that includes attainment of the goal automatically changes the lexical content of the verb. One could easily imagine Aktionsart prefixes of inception or limited duration, but the former are not attested, and the latter are attested only weakly with the prefix {po-}.

---

[42] Also example (99).

(199)   (и) рѣша сами в себѣ. **поищемъ** собѣ князя. иже бы володѣлъ нами. и судилъ по праву. (19)
'let us make a search (poiščem) for a prince who would rule over us...'

(200)   аще бо **поищеши** въ книгахъ м(у)др(о)сти прилѣжно. то обрящеши велику ползу д(у)ши своеи. (152)
'for if you (shall) search (poiščeši) diligently in the books of wisdom, then you will gain great benefit for your soul'

In neither (199) nor (200) is it absolutely clear whether {po-} actually has a temporal component or whether it instead modifies the verb's basic meaning (in particular, (199) lends itself to a future reading with a Modern Russian synonym *najti* 'find').[43]

All the other prefixed forms of *iskati* can be classified as paired verbs with only a tangential connection to the original simplex. Compare Sreznevskij's definitions of the verbs in (201)-(209): *doiskatisja — doiskat'sja* 'discover'; *iziskati — otyskat', najti, razsmotrět', priobrěsti, vybirat', otom'stit'* 'seek out, find, scrutinize, acquire, choose, avenge'; *priiskivati — dobyvat', priobretat', doiskivat'* 'attain, acquire, search out'; *sniskati — sobrat', skopit', priobrěsti, dostignut'* 'collect, amass, acquire, attain'; *vyiskivati — želat' zavladět'* 'desire to master'; *vzyskati — vzyskat'* 'exact, recover, censure'.

In none of the unsuffixed verbs is the notion of unfulfilled striving central, although it may be present under certain contextual conditions. In (201)-(204), for instance, attainment of telos is central.

(201)   не добра дань княже. мы **ся доискахомъ** оружьемъ одиною стороною (остромь). рекоша саблями. а сихъ оружье обоиду остро рекше мечь. си имуть имати дань на нас. (17)
'this tribute is no good, prince; we exacted (sja doiskaxom") [it] with a weapon sharp on one side, called a sabre, and their weapon, called a sword, cuts both ways; they will take tribute from us'

(202)   се ни въ чтоже есть. се бо лежить мертво. сего суть кметье луче. мужи бо **ся доищють** и болше сего. (199)
'this is nothing, for it lies dead; men-at-arms are better than this, for men will attain (sja doiščut') even more things [for you]'

(203)   и реч(е) имъ сберѣте аче и по горсти овса. или пшеницѣ. ли отрубъ. они же шедше ради **снискаша**. и повелѣ женамъ створити цѣжь. в немьже варять кисель. (128)

---

[43] On the other hand, Sreznevskij in fact defines *poiskati* as *iskat', domogat'sja, proizvesti slědstvie, razuznat'* 'search[I], solicit[I], pursue[P] an investigation, figure out[P]' with the last two meanings marked as questionable. He clearly sees it as primarily an imperfective verb with a prefix that is semantically and grammatically nearly empty, although both examples from the Primary Chronicle suggest a meaning closer to Modern Russian *poiskat'*, cf. Lixačev and Romanov 1950: 214, 303.

'and he said to them: collect a handful of oats, or wheat, or bran, and they, having gone, gladly *collected (sniskaša)* it; and he ordered the women to make a mash from which kissel-pudding is made'

(204) единою просих от Г(о)сп(одн)а. того **взищю**. да живу в дому Г(о)с(под)ни вся дни живота моего. (433)
'one thing I asked from the Lord *I will obtain (vziščju):* that I might live in the house of the Lord all the days of my life'[44]

In (205), by contrast, the negated exhortation leaves in doubt what the exact meaning is, but the possible conative function comes from the ambiguity of the context, not from the verb itself.

(205) **да не изищется** см(е)рть ихъ от князя. вашего. (48)
'*let* their death *not be sought/obtained (da ne iziščetsja)* from your prince'

(206) а землѣ Русьскѣи много зло створше. пролившe кровь х(ри)с(т)ьяньску. еяже крове **взищеть** Б(ог)ъ от руку ею (200)
'and having done much evil to the Russian land, having poured Christian blood, which God *will retrieve (vziščet')* from their hands'

It is not surprising, then, to see that these verbs create suffixed forms quite easily. A good example is the suffixed form *vziskaeši* in (207).

(207) не имаши бо града сде. но будущаго **взискаеши** вѣрою непобѣди-мою. и Б(о)жьею помочью. (392)
'for you will not seize a city here, but you *will obtain (vziskaeši)* the future one through indomitable faith and God's help'

Since the meaning 'find' is naturally protoperfective already in Old Russian, the suffixed forms express varying expansions of that concept. One expansion is repeated action in the past, as in (208).

(208) и дѣди ваши. трудом великим. и храбрьствомь. побарающа по Русьскѣи земли. ины земли **приискываху**. а вы хочете погубити землю Русьскую. (264)
'your grandfathers through great toil and bravery fought across the Russian land, and *acquired (priiskyvaxu)* other lands; and now you want to destroy/will destroy the Russian land'

Another expansion is negated striving in (209), which can also be construed as habit.

(209) да **не выискывати** было чюжего. ни мене в соромъ ни в печаль ввести. (254)

---

[44] Seen later in this chapter as example (306) and in chapter 5 as example (27).

'it would have been better *not to hunger (ne vyiskyvati)* for someone else's things, or lead me into shame or sorrow'

The verb *iskati*, then, shows numerous formal indications of protoimperfectivity, and should be classed as a protoimperfective verb despite its lexical placement in the telic category.

Conclusions. We can now address a question raised by the classification scheme in Maslov 1948. Maslov, following his pairability paradigm, lumps verbs of this subclass in with the *imperfectiva tantum,* whereas Kučera puts them in with telic acts. If Maslov's characterization holds for Old Russian, then the characteristics of *iskati* should make it more similar to statives and atelic actions. In fact, in that case we might expect natural conatives to resemble statives most closely, since both are very difficult to interpret as realizably telic, while atelic acts are—as we have seen—often easily reinterpreted as being telic. But although they share a bias against aspectual pairing, the patterns of prefixation and suffixation—in other words, the methods of aspectualization—are radically different for statives and conatives. Statives do not seem easily susceptible to perfectivization or grammatical reinterpretation of prefixes; conatives, on the other hand, show a high degree of perfectivity for prefixed forms and a well-developed secondary derivation system (see chart 4.12.1.1).

Chart 4.12.1.1. Features of statives, atelic acts, and conatives.

predicate type	simplex aorist	simplex future use	Aktionsart prefixes	spatial non-perfective prefixes	number of suffixed forms
stojati (state)	+	+	+/–	+	0
bljusti (atelic action)	+	+	+/–	–	1
iskati (natural conative)	–	–	–/+	–	3

Chart 4.12.1.1 suggests that conatives behave somewhat differently from atelic acts in Old Russian and quite differently from Old Russian statives. It shows the inherent difficulty in using pairedness as a predictor for the aspectual behavior of a verb, especially outside the Modern Russian period. It furthermore indicates that in this instance, Kučera's feature-based system is a more accurate predictor of aspectual behavior for the Old Russian period than is Maslov's system, which is based on aspectual pairedness.

4.13. HIGH TELICITY *(PASTI–PADATI)*

The simplex verb *pasti* exemplifies the membership of this class of predicates. The other simplex verbs analyzed in this chapter are all imperfective in Modern Russian; this verb, however, is perfective in Modern Russian. The simplex is attested twenty-six times in the Chronicles, often in the figurative meaning 'fall in battle, die' as found in (210) and (211).

(210) якож пр(о)р(о)къ гл(агола)ше **падете** пред врагы вашими. поженуть вы ненавидящии вас. и побѣгнете никому женущю вас. (222)
'as the prophet said: you *will fall (padete)* before your enemies; your enemies will pursue you; and you will flee with no one pursuing you'

(211) и быс(ть) сѣча велика. и одалаху Болъгаре. и реч(е) С(вя)тославъ воемъ своимъ. оуже намъ сде **пасти**. (69)
'and there was a great battle, and the Bulgars were winning, and Svjatoslav said to his warriors: here we must *fall (pasti)*'

Several times it is used in the expression *na nego pade žrebii* 'fate beset him', as in (212).

(212) на сего **паде** жребии по зависти дьяволи (82)
'fate *beset (pade)* him, thanks to the Devil's jealousy'

It also appears in the more common modern meaning 'fall down' with both people and churches. Four times it appears with the reflexive particle {sja}, always in this meaning.[45]

(213) в то же лѣт(о). **падеся** ц(е)ркы каменная Переяславли с(вя)таг(о) Михаила. (293)
'in the same year, the stone church of St. Mixail in Perejaslavl' *collapsed (padesja)*'

(214) азъ приемлю на вы плачь. домъ израилевъ **падеся** и не приложи въстати (99)
'I will bring mourning upon you; the house of the Israelites *fell (padesja)* and did not rise [again]'

These predicates show all the characteristics of protoperfectives. The non-past forms consistently represent future acts, as in (215).

---

[45] This usage is obviously not reflexive in the sense of an act performed on oneself, since 'fall' is intransitive, but should be lumped in with similar changes of position like Modern Russian *ložit'sja* 'lie down', *sadit'sja* 'sit down', *stanovit'sja* 'take a place standing' and Modern Czech *lehnout si* 'lie down', *sednout si* 'sit down'.

(215) мечемъ жребии на отрока и дѣвицю. на него же **падеть**. того зарѣжемъ б(ого)мъ (82)
'we will cast lots for the youth and the maiden; whomever it [the lot] *falls (padet')* upon, we will sacrifice that one to the gods'

The preterite forms are all aorists; they can mark a single act, as in (216) and (217).

(216) и **паде** мертвъ и людье разидошася. (181)
'and he *fell (pade)* dead, and the people dispersed'

(217) он же от многых ранъ **паде**. и тако скончася. (480)
'he *fell (pade)* from many wounds, and so met his end'

Sometimes they represent multiple acts construed as a summation, as in (218).

(218) Володимеръ же п(р)ебредъ рѣку с малою дружиною мнози бо **падоша** от полка его и боляре его ту **падоша**. (220)
'Volodimer forded the river with a small band, for many from his company *had fallen (padoša)* and his boyars *had fallen (padoša)* here'

The participle forms are all past participles representing single acts whose completion is followed by another act, as in (219) and (220).

(219) бѣ бо нетвердъ верою к нима и **падъ** ниць просяше прощенья. (182)
'for he had not been strong in his faith to them, and *having fallen (pad")* down, he asked for forgiveness'

(220) и вниде в ц(е)рк(о)вь с(вя)тыя Софья **падъ** на колѣну пред олтарем. нача молитися... (478)
'and he went into the church of St. Sophia; *having fallen (pad")* to his knees before the altar, he began to pray'

4.13.1. The derived form *padati*

We can compare *pasti* with *padati*, the unprefixed verb derived from it. This verb occurs seven times in the Chronicles: there are four imperfects, one non-past and two participles. All citations are given below. The progressive contexts in (221) and (222) indicate an action that exceeds the duration of the surrounding acts (in the first instance, a star shower; in the second, an earthquake).

(221) Посем же быс(ть) звѣздамъ теченье с вечера до заоутрья. яко мнѣти всемъ яко **падають** звѣзды. и пакы с(о)лнце без лучь сьяше. (165)
'then there was a star shower from evening until morning, for it seemed to everyone that stars *were falling (padajut')* and then the sun shone without rays'

(222) снесену бывшю корму и питью все то потре каменье дробное
сверху **падая**. (454)
'the food and drink was brought down, everything shook; *meanwhile* small
stones *fell (padaja)* from above'

Durative contexts frame an action limited in scope by surrounding acts; the focus is on the picture of an event over a limited duration, not on its completion.

(223) бяше чересъ гроблю мостъ ко врато(то)мъ граднымъ. тѣснячеся
другъ друга. пихаху въ гроблю. и спехнуша Ольга с мосту в
дебрь. **падаху** людье мнози. и оудавиша кони ч(е)л(о)в(ѣ)ци. (74)
'there was a bridge over the moat to the city gates; as they pushed each other,
they shoved [each other] into the moat, and they hurled Oleg from the bridge
into the ditch. Many people *fell (padaxu)*, and horses trampled on the men'

Example (224), for instance, is a description of a battle in progress.

(224) брани же велицѣ бывши. и мнозѣмъ **падающих** от обою полку. и
видѣвъ С(вя)тополкъ яко люта брань. и побѣже. (270)[46]
'it was a great battle, and there were many *falling (padajuščix)* in both
companies; and Svjatopolk saw how fierce the battle was, and fled'

Iterative contexts show repetition of the act, as in (225). In (226)—discussed also below as (255)—the context also has limited duration, because the sentence describes the weather conditions at a particular time, but the sequence of events emphasizes the repetition.

(225) и Б(ог)ъ неврежена мя съблюде. и с коня много **падах**. голову си
розбих дважды. и руцѣ и нозѣ свои вередих. (251)
'and God kept me from harm; and I *fell off (padax)* my horse many times,
broke my head twice, and hurt my arms and legs'

(226) бѣ бо яко мгла к земли прилегла. яко и птицам по аеру не бѣ лзѣ
лѣтати. но **падаху** на земли и оумираху. (447)
'for it was as if a mist hugged the earth, since even the birds could not fly
through the air, but *fell (padaxu)* to earth and died'

Particularly interesting are examples like (227).

(227) (и) побѣгоша наши пред иноплеменьникы. (и) **падаху** язвени предъ
врагы нашими. и мнози погыбоша (и быша)[47] мертви паче неже у
Трьполя. (221)
'and our men fled before the foreigners, and they *fell (padaxu)* wounded before
our enemies, and many perished, [and there were] more dead than at Tripoli'

---

46 The Academy ms. reads, more sensibly, *padajuščim*, to agree with *mnozěm* (dat. pl.).
47 This interpolation comes from the Radzivil and Academy mss.

In contrast to the aorist *pogyboša* 'perished', which sums up the fact that numerous people died in the battle, the imperfect *padaxu* indicates a repeated process conducted over a particular span of time: as they fled, people fell gradually before the enemy and eventually are counted among the dead. Obviously, in the meaning 'die' the predicate cannot be applied repeatedly to the same person; it is possible with the literal meaning 'fall down' in (225). Iterativity in the meaning 'die' comes only from the application of a single act to numerous people. This usage indicates a type of diffusion of the action to numerous parties which may be linked to the notion of "object distribution" presented earlier.[48] This diffusion is perceived as a mixture of iterativity and either durativity or progressivity.

This derived form thus looks protoimperfective, and we can assume aspectual pairedness for the verbs *padati–pasti* 'fall'. An interesting footnote to this is that the pair is partially defective in Modern Russian, with forms from *upasti* replacing the older *pasti* in the meaning 'fall down' and competing with it in other meanings. This trend toward the elimination of the simplex forms is notable in this group of verbs; indeed, the Old Russian of the Chronicles already indicates several roots where the simplex is not in common use (*opaliti* 'set afire', *odolěti* 'overcome', *poběditi* 'defeat', *uspěti* 'succeed', *iscěliti* 'heal', *razděliti* 'divide', *voskrěsiti* 'arise', *izlomiti* 'break', *preměniti* 'change'). Some roots still have simplex forms in the Old Russian of the Chronicles *(pustiti* 'permit', *roditi* 'give birth', *rubiti* 'build', *slati* 'send', *stretiti* 'meet', *vratiti* 'return', *gubiti* 'destroy', *miriti* 'pacify', *ložiti* 'lay, place') although in some cases the paucity of examples show that it is giving way to a prefixed form (*ložiti, gubiti*) or will do so by the Modern Russian period (*vratiti, stretiti,* also largely *slati*). The degree of this replacement is not surprising; high telicity and the bounding function of prefixes are quite similar, so prefixed forms may serve for many of these verbs as simply more emphatically telic forms.

4.13.2. Prefixed forms of *pasti*

The prefixed forms of *pasti* have several important semantic functions. As with the prefixes {s-}, {iz-}, they can amplify downward motion without adding to it; after all, the direction is already implied in the meaning 'fall' They can articulate the beginning point of the act; {ot-}, for instance, indicates what one falls away from. They can also articulate the end of the act; {v-} indicates what one falls into, and {pri-} indicates what one falls towards. One prefix, {o-}, indicates the surrounding of an object by other objects. Another, {na-}, has a meaning that is more figurative than literal; 'fall on' is usually used in the sense 'attack'.

There are also stylistic distinctions between prefixes in the case of {s-} and {iz-}. Neither significantly modifies the simplex verb's meaning, but there is a

---

[48] Starting from the premise that the theme of a verb is the complement that undergoes change, it should not be surprising to find that intransitive verbs show distributivity of the subject, which is both theme and agent, and transitive verbs show distributivity of both subject and object.

stylistic difference between them. The former describes concrete occurrences, as in (228), while the latter is used in a figurative sense, as in (229).

(228) **спаде** превеликъ змии отъ н(е)б(е)се. (214)
'a huge snake *fell (spade)* from the sky'

(229) женою бо первое **испаде** Адамъ из рая. (104)
'for it was first through woman that Adam *fell (ispade)* from paradise'

A third prefix used in similar contexts, {ot-}, has a slightly more specific meaning, since it focuses on the departure point of the fall or the deprivation of a particular state. Deprivation of grace is shown in (230) and (231), while in (232) this verb shows the moment of cessation.

(230) азъ створих ему **отпасти** Б(ог)а. (90)
'I made him *fall away (otpasti)* from God'

(231) дьяволъ прельсти Евгою Адама и **отпаде** рая. (104)
'the devil deceived Adam through Eve, and *he fell from (otpade)* paradise'

(232) и приспѣ к ним дружина вся. многое множство. наши же видѣвше ихъ оужасошася. и величанья своего **отпадоша**. (398)
'and the whole company joined with them, a numerous multitude; our men, when they saw them, were horrified, and *ceased (otpadoša)* their praises'

The two prefixes focusing more closely on the destination of the act have a similar semantic division. The prefix {pri-} focuses on the metaphoric goal of the act: the subjects fall down (possibly literally) at Christ's feet in order to show their recognition of his divinity.

(233) мы **припадаем** к нему гл(аголю)ще (119)
'we *fall down (pripadaem)* before him, saying...'

The prefix {v-}, in contrast to {pri-}, gives a more specific destination, such as (234) and (235), or a metaphorical destination, such as (236), (237), (243), and (244).

(234) и не обрѣтоша княжеѣ вои. и **впадоша** Олговичемъ в руцѣ. и тако изъимаша и. (304)
'and they did not find the prince's men, and *they fell into (vpadoša)* the hands of Oleg's men, and so they caught them'

(235) ровъ изры и ископа. и **впадеся** въ яму юже створи. (431)
'he dug up a ditch, and shoveled it out, and *he fell into* the pit that he had made'

(236)   И дошедъ велика дне. В(о)скр(е)с(е)нья по обычаю. празднова(въ) свѣтло. **впаде** в болѣзнь. разболѣвшю бо ся ему. и болѣвшю днии 5. (186)
'and having reached Easter Sunday—[and] having celebrated it joyfully, as was his habit—*he fell (vpade)* sick; then, having fallen sick, he was sick for five days'

(237)   видѣв же князя своего в велику бѣду **впадша**... гнаста по немъ. (324)
'when he saw his prince *fallen (vpadša)* into great misfortune... he chased after him'

The prefix {na-} is found in *napasti* with the meaning 'attack', as in (238) and (239).

(238)   и **нападе** на нь Куря князь Печенѣжьскии. (74)
'and Kurja the Pečeneg prince *attacked (napade)* him'

(239)   и се **нападоша** акы звѣрье дивии около шатра. (134)
'and they *attacked (napadoša)* like wild beasts around the tent'

It also has the meaning 'fall upon' in the sense of 'strike', as in (240). This last use is metaphorical, since the subject is an emotion (*užas"* 'horror'), making {na-} the only prefix that consistently modifies the meaning of the root in a substantial manner.

(240)   и оужасъ **нападе** на нь. и на воѣ его. (239)
'terror *fell (napade)* upon him and his soldiers'

Durative, progressive, and iterative contexts are found with derived prefixed forms. In (241), a state with clear endpoints is indicated, making it durative in nature.

(241)   обновлена быс(ть) ц(е)ркы с(вя)тая Б(огороди)ца в Суждали. яже **бѣ опадала** старостью. и безнарядьем. (411)
'the church of the Holy Mother of God in Suzdal', which *had been falling apart (bě opadala)* from old age and neglect, was renovated'

In (233) the context was progressive, but other derived verbs are found in iterative contexts, as in (242)-(244).

(242)   оже бо язъ от рати и от звѣри и от воды. от коня **спадаяся**. то никтоже вас не можеть вредитися. и оубити. понеже не будет от Б(ог)а повелѣно. (252)
'for since I [met no harm] from troops and animals and water and *falling off (spadajasja)* my horse, then no one can harm you or kill you unless it is willed by God'

(243) аще кто м(а)т(е)ре не послушаеть. в бѣду **впадаеть**. (63)
'whoever does not obey his mother *falls (vpadaet')* into misfortune'

(244) аще которыи братъ въ етеро прегрѣшенье **впадаше**. оутѣшаху
(188)
'if one of the brothers *fell (vpadaše)* into any kind of sin, they comforted [him]'

The prevalence of iterative forms may again be traceable to the lexical properties of the verb, which favor interpretations including the telos to those excluding it.

Conclusions. Unlike the other verbs we have examined here, *pasti* is an unprefixed protoperfective verb with a protoimperfective counterpart. This fact is not particularly surprising, since I have already established that very high telicity pushes predicates toward perfectivity (even when we might expect them to be protoimperfective by virtue of morphological features). The use of iteratives with derived forms is probably traceable to the high telicity of these predicates.

4.14. TELIC ACTS WITH NO SIMPLEXES (*UMERETI*)

The verb *umereti* 'die' is a slightly unusual choice for an example, because it does not have a simplex verb attested in the text. However, there are ample reasons for considering it here. All examples of the verb fall into this lexical subclass and provide interesting material for the distribution of derived forms. Furthermore, many verbs in this lexical subclass show only sparse attestations of the simplex form, so *umereti* is not atypical in this respect.

Umereti is attested sixty-three times in the text; the bulk of these attestations are aorists (thirty-two, or 51 percent). There are also a large number of perfects and forms with the perfect participle (ten, or 16 percent) and with the infinitive (eleven, or 17 percent). There are five non-past forms (8 percent), four past active participles (6 percent), and one imperfect (2 percent). Two out of the five attestations with the non-past of *umereti* appear in "if-then" sentences, as in (245).

(245) аще кто **оумреть** не оуря(ди)въ свое имѣнья... да възвратит имѣнїе к малым ближикам в Роус. (37)
'if someone (a Russian in Greece) *should die (oumret')* without having settled his affairs... let his property return to his youngest relatives in Russia'

One other—(246)—is a prediction:

(246) котопан же пришедъ Корсуню. повѣдаше яко в сии д(е)нь **оумреть** Ростиславъ. якоже и быс(ть). (166)
'...he reported that Rostislav *would die (oumret')* this day, which in fact did happen'

There are also two exhortatory usages (*da umret'* 'let him die'). All of the non-past usages have future modality.

The aorist, perfect, and infinitive usages all indicate a single, completed act, clearly "perfective" in nature. The perfect is used in (247) to indicate a state. In (248), the aorist reports a single act in a series. The infinitive in (249) also indicates a single, closed potential act.

(247) а конь **оумерлъ ес(ть)** а я живъ. (39)
'and the horse *has died (oumerl" es[t'])*, while I am alive'

(248) и выникнувше змиа (и)зо лба (и) оуклюну в ногу и с тог(о) разболѣс(я) и **умре**. (39)
'and the snake, having crawled out of the skull, bit him in the leg, and from this he got sick and *died (umre)*'

(249) лучи бы ми сде **оумрети**. (110)
'it would be better for me *to die* here'

One interesting usage of the verb is in (250)—earlier seen as (141)—where the imperfect tense is used. In this instance the imperfect indicates a repeated or habitual action that is perceived as completed each time.

(250) аще кто **оумряше** творяху трызно надъ нимъ. и по семь творяху кладу велику и възложахуть и на кладу м(е)ртвца. сожьжаху и посемь собравше кости. вложаху в судину малу. и поставяху на столпѣ... (14)
'when someone *died (oumrjaše)*, they would have a ceremony in his honor, and then they would make a large block and would place the dead man on the block, burn him up and then, having collected the bones, would put them in a small vessel and place it on a pillar'

4.14.1. The verb *umirati*

One test of the significance of this imperfect usage of *umereti* is to look at the distribution of forms with the suffixed verb *umirati*. Durative contexts are found, as (251) shows, with the pluperfect use of *umirati*. Here it is stated that 'before this no son *had died* before his father', framing that time with the epochal death of the son.

(251) и самъ съгорѣ ту Аронъ. и оумре пред о(т)цемъ. предъ симъ бо **не бѣ умирал** с(ы)нъ. предъ о(т)ц(е)мь. но о(те)ць предъ с(ы)н(о)мъ. (92)
'and Aaron himself burned up here, and died before his father did; for before this *no* son *had died (ne bě umiral)* before his father, but rather the father [had died] before the son'

The imperfect examples show a range of usages that focus on simultaneity, as opposed to sequentiality. However, in (252), the context is clearly iterative. The author describes people being attacked by demons; these attacks each time bring on death (potentially a slow, painful one, but this is not clear from context).

(252) аще кто вылѣзяше ис хоромины. хотя видѣти. абье оуязвенъ
будяше невидимо от бѣсовъ. язвою и с того **умираху**. (214-215)
'if anyone came out of the hut, wanting to see, he was immediately invisibly stricken by the devils with poison and *died (umiraxu)* from it'

Progressive contexts appear in (253)-(255); they describe conditions. Sometimes these conditions are juxtaposed with other simultaneous acts, as in (253). However, they need not appear with a second verb indicating simultaneity, as (254) shows; it is unimportant how many were dead at that particular point.

(253) многы кровы проливахуться межи ими. друзии же оуязвляеми **оумираху** (347)
'much blood was spilled between them, and others, being wounded, *were dying (oumiraxu)*'

(254) в си же времена мнози ч(е)л(о)в(ѣ)ци **оумираху** различными недугы. (215)
'in these times, many people *were dying (oumiraxu)* of various diseases'

(255) бѣ бо яко мгла к земли прилегла. яко и птицам по аеру не бѣ лзѣ лѣтати. но падаху на земли и **оумираху**. (447)[49]
'for it was as if a mist hugged the earth, since even the birds could not fly through the air, but fell to earth and *died (oumiraxu)*'

Although we can place these sentences in an iterative context, we need not do so; the context is more properly read as a progressive one that conveys a tableau at a certain moment in time. The import of this analysis is threefold. First, it shows an aspectual distinction in the past tense, with suffixed forms in progressive and durative contexts (to use Dostál's description, a view from inside the event) and nonsuffixed forms in iterative contexts (where each repetition of an event is rendered as a whole, promulgating a view from outside the event). Second, it indicates that iterativity is at least for this sort of verb not connected with imperfectivity; if anything, the canonical form of iterativity (repetition of discrete events) fits the protoperfective category best. Third, since all the events described are in the imperfect tense, tense must express a different aspectual distinction from verb-forming suffixes in this period.

This distinction between suffixed and nonsuffixed form is organized differently in the non-past. Gnomic usage (a type of generalized context) is possible, as in (256), where the message is that never at any point do the souls of the righteous face the possibility of death.

(256) пр(а)в(е)дн(ы)хъ бо д(у)ша **не оумирают**. (68)[50]
'the souls of the righteous *do not die (ne umirajut)*'

---

[49] Seen above as example (226).
[50] Other mss. have singular agreement with *duša* 'soul': *ne umiraet* 'does not die'.

Progressive and iterative contexts are also found with the non-past. Example (257), which emphasizes the manner of Christ's death, has a progressive context, as does (258), which indicates an action proceeding apace.

(257) ч(е)л(о)в(ѣ)къ есть кто оувѣсть яко Б(ог)ъ есть. яко ч(е)л(о)в(ѣ)къ **оумираеть**. (100)
'he is a man; who can know that he is God? For he *dies (oumiraet')* like a man does'

(258) мы того дѣля **оумираем** за Русьскую землю. и головы свои складываемъ. (345)
'for this reason we *are dying (oumiraem)* for the Russian land and laying down our heads [for it]'

Example (259) describes a state of affairs that obtains each time a death occurs.

(259) аще ли от наших **оумираеть** то носимъ к нашимъ б(ого)мь в бездну. (179)
'when one of ours *dies (oumiraet')*, then he is carried to our gods in the abyss'

The situation in (259) can be compared with the following sentence, from the same entry: *ašče kto* **umret'** *ot vašix ljudii, to v"znosim" est' na nebo* 'if anyone among your people *should die,* then he is carried up to heaven'. There is virtually no difference in context; if we choose to read the second as more connected or occasional in character, this is an interpretation imposed on us by aspect, not by context.[51]

An iterative context is found with the infinitive in (260).

(260) от сего начаша **оумирати** с(ы)н(о)ве предъ о(т)ц(е)мь. (92)
'from this time forth sons began *to die (oumirati)* before their father[s]'

There are a few attestations of this root with the prefixes {iz-} and {po-}, but they do not differ substantially in meaning or behavior from the pair *umirati–umereti*.

Conclusions. All the derived forms here show progressive or durative contexts, as expected, or at least do not exclude such a reading. Strongly telic acts already distinguish aspect, with iterativity being a context of perfectivity in the past tense; in the present tense iterativity is uncommon for protoimperfective verbs but not a reliable marker of perfectivity.

---

[51] The derived form here does suggest a certain simultaneity to the death and the descent of the soul into the abyss, but there is no specific contextual information to support this reading. For a fuller discussion of the problems of non-past "if-then" sentences, see chapter 5.

4.15. PUNCTUAL TELIC ACTS *(SUDITI)*

Predicates from the verb *suditi* fall into this class, along with a number of other predicates describing an act occurring mainly in the mind, with no measurable physical representation. Such acts are less prone to stative readings than punctual atelics (*viděti* 'see'), but share with them the ability to represent an action, telic or otherwise, as a momentary occurrence. Among these verbs are *grěšiti* 'sin', *soxraniti* 'preserve', *pomoči* 'help'. Several smaller, semantically specific groupings of verbs fit the lexical mold of this class, notably verbs of communication. These subtypes are not construed as distinct lexical classes, although it is interesting how the characteristics of the class as a whole are reflected in these groupings.

The verb *suditi* 'judge' is attested nineteen times in the Chronicles. There is one example each of an aorist, a perfect, a non-past, and an imperfect. In the non-finite forms there are eight infinitives or supines, four imperatives, two present participles and one past participle. The forms show a range of usages that align with both traditional "imperfective" functions and traditional "perfective" functions; at times these usages reflect the influence of tense, but often they do not. The preponderance of infinitive and supine forms means that many aspectual readings are conditioned not by grammar but by context.

The finite forms, few as they are, point to the aspectual ambiguity of the verb. The conditional mood in (261) takes a perfect participle in a generalized context (Modern Russian *sudil by*[I] '(who) would judge').

(261) поищемъ собѣ князя. иже **бы** володѣлъ нами. и **судилъ** по праву. (19)
'let us search for a prince who *would* rule over us and *judge (by sudil")* us according to the law'

The aorist *soudixom"* in (262) indicates that telos has been attained, indicating decisions taken several times (*mnogaždy*), perhaps at irregular intervals.[52]

(262) Наша свѣтлость болѣ инѣхъ хотящихъ еже о Бозѣ оудержати. (и) извѣстити такую любовь бывшоую межи хрестьяны и Роусю. многажды право **соудихомъ**... такую любовь оутвердити и извѣстити... (33)
'our serenity, above all desiring with God's help to maintain and proclaim such amity as exists between Christians and Russia, has often *deemed (soudixom")* it proper... to affirm and publicize this affection...'

---

[52] The Modern Russian translation has a perfective *rassudili* 'we judged' and has attached the iterativity to the previous phrase: 'the friendship which has existed more than once between Greeks and Russians'. This reading is odd, given the punctuation of the Old Russian text and the use of the participle *byvšouju* 'having been' instead of a form of *byvati* 'be (regularly)'.

Example (263), with the imperfect tense, expresses an occupation ('be a judge').

(263)   по сих же **судяше** Илии жрець. и (по) семь Самоилъ пр(о)р(о)къ. (97)
'after him Eli the priest *was judge (sudjaše)*, and after him the prophet Samuel'

In (261)-(263) an argument can be made that tense determines aspect; if *suditi* is weakly imperfective, then the perfectivizing aorist overrides this feature, the imperfectivizing imperfect supports it, and the conditional does neither. However, the non-finite examples reflect the same range of usages, while giving a few hints as to the eventual aspectual assignment of the verb. The imperatives can express a single instance of a judgment, as in (264)— Modern Russian *rassudi^P* 'make^P a decision'—or a generalized command or desire for the act of judgment, as in (265), where the Modern Russian translation has *davajte^I sud sirote* 'hear^I the plea of the orphan' for Old Russian *sudite sirotě*.

(264)   еда и мнѣ си(ц)е же створить. но **суди** ми Г(о)с(под)и по правдѣ. да скончается злоба грѣшнаго. (141)
'will he do the same to me? o Lord, *judge (sudi)* me by what is right, so that sinful evildoing might come to an end'

(265)   лишаемъ не мьсти. ненавидимъ. любо гонимъ терпи. хулимъ моли. оумертви грѣхъ. избавите обидима. **судите** сиротѣ. оправдаите вдовицю... (243)
'when robbed, do not seek revenge; when hated or persecuted, endure; vanquish sin; free those oppressed; *hear the plea (sudite)* of the orphan, give recompense to the widow...'

This ambiguity is in fact completely natural to the verb; we do not feel the need to impose on (266) one aspectual reading or another, since the judgment desired may be interpreted as being in a single instance or as part of an activity (although a single-event reading is suggested by the other predicates: *v"zbrani* 'hinder' and *primi* 'take').

(266)   **суди** Г(о)с(под)и. обидящих мя. възбрани борющимся со мною. прими оружье и щитъ. стани в помощь мнѣ. (478)
'*judge (sudi)*, o Lord, those who have offended me; hinder those who rise against me; take arms and shield, rise up in my defense'

In (267), an imperfective-like imperative is juxtaposed against a perfective-like non-past tense, parallel to the use of two different verbs in the first clause; aspect evidently does not play a central role in determining this verb's meaning.

(267)   еюже мѣрою **мѣри(те) възмѣриться** вам. и имже судомъ **судите судится** вам. (356)[53]

---

53   Matthew 7:2.

'you *will be measured (v"zmĕrit'sja)* by the measure with which you *measure (mĕrite)*, and you *will be judged (suditsja)* by the judgment with which you *judge (sudite)*'

The infinitive and supine add support to the nonaspectual assignment of *suditi*, using the simplex verb regardless of aspectual meaning. Example (268) refers to a single-time, completed action in the future.

(268) яко и сих ожидаеть. д(е)нь погибели их. егда придеть Б(ог)ъ **судитъ** земли. и погубять вся творящая безаконья. и скверны дѣющия. (86)
'when God comes *to judge (sudit")* the earth, and all who break the laws and commit abominations will perish'[54]

Suditi also appears in generalized processes that express duration or focus on the action regardless of result, as in (269)-(271). For instance, in (269), we learn that the Lord 'will come in glory *to judge* the living and the dead', clearly a more drawn-out process without a single definitive end result.

(269) прідеть же паки съ славою. **судити** живымъ и м(е)ртв(ы)мъ. (113)
'and again: "He will come in glory *to judge (suditi)* the living and the dead"'

(270) поставилъ же есть Б(ог)ъ единъ д(е)нь. в неже хощет **судити** пришедъ с н(е)б(е)се живымъ и м(е)ртв(ы)мъ. и **въздати** комуждо по дѣломъ его. (105)
'God has set a single day, on which, having come from Heaven, he will *judge (suditi)* the living and the dead, and *give (v"zdati)* to each according to his deeds'

(271) суд твои ц(а)р(е)ви дажь. и правъду твою с(ы)н(о)ви ц(е)с(а)р(е)ви. **судити** людемъ твоим в правду. и нищим твоимъ в суд. (467)[55]
'Give thy judgment to the king and thy righteousness to the king's son *to judge (suditi)* thy people with righteousness and thy poor with judgment.'

There are also contexts where either sort of interpretation is possible. In (272), Oleg leaves it unclear as to what this judgment consists of, a process or a single pronouncement; in (274), the verb *xotĕti* 'want' is used to form a compound future, but it is not clear whether *suditi* refers to a single judgment or to the process of judgment.

---

54 I disagree here with the Lixačev translation, which renders *sudit" zemli* as *sudit' narody* 'judge the peoples'. Far more likely is a reading in which God comes to judge (once) the earth (where the supine has a genitive singular complement); perhaps the translator was influenced by the modern assignment of *suditi* to the imperfective aspect.

55 Psalms 72:1.

(272) нѣс(ть) мене лѣпо **судити** еп(и)с(ко)пу. ли игуменом. ли смердом. (230)
'it is not fitting for a bishop *to judge (suditi)* me, nor for the priests, nor the commoners'

(273) пощади мя Сп(а)се... и егда сядеши **судити** дѣла моя... (256)
'spare me, o Savior... when you sit *to judge (suditi)* my deeds...'[56]

(274) помилуи мя Г(о)с(под)и помилуи егда хощеши **судити**. не осуди ме(не) въ огнь. (256)
'have mercy on me, o Lord; have mercy when you *(shall) judge (suditi)* me; do not condemn me to the fire'

The higher incidence of imperfective-type examples points in the direction of imperfectivity (unsurprisingly so, since *sudit'* is imperfective in Modern Russian), but perfective-type meanings are often present or possible. (Some such features of *sudit'* are present in Modern Russian as well; it is not clear whether they extend to this lexical class as a whole.)

Present and past participles lead to the same conclusions, the former representing an act in progress (as in (275) and (276): Modern Russian *tvorjaščij*[I] *sud* 'holding[I] court', *dajuščij*[I] *sud* 'passing[I] judgment') and the latter representing completion, as in (277).

(275) аще есть плод праведника. и есть убо Б(ог)ъ **судяи** земли. (242)
'if there is a reward for the righteous man, then it is God, *who judges (sudjai)* the earth (the nations)'

(276) и разумѣите и видите яко азъ есмъ Б(ог)ъ. испытая с(е)рдця. и свѣдыи мысли. обличаяи дѣла. опаляяи грѣхы **судяи** сиротѣ. и оубогу и нищю. (255)
'understand and see that I am God, testing hearts and knowing thoughts, exposing deeds, incinerating sins, *giving justice (sudjai)* to the orphan and the pauper and the lowly'

(277) **судившю** Ярославу тако. ... (452)
'Jaroslav *having decided (sudivšju)* as follows: ...'

4.15.1. Prefixed verbs from *suditi*

In contrast to the verb *suditi*, its prefixed forms all show signs of perfectivity. As is typical for this group, multiple forms with similar meanings are in competition: *osuditi* 'condemn', *posuditi* 'pass judgment, violate, undo', *rassuditi* 'pass judgment, decide, assign'. No derived forms of *suditi* are found in the

---

[56] The syntax is unclear here, so I have followed Lixačev in eliminating the word 'and'.

Chronicles. The non-past forms in (278) and (279) both indicate single, unitary acts that are linked in a chain to other events.[57]

(278) грѣшныи бо и сдѣ по грѣху мучится. а на судѣ Б(ож)ии **осудится** в муку. (356)
'for the sinner is even here tortured by sin, and on the Day of Judgment *will be condemned (osuditsja)* to torture'

(279) аще кто сего **посудить** да будеть проклять. (124)
'if someone *should violate (posudit')* this, let him be cursed'

Example (280) shows expectation of a one-time, future act.

(280) да како мя с тобою Б(ог)ъ **россудит**. якож и бысть. (482)
'however God *shall decide (rossudit)* about you and me, so it shall be'

In (281) and (282), *rassuditi* likewise refers to a single, completed act.

(281) рекоша ему Новгородци. оударилъ еси пятою Новъгородъ и шелъ еси былъ на стрыя своего на Михалка. поваблень Ростовци. да оже Михалка Б(ог)ъ поялъ. а с братомъ его съ Всеволодомъ Б(ог)ъ **росудилъ** тя чему к намъ идеши. (382)
'the Novgorodians said to him: you brought Novgorod under your heel and would have gone against your uncle Mixalko, warned by the Rostovites that God had taken Mixalko, and God *has decided between (rosudil")* you and his brother Vsevolod; so why do you come to us?'

(282) Батыи же почтивъ я. ч(е)стью достоною. и отпустивъ я. **расудивъ** имъ когождо в свою о(т)чину. (470)
'Batyj, having greeted them with great honor, released them, *having assigned (rasudiv")* them each to his own territory'

In two examples, Old Russian has a prefixed protoperfective, where Modern Russian might lead us to expect a protoimperfective. In (283), the negated prefixed form *ne osudi* refers to the negation of a single event; a Modern Russian imperfective (e.g., *ne osuždaj*) is required for general prohibitions of this sort, with the perfective having more of an immediate force or functioning as a warning not to do something (medieval Russians were, needless to say, not in the habit of issuing warnings to God).

(283) помилуи мя Г(о)с(под)и помилуи егда хощеши судити. **не осуди** ме(не) въ огнь. (256)

---

[57] It is debatable whether they represent future actions or not; the matter of "if-then" sentences and related sentence types is discussed in more detail in chapter 5. It is sufficient to say that these forms indicate potential acts, if not definitely future ones.

'have mercy on me, o Lord; have mercy when you (shall) judge [me]; *do not condemn (ne osudi)* me to the fire'

This discrepancy is best perceived not as an example of anaspectuality, but of differing scopes of aspectuality. The Old Russian negated imperative seems to occupy the same place as the Old Russian affirmative imperative; that is, aspect is only used to describe the temporal character of the act and not various discourse properties connected with the performance of the act—as is the case in the Modern Russian imperative.

The second example of this sort is (284), where the Old Russian text has a protoperfective imperfect *osudjaše* in a chain of repeated events. Here, once again, the act, regardless of whether it is repeated or not, is perceived as being discrete and complete on each occasion, hence the use of a protoperfective.

(284)   аще кого видяше ли шюмна. ли в коем зазорѣ **не осудяше** но вся на любовь прекладаше. (264) [58]
'Whenever he saw someone angry or shamed, he *did not condemn (ne osudjaše)* him but reconciled them all'

A preliminary conclusion about iterative usage is that Old Russian aspect comments exclusively on the character of the act; repetition can be expressed by either protoperfectives or protoimperfectives, depending on whether the individual performances of the action can be summed up as a process (protoimperfective) or whether their discreteness is important to the surrounding acts (protoperfective). Modern Russian aspect, by contrast, pays less attention to lexical aspectual features and more to contextual concerns. The nature of iterative sentences in Old Russian and their relation to Modern Russian is discussed at greater length in chapter 5.

A side effect of the discrepancies seen in (283) and (284) is that the prefixed form is used more widely in Old Russian than in Modern Russian, articulating lexical and aspectual features about the progress of an act through time where Modern Russian pays more attention to discourse concerns and consistency of aspectual assignment throughout a sentence.

Conclusions. The verb *suditi* presents evidence for a category of verbs that is not so much biaspectual as anaspectual or aspectually indifferent. Testament to this is its widespread vacillation in aspectual usage and a large number of forms that support both a protoperfective and a protoimperfective reading. Biaspectuality assumes a basic adherence to an aspectual system; forms regularly take on set aspectual functions that are clear in context. This verb exhibits a different sort of behavior, which is best explained by assuming lack of participation in such an organized system of functions.

Because *suditi*, although a perfectly secular Old Russian verb—see in particular (261), (262), (272) and (284)—is most often found in religious contexts and

---

[58] The Radzivil and Academy mss. have the derived form *osužaše*. Seen also as example (121) in chapter 5.

quotations from Scripture, it is appropriate to question whether or not other verbs without this religious overtone will still behave anaspectually. To test this, I will examine two other verbs from this group: *prositi* 'ask, request' and *kazati* 'say, teach, instruct, point'.[59]

4.16. COMMUNICATIVE ACTS *(PROSITI)*

The verb *prositi* 'request, ask (a favor)' also ranks high on the list of anaspectual verbs. There are fifty-seven attestations of *prositi* in the Chronicles; twenty-four of them (42 percent) are present participles, showing a decided slant toward Modern Russian imperfective usage; in the remainder, however—noticeably the aorist, infinitive, and imperative—usage tends toward the protoperfective. The non-past shows evidence of both imperfective-like and perfective-like features.

4.16.1. Participles of *prositi*

Consider the participle forms in (285)-(288), which seem to show the participle expressing ongoing action simultaneous with another act. A closer look at these examples reveals that not all of them necessarily do so. Examples (285) and (286) express action subsequent to a single act, while (287) and (288) express action performed in the same time frame as another act (although not necessarily simultaneously!) or in sequence with an iterated act. In (285), the participial form has a future modality; the mission first arrives and then states a request, or arrives in order to make a request; (286) is similar but with an aorist, not a perfect.

(285)   се преслалася ко мнѣ Словѣньска земля. **просящи** оучителя собѣ. (26)
'behold, the Slavic land has sent to me, *asking (prosjašči)* for a teacher for itself'

(286)   приде с дружиною своею **прося** оу него бл(а)г(о)с(ло)в(е)нья и м(о)л(и)твы. (157)
'he came with his company, *asking (prosja)* him for blessings and prayers'

The sequencing is clear from the semantics of the verbs *prositi* 'ask', *preslatisja* 'be sent over', *prijti* 'arrive'; a strict simultaneous reading placing the request at the same time as the trip or the arrival is nonsensical. In (287) and (288), it is not clear whether the emissaries go only once to plead their case or whether emissaries are sent several times, each time arriving and then pleading their case.

(287)   и сѣдя ту посылаше к Олгови мира **прося**. (238)
'and staying here, he sent to Oleg, *asking (prosja)* for peace'

---

[59] The latter belongs only partially in this class, as will be discussed in section 4.17.

(288) В тож лѣт(о) приходи еп(и)с(ко)пъ Черниговьскыи Пердурии. Ко Всеволоду Гюргевичю Володимерю мира **прося** оу него. абы оумирити его с Рязанци... (404)
'in the same year the Bishop of Černigov, Perdurij, came to Vsevolod Gjurgevič in Volodimer', *asking (prosja)* him for peace, in order to reconcile him with the Rjazanites...'

Either way, in (287) and (288), the sending or arriving precedes the request. Future modality is possible here, but because of the possible iterative reading, it is not as strong, since iterativity reduces the impact of the sequencing. Characteristic of participles in this class, then, is weak sequencing (with protoperfectives) and iterativity (with protoimperfectives).

4.16.2. Non-past forms of *prositi*

Compare this now to the non-past tense examples. Future modality occurs in two of the nine attestations and is possible in several others. Moreover, the possibility of a gradient of tense uses, from present to future with a range of fuzzier examples in between, is important. In (289)-(291), *prositi* has a present sense, although a future reading is not impossible.

(289) но мало оу васъ **прошю**. даите ми от двора по 3 голуби да 3 воробьи. (59)
'but *I ask (prošju)* of you a small thing: give me from each building three pigeons and three sparrows'

(290) и прошенья егоже азъ **прошю** дажь ми. (466)
'and the request which I *ask (prošju)* for, grant me'

(291) **просимъ** оу тобе с(ы)на княжитъ Новугороду. (415)
'*we ask (prosim")* you for your son to rule in Novgorod'

In (292), the 3. sg. non-past form *prosit'* may have a future sense, parallel to the form *lišit'*.

(292) егоже бо ч(е)л(о)в(ѣ)къ **просить** у Б(ог)а всѣм с(е)рдц(е)мь то Б(ог)ъ его **не лишить**. (378)
'what man *asks (prosit')* God for with all his heart, God *will not deprive (ne lišit')* him of'

Finally, in (293) and (294), *prositi* is more clearly future (note the Modern Russian translations *poprosit*[P] 'he will ask[P]', *poprosim*[P] 'we will ask[P]').[60]

---

[60] The presence of conditional sentences in (292) and (293) makes the sense of the verb form in the protasis difficult to assess. For a discussion of conditional sentences, see section 5.2.4.

(293) тогда аще **просить** вои оу нас князь Рускии. да воюеть. да дамъ ему елико ему будеть требѣ. (51)
'then if the Russian prince *asks (prosit')* us for troops in order to make war, then I will give him as many as he needs'

(294) Половци же слышавше яко идет Русь. собрашася бе-щисла. и начаша думати. и рече Оурусоба **просим** мира оу Руси. (278)
'Countless Polovtsians, having heard that Russia was coming, met and took counsel, and Urusoba said: "*let us ask (prosim)* Russia for peace"'

4.16.3. Infinitives of *prositi*

Infinitive complements show the same range of possibilities. Progressive contexts like (295)-(297) are consonant with Modern Russian usage of this verb.

(295) и почаша Греци мира **просит(и)**. (30)
'and the Greeks began *to beg (prosit[i])* for peace'

(296) да аще мя **просити**. право то пришлите мужа нарочиты. (56)[61]
'and if you are *to ask (prositi)* for my hand properly, send your best men'

(297) видѣв же Мстиславъ вои множство около города. и не быс(ть) ему помочи ни откуду же. и нача **просити** пути оу него. и Всеволод цѣлова к нему кр(е)стъ и да ему путь. (429)
'when Mstislav saw the multitude of soldiers around the city, and there was no help for him from anywhere, he began *to ask (prositi)* him for clear passage, and Vsevolod swore an oath with him, and let him pass'

However, the reflexive *prositi sja* in (298) indicates a single, future occurrence (the Modern Russian translation has *otprosit'sja*^{P} 'ask^P to take leave' here).

(298) и посем хотях **проситися** оу С(вя)тополка. и оу Володимера. ити на Половци. (266)
'and then I wanted *to ask (prositisja)* Svjatopolk and Volodimer to go against the Polovtsians'

Unlike *suditi*, *prositi* also has an unprefixed suffixed form *prašati*, which appears only once in the Chronicles.

(299) посемь же поча **прашати** его. что ради боятся его. (179)
'afterwards he started *to ask (prašati)* him why they were afraid of him'

---

[61] The other mss. have the more plausible form *prosite*, yielding a reading: 'if you are asking for my hand in truth...' This reading makes more sense, but I did not think use of the infinitive here was so clearly in error as to warrant amending it.

As opposed to the other phasal uses of the infinitive found in (295) and (297)—'ask for peace' and 'ask for free passage'—the request in (299) is a specific sentence, meaning that we are more likely to perceive the progression of this action in time as being a repetition of the same question instead of a single process. Such a reading fits with my earlier observation about another unprefixed derived verb—*stavljati* (see section 4.10).

4.16.4. Past tense forms of *prositi*

The thirteen past tense forms of *prositi* include 9 aorists (69 percent) and 4 imperfects (31 percent). In (300), the subject is the saintly life of a member of the monastery. The context is iterative.

(300) добрии ч(е)л(о)в(ѣ)ци... приходяще к нему **просяху** оу него бл(а)г(о)с(лове)нья. (157)
'good people, coming to him, *asked (prosjaxu)* him for his blessing'

Similarly, (301) tells of a sickness that the holy apostles and fathers request, a context either general or iterative in nature.

(301) быс(ть) ему болесть зла. еяже болѣзни **просяхуть** на ся с(вя)тии ап(о)с(то)ли. и с(вя)тии о(т)ци оу Б(ог)а. (366)
'he had a terrible sickness, which sickness the holy apostles and the holy fathers *ask (prosjaxut')* God for'

Examples (302) and (303) are by contrast durative contexts. In (302), the metropolitan in question is asking for forgiveness once he falls down; in (303), the time period covered by the verb is limited.

(302) бѣ бо нетвердъ верою к нима и падъ ниць **просяше** прощенья. (182)
'for he had not been strong in his faith to them, and having fallen down, he *asked* for forgiveness'

(303) м(и)л(о)стнями и вѣрою очищаются грѣси. тѣмже и не погрѣши надежи. егоже **просяше** оу Б(ог)а. (466)
'Through offerings and faith, sins are cleansed; thus do not lose hope for what you *have asked (prosjaše)* from God.'

Examples (304)-(307), with the aorist, are summarized single acts, describing a single event regarded without respect to duration. In (304) and (305), the request is in a chain of events.

(304) сь посла к Роговолоду. и **проси** оу него дщере за Володимера. Он же реч(е)... (299)
'that one sent to Rogovolod and *asked (prosi)* him for his daughter for Volodimer. He [Rogovolod] said that...'

(305) кре́ститися **проси́ша**. и покори́тис(я) Гре́ком. (19)
'they *asked (prosiša)* to be baptized, and to submit to the Greeks'

Examples (306) and (307) sound more like perfects than an aorist, but also describe single, completed acts.

(306) еди́ного **проси́х** от Г(о)с(под)а того́ взищю́. да жи́ву в дому́
Г(о)с(под)ни вся дни живота́ моего́. (433)
'*I asked (prosix)* the Lord for only one thing which I will obtain: that I may live in the house of the Lord all the days of my life' [62]

(307) живота́ **проси́** оу тебе́ и далъ ему́ еси́. долготу́ дни в вѣкы вѣку.
(421)
'*he asked (prosi)* life of thee; thou gavest it to him, length of days for ever and ever' [63]

4.16.5. Prefixed forms of *prositi*

There are numerous prefixed forms of the verb *prositi*, most formed on the suffixed *prašati*. Some of them are fairly close in meaning, such as *vprašati, vprositi, uprašati, suprašati*. The verb *isprositi*, on the other hand, when compared with *prositi* more resembles the relationship found between natural conatives and their prefixed forms; it is used in the meaning 'receive something, having asked for it', and in its reflexive form *isprositi sja* has a meaning identical to that seen with *prositi sja* in (298) above. Similarly the verb *sprašati sja* appears in the meaning 'take counsel, decide on a course of action'. All examples appearing in the Chronicles of these verbs are reproduced below.

The simple prefixed verbs do not pose a problem. All the acts they refer to are completed single events, a viewpoint associated with the perfective aspect. By these criteria, *isprositi* and *isprositi sja* are protoperfective, as seen in (308)-(312). In (308), two men '*received leave to go* to Constantinople', after which they 'set off along the Dnepr'. The pluperfect *isprosil"sja bjaše* 'having received leave to go' in (309) carries a similar force.

(308) и та **испроси́стася** ко Ц(а)рюго́роду с ро́домъ свои́мъ. и поидо́ста по Днѣпру́. (20)
'and these two *received leave to go (isprosistasja)* to Constantinople with their tribe, and they set off along the Dniepr'

(309) по́иде проти́ву им. **испроси́лъся бя́ше** оу Святосла́ва. (395)
'and he set off against them; he *had received leave to go (isprosil"sja bjaše)* from Svjatoslav'

---

[62] Seen earlier in this chapter as example (204) and in chapter 5 as example (27).
[63] Psalms 21:4.

Examples (310)-(312), which are typical nonreflexives, sandwich the peace attained between other acts, forcing the aorist to be read as one complete event.

(310) и посла с покореньем къ Ярополку. и **испроси** миръ. и цѣловаша ч(е)стныи кр(е)стъ. и створи миръ. (306)
'and he sent humbly to Jaroslav, and *received* the peace *he sought (isprosi)*, and kissed the holy cross, and made peace'

(311) Георгии князь Володимеричь. **испроси** у брата своего Ярополка Переяславль. а Ярополку вда Суждаль... (302)
'Prince Georgij Volodimerič *received (isprosi)* Perejaslavl' from his brother Jaropolk, and he gave Suzdal' to Jaropolk...'

(312) и проси оу него дщери за своего сыновца. за С(вя)тослава. и **испроси** оу него помочь. и посла к нему с(ы)на своего Изяслава со всѣм полкомъ. (350)
'and he asked for his daughter for his nephew Svjatoslav, and he *received (isprosi)* help from him, and he sent his son Izjaslav to him with a whole company'

The evidence for *vprositi* is slimmer, but in its single aorist attestation in (313) it also appears to be protoperfective.

(313) и **впроси** воды. они же даша ему. и испи воды. (261)
'and he *asked (vprosi)* for water; they gave it to him, and he drank of the water'

If the Russian aspectual system is fully developed by this time, we would expect verbs formed on the derived base *-prašati* to be clearly protoimperfective. However, *-prašati*, like the simplex *prositi*, is also anaspectual when prefixed. The progressive reading found in (314), with the pluperfect tense, is normal for a derived verb (see the discussion of (299) above).

(314) **бѣ** бо **въпрашал** волъхвовъ (и) кудесникъ. от чего ми ес(ть) смерть. и реч(е) ему... (38)
'for *he had been querying (bě v"prašal)* the soothsayers and magicians: what will I die of? And they told him...'

(315) призвавъ книжникі и старци людьския. и **въпраша** их кде Х(ристо)съ ражается. Они же рѣша... (102)[64]
'having summoned the learned men and elders of the people, he *queried (v"praša)* them: where is this Christ being born? And they said...'

The aorist in (315) can also—marginally—be read in a progressive or iterative context: 'he *would ask/was asking* them where Christ was being born'. This only works if the derived form shows that the men whom Herod summoned were each

---

[64] The Academy ms. has a 3. sg. imperfect *voprošaše*.

asked individually or over a period of time. However, note that in (316), the prefixed derived past participle *sprašav"sja* refers to a single, completed event.

(316) а Вячеславъ **спрашавъся** съ Всеволодом. отда Переяславль Изяславу Мстиславичю. (310)
'and Vjačeslav, *having taken counsel (sprašav"sja)* with Vsevolod, gave Perejaslavl' to Izjaslav Mstislavič'

This pattern holds as well for the aorist in (317)—as well as (318) and (319).

(317) оузрѣста на горѣ градок и **оупращаста** и рѣста, чии се градок? (20)[65]
'they saw a small town on the hill and they *asked (oupraščasta)* and said: whose town is that?'

The perception of these verbs as perfective, imperfective, or ambiguous varies with the tense and mood employed. Past tense forms and past participles describe either a single question or a series of similar questions directed at members of a group to elicit a single answer or identical answers, as in (318) and (319), as well as (316) and (317). The ambiguity is summed up in the English translation of the aorist *vpraša* in (318). A summary of multiple events may result, although this sense may be weak enough to allow nonsummative readings, as in (314) and (315).

(318) бѣ же единъ старець не былъ на вѣчи томь. и **впраша** что ради вече было. и людье повѣдаша ему... (127)
'there was one old man who was not at the council, and *he asked/was asking (vraša)* why a council had been called, and the people told him...'

(319) а полонъ свои отяша. **впрашаша** же и тѣхъ много ли вашихъ назади еще. (360)[66]
'and they took their prisoners away, and *they asked (vprašaša)* them: are there still many of your people back there?'

In contrast to these protoperfective or distributive uses, the non-past forms, present participles and infinitives are found in iterative, progressive or durative contexts, as in (320)-(322). The present participle in (320) is in both a progressive and an iterative context (a repeated request simultaneous with being driven about).

(320) повелѣ... возити по городу **въпрашающим**. кде болнии и нищь не могы ходити. тѣм раздаваху на потребу. (126)
'he ordered...to be taken around the city, *asking (v"prašajuščim)* where the sick and poor unable to walk were, and gave them what they needed'

---

[65] Other mss. have *v"prašasta, uprošasta*, which are derived forms with dual agreeement.
[66] The Radzivil and Academy mss. have the imperfect 3. pl. *v"prašaxu*.

In (321), by contrast, the context of *nača vprašati* 'he began to ask' is more clearly progressive, since what follows is a lengthy question and diatribe.

(321)   и пришедшю ему. нача **впрашати** его Володимеръ. то вѣдѣ яла вы рота. многажды бо ходивши ротѣ воеваете Русскую землю. то чему ты не казаше с(ы)н(о)въ своихъ и роду своего не преступати роты... (279)
'and having come to him, Volodimer began *to ask (vprašati)* him: has not this oath truly ruined you? For having taken this oath, many times you made war upon the Russian land; so why do you not tell your sons and family not to break oaths...'

Example (322) is similar, since the process of asking in the non-past summarizes a process described earlier.

(322)   тако **съупрашаются** со слезами родъ свои повѣдающе и въздышюче. очи возводяще на н(е)бо к Вышнему свѣдущему тайная... (225)
'in this way *they ask each other (s"uprašajutsja),* talking tearfully about their homeland, sighing, raising their eyes to the sky to the Highest one who knows all secrets...'

The imperative *vprašai* 'ask' in (323) is ambiguous. Either interpretation—an emphasis on the action itself, regardless of completion, or an emphasis on the completion of the action—is possible.

(323)   иди **впрашаи** е ли Михаль в кельи. (191)
'go *ask (vprašai)* if Mixal' is in his cell'

It remains to be seen whether this distribution of contexts is played out in any other verbs of this class. If so, it would indicate that although simple prefixed predicates in this class are protoperfective, the simplex verbs and derived verbs do not have any consistent grammatical aspectual assignment, and that it is the function of the tense or context to provide it.

Conclusion. Although *prositi* is clearly telic in its usages, it behaves much more like *vidĕti*, which is generally held not to be telic. A range of usages that do not seem to correspond to strict aspectual distinctions, plus a set of prefixed derived verbs that show ambiguous aspectuality, place it in the camp of anaspectual verbs.

4.17. DEGREES OF PUNCTUALITY *(KAZATI)*

Some verbs have a range of meanings that, while all related and (arguably) part of the same field of meaning in Old Russian, straddle lexical categories. A good example is *kazati* 'teach, instruct, say, point.' In its first two meanings it falls into the category of telic acts *(staviti),* but in its third and fourth meanings it describes a communicative act, placing it among the punctual telics (*prositi*). This explains the wide variety of forms found with this verb and the diversity of its prefixed forms.

In the meaning 'say', *kazati* indicates a single, definite utterance, as seen in the perfect tense forms in (324) and (325).

(324) гл(аго)л(и)те что вы **казалъ** ц(а)рь. (53)
'tell us what the tsar *has told (kazal")* you'

(325) мы вѣдаем. аже того брат твои **не казалъ**. ни велѣлъ творити. но мы хочем оубити Игоря. (317)
'we know that your brother *has not said (ne kazal")* this, nor ordered it to be done, but we want to kill Igor''

The infinitive *kazati* is used in (326) with a meaning that is somewhat broader in scope, indicating either a single utterance or the act of speaking about this monstrous deformation.

(326) на лици ему срамнии оудове. иного нелзѣ **казати** срама ради. (164)
'on its face were like unto private parts; shame forbids *saying (kazati)* more than this'

In (327), *kazati* has the meaning 'point' and the 3 pl. non-past *kažut'* is used to suggest ongoing or repeated action simultaneous with other actions.

(327) и есть не разумѣти языку ихъ. но **кажють** на желѣзо и помаваютъ рукою просяще желѣза. (235)
'and there is no understanding their language, but *they point (kažut')* to iron and wave their hands, asking for iron'

In the meaning 'point', however, *kazati* also represents a single act of unspecified duration, presumably one concurrent with the speakers' pronouncement, as with the aorist in (328).

(328) они же **казаша** рекуще. поидѣте по свою брат(ь)ю. али мы идем по свою брат(ь)ю к вам. (399)
'and they *pointed (kazaša)*, saying: follow your brothers, and we will follow our brothers to your land'

Kazati can also be used in this meaning in explicitly progressive contexts, as with the present verbal adverb in (329).

(329) вследуя нравом ихъ. и оученью. но токмо бо словом оуча но и дѣлом **кажа**. (457)
'following their morals and teachings, not only teaching with words but also *showing (kaža)* with deeds'

In the sense 'teach, instruct, punish', *kazati* often appears in generalized contexts, as in (330)-(333), respectively non-past, infinitive, aorist and non-past forms

(330) **кажеть** бо ны добрѣ бл(а)гыи Вл(а)дыка (224)
'for our blessed Lord *teaches (kažet')* us well'

(331) тако подобаеть бл(а)гому Вл(а)д(ы)цѣ **казати**. (224)
'it is fitting for the blessed Lord *to teach (kazati)* thus'

(332) се бо на ны Б(ог)ъ попусти поганым. не яко милуя ихъ но насъ **кажа**. да быхомъ ся востягнули от злых дѣлъ. (222)
'for behold, God loosed the pagans on us, not because he loved them, but *because he was punishing (kaža)* us, so that we might pull ourselves up from evil deeds'

(333) не вѣдуще яко Б(ог)ъ **кажеть** рабы своя. напастми ратными.... (233)
'not knowing that God *punishes (kažet')* his servants with the misfortunes of war...'

However, this usage of *kazati* is also found in a durative context with the imperfect in (334), referring to a potential action over a period of time in the past.

(334) многажды бо ходивши ротѣ. воевасте Русскую землю. то чему ты **не казаше** с(ы)н(о)въ своихъ. и роду своего не преступати роты. но проливашет кровь х(ре)с(т)ьяньску. (279)
'Many times, having taken an oath, you made war on the Russian land; why then *did you not instruct (ne kazaše)* your sons and your family not to break an oath, but (instead) poured Christian blood?'

These non-past forms with only present usages indicate a verb that tends strongly toward the protoimperfective, at the same time as its punctual meanings suggest a strong protoperfective bent reflected in the aorist usages of *kazati*.

The prefixed forms from *kazati* are unusual in that separate suffixed forms exist for the non-past and the present participle. The form *nakazati* serves as the infinitive for both *nakažu* and *nakazaju*.[67] The aorist in both cases is *nakaza*; the perfect is *nakazal*.[68] There are six such prefixed verbs in the Chronicles; three—

---

[67] There are two possible viewpoints here. One is that these forms indicate the existence of two separate verbs, isomorphic in all but the non-past tense and present participle; the other is that there exists only a single verb with two participles and two non-past tenses. The second variant is simpler and thus less troublesome—as long as the stipulation is made that the purpose of having two non-past tenses *is not there to distinguish present from future, but to distinguish different sorts of acts*. For a further discussion of this point, see section 3.4.3.

[68] If there were two separate verbs, one might expect forms like aorist *nakazaja*, perfect *nakazajal*, infinitive *nakazajati* to develop in Old Russian; however, there are no traces of them in this text.

predpokazati, prikazati, prokazati—are attested only sporadically, and I will examine the other three—*nakazati, pokazati, skazati*—below.

4.17.1. *Nakazati* and related forms

The verb *nakazati* appears in the Chronicles in several meanings: 'teach, instruct', 'order', 'chastise', 'punish'.[69] In the meaning 'teach, instruct', *nakazati* can summarize the results of teaching, as with the perfect *nakazal"* in (335).

(335)   вы же чада Б(о)жья послушаите оученья и не отрините наказанья ц(е)рк(о)вн(а)го. якоже вы **наказалъ** Мефодии оуитель вашь. (27)
'you, o child of God, obey the teachings, and do not reject the instructions of the church, as your teacher Methodius *has taught (nakazal")* you'

In (336) the participle *nakazav"* 'having instructed' shows the completion of a set course of instruction and is parallel to the form *naoučiv"* 'having taught', a protoperfective:

(336)   **наказавъ** его и наоучивъ чернечьскому образу. и реч(е) ему иди в Русь опять... (156)
'having instructed (nakazav") him and taught him the monastic way of life, he said to him: go back to Russia...'

In (337), however, the focus is on process, not result. Here the progressive use of conditional *nakazal" by* is parallel to *poučal" by* 'would teach', which also focuses on process.

(337)   и нѣс(ть) оу насъ оучителя. иже **бы** ны **наказалъ** и поучалъ насъ. (26)
'we have no teacher who *could instruct (by nakazal")* and teach us'

Imperfect tense forms of *nakazati* express a general tendency in the meaning 'teach', as in (338).

(338)   такоже и старѣишии имя(ху) любовь к меншимъ. **наказаху** оутѣшающе. яко чада възлюбленая. (188)
'the elders had love for the younger ones; *they taught (nakazaxu)* them, comforting them like beloved children'

In the punctual meaning 'warn, instruct', they express a repeated act of no real duration, as in (339).

(339)   и аще кого видяше в помышленьи. обличаше и втаїнѣ и **наказаше** блюстися от дьявола. (190)

---

[69] I did not count occurrences of this verb, since it would be skewed by the frequent repetitions of the Biblical quotation in (346).

'and if he saw anyone lost in thought, he would confront him in private and *instruct (nakazaše)* him to beware of the devil'

The present verbal adverb *nakazaja* is used in (340) to indicate the simultaneity of two acts (here, as usual, the second act is *utěšaja* 'comforting').

(340) оутѣшая и **наказая** приходящая к нему. другоиця в домы ихъ приходя. и бл(а)г(о)сл(о)в(е)нье имъ подавая. (212)
'comforting and *instructing (nakazaja)* those who came to him; at other times going to their houses and giving them his blessing...'

The sole example of *nakazati* in the meaning 'order' is a completed one found as a past participle in (341):

(341) **наказавшю** князии кр(е)ста ч(е)стнаго не преступати. и старѣишаго брата чтити. а злых ч(е)л(о)в(ѣ)къ не слушати. (377)
'having ordered (nakazavšju) the princes not to break a sacred vow and to honor their elder brother and not to listen to evil men...'

The meaning 'punish' is likewise used to indicate a single, completed act. It appears in the perfect, non-past, aorist and infinitive in this usage, as found respectively in (342)-(345). Notably, this single act does not necessarily indicate futurity in the non-past in (342).

(342) бѣда оупространися. праведно и достоино есть. тако **да накажемься**. тако вѣру имем. (223)
'the misery spread; it is right and fitting *that we be so punished (nakažem"sja)*; in this way we will gain faith'

(343) да доколе Б(ого)ви терпѣти над нами. за грѣхы наведе на них. и **наказалъ** по достоянью рукою бл(а)говѣрнаго князя. (382)
'and so long as God will suffer us, he brought down [punishment] on them, and *has punished (nakazal")* them as they deserved at the hand of the faithful prince'

(344) тако и сия людi Новгородьскыя **наказа** Б(ог)ъ. и смѣри я дозѣла. за преступленье кр(е)стное. (362)
'so did God *punish (nakaza)* the people of Novgorod and humble them for their trespass of the cross'

(345) того ради всем(и)л(о)ст(и)выи Б(ог)ъ хотя погубити. и **наказати** безбожныя с(ы)ны... (446)
'for this reason the all-merciful God, wanting *to* destroy and *punish (nakazati)* the godless sons...'

Example (346) has a progressive use of *nakazati* in the sense 'instruct, teach' (present verbal adverb) and a summarizing one in the sense 'punish' (imperative).

(346) и Д(а)в(и)дъ пр(о)рокъ гл(аголе)ть. **наказая накажи** мя Г(о)с(под)и.
но см(е)рти не предажь мене. (405)
'and David the prophet says: *in instructing me (nakazaja), chastise (nakaži)
me, o Lord, but do not give me over to death*'[70]

The explicitly derived forms *nakazaja, nakazaju* are thus limited to contexts that are easily understood to express duration, and the imperfect tense serves a different function, stressing repetition of discrete acts. However, this difference might rather result from the meanings of the verbs found in these contexts. When *nakazati* is used atelicly (for general instruction or teaching), the context is interpreted as progressive or durative; when it is used with a punctual meaning (for a particular utterance), the context is more likely to be perceived as iterative.

The single example of *nakazyvati* in (347) is found in an exhortation to proper behavior, indicating what a person generally should do. The simultaneous *utěšati* 'to console' also gives the context a strong progressive element. The infinitive *nakazyvati* appears with the nonpunctual meaning 'teach, instruct'.

(347) подобаеть черноризцем... образ бывати собою. въздержаньем и
бдѣньемь. хоженьем и смѣреньем. **наказывати** менша и оутѣшати
я. (184)
'it is fitting for a monk... to be an example himself of restraint and vigilance,
industry and humility, *to instruct (nakazyvati) the lesser and to comfort them*'

Compare this to the single attested infinitive of *nakazati* in (345), which means 'punish' and follows the verb *xotěti*, thus expressing a desire for a single act in the future. This indicates that as the examples above suggest, the root *kazati* is nonaspectual; it takes on the character of whatever tense is attached to it or whatever context it is in. To lessen the punctual meaning of the infinitive, a clearly derived form is used, giving it a more general sense.

4.17.2. *Pokazati* and related forms

The verb *pokazati* is also more semantically heterogeneous in the Old Russian period. In addition to the meaning 'show' found in Modern Russian, it can mean 'teach, instruct' or 'express'. For aorist, infinitive, and perfect or past participles, the verb form is easily read as a single, unified act but does not always mandate such a reading; in this sense the verb resembles other punctual verbs like *suditi* 'judge', *viděti* 'see', *diviti sja* 'be surprised', which had a high degree of variation in meaning and form.

In (348) and (349), the aorist event happened once and was completed.

(348) но възведе и на гору Вамьску. и **показа** имъ землю обѣтованую. и
оумре Моисии ту на горѣ. (96)

---

70 Cf. Psalms 118:18. "The Lord has chastened me sorely, but He has not given me over to death."

'but He led him up onto Mount Pisgah, and *showed (pokaza)* him the promised land, and Moses died there on the mountain'

(349) Ярославъ же сѣде Кыевѣ. оутеръ пота с дроужиною своею. **показавъ** побѣдоу и троудъ великъ. (146)
'Jaroslav settled in Kiev, and finished his work with his followers, having *proved/shown (pokazav")* his victory and great labor'

In (350), the infinitive refers to a tour of the church—in other words, a longer period of time summed up as a unified whole.

(350) и пристави к ним моужи свои. **показати** им ц(е)рк(о)вноую красотоу. и полаты златыа. и в них соущаа богатество... (38)
'and he assigned his men to them *to show (pokazati)* them the beauty of the church, and the golden rooms and the riches contained therein...'

Most examples of *pokazati* bear the meaning 'show, point out'. Only (351) retains the meaning 'teach', with the present verbal adverb.

(351) Намъ **показая** постное время. постомь ап(о)ст(о)ли искор(ен)иша бѣсовьское оученье. (185)
'*in teaching (pokazaja)* us about the fasts, with fasting the apostles rooted out the demons' teachings'[71]

Other meanings of *pokazati* are found in set phrases in (352) and (353). The perfect used in *pokazal est' pobědu* in (352) means not 'has shown victory' but 'has shown the way to victory'. In (353), the past verbal adverb phrase *pokazavše emu put' ot sebe* does not mean that the Poles politely showed Izjaslav the route out of Poland; it means that they led an attack against him (and possibly collected his booty along the way). Both meanings summarize a completed event.

(352) такоже и Г(о)с(под)ь нашь **показал** ны **есть** на врагы побѣду 3-ми дѣлы добрыми избыти его. и побѣдити его. (243)
'in this way our Lord *has shown (pokazal est')* us to victory over our enemies, to get rid of him by three good deeds and vanquish him'

(353) Изяслав же иде в Ляхы со имѣнием многым. гл(агол)я яко симь налѣзу вои. еже все взяша Ляхове оу него. **показавше** ему путь от себе. (183)
'Izjaslav went to Poland with many goods, saying: with this I will find soldiers. The Poles took all of this from him, *having driven (pokazavše)* him from their land'[72]

---

[71] I assume here that the variant *iskoreniša* found in the Radzivil and Academy mss. is correct, since I find no recorded meanings for the Laurentian *iskoriti*.

[72] This order of events is unusual (we would expect them to first take the spoils, then banish the spoiler), but the only alternative is to read *i pokazaše emu put'* 'and he was

The *pokažju*-type forms are for the most part future in meaning, as in (354).

(354) изиди из дому о(т)ца своего. в землю в нюже ти **покажю**. (92)
'go forth from your father's house into the land which I *will show (pokažju)* you'

However, they can also indicate single acts perceived as a unit, without reference to an absolute time frame, as in (355).

(355) о том аще оукраден боуд(е)ть челядинъ Роускыи. или оускочит или по нужи продан боуд(е)ть. и жаловати начноут Роус. (да) **покажеться(я)** таковое от челядина. и да поимуть (и) в Роус. (36)
'...if a Russian commoner be stolen or run away or be forcibly sold and Russia begins to complain, *let it be proved ([da] pokažet'sja)* about the commoner, and let them take him back to Rus'

The *pokazaju*-type participles in (356)-(357) are in progressive contexts. In (356), the activity of 'showing' is reduced to a more stative meaning (i.e., the beauty of the church *was visible* to them); the meaning in (357), 'demonstrating', retains a more active meaning.

(356) и поставиша я на пространьнѣ мѣстѣ. **показающе** красоту ц(е)рк(о)вную. (107)
'and he placed them in a spacious location, *showing (pokazajušče)* [them] the beauty of the church'

(357) но на ся перея печаль братню. **показая** любовь велику. свершая ап(о)ст(о)ла гл(аголю)ща... (203)
'but he took his brother's woes upon himself, *showing (pokazaja)* his great love, fulfilling the words of the apostle, who said...'

The non-past *pokazajut'* in (358) indicates a repeated act, although its co-occurrence with other acts makes a progressive reading possible as well.

(358) Анг(е)лъ бо приходит кдѣ бл(а)гая мѣста. и м(о)л(и)твении домове. и ту **показають** нѣчто мало видѣнья своего. яко мощно видѣти ч(е)л(о)в(ѣ)к(о)мъ. (284)[73]
'for the angel comes to blessed places and prayerful homes, and here they *show (pokazajut')* some little bit of their appearance, so that people may see'.

Compare the *pokazaju*-forms with the forms that have a {-v-} suffix, all of which appear in progressive or durative contexts. In (359) and (360), the participle

---

driving them out' with the Radzivil and Academy mss., or assume that both are an error for *i pokazaša emu put'* 'and they drove him out'.

[73] The Radzivil and Academy mss. have *pokazujut'*, with a different imperfectivizer.

indicates an act co-occurring with some other act. In (359) this act takes on a stative quality.

(359) и повѣси щит свои въ вратех. **показоуа** побѣду. (32)
'and he hung his shield on the gate, *showing (pokazouja)* his victory'

In (360) it represents a highly telic type of instruction that is in progress (i.e., showing as a type of teaching, but one that implicitly leads to understanding).

(360) и пристави к ним моужи свои. показати им ц(е)рк(о)вную красотоу... оучаще я к вѣре своеи. и **показующе** им истиную вѣроу... (38)
'and he added his men to them to show them the beauty of the church... instructing them in their faith, and *showing (pokazujušče)* them the true faith'

In (361), the reason for a derived form is less clear; the context of the non-past form is virtually identical to that of (355). It is possible that the process involves numerous brocades, and is thus specified as having some innately long duration (compared to the process of obtaining a seal), but this is not clear from the sentence.

(361) и от тѣхъ паволокъ аще кто крьнеть. **да показываеть** ц(а)р(е)ву мужю. и то е запечатаеть и дасть имъ. (49)[74]
'and if someone should buy of these brocades, then *let him show (da pokazyvaet')* [them] to the emperor's man, and he will place a seal on them and give it to him'

Unlike *nakazati*, which had the full range of tenses available, *pokazati* does not have imperfect tense forms attested in this text. Instead, imperfects appear only with the suffixed forms *pokazovati* and *pokazyvati*, as seen in (362) and (363).

(362) и се рекъ показа Володимеру запону. на неиже бѣ напис(а)но судище Г(о)с(под)не. **показываше** ему. о десну пр(а)в(е)дныя в весельи, предъидуща въ раи. а о шюю грѣшники идуща в муку. (106)
'and having said this, he showed Volodimer the curtain on which the Lord's court was described; *he showed (pokazyvaše)* him the righteous on His right hand joyously approaching Paradise, and on His left hand the sinners going to their torment'

(363) тако и се явленье нѣкоторое **показываше**. емуже бо быти и быс(ть). (285)
'thus this vision *showed (pokazyvaše)* something which was to be and [which then] took place'

---

[74] The Radzivil and Academy mss. have *pokazuet* for *pokazyvaet'*, with a different imperfectivizing suffix, and *kupit'* for *kr'net'*.

In (362) the derived form presumably indicates a description of marked length: Volodimer is shown *(pokaza)* a curtain with an allegorical tableau of the Lord's court, and the derived imperfect *pokazyvaše* indicates how the philosopher pointed out each detail of it to Volodimer.[75] In (363) the imperfect *pokazyvaše* is used in a durative context, about an action that took place over a period of time and that was just described to the reader. The relegation of these forms to the derived verb, plus the frequency of the aorist with *pokazati* (12 out of a total 24 forms of *pokazati*) makes *pokazati* seem more protoperfective than does *nakazati;* again, this is not surprising, considering the nature of the act. There is no discernible difference in meaning between *pokazovati* and *pokazyvati;* the existence of doublets may be simply an indication of the uncertain status of these derived verbs in the morphology of the period.

The relations in this text between simplex, simple prefixed, and derived prefixed verb differ fundamentally from that found in the modern language. In Modern Russian, *kazat'* is rarely used; instead, the verbs *pokazyvat'–pokazat'* and *nakazyvat'–nakazat'* form aspectual pairs. The data from this text suggest that the basic aspectual relationship in Old Russian was between simplex and simple prefixed form. The derived forms (e.g., *nakazaju, nakazyvaju*) appear in contexts specifically expressing simultaneity or duration; these forms certainly bear an aspectual relationship to the simple prefixed forms, but this relationship is one of duration vs. lack of it, rather than being concerned with the telos of the act.

Furthermore, the potential for expressing iteration does not seem to be a function of form so much as it is one of lexical meaning. Derived forms of punctual acts tend to be interpreted iteratively; derived forms of nonpunctual acts tend to be interpreted progressively or duratively.

4.17.3. *Skazati* and related forms

The last remaining verb in this group is *skazati* 'tell, say, describe'. Unlike *nakazati* and *pokazati*, both of which retain the meaning 'teach' from the simplex verb, *skazati* shows no traces of this meaning in the Chronicles. Instead, it has in common with *kazati* the meaning 'say' and seems to be used most often as a synonym of the simplex verb. It would be difficult to prove an aspectual relationship between the verbs; as we saw above, *kazati* has anaspectual characteristics, and *skazati* is if anything more confusing due to the plethora of non-past forms. However, the evidence does suggest that *kazati* leans toward imperfectivity, while *skazati* leans toward perfectivity, based on the number of forms in imperfective-like and perfective-like contexts. Aspectual characteristics are stronger with *skazati*, although it is contradicted by the presence of the derived present tense forms in {-aju}, etc. The special relationship between *kazati* and

---

[75] A Modern Russian translation of the Primary Chronicle uses the perfective *ukazal* 'pointed'.

skazati is suggested by the fact that at this point no derived forms parallel to *pokazyvati, pokazovati, nakazyvati* are found in this text.[76]

In contrast to forms of *kazati,* the forms *skazaju,* etc. are used to mark an oft-repeated tale or story. The context is generalized; however, the semantics of this verb ('recount') make it somewhat more process-oriented than the simplex. Note the use of *jako* 'how' after the non-past in (364); this construction, indicating that a description follows, does not appear with the simplex *kazati* in this text.

(364) якоже **сказають**. яко велику честь приялъ от ц(а)ря. (10)
 '...*they tell (skazajut')* how he received great honor from the king'

The {-aju} forms of *skazati* can also indicate a story that is told in a book, as with the non-past form *skazaet'* in (365).

(365) си суть людье заклепении Александром Македоньскым ц(е)с(а)-р(е)мь. якож **сказаеть** о них Мефоди папа Римскыи. (235)
 'these are the people imprisoned by King Alexander of Macedon, as Methodius the Roman pope *says (skazaet')* about them...'

They can also introduce an ongoing story; that is, one that appears in a progressive context, as with the participial forms in (366). Example (367) similarly has a progressive context for the participle *skazajušče* 'describing'.

(366) и много гл(агола)ша **сказающе**. от начала миру. о бытьи всего мира. **суть** же хитро **сказающе**. и чюдно слышати их. (106)
 'and they spoke a great deal, *telling (skazajušče)* from the beginning of the world about the whole world's existence, and *they spoke (sut' skazajušče)* so cleverly that it was wondrous to hear them'

(367) и поставиша я на пространьнѣ мѣстѣ. показающе красоту ц(е)-рк(о)вную. пѣнья и службы архиерѣиски престоянье дьяконъ. **сказающе** имъ служенье Б(ог)а своего. (107)
 'and they placed them in a spacious location, showing [them] the beauty of the church, the singing and the services of the archpriests, and the duties of the deacons, *describing (skazajušče)* to them the services for their God'

The forms *skažu* etc. on the other hand, indicate a single act summed up as a whole, as in (368). The use of *pred družinoju* 'before the company' indicates a duration inherent in *skažite* 'tell (imperative)' that is minimized or suppressed in this form.

---

[76] Not to say that such forms will not soon exist in Old Russian. They are quite numerous in fifteenth-century texts, and Sreznevskij lists one form of *skazovati* from the twelfth century, but the bulk of his examples are from the fifteenth century and later. In the period considered here, the dearth of derived forms of *skazati* could stem from the viability of the simplex verb *kazati* in the meaning 'tell, recount'.

(368) реч(е) Володимеръ се придоша послании нами мужи. да слышимъ
       от нихъ бывшее и реч(е) **скажите** пред дружиною (108)
       'Volodimer said: here come the men we sent; let us hear from them what has
       happened, and he said: *tell (skažite)* [your story] before the company'

Example (369) also sums up a lengthy recitation from beginning to end with a single non-past form.

(369) се же не свѣдуще право гл(аголе)ть. яко кр(е)ст(и)лься есть в
       Киевѣ. а инии же рѣша (в) Василиви. друзии же инако **скажють**.
       (111)
       'those who do not know the truth say that he was baptized in Kiev, and others
       said in Vasiliv'; still others *will tell (skažjut')* [it] differently'

Non-past forms like *skažju* 'I (will) say' also indicate events of varying placement in the future. Some indicate an act that will become narrative immediately, as in (370).

(370) О оубьеньи Андрѣевѣ: В то же лѣт(о) оубьенъ быс(ть). великыи
       князь Андрѣи. с(ы)нъ великаго князя Георгия. внукъ Мономаха
       Володимера. оубьенье же его послѣди **скажем**. (367)
       'About the murder of Andrej. In that year Grand Prince Andrej was murdered,
       the son of Grand Prince Georgij, the grandson of Volodimer Monomax, whose
       death we *will* subsequently *recount (skažem)*'

However, the retelling need not follow immediately, but may be at a greater distance from the warning, as in (371).

(371) а о Феодосовѣ житьи (п)акы **скажемъ**. В лѣт(о) 1052. Преставися
       Володимеръ с(ы)нъ Ярославль... (160)
       'and we *will tell (skažem")* about Theodosius's life later. In the year 1052,
       Volodimer, son of Jaroslav, died...'

The future act may also be predicated on a preexisting condition, as in (372). In this instance, it opens the way for a lengthy story.

(372) аще хощеши послушати да **ска(жю)** ти. из начала. чьсо ради сниде
       Б(ог)ъ на землю. (87)
       'if you wish to hear [it], then I *will tell (ska[žju])* you from the beginning for
       what reason God came down upon the earth'

The aorist and infinitive forms of *skazati* in (373)-(378) generally fall in line with the *skažu*-type meanings, not with the progressive and generalized contexts where the *skazaju* forms are found. In numerous instances, the aorist summarizes a speech or description, as in (373)-(375). In (373), for instance, a prior message is referred to.

(373) и созва философы вся. и **сказа** имъ рѣчи вся Словѣньскихъ князь. и реша Философи... (26)
'and he called all his philosophers together and *recounted (skaza)* to them the speeches of all the Slavic princes, and the philosophers said...'

(374) а остатокъ бьеных тѣх. бѣжаша дружинѣ своеи. гдѣ бяху переже вѣсть послали. и **сказаша** имъ свою погыбель. (398)
'and the remainder of the beaten ones fled to their companies where they had earlier sent news, and *told (skazaša)* them of their decimation'

(375) и створиша миръ якож в прежнее лѣт(о) **сказахъ**. (273)
'and they made peace, as I *told about (skazax")* in last year['s entry]'

The infinitive frequently has the same function, summarizing a potential description, as in (376).

(376) Се же хощю **сказати** яже слышах преж сих 4 лѣт. яже **сказа** ми Гюрятя Роговичь. Новгородець. (234)
'Here I want *to tell (skazati)* what I heard four years ago, which Gjurjata Rogovič the Novgorodian *told (skaza)* me'

The negated infinitive is used in (377) to indicate an inability to fully, completely, or adequately describe an event; the action negated is thus perfective-like.

(377) оукраси св(ят)ую ц(е)рк(о)вь... иконами многоцѣньнами. ихже нѣс(ть) мощи и **сказати**. (458)
'he decorated the holy church...with invaluable icons, which it is not possible even *to describe (skazati)*'

The infinitive is, however, occasionally used in a more general sense. In (378) it lends a sense of completion to the act, but also could imply a lengthy act, albeit one summarized to some extent.

(378) и послѣте ны учителя. иже ны могуть **сказати** книжная словеса и разумъ их. (26)
'send us teachers who can *tell (skazati)* us the words of the Book and their meaning'

Conclusions. The multiplicity of meanings and lexical classes has a traceable impact on the development and distribution of prefixed forms. Those lexemes prone to more processual readings, like *nakazati* and its derivatives, are more likely to find imperfective-like contexts and tense forms appearing with the base *nakaza-*. Those with a less obvious processual reading and less semantic connection to the simplex verb, like *pokazati* and its derivatives, are more likely to have a greater range of derived forms. There is also a greater chance that the base form *pokaza-* will be read as protoperfective, thanks to the punctual nature of the act. The verb *skazati*, which also has a tendency toward punctuality, is further influenced by its similarity with the meaning of the simplex verb *kazati,* and if *skazati* can be said to have an aspectual "partner" in this text, then the only verb that fits this description is the simplex *kazati*. Certain processual vs. nonprocessual distinctions are expressed by the specialized forms *skazaju* etc.

The semantics of the individual verbs—as well as their relations to the semantics of the simplex from which they are formed—play an important role in determining the aspectual properties and the range of forms available to each verb in this text.

4.18. HYPERTELIC ACTS

Hypertelic predicates include telos within their limits. For the purpose of this study (which classes acts according to the possibility of duration and telos), the only acts that will be discussed under this heading are semelfactives.[77] **Semelfactives** are predicates whose action is by nature so instantaneous that it cannot be perceived as a process. A series of these actions will, however, often be perceived as a seamless whole, although it is made up of discrete acts. They are represented in Old Russian and Modern Russian by simplexes and verbs suffixed with {-nu-}, as well as by prefixed verbs.

Other verbs—a classic example is the modern pair *prixodit'* –*prijti* 'arrive'—are not "instantaneous" acts in the same sense but nonetheless cannot be conceived of as a process. The imperfectives of such verbs are in a sense defective; they occur in iterative contexts, not progressive or durative ones, and only by extending the concept of iterativity can they appear in generalized ones.

This latter type, however, is always formed by prefixation in both Old Russian and Modern Russian; since there are no simplexes to discuss, such verbs will appear under the appropriate heading.

4.19. SEMELFACTIVES *(STRĚLITI)*

The verb *strěliti* 'shoot' expresses a single, swift, indivisible act; it is attested three times in the Chronicles. Its unprefixed derivative, *strěljati*, is attested fifteen times. One prefixed form is used, *rasstrěljati*, which is attested three times.

This verb behaves like a protoperfective in (379)-(381). The aorist in (379) indicates that someone loosed a single arrow with a message attached.

(379) и (се) мужь Корсунянинъ **стрѣли** имянемъ Настасъ напсавъ сице на стрѣлѣ. (109)
'and a man from Korsun named Nastas *loosed a shot (strěli),* having written this on the arrow...'

---

[77] In a more complete description of the verbal system, such as that given by Kučera, this class would include all perfective-type verbs, since they include the attainment of telos, and there would have to be subclasses of hypertelicity.

In (380), one round of arrows is probably loosed, since the past participle is portrayed as a quick act, after which the archers take flight from the Huns.

(380) и **стрѣливше** побѣгнуша предъ угры. (271)
'and, *having shot (strělivše),* they fled before the Huns'

In (381), the subject has notched his bow—intending to fire (infinitive) at least once—when he is struck down.

(381) Мстиславу же хотящю **стрѣлити**. снезапу оударенъ быс(ть) подъ пазуху стрѣлою. (272)
'Mstislav, intending *to shoot (strěliti),* was suddenly shot under the bosom by an arrow'

As opposed to other verbs with unprefixed derivatives, *strěliti* is less common than the derived form, *strěljati*. This is certainly due to the nature of the act; any expression of process will require the derived form, not the semelfactive form.

Virtually all the examples of *strěljati* occur in imperfective-like contexts. In this class of verbs, however, all progressive, durative and general contexts contain iterativity as an essential component; no prolongation of the act can be found that does not also involve a repetition of the semelfactive event. The present participles in (382)-(384) are in progressive contexts, showing multiple simultaneous acts.

(382) Печенѣзи оустремишася на нь. **стрѣляюще** его. (66)
'the Pečenegs headed towards him, *shooting (strěljajušče)* at him'

(383) единою поступиша к граду под вежеми. овѣм же бьющим с града. и **стрѣляющим** межи собою. идяху стрѣлы акы дождь. (271)
'once they approached the town underneath the towers, some fighting from the town, and [others] *shooting (strěljajuščim)* between themselves; arrows flew like rain'

(384) наши же... поидоша противу имъ **стрѣляюще** я. (445)
'our men... went against them, *shooting (strěljajušče)* at them'

However, the context in (385) is durative, the past participle being temporally limited by the adverbial phrase *do večera* 'until evening' and the following actions.

(385) **стрѣлявшим** же **ся** им до вечера. и възвратившася опят. (333)
'*having shot at each other (strěljavšim sja)* until evening, they retreated back...'

In (386), Andrej is laying out his plans for the coming battle; the supine *strěljatsja* indicates inceptivity (i.e., that they will begin to fire on their enemies) but also implies that shooting will continue for a while (and is thus to a certain extent both progressive and iterative).

(386) тако створим. атъ язъ почну д(е)нь свои. поим же дружину свою и ѣха подъ городъ. вышедшимъ же пѣшимъ из города **стрѣлятся** и поткну⁷⁸ на нь с дружиною своею и с Половци... (339)

' "let us do it this way: I will start the day." Having taken his company, he rode up to the town. Those who came out of the town on foot *to shoot (strěljatsja)* fell on him and his company and the Polovtsians...'

Example (387) is an imperative in a generalized context (an exhortation not to shoot at all, or a general prohibition).

(387) а посем рекоша Татарове Володимерцем. **не стрѣляите**. (461)
'and then the Tatars said to the people of Volodimer: *do not shoot (ne strĕljaite)!*'

The difference between lexical and contextual iterativity is made clear in (388); lexical iterativity is present, of course, but so is contextual iterativity, as the scene is repeated several times, hence the imperfect *strĕljaxu*.

(388) ихже емше овѣхъ растинаху. другия аки страни поставляюще. и **стрѣляху** въ ня. измахуть опакы руцѣ съвязывахуть. гвозди желѣзныи посреди главы въбивахуть ихъ. (44)
'and having seized them, they crucified some of them; and, setting others to one side, *they shot (strĕljaxu)* into them, seized them, tied their hands in back, [and] drove iron nails through their head[s]'⁷⁹

The derived prefixed verb *rastrĕljati* is less clearly protoimperfective. Examples (389) and (390) are respectively progressive and iterative contexts, but (391) is without doubt a protoperfective event. Once again we can look to object distribution for an explanation. All the forms show the distribution of a set of actions over a set of patients (a number of people shoot a number of other people), and this act can be perceived either as in progress at the time, as with the imperfects in (389) and (390), or as a bounded event in a series, as with the aorist in (391).

(389) овѣхъ посекаху дроугиа же мучахоу. иныя же **растреляхоу**. а дроугыя в море вметахоу. (30)
'some they cut up, others they tortured, still others *they shot (rastreljaxou)* and yet others they threw into the sea'

(390) ихже емше овы растинахуть. другыя же стрѣлами **растрѣлаху** в ня. а ини опакы руцѣ связывахуть. (460)
'when they seized them, they crucified some of them; for others, *they shot (rastrĕlaxu)* into them, and tied their hands in back'

---

⁷⁸ The account is somewhat confused here; I am reading *potknu* as if for *potknuša* 'they fell (aorist 3 pl.)' to make some sense out of the narrative.

⁷⁹ This sentence, which first appeared as example (143) above, is discussed in greater detail as example (124) in chapter 5.

(391) а заоутра по зори повѣсиша Василя. и Лазаря. и **растрѣляша** стрѣлами Василковичи. и идоша от града. (268)
'and in the morning after sunrise they hanged Vasilij and Lazar', and *shot (rastrěljaša)* Vasilij's men with arrows, and left the city'

In fact, this verb seems analogous to *rasstavljati* in section 4.10, in which the prefix {raz-} is used as a perfectivizer regardless of the suffixation. The variation in usage will, in this case, eventually be resolved in favor of the perfective aspect, since *rasstreljat'* is perfective in Modern Russian.

Conclusions. Semelfactives behave much like verbs of the highly telic category, except that iterativity is an added component of all the derived forms' progressive, durative and generalized contexts due to the verbs' lexical meaning.

4.20. PRELIMINARY CONCLUSIONS ABOUT ASPECT

This initial review of several verbs from the Primary Chronicles and the Suzdal' Chronicles has suggested a number of ways in which Old Russian aspect differs from Modern Russian aspect.

4.20.1. Contextual factors and the genesis of aspect

Foremost among these is the influence of context on aspect, which is considerable in Old Russian. First, we have seen that iterativity, which is often considered an automatic trigger for the imperfective aspect in Modern Russian, is compatible with all sorts of forms in Old Russian, depending on the lexical contour of the event. This matter will be taken up in more detail in chapter 5.

If iterativity falls outside the category of protoimperfective verbs, then we must look to progressive and generalized contexts as the most strongly protoimperfective contexts in the earliest stages of Russian aspect. This study strongly supports the conclusions of Maslov that the perfective and imperfective aspects did not arise from complementary categories, such as determinate vs. indeterminate verbs, or progressive vs. non-progressive aspects, but rather result from the convergence of two related and overlapping categories, such as *realized telicity* in the case of the perfective and *duration* in the case of the imperfective. It furthermore suggests that the perfective aspect was the more clearly defined in Old Russian, and that the set of functions and usages we now call "imperfectivity" had not yet coalesced but was far more differentiated by lexical class than it is now.

One fact was mentioned in passing that deserves to be reiterated: while simplex and derived forms are usually found in progressive or general contexts when their predicates are nonpunctual telics (like those from *staviti* 'build'), the nonpunctual telic predicates (like *prositi* 'ask' and its derivatives) tend to appear in iterative contexts, not progressive ones.[80]

---

[80] This tendency is not as clearly marked with derivatives of *kazati*, due to wider variation—from punctual to nonpunctual—in the meanings of this verb.

Furthermore, the large number of aspectually neutral verbs means that context plays a large role in determining whether the action is perceived as reaching its limit or not. For these verbs, the aspect is far less important than the tense (see section 4.13 and discussion of *ostaviti* in section 4.10.6) and other external factors in determining the meaning.

4.20.2. The place of lexical aspect

One of the points that comes through most strongly in the analysis presented above is the lack of a single factor controlling aspectual assignment and function in Old Russian. Unlike in Modern Russian, we cannot look to a system of grammatical aspect characterized by a binary opposition. Nor can we replace this with another binary opposition of determinate vs. indeterminate; the data above contradict any such simple protoaspectual system. Instead, we find a sliding scale of lexical groupings that demonstrate different affinities for aspectual behavior. Chart 4.20.2.1 organizes the distribution of aspectual affinities for the verbs treated in this chapter.[81]

Chart 4.20.2.1. Aspectual affinities of various Old Russian verbs

Protoperfective	sobljusti, umereti, povoevati, streliti, isprositi, uvideti, udiviti sja, -suditi, -iskati, -staviti
Largely protoperfective (but with anaspectual traits)	skazati, pokazati, rasstavljati, vosstavljati
Nearly anaspectual (but with protoperfective traits)	ostaviti, nakazati, vprašati, sprašati
Anaspectual	prositi, suditi, kazati, knjažiti, diviti sja
Anaspectual (but with protoimperfective traits)	stojati, videti, voevati, rasstreljati
Largely protoimperfective (but with anaspectual traits)	ostojati, etc., bljusti, staviti
Protoimperfective	sobljudati, iskati, umirati, streljati, divovati sja, udivljati sja, -iskivati, -stavljati

---

[81] The scale proposed here should be completely gradual, with each verb occupying its own slot on the cline, but for the sake of simplicity and easy comparison I have arranged the verbs into groups with more or less similar behavior.

As noted earlier, there is no simple way to define these distributions. To review earlier conclusions, I stated that a classification by aspectual pairability à la Maslov does not necessarily give us either a logical classification by telos or a system that reflects the distribution of forms and meanings in Old Russian. For this reason I chose to separate natural conatives from the atelic class, which implies redefining telicity to include not only telic points that are realizable but also those that are clearly unrealizable.

This argument about the centrality of process for the imperfective aspect has implications for the rest of the telic predicates as well. Telic predicates show a wide distribution of usages, with some simplexes tending towards imperfectivity and some towards perfectivity. As mentioned above, the crucial factor here may be the basicness or centrality of the process. In some predicates a notion of completion is more basic or natural to the action, while in others process is more basic or neutral. In a third group, more variation is seen, and in a fourth group result precedes any notion of process. At the very simplest, then, the factors that create various lexical groups include the presence or absence of telicity and the centrality of process. I do not think it will be possible to reduce these factors to a single one, and it may prove necessary to add further ones. This analysis points in the direction of a more detailed reconciliation of the grammatical notion of aspect and lexical categories.

4.20.3. The expansion of both Old Russian aspects

Another related issue is the status of the protoperfective verbs considered in this chapter. In at least three separate cases *(podiviti sja* 'be amazed', *povoevati* 'fight a battle, win a war, conquer', *uvidĕti* 'see, glimpse') the verbs indicated, while clearly protoperfective, had a much narrower range of functions and usages than do modern perfectives. This ties in nicely with the observation that Old Russian had far fewer prefixes causing pure perfectivization and far more causing Aktionsart modifications, spatial limitations, and more fundamental shifts of basic lexical meaning. In all three of these cases, verbs that appear originally to have had a substantially different meaning have been gradually deprived of their initial primary functions and have come mainly to serve as the protoperfective component of a newly protoimperfective verb. For these verbs, contrary to Maslov and Borodič,[82] the protoimperfective represents a narrowing of the verb's original use while the

---

[82] Both Maslov and Borodič, in their historical analyses, conclude that the perfective aspect develops out of an earlier category *(opredelennost'* 'determinacy' for Borodič, *predel'nost'* 'terminativity' for Maslov) as a narrowing of its functions, while the imperfective aspect develops out of a different category *(neopredelennost'* 'indeterminacy' for both scholars) as a broadening of its functions. The difficulty here is in the "narrowing" statement, not in Maslov's interpretation of telicity (or, more precisely, realized telicity) as the basis for the perfective; I would prefer to see both the perfective and imperfective aspects in a general state of expansion throughout the Old Russian period, as opposed to a picture in which the imperfect expands while the perfective contracts.

protoperfective takes on wider usage as a member of the aspectual opposition. This replacement of lexical meaning with grammatical function is characteristic of morphological units, according to Traugott 1982, and the fact that this process seems to take place mainly with atelic acts bears further witness to the lexically dependent character of Old Russian aspect.

Lexical groups are crucial to spreading the applicability of the protoimperfective aspect through the various contexts discussed above. If we assume that iterativity at some point becomes a marker of imperfectivity whereas in the Chronicles it clearly is not, the question is how and why this shift could have taken place. This matter will be taken up in greater detail in chapter 5 and subsequent discussions.

5. More Issues from the Chronicles

5.0. INTRODUCTION

In the last chapter, I used a detailed exegesis of a few verbs in the Chronicles to set up a probable aspectual system for Old Russian. I presented the evidence as synchronic data; that is, I treated the Chronicles as if they were a single text written in a more or less uniform style. This approach yielded a broad base of examples and a grasp of the overall usage patterns of each verb, but also allowed me to propose hypotheses about the state of aspect represented in the text.

Such hypotheses, of course, represent only the beginning of a study. First, I have yet to prove that these hypotheses do in fact apply to the verbal lexicon at large; for this purpose, I will draw examples from the remaining verbs in the database. Second, the relationship between aspect and certain contexts needs to be fleshed out, as well as how these usage patterns relate to the previously defined lexical classes. Third, the fact remains that the Chronicles were certainly not written as a single unified work but represent rather the labor of various chroniclers and numerous scribes over several hundred years. As such, the Chronicles may contain historical strata that differ as regards the development of aspect. While this last point is of secondary significance in this study, it will at points have an effect on the way I interpret the data.

5.1. OVERVIEW OF CHAPTER STRUCTURE

In this chapter, I will round up the factors influencing aspectuality discussed in the previous chapter and briefly treat them feature by feature, instead of verb by verb. To determine the aspectuality of a simplex verb, I used four criteria: the temporal assignment of the non-past form, the usage patterns of the infinitive, the distribution of form and meaning in the preterite tenses, and the apparent aspectual assignment of prefixed forms of the verb. In sections 5.2 through 5.5 following, the first three of these criteria will be examined from the point of view of different lexical classes to further strengthen the argument that aspect has a clear grammatical shape only in certain parts of the Old Russian verbal system in this period.[1]

The remainder of the chapter treats a number of other features of the verbal system that interact closely with aspectual assignment and lexical class. Section 5.6

---

[1] The fourth criterion, prefixation, is treated in section 5.7.

explores lexical classes and their interaction with the imperfect tense. In sections 5.7 through 5.9, I will consider the phenomenon of prefixation and its effect on aspectual formation; the late appearance of simplex verbs in the text; and the competition betwseen suffixed verbs and simplex verbs. (The usage patterns of motion verbs and their prefixed forms will be treated under prefixation in section 5.7.) Some of these factors appear only at certain points in the text. Where there is reason to suppose that chronology plays a role, this contention will be investigated.

5.2. ASPECTUALITY IN NON-PAST FORMS

The crucial status of the non-past tense in determining aspect is evident in discussions of both Modern Russian and Old Russian. One of the chief claims for aspect as a Modern Russian grammatical category is the difference of inflectional patterns for perfective and imperfective verbs. The clearest of these is the presence of a periphrastic future tense that can be formed only from imperfective verbs (thus, *budu čitat'^{I}* 'I will be reading^I' or even *budu pročityvat'^{I}* 'I will be reading through^I' are grammatical, but **budu pročitat'^{P}* is not). The most straightforward way to prove that Old Russian has a regular aspectual system would be to find a similar feature.

From a look at the Old Russian data, however, it is clear that this inflectional support for aspect is lacking: Old Russian does not have a synthetic future tense sensitive to aspect. It has periphrastic constructions with *imati* and *xotěti*, but these are less helpful, since both protoperfective and protoimperfective forms can follow. Another possibility, then, for proving the grammaticality of aspect in Old Russian is to propose that regular distinctions in function show the presence of grammatical rules. Under this assumption, the non-past tense of a protoperfective verb should express future action, while the non-past tense of a protoimperfective verb should express present or timeless action.[2] While there is support for this claim, it is far from universal. Acts that are both telic and nonpunctual do have a morphological reflection similar to their Modern Russian one, with presentness and futurity in the non-past correlating with aspectual assignment. For acts that are punctual and/or atelic, presentness and futurity are not delimited by complementary verb forms in Old Russian and do not correlate with any sort of aspectual description.

5.2.1. Nonpunctual telic acts with non-past forms

Telic acts in Old Russian have roughly the same distribution of forms found in Modern Russian: non-past forms of protoperfectives express futurity, and non-past forms of protoimperfectives express presentness. There are occasional exceptions, but these mostly fall into regular patterns that indicate differences in context or syntax between Old Russian and Modern Russian.

---

[2] Of course, if we were looking at Old Russian protoperfectives, we would want to allow for the possibility of a form like the Modern Russian *nagljadno-primernoe značenie* 'exemplary meaning', where perfectives express irregularly repeated acts.

Non-past forms are far less common than preterite forms in the Chronicles and are found in a limited number of contexts. They are most often found in reported or direct speech. Given this smaller corpus, I decided not to limit the samples to simplex verbs, so prefixed and suffixed verbs are included as well.

Non-past forms with present meaning usually describe an ongoing action in this text. Example (1), from the epigraph to the Primary Chronicle, refers to the reader.

(1)   а иже **чтеть** книгы сия. то буди ми въ м(о)л(и)твахъ   (286)
        'he who *reads (čtet')* these words, let him remember me in his prayers'

Similarly, (2) describes the activity the addressee is engaged in, and (3) is a speech act ('we *bow* to you' = 'by saying this we submit to you').

(2)   ты княже чюжея земли **ищеши** и блюдеши. а своея ся охабивъ.   (67)
        'you, o prince, *are searching for (iščeši)* and watching over another's land, while having abandoned your own'

(3)   а нонѣ не имѣи на нас гнѣва. аще есмы воевали на своего брата оже нас не слушаеть. а тобѣ **ся кляняем**. а мужѣ твои пущаем (403)
        'and now do not have anger toward us; for if we made war on our brother who does not obey us, still we bow *(sja klanjaem)* to you, and release your men'

Example (4) also has a progressive reading, although this action is synchronized with a past action.

(4)   начах тужити еда како на страну **копаемъ**.   (210)
        'I began to despair that we *were digging (kopaem")* to one side [of it]'

More generalized statements appear in (5) and (6), respectively about the nature of demons and what heaven is like.

(5)   а бѣси на злое всегда **ловять**.   (135)
        'and demons always *hunt (lovjat')* [men] for evil'

(6)   но скрываите собѣ скровище на н(е)б(е)сѣх. идеже ни тля **тлить** ни татье **крадуть**.   (125)
        '...but lay in treasures for yourself in Heaven, where no moth *corrupts (tlit')*, nor do thieves *steal (kradut')*' [3]

Similar in character is (7); 'they *deceive (lžjut')* God and you as well' does not mean the action is occurring at the moment of speech, but rather presents a universal fact: that it is the habit of demons to deceive.

(7)   они княже Б(ого)ви **лжють** и тобѣ.   (386)

---

[3] Matthew 6:19.

All attestations of these verbs in the non-past are found with a present or gnomic sense, and this generalization holds for all similar verbs that represent telic acts, so long as these actions do not have a punctual reading. The apparent exceptions are of two sorts. First, a verb with the exhortative *da* can have a future sense even where we might otherwise expect a present reading. Second, a verb that is usually read as telic can have an atelic reading. In this case, the non-past reading cannot be predicted based on the usual telic usage.

In (8), the "if-then" clause shows future modality; it would be hard or impossible to give it a present reading, since it is predicated on an eventuality. The use of *pišju* instead of *napiš(j)u* is troubling, unless it is read as a periphrastic imperative, a way of expressing the signatory's obligations in a hypothetical future.

(8) аще ли **хотѣти начнеть** наше ц(а)р(с)тво от васъ воина противящаяся намъ. **да пишю** къ великому князю вашему. и **послеть** къ намъ елико же хочемъ. (52)[4]

'if our kingdom *should begin to want (xotěti načnet')* troops from you against our enemies, *let me write (da pišju)* to your grand prince, and *he will send (poslet")* us as many as we want'

This usage occurs only with simplex verbs, perhaps because they have a wider range of meaning than the suffixed verbs, and can thus accommodate a one-time, completed act in the way that suffixed verbs cannot. A similar use of *da* with the verb *voevati* 'make war' is seen in (9).

(9) тогда аще просить вои оу насъ князь Рускии. да **воюеть**. да дамъ ему елико ему будеть требѣ. (51)

'then if the Russian prince asks us for troops *so he might make war (da vojujet')*, I will give him as many as he shall need'

The future modality of (9) can also be pinned to the predicate's lexical class, which is atelic (the prince wants men to fight; no goal is specified or implied).

The second sort of exception (for verbs in this group expressing future meaning) appears in (10), where the "if-then" structure indicates futurity with the verb *praviti*, usually classed as protoimperfective and telic.

(10) да аще сего **не правимъ**. то болшее зло встанеть на нас. и начнет брат брата закалати. и погыбнеть земля Руская. (262)

'if *we do not fix (ne pravim")* this, then a greater evil will descend upon us, and brother will begin to stab brother, and the Russian land will perish'

Because in this instance *praviti* does not mean 'direct, lead' but rather 'fix, amend', this reading is therefore punctual, and the simplex can express futurity.[5]

---

4 Discussed also below as example (177).
5 The particle *da* cannot form an imperative in this example; rather, it means 'and'. Unlike the usage of *da* in (8) and (9), there is no sense of future modality attached to the

So far, the "if-then" constructions I looked at have all clearly shown futurity in both parts, but this need not be the case. If the context does not clearly indicate present or future, the potential aspect of verbs in the sentence is often mixed. (Sentences of this type will be discussed more fully in section 5.2.4 below.) Consequently, I have avoided using such clauses in the examples below of futurity; this substantially limited the sample size, since most attestations of "future" events are in fact conditional statements whose futurity is ambiguous.

Examples (11)-(17) all contain telic acts with a future sense. There does not seem to be a substantial difference between simplex verbs and prefixed verbs in this case; verbs like *pasti* 'fall', *plěniti* 'imprison', and *stupiti* 'step, set foot, enter' reliably indicate futurity for non-past forms, as can be seen in (11)-(13).

(11) реч(е) аще можеши противитися мнѣ то се есмъ здѣ. ουже **плѣню** твою (землю). (478)
'he said: if you can resist me, then I am here; already I *will take* your land *captive (plěnju)*'

(12) от Г(осподнь)а стопы ч(е)л(о)в(ѣ)ку исправятся. егда **ся падеть и не разбьетьс(я)**. яко Г(о)с(под)ь подъемлеть руку его. (242)
'man's steps shall be directed by the Lord; if *he should fall (sja padet')*, he will *not be crushed (ne razb'et's[ja])*, for the Lord will hold up his hand'

(13) аще ли не хочета. то нам неволя зажгоша град свои **ступим** в Гречьску землю. (173)
'if you will not [do this], then, against our will, having burned our town, we *will head for (stupim)* the Greek land'[6]

In (13), the action is also imminent. Prefixed verbs express futurity, predicated on certain preconditions in (14).

(14) да аще мя просити право то пришлите мужа нарочиты. да в велицѣ чти **приду за** вашь князь. еда **не пустят** мене людье Киевьстии. (57)[7]
'and if you are to ask for my hand properly, then send your best men, and in great honor I *will marry (pridu za)* your prince, for otherwise the people of Kiev *will not release (ne pustjat)* me'

(15) да бы ны оупередити до Гюргя. а любо и **проженем**. ли **примирим** к собѣ. (342)

---

particle in (10). This explanation also takes care of Ruzicka's claim that *praviti* is nonaspectual in Old Russian (1957: 28), as mentioned in section 3.5.2.

[6] I read *zažegše* with the Radzivil and Academy mss. instead of the Laurentian's *zažgoša*.
[7] The Radzivil and Academy mss. have *da ašče mja* **prosite** 'and if you *ask*', which makes more sense here.

'let us go first to Gjurgij, and either we *will drive (proženem)* him *out*, or we *will ally (primirim)* him with us'

(16) егда кто вѣсть кто **одолѣеть** мы ли онѣ ли. (46)
'when who knows who *will prevail (odolěet')*, we or they'

(17) и **наполнятся** гумна ваша пшеницѣ. (169)
'and your barns *will fill (napolnjatsja)* with grain'

The few instances where temporal assignment is unclear are in iterative contexts and will be discussed later. Non-past forms of telic nonpunctual predicates, then, show temporal assignment that correlates with modern aspectual assignment. It suggests that these verbs behave like protoperfectives if futurity is expressed and like protoimperfectives if a present or gnomic sense is expressed. This hypothesis will be tested further in coming sections.

5.2.2. Atelic acts with non-past forms

While fewer verbs express atelic acts than telic acts, the frequency of atelic acts and their centrality in the lexicon make them indispensable to a study of aspect. Most atelic predicates are found with imperfective verbs in Modern Russian. The distribution of non-past usage, however, does not correspond strictly to this tentative aspectual assignment. Instead, verbs in this category express either presentness or futurity. Most verbs have a bias in one direction, but this is a tendency, not a rule.

While the Old Russian verb *biti* 'hit, strike' is not atelic, the reflexive form has the meaning 'fight, do battle', which is atelic. Of eight examples of *biti sja* in the non-past, five have future meaning of the sort shown in (18)-(21). Sometimes the future character is implied by context, as in (18), which is a prediction.

(18) и реч(е) Редедя ко Мьстиславу. не оружьемь **ся бьевѣ**. но борьбою. и яста ся бороти крѣпко. (147)
'and Rededja said to Mstislav: not with arms *will we fight (sja b'evě)*, but by wrestling; and they began to wrestle fiercely'

(19) даи княже оружье и кони. и еще **бьемся** с ними. (170)
'o prince, give us guns and horses, and we *will keep fighting (b'emsja)* them'

In (19), the action is pinned on a contingency which functionally is similar to an "if-then" clause. Example (20) presents two options, one with a protoperfective *stvorim* 'we will make', the second with the form *b'emsja* 'we (will) fight'.

(20) а любо с ним миръ створим. али с ним **бьемся**. (315)
'either we will make peace with them, or we *will fight (b'emsja)* with them'.[8]

---

8   This could also be read as a 1. pl. imperative, but note that in this case, we have to account for the fact that Old Russian does not distinguish the 1. pl. imperative of a

(21) Оугри же пьяни величахуться рекуще. аще на ны придут **бьемся** с нимь. (336)
'if they march on us, we *will fight (b'emsja)* them'

Slightly more problematic is (21), since it presents an "if-then" condition, but the single-time, future sense of the sentence is evident. Example (22) has a progressive context with presentness shading into futurity (cf. the Modern Russian translation: *ne budem bit'sja za nix* 'we will not fight for them/let us not fight for them').

(22) и рѣша Д(а)в(и)дови. выдаи мужи сия. **не бьемъся** за сихъ. а за тя битися можем. (268)
'and they said to David: give up these men; we *will not fight (ne b'emsja)* for them, but for you we can fight'

Similar vacillation between future and present for stative predicates can be seen with other verbs. A present or gnomic sense—as expected—is seen in (23)-(26). In (23) the stative *žiti* 'live' is used; in (24), the perpetual fear of demons is described.

(23) иже **жиоуть** въ странахъ полунощныхъ. (11)
'those who *live (žiout')* in the northern countries'

(24) бѣси бо Б(ог)а **боятся** (135)
'for devils *are afraid (bojatsja)* of God'

(25) Половци законъ **держать** о(те)ць своих. кровь проливати а хваляще о сихъ. (16)
'The Polovtsians *hold (deržat')* to the law of their fathers: to pour blood and revel in these things'

(26) а ты **держишь** ворогы своѣ просты. а се ворози твои и наши Суждалци. и Ростовци. любо и казни. любо слѣпи. али даи нам (385)
'and you *leave (deržiš')* your enemies free; either punish these enemies of yours and ours, the Suzdalites and the Rostovites, or blind them or give them to us'

Futurity is seen in (27), although this could easily be blamed on the presence of an exhortative *da* and the formulaic quality of the statement.

(27) единою просих от Г(о)сп(однь)а. того взищю. **да живу** в дому Г(о)с(под)ни вся дни живота моего. (433)

---

protoperfective like *stvorim* from that of *biti sja*. Modern Russian distinguishes between perfective imperatives, in which the non-past stands alone as in Old Russian, and imperfective imperatives, which require a compound form with *budem* or *davaj(te)*.

'one thing I asked from the Lord I will obtain: *that I might live (da živu)* in the house of the Lord all the days of my life'[9]

(28) и аще мя вдасть Ляхом **не боюся** см(е)рти. (266)
'if you betray me to the Poles, I *will not fear (ne bojusja)* death'

Example (28), however, clearly refers to an impending act, hence its future modality. The picture in (29) is more complicated.

(29) но первомоу убо словоу. да оумиримся с вами Грекы. **да любим** друг друга от всеа д(у)ша и изволениа. и не вдадим елико наше изволение быти от соущих. по рукою наших (князь) свѣтлых. никакомоу соблазну или винѣ... (33)
'but by our first word, let us make peace with you Greeks, *and let us begin to love/that we might love (da ljubim)* each other with all our hearts and wills, and inasmuch as it is in our power, we will not permit any deception or crime from those under the direction of our serene princes...'

Although I have already hypothesized that *da* plus the indicative forms an exhortation, the situation here can be read differently. The two other predicates in the sentence indicate acts with clear inception points: 'make peace' and 'permit, give in'. If we read *ljubim* this way, an inceptive component is added to it that it lacks in Modern Russian (hence Lixačev's translation *stanem^P ljubit'* 'we will begin^P to love'). The hint of inceptivity in the Old Russian form suggests that more is going on here than a simple present-to-future transformation.

The clearest and most interesting examples are (30) and (31). Example (30) presents a speech act in a progressive context.

(30) **молим ти ся** раби твои. (256)
'*we,* your slaves, *pray (molim sja)* to you'

(31) пошли ты моуж(а) своег(о). ко свату своему. а я слю своег(о) моуж(а). ко о(т)цю и г(оспод)ноу великому князю Всеволоду. и ты ся моли. и я **ся молю**. абы ти дал Киевъ опят. (419)
'you send your man to your child's father-in-law, and I will send my man to my father and lord, the grand prince Vsevolod; you pray, and I *will pray (sja molju)* too that he return Kiev to you'

In contrast, the futurity of the second clause in (31) is easy to establish, since the form *molju sja* 'I (will) pray' is parallel to the imperative *moli sja* 'pray!', with the bipartite conjunction *i... i...* 'both... and...' suggesting that both actions will be performed at the same time. The atelic act of praying is summed up here in a single moment. This usage of *moliti sja* verges perilously on being not atelic, but rather telic and punctual, de-emphasizing prayer as action and emphasizing prayer as an

---

[9] Seen in chapter 4 as examples (204) and (306).

act of communication. In this way, a link appears between the atelic and telic punctual classes that will be of interest later in this discussion.

5.2.3. Punctual telic acts with non-past forms

Punctual telic acts, unlike nonpunctual telic acts, have a distribution similar to atelic acts. Simplex verbs are either present or future in sense, regardless of expected aspectual assignment. Examples are infrequent, but indicate future meaning about a quarter of the time where present meaning is expected (based on Modern Russian assignment), and vice-versa. Future sense is more common with verbs representing abstract, punctual acts, such as (32)-(34).

(32)   и возму землю Лядьскую. и **мьщю** Русьскую землю. (266)
        'I will take the Polish land, and *will avenge (m'ščju)* the Russian land'

(33)   яко кровь с(ы)н(о)въ своихъ мщаеть и **мстить**. (268)
        'for he avenges and *will avenge (mstit')* the blood of his sons'

(34)   аще **ся миришь** с братьею своею. а мои люди чему выдаешь. (403)
        'if you *should make peace (sja miriš')* with your brothers, then what will you betray my men to?'

However, future meaning is also possible with communicative acts; note the form *slju* 'I (will) send' in (31) above, which we would expect to express present meaning, but has a future sense instead ('send' is a communicative act in that it means 'give a message to someone and a directive to leave'). Likewise, in (35), *čto otvěščaete* can mean either 'what *will* you *answer?*' or 'what *do* you *answer?*'

(35)   да что оума придасте. что **отвѣщаете**. (107)

Punctual abstract acts like *m'stiti* 'avenge' and *javiti sja* 'appear' can also have a present or gnomic sense, as in (36) and (37).

(36)   не **мьстить** бо Г(о)с(под)ь дважды о томь. (224)
        'for the Lord *does not punish (ne m'stit')* twice for the same thing'

(37)   и боуд(е)ть казнь. якож **явитьс(я)** согрешенье о сем. (34)
        'the punishment will be according to what the transgression *shall appear to be (javit'sja)*'

Both (36) and (37) can correspond to an English future tense, but only with the same gnomic sense. Communicative acts often appear either in progressive contexts, as in (38), which is a speech act, or in generalized contexts, as in (39).

(38)   имуще помощницю в печали и в болѣзни. и от злых всѣх. и тебе **славлю** препѣтая. (255)

'having a helper in sorrow and sickness and against all evils, I *glorify (slavlju)* you in song'

(39)   и рѣша бояре и старци. вѣси княже яко своего никтоже не **хулить** но **хвалить**. (107)
'and the nobles and elders said: you know, o prince, that no one *disparages (xulit')* what is his, but rather *praises (xvalit')* it'

In (39), Volodimer's advisors warn him that he will not be able to make an informed decision about his religion simply from listening to the various religions' emissaries. A more curious example, showing the slippery nature of communicative verbs, is (40).

(40)   Кыяне же рекоша. князь нас **вабить** к Чернигову. (317)
'the Kievans said: the prince *invites (vabit')* us to Černigov'

Here, the non-past signals neither that an invitation is in progress nor that one is expected or generally held to exist. Rather, an invitation was proffered in the past, and it is held to be in force up to the present moment. In a way, the non-past reflects a state rather than an act at this point in the narrative, underscoring another connection between the atelic and punctual telic classes.

5.2.4. Conditional sentences

As mentioned earlier, certain "if-then" conditions do not have a clear future or present sense. These conditions usually describe the result of some potential action, but not an action that is likely to happen just once. Instead, the result will obtain whenever the condition is met; the application of the result is viewed as a law. Therefore, the condition is neither obviously present nor obviously future. The law is currently in effect and thus describes conditions that apply generally in the present, but the way it is stated can also describe one future act and its result. Because a number of treaties and exhortations are found near the beginning of the Primary Chronicle, the data come predominantly from these early sections; however, this seems to be more a stylistic function than a temporal one, since scattered examples are found further on as well.

In this situation, Old Russian, like Modern Russian, does not use aspect to distinguish tense as such. However, Old Russian verbs are more likely to respect lexical groupings in their choice of forms than are Modern Russian verbs, where aspectual consistency is more important. A typical formula for such sentences is found in (41). A predicate in the non-past forms the protasis *(ašče xto xulit'...* 'if anyone should speak ill of the Slavic writings...'), and a predicate preceded by the exhortatory *da* forms the apodosis *(da budet' otlučen...* 'let him be excluded from the church').[10]

---

10   A *protasis* is the 'if' clause of a conditional sentence; an *apodosis* is the 'then' clause.

(41) да аще хто **хулить** Словѣньскую грамоту **да будеть** отлучен от ц(е)ркве. дондеже **ся исправять**. (27)[11]
'and if anyone *should speak ill* of the Slavic writings, *let him be excluded* from the church until he *corrects himself*'

If the protatic predicate is punctual, as in (41) and (43), or atelic, as in (45) and (47)-(49), it will be a protoimperfective or anaspectual form. If the protatic predicate is a nonpunctual telic act, it is more likely to be a protoperfective, as in (44) and (46). There is no prohibition against combining these forms, as in the protasis of (42), where a nonpunctual telic act is protoperfective (*ruku ne dadjat'* 'they will not surrender') and an atelic act is protoimperfective (*protivjatsja* 'they will resist').

(42) аще руку **не дадять** и **противятся**. ди[12] оубьени **будуть**. да **не изищется** см(е)рть ихъ от князя. вашего. (48)
'if they *do not surrender*, and *resist* us, then they will be killed, and their death *will not be sought* from your prince'

Since the exhortatory *da* in the apodosis implies future action, the predicate following it does not need to offer a value for tense; instead it reflects the form most basic to its meaning, a difference that is either aspectual or lexical, depending on the reading of the facts. In some cases a form implying future reading is easily available—as in (41)-(44). The form emphasizes not absolute futurity but relative futurity or temporal distance: the fact that the act in the apodosis is contingent upon the protatic condition and follows it. This is the case in (43). A similar account with nonpunctual telic predicates can be seen in (44).

(43) аше **лучится** кому от лодьи оубеену быти. от нас Роус. или что взято любо **да повинни будуть** то створшии. прежереченною епитемьею. (36)
'if one of us from the boats, from Russia, *should happen* (*lučitsja*) to be killed, or something taken, then those who did it *will be subject* (*da povinni budut'*) to the aforementioned punishment'

(44) аще кто **оубьет** или хрестьанина Русинъ. или хрестьянинъ Роусина. **да оумрет** идѣже аще **сотворит** оубiиство. (34)
'if a Russian *should kill* (*oub'et*) a Christian, or a Christian a Russian, *let him die* (*da oumret*) where he *commits* (*sotvorit*) the murder'[13]

If the predicate is atelic, however, it need not find expression in a protoperfective form. Instead, a simplex verb is adequate to the task, and temporal

---

[11] The Academy and Radzivil mss. have the more logical 3. sg. *ispravit'*, but without the reflexive; the Troitskij ms. had *ispravit'sja*, which makes the most sense.
[12] The Academy and Radzivil mss. have, more comprehensibly, *da*.
[13] Literally, 'where he *shall commit* the murder', once again emphasizing the dependency of this punishment on the occurrence of the protasis.

distance is derived from *da*. The easy compatibility of simplex atelics with protoperfectives can be see in the apodoses of (45) and (46). For an example of atelic simplexes in the protasis, note (45): *est'* 'is', *deržit'sja* 'be held'. Example (46) has an atelic simplex in the apodosis: *mnit'sja* 'be assumed'.

(45)   ащел(и) **ес(ть)** неимовит сотворивыи оубои. и оубежавъ **да держитьс(я)** тяжи. дондеже обрящеть(ся) и **да оумреть**. (34)
'if the man who committed and fled a murder *has (es[t'])* no property, *let* him *be held (da deržit's[ja])* until the matter is resolved, and then *let* him *die (da oumret')*'

(46)   аще **обрящетьс(я)**. ли Русинъ. ли Греченинъ **да възратят** искупное лице въ свою сторону. и **возмоут** цѣну ег(о) коупящіи. или **мнитьс(я)** в коуплю наднь челядинаа цѣна. (36)
'if a Russian or Greek *should be found (obrjaščet's[ja])*, *let* them *return (v"zvratjat)* the captured person to his side, and the buyer *will pay (vozmout)* a price for him, or *there will be assumed (mnit's[ja])* as his ransom the price for a commoner'

Examples (47)-(49) are different from the remaining examples. They do not have an exhortatory *da* in the apodosis; instead of reflecting sequential acts, they imply a causality that is logical, not temporal. The likelihood of an exclusively future reading is low; anaspectual and protoimperfective forms predominate in generalized, repeated, or progressive contexts. The single protoperfective form in this group, *poxvalit'* in (48), is a further result of the apodosis and thus may be more circumscribed or limited by virtue of its distance from the present.

(47)   аще бо наказанья **терпите**. яко с(ы)номъ вамъ **обрѣтается** Б(ог)ъ. (371)[14]
'if you *endure (terpite)* discipline, God *treats (obrětaetsja)* you as sons'

(48)   **хощеши** ли ся власти не бояти. злаго **не твори**, и **похвалить** тя. аще ли зло **творишь боися**. (422)
'if you *want (xoščeši)* not to fear power, then *do (ne tvori)* no evil, and He *will praise (poxvalit')* you; if you *do (tvoriš')* evil, then *be afraid (boisja)*'

(49)   аще кто **пьет** или **ясть**. то все въ славу Б(о)жью. (85)
'if anyone *drinks (p'et)* or *eats (jast')*, then it [is] all for the glory of God'

A nice minimal pair is offered by (41) and (49). Example (41) has sequential acts, favoring a punctual reading of both verbs, whereas (49) has simultaneous acts, favoring an atelic reading of all predicates (including, of course, the zero copula in the apodosis). The difference between ongoing, simultaneous acts and sequenced

---

14   Alternatively, in the Radzivil and Academy mss., *jako synom" svoim"* (from Hebrews 12:7).

acts with clear beginnings and endpoints gives the rationale for the future tense *budet'* 'will be' in (41) and the present tense zero copula in (49).

To summarize: A condition is often constructed so that its effects can be invoked in the present time or reserved for the future. Verbal aspect and lexical features do not indicate presentness or futureness in Old Russian "if-then" sentences of this sort; instead, they indicate the relationships between the acts and the shape of each individual act. This distinction is clearly an aspectual one, but in Old Russian **it need not be encoded in an aspectual marker on the verb if it is already lexically or contextually evident.**

Furthermore, context—particularly words like *da*—frequently gives clues as to the way the acts are related to each other in time and to the present; in other cases, the simple presence of a conditional construction may indicate sequentiality. If sequencing is strongly indicated by context, the predicates may encode this sequencing only weakly, with forms that have little aspectual value. Where sequencing or simultaneity is necessary but largely absent from context, it will usually be clearly marked by verb forms with a strong aspectual value derived from their grammatical aspect or their lexical aspect. A good example of a verb form marking sequence is the telic predicate *poxvalit'* 'he (will) praise' in (48), which indicates an act subsequent to the apodosis *zlago ne tvori* 'do no evil'.

5.2.5. Summary of findings on the non-past

There are two different non-past usage patterns in the Chronicles. The first pattern includes predicates that regularly use the non-past to indicate futurity (protoperfective predicates), and predicates that regularly use the non-past to express present or gnomic events (protoimperfective predicates). These distinctions correspond to the expected aspectual assignment of the verb. I hypothesize that these predicates are aspectual, and that each is assigned to one particular aspect, whose feature in the non-past system is that it indicates the tense of the form as future or present. These predicates belong to lexical classes that are both telic and nonpunctual.

Acts that are atelic and/or punctual have another pattern. Non-past forms can be either future or present; for any given predicate, one sense typically predominates but does not exclude the other. The usage found does not always coincide with the expected aspectual assignment of the verb; some *(deržati* 'hold') are predominantly present, while others *(biti sja* 'fight') are predominantly future. It may be that the limited number of attestations—and their frequency in certain set expressions—exaggerates these tendencies, and that all predicates of these classes have an equal possibility of future or present realization.

It seems curious at first glance that the three largest classes of predicates in this anaspectual pattern—nonpunctual atelic, punctual atelic, and punctual telic—are defined by the presence or absence of two features, telicity and punctuality, and yet they are not marked the same way for either of these features. Statives and atelic actions are atelic and nonpunctual; the third class, made up of abstract acts and communicative acts, is telic and punctual. However, I have demonstrated a number of links between these classes. A communicative act, once complete, may function as a state; taken as an indivisible series of acts, it may be seen as an atelic process. Furthermore, the small but high-frequency class of atelic punctuals *(viděti* 'see', *slyšati* 'hear', *diviti sja* 'be surprised') serves as another link. Atelicity and punctuality favor anaspectuality; telicity and nonpunctuality favor aspectuality.

Certain "if-then" sentences have a different logic of construction that defies labels like "present" and "past." Often the condition is both a statement of current fact and a warning at the same time; lexical and contextual features interact in such sentences to produce a semblance of "grammatical aspect" that is in fact sentential, rather than purely verbal, in nature.

5.3. ASPECTUALITY IN THE INFINITIVE MOOD

The infinitive and supine are promising categories for assessing the reflection of aspect in the verbal system. In the non-past and preterite systems, it is constantly necessary to filter out the effects of tense in order to look at aspect; in the infinitive mood,[15] this is not the case. Nor are the infinitive or supine subject to other partially aspectual distinctions, like those found in participles. It will be easier, then, to ascertain whether a form reflects one or another protoaspect when it is an infinitive or supine.

For the purposes of this analysis, I will ignore any semantic difference between the infinitive and supine forms and ascribe it to their differing contexts, i.e. I will assume that any semantic properties of Old Russian supines as distinct from infinitives can be said to stem from their position as complements of a motion verb. The most frequent contexts for infinitives are: following a phasal verb *(načati* 'start', *končati* 'end'); following a modal predicate *(xotěti* 'want, will', *moči* 'be able', *iměti* 'have, will', *godno* 'it is proper'); to express necessity or prohibition without a modal form; to express possibility or impossibility after the verb *byti* 'be'; to express varying degrees of commands or suggestions contained in a communicative act *(nakazati* 'teach, preach', *poveléti* 'order'). These contexts present ample possibilities for a range of aspectual meanings and functions.

5.3.1. Nonpunctual telic acts in the infinitive mood

Infinitives and supines of nonpunctual telic acts have a distribution of usage in the infinitive mood that corresponds to their expected aspectual assignment. Protoperfectives describe a single act brought to completion or conceived of as a whole; protoimperfectives describe an act given duration, one not specifically completed or finished, or one repeated in an open-ended series.

The protoperfective forms in (50)-(55) describe actions that occur once or are summarized as a whole. In (50), the successful sending of news was impossible; the

---

[15] For lack of a better category to include the infinitive and the supine, I use the term "infinitive mood." I rejected the term "nonfinite" on the grounds that it includes participles and imperatives as well.

phrase *ne bě l'zě...ni věsti poslati* 'nor was it possible..to send a message' indicates not whether it was possible to make an effort to leave or to send out a messenger, but that the entirety of the action—getting out of the city and sending a message that would reach its goal—was impossible.

(50)   не бѣ льзѣ изъ града **вылѣсти**. ни вѣсти **послати**. (65)
'it was not possible *to leave* the town, nor *to send* a message'

(51)   а самъ мысля **оубити** Ярополка. гражены же не бѣ льзѣ **оубити** его. (77)
'and he himself was thinking of *killing (oubiti)* Jaropolk; but [on account of] the citizens it was not possible *to kill (oubiti)* him'

A similar situation is found in (51), where undoubtedly an attempt at killing Jaropolk was made; however, the act was a failure. This inclusion of action and attainment of telos can also be seen in (52).

(52)   оутро же повелѣ **послати** по Печенѣгы. (128)
'in the morning he ordered *to send (poslati)* to the Pečenegs'

Here, there may have been numerous emissaries and messages going out, but it is not the process of sending them that is important, but the attainment of the entire act, telos included. The attainment of a single telos is also implied in (53)-(55).

(53)   Каинъ и хотяше **оубити** и. и не оумяше. како **оубити** и. (89)
'Cain wanted *to kill (oubiti)* him, and he did not know how *to kill (oubiti)* him'

(54)   они же кликнувше поидоша **оубитъ** Игоря. (317)[16]
'and with a yell they went *to kill (oubit")* Igor''

(55)   и молви ему тако. оже хощеши **послати** мужь свои. и воротится Володимеръ. то вдам ти которои ти городъ любъ. (265)
'and they told him: if you *send (xoščeši poslati)* your men, and Volodimer should return, then I will give you whichever city you want'

In contrast, simplex and derived representations of nonpunctual telic acts express actions that lack this external perspective on the act. Instead, the act is viewed as articulated, either by focusing on the process or on the numerous component acts that make up a repetitive chain.

The verbs *počati, načati* 'begin' are followed only by the protoimperfective forms *posylati, slati, prisylatisja* 'send', *sobirati* 'collect', *brati* 'take, collect' as in (56)-(60). The protoperfective forms *sobrati* 'collect', *poslati* 'send' do not appear after *načati*. All of these protoimperfectives can thus appear in progressive contexts, although the acts they represent are not quite identical in lexical shape.

---

[16] The Radzivil and Academy mss. have, interestingly enough, *ubivati*.

Derived forms like *posylati, sobirati* often describe an action that is highly articulated, one that is composed of a number of distinct smaller acts.

(56) начаша скотъ **събирати**. от мужа по 4 куны. а от старость по 10 грив(ен). а от бояръ по 18 грив(ен). (143)
'they began *to collect (s"birati)* money, four kunas from each man, and ten grivnas from the elders, and eighteen grivnas from the boyars'

(57) и **посажа** посадники по городом. и дани поча **брати**. (237)
'and he *placed (posaža)* representatives in the towns, and began *to collect (brati)* taxes'

In (56), the emphasis is on the amount paid by each person, while in (57), although the idea of collection from various sources is still present, the emphasis is on the establishment of an overall process. Slightly closer are (58) and (59), where the difference between *slati* and *prisylati sja* is barely detectable (aside from the presence of a reflexive; for more on reflexivity with these verbs, see section 5.9.5).

(58) и поча Володимеръ **слати** къ Игореви река. оже мя с братомь оумиришь. то по его см(е)рти помогу ти г Кыеву. И Игорь нача молитися. ко Всеволоду. и молбою. и гнѣваяся. река не хочеши ми добра. про что ми обреклъ еси Кыевъ. (312)
'and Volodimer began *to send (slati)* to Igor', saying: reconcile me with my brother, and after his death I will help you to [the throne of] Kiev. And Igor' began to entreat Vsevolod with prayers and wrath, saying: you wish me no good; why have you denied me Kiev?'

(59) тое же зимы **присылатися** нача Изяславъ. къ Андрѣеви река. брате въведи мя къ о(т)цю в любовь. и присылаше к нему розирая нарядъ его. и како строить городъ... (329)
'that winter Izjaslav began *to send (prisylatisja)* to Andrej, saying: brother, reconcile me with our father. And he sent to him, observing his [brother's] host and how he was building a stronghold...'

Example (58) is more unified in its perspective on the action; once Igor accepted Volodimer's plea (however many times Volodimer contacted him before he did so), Igor took up his cause. The opposite conclusion seems true about (59), where the focus is on Izjaslav's motivations during the period when he sent emissaries to Andrej. Once more, articulation of the derived form plays a role in the choice of form.

An articulated set of events appears in (60), where the prophets sent down are many in number and are dispatched at widely varying times.

(60) и нача Б(ог)ъ **посылати** к нимъ пр(о)р(о)ки. (97)
'and God began *to send (posylati)* prophets to them'

For the other infinitival contexts, verbs are used according to the aspect corresponding most closely to the given context. Thus with *povelě* 'he ordered', the verb can be imperfective *(sobirati)* when it refers to an ongoing process, as in (61).

(61) и повелѣ **сбирати** вои от мала до велика. (201)
'and he ordered *to assemble (sbirati)* the troops from the smallest to the largest'

However, as in (52) above, *poveleti* also appears with protoperfective predicates, indicating a single action viewed as a completed whole. Example (62) is a generalized truth or rule; the highly telic act *ubivati* 'kill' is used to show the regularity and frequency of this act.

(62) етеръ же законъ Халдѣемъ (и) Вавилонямъ. м(а)т(е)ри поимати. съ братними чады блудъ дѣяти и **убиватi** (15)
'and the Chaldeans and Babylonians have their own laws: to sleep with their mothers, to fornicate with their brothers' children and *to kill (ubivati)*'

Example (63) is difficult to explain; the use of a derived form *posylati* 'send' with a singular noun *gramotu* 'letter' is unexpected.

(63) ношаху сли печати злати. а гостье сребрени. ныне же увѣдѣлъ есть князь нашь. **посылати** грамоту ко ц(а)р(с)тву нашему. иже посылаемы бывают от нихъ (посли) и гостье да приноситъ грамоту пишюче сице... (48)
'emissaries carried gold seals, and guests silver; now our prince has ordered *to send (posylati)* a letter to our kingdom; let the emissaries and guests who are sent by them bring a letter, reading [lit. writing] as follows...'

The Radzivil manuscript's variant reading offers one resolution: *nyně uvěděl est' knjaz' naš' posylati gramoty...* 'now our prince has ordered *letters* to be sent...'. The use of the infinitive and in particular of the form *posylati* is then easily explained as reported speech that orders the repeated performance of an action; regardless of the grammatical number of the object, it is clearly to be read as plural.[17]

To summarize, infinitive usage for nonpunctual telic acts is constrained by aspectual assignment. It is relatively easy to find contexts in which a protoperfective predicate and a protoimperfective predicate can both be found, where each expresses a different set of functions. A protoimperfective predicate conveys an articulated event; a protoperfective predicate conveys a nonarticulated event, containing both process and attainment of telos. Within the protoimperfective category, there is a competition between more and less articulated acts. This competition suggests that perhaps the lexicon is not as neatly partitioned

---

[17] Further proof of this point is that the Academy ms. has no direct object. Example (63) is also discussed later as example (213).

into pairs as it is nowadays, and that, for instance, a verb like *poslati* may sometimes be paired with *slati* and sometimes with *posylati* depending on the degree of articulation of the act (i.e. depending on where it falls within the nonpunctual telic class of predicates).

5.3.2. Atelic acts in the infinitive mood

Atelic acts do not have the same distribution of forms found with the nonpunctual telic class. Instead, infinitives and supines of these verbs vary widely in meaning and potential aspectual class.

Atelic predicates express acts of any shape and duration, regardless of which aspect might be associated with that meaning in Modern Russian. Even more interesting, there are acts where neat definitions of meaning seem irrelevant.

The infinitive *mněti* 'seem' in (64) and (65) occurs in a durative context, because the state lasts as long as people look or the phenomenon continues. From the perspective of the writer, these appearances are bounded in time; obviously, the world did not come to an end, as the people must have soon realized.

(64) и быс(ть) черно. по земли же и по хоромом. снѣгъ. **мнѣтиж** всѣм ч(е)л(овѣ)к(о)мъ зряче. аки кровь прольяна на снегу. (419)
'...and the snow was black upon the earth and the buildings, *so as to seem (mnětiž)* to all the people watching as if blood was poured on the snow'

(65) оторгаху бо с(я) звѣзды на землю. **мнѣти** вид(я)щим я. яко кончину. (419)
'the stars were flung to earth, *to seem (mněti)* to those seeing them like the end [of the world]'

(66) да доколѣ Б(ого)ви **терпѣти** над нами. за грѣхы наведе на них и наказалъ по достоянью рукою бл(а)говѣрнаго князя. (382)
'and so long as God *was to suffer (terpěti)* us, he brought down [punishment] on them, and punished them as they deserved at the hand of the faithful prince'

A similar reading is seen in (66), where the sufferance of God is bounded temporally.

Progressive contexts, the boundaries of whose actions extend beyond the narrative time frame, are found in (67) and (68) with *načati* 'begin'.

(67) и **плакатися** нача попадья. яко мертву сущю оному и очюти плачь. (261)
'the priest's wife began *to cry (plakatisja)*...'

(68) Игорь... нача **мыслити** на Деревляны. хотя примыслити большюю дань. (54)
'Igor'...began *to plot (mysliti)* against the Derevlians, wanting to receive a bigger tax'

But other contexts are ambiguous: it is difficult to say whether they refer to an act with explicit duration or one summed up entirely without respect to process. Thus (69) with *protiviti sja* can refer to a process that occupies a span of time or one that sums up the act in a single point; 'he could not *struggle* against them' or 'he could not *resist* them' are equally valid readings.

(69) Мстиславъ же видѣвъ множьство вои. и не возмогъ **противитися** имъ затворися в городѣ. (347)
'Mstislav, having seen the multitudes of soldiers and having been unable *to resist/struggle against (protivitisja)* them, locked himself in the city.'

Similar double readings can be advanced for (70) and (71).

(70) и мысляшеть **противитися** Юргу брату своему. (452)
'and he planned *to oppose (protivitisja)* Jurgij his brother'

(71) аще можеши **противити** мнѣ то се есмъ здѣ. (478)
'if you can *stand against (protiviti)* me, then I am here'

In (72), *mysliti* 'think, plot' could characterize one single thought that occurs to one while riding or the entire chain of thought.

(72) та бо есть м(о)л(и)тва всѣх лѣпши. нежели **мыслити** безлѣпицю ѣздя. (245)[18]
'for that is the best prayer of all, rather than *think of (mysliti)* trifles while riding'

(73) веля имъ **оучити** люди. понеже тѣмь есть поручено Б(ого)мь. (153)
'directing them *to instruct (oučiti)* the people, since this is what God commanded of them'

In (73), Jaroslav commands the priests to '*instruct* the people', but once again, the scope and direction of this command is never directly interpreted as formally bounded and complete—a limited directive—or as expansive and process-oriented (the more likely reading). Example (74) is also ambiguous, but in the other direction: it does not clarify whether the speaker makes a specific entreaty to his father or whether he intends to impress his father with his general filial devotion (i.e. prayer directed elsewhere);[19] in this instance, the former seems more likely.

(74) иди ис Суждаля Мурому а в чюжеи волости не сѣди. и азъ пошлю **молится** з дружиною своею къ о(т)цю своему. и смирю тя со о(т)ц(о)мь моим. (237)

---

[18] Discussed below also as example (156) and example (203).
[19] For this to be true, the complement *k otcu svoemu* 'to my father' would have to be an object of the finite *pošlju* 'I will send' instead of the supine *molitsja* 'to pray, entreat'.

'Go from Suzdal' to Murom, and do not stop in anyone else's land; and I will send with my company to my father *to pray (molitsja),* and I will reconcile you with my father'

To summarize, atelic acts show a much broader range of uses in the infinitive and supine than do nonpunctual telic predicates. Not only can atelic acts express meanings and functions associated with either protoaspect, but in a large variety of cases, they do not express any one single meaning tied to a single protoaspect, but leave open a range of possibilities that are completely unconnected with aspect. The evidence strongly suggests that these predicates are not aspectual in character.

5.3.3. Punctual telic predicates in the infinitive mood

Punctual telic predicates follow the pattern laid out for atelic acts above, in that they do not show a strict separation of meaning and function by aspect. Instead, the forms show that each verb appears in a wide range of predicates in varied contexts without following aspectual guidelines. Some forms occur in marked progressive contexts, such as (75)-(77) with the verbs *počati, načati* 'begin'.

(75) и наоутрия придоша Печенѣзи. почаша **звати** нѣ(сть) ли мужа. се нашь доспѣлъ. (123)
 'and the next day the Pečenegs came; they began *to call (zvati):* is there no man [here]? Ours is ready!'

(76) не даите пакости дѣяти... да не **кляти** вас начнуть. (246)
 'do not let evil things occur... and they will not begin *to curse (kljati)* you'

(77) егда **ся** начаху **каяти**. и помиловашеть их (и) егда избавяшеть ихъ. паки оукланяхуться. на бѣсослуженье. (97)[20]
 'when they would begin *to repent (sja kajati),* he would take mercy on them; (and) when he redeemed them, again they veered off into demon worship'

Other contexts mark the act as completed or considered as a whole, such as (78)-(82). Notably, some verbs which are Modern Russian imperfectives express a perfective-like act here, as in (78). Here the reading 'treat' without reference to a final cure does not particularly make sense; people expected instantaneous cures from holy men. Similarly, the use of *vrediti (sja)* 'harm' in (79) suggests a unitary act.

(78) приде в Суждаль к с(вя)тому Дмитрию. в свою келью. хотя **лѣчити** свою немочь. (452)
 'he came to Suzdal' to the holy Dmitrij's cell, wanting *to cure (lečiti)* his sickness'

---

[20] This sentence is discussed further as example (132) below.

(79) то никтоже вас не можеть **вредитися**. и оубити. понеже не будет
от Б(ог)а повелѣно. (252)
'for no one can *harm (vreditisja)* you or kill you unless it is God's will'

The two infinitives following *xotěti* 'want, intend' in (80) and (81) also indicate single, whole acts.

(80) и разумѣ яко хотят и **слѣпити**. (260)
'and he understood that they want[ed] *to blind (slěpiti)* him'

(81) поиде на Греки въ лодьях и на конихъ хотя **мьстити** себе. (45)
'he went against the Greeks in boats and on horse, wanting *to avenge (m'stiti)* himself'

(82) но да сими словесы пославше бяше переди. брат ко мнѣ **варити**
мене. (253)
'but with these words, my brother had sent ahead to me *to warn (variti)* me'

Still others, such as (83)-(85) cannot be committed to either perspective; the action can be seen as either a unified whole, as a series of acts, or as articulated acts (i.e. that have duration or repetition). Example (83), for instance, is open to any of these three interpretations of 'call'.

(83) он же повелѣ **звати** братью всю. (186)
'he gave the order *to call (zvati)* all the brothers'

(84) и рѣхъ **не хвалитися** поганым. (249)
'and he said: the heathens are *not to be praised (ne xvalitisja)*'

(85) мнѣ ни о чем же буди **хвалитися**. токмо о кр(е)стѣ Х(ри)с(то)вѣ.
(439)[21]
'far be it from me *to glory (xvalitisja)*, except in the cross of Christ'

The above examples can be divided into forms of communication, like *zvati* 'call', *variti* 'warn', *xvaliti sja* 'praise' and *kajati sja* 'regret, repent', and abstract punctual acts like *vrediti (sja)* 'harm', *lěčiti* 'treat, cure', *m'stiti* 'avenge'. The former have great plasticity of meaning, running the gamut from single, durationless acts to repeated or ongoing acts, as in (86).

(86) и повелѣ трость держати ч(е)л(овѣ)комъ. и ходити по городу и
звати. тростем трясомом. бес комара граду. (40)
'and he ordered that people hold their stick[s], and that [they] walk around the city, and *call (zvati)*, shaking their stick: no mosquitoes for the city!'

---

[21] A paraphrase of Galatians 6.14.

The latter are more restricted in their infinitive and supine usage, rendering mostly single, durationless acts, as in (87)-(88).

(87)   азъ бо Ляхом много зла творих. и хотѣлъ е(смь) створити и **мстити** Русьскѣи земли. (266)
'I did much evil to the Poles, and I wanted to do [it] and *to avenge (mstiti)* the Russian land'

(88)   и ц(е)с(а)рь яша Девгенича. и повелѣ и **слѣпити**. (227)[22]
'the king seized Devgenič and ordered him *blinded (slĕpiti)*'

Given that in Modern Russian these verbs are imperfective, this finding is surprising as well.

In summary, the punctual telic acts do not behave predictably with respect to aspect. In many places, their functions are associated exclusively with the perfective in Modern Russian, when, given the morphological evidence and Modern Russian facts, we would expect the verbs to be imperfective. In numerous other instances, no clear aspectual assignment is possible even for isolated contexts. Punctual telics behave more like atelics than like nonpunctual telics with respect to aspect: they appear not to be subject to the semantic constraints associated with grammatical aspect.

5.4. ASPECTUALITY IN PRETERITE FORMS

The Old Russian preterite tense system is the most complex and the most informative of the systems I have discussed. Because it offers three tenses that situate an act in the past (without even including the various pluperfect forms), it therefore has the potential to encode more information in the verb form itself than other systems (non-past and infinitive) do. It is also the most problematic of the verbal systems, since the precise functions of the Old Russian preterite tenses and the significance of the Old Russian three-way division between aorist, imperfect, and perfect is still the subject of much debate. Furthermore, as more information is encoded in the preterite verb form, correspondingly less information needs to be encoded in the context, making a correct reading of the tense form all the more crucial. I will confine my remarks here to a few notes about the features of the aorist and imperfect tenses and what information they yield about aspect in these texts.[23]

While the Old Russian aorist may show instantaneous or completed action, especially with telic acts, it plays a different role with atelic acts and some punctual telics. For the latter groups, the aorist describes acts regardless of length or

---

[22] The Radzivil and Academy mss. diverge considerably from the Laurentian ms. here.
[23] For reasons of space I will leave aside the perfect tense. Its relationship with aspect is discussed in Forsyth 1972, which formulates an elegant hypothesis about the conjunction of the rise of the perfect and the rise of aspect in Old Russian. This hypothesis and others about the interaction of tense and aspect are discussed in detail in chapter 3.

completion. The evidence for this can be found in the previous chapter. A basic function of the Old Russian aorist, then, is the *summarizing* of an act.[24] This function matches well with punctual acts and explains the preponderance of aorist forms with these simplexes. Notably, while the proportion of imperfects with time limitations in these groups is much lower than that of aorists, it does constitute a significant percentage of the sample, meaning that we cannot simply ascribe the limiting of time (a durative function) entirely to the aorist and leave progressive functions to the imperfect. The aorist reliably indicates *completion* and *sequencing* only for nonpunctual telic acts.

As we have seen, nonpunctual telic acts from protoperfective verbs like *pasti/padu* 'fall' rarely have imperfect forms. The imperfect of such a verb, when it appears, expresses *repeated action;* most imperfects are found with the corresponding protoimperfective verb *padati,* where they can express either repetition or *duration.* This situation does not hold for punctual telic acts; nor does it hold for atelic acts, where iteration and indications of duration can blur together.

The usage of aorist and imperfect tenses, then, is not simply a matter of setting out a few well-defined functions; the precise semantic boundaries of these forms vary depending on the lexical shape of the act.

5.4.1. Nonpunctual telic acts in the preterite

Nonpunctual telic acts have two patterns of preterite usage. One set of verbs expresses past acts predominantly in the aorist; the acts are interpreted as closed, completed events. The occasional imperfect form is interpreted as denoting an iterated, completed act, usually in a string of other events. Another set of verbs expresses past acts predominantly in the imperfect. These imperfects express action not bounded by limits imposed in the predicate; the limits, if there are any, come from context. The act is often found in progressive or durative contexts, although the context can be read as generalized or iterated if it is the occurrence of the act and not the results of it that are important.

The predicates in these sentences all express acts that are seen as finished or whole. Sometimes this effect is achieved by looking at the act in retrospect and explicitly summarizing it, regardless of its final state, as in (89).

(89) и **созда** столпъ то за 40 лѣт. и не свершенъ быс(ть). (5)
 'and *it took him* forty years *to build (sozda)* that pillar, and it was not finished'

In other cases, it is the chain of actions that shows the completed character of the aorists, as in (90)-(93).

---

[24] This is not its only function, but note that the "perfective" feature of completion can be a side effect of the summative marking in the aorist, although it need not be. A fuller discussion of the Old Russian aorist can be found in van Schooneveld 1959.

(90) **взяша** главу его. и во лбѣ его **съдѣлаша** чашю. **оковаше**[25] лобъ его. и пьяху по немь. (74)[26]
'they took (vzjaša) his head, and in his skull they fashioned (s"dělaša) a chalice, bronzed (okovaše) his skull and drank from it'

(91) Въ лѣт(о) 6499 Володимеръ **заложи** градъ Бѣлъгородъ. и **наруби** въ не от инѣхъ городовъ. (122)
'in the year 991, Volodimer founded (založi) the town of Bělgorod, and assembled (narubi) in it [people] from other cities'

(92) и быка **пустиша**. и **побѣже** быкъ мимо и. (123)
'and they loosed (pustiša) the bull, and the bull ran (poběže) by them'

(93) егда бо **прокопахъ послахъ** к игумену. (211)
'for when I broke through (prokopax"), I sent (poslax") to the priest'

In (90), for instance, the enchaining of these actions shows their closed, finite character. Following Maslov 1954, we can also distinguish events in series where the link is created explicitly by a conjunction, as in (93). Sometimes, however, these same verbs we have just seen in the aorist occur in the imperfect tense, where they represent the regular completion of an act in a series, as in (94).

(94) аще ли вержаше на другаго. и не прилняше к нему цвѣтокъ. стояше крѣпок в пѣньи. дондеже **отпояху** оутренюю. и тогда **изидяше** в кѣлью свою. (190)
'if [the demon] threw [a flower] at someone else, and the flower did not stick to him, he stood firm as he sang, until they had finished singing (otpojaxu) matins, and then went off (izidjaše) to his cell'

Here, an older monk has a vision to explain why some monks seemed to be overcome by dizziness and had to leave matins early for a few extra winks, while others did not; he saw a demon that cast flowers at the monks. If the flower stuck to a monk, he would suddenly feel confused and walk out; if it failed to stick, the monk stayed until he had *sung through* (imperfect protoperfective) the service, at which point he could *leave* (imperfect protoperfective). The strict temporal ordering here enjoins the use of a protoperfective verb; the regular character of the action makes the imperfect tense appropriate.

A nice minimal pair is found in (95) and (96). The negated aorist of *propustiti* 'let through' in (95) indicates that, contrary to expectation, the Polovtsians' emissaries to Vsevolod were not allowed to return when their mission was over.

(95) **послали** бо **бяхуть** послы ко Всеволоду. и **не пропустиша** их опять. (296)

---

[25] The Radzivil and Academy mss. have the participle *okovavše*. The 3. sg. imperfect here is quite likely a scribal error for the 3. pl. aorist *okovaša*.

[26] Discussed further below as example (185).

'for they *had sent (poslali bjaxut')* emissaries to Vsevolod, and they *did not let (ne propustiša)* them back in'

(96) а Алтунопа **възвратяшеться** вспять. и **не допустяху** Оугрѣ опять. и тако множецею оубивая. **сбиша** ѣ в мячь. (271)
'and Altunopa *returned (v"zvratjašet'sja)* back, and they *did not let (ne dopustjaxu)* the Huns back, killing so many that they *pounded (sbiša)* them into a heap'

A single attempt or expectation is cancelled in (95). In contrast, (96) is a battle scene, where consecutive attempts to break through are met each time with resistance. The iterative context prompts the use of the imperfect tense with verbs emphasizing completion.

A second behavior pattern for these verbs occurs with nonpunctual telic acts that focus on action, regardless of whether the act is completed or not. In (97)-(100) are derived forms of some verbs seen in (89)-(96). The semantic differences between the derived and nonderived forms stem from the ability of the former to appear in progressive contexts along with a strong telic component. In (97), the telic predicate *otpěvati časy* 'sing (through) the (liturgical) hours' is juxtaposed with the atelic action *moliti sja Bogu* 'pray to God'.

(97) и приходя с Берестового **отпѣваше** часы и **моляшеся** ту Б(ог)у втаинѣ. (156)
'and coming [there] from Berestovoe, *he would sing (otpěvaše)* the hours and *pray (moljašesja)* to God in secret'

The author had three options here to convey the meaning 'sing the hours': a simplex verb in the imperfect *(pojaše časy)*; a simple prefixed verb in the imperfect *(otpojaše časy)*; and a prefixed derived form in the imperfect *(otpěvaše časy)*. The first option does not state definitively that the hours were sung through; in other words., it lacks a defined end or telos for the event. The second option would imply repeated completion of the hours, with no duration considered apart from the attainment of the goal. Only the final choice combines both telicity and duration, allowing the act to show both that the singer completed the required songs and that the act of singing has a parallel durative value to that of praying.

Example (98) presents a problematic combination of verbs. In it, Volodimer celebrated his victory for eight days and then returned to Kiev.

(98) Празднованъ князь днии 8. И **възвращашеться** Кыеву на Оуспенье с(вя)тыя Б(огороди)ца. и ту пакы **створяше** праздник великъ. сзывая бещисленое множство народа. (125)
'Having celebrated for 8 days, the prince *returned (v"zvraščašet'sja)* to Kiev on the [Feast of the] Assumption of the Holy Mother of God, and there again *celebrated (stvarjaše)* a great holiday, inviting an innumerable number of people'

The use of the imperfect here along with the prefixed derived stem {v"zvrašča-} must indicate that the process of his return coincided with a holiday celebration that was already in progress. The use of the unusual derived verb *stvarjati* introduces telicity into the portrayal of the festivities. The simplex predicate *tvoriti prazdnik* 'celebrate a holiday' would have implied an atelic act in progress. With the suffixed *stvarjati prazdnik,* the celebration is presented as a telic event, one with a natural sequence from beginning to end, and the process of Volodimer's return coincides with a portion of this sequence.[27]

Example (99) seems at first to be a cut-and-dried case of simultaneous actions.

(99)   не возмогоша всего полона отнести. но овых **сѣчаху**. а иных множство **пущахут** опять в своя си. (449)
'they could not carry off all the prisoners, but *executed (sěcaxu)* some, and a multitude of others they *permitted (puščaxut)* to return to their homes'

However, the predicate *puščaxut* occupies a different lexical class than the prefixed forms seen above. While it could conceivably represent an iterated act (numerous people were individually released), it more likely represents a state (permission existed for some people to return home).[28] Interestingly enough, no imperfects from prefixed derived forms of *-pustiti* are found in these texts.

Example (100) is in a durative context: while Mstislav remained in Suzdal', he sent messages to Oleg. The iterativity of the act (multiple sendings are implied) is subordinate to its durative character, which is bounded by Oleg's deceitful reply that he will make peace with Mstislav.

(100) а Мстиславъ приде Суждалю и сѣдя ту **посылаше** к Олгови мира прося. (238)
'and Mstislav came to Suzdal', and ruling there, he *sent (posylaše)* to Oleg, asking for peace'

This example could also be read as conative if the larger context is invoked, implying that the missives were doomed due to Oleg's malevolent intentions, but given the clear limits emphasized in *sědja* 'ruling' this seems overwrought.

To summarize the evidence from telic, nonpunctual acts: some verbs show a proclivity for *aorist* usage to express *summarized acts,* where summary equals *attainment of the goal,* or (rarely) *completion of the action regardless of goal.* Where these verbs have *imperfect* tense forms, they indicate *repeated attainment of*

---

[27] Another interpretation hinges on a sentence that appears a few lines down: *i tako po vsja lěta tvorjaše* 'and he did it this way each year'. Volodimer, as it turns out, was so enchanted by the success of his first celebration that he made a habit of it. In this case, the repetitive character of the celebration—in retrospect—could have influenced the author or scribe to use these verb forms.

[28] A good Modern Russian equivalent might be the verb *razrešat'* 'permit', which can have a telic meaning, but more often has an atelic one in predicates like *ne razrešaetsja* 'it is not permitted'.

the goal, usually in a *sequence of acts.* Other verbs, like those in (97)-(100), have only imperfect forms in the Chronicles; these imperfects occur in *progressive or durative contexts.* If iterativity is involved, it is subordinate to a greater time constraint, and the multiple acts are viewed as parts of a whole, unbroken act.

These two patterns are consistent with strict aspectual assignment, since the first group conforms to protoperfective norms and the second to protoimperfective norms. A single lexical entry (e.g., 'fall') is expressed by two verbs with differing preterite tense distributions and, where there is overlap, different functions assigned to those tenses depending on which verb is used. Already, for the protoimperfective group, a certain heterogeneity of purpose can be seen: protoimperfective predicates can express both unbounded and bounded duration. From the second context—goal-oriented motion circumscribed by time limits—comes the Modern Russian conative function of these predicates, seen here only occasionally and subordinated to the durative function of the context.

Furthermore, the usage of derived forms shows them to be lexically more homogeneous than the simplex verbs they came from. Because the presence of prefixes imposing a boundary or limit on the act prompts the development of these new, process- and repetition-oriented forms, the acts they describe are overwhelmingly telic in nature. It is in this nonpunctual telic group that we first see the possibility of assigning protoimperfectivity and protoperfectivity not only to certain *predicates,* but to entire *verbs* as well, since all of these verbs' predicates fall within a single lexical group.

5.4.2. Atelic acts in the preterite

Atelic acts do not have the same neat distribution of preterite tense forms as the nonpunctual telic acts do. Here single lexical units are not often distributed over two or more verbs with complementary usage patterns; instead, a single verb displays all the forms required for all possible functions.

All three verbs seen here—*deržati* 'hold, keep', *dumati* 'think, take counsel', *plakati sja* 'cry'—are found with both aorist and imperfect forms. In none of these verbs does one tense rule out the appearance of the other; *plakati sja* is attested by seven imperfects versus twenty-eight aorists, a ratio of 1:4; *deržati* is found in the imperfect four times and in the aorist four times, for a ratio of 1:1; *dumati* appears twice in the imperfect and once in the aorist, for a ratio of 2:1.

Deržati has a range of durations. The aorist conveys indeterminate duration summed up in a single form, as in (101).

(101)   Всеволодъ же посла по них и вороти еп(и)с(ко)па с ними. и **держа**
и с еп(и)с(ко)п(о)мъ. (308)
'Vsevolod sent after them and sent back the bishop with them, and *held (derža)* them with the bishop'

The imperfect, meanwhile, occurs in a progressive context, as in (102), describing the faith the Varangian held at the time he arrived.

(102) Варягъ то пришелъ изъ Грекъ **держаше** вѣру х(р)ес(т)яньску. и бѣ оу него с(ы)нъ красенъ лицем и д(у)шею. (82)
'a Varangian came from the Greeks; he *held (deržaše)* the Christian faith, and he had a son fair of face and soul'

The imperfect also appears in a durative context in (103), where its duration is limited to the time Boris was ruler.

(103) Борису Жидиславичю воевода бѣ в то время. и нарядъ весь **держаше**. (364)
'Boris Židislavič was the warlord at that time, and *held (deržaše)* command'

Likewise, the act of thinking can be summed up with an aorist, regardless of actual duration, as in (104):

(104) наши же слышавше **думаша** оже дамы симъ животъ а Половець много есть назади. а нас есть мало (359)
'our men, having heard this, *thought (dumaša)* that: we will give up our lives here, and there are many Polovtsians behind, and we are few'

Dumati is also used in the imperfect to indicate an ongoing act, as in (105).

(105) и не припустяху его к собѣ. но особь **думаху** о Д(а)в(и)дѣ. и сдумавше послаша к Д(а)в(и)ду мужи своѣ. (274)
'they did not let him in to see them, but *took counsel (dumaxu)* especially about David, and having reached a decision, sent their men to David'

(106) князь Глѣб... въсхотѣ к нимъ ити на снем. и реч(е) посломъ Половецьскымъ. иду к вам. и **думашеть** з дружиною своею о том. г которым поидемъ передь. (358)
'...and he said to the Polovtsian emissaries: I will come to you; and *he conferred (dumašet')* with his company: which ones will we go to first?'

In (105), Oleg's refusals to see David contrast with the fact that simultaneously he and his allies are thinking about David. In (106), Gleb is concerned about the fact that he has two meetings planned with opposing camps of Polovtsians, and these worries form a background to his spoken decision to the second group of Polovtsians. In both (105) and (106) the imperfect form of *dumati* is followed by a form of *sdumati* 'decide, resolve', underscoring the atelic character of the preceding act.

The verb *plakati sja* is often used in the aorist to indicate that someone was mourned for the prescribed duration in the appropriate manner, as in (107).

(107) и **плакашася** людье вси плачем великим. и несоша и погребоша на горѣ. еже гл(аголе)ться Щековица. (39)
'and all the people *mourned (plakašasja)* with a great lament, and they carried him and buried him on the mountain...'

(108) и слезъ достоино. Всеволодъ и Мстиславъ. с дружиною своею. и вси гражане **плакахуся** зряще. Володимера. (461)
'and Vsevolod and Mstislav with their companies and all the citizens *cried (plakaxusja)* manifold tears, seeing Volodimer'

When the perspective changes slightly, and the crying is presented as a tableau, as in (108), the imperfect is used to give a greater sense of immediacy and ongoing action concomitant with seeing Volodimer.

In conclusion, the aorist and imperfect tenses are used differently with atelic predicates than they are with nonpunctual telic predicates. Instead, the same verb is found with both tenses, and the differences in function between aorist and imperfect reduce down to a continuum between bounded and open-ended acts.

5.4.3. Punctual telic acts in the preterite

Punctual telic acts have the same distribution as atelic acts: a range of past tense action types, from summative to prolonged, are conveyed with the same verb using different tenses.

As with punctual telic infinitives, punctual telic preterite forms lean toward either summarizing or iterativity; this is reflected as a predominant use of either the aorist or the imperfect. The usage in the past tense, however, need not be identical to the usage found for the infinitive. Examples are few for each verb, but the overall pattern is clear: predicates describing abstract actions *(grěšiti sja* 'miss', *slěpiti* 'blind', *vrediti* 'harm') appear in the aorist, while predicates describing communication *(l'stiti sja* 'deceive', *zvati* 'call', *kljati sja* 'swear', *braniti* 'forbid', *variti* 'warn') appear in either the aorist or the imperfect. Examples (109)-(114) describe acts of uncertain but most likely short duration, summed up in an aorist form. Some, like (109)-(111), are certainly momentary in nature.

(109) единъ **грѣшися** Яня топоромъ. Янь же оборотя топоръ оудари и тыльемь. (176)
'one *missed (grěšisja)* Jan' with his axe; Jan', turning the axe around, hit him in with the blunt end of it'

(110) и хотя оударити в око. и **грѣшися** ока и перерѣза ему лице. (261)
'and wanting to strike him in the eye, he *missed (grěšisja)* the eye and cut open his face'

(111) и с коня много падах. голову си розбих дважды. и руцѣ и нозѣ свои **вередих**. (251)
'and I fell many times from my horse, broke my head open twice, and *injured (veredix)* my arms and legs'

The form *veredix* 'injured' in (111) suggests that Vladimir injured his hands and legs more than once, making a limited iterative reading warranted. In some cases, however, the aorist clearly summarizes the repetition of actions spread over time, as in (112) and (113). The other appearance of *veredix* in (114), like the form in (111), gives no indication of overt repetition, but the context—a summary of Vladimir's youth—makes an iterative or durative reading necessary.

(112) и слѣпиша Руси много. (154)
'and they *blinded (slěpiša)* many Russians'

(113) и пришед Мьстиславъ исѣче иже бѣша высѣкли Всеслава. числом 70 чади. А другыя слѣпиша. другыя же без вины погуби не испытавъ. (174)
'and when he arrived, Mstislav *executed (isěče)* seventy people who had freed Vseslav, and others *they blinded (slěpiša)*; still other innocents *he killed (pogubi)* without investigating'

(114) в оуности своеи вередих. не блюда живота своего. ни щадя головы своея. (251)
'in my youth I *misbehaved (veredix)*, neither guarding my own life, nor protecting my own head'

Communicative acts in the aorist are often perceived as unified wholes, regardless of their actual duration, as in (115)-(117). Example (115), for instance, yields no information about the duration of the act or whether it was repeated.

(115) понеже звахъ вы и не послушасте мене. (63)
'for I *called (zvax")* you and you did not heed me'

In (116), whether this swearing was repeated several times or only once is unclear from the context.[29]

(116) сему Д(а)в(и)ду кляся Б(ог)ъ. яко от племене его родити с(я) Б(ог)у. (97)
'God *swore (kljasja)* to David that God would be born of his tribe'

Example (117) is similar in that it apparently represents a single act *(varix* 'I warned') conveyed by a simplex. The Modern Russian translation respects this with a perfective form *predupredil* ('I warned').

(117) сими бо словесы варих тя переди егоже почаяхъ от тебе... (253)
'with these words *I warned* you ahead of time what I expect from you'

However, communicative acts also appear in the imperfect. In this case their context may be explicitly iterative, as in (118) and (119), where the interdiction is presented as an act that is certainly repeated regardless of effect.

---

[29] The Modern Russian translation uses the biaspectual verb *obeščat'* 'promise'.

(118) но аще кто хотяше кр(е)ститися **не браняху** но **ругахуся** тому.
(63)
'but if someone wanted to be baptized, *they did not forbid (ne branjaxu)* it but *mocked (rugaxusja)* him'

(119) многажды **браняшеть** ѣсти мясъ. въ Г(о)с(по)дьскыѣ праздьникы.
(354)
'many times *he forbade (branjašet')* the eating of meat on the Lord's holidays'

However, it may also be implicitly iterative, as in (120), where two actions occur in the same environment, but need not be simultaneous.

(120) се бо лукавьствоваше на князя своего лестью. и паки языки своими **льстяхуся**. (76)[30]
'for he plotted evil against his prince with deception, and further: they *told lies (l'stjaxusja)* with their tongue[s]'

Examples (118) and (119) raise a further issue. In my analysis of nonpunctual telic acts, I stated that interruption of a process—i.e., interruption of progress toward the telos—occasionally, but not always, yields a conative reading. In these examples, however, which represent punctual telic predicates, conativity is conveyed by repetition of completed acts; the only conceivable reason for their repetition is their failure to have an effect. (As will be seen in section 5.6, this is usually represented in Old Russian by an imperfect protoperfective when the act is nonpunctual telic.)

The telic–atelic distinction, which played such a crucial role in creating a perfective and imperfective aspect for nonpunctual predicates, seems less interesting for punctual telic acts. Instead, the difference between protoperfective and protoimperfective verbs rests on the status of the act's result. Both (118) and (119) can have a conative reading: it follows that for communicative acts, the salient difference between the protoperfective form and the non-aspectual form (the "non-perfective" form in chart 5.4.3.1) is the presence of a response to the act. It is repeated requests, rather than the prolongation of the process, that trigger conative readings.

In summary, punctual telic predicates take either aorist or imperfect forms in the preterite system. The forms are found in a wide variety of contexts; their meaning and distribution is not limited by a grammatical aspectual system. Interestingly enough, they are less likely than nonpunctual telic predicates to be found in contexts showing an act with explicit duration; instead, they are more likely to be found in contexts that are explicitly iterative or that situate multiple acts within a single time frame without specifying simultaneity. Conativity for these acts is linked with fruitless repetition of an act rather than with lack of completion.

---

[30] The clause following *i paki* is a scriptural citation; since strict agreement is not necessary, the plural verb is not incompatible with the singular one in the first clause.

Chart 5.4.3.1. Comparing punctual telic and nonpunctual telic forms

	For non-completed acts	For completed acts	In iterative contexts	In durative or progressive contexts	Conative effect seen when
Nonpunctual telic acts (*staviti*)	use proto-I form	use proto-P form	use proto-P (or proto-I) form	use proto-I form	proto-I form used in durative or progressive context
Punctual telic acts (*prositi*)	use non-P form	use non-P form	use non-P (or proto-P) form	use non-P form	non-P form used in iterative context

5.5. ASPECT AND LEXICAL CLASS SUMMARIZED

In the preceding three sections, I presented evidence for and against aspect as a grammatical category in Old Russian. The results were consistent: in each category, acts which were telic and nonpunctual were expressed according to an aspectual grammar similar (but not identical) to that of Modern Russian. Each of the verbs involved expressed only a few of the functions available in the verbal system; another verb, usually one related by suffixation, was used to express the balance of these functions. In the non-past tense, the primary distinguishing feature was the form's ability to express either future or present meaning; in other situations, it was the act's ability to appear with completed or uncompleted meaning.

Atelic predicates and punctual telic predicates did not exhibit the same sharp limitations on usage. Instead, all tenses and functions were found with forms of a single verb. For punctual verbs, distinctions were made far more often between iterative and noniterative acts. The logical conclusion is that aspect in its modern form or sense did not extend to all corners of the lexicon in Old Russian; its application was limited to nonpunctual telic acts at the time of the Chronicles.

Since I have established that perfectivity exists in some form at this stage of Old Russian, I still need to address directly Forsyth's claim (1972: 496) that the absence of (proto-) perfectivity indicates, by the nature of binary privative oppositions, a (proto-) imperfective aspect. To this statement I would oppose Timberlake's claim (1982: 307) that a category which lacks an invariant with predictive value is not of much use.[31] If anything, the usage patterns of Old Russian verbs which are "nonperfective" are even more heterogeneous than those of Modern Russian verbs.

I have shown that for Old Russian, lexical groupings consistently predict the behavior of these "nonperfectives," while binary aspectuality, by creating a sort of "junk category" called the imperfective, fails to do so. It might be more accurate to

---

[31] For a more thorough discussion of these views in Forsyth 1970, 1972 and Timberlake 1982, see sections 2.1.1, 2.4.1 and 3.2.8.

say that Old Russian has one protoperfective aspect, and several protoimperfective aspects determined by lexical class that have little in the way of shared usage patterns. I have taken this one step further in refusing to acknowledge the commonality of these multiple protoimperfective aspects simply on the basis of historical determinism; that is, the fact that they will coalesce into an imperfective aspect at a later date does not warrant automatically making such a distinction for this stage of Old Russian.

What are the implications of having a partially operative system of grammatical aspect that operates only within a larger, lexical aspectual framework lacking clear morphological divisions? Once the concept of a "default imperfective" is rejected, "grammatical aspect" in the Modern Russian understanding of the term (a binary opposition) must be rejected for Old Russian, because it cannot exist until an overwhelming majority of verbs in the lexicon (and at the very least, virtually all the verbs in the language's core lexicon) can be labeled with one of two meaningful labels.[32] Yet there is no doubt that a type of grammatical aspect exists in Old Russian as a limited distinction functioning within certain lexical predicate classes, perhaps much the same way as a "determinate–indeterminate" distinction exists for Modern Russian unprefixed motion verbs but not elsewhere in the verbal system.[33]

As I have shown, when I classify verbal acts by lexical type, I am not classifying whole verbs but only their predicates, since a single verb may have multiple lexical assignments.[34] In doing so, I reject for Old Russian a fundamental principle of the Modern Russian aspectual system proposed by the grammatical aspect school: that aspect is assigned on the level of the verb. Instead, in Old Russian, degrees of aspectuality depend on the lexical classes of verbal predicates; they are a feature of the lexical submeanings expressed in each predicate, and to the extent that the complements of a verb help define the lexical class of a predicate, aspect is a feature of the context of the sentence as well. I will explore this claim more thoroughly later in this chapter.

5.6. SPECIAL USES OF THE IMPERFECT TENSE

Having discussed the distribution of aspect in the lexicon, I will now turn to its distribution in various types of sentences or contexts. One question I have so far avoided is the polysemous usage of the imperfect tense. Structuralist studies of early Slavic aspect suggested that in the preterite tense system, the aorist is the unmarked past tense while the imperfect is the marked tense. However, in the analysis presented here, the imperfect has been seen with a number of greatly

---

[32] Here "meaningful" means that the label has predictive value for the morphology and usage patterns of each verb.
[33] This comparison is purely structural and not at all relevant to the semantics of determinacy or aspect.
[34] An example is *sdelat' zadanie* 'do an assignment', which is nonpunctual, vs. *sdelat' zamečanie* 'make a comment', which is punctual. See the discussion of Maslov 1948 in section 2.2.1.

varying functions; the variations in imperfect function are certainly as great or greater than the variations in aorist function. Such wide variation should be characteristic only of the "unmarked" member of a pair, not the "marked" member; a new explanation is evidently needed.

It was mentioned earlier that a number of contextual features map directly into one or another aspect in Modern Russian; for instance, phasal verbs (i.e., *načinat'– načat'* 'begin', *prodolžat'–prodolžit'* 'continue', *končat'–končit'* 'finish') require an imperfective complement (or, where that is not possible, a biaspectual complement). This particular feature holds for Old Russian as well, but such clear-cut situations are not as numerous as they are in Modern Russian. For instance, in Modern Russian, an iterative context normally triggers the use of the imperfective aspect, unless the iterative sequence is irregular in its occurrence or the speaker wishes to focus closely on the sequencing of the events, in which case a chain of perfectives can appear.[35] However, it is well known that the imperfect tense in Old Russian was ordinarily used with one or more protoperfective verbs to express iteration, especially in chains of events. From a Modern Russian perspective, this lamentable lack of consistency certainly appears to be a deficiency or a major exception in the aspectual system, but the problem is rather in using a Modern Russian perspective on aspect. In Old Russian, iterativity is not a context that automatically conditions the use of either aspect; the connection between iterativity and aspect is a later development. Instead, acts that are regularly repeated appear routinely with protoperfective verbs.

Jurij Maslov analyzed the meanings of these perfective imperfects in his 1954 article "Imperfekt glagolov soveršennogo vida v slavjanskix jazykax" ("The Imperfect of Perfective Verbs in Slavic Languages"). Maslov's findings are by and large congruent with my own, although they differ in a few details. Maslov notes that we expect imperfective imperfects to be the norm, and he outlines their usage in older and modern Slavic languages. Imperfective imperfects convey four basic meanings: simultaneity, repetition, conativity, and nonindicative modality. The first two meanings he sees as basic to the imperfect; the last two are later, derived phenomena (Maslov 1954: 71). Maslov sets himself the task of carving a separate place for the perfective imperfect within this relatively wide range of meanings.[36]

Starting from the premise that, contrary to prevailing opinion, aspect had only begun to take shape in the grammar of Prehistoric Slavic and reached completion only in the individual daughter languages, Maslov states that the forms we now call "perfective imperfects" appear for three reasons: first, because some verbs we now label "perfective" were not in fact aspectual at the time, leading us to confuse aspectual indifference with perfectivity; second, that the imperfect tense's meaning

---

[35] This is a gross oversimplification of the Modern Russian evidence, but it will suffice for present purposes.

[36] Despite his insistence that "perfective" and "imperfective" meant very different things in Old Russian than they do today, Maslov still labels his Old Russian forms with these Modern Russian terms, presumably for the sake of convenience. I will retain Maslov's terminology for the discussion of this article.

had been somewhat diluted by the time written texts first appeared, so that in them it tended to fall together with the aorist's meaning; and third, that the imperfect of perfective verbs is in certain instances normal and explainable, conveying a different shade *(ottenok)* of meaning from the imperfect of other verbs (1954: 73, 78).

Maslov concentrates on this third group of "normal" perfective imperfects, classifying them under the umbrella of an iterative perfective *(kratno-perfektivnyj)* usage. Within this category he defines three subtypes: paired iterative *(kratno-parnyj)*, linked iterative *(kratno-cepnoj)*, and bounded iterative *(kratno-predel'nyj)*. Paired iterative usage brings two or more events into strict linear succession; one event or set of events cannot begin until another event or set of events has transpired. The two sets are related by conjunctions like *egda že* 'when, whenever' or *ašče kto* 'if someone (should)'. Linked iterative usage does not have the same clear reflection in the syntax; instead, the fact of sequencing is deduced logically from the position of acts in a chain. Bounded iterative usage uses one event to mark a boundary or limit *(predel)* for the unfolding of the other event; it is typically marked with the conjunction *dondeže* 'until' (1954: 81-82, 89-91).

Comparing these perfective imperfects to imperfective imperfects, Maslov notices some cases where there is a clear semantic differentiation between the perfective and the imperfective forms. In these instances, the imperfective represents simultaneity or extended duration. In other cases, Maslov can find no clear semantic differentiation; the imperfective imperfect seems to have the same bounded iterative function he ascribes to the perfective imperfect. Maslov looks at these last examples through the lens of language change, and claims that when an imperfective imperfect expresses a bounded, repeated act, then it is a historically innovative form, which, in absorbing the function of the old perfective imperfect, shows how the new aspectual system of paired and grouped verbs is replacing the older aspectual system, where tenses expressed these distinctions.

Finally, Maslov suggests that sentences with strings of imperfects can be converted in Old Russian to sentences with strings of non-past forms, and that these conversions observe the aspectual distinctions in the original sentence. In Maslov's view, then, the Old Russian perfective imperfect has two successors that are directly reflected in the structure of Modern Russian. The first possibility is that the perfective imperfect string is transformed into an imperfective imperfect string. This conversion is seen in copyings of older texts. Eventually the imperfect is given up altogether, and the result in Modern Russian is a string of imperfective verbs in the past (formerly the perfect) tense. The second possibility is that the perfective imperfect string is transformed into a perfective non-past string. Evidence of such structures appears in every Old Russian text; the corresponding feature in Modern Russian is a string of perfective verbs in the non-past tense, with an obligatory marker indicating that the action is a repeated past string (often *byvalo* 'it used to be that').

Each of these two Modern Russian corresponding structures, according to Maslov, retains part of the semantic load of the old perfective imperfect within the verbal form but also gives a portion of that load over to other parts of the sentence. The first transformation (perfective imperfect becomes imperfective imperfect and then imperfective perfect) retains the iterativity of the original structure but fails to express the internal ordering and structure of the events. This internal ordering can then be picked up by context, if need be. On the other hand, the second transformation (perfective imperfect becomes perfective non-past) maintains the internal ordering and bounding imposed by perfectivity but loses the ability to express iterativity. The repetitive feature is shunted onto an obligatory extra phrase or word (1954: 87-88).

There are only a few points to quibble with in Maslov's analysis. First, more could be made of the fact that lexical factors can determine behavior in iterative contexts. Maslov hints at this when he says that sometimes an imperfective verb is necessary to mark "extended duration." It would be more accurate to say that the "imperfective" verb is necessary because the event cannot be conceived of as momentary, suggesting that duration is inherent in the definition of the act. Maslov's condition can be reformulated to read: a protoimperfective or anaspectual verb is necessary when the act is nonpunctual or when duration is an essential component of the definition of the act.

Second, while Maslov is correct in making the connection between the Old Russian perfective imperfect and the Modern Russian perfective non-past with *byvalo,* it is not clear whether he believes that all instances of iterative perfective acts in Old Russian therefore represent stages of this transformation. Certainly many non-past iterative acts do not represent acts in the past; instead, they represent acts in an indefinite present-future (as seen in section 5.2.4), and thus it might be more fruitful to look at the Modern Russian perfective non-past with *byvalo* as a convergence of two separate Old Russian structures exclusively in the arena of tense. The *byvalo* construction and others like it, however, maintain their separateness from other perfective non-pasts even in Modern Russian, because they must periphrastically mark the act as belonging in the past. This interpretation is supported by one of Maslov's own observations: that *byvalo* constructions require a chain of events, and a single perfective non-past act cannot combine with *byvalo* to express a repeated, perfective act (1954: 92n). Modern Russian does allow single perfectives to suggest iterativity when a non-past context is involved, as in Kučera's example: *raz v god on pravdu skažet*^{P} 'once a year he tells^P the truth' (1983: 178). This additional differentiation between perfective non-pasts representing past events and non-past events does suggest that these structures have different sources, and are not simply extensions of a single non-past function.

It is not necessary to repeat Maslov's classification of Old Russian sentence types on the evidence from the Chronicles; his analysis covers many of the interesting examples from these texts and sorts them into the correct types We can revisit the evidence, however, and determine how the usage and meaning of the imperfect tense reflects lexical distribution and how it contributes to a general picture of iterated action in Old Russian. Two examples from the Chronicles are reproduced as (121) and (122).

(121) аще кого **видяше** ли шюмна. ли в коєм зазорѣ **не осудяше** но вся на любовь **прекладаше**. (264)[37]

'whenever *he saw (vidjaše)* someone angry or shamed, *he did not condemn (ne osudjaše)* him but *reconciled (na ljubov' prekladaše)* them all'

(121a) *tr:* Когда **видел** кого разбушевавшимся или опозоренным, **не осуждал** того, но всех **примирял** и **утешал**. (377)

(122) аще кто **оумряше творяху** трызно надъ ним. и по семь **творяху** кладу велику и **възложахуть** и на кладу м(е)ртв(е)ца. **сожьжаху**. и посемь собравше кости. **вложаху** в судину малу. и **поставяху** на столпѣ. (14)[38]

'when someone *died (oumrjaše), they would have (tvorjaxu)* a ceremony in his honor, and then *they would make (tvorjaxu)* a large block and *would place (v"zložaxut')* the dead man on the block, *burn* him *up (sož'žaxu)* and then, having collected the bones, *would put (vložaxu)* them in a small vessel and *place (postavjaxu)* it on a pillar'.

The forms in (121) and (122) can be grouped by their lexical class and context. Those acts where the context does not impose a necessary or specified limit—*vidjaše* 'saw', *tvorjaše tryzno* 'had a ceremony'—are simplexes. Those that are clearly completed acts—*v"zložaxut'* 'placed', *sož'žaxu* 'burned up', etc.—are prefixed protoperfectives, with the exception of *tvorjaxu kladu* 'made a block'. In Old Russian, repetition is expressed most easily by focusing on the telicity of each act; telic acts show a propensity to be expressed as protoperfective.[39] The presence of an iterative context does not automatically condition the use of one aspect or another; rather, the lexical features of the act and the requirements of the context determine which form will be used. In later manuscripts, changes are made that bring these examples more closely into line with Modern Russian usage: protoperfective imperfects are replaced either by the corresponding suffixed imperfectives *(osužaše, sožigaxu, vlagaxu,* etc.) or by non-past forms, recalling the Modern Russian exemplary meaning *(vozložit', vozložat')*. No changes are made to verbs where no limit is imposed, suggesting that the reanalysis touched only those predicates that were marked for aspect.

Similar analyses can be imposed on other examples of iterated acts. This is clearest when the strings of iterated acts are uniform in aspect. Most of the imperfects in (123)-(126) come from predicates that are either clearly protoperfective or clearly protoimperfective, since they are nonpunctual and telic. The protoimperfectives are derived prefixed forms, but here they need not define

---

[37] Appeared as example (284) in chapter 4.
[38] Appeared as examples (141) and (250) in chapter 4.
[39] Although for punctual acts, the evidence is less clear. The only suffixed imperfective here, *prekladaše,* is a punctual act. Evidence from later texts suggests that derived forms are important in the punctual telic class for expressing clear repetition, and (121) supports this conclusion.

actions that occur simultaneously in the literal sense; instead, the actions can be iterative but interleaved in such a way as to lack any precedence or ordering, or actions presented as logical, not temporal, alternatives, as in (123).

(123)   они же пр(о)р(о)ки **избиваху**. другия **претираху**. (87)
        'some prophets *they killed (izbivaxu)*, while others *they tortured (pretiraxu)*'

The killing and the torturing need not take place at exactly the same time; these are two alternate fates, and the use of imperfects presents them as such. In fact, these two types of actions have different lexical contours. *Izbivati proroki* 'kill the prophets' is highly telic and nonpunctual; *pretirati proroki* 'torture the prophets' is an atelic action and thus only marginally aspectual at best. Example (124) is closer to a classic protoimperfective imperfect string, in that the actions all occur in a clearly bounded time frame preceded by the start of the battle and followed by a description of the havoc it wrought.

(124)   ихже емше овѣхъ **растинаху**. другия аки страны поставляюще. и **стрѣляху** в ня. **изимахуть** опаки руцѣ **съвязывахуть**. гвозди желѣзныи посреди главы **въбивахуть** ихъ. (44)[40]
        'and having seized them, *they crucified (rastinaxu)* some of them; and, setting others to one side, *they shot (strěljaxu)* into them, *seized (izimaxut')* them, *tied (s"vjazyvaxut')* their hands in back, [and] *drove (v"bivaxut')* iron nails through their head[s]'

Still, there is an interesting nested set of problems here. In the first place, we are presented with two alternative and thus somewhat simultaneous scenarios, similar to (123). The scenarios are outlined in chart 5.6.1.

Chart 5.6.1. Scheme of acts for (124).

Scenario 1	*or*	*Scenario 2*
rastinaxu ix	(ili)	strěljaxu v nja
		rucě izimaxut' opaki
		svjazyvaxut' rucě
		v"bivaxut' gvozdi

However, the second scenario does have a more rigid ordering of items. The need for protoimperfective predicates on the right to show simultaneity with *rastinaxu* is balanced by the need to maintain order within the series, which would best be done with protoperfective predicates.

---

[40] This sentence is also discussed as examples (143) and (388) in chapter 4.

There is a further level of difficulty. Within the ordering of items on the right, there is a great deal of leeway for either a distributive or a strict iterative reading. In other words, either all the men were shot at, then they were all taken out again, all had their hands tied, and all had nails driven into their heads, or these acts could have been performed at random on individual men at various times, meaning that while some men's hands were being tied, others were having nails driven into their heads—a progressive reading. It is at this level that I locate the motive for the derived prefixed forms on the right, which suggest that, regardless of the order in which each man had these tasks performed on him, the actions went on in the same time frame, within the larger picture of the battle.

The fact that these derived forms are also prefixed helps to explicate these multiple layers of progressive and iterative contexts. Theoretically, the writer also had recourse to simplex verbs like *vjazati* 'tie', *brati* 'take, seize', *biti* 'hit'. The use of derived prefixed forms, however, strikes a balance between strongly expressed progressivity and strong telicity that implies repeated completion.

Examples of protoperfective predicates in the imperfect tense are clearer. In (125), the strongly telic *pod"p'jaxut'sja* 'they had a drink' is a necessary precursor to *nač'njaxut' roptati* 'they began grumbling'. In (126), the punctual telic forms *povelěvaše* 'he ordered' and *prixodjaše* 'he came' suggest iterativity. The following predicates in the sentence are all protoperfectives that express a repeated sequence of events.

(125) егда же **подъпьяхуться начьняхуть** роптати на князь гл(агол)юще... (126)
'when they *had had a drink or two (pod"p'jaxut'sja),* they *would begin (nač'njaxut')* to grumble about their prince...'

(126) аще кто...**приходяше** в манастырь к бл(а)ж(е)ному Феодосью. **повелѣваше** сему Дамьянъ м(о)л(и)тву створити болящему. и абье **створяше** молитву. и масломь **помазаше**. и **приимаху** ицѣленье приходящии к нему. (189)
'If anyone...*came (prixodjaše)* to the monastery to the blessed Theodosius, he *would order (povelěvaše)* Damian to say a prayer for the sick man, and immediately, he *would say (stvorjaše)* the prayer, and *would smear (pomazaše)* [him] with oil, and those who came to him *received (priimaxu)* healing'

A more curious problem arises with the verbs *umykati* and *umykivati* 'seize for marriage'. Both are attested in close proximity in the Primary Chronicle, with no apparent difference in meaning or usage; furthermore, Sreznevskij defines both of them as *poxiščat' ili uvozit' děvicu dlja braka* 'abduct[I] or carry off[I] a maiden for purposes of marriage' and lists only the two examples from the Primary Chronicle to support this definition.

(127) а Древляне живяху звериньскимъ образомъ. жиоуще скотьски. оубиваху другъ друга. ядяху вся нечисто. и брака оу нихъ **не бываше**. но **умыкиваху** у воды д(ѣ)в(и)ця. (13)

'and the Derevlians lived like animals, carrying on like cattle: they killed one another, ate all manner of unclean foods, and there *were no (ne byvaxu)* marriage ceremonies among them, but they *would carry off (umykivaxu)* maidens by the water'

(128) и браци **не бываху** въ них. но⁴¹ игрища межю селы. **схожахуся** на игрища на плясанье. и на вся бѣсовьская игрища. и ту **оумыкаху** жены собѣ. с неюже кто **съвѣщашеся. имяху** же по двѣ и по три жены. (14)
'and there *were no (ne byvaxu)* marriage ceremonies among them, but rather a party among the villages: they *would meet (sxožaxusja)* for the party, for dancing and all kinds of demonic carousing, and there they *would carry off (umykaxu)* women for themselves with whom each *had* already *made an agreement (s"věščašesja)*, for they *had (imjaxu)* two and three wives each'

Example (127) stresses regular alternatives, as opposed to simultaneous acts: the Derevlians, unlike normal people, did not have marriages, as they *would carry off* maidens instead. Example (128), however, suggests that *umykati* is most likely protoperfective. First the Radimičians (for instance) *would meet* (a derived prefixed verb, protoimperfective, sets the scene) and there they *would carry off* women who had previously *agreed* to this (the form *s"věščašesja* is punctual, suggesting anaspectuality). The last form, *imjaxu,* is part of a more general statement to the effect that the Derevlians each had two or three wives, and is not connected with the explanation of how those wives were obtained.

Clearly, it is not sufficient for this analysis to take into account only the aspect of the predicates involved. Instead, we have to account for the lexical scope of the predicate as well, since that often offers some clues as to verbal behavior. It is worth looking at a few more complex examples to see if they bear out this hypothesis, such as (129).

(129) да егда в ц(е)рк(о)вь **внидяшеть. и слыша** пѣнье и абье слезы **испущашеть.** (295)
'and when he *entered (vnidjašet')* the church, he *heard (slyša)* the singing and immediately *shed (ispuščašet')* tears'

Example (129) presents three predicates: protoperfective imperfect *(vnidjašet')*, then anaspectual aorist *(slyša)*, then protoimperfective imperfect *(ispuščašet')*. The protoperfective *vnidjašet'* 'entered' is not hard to explain à la Maslov: strict ordering requires a protoperfective form. The appearance of the participle *slyša* 'hearing' is not surprising: verbs describing punctual atelic acts can also express inception or a momentary action. The use of an imperfect *ispuščašet'* 'loosed, expressed' is more difficult to justify. We would expect *ispuščati* to have nonpunctual, telic predicates that would be aspectually protoimperfective, and the plural noun *slezy* 'tears' seems to confirm this reading. However, if the predicate

---

41 Found in the Troitskij, Academy, and Radzivil mss. instead of the Laurentian's *i.*

ispuščati slezy 'shed tears' is considered a synonym for *plakati (sja)* 'cry', the question of aspect becomes moot; the predicate is atelic. The form found in (129) can be read with inceptive meaning, which is perfectly acceptable for an atelic predicate.

As a lexically anaspectual predicate, *ispuščati slezy* does not fall under one of Maslov's sentence types. Instead, it prompts a revision of one of his other statements: that some imperfects are unexpectedly found with "perfective" verbs because those verbs are not yet truly protoperfective. Once I have already defined a few contexts in which protoperfective verbs are expected with the imperfect tense, it is only a small step to make the further claim that some imperfects are unexpectedly found with "imperfective" verbs simply because these verbs are not yet "imperfective."

Revising this statement to fit with a lexical account, I can state that **sometimes we find protoimperfective predicates where a protoperfective one is expected; this situation reflects the fact that not all predicates of modern-day imperfective verbs are in fact protoimperfective in Old Russian.** In example (129), by Maslov's account, a protoperfective imperfect would be expected. The appearance of an apparent protoimperfective imperfect is due to the fact that the lexical contour of the predicate, not the verb as a whole, determines aspectual assignment or the lack thereof.

In (130), there are two aorists *(idě* 'they [sic] went'; *mnogy c(e)rkvi zapališa ognem'* 'they *set fire* to many churches') with an imperfect sandwiched in between them *(požigaxu sela i gumna* 'they torched villages and barns'). This situation is easier to explain: the aorists carry the narrative forward, while the derived prefixed imperfect describes occasional, repeated action along the way.

(130)   **идѣ** лукавии с(ы)н(о)ве Измаилеви **пожигаху** села и гумна. и многы ц(е)ркви **запалиша** огнемь. (223)
        'and the treacherous sons of Izmail *torched* villages and barns, and *set fire* to many churches'

Example (131) has two seemingly identical acts expressed with imperfects, one from a prefixed protoperfective *(posvětjaše* 'lit up, flashed'), and the other from a simplex protoimperfective *(bleščašet'sja* 'flared, fired, flashed').

(131)   и быс(ть) сѣча силна. яко **посвѣтяше** молонья. **блещашеться** оружье. и бѣ гроза велика. и сѣча силна и страшна. (148)
        'and there was a fierce battle, for lightning *flashed*, weapons *shone*, and there was a great storm, and a fierce and terrible battle'.

The difficulty here is that the events should not be strictly ordered. The verb *posvětjaše* 'lit up, flashed' must be either inceptive or durative, but here the protoperfective also indicates sharply delimited and possibly occasional repetition of the event, in contrast to the form *bleščašet'sja* 'flared, fired, flashed', which is protoimperfective and here conveys an act that is ongoing.⁴² This example suggests that a single imperfect with progressive properties is enough to imply simultaneity; other imperfect acts in the sentence can express varying degrees of regularity, duration through aspectual or lexical distinctions without altering the simultaneity of the acts.

In (132), three protoperfective predicates—*načaxu* 'they began', *pomilovašet'* 'he took mercy', *izbavjašet'* 'he forgave'—are followed by a derived prefixed form, *ouklanjaxut'*.

(132)   егда ся **начаху** каяти и **помиловашеть** их (и) егда **избавяшеть** ихъ. паки **оукланяхуться**. на бѣсослуженье. (97)⁴³
'when they *would begin* to repent, he *would take mercy* on them; when he had *redeemed* them, they *would* again *veer off* into devil worship'

The sentence's two apparently parallel structures, both with "when–then" clauses, seem to be violated by the final verb form. If we consider the possible meanings of *uklanjati sja* 'fall (away from God, into sin)', however, the source of the problem becomes clear. The protoperfective *ukloniti sja* is inceptive, meaning the choice between *ukloniti sja* and *uklanjati sja* is a matter of marking inception vs. state.⁴⁴ The form *uklanjaxut'sja* shows that a general tendency—an inclination toward evil—was interrupted periodically by cycles of repentance and salvation.

Maslov's system of clear-cut definitions and sentence types forms a solid basis for understanding the imperfect tense in Old Russian. It successfully demonstrates the regularity of protoperfective verbs in the imperfect tense but is less successful at explaining certain mixtures of aspectual and anaspectual forms that frequently crop up in the Chronicles. To account for these anomalous forms, we have to add more weight to contextual and lexical factors, which Maslov only hints at. Furthermore, the sentence structures Maslov proposes are useful as guidelines, but the actual language situation also presents far more complex and ambiguous settings, where the apparently capricious choice of forms may be motivated by a number of possible interpretations of the relations between the acts.

5.7. CHRONOLOGY AND PREFIXATION

Prefixation has figured prominently in my discussion of aspect and aspectualization. It is worth taking a few moments to recap the generally accepted

---

42   The Modern Russian translation suggests that the weapons lit up in the glare of the lightning; this is a temporal reading of *jako* 'as, while', where I chose a logical reading 'for'. Weapons, after all, can 'flash' at any time; this is a conventional way of saying that they were seen or used. In either reading, there is a clear difference between the occasional, singular flashes of lightning and the geographically random, dispersed nature of the weapons' illumination.
43   Appeared above as example (77).
44   The forms of *ukloniti sja* attested in the Chronicles support an inceptive reading for this verb.

facts about prefixation in Old Russian and those that have been proposed so far in this study. Old Russian verbal prefixes have two basic effects on the verb: they either comment on the location or configuration of the theme (a spatial function) or on the unfolding of the act itself (a telicizing or "perfectivizing" function). In both types, a deformation of the simplex's meaning is permissible; this deformation is more common with the telicizing function but is also found with the spatial function. With motion verbs, the effects of prefixes are in between these two classes: they telicize (to a certain extent) as well as commenting on the positioning of the theme.

Certain prefixes have been held to have a pure perfectivizing function; in other words, when they add telicity to an act, they do not modify the configuration of the act in any other way. These examples are sporadic and constitute a subclass of the telicizing function.

The **spatial function** of prefixation has long been recognized in Old Russian, although it is usually classified simply as an irregularly occurring phenomenon. It has been shown in this study that stative predicates undergo spatial prefixation regularly, while in large measure avoiding telicizing prefixation; prefixes on statives simply mark space, without any imposition of greater telicity. Atelic punctual predicates *(viděti* 'see') can also have this sort of prefixation.

The **telicizing function** of prefixation effects a change to the basic meaning of the predicate that also entails a change in its telicity. Stating the change in this fashion—as a modification to lexical shape, rather than to aspect—has advantages. Even a cursory look at Old Russian texts shows that the functions we associate with perfectivity for the most part go hand in hand with the prefixation of a simplex verb. However, it is not necessary that this connection be a direct one. It is more accurate to see the semantics of prefixation as a two-step process: prefixation often imposes a greater sense of motion toward a goal, increasing the telicity of the act. Such highly telic acts are most naturally protoperfective where and when aspect is established.

A corollary to this point is that increases in telicity are not always easily discernible; highly telic acts, and particularly punctual telic acts, are least susceptible to major usage changes based on "perfectivizing" prefixation, because their telicity and potential for punctuality is high already. In these verbs, behavioral differences between simplex and prefixed predicates may be minimal, or the prefixed verb's range of meaning and usage may be more limited than the simplex's.

The **spatial-telicizing function** of prefixation found with motion verbs are discussed at the end of section 5.7.2.

The **pure perfectivizing function** of prefixation transforms a non-perfective predicate into one that functions as a perfective with no change to the predicate's meaning or lexical class. There is substantial disagreement about the appropriateness of this category for Modern Russian, let alone for Old Russian, and it will be important to either justify or disprove the existence of such prefixes in Old Russian.

5.7.1. Spatial prefixation

There are a number of sentences from the Primary Chronicle that are often cited to prove the general lawlessness that prevails in the Old Russian aspectual system. Example (133) is the best known of them.

(133) Днѣпръ бо **потече** из Оковьскаго лѣ(са) и **потечеть** на полъдне а Двина ис тогоже лѣса **потечет**. а **идеть** на полунощье и **внидеть** в море Варяжьское. ис того же лѣса **потече** Волга на въстокъ. и **вътечеть** семьюдесять жерелъ в море Хвалисьское. (7)
'for the Dnieper *rises (poteče)* in the Okovskij forest, and *flows (potečet')* to the south, and the Dvina *rises (potečet)* in the same forest, and *goes (idet')* to the north, and *empties (vnidet')* into the Baltic Sea; from that same forest the Volga *runs (poteče)* to the east, and *flows (v"tečet')* through seventy mouths into the Caspian Sea'

This is a well-known geographical description from the Primary Chronicle, and the use of prefixed determinate verbs to convey a general truth has bothered many researchers. The prefixed forms above differ from the unprefixed determinate forms, like *idet'* 'it goes', only in that they show direction or inception. (Direction is shown in the case of the prefix {v-}: *vnidet'* 'it enters', *v"tečet'* 'it flows in', and inception in the case of the prefix {po-}: *poteče* 'it rises/begins'.) In many instances, though, prefixed motion verbs do behave just as expected from Modern Russian, as in (134).

(134) и реч(е) **поиду** в Русь **приведу** боле дружинъ. (71)
'and he said: *I will go (poidu)* to Russia [and] *will bring (privedu)* more troops'

Prefixed non-past forms have future sense in (134) and indicate an act viewed as a whole, which we associate in Modern Russian with perfectivity. This behavior pattern is consistent enough that works on Old Russian aspect have posited an exceptional class of geographical descriptions to account for exceptions like (133).[45] Intuitively this is not a satisfying answer.

To put these usage patterns in perspective, I will examine a few unprefixed verb forms. Sometimes an unprefixed verb represents an act in the present, as with the form *idut'* 'they are coming' in (135).

(135) и посла пред ними слы гл(агол)я сице. ц(а)рю се **идуть** к тебѣ Варязи. не мози их держати въ градѣ. (79)
'and he sent emissaries ahead of them, saying: hark, the Varangians *are coming (idut')* toward you; do not try to hold them in the city'

---

[45] Ruzicka 1957 does this explicitly; more cautious researchers like Kuznecov seem reluctant to allow it a separate class. See the relevant discussions in chapter 3.

In (135), *idut'* 'they are coming' expresses an ongoing action in a single direction. This does not have to be the case, however, as in (136), where the form *lězu* expresses intention to perform an act immediately ('I will go' instead of the expected 'I go'), parallel to the prefixed form *narjažju* 'I will arrange, make arrangements'.

(136) И реч(е) С(вя)тополкъ посѣдита вы сдѣ. а язъ **лѣзу наряжю**. и лѣзе вонъ. (259)
 'and Svjatopolk said: you stay here, and I *will go* and *arrange things;* and he went out'

Example (136) shows that the non-past of these predicates can express at least certain kinds of futurity. This should not be surprising, since the same phenomenon occurs in Modern Russian with exactly these verbs.

The only forms where the non-past meaning is atypical by Modern Russian standards are thus those of (133). However, the problem disappears if these verbs are analyzed by lexical predicate class. Examples (134)-(136) all have telic predicates, showing striving toward a goal; only (133) uses these forms as atelic predicates, interpreting motion verbs as unchanging states. As such, these prefixed forms are not protoperfective; instead, they have stative interpretations like those suggested in chapter 4 for prefixed verbs like *prederžati* 'be in charge of', *predležati* 'lie prior to', *pristojati* 'support, back up'.

5.7.2. Telicizing prefixation

Much telicizing prefixation in Modern Russian falls into the category we call Aktionsart prefixation: that is, the prefix makes changes to the temporal shape of the act, limiting it in some way, while leaving unaltered the act that the verb describes. In the Old Russian of the Chronicles, it appears that some Aktionsart functions of prefixation are quite ancient, while others are more recent. In particular, the association of a prefix with a single, predictable Aktionsart meaning is not common and is only found in the later part of the Chronicles.

Inception is clearly the oldest Aktionsart function marked by prefixes. In the Chronicles, it is found most often with {po-} and {v"z-}, although these are not the only means of indicating inception. Simplex verbs that express atelic acts can often express a corresponding inceptive act as well when the context is clear enough. The appearance of the prefix {za-} as a regular marker of inception is found quite early in the Chronicles with certain verbs. One reason for this may be that {po-} had several additional uses besides its inceptive function, including the sense 'complete, finish off'. With the verb *žeči* 'burn (trans.)', for example, both forms in {po-} and {za-} are found from the earliest dates in consistent proportions, with the former being far more frequent than the latter. But {po-} does not always express a clear inceptive meaning; sometimes it indicates completion or totality. This is probably the case in (137), where it fits in the middle of a list of destructive accomplishments attributed to Igor's army and their Byzantine opponents.

(137) много же с(вя)тыхъ ц(е)рквии огнемъ предаша. манастырѣ и села **пожьгоша**. и именья немало (от) обою страну взяша. (44)
'they consigned many holy churches to flames, *burned (pož'goša)* monasteries and villages, and took no small amount of property from both sides'

However, contrast this with (138), where the same verb form fits in a chain of events, making it more likely to represent the initial setting on fire of the gates. It appears that the precise function of the prefix {po-} is generated by the context, not merely by its attachment to a particular root.

(138) Володимеръ же приступи ко вратомъ в(о)сточнымъ. от Стрежени и отя врата. и отвориша градъ околнии. и **пожгоша** и. людемъ же вбѣгшим въ дънѣшнии градъ. (201)
'Volodimer advanced to the eastern gates from Strežen' and seized the gates and they opened the outer town, and *burned (požgoša)* it; the people ran into the lower town'

In contrast to the murky state of affairs with {po-}, the prefix {za-} regularly represents initiation of an action, as in (139) and (140).

(139) они же **пережьгоша** истопку. и влѣзоша Деревляне. начаша ся мыти. и запроша о нихъ истобъку. и повелѣ **зажечи** я от двери. ту изгорѣша вси. (57)
'and they *fired up (perež'goša)* the bath, and the Derevljane went into it [and] began to wash themselves, and they locked the bath on them, and [she] ordered *to set* them *afire (zažeči)* from the doors, and all of them burned to a crisp'

(140) Быс(ть) пожаръ в Володимери городѣ... в полъночи **зажжеся**. и горѣ мало не до вечера. ц(е)рквии изгорѣша 14 а города половина погорѣ. (409)
'There was a fire in the city of Volodimer'... it *began (zažžesja)* at midnight and burned almost until evening; fourteen churches burned down and half the city was incinerated'

In (139), Olga takes revenge on her enemies by offering them a hot bath. Once they are inside, she has the bathhouse torched from the outside, and the fact that *zažeči* refers to the beginning of the fire is clear from the following phrase *ot dverii* 'from the doors'. Example (140) has a clear sequence of actions in which *zažžesja* denotes when the fire was set, while the course of the fire and its results are given later in the sentence.

Part of the difficulty with *žeči* comes from the fact that its meaning ('cause to burn, set alight') is inherently highly telic and suggests the beginning of a process; in this sense, neither prefix contributes much to the meaning of the verb. (Note that the reflexive form in (140) is most easily read as a passive transformation, indicating action directed at oneself—'the fire was set'—not as an intransitive transformation of the transitive predicate—'the fire flared up'.) A more interesting test case will be *gorěti* 'burn', which is usually intransitive in meaning and forms an atelic predicate more easily. Once again, the degree of inception in the prefixes {po-} and {v"z-} is relatively weak. Virtually all examples that can be inceptive can also be read as indicating completion or exhaustion, as in (141) and (142).

(141) и тако **възгарахуся** голубьници. ово клѣти. ово вежѣ. ово ли одрини. и не бѣ двора идеже не горяще. и не бѣ льзѣ гасити. вси бо двори **възгорѣшася**. (59)
'and in this manner, the pigeon-coops and cages and towers and sheds *burst into flame (v"zgaraxusja)*, and there was not a courtyard that was not burning, and it was not possible to put it out; all the courtyards *burst into flame/burned up (v"zgorěšasja)*'

(142) Ярославъ иде (в Киевъ). и **погорѣ** церкви. (142)
'Jaroslav went (to Kiev) and *burned down/set fire to (pogorě)* the church'

Sometimes the exhaustive character of the prefix is even explicit, as in (143).

(143) мало остася города. а все **погорѣ**. и товара **погорѣ** множство бещислено. (453)
'little remained of the city, and everything *burned (pogorě)*; and an uncountable quantity of merchandise *burned (pogorě)*'

In fact, the best indicator of inception for this verb seems to be the affix {roz- -sja} as seen in (144):[46]

(144) в едину бо нощь **вжегъ** пещь выстобцѣ оу пещеры. яко **разгорѣся** пещь. бѣ бо утла. и нача палати пламень оутлизнами. (196)
'one night he *lit (vžeg")* the stove in the hut near the cave, when the stove *caught fire (razgorěsja)*, for it was cracked, and the flame began to burn through the cracks'

Furthermore, the form *zagorěti* is absent from the Primary Chronicle. It appears only in the Suzdal' Chronicle, as in (145).

(145) и на ту нощь **загорѣся** городъ. (308)
'and that night the city *caught fire (zagorěsja)*'

What can we make of the distribution of forms and meanings found in (141) through (144)? First, inception in Old Russian need not be a separate, abstract meaning encoded in the prefix. Instead, it may stem from a reinterpretation of a different function that happens to react with the semantics of the predicate in question to produce an inceptive effect. Thus, the prefix {v-} has a basically spatial

---

[46] It is conceivable that the prefix in *vžeg"* is actually a contracted form of {v"z-}. However, this particular predicate *(vžeg" pešč'* 'lit the stove') is not attested elsewhere in the Chronicles, and there are no semantically similar forms from *vozžeči* 'light' to support this interpretation.

or telicizing function, but with the verb *žeči* it acquires an inceptive function as well (as if fire is somehow 'set into' an object). A similar inceptivity is seen later in the same example with the prefix {raz-}, where spreading fire reinforces the notion of flames bursting out all over. For this particular verb, the prefix {v"z-} may be less successful at connoting inception, because rising flames already indicate that the fire is well underway. Second, the dependency of time-limitation features on spatial features suggests that Aktionsart prefixes may have been even more numerous and idiosyncratic in their application in Old Russian than they are in Modern Russian. The late appearance of {za-} as a reliable inceptive prefix for this verb may indicate that this prefix is spreading gradually through the lexicon in this era.

It is important to note that not all verbs with apparently inceptive prefixes have the same range of meanings and usages as the simplexes they are formed from. A good example is the verb pair *ljubiti–v"zljubiti* 'love–find love for'. The simplex *ljubiti* is used foremost to express relations between people (husbands for wives, brothers for each other, parents for children). It also describes religious sentiments, such as man's love for God and God's love for man. Rare examples describe love for an abstract concept (truth, justice). The prefixed form *v"zljubiti* is used almost exclusively to describe the last two sorts of love. As such, its meaning is more intimately bound with faith than is the simplex's. For love between people, the periphrastic expression *stvoriti ljubov'* 'bring about love' is often used. This expression emphasizes a different semantic component of the Old Russian word, which can imply both love and friendly (peaceful) relations when used about rulers; this decidedly secular connotation is notably absent from the examples of *v"zljubiti*.

A different Aktionsart function, expressing fulfillment, exhaustion or satiation of an act, is found with the prefixes {do-} and {ot-} in Modern Russian. This use of the prefix {do-} appears in the Chronicles from an early date, but its use multiplies greatly later on. For instance, it appears a total of fourteen times in the Primary Chronicle's 286 pages, but in the Suzdal' Chronicle it appears twenty-six times in 200 pages. Other prefixes, such as {ot-}, {vy-} and {iz-}, which can have a similar function, are far less common. These prefixes, of course, are multifunctional, more often expressing direction or even location in these texts. For instance, I found only three verbs with {ot-} that express an exhaustive meaning; for one of these, *otstojati,* I found two different uses.

(146) оусты же чтуть мя а с(е)рдце ихъ далече **отстоить** мене. (169)
'with their lips they honor me, but their heart *stands* far *from (otstoit')* me'[47]

(147) видѣ старець се. по обычаю бо сему старцю. **отстоявшю** оутренюю предъ зорями. идоша по кѣльямъ своимъ. (190)
'and the old man saw this: as was this old man's habit, when he had *stood through (otstojavšju)* matins before dawn, they [the monks] would go to their cells'[48]

---

47 Matthew 15:8 and Mark 7:6. Also appeared as example (79) in chapter 4.
48 Overlaps with material in example (82), chapter 4.

The function of the prefix in (146)—the example is a scriptural quote—is unambiguously spatial, and the prefix plays no aspectual role. Only in (147) does *otstojati* clearly mean 'stand until the end of something'. Given the differing styles of the texts and their closeness in the manuscript, no clear temporal conclusion can be drawn about these uses of {ot-}. Still, it is noteworthy that a single verb could be used both telically and atelically with the same prefix, where the prefix had both spatial and telicizing functions. It may be that the change in function from distal prefixation to telicizing prefixation preserved some of the negative connotation of distance seen in (146). If distance is reinterpreted as a lack of possession, it is understandable how the telicizing function of {ot-} came to be exhaustive, as against {do-}, which is more likely to express fulfillment.[49]

A similarly early stage of development can be observed with the prefix {na-}, which in Modern Russian can have an exhaustive meaning with distinct negative connotations *(nadelat'^{P}* 'screw something up^P by overdoing it'). This meaning is absent from the Chronicle's attested forms with {na-}. In some instances, {na-} has lost its function and become lexicalized (as in *nadějati sja* 'hope'); otherwise it often accompanies verbs denoting the filling of an object or person *(nalijati* 'pour into', *napitati* 'feed up', *napolniti* 'fill up', *nasytiti* 'satiate'). In the Chronicles, traces of a spatial function remain along with telicizing prefixation in the verbs *navjazati* 'tie onto', *naskakati* 'jump onto'.

There are sporadic indications in the Chronicles that prefixed verbs with an early provenance are more likely to retain the aspectual ambiguity of the simplex form, while prefixed forms found only later in the Chronicles are clearly protoperfective. Such is the case with prefixed forms of *metati* 'cast, hurl'. The simplex shows considerable ambiguity itself, with forms like *žreb'i metavše* 'having cast lots' having a completed meaning, vs. *aky dožd' kamen'e metaxu na n'* 'like rain they hurled stones upon him', where the predicate is clearly an iterative semelfactive (an uninterrupted repetition of durationless actions perceived as a process). Forms attested early in the Primary Chronicle, such as *vmetati* 'cast or hurl into' and *otmetati* 'cast or hurl off', have the same variation in meaning, while those found only at the end of the Suzdal' Chronicle, like *nametati* 'heave onto', *pometati* 'throw', and *smetati* 'hurl off, sweep off' are attested only as completed acts. This unusual state of affairs may in two different senses be a reflection of the relative paucity of semelfactive iteratives. First, the small number of these forms means that there are few verbs with enough forms attested to make reliable generalizations. Second, because they are a small group of predicates, the semelfactives may tend to assimilate to the more common and productive nonpunctual telic pattern, in which prefixing a verb that indicates a process yields a completed act. This model explains the pattern of *nametati, pometati,* and *otmetati* as a gradual regularization of the prefixation process, making it more uniform in its effect across the various lexical groups. If this model is correct, it confirms that early Old Russian already made partial use of a productive process in which

---

[49] Incidentally, Modern Russian maintains both these meanings of *otstojat'*: one perfective and exhaustive, one imperfective and spatial.

prefixation also added telicity and thus perfectivity, and that in the eleventh to fourteenth centuries this process was being extended from the telic nonpunctual predicates to other parts of the verbal system.

5.7.3. Prefixation and motion verbs

Having established the atelic nature of acts like *rěka v"tečet'* 'the river flows in' as the reason for their prefixes' failure to perfectivize the whole predicate, it is only a small step to asking if we can make the same claim for indeterminate motion verbs like *xoditi* 'walk (regularly, habitually)', *ězditi* 'ride (regularly, habitually)'. After all, in Modern Russian, indeterminate verbs are often atelic and their prefixed forms usually appear in durative, progressive, or iterative contexts and do not represent instantaneous or summarized acts. It is worth seeing if the same situation holds for Old Russian.

Since I did not collect data on motion verbs comprehensively from the Chronicles, my data are drawn from two sources. First, a search through my data turned up numerous forms of indeterminate motion verbs in the citations for other verbs. These attestations, since they appeared randomly, should be representative, although I will not attempt to extract any numeric comparisons from them. In all these examples (with one exception) the indeterminate verbs stand for an atelic action: motion described simply as motion, without a goal. The predicates can have the argument *po* + dative case noun phrase, indicating undirected motion within a certain area, as in (148)-(150).

(148) и повелѣ трость держати ч(е)л(овѣ)комъ. и **ходити** по городу и звати. тростем трясомом. (40)
'and he ordered that people hold their stick[s], and that [they] *walk (xoditi)* around the city, and call, shaking their stick'

(149) и поча **ходити** по дебремъ и по гора(мъ) ища кдѣ бы ему Б(ог)ъ показалъ. (156)
'and he began *to walk (xoditi)* through wildernesses and mountains, looking for the place God would show him'

(150) повелѣ пристроити кола (и) въскладше хлѣбы. мяса, рыбы... **возити** по городу въпрашающим. кде болнии и нищь не могы ходити. тѣмъ раздаваху на потребу. (126)
'he ordered [them] to make ready the carts (and), having loaded on breads, meat, fish... *to drive (voziti)* [these things] around the city, asking where the sick and poor were who could not walk, and they gave them what they needed'

Similarly, the predicate *ězdja v"zle bereg"* 'riding along the bank' in (151) indicates motion within a limited area, without regard to starting and ending points.

(151) воевода нача С(вя)тополчь **ѣздя** възлѣ берегъ. оукаряти Новгородцѣ... (142)

'Svjatopolk's commander began, *riding* along the bank, to mock the Novgorodians'

Sometimes the indeterminate motion verb conveys ability to perform an action without regard to goals or endpoints, as in (152) and (153).

(152) и нача чюдеса велика творити. м(е)ртвия въскр(ѣ)ш(а)ти. прокаженыя очищати. хромыя **ходити**. слѣпымъ прозрѣнье творити. (103)
'and he began to do great miracles: to resurrect the dead, cleanse the afflicted, make the lame *walk (xoditi)* [and] the blind clear of sight'

(153) и посем наоучи на тряпезницю **ходити**. и посажашеть и кромѣ брат(ь)и. (и) положаху пред ним хлѣбъ... (194)
'and afterwards he learned *to go (xoditi)* to the refectory, and they sat him separately from the brothers, and placed bread before him...'[50]

Example (154) expresses the negation of this: an order is given forbidding a horse to be brought into the prince's presence.

(154) и повелѣ кормит (и) и **не водити** ег(о) к нему. (38)
'and he gave orders to feed [the horse] and *not to bring (ne voditi)* it to him'

In some instances, the atelicity of the predicate is bolstered by other analogous atelic or explicitly iterative predicates in the sentence, as in (148): *deržati... i xoditi po gorodu* 'to hold... and *to walk* about the city'; in (152): *nača... m(e)rtvija v"skr(ě)š(a)ti. prokaženyja očiščati. xromyja xoditi* 'he began... *to raise* the dead, *cleanse* the afflicted and make the lame *walk*'; and in (154): *povelě kormit(i) i ne voditi ego k nemu* '[he] gave orders *to feed* [it] and *not to bring* it to him'.

My sampling included only one aorist form each for the verbs *xoditi* and *voditi* indicating a telic act.

(155) приде на холмъ. кде стояше Перунъ. покладоша оружье свое и щитъ и золото. и **ходи** Игорь ротѣ и люди его. елико поганыхъ Руси. а хр(ест)яную Русь **водиша** ротѣ. в ц(е)ркви с(вя)т(а)го Ильи. (54)
'and they came to the hill where Perun stood, and they put down their arms and shield[s] and gold, and Igor' *took an oath (xodi rotě)*, and his people, as many as were pagans from Russia; and they *administered the oath (vodiša rotě)* to the Christian Russians in the church of St. Ilja'

This anomaly is easily explainable, since the predicates *xoditi rotě* and *voditi rotě* mean respectively 'take an oath' and 'administer an oath'. These predicates are telic, and thus the aorist with these indeterminate verbs expresses a summation of

---

[50] In the English translation I follow two divergences in the Radzivil and Academy mss.: *naučisja* for *naouči* and *posažaxu* for *posažašet'*.

numerous oaths taken and administered (iteration is also implied in the phrase *eliko poganyx" Rusi* 'as many as were pagans among the Russians').

My second source for indeterminate forms was the *Poučenie Vladimira Monomaxa,* which is interpolated into the Laurentian manuscript under the entry for 1096 (pp. 240-252 in the *Polnoe sobranie russkix letopisej).* This text yielded an abundance of forms whose usage is different from those in the rest of the text.[51] Of these examples, only (156) and (157) show motion as an atelic action. The form *ězdja* 'while riding' in (156) is a background activity, showing process but no direction or goal. Somewhat similar is the second occurrence of *xodiv"* in (157), which means 'spend time travelling'.(Modern Russian imperfective *proxodil).*

(156) та бо есть м(о)л(и)тва всѣх лѣпши. нежели мыслити безлѣпицю **ѣздя**. (245)[52]
'for that is the best prayer of all, rather than think of trifles *while riding (ězdja)*'

(157) та посла мя С(вя)тославъ в Ляхы. **ходивъ** *(ходил)* за Глоговы. до Чешьскаго лѣса. **ходивъ** в земли ихъ 4 мѣсяци. (247)
'Svjatoslav sent me to the Poles, and I *went (xodiv")* past Głogów to the Czech Forest, *having travelled (xodiv")* in their land for four months'

A second type of usage is the round-trip also indicated in (157); Vladimir writes that Svjatoslav sent him to Poland, from where he made a trip into the Czech Forest. In the next sentence he is back in Poland, and then we learn that he went to Turov afterwards. The round-trip sense (modern *xodil)* is in some ways similar to the atelic meaning mentioned earlier, in that the former suggests motion that begins and ends at the same point, while the latter can suggest motion that takes place all within a single area. It might therefore be tempting to say that round trips are atelic, because regardless of the fact that there is a prescribed journey involved, it ends in the same place it started, giving it the same lack of effect as an atelic act. However, this interpretation confuses *telicity,* which is lexical, with *result,* which is a discourse feature; an evaluation of an act's effectiveness cannot determine its telicity, which should be an objectively observable phenomenon. The fact is that a one-way trip with an endpoint is telic; a round trip, therefore, is still telic, since the trip follows a planned trajectory, first approaching its midpoint and then its endpoint. The predicate *xodiv" za Glogovy do Češ'skago lěsa* 'having gone beyond Głogów as far as the Czech Forest' is telic, since a goal is present.[53]

---

[51] The impetus for using the *Poučenie* was a comment by Ruzicka (1957: 23): "Die indeterminierten Simplicia treten kaum an oder über die Grenzen des imperfektiven Aspekts, auch im Aorist nicht, der durchaus vorkommt, besonders häufig in der 'Poučenie' Monomaxs." (However, the conclusion of Ruzicka's statement—that aorists of motion verbs are still clearly imperfective—is, in my opinion, not correct.)

[52] Discussed earlier as example (72), and further on as example (203).

[53] Seeing all round trips as telic provides a clue to one puzzling aspectual pair in Modern Russian: *xodit'–sxodit'* 'make a round trip'. In this telic meaning, the verb *xodit'* is

Once it is clear that the predicate is telic, the various semantic components and their reflection in the sentence fall into place: the verb chosen *(xoditi* vs. *idti)* shows the indeterminate vs. determinate distinction (here multiple directions vs. a single direction); the presence or absence of a destination and the tense form mark the indeterminate predicate as atelic or telic, since a telic predicate is likely to have an aorist form or past participle, and an atelic predicate is likely to have a non-past or imperfect form or a present participle. A combination of indeterminacy and telicity thus gives us the reading 'round trip'. The presence or absence of result is not marked in the verb form; instead, it comes from the context at large. This analysis holds equally well for (158)-(160). In all three examples, an indeterminate verb in the aorist indicates the entirety of a trip, both outward journey and return.

(158) тои пакы **ходихомъ**. том же лѣт(е). со о(т)ц(е)мь и со Изяславомь биться Чернигову. с Борисомь. и побѣдихомъ Бориса и Олга. (248)
'then *we went (xodixom")* again that year with my father and Izjaslav to Černigov to fight Boris, and we vanquished Boris and Oleg'

(159) а въ Вятичи **ходихом** по двѣ зимѣ. на Ходоту и на с(ы)на его. и до Корьдну **ходихъ** 1-ю зиму. и пакы по Изяславичихъ за Микулинъ. и не постигохом ихъ. (248)
'and *we went (xodixom)* among the Vjatičians two winters against Xodot and his son: the first winter *I went* (xodix") to Kor'dno, and then after Izjaslav's men and against Mikulin, but we did not overtake them'

(160) и **ходихом** за Супои и ѣдучи к Прилуку городу. и срѣтоша ны внезапу Половечьскыѣ князи 8 тысячь. (248)
'and *we went (xodixom)* past the Supa and [were] riding to the town of Priluk, and suddenly the Polovtsian princes [with] eight thousand [men] met us'

To sum up the evidence from unprefixed indeterminate verbs like *xoditi, ězditi* 'go': as with the determinate verbs *idti, exati* 'go', the predicates of these indeterminate verbs can be either telic or atelic.[54] Just as atelic determinates are rarer than telic ones, so are telic indeterminates rarer than atelic ones. However, the preponderance of atelic uses for these verbs suggests that a majority of the prefixed indeterminate forms we will find will not be protoperfective. To check this

---

imperfective but highly articulated, since it supposes at least two stages to the journey; the only prefixed form clearly related to this round-trip sense is *sxodit'*, which is also the only commonly used prefixed form of *xodit'* perceived as perfective. (The difference is even clearer with the perfective *s"ezdit'*, which is the only commonly used verb formed by attaching a prefix directly to the indeterminate stem *-ezdit'* instead of to the stem *-ezžat'*, which is derived from *-ezdit'*.)

[54] This fact creates further difficulties for the theories of Borodič and her adherents, who insist that the determinate–indeterminate opposition and the telic–atelic opposition are one and the same.

assumption, I will examine a number of indeterminate verbs with prefixes. I will not examine abstract compounds like *provoditi* 'spend, conduct' in (161).

(161)   и поучивъ ихъ како **проводити** постное время. в м(о)л(и)твахъ нощныхъ и дневныхъ. блюстися от помыслъ скверньныхъ. (183)
'and having taught them how *to spend (provoditi)* the fast days in nightly and daily prayers to guard themselves against vile thoughts...'

This example is introduced as a reminder that some prefixes on indeterminate verbs induce a shift to an abstract meaning; although abstract acts can also be aspectual, their development appears quite different. Of the remaining, nonabstract examples, some express an action captured as a process, like the solar eclipse described in (162).

(162)   и въ с(о)лнци оучинися яко м(е)с(я)ць. из рогъ его яко угль жаровъ **исхожаше**. (396)
'and in the sun it became like the moon; *it radiated (isxožaše)* like hot coal from its horns'

Present participles and verbal adverbs can perform a similar function, as in (163), or they can appear in iterative contexts, as in (164).

(163)   много бо попеченье створи о ц(е)ркви с(вя)тыя Б(огороди)ца... д(е)нь от дне начиная. и **преходя** от дѣла в дѣло. (459)
'for he expended much effort on the church of the Holy Mother of God... starting each and every day, *going (prexodja)* from one matter to the next'

(164)   и на заоутреню **входя** преже всѣм. стояше крѣпко и неподвижимо. (195)
'and, *entering (vxodja)* at matins before everyone else, he stood firmly and immovably'

A progressive context appears in (165), where the treaty supposes a contingency consisting of two simultaneous actions (on their way to the Greeks, the Black Bulgars might make war in the land of Korsun). The form is non-past, 3 pl.

(165)   а о сихъ оже то **приходять** Чернии Болгаре. (и) воюють въ странѣ Корсуньстѣи. (51)
'and on these matters: if the Black Bulgars *are coming (prixodjat')* [to Greece], and are making war in Korsun...'

In one case—(166)—the verbal adverb in the phrase *ne vyxodja iz pečery* 'without leaving the cave' is in a durative context limited by a time expression.

(166)   ...ископа печеру... в неиже сконча животъ свои. живъ в добродѣтели. **не выходя** ис печеры. лѣт 40 никдѣже. (158)

'he dug out the cave... in which he ended his life, having lived a life of good deeds, *without* ever *leaving* the cave in forty years'

Sometimes the prefixed forms refer to a regular sequence of repeated events, as in (167). Here the treaty stipulates how the Russians shall conduct their trade business with the Greeks; the predicate has *da* 'let' plus a 3 pl. non-past form.

(167) **да входять** в городъ одинѣми вороты... и да творять куплю. якоже имъ надобѣ. паки **да исходять**... (49)
'let them have entrance (da vxodjat') to the city through one gate... and let them do whatever business they need, and then *let them leave (da isxodjat')*...'

Example (168) is similarly iterative, since the substantivized participle *prixodjaščaja* 'those who come' indicates that there were numerous visitors to the church. The imperfect *priĕzdjaxu* 'they came' in (169) indicates that the army went out to do battle several times, an iterative use of the imperfect tense.

(168) и вся **приходящая** изъ окр(е)стъных град. в с(вя)тую зборную ц(е)рк(о)вь с(вя)тыя Б(огороди)ца. ово послушающе оученья его еже от с(вя)тыхъ книг. ова же хотяще видѣти оукрашенья с(вя)тыя ц(е)рькви... (458)
'and all *those who came* from the surrounding towns to the holy cathedral of the Holy Mother of God either listened to his teachings, which are from the holy books, or wanted to see the adornments of the holy church...'

(169) и перебродися оу Заруба. и сташа оу Мажева селца товары. оттолѣ же **приѣздяху** к городу биться. (335)
'and he forded the river at Zarubo, and they stopped near Maževo, a trading town, from which they *would come* to the city to fight'

Different and more troubling are the usages found in (170) and (171), with the aorist 3 pl. *prixodiša* and the perfect 3 pl. *prixodili sut'*.

(170) се слышавше Жидове Козарьстии. придоша рекуще слышахомъ яко **приходиша** Болгаре. и х(ри)с(т)еяне оучаще тя. (85)
'having heard this, the Kozarian Jews arrived, saying: we heard that the Bulgars *came (prixodiša)* here, and the Christians, instructing you'

(171) слышахомъ яко **приходили суть** Болгаре. оучаще тя прияти вѣру свою. (86)
'we heard the Bulgars *have come (prixodili sut')* here, teaching you to accept their faith'

Both are statements made by ambassadors to Vladimir as he is choosing what faith to join, and both clearly indicate a single visit without respect to duration. How to explain this use of the verb *prixoditi?* The answer hinges on the conditions for telicity in unprefixed forms: the forms *prixodiša, prixodili sut'* represent a round-trip journey, corresponding to the telic usage of the verb *xoditi* seen above in (157)-(160). If these forms display signs of perfectivity, then that is in keeping with the fact that Old Russian telic predicates become protoperfective when prefixed.[55]

There are several examples of durative uses of the prefix {po-}. In these instances, the prefixed form indicates a future act explicitly limited in time, as in (172) and (173). In (172), Igor changes his mind and decides to return to collect more taxes. The act is limited in time but does not indicate a specific direction. In (173), Vladimir Monomax is deciding which course to pursue; interestingly enough, 'go hunting' is conveyed with a simplex verb *(na lov" ěxati)* while 'collect taxes' is conveyed with a prefixed derived verb that needs no complement *(poězditi)*. Both forms are rendered by the determinate imperfective *exat'* in Modern Russian. The verbs, although limited in duration, are not necessarily protoperfective: the contrasting options open to Monomax in (173) are protoimperfective in nature, suggesting that all the infinitives may have an open-ended reading.

(172) Идуще же ему въспять. размысливъ реч(е) дружинѣ своеи. идѣте сь данью домови. а я возъвращюся **похожю** *(пособираю)* и еще. пусти дружину свою домови. (54)
'As he was going back, he changed his mind and said to his company: go home with the tax revenues, and I *will* return and *collect* some more *taxes (poxožju)*. He released his company [to go] home'

(173) и сѣдше думати с дружиною. или люди оправливати. или на ловъ ѣхати *(ехать)*. или **поѣздити** *(ехать)*. или лечи спати. (247)
'and having sat down he took counsel with his company: either to send people off, or to go hunting, or to *collect taxes (poězditi)*, or go to sleep'

This wide range of meanings and usages stems from the nature of prefixes used with motion verbs and the substantial semantic problems that arise when an indeterminate motion verb accepts a prefix. Pure spatial prefixation (i.e.,

---

55 In Modern Russian, we would say that the lack of evident result is what causes the use of a derived form *(prixodili)* as opposed to a perfective one *(prišli)*. The prefixed forms, derived and nonderived, are paired in an aspectual opposition. In Old Russian, however, the "pairing" apparently makes reference to the simplex verbs instead, i.e., it is lexical not aspectual. To use examples: *prijti* is a spatial-telicizing modification of *idti*, and *prixoditi* is a spatial-telicizing modification of *xoditi*. Thus *prijti* marks a journey in one direction (the direction is marked by the prefix), because *idti* also indicates a unidirectional journey; *prixoditi* indicates a round trip (again, the prefix marks the direction of the trip) because *xoditi* can indicate a round trip. It also stands to reason that where *idti* and *xoditi* are atelic, corresponding prefixed forms will also be atelic.

Of course, later a reanalysis takes place in which *prijti* and *prixoditi* become paired, and it is then that the single direction of the former becomes contrasted to the round trip of the latter, leading to the new "result vs. lack of result" opposition—which, incidentally, ties in with other emerging features in the aspectual system.

prefixation that indicates only a space in which the action took place) is uncommon with motion verbs, although such prefixes are occasionally encountered, as in (174).

(174) възведъ очи свои. позрѣ по братьи. иже стоять поюще по обѣма странама. видѣ **обиходяща** бѣса. въ образѣ Ляха в лудѣ. и носяща в приполѣ цвѣткы (190)
'having raised his eyes, he looked around at the brethren, who stood singing on both sides [and] saw a demon *walking around (obixodjašča)* in the guise of a Pole in a garment, and wearing flowers in the flap'

What motion verbs often have, however, are prefixes with a directional function like the ones seen in (162)-(171)—that is, prefixation that indicates a change to the goal of the act. This directional prefixation is normally telicizing, unlike the spatial prefixation in *otstojati* 'stand far away', *obderžati* 'grip', etc. seen in chapter 4.

However, indeterminate motion verb predicates behave differently from other atelic and telic predicates in important ways. Directional prefixes on motion verbs add a goal, but the indeterminate motion verbs usually form highly atelic predicates, rarely expressing direction and focusing attention instead on the mechanics of the action. The result is that prefixed indeterminate forms usually end up expressing direction, and thus acquire telicity, but the sense of "motion in progress" or "motion as habit" is retained, preventing the form from being labelled protoperfective. Only where telicity is evident in the original indeterminate form (as with round trips) does the heightened telicity of the prefixed form cause it to be perceived as protoperfective. This information is summarized in Chart 5.7.3.1.

The chart shows that while there are clearly semantic differences between the types of prefixes compared, there is no consistent aspectual behavior pattern discernible from the type of prefix. A far greater degree of correlation is found between aspectual behavior and the lexical class of the predicate, with the division between telic and atelic predicates providing the main distinction.

There is one place where, according to the chart, the lexical classification fails to predict the effect of prefixation. Some verbs, when prefixed in such a way that their meaning changes fundamentally, become protoperfective *(bljusti* 'watch over' > *sobljusti* 'preserve') while others do not *(stojati* 'stand' > *predstojati* 'attend to, serve'). This is more a failure in the nature of the chart than anything else; the chart, after all, is based on divisions into predicate groups. The pairs given above are related primarily morphologically, not lexically, so that relating *predstojati* back to an "original" atelic predicate of *stojati* (or *sobljusti* back to an atelic predicate of *bljusti)* is difficult, if not impossible, to justify.

Atelic predicates from indeterminate motion verbs, then, form a grammatical "bridge" between telic acts and other atelic acts. As with the telic predicates, prefixes increase telicity, but in the atelic predicates, this prefixation often fails to cause perfective-like behavior.[56] The perfectivizing feature of telicizing prefixes only holds for telic acts.

---

[56] Hence I term these prefixes "telicizing," not "perfectivizing."

Chart 5.7.3.1. Comparison of prefix function and lexical class

Prefix function	Atelic predicates (non-motion)	Atelic indeterminate motion	Telic indeterminate motion (round-trip)	Telic predicates (non-motion)
Spatial	common; no asp. change; spatial change *pristojaxu k nemu muži*	rare (can shade into category below); no asp. change; *viděobixodjašča běsa*	semantically impossible (round-trip implies actual motion)	not found
Telicizing with direction	semantically impossible (non-motion means no direction)	common; no asp. change; semantic change *prexodja ot děla v dělo*	common; asp. change (?); semantic change *prixodiša Bolgare*	common; asp. change; semantic change *vpisax mnogo slovesa*
Abstract telicizing	rare; some asp. changes; semantic change *sobljudi mja; predstojaše*	rare; no asp. change; semantic change *provoditi vremja*	not found	common; asp. change; semantic change *oustavi dani*

5.7.4. Pure perfectivizing prefixation in Old Russian

The existence of pure perfectivizing prefixation is not universally accepted for Modern Russian, let alone for Old Russian. Numerous scholars have insisted that in fact the verbs in so-called Modern Russian pairs like *pisat'–napisat'* 'write', *delat'–sdelat'* 'do, make' have slightly different meanings derived from a residual lexical meaning in the prefix.[57] This viewpoint is even more widespread for Old Russian; most handbooks and articles claim that the development of simplex-to-prefixed pairs comes only in the final stages of aspectual development, possibly as late as the eighteenth century (if at all). In this section, I will examine two Old Russian verb pairs that are likely candidates for aspectual pairhood and ascertain how well they meet the various criteria established here. The pairs are *pisati–napisati* 'write' and

---

57 See the discussion of Isačenko 1960 in section 2.3.2.

dělati–sdělati 'make'.⁵⁸ In both instances, the simplex verb is usually used telically, so we would expect the prefixed form to be protoperfective and the simplex form to be protoimperfective. The proof will have three components: satisfactorily establishing the protoperfectivity of the prefixed form; showing that it consistently has the same lexical meaning as the simplex verb; and determining that the simplex verb itself appears only in contexts not available to the prefixed verb.

For Modern Russian I might require a more stringent proof—that for all predicates of the simplex there is a corresponding predicate with the identical prefixed form—but this seems extreme for Old Russian, where some of those predicates (if atelic and/or punctual) by definition do not participate in the aspectual system.⁵⁹

The pair *pisati–napisati* 'write' is amply attested in the Chronicles. The reflexive simplex in (175) refers to a state.

(175) яко **пишется** в лѣтописаньи Гречьстѣмь (17)
'as *is written (pišetsja)* in the Greek chronicles'

It can also refer to writing as a telic act, as in (176) and (177).

(176) и нача... писець **писати** гл(аго)ла сице. (72)⁶⁰
'and the scribe began *to write (pisati),* saying as follows...'

(177) аще ли хотѣти начнеть наше ц(а)р(с)тво от васъ воина противящаяся намъ. **да пишю** къ великому князю вашему. и послеть к намъ елико же хочемъ. (52)⁶¹
'if our kingdom should begin to want troops from you against our enemies, *let me write (da pišju)* to your grand prince, and he will send us as many as we want'

Sometimes the simplex is found in a generalized context, as in (178).

(178) а силнии **пишють** правду (152)
'and the strong *write (pišjut')* the laws'

Examples like (178) are atelic, indicating occupation rather than specific actions. The verb *pisati* in the non-past tense indicates a present act (or a future act with the particle *da)* and in the infinitive expresses generalities or action in progress.

---

58 I could easily add a third pair: *tvoriti–stvoriti* 'make, create'. However, this verb is so common and is used in such widely varying types of predicates that a thorough analysis of it would require more space and time than circumstances warrant.
59 I think this criterion may be too demanding even for Modern Russian, which calls into doubt whether Modern Russian truly has aspectual "verbs" as opposed to aspectual "predicates," but this is a different kettle of worms.
60 The Laurentian ms. has *nača pisec' pisec' psati,* with an obvious scribal error.
61 This sentence appeared earlier in this chapter as example (8).

The verb *napisati* does not express the stative meaning seen above or an inceptive meaning corresponding to it. Instead, it expresses the completion of telic action, as in (179)-(181).

(179) се же **написахъ** и **положихъ**. в кое лѣто почалъ быти манастырь. и что ради зоветься Печерьскыи. (160)
'I *wrote (napisax")* this and *set down (položix")* in what year the monastery came to be, and why it is called the Monastery of the Caves'

(180) **написах** ти грамоту. аще ю приимеши с добромь. ли с поруганьемь. свое же оузрю на твоем писаньи. (253)
'I *wrote (napisax)* you a letter; whether you accept it with good will or malediction I will see in your writing'

(181) аще ли оубѣжавше в Русь придуть. мы **напишемъ** ко князю вашему. яко имъ любо тако створять (48)
'if someone, having fled, comes to Russia, we *will write (napišem")* to your prince, so they might do as they please with him'

These usage patterns correspond closely to those of the simplex, except that they construe the act as completed or closed. The prefixed form is found primarily in the aorist; it is also attested in the non-past with a future reading, the past participle, and the imperative. One infinitive usage describes a completed act. Even if we try to give {na-} a specialized meaning, such as 'set down in written form', we have to reckon with examples like (177), which show the same meaning for the simplex.

The distribution of forms for these two verbs strongly resembles that of an aspectual pair. If we allow the pair to cover only telic predicates of *pisati,* then we have at least a partial aspectual opposition covering a vast majority of attested forms of the verbs.

The simplex verb *dělati* can represent an ongoing action, whether immediately in progress or generalized, as in (182)-(184).

(182) и **дѣлають** нивы своя и землѣ своя. (58)
'and *they tend (dělajut')* their fields and their land'

(183) брат(ь)я что тако **дѣлаете**. не дивно оже ны быша погании воевали. а се нонѣ хочете брату своею оубити. (401)
'brothers, what *are you doing (dělaete)?* Is it not strange that the heathens were fighting us, and yet now you want to kill your own brothers?'

(184) аще бы ч(е)л(о)в(ѣ)к(о)мъ Б(ог)ъ реклъ на н(е)бо столпъ **дѣлати**. то повелѣлъ бы самъ Б(ог)ъ словомъ (91)
'if God had told men *to build (dělati)* a tower to heaven, then God would have ordered it with his own word'

Dělati appears as an infinitive and non-past form with present sense and as a present participle in progressive contexts.

The prefixed verb *sdělati* is used to indicate actions of the same meaning viewed as complete or closed, as in (185)-(187).

(185) и оубиша С(вя)тослава. (и) взяша главу его. и во лбѣ его **съдѣлаша** чашю. оковаше лобъ его. и пьяху по немь. (74)[62]
'they killed Svjatoslav, and took his head, and in his skull *they fashioned (s"dělaša)* a chalice, bronzed his skull and drank from it'

(186) егда **сдѣла** ковчегъ. и реч(е) Г(о)с(под)ь Ноеви (90)
'when *he built (sděla)* the ark, then the Lord said to Noah...'

(187) а си б(о)зи что **сдѣлаша**. сами дѣлани суть (82)
'and what *have* these gods *done (sdělaša)*; they are only creations'

The verb *sdělati* appears predominantly in the aorist, with one example being a past participle. Altogether, *dělati* and *sdělati* function quite well as complementary parts of an aspectual pair.

I see only one cogent argument against treating these pairs as aspectual. In both instances, the prefixed form can be said to add an Aktionsart "resultative" or "completive" meaning to the predicate as well as simply forcing a change in perspective. However, this Aktionsart meaning is only marginally stronger in Old Russian than in Modern Russian, where these pairs are routinely accepted as equivalent to the canonical suffixed pairs. Furthermore, although Old Russian lacks the result-oriented nature of Modern Russian aspect, the existence of lexical oppositions alongside or instead of grammatical ones was characteristic of Old Russian aspect, and I see no reason to say that these pairs were further from the Old Russian aspectual "norm" than many others.

It remains to explain how these aspectual pairs fit into the developing aspectual system. If aspect is in fact in the process of developing at the time and is already well-established for nonpunctual telic acts, the development of these aspectual pairs in the accretive subgroup (predicates expressing action that by nature accrues irretrievably, regardless of result) could have been a side effect, an interaction of the lexical properties of the subgroup with the growing tendency to channel the usage of telic acts into two patterns ascribed to paired verbs. Instead of being a late addition to the aspectual system, then, these pairs represent holdovers from a partially productive pattern during the formative period of aspect. This hypothesis accounts more satisfactorily than does the traditional explanation for the sporadic character of these pairs, the residue of Aktionsart meaning sometimes perceived for the prefixed member, and their association with a single lexical subgroup. After all, the feature associated with the spread of aspect in the later period is the extraordinary

---

[62] See the discussion of this sentence above as example (90).

productivity and overgeneralization of imperfectivizing suffixes—which is hard to reconcile with the creation of occasional pairs using varied prefixes.

5.8. LATE APPEARANCE OF SIMPLEXES

If, as is widely claimed, suffixation of verbs and aspectualization of the verbal system go hand in hand, then the interaction between simplexes and suffixed verbs should be of interest in a period when aspect was just forming. The Chronicles show evidence for two sorts of developments. First, suffixed forms can appear relatively early and simplex verbs only later. This could be an example of deprefixation *(dépréverbation),* as explored in Vaillant 1946. Second, the texts can reflect a competition and division of turf between simplex and suffixed forms with virtually identical meaning.

Some simplex verbs do not appear until late in the text, or fail to appear at all, while prefixed and suffixed forms of these verbs are found. A classic example discussed in chapter 4 is the root *mereti* 'die', which is found in the Chronicles only with the prefixes {u-}, {po-} and {iz-}. A more curious, if also well-known example, is the root *čistiti,* which is found only in the compounds *očiščati–očistiti* 'cleanse'. Modern Russian also has a simplex verb *čistit'* 'clean'. This could conceivably be an example of deprefixation, an idea proposed by Vaillant in which an initial syllable similar in form to a prefix[63] is reanalyzed as being one. Deprefixation can be a form of imperfectivization, and it is fairly difficult to recover except by extensive scouring of texts, unless the newly deprefixed verb is clearly missing material that was formerly in root-initial position. In the case of *očiščati–očistiti* I hesitate to invoke deprefixation, because the prefixed verb is used only in a specialized meaning—'cleanse' in the religious sense. Looking at a verb with similar meaning *(myti* 'wash') we find that the verb pair *omyti–omyvati* 'wash clean' is used predominantly with abstract, religious complements *(grěxy* 'sins', *pregrěšen'ja* 'transgressions'; *krov'* 'blood' in the Macbethian sense). The lack of a simplex form *čistiti* may simply be a reflection of the texts' subject matter.

An easier nut to crack is the use of the verb *čtiti* 'honor, pay respects', which first occurs two-thirds of the way through the Primary Chronicle (in the entry for 1066, p. 166) and the bulk of whose attestations are in the final forty pages of the Suzdal' Chronicle. Here, however, no suffixed forms are attested, and the prefixed form *počtiti* 'pay respects' has roughly the same distribution. The semantics of the verb hold the key here: the initial usages mean simply 'honor', while the later ones concern the paying of tribute as a form of honor or respect. Here language reflects history—the advent of the Golden Horde—in introducing a usage heretofore sporadic or nonexistent.

The simplex verb *slaviti* 'praise' also shows a marked increase in usage in the Suzdal' Chronicle: it appears twice in the Primary Chronicle entry for 986, twice in the entry for 1096, and then an additional twelve times in the Suzdal' Chronicle.

---

63 Many of these initial segments were originally nominal prefixes, meaning the original verb was formed by denominalization and retained the prefix in its formation.

However, this sudden prosperity is easy to understand Of the twelve attestations in the Suzdal' Chronicle, five occur with the phrase *razidošasja slavjašče B(og)a* 'they dispersed, praising God' and five more occur with the phrase *xvalja i slavja* 'praising and glorifying'. There may be a cultural or religious explanation for the increased usage of these fixed phrases, but it is linguistically insignificant and will only deform the analysis.

One example for which deprefixation seems more likely, however, is the root *miriti* 'make peace'. While prefixed forms *umiriti (sja)* and *smiriti (sja)* are attested from the earliest dates with roughly the same meaning, in the Suzdal' Chronicle unprefixed forms with roughly equivalent perfective-like function begin to be found, especially in direct quotations. Without resorting to deprefixation, we could invoke a spoken vs. literary dichotomy or a dialect difference, referring to the more conservative language of northern Russia that appears consistently in the Suzdal' Chronicle and is mixed with southern Russian forms in the Primary Chronicle.

From what is known of the morphological development of aspect in Slavic languages, one would expect simplex forms to be more archaic than prefixed ones. Predictably, then, there are few examples of simplex verbs whose attestations increase over time instead of decreasing. Such examples occur only sporadically and can often be attributed to a variety of other factors, including semantic changes in the predicates and the particular lexicons or styles of the texts involved.

5.9. DEVELOPMENT OF SUFFIXED FORMS

The development of suffixed verbs from prefixed verbs accompanies the gradual building of the Modern Russian aspectual system. In fact, the mere presence of these suffixed forms in Old Russian texts has often been invoked as proof that a regular aspectual system already existed in Old Russian. However, the Chronicles have a considerably more complex set of interactions between existing suffixed forms and the other forms—simplex and prefixed—that coexist with and to a certain extent compete with them. In various places, we observe that suffixed forms compete with simplexes and become more common in contexts where formerly simplexes predominated, or alternately we notice a rationale developing for semantically or contextually differentiating the simplex from the suffixed form. This sort of interaction testifies that grammatical aspect in Old Russian is still in the process of formation.[64]

A large number of verbs in the Chronicles have suffixed forms from an early date in the texts; conversely, there are also many that never show signs of

---

[64] Another interesting indicator of the development of suffixed forms is the contextual competition between the prefixed forms of a verb with and without derivational suffixes. However, I have dealt with this phenomenon earlier in this chapter (see particularly the discussion of the imperfect tense and the non-past tense in sections 5.6 and 5.2.4 respectively), so it will not be taken up again here.

suffixation.65 A smaller group of verbs have simplex forms and competing compound forms with very similar meanings. These conflicts are resolved primarily in three ways. First, the simplex form may give way to the compound form. Second, a semantic differentiation may develop between the compound forms and the simplex forms. Third, the simplex may come to be used in different contexts from the compound form, while retaining the same basic meaning.66 I do not claim, based on the evidence from these texts, that it is possible to establish a definitive chronology for the suffixation of any one verb; on the other hand, I will show that in general terms, suffixation was a process more limited in scope for the composers of these texts than it is for the Modern Russian writer.

I will consider a number of pairs of verbs in this section. Each pair has forms that are more or less synonymous and, if there is a complementary distribution of forms by meaning or usage, then that distribution is not a classic aspectual distribution as defined elsewhere.67 The pairs are: *množiti sja~umnožati (sja)* 'multiply, become (or make) numerous', *koriti (sja)~ukarjati* 'mock, scorn, abuse', *krěpiti (sja)~ukrěpljati* 'strengthen, fortify (oneself)', *mysliti~pomyšljati* 'think, plot', *slati (sja)~posylati (sja)* 'send'. Their predicates do not fall into any single lexical class.

5.9.1. The verbs *množiti sja, umnožati (sja)*

The verb *množiti sja* 'multiply' is found only once in the Chronicles; the suffixed *umnožati (sja)* is found three times in a single passage and once elsewhere. The context for *množiti sja* in (188) is progressive but can be understood as a general truth that occurs all over the country.

(188) и при семь нача вѣра х(ри)с(т)ьяньска плодитися. и раширяти. и церноризьци почаша **множитися**. и манастыреве починаху быти. (151)

'and at this time our Christian faith bore fruit, and spread, and the monks began *to multiply (množitisja)*, and monasteries came into being'

This interpretation makes the process less focused than in (189)-(191), where the current growth in a single monastery is the subject of concern.

---

65 The verb *moliti (sja)*, for instance, means 'pray' when used reflexively in these texts and 'implore' when used transitively. Modern Russian uses the suffixed form *umoljat'* for the latter meaning. See chapters 6, 7 and 8 for more examples of this type.

66 This third resolution seems to me an inherently unstable one, and it may be—both in Old Russian and in Modern Russian, where the same phenomenon is occasionally seen—that it is merely a phase that precedes discarding the simplex altogether.

67 The wording here is designed to weed out "competition" between verbs which are probably paired aspectually, such as *javljati sja–javiti sja* 'appear'. This approach allows us to avoid numerous analyses which would be trivial and are, in effect, addressed elsewhere in this work.

(189) и нача Б(ог)ъ **умножати** черноризцѣ. м(о)л(и)тв(а)ми с(вя)тыя Б(огороди)ца. и съвѣтъ створиша брат(ь)я со игуменомь. поставити манастырь (158)
'and God began *to multiply (umnožati)* the monks through the prayers of the Holy Mother of God, and the monks took counsel with the Father Superior to build a monastery'

(190) и рѣша о(т)че брат(ь)я **оумножаются**. а хотѣли быхомъ поставити манастырь. (158)
'and they said: o father, the brethren *are multiplying (oumnožajutsja)*, and we would like to build a monastery'

(191) река тако княже мои. се Б(ог)ъ **умножаеть** брат(ь)ю а мѣстьце мало. (158)
'saying thusly: o my prince, behold, God *is multiplying (umnožaet')* the brethren, and there is little room for them'

In (189), the suffixed form occurs with an instrumental complement ('through the prayers of the Holy Mother of God'), intensifying the progressive nature of the context. The more telic nature of the suffixed form is evident also in (192), where a past participle *(umnožavši)* is used.

(192) аще ли почнеть не оуправляти дани. да изнова из Руси совкупивше вои **оумножавши**. поидемъ Ц(а)рюгороду (72)
'if they begin not to send their tribute, then, having collected the troops *whose number we have increased, (oumnožavši)* let us go against Constantinople'

5.9.2. The verbs *koriti (sja), ukarjati*

The verbs *koriti (sja)~ukarjati* 'scorn, mock, abuse' are sparsely attested, so it is difficult to draw conclusions about the semantic ranges of the two verbs. These texts have only one form—the simplex—that is reflexive; it seems merely to indicate a stronger, perhaps more emotional act than the nonreflexive simplex, a feature that is in keeping with reflexive usage in Modern Russian. There are clear differences in context between the simplex and the suffixed form. The simplex in (193) indicates a generalized truth; it introduces a standard joke the Russians make about the Radimičians.

(193) и посла и Володимеръ передъ собою Волчья Хвоста. сърѣте е на рѣцѣ Пищанѣ. и побѣди Радимичѣ Волъчии Хвостъ. тѣмь и Русь **корятся** Радимичемъ гл(агол)юще. Пищаньци волчья хвоста бѣгають. (84)
'and Volodimer sent Wolftail out ahead; they met him on the River Piščan, and Wolftail beat the Radimičians. The Russians *mock (korjatsja)* the Radimičians with this, saying: the Piščancians run from a wolf's tail'

(194)   Изяславъ же сего не послуша. и нача(ша) люди его **корити**. (171)
        'But Izjaslav did not listen to this, and the people began *to revile (koriti)* him'

In (194), *koriti* represents an action in progress, but one that is not further explicated. In (195) and (196), by contrast, the suffixed form is used when the entire taunt is repeated.

(195)   и воевода нача С(вя)тополчь ѣздя възлѣ берегъ. **оукаряти**
        Новгородцѣ гл(агол)я. что придосте с хромьцемь симь. о вы
        плотници суще. а приставимъ вы хоромомъ рубити нашимъ. (142)
        'Svjatopolk's commander began, riding along the shore, *to mock (oukarjati)* the Novgorodians, saying: why have you come with this cripple? Oh, you're carpenters! We'll set you to building our houses!'

(196)   и воевода. именемь Буды. нача **укаряти** Болеслава гл(агол)я. да то
        ти прободемъ трѣскою черево. твое толъстое. бѣ бо Болеславъ
        великъ и тяжек. яко и на кони не могы сѣдѣти. (143)
        'and a commander named Budy began *to taunt (ukarjati)* Boleslav, saying: we'll run a stake through your fat belly; for Boleslav was so big and heavy that he could not sit on a horse'

Example (197) uses the suffixed verb in a more explicitly progressive context, where numerous acts—including stealing icons, burning doors, and slandering God and the Russian religion—occur simultaneously (or, alternatively, 'slandered' encapsulates all the other defilements—a type of logical simultaneity).

(197)   влѣзше в притворъ оу гроба Ѳеодосьева. емлюще иконы зажигаху
        двери. и **оукаряху** Б(ог)а и законъ нашь. (233)
        'having come in through the opening near Theodosius's grave, and grabbing the icons, they set fire to the doors, and *slandered (ukarjaxu)* God and our law'

The suffixed verb is restricted to more explicitly progressive contexts, although the simplex is also used this way, as in (193). The simplex is thus broader and more general in its application, while the derived form is reserved for special emphasis on the duration or quality of the process.

5.9.3. The verbs *krěpiti (sja), ukrěpljati*

Another pair with the prefix {u-}, *krěpiti (sja)~ukrěpljati* 'strengthen, fortify (oneself)', has a different distribution of forms. The reflexive, which once again appears only with the simplex form, appears in a generalized context, as in (198).

(198)   град свои схрани. Д(е)в(и)це М(а)т(ер)и ч(и)стая. иже о тебѣ вѣрно
        ц(а)рствуеть. **да** тобою **крѣпимся** и тобѣ ся надѣет. побѣжает зся
        брани. испромѣтает противныя. и творить послушенье. (255)
        'o pure Virgin Mother, preserve your city, which faithfully endures through your help, *that we may be strengthened (da krěpimsja)* through you, and have

faith in you; may it overcome all obstacles, overthrow those opposing it, and live in obedience'

The non-reflexive form can appear in this same generalized context, as in (199). However, it is also be used progressively in (200), where Alexandr boosts his men's spirits with a speech that follows in the text.

(199) Ахматъ оставя брата своя 2 блюсти и **крѣпити** свободъ своих. и самъ не смѣ оставити в Руси. (481)
'Axmat, leaving his two brothers *to* guard and *strengthen (krěpiti)* their freedoms, could not remain in Russia'

(200) он же выиде изъ ц(е)ркве утирая слезы и нача **крѣпити** дружину свою и реч(е) не в силах Б(ог)ъ но в правдѣ. помянем Пѣснословца. си во оружьи. си на конех мы же во имя Г(о)с(под)а Б(ог)а наш(е)го призовем. (478)
'he left the church, wiping away his tears, and began *to encourage (krěpiti)* his men; and he said: God is not in strength but in truth. Let us remember the Psalmist: some [call] upon chariots, some upon horses; but we shall call upon the name of our God the Lord'

This progressive use overlaps with that of the suffixed form, which appears in similarly explicit progressive contexts in (201) and (202).

(201) видѣвъ же и Половци стояща назадѣ. и к тѣмъ гна. и много имъ молвивъ и **оукрѣпляя** на брань. и оттуду ѣхавъ полкъ свои оукрѣпивъ. (333)
'having seen the Polovtsians standing in back, he sped over to them, and having said many things to them and *encouraging (oukrěpljaja)* them to battle, from there he went and encouraged his regiment'

(202) Володимеръ же Б(о)жьею помочью и с(вя)тое Б(огороди)ци. и дѣда своего с(вя)тог(о) м(о)л(и)твою оукрѣпляем и о(т)ца своего. поиде противу им. (395)
'Volodimer, *being strengthened (oukrěpljaem)* with the help of God and the Holy Mother of God, and the prayer of his holy grandfather and his father, went against them'

It is interesting (although hardly conclusive) that in addition, both these verbs make a relatively late appearance in the text. The simplex appears once near the end of the Primary Chronicle and twice in the Suzdal' Chronicle; the suffixed form appears only in the Suzdal' Chronicle. (The other attested forms of this root—*krěpljati, okrěpiti,* and *ukrěpiti*—also conform to this pattern.) It is possible that this set of verbs, or at least the existence of suffixed forms with this stem, is newer to the language, meaning that the developments above represent an earlier, more fluid stage in the differentiation of simplex and suffixed forms.

5.9.4. The verbs *mysliti, pomyšljati*

The verb pair *mysliti~pomyšljati* 'think, plot' is found more often than other pairs examined so far. The simplex is attested thirteen times, the suffixed form seven times. With this pair, the simplex appears in a wider range of contexts than the suffixed form. Sometimes it appears in a generalized context, as is the case in (203) and (204).

(203) аще бо инѣх м(о)л(и)твъ не оумѣете молвити. а Г(о)с(под)и помилуи зовѣте бес престани втаинѣ. та бо есть м(о)л(и)тва всѣх лѣпши. нежели **мыслити** безлѣпицю ѣздя. (245)[68]
'and if you do not know how to say any other prayers, then say "Lord have mercy" over and over again to yourself; for that is the best prayer of all, rather than *think (mysliti)* of trifles while riding'

(204) анг(е)лъ бо ч(е)л(о)в(ѣ)ку зла не створяеть. но бл(а)гое **мыслить** ему всегда. (135)
'an angel does not do a man any harm, but always *thinks (myslit')* of what is good for him'

In these examples, it is impossible to assign duration or continuity to the act; 'thinking about trifles' in (203) and 'thinking of what is good' in (204) could be either a state or a regular repetition construed as such. In (205), the context of *mysljat'* is nominally progressive but more likely indicates a characteristic of those described (they have hatched a plot but may not be thinking of it right now).

(205) то суть неистовии. иже приемше от князя или от господ(и)на своего ч(е)сть ли дары. ти **мыслять** о главѣ князя своего. на пагубленье. (77)
'these are cruel men, who, having received from their prince or lord his respect or gifts, *plot (mysljat')* against their prince to kill him'

A similar progressive or general context is seen in (206).

(206) ты **мыслѣши** на наю. и поганым помагати хощеши. (230)
'you *are plotting (mysliši)* against us, and want/intend to help the heathens'

A more explicitly progressive context appears in (207), where after the Jews' visit to Vladimir, he expresses his surprise that they expect him to embrace a religion whose adherents are being punished by their God.

(207) аще бы Б(ог)ъ любилъ васъ и законъ вашь. то не бысте росточе(ни) по чюжимъ землямъ. еда намъ то же **мыслите** прияти. (86)
'if God loved you and your ways, then you would not be dispersed among foreign lands; *do you expect (myslite)* us to accept this as well?'

---

[68] Discussed earlier as examples (72) and (156).

As for the valences of the verbs, the simplex can take a direct object, an infinitive, or a locative object with the prepositions *na* 'on, against' and *o* 'about'. I found one example with the construction *mysljaše kde by žiti* 'he was wondering where to live', which appears to be a cross between the infinitive construction and a truly independent clause.

The suffixed verb *pomyšljati* is used in the same two meanings 'think, plot' as the simplex but appears in a more restricted set of contexts. It can appear with a dependent clause that has its own subject, as in (208), which has an unequivocally progressive context.

(208) и нача **помышляти**. яко избью всю братью свою. и прииму власть Руськую единъ. (139)
'and he began *to plan (pomyšljati)* that: I will kill all my brothers, and take power in Russia alone'

The verb can also appear with an infinitive complement, as in (209) or a dependent clause construction, as in (210). Both are progressive contexts, indicating the subject's state of mind at a particular moment in time.

(209) не всхотѣ сего (послушати) но паче **помышляше** и Новъгородъ переяти. (238)
'he did not want (to obey) this, and instead still *thought (pomyšljaše)* about capturing Novgorod'

(210) **помышляю** како стати. пред страшным Судьею. каянья и смѣренья не приимшим межю собою. (252)
'I *wonder (pomyšljaju)* how to come before the Final Judgment without your having repented and made peace between yourselves [i.e., my heart, body and soul]'

There is a large degree of overlap in usage between the simplex and the suffixed form. Both are found in garden-variety progressive contexts, although those with fully elaborated dependent clauses seem to be restricted to the suffixed form. Progressive contexts that shade into generalized contexts—and the generalized contexts themselves—are the province of the simplex verb. Activities that lexically place greater emphasis on the activity of thinking, as in (210), are conveyed by derived forms.

5.9.5. The verbs *slati (sja), posylati (sja)*

The verbs *slati (sja)~posylati (sja)* 'send' survive into Modern Russian as virtual synonyms, although the former is often reserved for abstract objects *(slat' privet* 'to send one's greetings'). These two verbs are amply attested in the Chronicles. However, an abstract–concrete distinction is not supported by the Old Russian data. Inanimate themes are more common with the suffixed form, especially when found in the plural. *Korabli* 'ships' in (211), *dari* 'gifts' in (212), *gramoty* 'letters' in (213)[69] are found with *posylati*.

(211) да посылають въ Греки. къ великимъ ц(а)р(е)мъ Гречьскимъ корабли. елико хотять со слы и с гостьми. (48)
'*let them send* (*da posylajut'*) as many ships as are wanted to Greece to the great Greek emperor with emissaries and guests'

(212) и дари свыше **посылаются**. нынѣ и прис(н)о в бесконечныя вѣкы аминь. (394)
'and gifts *are sent* (*posylajutsja*) from above, now and forever and unto the endless ages, amen'

(213) нынѣ же увѣдѣлъ есть князь нашь. **посылати** грамоту ко ц(а)р(с)тву нашему. (48)
'now our prince has ordered *to send* (*posylati*) a letter to our kingdom'

However, *med"* 'honey' in (214) is found with *slati*. Notably, this is the only example of a mass noun with these verbs.

(214) ибо брашно свое и медъ по улицам на возѣхъ **слаше** болным. (368)
'for he *would send* (*slaše*) his food and honey on carts around the streets to the sick'

Sending people as emissaries is more commonly conveyed by the simplex form, as in (215).

(215) да се Василю **шлю** тя. иди к Василкови... (265)
'and thus, Vasilij, I *am sending* (*šlju*) you; go to Vasilko...'

The simplex likewise indicates the sending of emissaries in (216), (217), (221) and (222).

(216) Кияне **слются** къ Володимеру. гл(агол)юще... (77)
'the Kievans *send* (*sljutsja*) to Volodimer, saying...'

(217) и нача к ним **слати** князя Д(а)в(и)да Муромскаго. и Михаила Борисовича мужа своего. (431)
'and he began *to send* (*slati*) to them Prince David Muromskij, and his man Mixail Borisovič'

However, the derived verb can also be used for this purpose, as in (218). This sending is more occasional and sporadic, and occurs over a longer time period, than the missives in (215) through (217), (221), and (222).

---

[69] A plural sense is clearly intended here, whether or not a plural form is required. See example (63) for a fuller discussion of this problem.

(218) и нача Б(ог)ъ **посылати** к нимъ пр(о)р(о)ки. (97)
 'and God began *to send (posylati)* prophets to them'

Neither *slati* nor *posylati* requires a direct object; they can appear with only the preposition *k* 'to' or *po* 'after', obscuring whether the message was sent in written form or orally with the messenger. A case in point is (219).

(219) аще братъ етеръ выидяше из манастыря. вся брат(ь)я имяху о томь печаль велику. **посылаючи** по нь призываху брата к монастырю. (189)
 'if any brother should leave the monastery, all the brethren would be deeply sorrowed over this; *sending (posylajuči)* after him, they would summon the brother [back] to the monastery'

As for contextual differences, these are also hard to find. Iterative contexts are more common with the suffixed form, as seen in (218)-(220).

(220) и сѣдя ту **посылаше** к Олгови мира прося. (238)[70]
 'and reigning there, *he sent (posylaše)* to Oleg, asking for peace'

However, iterative contexts are also found with the simplex, as in (217) and (221).

(221) **шлющим** же имъ межи собою. (326)
 '*sending (šljuščim)* messengers back and forth'

Surprisingly, actions in progress or imminent at the moment of speech are found with the simplex, as in (215) and (222), but never with the suffixed form.

(222) азъ есмъ м(е)н(ьш)ии тебе **слися** к отцю моему. а дружину юже еси заялъ вороти. а язъ тебе во всемъ послушаю. (238)
 'I am younger than you; *send (slisja)* to my father, and return the company which you seized, and I will obey you in every matter'

The meaning of the reflexive particle {sja} differs depending on whether it is used with the simplex or the suffixed form. The reflexive particle, when attached to *slati* as in (216) and (222), refers back to the sender, without respect to theme; it may sometimes imply that the sender is also the messenger, but this does not hold as a rule, and it more probably refers to the sender's degree of interest in the message. When attached to *posylati* as in (212), the reflexive particle refers to the theme—that which is sent. Reciprocity is expressed periphrastically, as in (221): 'they sent [messages] to one another'. This distinction reflects the suffixed form's tendency to have plural or multiple themes. Nonreflexive forms indicate that the sender and the messenger are different.

---

[70] The text of this example is followed by that of (222).

5.9.6. Conclusions about simplexes and derived verbs

The results of this survey of competition between simplex and suffixed forms are not uniform. Some pairs were shown to have a clear-cut distribution into those found in progressive (suffixed) and nonprogressive (simplex) contexts. Other pairs had a suffixed verb that was limited to progressive contexts but without excluding the simplex from them. Finally, one pair showed near complete overlap in most categories, with the progressive contexts being reserved for the simplex.

The first two developments are easy to reconcile. The dating of the suffixation process for the individual simplex verb and the peculiarities of any given verb's semantics may explain why some verb pairs exhibit complementary distribution of forms and others exhibit overlapping distribution of forms. The example of *slati~posylati* 'send' shows that distribution by context type is not the only possible resolution of this competition; a distribution by object type may eventually prevail instead. In this instance, such a distribution is enabled by the numerous types of objects available; no such diversity of direct object types can be found, for example, with lexical items like 'scorn' or 'think'.

5.10. CONCLUSIONS

In this chapter, I have expanded on the analysis of data from the Primary Chronicle and Suzdal' Chronicle begun in chapter 4. This expansion went in three basic directions. First, I increased coverage of lexical classes to include material from a wider variety of verbs, including motion verbs. Second, I approached the interaction of contextual and lexical factors in a more comprehensive manner to account for troublesome situations such as repeated past contexts and conditional contexts. Third, I looked at the interaction of morphology and semantics in the formation of aspect by analyzing the semantics of prefixation and suffixation. A brief summary of my findings follows.

Lexical classes. The additional material presented in this chapter supports the hypothesis put forward in chapter 4: that aspect did not in fact encompass the entire Old Russian verbal system, and that lexical classes can be used to determine which verbs were aspectual and which anaspectual. Furthermore, the structures proposed for aspectuality and anaspectuality can be applied with equal success to motion verbs, explaining the apparent anomalies in their development.

One troublesome feature of the lexical class hypothesis is that lexically dissimilar predicates (punctual telics and nonpunctual atelics) are both read as anaspectual. I examined the connections between these two classes and gave some justification for their similar behavior patterns.

Context. Examining the Old Russian non-past and imperfect tenses provided substantial evidence that aspect in Old Russian did not exhibit the same degree of automatic assignment in various contexts. Instead, lexical features and external contextual features often contributed to the choice of form. In the non-past, what appeared to be a "present vs. future" distinction can be reanalyzed as something less clearly aspectual: a distinction between immediate and remote concerns, combined with other lexical and contextual features.

In the imperfect tense, Maslov's findings served as a basis for my discussion of imperfect usage. Old Russian lexical classes were found to have a strong influence on the type of forms that appeared, and contextual features, such as the introduction of conative function in certain lexical classes, were also seen to play a role. Old Russian clearly does not reckon iterativity as a context requiring protoimperfective verbs.

Morphology. Prefixation is a more complex process in Old Russian than in Modern Russian, with the results of prefixation depending on lexical predicate assignment. Suffixation increases the processual component of action, although numerous features from the lexicon and context interfere with this development, and the differentiation between suffixed and simplex forms is played out in the texts. In both features of the morphology discussed here, diachronic approaches to the material are occasionally of use; where appropriate, they support the conclusions drawn elsewhere.

6. The Journey Across Three Seas

6.0. INTRODUCTION

The Journey Across Three Seas is a late fifteenth-century text whose introduction tells us it was written by one Afanasij Nikitin, a merchant of Tver'. The text takes the form of notes on Nikitin's journey to India: it records both the itinerary and the exotic things Nikitin saw along the way, as well as some of the more mundane details of Indian and Middle Eastern life. Unlike the other authors in this survey, Nikitin had no particular religious or political axe to grind, and consequently, his text has a far less formal, more colloquial feel than the other texts. This is not to say that the text is entirely free of high-minded, didactic moments; Nikitin often refers to the trials of a Christian in heathen lands, and, consciously or unconsciously, he took as his literary model the more pious accounts of pilgrimages to the Holy Land that were popular at the time. At these points, the language becomes more baroque and imitative of Church Slavic texts. By and large, however, the text is written in a down-to-earth idiom. There are frank descriptions of Eastern mores and numerous notes about prices and marketing practices, all of which might have been of concern to Russians travelling east.

This idiom is also reflected in the text's language, which is less conservative than that of other texts in this survey. The sentences are structured paratactically rather than hypotactically, with a minimum of participles and subordinating conjunctions. The perfect is the ordinary mode of past tense narration, although aorists appear in certain episodes and with certain familiar verbs. Nikitin's language, then, is closer to popular speech in two ways: it is both linguistically progressive and stylistically more conversational, lacking many of the archaic elements that characterize Russian narrative writing of the time, but also appropriately less formal, in keeping with his subject matter. However, it is not always possible to disentangle linguistic concerns from stylistic ones, so I will not automatically label nonstandard or nonliterary features in this text as "innovative."

From an aspectual standpoint, the *Journey* presents us with a picture that differs from the modern system of aspect and the system presented for the Chronicles in a number of respects. As might be expected, the aspectual system of the *Journey* has fewer derived forms than does Modern Russian, but yet shows more evidence for a grammatical aspectual system across lexical groups than do older texts.

The most apparent difference between the Old Russian of this text and Modern Russian is the relative infrequency of derived forms; Nikitin favors simplex protoimperfective verbs or protoperfective verbs in many situations where Modern Russian uses secondary imperfectives. When the verbs are considered from this point of view, they fall into three behavioral categories, which are dealt with in turn. The first group, discussed in section 6.1, concerns the distribution of simplex protoimperfectives in Old vs. Modern Russian. Section 6.2 takes up the distribution and usage of unprefixed derived protoimperfectives in Old Russian; section 6.3 treats the usage of prefixed derived protoimperfectives in Old Russian.

Another difference between Old and Modern Russian is examined in section 6.4, which discusses the use of protoperfective forms in what Modern Russian terms "imperfective" contexts. The contextual evidence from sections 6.1 through 6.4 is summarized in section 6.5.

Section 6.6 compares the evidence for lexically-prompted aspectual behavior in the *Journey* with that found for the two earlier texts, the Primary Chronicle and the Suzdal' Chronicle. Evidence for lexical classification is still present, although it does not have the same far-reaching effects it did in the earlier texts.

For the *Journey*, I entered every verb form (excluding forms of *byti* 'be') into a database, along with its equivalent in Modern Russian in the translation, for a total of nearly 700 forms. I then classified all the forms found in imperfective-type contexts—regardless of the apparent aspectual assignment of the Old Russian verb[1]—according to contextual usage and lexical class.

6.0.1. Explanation of contexts

The contexts for usage of imperfective verbs are derived from those proposed in Timberlake 1982 and Maslov 1973.[2] Modern Russian imperfective verbs occur primarily in four contexts. **Iterative contexts** indicate recurring situations. These can be explicitly iterative (i.e. containing a key word like *mnogaždy* 'many times') or implicitly iterative (i.e., "each time *x* occurs, then *y* occurs.") Excluded from this group are conditional sentences whose occurrence is only projected, not attested (i.e., "should *x* occur, then *y* shall occur"). **Durative contexts,** following Timberlake, indicate acts with duration whose scope is encompassed by the perspective of the narrator. Durativity can be stated explicitly with phrases like *desjat' dnej, dolgo, mesjac* 'ten days, a long time, a month', or it can be implied by framing the predicate with events that mark a beginning and end to the action. **Progressive contexts** contain acts which extend beyond the immediate perspective of the narrator. An example from Nikitin is *Is Platany esmja pošli na more, i větr" nas strěčaet zlyj, ne dast" nam po morju xoditi* 'From Platana we set out upon the sea, but a cruel wind *meets* us; it would not let us sail the sea' (17). Here two attempts to begin a trip are set against the background of bad weather, whose endpoints are never made clear. Some progressive contexts do not place the verb form in such clear relief against a protoperfective but imply it by comparison to other acts mentioned nearby in the text.

There is also a set of contexts—the most heterogeneous and therefore the hardest to define—that portray a general truth about an act. These can take the form

---

[1] Modern Russian usually considers iterativity and conativity to be imperfective contexts, so I included such forms in my data. However, as I will show in this chapter, Nikitin often used perfective forms in these contexts, and deciding when he could do so contributes substantially to this analysis.

[2] The explanation given here expands slightly on that found in section 1.5.

of the narrator's own observations or of universally accepted phenomena, which the narrator relays but cannot vouch for from his own experience. These **generalized** contexts lack the clear boundaries between acts that characterize iterative contexts and offer no surety that the action was in progress at any point in time relative to the narrator's time frame. Instead, they establish a condition whose current status is less important than the larger situation it stands for. Examples from Nikitin are *v Kuluri že roditsja axik′* 'sard originates in Kuluri'; *ljudi xodjat nagi* 'people walk around naked'. In both of these examples, it is not important whether or not sard is actually being mined at this moment or whether people are right now walking naked in the streets; instead, a larger picture (geographic or moral, in these cases) is being painted that has no particular relation to the narrative time frame. This type of context is markedly similar to, but does not necessarily coincide exactly with, lexical categories of stative and atelic action predicates.

I chose in this study to treat these contextual "categories" as contextual **properties**; in other words, each attestation can exhibit one or more of these contextual properties. This approach seemed warranted, given the subject matter; Nikitin's text is less than crystal clear in its syntax and, like other medieval texts, its narrative occasionally defies analyses grounded in modern reading conventions. Consequently, it is not always possible to assign one and only one reading to a particular verb form. What starts off as an account of a battle may drift into a description of someone's army, and the resulting ambiguity makes it difficult to classify the context as progressive or generalized. Moreover, some contexts defy clear classification and have elements of more than one contextual type in them. A description of a ritual that is clearly composed of a series of repeated actions can be both general in its scope (a description of a culture) and iterative in its particular manifestation (a description of a series of repeated acts), and might also contain progressive elements, if there is a strong sense that, as he writes, the narrator is mentally replaying a scene he witnessed or describing events that happened simultaneously. Treating these categories as nonexclusive properties of a context gives appropriate latitude to the semantic possibilities of the original text.

Lexical properties of the verbs are classified according to a system developed from Kučera 1983, Maslov 1948, and Timberlake 1984, as laid out in chapters 1 and 2. States and activities are considered separately, and activities are defined as **telic** and **atelic** (the presence or absence of a goal for the act). Attention is give to the **punctual–nonpunctual** opposition derived from Maslov 1948. Motion verbs will be treated separately using the same set of criteria.

6.1. OLD RUSSIAN SIMPLEXES

A consistent feature of Nikitin's text is the use of simplex verbs that no longer exist in Modern Russian or are archaic in the meaning he employs. Examples (1)–(7) show verbs in this text that are replaced in Modern Russian by derived imperfectives from the same stem. In (1), Old Russian *gadati* 'guess' is used.

(1) А Великаго дни и въскресения Христова не въдаю, а по при-
мътамъ **гадаю** Великъ день бывает християньскы первие бесер-
меньскаго баграма за девять дни или за десять дни. (10)
'And I do not know when Easter and the Resurrection of Christ is, and by signs
I deduce (gadaju) that Christian Easter precedes the Muslim Bairam by nine or
ten days.'

Although Modern Russian retains this verb, according to dictionaries it is archaic in the meaning 'guess' and retains only the meaning 'foretell'. 'Guess' is best translated in Modern Russian by *dogadyvat'sja*, the derived prefixed imperfective; the range of meanings available to the simplex has shrunk, while that of the derived form has expanded.

A similar problem of polysemy occurs in (2), where the modern translator chose the derived form *podsteregaet* to translate Old Russian *sterežet* 'lies in wait'.

(2) Ту наѣхали на нас три татарины поганые и сказали нам люивыя
въсти: «Кайсым салтан **стережет** гостей в Бузани, а с ним три
тысящи татар.» (5)
'Here three Tatars met us and gave us false reports: "Sultan Kaisim *lies in wait
(sterežet)* for merchants at Buzan, and with him (are) three thousand Tatars." '

While the Modern Russian simplex can still mean 'lie in wait for', it has a number of additional meanings (also 'protect, guard') which could have made the sense of the sentence ambiguous; the use of a derived imperfective renders the notion of constant watchfulness unambiguously. One Modern Russian translation retains forms of the simplex *sterec'*, indicating its viability in the modern language. (The reflexive *sterec'sja*, however, has largely been supplanted by the derived imperfective *osteregat'sja* in the modern language.)

In (3), Old Russian *zovut* 'they call, name' is supplanted in the Modern Russian translation by the derived imperfective *nazyvajut* 'they call'. This example reflects the fact that Modern Russian *zvat'* is generally restricted to people; things and classes are most often named with *nazyvat'*, a clear change from the Old Russian period. (One archaizing translation, not surprisingly, retains *zvat'*.[3])

(3) А тѣ волы аччей **зовут**. Индѣяне же вола **зовут** отцем, а корову
материю. (10)
'And the bulls *are called (zovut)* "ačče". The Indians *call (zovut)* the bull their
father, and the cow their mother'[4]

(4) А кто у них умрет, ини тѣх **жгут** да и попел сыплют на воду. (10)
'And when one of them dies, the others burn *(žgut)* them, and spread the ashes
on the water'

---

[3] See the discussion of translations in section 1.0.3.
[4] See the discussion of examples (19) and (20) below.

In (4), the form *žgut* 'they burn' is used in the sense 'burn up', where the Modern Russian translation has *sžigajut* 'they burn up'. While the simplex apparently doubled in Nikitin's idiom as the general verb 'burn' and an iterative rendering of the more telic 'burn up', the Modern Russian preference for a derived form indicates that the modern simplex may not adequately describe a highly telic event.

In (5), where Nikitin describes how to ride an elephant, he uses the simplex form *pravjat* 'they direct, lead, order', where the Modern Russian translation has the derived form *napravljajut* 'they direct, steer'.

(5) Да человѣкъ седит в доспѣсе промежу ушей, да крюк у него желѣзной великой, да тѣм его **правят** (13)
'And a man in armor sits between the ears, and he has a large iron hook, with which *they direct (pravjat)* it'

The modern verb *pravit'* 'make corrections, straighten, prepare for use' is much narrower in meaning than Old Russian *praviti*; among the twenty definitions Sreznevskij gives for this verb are those indicating leading, ruling, fulfilling, and directing. The meaning 'direct' occurs frequently on Sreznevskij's list, and this frequent meaning has transferred in Modern Russian to a prefixed derived imperfective with narrower meaning, seen here as *napravljajut* 'they direct'.

Examples (6) and (7) likewise show greater lexical specificity in the modern use of derived imperfectives. Old Russian has simplex *brejut* 'they shave', *vjažut* 'they tie', where Modern Russian has derived *sbrivajut* or *sbrevajut* 'they shave off' and *privjazyvajut* 'they tie up to'.

(6) Да у бутхана **бреются** старые и молодые, жонки и девочки. А **бреют** на себѣ всѣ волосы — и бороды, и головы, и хвосты. (9:[5]
'And in the But-khan's house both the old and the young *shave (brejutsja)*, both women and girls. And they *shave (brejut)* all their hair—beards, heads and tails'

(7) А к слоном **вяжут** к рылу да к зубом великие мечи по кентарю кованых... (8)
'And *they tie (vjažut)* large iron swords a kentar in weight to the elephants' heads and tusks'

The verbs *privjazyvat'* 'tie onto' and *sbrivat'/sbrevat'* 'shave off' are more telic and more specific about the direction of the action than their Old Russian counterparts in the text, *vjazati* 'tie' and *briti* 'shave'. Modern Russian translations use the prefixed forms despite the fact that the modern language retains simplex verbs with the same meanings as the Old Russian forms. Although the prefixed

---

5   The meaning of *xvosty* 'tails' is unclear here; it might mean 'rears', but Lur'e speculates it may have been accidentally interpolated into the ms., since it appears often in the preceding text.

forms at least nominally show direction, this function is not particularly strong, since it is partially redundant: one always shaves something off, never on; and 'tying' usually means 'tying to something'. The prefixes therefore use this directional component as a metaphor for marking the boundary of the act, making it more telic, and this is their primary function.

Chart 6.1.1 shows verbs used by Nikitin that are replaced in Modern Russian (MoR) by a corresponding prefixed derived imperfective. The two patterns above are reflected in the chart. For certain verbs the meaning in which Nikitin uses the simplex protoimperfective has narrowed in use in Modern Russian or no longer occurs in Modern Russian. Examples are *zvati* 'name', which is replaced by *nazyvat'* for things; *gadati* 'guess', which is largely supplanted by *dogadyvat'sja;* and *praviti* 'direct, lead', which is replaced by *napravljat'* in this sense.

Nikitin also has one verb—*divovati sja* 'be surprised'—that is an unprefixed derived protoimperfective unattested in the modern language. The simplex verb *diviti sja* from which it is derived is also considered variously old-fashioned or a mark of uneducated speech in the modern language, which takes as normative the prefixed derived imperfective *udivljat'sja,* formed with an {-aj-} suffix.

In other cases, the simplex form is still in use, but Modern Russian in certain contexts prefers the greater degree of specification and/or telicity offered by the prefixed secondary imperfective. Examples are *privjazyvat'* 'tie to, tie up' for Nikitin's *vjazati; podsteregat'* for *stereči* to specify 'lie in wait'; *sbrivat'* 'shave off' for Nikitin's *briti;* and *sžigat'* 'burn up' for Nikitin's *žeči*.

These last four verbs are found in generalized contexts, and it is specifically here that Old Russian relies more heavily on simplexes than does Modern Russian. From a contextual standpoint, Modern Russian has extended the scope of secondary imperfectives farther than it had in Nikitin's time. The evidence for derived forms in the Old Russian text is in sections 6.2 and 6.3.

6.2. UNPREFIXED DERIVED FORMS IN OLD RUSSIAN

There are two patterns typical for verbs with unprefixed derived protoimperfectives. The first, seen in (8)-(11), is exemplified by the pair *pustiti-puskati* 'release'. The protoperfective only appears when prefixed, as in (8) and (9).

(8)   И **отпустил** мя доброволно. (5)
        'And *he released (otpustil)* me willingly'

(9)   И тут судно наше меншее[6] пограбили и четыре головы взяли
        рускые, а нас **отпустили** голыми головами за море, а вверхъ нас
        не пропустили вѣсти дѣля. (6)
        'And here our smaller ship was robbed and *they* took four Russians [prisoner]
        but *released* (otpustili) us bare-headed beyond the sea, and *didn't permit (ne
        propustili)* us upriver so the news would not be heard'

---

6   Lur'e corrects *menšee* 'smaller' to *bolšee* 'bigger' here according to the Troickij ms. to
    preserve the logic of the narrative.

Chart 6.1.1. Fifteenth-century simplex protoimperfectives that are twentieth-century derived imperfectives in the Journey

simplex verb	prefixed perfective	unprefixed derived imperfective	modern prefixed derived imperfective	iterative	general	progressive	durative
брити			сбривать		1		
(дивити ся)		диковати ся	удивляться	1			
звати			называть		1		
правити			направлять		1		
воевати			завоёвывать		1		
вязати	привязаны, повязаны		привязывать	1			
крыти (ся)			скрывать(ся)		2		
жечь	пожечи, сожечи		сожигать	1			
стеречи			подстерегать			1	
гадати			догадываться			1	
(нудити)	понудити		понуждать	.5			.5

NOTES: Most of the above paired Old and Modern Russian verbs appeared only once in the given text. A few appeared more than once. Where the entries had varying contexts, the number of each type of context is listed. Half a point means a verb could be read as belonging to either context. A verb form in parentheses means it was not attested in this text.

FEATURES: For all verbs on this chart:
Imperfective simplex verbs do not have secondary imperfectives in the *Journey*.
Modern Russian verbs have derived imperfectives from the same root.
Iteration can be expressed periphrastically with a perfective verb and an adverb.

The protoimperfective appears only unprefixed, as in (10) and (11). The imperfectivizing suffix is {-aj-}, which is overwhelmingly used in this group.

(10) Да пѣших **пускают** наперед, а хоросанцы на конех да в доспѣсех, и кони и сами. (8)
'And *they send (puskajut)* footsoldiers up front, and the Xorosanites on horses and in armor, both they and their horses'

(11) А гарипов **не пускают** въ град. (9)
'And *they do not allow (ne puskajut)* foreigners into the city'

The second pattern is shown in (12)-(14), which occur with the verb *piti* 'drink.' This verb appears in derived form in generalized or durative contexts, as in (12).

(12) А жити в Гундустани, ино вся собина исхарчити, занеже у них все дорого: один есми человѣкъ, ино по полутретья алтына на харчю идет на день, а вина **есми не пивал**, ни сыты. (14)
'And to live in Hindustan is to exhaust all one's means, because everything is expensive: I am only one man, but two and a half altyns a day go toward food, although *I drank neither (esmi ne pival)* wine nor honey-water'

It also occurs in the past tense as a categorical denial, although apparently this form is not obligatory in this sense; contrast (12) with (13), where an explicit duration is given in the text.

(13) А град же взял индийской меликъчанъ хозя, а взял его силою, день и нощь бился з городомъ 20 дни, рать **ни пила**, ни ѣла, под городом стояла с пушками. (16)[7]
'And the Indian khan Melikčan took the city, and took it by force; day and night he fought with the city for twenty days, the company *neither drank (ni pila)* nor ate, [but] stood outside the city with cannons'

(14) Да жонки пѣшие наги, а тѣ воду за ними носят **пити** да подмыватися, а одинъ у одного воды **не пиет**. (15)
'And the women walk around naked, and they carry water around with them *to drink (piti)* and wash with, and they *do not drink (ne piet)* each other's water.'

In (14), the simplex appears as an infinitive and a non-past form in a generalized context. No prefixed verbs with *piti* are attested in the text. The imperfectivizing suffix is {-vaj-}, found in the unprefixed group with only one other verb, *byvati* 'be (regularly, habitually)'.

Chart 6.2.1 shows two major subgroups of verbs with unprefixed derived forms. The first group contains the verbs *pivati* 'drink', *byvati* 'be (regularly, habitually)', *slyxati* 'hear' and *vidati* 'see', all of which are protoimperfectives.

---

[7] Appears below as example (26).

Chart 6.2.1. Unprefixed derived forms from unprefixed simplex verbs in the Journey.

simplex verb	prefixed perfective	unprefixed derived imperfective	prefixed derived imperfective	iterative	general	progressive	durative
пити		пивати					1
быти		бывати		1	1		
(слышати)		слышати				1	
видѣти	увидети	видати					1
(лишити ся)		лишати ся		1			
(пустити)	отпустити, пропустити	пускати		1	1		
срѣтити		срѣчати					1
(явити ся)		являти ся		2		1	
(-стрѣлити)	застрѣлити	стрѣляти		2		1	
(яти)		имати	подымати, поимати	1			
(-клонити ся)		кланяти ся					
(-ронити)		роняти		.5	.5		

FEATURES: Imperfective simplexes (top section) derive unprefixed imperfectives using {-ivaj-} or -{jaj-}
Perfective simplexes (middle section) derive unprefixed imperfectives using -{aj-} or {-jaj-}
All sections: prefixed perfectives and prefixed imperfectives are rare.

NOTES: Most Old Russian verb sets appeared only once in the given text. Where multiple entries had varying contexts, the number of each type of context is listed. Half a point means the form could belong to either context. Forms in parentheses are unattested. The last two entries are paired irregularly in Modern Russian (кляняться–поклониться; ронять–уронить; this text gives no evidence for classifying the hypothetical simplex verbs as pf. or impf. In Modern Russian, simplex verbs of this sort can have different meanings and belong to different pairs than their derived impfs.

The second group of verbs in Chart 6.2.1 contains verbs which are either protoperfectives or are unattested in their simplex forms in the modern language. Notably, these groups also break down by derivational pattern; those based on protoperfectives use the suffixes {-aj-} and {-jaj-}, but those based on protoimperfectives can use either the {-vaj-} or the {-aj-} suffix. A single verb *žaliti* 'complain, pity, concern oneself' uses the {-ovaj-} suffix, which is no longer productive in Modern Russian as an imperfectivizer. These verbs are found mostly in generalized contexts but can also be progressive *(javljati* 'appear', *vidati* 'see' and *slyxati* 'hear') or weakly iterative (*lišati sja* 'be deprived').

In all likelihood, this distribution reflects a secondary trend in Old Russian that is only dimly visible in the *Journey:* the {-vaj-} suffix is not only an aspectual marker but also comes into use as a general marker of repetition and emphasis with unprefixed verbs. The {-aj-} suffixes evidently could also be used this way, but their usage is restricted to the verbs *vidati*, *slyxati* in this text; other unprefixed verbs appearing with this suffix are protoimperfectives *(puskati* 'permit', *srěčati* 'meet', *javljati sja* 'appear') corresponding to simplex protoperfectives. The {-aj-} suffixes are therefore connected with established older derivations that by now create an aspectual distinction similar to that of Modern Russian, while the {-vaj-} suffixes are seen in this text on the brink of what will be a tremendous expansion in productivity, during which habitual, occasional, or emphatic forms like *pival, byval* will coexist alongside standard prefixed derivations creating Modern Russian-type aspectual distinctions.

6.3. PREFIXED DERIVED FORMS IN OLD RUSSIAN

The text also has prefixed derived protoimperfectives, yet in many cases the domains of these derived protoimperfectives are substantially more limited than they are in Modern Russian. A good example of the limitations on usage of derived protoimperfectives is the use of the infinitive *kryti* 'to close, cover, conceal', which appears three times as a simplex protoimperfective in (15) and (16). Twice the Modern Russian translation has a prefixed derived infinitive *skryvat'* 'to conceal'.

(15) И они же не учали ся от меня **крыти** *(скрывать)* ни о чем... ни жонъ своихъ не учали **крыти** *(скрывать).* (22-23)[8]
'And they did not begin *to hide* anything from me... nor did they begin *to hide* their wives from me.'

(16) Индѣяне же не ѣдят никоторого же мяса... А от бесермен **крыются**, чтоб не посмотрил ни в горнець, ни в ѣству. (10)
the Indians do not eat any sort of meat.... and *they hide* from Muslims, so [t]he[y] do not look into their pot or at their food'[9]

---

[8] This quote comes from a passage in the Troickij ms. not found in the Ètterov ms. (Both versions are given in Lur'e's edition of the *Journey.)*
[9] The shift in subject from plural to singular (gen. pl. *besermen* in the first clause is followed by sg. *čtob ne posmotril* in the second) would sound awkward here, so I have

However, there is only one prefixed derived form of *kryti* in this text, in (17).

(17) А толко посмотрит, ино тое ѣствы не едят. А едят, **покрываются** платомъ, чтобы никто не видѣлъ его. (10)
'And if one looks, the other will not eat that food. And (when) they eat, *they cover themselves (pokryvajutsja)* with a cloth, so that no one might see them [lit. him].'

The simplex verb forms are used in generalized contexts; only in the final example is the context iterative ('whenever they eat, they *cover themselves...*'), and it is this context that the derived form is found. A further division seems to be semantic: the derived form means 'hide' in the very literal sense of covering oneself, as seen in (17), while the simplex has both this concrete manifestation, as seen in (16), and more metaphorical uses of the word 'hide' in the sense of 'keep invisible' or 'keep quiet about something', both of which are found in (15). These metaphorical uses are conveyed in Modern Russian by the verb *skryvat'*; the *Slovar' russkogo jazyka v četyrëx tomax* lists primarily the aforementioned concrete meanings for *kryt'*, while the meaning *tait', ne obnaruživaja, prjača* 'keep secret, not disclosing, hiding' is given as archaic.[10]

The verb *zvati* 'call, name' exemplifies another limitation on the use of the derived protoimperfective. In (18), the derived protoimperfective appears as *prizyvati* 'call upon', with a meaning different from that of the simplex verb.

(18) Да молился есми Христу вседрьжителю, кто сотворил небо и землю, а иного есми не **призывал** никоторого именем, богъ олло, богъ керим... (11)
'And I prayed to Christ the Almighty, who made heaven and earth, and no other *did I call (ne prizyval)* by any such name, Lord Allah, merciful God...'

The derived form *ne prizyval* in (18) represents an action that is more telic than the simplex *zvati*; all meanings of Old Russian *prizyvati* and Modern Russian *prizyvat'* imply that some action is required of the person called upon. Here, then, the Old Russian and Modern Russian agree in choosing a derived form to express an act which differs substantially in its lexical shape. Where Modern Russian has *nazyvajut* 'call' in (19)-(21), though, the older text has only the simplex verb, indicating that this restriction of the simplex verb's domain at the expense of a

---

rendered both clauses in the plural. Apparently this shift of subjects did not sound unnatural to Nikitin; it also appears, for instance, in (17).

10 This meaning is also archaic for the reflexive *kryt'sja*; however, Modern Russian *kryt'sja* still retains a hint of the figurative meaning in Old Russian *krytisja: zaključat'sja v čem-libo, ne obnaruživajas'; tait'sja* 'consist of something not revealed; be hidden'. Note that the Modern Russian usages cited imply some sort of covering, metaphorical or not, while the examples of *kryti sja* in Nikitin do not.

prefixed derived imperfective is a later innovation. Examples (19) and (20) refer respectively to a citation in a foreign language and the assignment of a title.

(19) А тѣ волы аччеи **зовут**. (10)
      'And they *call (zovut)* bulls "ačče" '

(20) Индѣяне же вола **зовут** отцем, а корову материю. (10)
      'The Indians *call (zovut)* the bull their father and the cow their mother'[11]

Example (21) treats naming as the assigning of an attribute, in this instance a false attribute.

(21) А сыто жидове **зовут** Шабат своими жидовы, а то лжут; а шаибатене не жидова, ни бесермена, ни кристьяне, иная вѣра индийскаа... (12)
      'and the Jews *call (zovut)* Šabat their own, Jews, but they lie; the people of Šabat are not Jews nor Muslims, nor Christians, but another Indian faith'

However, in contrast to the situation with Old Russian *kryti* and Modern Russian *kryt'~skryvat'* seen above, the difference between Old Russian *zvati* and Modern Russian *zvat'~nazyvat'* is not clearly divided into concrete vs. metaphorical usage. Instead, the difference is in the nature of the theme (human vs. nonhuman), which is only a "metaphorical" difference inasmuch as the naming of people may be more canonical than the naming of nonhumans, or the giving of proper names may be more canonical than the giving of generic names, as in (19)-(20), or of attributes, as in (21).[12] Lexically, the nature of the action—"naming"—remains the same for both *zvat'* and *nazyvat'*.

A different motive can be found for the use of the derived form *razbivati* in Nikitin's text. In (22) and (23), this verb appears in Modern Russian translations as *razbojničat'*, 'be a pirate'.

(22) А пошлин много, а на море разбойников много. А **разбивают** все кафары, ни крестияне, не бесермене: а молятся каменым болваном, а Христа не знают, ни Махмета не знают. (8)
      'And there is much tribute/taxes (to be paid), and there are many robbers on the high seas. And all the Kafars *are robbers (razbivajut)*; they are neither Christians nor Muslims, but pray to stone figures, and they know neither Christ nor Mohammed.'

(23) Меликътучар два города взял индийскых, что **разбивали** по морю Индийскому. (14)
      'Meliktučar took two Indian cities, which *had been robbing (razbivali)* [ships] on the Indian Sea.'

---

[11] Examples (19) and (20) were presented earlier as example (3).
[12] Another such theme-based distinction between simplex and derived verbs in Old Russian was seen with *slati~posylati* 'send' in section 5.9.5.

The prefixed protoperfective *razbiti (sja)* 'break, wreck; be wrecked' is used in a completely different sense, as seen in (24) and (25); its semantic connection to the derived form is tenuous at best (robbery is a form of wreckage). In (24) the usage is impersonal, with the weather probably causing the act. In (25) the reflexive form indicates an action performed on the ship by unknown forces.

(24) А въстала фуртовина на море, да судно меншое **разбило** о берег. (6)
'And a storm came up on the sea, and the smaller ship *was dashed (rozbilo)* against the shore.'

(25) «судно **ся** (мое) **розбило** под Тархи, и твои люди, пришед, людей поимали, а товаръ их **пограбили**...» (6)
' "(My) ship *was wrecked (sja rozbilo)* near Tarxi, and your men, once they came, seized (my) men and *robbed (pograbili)* them of their goods..." '

The protoperfective verbs most closely approximating the meaning of *razbivati* are *razgrabiti* and *pograbiti* 'rob', which appear several times in this text. Even so, they describe the act of robbery, not the condition of being a robber (see (25), which has a direct object: *tovar" ix pograbili* 'they stole their wares'). This state of affairs is admitted by Sreznevskij's data: the two examples of *rozbiti*[13] with the meaning 'steal, rob' come from the thirteenth century, while the three examples of *razbivati* and *rozbivati* with this meaning come from the fourteenth and fifteenth centuries, all of the latter expressing an atelic meaning 'rob habitually, be a robber'.

The simplex *biti* 'beat, strike, fight', while widely used with various meanings in medieval texts, rarely appears in this text, and never with a meaning remotely like 'rob'. One example of the simplex is the atelic use of *biti sja* found in (26).

(26) А град же взял индийской меликъчанъ хозя, а взял его силою, день и нощь **бился** з городомъ 20 дни, рать ни пила, ни ѣла, под городом стояла с пушками. (16)
'And the Indian khan Melikčan took the city, and took it by force; day and night *he fought (bilsja)* with the city for twenty days; the company neither drank nor ate, but stood outside the city with cannons.'[14]

This lack of correspondence between the unsuffixed and suffixed forms is mirrored elsewhere in this family of verbs, as seen with *pobiti* 'kill' and *pobivati* 'defeat' in section 6.4 below. It may indicate a problem in the aspectualization process, namely that at this stage, suffixes occasionally do more than simply change the aspect of a verb. While a verb's aspect does clearly change when it is suffixed, changes of meaning can also take place, which prevent strict aspectual pairing. (Further evidence for this process is presented in chapter 7.)

---

13 No examples with this meaning are listed under *razbiti*.
14 Example (26) appeared earlier as example (13).

The form *razbivati,* then, is an aspectual singularity in this text, despite sharing a root and a prefix with *razbiti* and the root and aspect of *biti*. No morphologically related form shares this meaning with it. Perhaps the prefix is best interpreted as a deformation of a spatial meaning ('beat all over the place' = 'be a robber') for the suffixed form, as opposed to the Aktionsart meaning it takes on in the unsuffixed form ('beat thoroughly' = 'wreck'). This differentiation according to telic or atelic meaning of the root recalls the variations in prefixal meaning for telic and atelic predicates seen in earlier chapters.

Predicate valences also reflect these differences in meaning. Both *biti* and *razbiti* normally require a direct object or a reflexive form in this text, while *razbivati* does not.[15] In one use of *razbiti*—in (24)—the agent remains unspecified, yielding a sense similar to Modern Russian impersonal sentences; in (25) the reflexive form suggests an unnamed group or force is responsible, and the ship is the object of the action (though in the nominative case). The verb *razbivati*, however, never appears with an accusative object, or indeed any kind of object besides prepositional phrases of location. New derived forms can thus observe different combinatory and grammatical rules than the verbs they sprang from.

Chart 6.3.1 and 6.3.2 list prefixed verbs that have derived protoimperfectives attested in the text. There are thirteen such verbs in the work, eleven of which use suffixes with {-v-}. Of the eleven {-vaj-} verbs, three are formed from the simplex verb *biti* 'hit, beat.' The non- {-vaj-} verbs are three in number: *vpadati* 'fall', *posylati* 'send', and *prodajati* 'sell' (which has derived protoimperfectives of both types), and they use {-aj-} suffixes ({-aj-} or {-jaj-}). *Prodati* 'sell' is certainly by the time of this text divorced completely in meaning from the simplex *dati* 'give', meaning that it has a behavior pattern more like that of a simplex verb.

A majority of the prefixed derived verbs in this text are in iterative contexts; the remainder are distributed across the remaining three types of contexts. For many of the remaining forms, however, it is possible to find a way to interpret the reading as iterative: for instance, some verbs describe actions that imply iteration when a prolonged period of time is specified. An example is the relationship between the verbs *kazati, skazati,* and *skazyvati,* which all mean 'say'. The finite forms of *skazyvati* are used in the 3. pl. in this text, and mean 'they said/they say', as in (27) and (28). As (27) shows, this usage is identical to that of the simplex *kazati,* although (28) suggests that a more processual reading is also possible. Modern Russian uses forms of *govorit'* 'say' in all these instances.

(27)   Да о вѣрѣ же о их распытах все, и оны **сказывают**: вѣруем въ Адама, а буты, **кажуть**, то есть Адамъ и род его весь. (23)[16]
       'And I asked all of them about their faith, and *they say (skazyvajut):* we believe in Adam and the Buty; *they say (kažut'),* that is Adam and all his descendants.'

---

[15] One regular exception is the expression *biti čelom* 'petition', which appears with a dative complement instead of an accusative, but this is clearly a fixed phrase which must be treated separately from other instances of the verb *biti*.

[16] This quote comes from a passage in the Troickij ms. not found in the Ètterov ms.

Chart 6.3.1. *Fifteenth-century simplex verbs with derived forms in the original text of the Journey.*

simplex verb	prefixed perfective	unprefixed derived imperfective	prefixed derived imperfective	iterative	general	progressive	durative
звати			призывати	**d-1**	**d-1**, s-3		**d-1**
(-пасти)	впасти		впадати	**d-1**			
(яти)		имати	подымати	**d-1, s**			
(валяти)			разваляти	**d-1**			
(-слати)	послати прислати отслати		посылати	**d-1**			
бити	побити, розбити выбити убити		побивати разбивати обивати	**d-2** — **d-2**	s-3 **d-1**	s-1 **d-1**	s-2
крыти (ся)	покрыти		покрывати ся	**d-1**, s-1	s-2		
(мыти)			подмывати ся омывати	**d-1** **d-1**			
(пополоскати)			пополаскивати	**d-1**			
казати (ся)	сказати		сказывати	**d-1.5**	**d-2**, s-2	**d-1**	
писати	— написати		записывати	**d-1**			s-1
(искати)	обыскати		обыскивати			**d-1**	

NOTES: Some Old Russian verb sets appeared only once in this text.; some appeared more often. Where entries had varying contexts, the number of each type of context is listed. Half a point means a verb could be read as belonging to either context. Forms in parentheses were not attested in this text. The number of simplex forms (s) and derived imperfective forms (d) is given.

Chart 6.3.2. Anomalous verb sets with derived prefixed forms in the Journey.

simplex verb	prefixed perfective	unprefixed derived imperfective	prefixed derived imperfective	iterative	general	progressive	durative
дати	продати, удати, раздати	давати	продавати = продаяти	**p-1** **p-1**, u-5	**p-1** **p-7**, u-3		**p-1** **p-1**
(дети)			въздевати	**p-1**			
(жалити (ся))	сжалити ся	жаловати ся	пожаловати	u-1			

NOTES: These verb sets are anomalous for several reasons. In the first place, the relation between the prefixed (p) and unprefixed (u) forms may be obscured. This leads to verbs like давати-дати and продавати-продати being treated as entirely separate verb sets. The difference between девати-дети and въздевати-въздети is equally distant. The last set is arranged in a different manner; the verb пожаловати is actually a perfective, and its corresponding imperfective is жаловати , not пожалити. While the strict placement of пожаловати is evident even in this text, and speaks for the idea that жаловати may be denominal (<жалоба 'complaint') and not derived from the simplex жалити, which has the same root.

(28) Мене залгали псы бесермены, а **сказывали** всего много нашего товара, ано нѣт ничего на нашу землю... (8)
'Those curs, the Muslims, deceived me, and *told of (skazyvali)* many of our wares, but there is nothing here for our country...'

However, forms of *skazyvati* can also mean 'it was said at the time', which is used parenthetically in (29) and (30).

(29) А держит, **сказывають,** семь темъ от меликъточара. (7)[17]
'And he holds from Melikotočar, *they say (skazyvajut')*, seventy thousand troops.'

(30) А рати их, **сказывают,** велми много, а язык у них есть свой. (9)
'and their army [the monkeys'], *they say (skazyvajut)*, is very large, and they have their own language.'

The context for *skazyvati* is thus iterative in (27) and (28) but durative or progressive in (29) and (30). Identifying the speech act with its consequences is a common phenomenon in language but creates problems for contextual classification: it is difficult to tell when a generally accepted statement is to be read as simply the prevailing wisdom of the moment—a generalized context—and when it actually represents repetition of a statement or duration of a state.

Acts expressed with the prefixed form *skazati* represent a single recounting of a story or position. Note, however, that in (31) and (32), *skazati* appears with a direct object: *skazati věru svoju* 'tell of one's faith' in (31), and *skazati lživye věsti* 'give false reports' in (32).

(31) и **сказах** имъ вѣру свою, что есми не бесерменинъ, исаядениени есмь, християнинъ, а имя ми Офонасей, а бесерменьское имя хозя Исуфъ Хоросани. (22)[18]
'And *I told (skazax)* them of our faith, that I am not a Muslim, but a follower of Jesus, a Christian, and my name is Afanasij, and my Muslim name is khan Isuf Xorosani.'

(32) Ту наѣхали на нас три татарины поганые и **сказали** нам лживые вѣсти: «Кайсым салтан стережет гостей в Бузани, а с ним три тысящи татар». (5)
'Here three pagan Tatars met us and *gave (skazali)* us false reports: "Sultan Kajsim lies in wait for merchants at Buzan', and with him (are) three thousand Tatars."'

---

[17] The verb form *skazyvajut'* appears in the Troickij ms. but not in the Ètterov ms., although the rest of the sentence is present.

[18] This quote comes from a passage in the Troickij ms. not found in the Ètterov ms.

This matches the usage found in (28) *(skazyvali vsego mnogo našego tovara* 'told of much of our merchandise'), but not with (27), where the derived form introduces indirect discourse without a nominal object, or with (29) and (30), where the derived form is parenthetical. Sreznevskij confirms these restrictions of the protoperfective *skazati,* listing mainly examples with direct objects. Those examples of *skazati* that introduce indirect discourse either have a direct object as well (as in (31), which is rare) or use an interrogative as a conjunction *(a tot" stav" skažet, kak" pravo pred B(o)gom"* 'and that one, having stood up, will tell how the law is before God'). In Nikitin's text, the derived form —although generally more restricted than the simple prefixed form *skazati*—has acquired usages and meanings not found with the simple prefixed form, indicating a relationship between the forms that is both aspectual and secondarily lexical.

Another problematic area is the description of verb sequences that convey a general behavior pattern, but contain strong hints of iterativity. Almost all of Nikitin's descriptions of Indian behavior fall into this category. Stretching the definition of iteration encompasses nearly all of these situations. In the company of protoimperfective verbs, even if merely describing a single occurrence of a habit, an analogy is drawn to iterative strings. In fact, these derived forms do seem to occur nearly exclusively when other protoimperfective verbs are present nearby.

This broadly defined iterative context can therefore act as a trigger for the use of protoimperfectives derived with {-vaj-}. Such sentences may have explicit iterative adverbs like *mnogo* 'much', *často* 'often', or may use a construction of the type "whenever *x* is done, then *y* is done."

6.4. OTHER STRATEGIES FOR CONVEYING ITERATIVITY

There are many indications in this text, however, that use of a protoimperfective verb was not the only strategy open to Nikitin in iterative contexts. A good example, in contrast to the one provided for *razbivati* 'be a pirate' above, is the pair *pobivati–pobiti.* This pair appears in the text with two different meanings, which have correspondingly different results in iterative contexts. In the meaning 'defeat, triumph over' the derived form is found. However, it does not appear in the meaning 'murder, kill'. Instead, at the end of a protoimperfective string, a protoperfective verb appears. In (33), when describing the monkey tribes of India, the author cannot resort to the simplex without drastically altering the meaning—*pobiti* 'kill (pf.)' vs. *biti* 'beat (impf.)'—and also avoids the derived protoimperfective. He resorts to a prefixed protoperfective, letting the prior string of protoimperfectives carry the weight of iterativity in the context: [19]

---

[19] The Modern Russian translation, by contrast, contains a perfective in the protasis, but all imperfectives in the apodosis: *Esli kto obez'jan obidit^P, oni žalujutsja^I svoemu knjazju, i on posylaet^I na obidčika svoju rat; i oni, k gorodu pridja, doma razrušajut^I i ljudej ubivajut^I.* Two native speakers of Russian, faced with the text of this example, allowed either *obidit^P* or *obižaet^I* in the protasis, depending on whether the injury occurs once

(33) А обезьяны, то тѣ живут по лѣсу. А у них есть князь обезь-
яньскый, да ходит ратию своею. Да кто **замает**, и они **ся жалуют**
князю своему, и он **посылаеть** на того свою рать, и оны, пришед
на град, дворы **развалают** и людей **побьют**. (9)
'And as for the monkeys, they live in the forest. And they have a monkey
prince, and he travels with his company. And when someone *injures (zamaet)*
them, they *complain (sja žalujut)* to their prince, and he *sends (posylaet')* his
warriors against that person, and, having come into the city, they *knock down
(razvaljajut)* houses and *kill (pob'jut)* people.'

There is no possibility here of invoking a difference in lexical class; both
meanings cited, 'defeat' and 'kill', are highly telic. Instead, we might appeal to the
more highly aspectualized nature of sequenced acts in Old Russian to explain the
failure to imperfectivize in (33); a derived form would overemphasize the process
when it is the result (death) that is the primary issue. In (34), the context indicates
that the outcome of any one battle between Meliktučar and his enemies is irrelevant,
and the numerous victories and defeats are part of an ongoing process.

(34) А меликътучар седит на 20 тмах; а **бьется** с кафары 20 лѣт есть, то
его **побивают**, то он **побивает** ихъ многажды (7)
'And Meliktučar has 200 thousand (warriors), and he *has been fighting
(b'etsja)* with the Kafars for twenty years: sometimes *they beat (pobivajut)*
him, many times he *beats (pobivaet)* them.'

(34a) tr: ...и они его не раз **побеждали**, и он их много раз **побеждал**.
(46)
'and they *beat (pobeždali)* him more than once, and he *beat* them many times.'

The purpose of the sentence is to show how many times they have fought and
that the outcomes are balanced between one side and the other. At this point in Old
Russian, this particular derived form implies an outcome, but it cannot set the
conditions for a sequence of events; in fact, it occurs in a context where a sequential
reading is disallowed.

Compare (34) to (33), where the monkeys' murdering of humans does in all
probability follow the previous actions in the sentence. Here, both suffixed and
unsuffixed forms are found. The suffixed forms *(zamaet* 'injures', *žalujut sja* 'they
complain', *posylaet* 'sends') focus on repetition of this hypothetical precursor to the
monkeys' attacks on human settlements; the unsuffixed acts *(prišed* 'having come',
pob'jut 'they [will] kill') show temporal distance from the suffixed forms and
indicate temporal sequencing of acts. One suffixed form, *razvaljajut* 'tear down', is
wedged between unsuffixed forms and focuses more on the process—the monkeys'
destructive capabilities—than on the results of their actions.

each time or occurs constantly, but agreed on the necessity of having imperfectives
everywhere else.

At this point, it is worth comparing these Old Russian iterative strings to the Modern Russian "graphic-exemplary" meaning *(nagljadno-primernoe značenie)* of the perfective aspect. The graphic-exemplary usage, which is said to indicate irregular or occasional repetition, focuses attention on the completeness of each instance of the series; it is contrasted to an imperfective rendering of the situation, in which repetition and continuity can blend together. Examples of the modern graphic-exemplary perfective are given in Rassudova (from the 1984 translation of Rassudova 1982; English glosses have been emended where necessary).

(35) Он каждому **поможет**^{P}.
'He'll *help*^{P} *(pomožet)* anyone.' (114)

(36) Бывает, что и **не заметишь**^{P} ошибку сразу.
'Sometimes you *won't* even *notice*^{P} *(ne zametiš')* the mistake immediately.' (116)

(37) Ну всегда что-нибудь да **забудешь**^{P}, чего-нибудь **не предусмотришь**^{P}, **приходится**^{I} все переделывать.
'You can always *forget*^{P} *(zabudeš')* something; you may *not foresee*^{P} *(ne predusmotriš')* something, and then you *have*^{I} *(prixoditsja)* to do everything over again.' (117)

(38) У меня часто **бывает**^{I} так: **кажется**^{I}, что уже все понятно, а **начну**^{P} делать — и опять **появляются**^{I} вопросы.
'With me it often *happens*^{I} *(byvaet)* like this: everything *seems*^{I} *(kažetsja)* clear, but I'll *start*^{P} *(načnu)* to do it—and questions *come up*^{I} *(pojavljajutsja)* again.' (116)

If the possibility exists in Modern Russian for such constructions, it is not surprising to find them in Old Russian texts. What is unusual is the variety of constructions available in this text. In Rassudova's examples, a switch from imperfective to perfective can occur, but there is a clear division between perfective and imperfective parts of a sentence. Perfectives are not sandwiched between two imperfective verbs, as in (39) below—unless a clear pause is indicated, as in (38).

If one believes the accounts found in Rassudova and Forsyth, there is a clear semantic difference in Modern Russian between the strings of perfectives that create a graphic-exemplary context and the standard use of imperfectives for iteration (Forsyth 1970: 171-177).[20] This clear division between a graphic-exemplary usage and a continuous iterative usage is missing from the Old Russian examples (see (33) and (39)). Instead, where Modern Russian prefers that all verbs in a clause have the same aspect, which then indicates the kind of iterativity in question, Old Russian aspectual assignment depends more on the nature and context of each act; it uses

---

[20] However, if Modern Russian translations of Old Russian texts are any indication, this hard-and-fast rule of Modern Russian grammatical aspect is far less strict than Rassudova believes.

protoperfectives for sequencing while suffixed protoimperfectives show both sequenced and nonsequenced iteration.

As an example of this system, the protoperfective form *dotyčjut* 'they (will) touch' in (39) is surrounded by the protoimperfectives *sja klanjajut* 'they bow' and *ne govorit* 'he [sic] does not speak', so that its iterativity is suggested by context.

(39) Пошел или пришелъ, ини **ся кланяют** по-чернеческыи, обе руки до земли **дотычют**, а **не говорит** ничего. (10)
 'And leaving or entering, they *bow (sja klanjajut)* like monks, *touch (dotyčjut)* both hands to the ground, and *he doesn't say (ne govorit)* anything.'

This is a practice acceptable enough in Old Church Slavic, and normal in languages like Czech, where the lexical meaning of the one-time act takes precedence over the iterativity of the action.[21] It is rarely acceptable in Modern Russian, however, especially in mid-sentence, and both translations have an imperfective verb *(kasaetsja* 'he touches'). These examples suggest that in Nikitin's Russian, although iterativity is already seen as an acceptable and desirable place to have derived protoimperfectives, it is not yet a necessary and sufficient reason for using them.

In his 1954 article "Imperfekt glagolov soveršennogo vida v slavjanskix jazykax" ("The Imperfect of Perfective Verbs in the Slavic Languages"), which was discussed in section 5.6, Jurij Maslov analyzed the meanings of the imperfect tense used with verbs of the perfective and imperfective aspects. Maslov hypothesized that originally in Old Russian and other Slavic languages in their oldest recorded states, the use of an imperfect form with a verb of perfective aspect indicated sequencing of acts, while the use of an imperfect form with a verb of imperfective aspect indicated simultaneity of acts. This system already shows signs of strain in Old Russian, he says, and is eventually supplanted by two alternate systems. In the first, derived imperfectives replace the prefixed perfectives, and the final result is iterative strings in the old perfect tense where sequencing is implied but not clearly marked by the verb form. In the second, perfective non-past forms replace the perfective imperfects, and the past nature of the acts is suggested periphrastically with expressions like *byvalo* 'it used to be that'. Examples (33), (34), and (39) lend support to Maslov's hypothesis, suggesting that the model for this second change in the preterite system may have come from the non-past system, which was evidently undergoing reinterpretation along the same lines.

Example (40) with the verb *ponuditi* 'request, convince' suggests that durative action can be expressed equally well with a protoperfective verb and a word like *mnogo,* especially when the action ends in failure.

(40) Бесерменин же Меликъ, тот мя **много понуди** в вѣру бесерменьскую стати. (13)
 'The Muslim Melik *often urged (mnogo ponudi)* me to take the Muslim faith.'

---

21 See Eckert 1984 on the comparison between Russian and Czech aspect.

Modern Russian requires an imperfective here to express the notion of repeated or continuous action ending in failure (*sil'no ponuždal* 'strongly urged'); the emphasis in Nikitin's text would seem to be on the repetition of a single action at several discrete occasions.[22] One can conclude that conativity does not regularly trigger use of the Old Russian protoimperfective aspect.

6.5. SUMMARY OF CONTEXTUAL FACTORS

To summarize the data examined so far, I will first consider the distribution of verbal suffixes in derived forms. Second, I will relate the distribution of derived forms to context features. (A third area, the constraints that lexical groupings of verbs place on the process of imperfectivization, will be examined in section 6.6.)

Aspect in Nikitin's work already displays some modern characteristics. From older forms in {-aj-} and {-jaj-} there are more unprefixed derived protoimperfectives than there are prefixed derived protoimperfectives *(prizyvati* 'call upon', *vpadati* 'fall into', *podymati* 'raise', *razvaljati* 'destroy', *posylati* 'send'). Prefixed derived protoimperfectives in {-vaj-} are well-represented. For Nikitin, this is the most productive derivational suffix for prefixed verbs.

These derived forms, however, do not occur everywhere we might expect an imperfective counterpart to a prefixed protoperfective; these new verbs are largely limited to iterative and progressive contexts or—in some instances—to particular meanings of the verb. Use of the protoimperfective aspect is not yet a requirement in iterative contexts, and it continues to coexist with other forms, including periphrastic expressions and context induced from surrounding protoimperfectives. Context thus plays a much larger part in Nikitin's Russian than it does in Modern Russian in determining the possibility that a given form will imperfectivize.

Chart 6.5.1 summarizes this material, showing the verbs involved in this work and their respective ability to imperfectivize in Modern and Old Russian. The verbs *zvati* 'call' and *kryti* 'cover' are represented in "in-between" states, and the clear movement of verbs in the chart is toward the right hand side, i.e. verbs that do not have derived imperfectives in the situations given eventually acquire that ability as the protoimperfective aspect becomes necessary in more and more contexts, and the derived forms usurp meanings originally attached to simplexes.

It is also useful to consider the contextual distribution of the verb types discussed above. Chart 6.5.2 (following pages) shows the distribution of forms in each context type. Derived forms and other anomalous forms are given as a percentage of the total number of forms in that context. (The numbers in any column do not add to 100 percent because most forms in any context were nonanomalous simplex forms.) Chart 6.5.3 (following pages) shows the distribution of contexts in each morphological class. The number of forms in each context is given as a percentage of the total number of forms in that morphological class. (Here the numbers do make 100 percent, adding across the rows.)

---

[22] Two native speakers of Russian both chose *sil'no ponuždal* as opposed to **sil'no ponudil*, supporting the translator's decision.

Chart 6.5.1. Susceptibility of verbs to suffixation

GROUP A VERBS (No derived form in the Old Russian text)	GROUP B VERBS (derived form is unprefixed)	GROUP C VERBS (derived form has prefixed forms)
крыти (some meanings)	———————>	крыти/покрывати
звати (some meanings)	———————>	звати/призывати
жечи	стреляти†	посылати
дѣлати	давати†	продавати
ставити	кланяти ся†	разбивати, побивати, обивати
вязати	пускати†	пополаскивати
правити	лишати†	сказывати
бритися	роняти†	подмывати, омывати
гадати	являти†	обыскивати
блюсти	стрѣчати†	въздевати
воевати	бывати	разваляти†
стеречи	пивати	впадати†
	слыхати	подымати†
	видати	

|<------- extent of imperfectivization in Nikitin ------->|

|< ------------------ extent of imperfectivization in Modern Russian -------------------- >|

† *simplex verb is protoperfective*

Of the forms found in iterative contexts (Chart 6.5.2), a comparatively large proportion (12.8 percent) have forms with {-vaj-} suffixes. Progressive contexts had {-vaj-} verbs in 8.6 percent of the forms examined, and durative and generalized contexts had respectively 2.5 percent and 3.2 percent.

Verbs with {-aj-} suffixes showed a similar spread (15.5 percent for iterative contexts, 8.6 percent for progressive contexts, 7.9 percent for generalized contexts, and 4.9 percent for durative contexts).

Protoperfective verbs translated by a Modern Russian imperfective are, understandably, much better represented in iterative contexts (6.6 percent of all verbs) than in the progressive (1.4 percent) or the durative (1.2 percent) contexts. There was only one generalized context example with these verbs.

For instances where an Old Russian simplex verb appeared in the Modern Russian as a prefixed derived imperfective, the figures were weighted toward the progressive context, in which 5.7 percent of its examples displayed this correspondence. The figures were 2.7 percent and 3.8 percent for the iterative and generalized contexts, respectively; there were no durative examples with this correspondence.

Chart 6.5.2. Contexts. Percentage of forms per context by morphological features (the balance in each column is simplexes.)

context type—> type of verb	iterative (113 attestations)		progressive (35 attestations)		durative (81 attestations)		generalized (158.5 attestations)	
derived impf. verb with {-vaj-} suffix	14.5/113 =	12.8	3/35 =	8.6	2/81 =	2.5	5/158.5 =	3.2
derived impf. verb with {-aj-} suffix	17.5/113 =	15.5	3/35 =	8.6	4/81 =	4.9	12.5/158.5 =	7.9
OR pf. = MoR impf.	7.5/113 =	6.6	.5/35 =	1.4	1/81 =	1.2	1/158.5 =	0.6
OR simplex impf. = MoR derived impf.	3/113 =	2.7	2/35 =	5.7	—		6/158.5 =	3.8

Chart 6.5.3. Morphology. Percentage of forms with a certain morphological feature found in each imperfective context.

context type—> type of verb	iterative		progressive		durative		generalized	
derived impf. verb with {-vaj-} suffix (24.5 contexts)	14.5/24.5 =	59.2	3/24.5 =	12.2	2/24.5 =	8.2	5/24.5 =	20.4
derived impf. verb with {-aj-} suffix (37 contexts)	17.5/37 =	47.3	3/37 =	8.1	4/37 =	10.8	12.5/37 =	33.8
pf. verb in OR = impf. verb in MoR (10 contexts)	7.5/10 =	75.0	.5/10 =	5.0	1/10 =	10.0	1/10 =	10.0
OR simplex impf. = MoR derived impf. (11 contexts)	3/11 =	27.3	2/11 =	18.1	—		6/11 =	54.5

NOTE: Half points occur because some forms are both durative and iterative, both progressive and general, etc.
abbreviations: OR = Old Russian; MoR = Modern Russian

Considering the distribution of each morphological class of verb yields similar statistics. In Chart 6.5.3, more than half of the {-vaj-} verbs (59.2 percent) can be found in iterative contexts; the other categories each have between 8 and 20 percent of these verbs. For {-aj-} suffixes, the largest number are found in iterative and generalized contexts (47.3 percent and 33.8 percent respectively), followed by durative (10.8 percent) and progressive (8.2 percent) contexts. All but three of the protoperfective verbs represented by an imperfective in Modern Russian are in clearly iterative contexts. Simplex protoimperfectives represented by a prefixed derived imperfective in Modern Russian are more heavily weighted toward the generalized category, with 54.5 percent in generalized contexts, 27.3 percent in iterative contexts, 18.1 percent in progressive contexts. (None appeared in durative contexts.)

The evidence shows, then, that {-vaj-} verbs were clearly most common in iterative contexts and that a significantly higher percentage of all iterative contexts were occupied by these verbs. One can expect that protoimperfective {-vaj-} verbs are most productive in the iterative context in the fifteenth century, and their usage gradually spreads to other contexts on the way to the Modern Russian pattern of distribution.

Although a plurality of {-aj-} verbs are found in iterative contexts, the large number of forms in generalized context (over one-third) is notable. It indicates that while {-aj-} verbs are often found in iterative contexts in the fifteenth century, they differed from the {-vaj-} verbs in that their semantic range was somewhat wider. When the sheer numbers are considered, the results are more striking: there were more than twice as many {-aj-} verbs in generalized contexts as there were {-vaj-} verbs (12.5 to 5).

The preponderance of generalized context verbs that are simplex in Old Russian but secondary imperfectives in Modern Russian is not surprising. Lack of external (contextual) motivating factors for the secondary protoimperfective is most likely to occur in the generalized context; iterative contexts and to a certain extent progressive and durative contexts provide impetus for the use of a derived form. In these contexts, many of the derived verbs that we expect to see in Modern Russian are already in use, but their use may not yet have spread to the generalized context.

6.6. REMNANTS OF LEXICAL ASPECT

We have already seen in the *Journey* that certain lexical features—for instance, lexical differentiation between prefixed forms and derived forms created from them, and peculiarities of communicative acts—have an influence on the way forms are used and developed in this text. Using categories from Kučera 1983, Maslov 1948, and Timberlake 1984, I determined that more general lexical classes also provide useful indications of how predicates behave in the text, although the distinctions are less important than they were for earlier texts. The specific adaptation of these categories is outlined in section 2.7.

An interesting distinction between telic and atelic forms appears when the text is compared with its translation. Nine forms are Old Russian protoimperfectives that correspond to Modern Russian perfectives; of these, eight are atelic predicates. Twenty-two forms are Old Russian protoperfectives that correspond to Modern Russian imperfectives; of these, all but one are telic.

The examples in which an Old Russian protoperfective is translated by a modern imperfective are more numerous, although less central for my purposes here; the interesting mismatches in this direction concern the portrayal of iterative events and were examined in section 6.4. It is not especially surprising to note that all the predicates in this group are telic; atelic protoperfectives are not possible, unless states of limited duration like modern *postojat'* 'stand for a while' are counted, and these forms are not found in Nikitin's text.

The protoimperfectives in the Old Russian text are replaced by forms with an explicit Aktionsart meaning. In (41), the Old Russian uses a simplex in the phrase *tebě... ne boronju* 'I will not hinder you'.

(41) А что будет тебѣ надобе у меня, и ты ко мнѣ пришли, и яз тебѣ, своему брату, **не бороню**. (6)
'And whatever you need from me, you just send to me, and I *will not hinder* you, my brother'

(41a) *tr:* А что тебе от меня нужно будет, и ты ко мне присылай, и я тебе, брату своему, ни в чем **перечить не стану**. (44)

The non-past form indicates a future act, despite its apparent imperfectivity (Sreznevskij defines *boroniti* as *měšat'*, *prepjatstvovat'*, *zaščiščat'* 'hinder, impede, defend', all of which are listed in imperfective forms), as is clear from the context in which it appears. Xasan-bek's message to his brother-in-law concerns Nikitin and his shipmates; he offers his relation that 'whatever you shall need from me' as a consequence of their release, 'send me a message, and I will not hinder you'. The context situates the actions in the future; the use of a simplex after the imperative 'send' shows that in this text, simplexes, especially those that are nonpunctual and stative, still have the possibility of shifting temporal assignment between present and future. Examples of this sort are not numerous, but are still notable when they occur.

The Modern Russian translation in (41a) cannot use an imperfective form. In addition, the imperfective imperative *prisylaj* 'send' is used instead of the perfective, suggesting both the higher degree of politeness available with a Modern Russian imperfective imperative and the possibility of repeated sendings. Any "futurity" in the imperfective is conveyed by context. However, the second verb in the clause needs to suggest both the ongoing nature of the act and the fact that it occurs in the future; (41a) solves this problem by giving the phrase an inceptive cast: *perečit' ne stanu* 'I will not move to thwart you'. This example highlights the problems in trying to express futurity and imperfectivity in a single form. In Old Russian, the lexical shape of the act predominates; in Modern Russian, the inceptive quality of the act places it clearly in the future, anterior to the sending of the message, meaning that temporal assignment predominates over lexical shape. It could also suggest that the Old Russian form *boronju* has more plasticity in its ability to express inceptive meaning than do the corresponding Modern Russian forms.

Unlike the Chronicles, which had enough data to suggest conclusions about the aspectuality of these forms, the *Journey* does not have other examples of this sort. It is hard to say whether the appearance of a protoimperfective here is the result of broad aspectual indifference in this lexical class or a more specific problem resulting from the intersection of lexicalized duration and future time.

Example (42) presents a mismatch between the Old Russian protoimperfective *pečalovati* (Sreznevskij defines it as *zabotit'sja* 'take care of, worry about') and the Modern Russian perfective *poxlopotat'* 'petition, intercede'. Both are in the subjunctive, suggesting an act that is desired as a result of their arrival.

(42)   А били есмя челом Василию Папину да послу ширваншину Асан-бѣгу, что есмя с нимъ пришли, **чтобы ся печаловал** о людех, что их поимали под Тархи кайтаки. И Асанбѣг **печаловался и ѣздил** на гору къ Булатубегу. (6)
'And we petitioned Vasilij Papin and the emissary of the širvanšax Xasan-bek, whom we had come with, *that he take care (čtoby sja pečaloval)* of the people whom the kajtaks had seized near Tarxi. And Xasan-bek *took up our cause (pečalovalsja)* and went to the mountain to Bulat-bek'

(42a) *tr:* И я бил челом Василию Папину и послу ширваншаха Хасан-беку, с которым мы пришли — **чтоб похлопотал** о людях, которых кайтаки под Тарками захватили. И Хасан-бек **ездил** на гору к Булат-беку **просить**. (44)[23]

The Modern Russian in (42a) suggests that they petitioned Xasan-bek to intervene once (perfective) on their behalf, or that they expected him to begin doing so (inceptive). The Old Russian protoimperfective apparently adequately conveys the open-ended future process; the Modern Russian makes inception explicit.

The second sentence of (42) gives another clue as to why this is possible: the Old Russian verb *pečalovati sja* apparently has a range of meanings from the atelic 'take care of' to a punctual, telic meaning 'ask, petition'. The Modern Russian conveys this range of possibilities either by using a perfective, as in the first sentence of (42a), or by using an imperfective infinitival complement, as in the second sentence of (42a). An imperfective infinitive as the complement of a motion verb has a certain amount of inceptivity built in via context, which the Old Russian seems to convey without needing the explicit context *(pečalovalsja i ězdil* having

---

[23] The reading in Lur'e's translation *ja bil* 'I petitioned' apparently comes from the Troickij ms.; the Ètterov ms. has a plural form.

the meaning 'took up our cause and went', rather than 'went to plead our cause', as in the translation).[24]

Example (43) has yet another atelic predicate—*xoščet* 'wants'—translated by an inceptive form, *zaxočet* 'is seized by a desire'.

(43)   Ино, братие рустии християня, кто **хощет** поити в Ындѣйскую землю, и ты остави вѣру свою на Руси, да воскликнув Махмета да поити в Гундустаньскую землю. (8)
'So, my Christian Russian brethren, whoever *wants (xoščet)* to go to the Indian lands, leave your faith behind in Russia, and, having embraced Mohammed, then go to Hindustan'

(43a)   *tr:* А так, братья русские христиане, **захочет** кто идти в Индийскую землю — оставь веру свою на Руси, да, призвав Мухаммеда, иди в Гундустанскую землю. (47)

Once again, the Old Russian form in (43) can indicate a range of temporal possibilities from present to past, while the Modern Russian form in (43a) is more explicitly future in orientation and suggests single, occasional events. (The structure of the Modern Russian protasis *zaxočet kto* 'should anyone want', with no explicit "if" and a reversal of normal word order, supports this interpretation.)

Since chapters 4 and 5 stressed the status of atelic predicates, it will be useful to see if the same generalizations hold for the *Journey*. One familiar test case is the verb *viděti* and related forms, which were used as an example of punctual atelic predicates. They appear six times in this text. It is difficult to discern a difference in meaning between the suffixed predicate *ne vidali nikogo* 'we saw no one' in (44) and the simplex *ne viděx ničego* 'I saw nothing' in (45).

(44)   И Казань есмя проѣхали добровольно, **не видали** никого, и Орду есмя проѣхали, и Сарай есмя проѣхали. И вьѣхали есмя в Бузанъ. Ту наѣхали на нас три татарины поганые и сказали нам лживые вѣсти... (5)
'And we travelled freely through Kazan'; *we saw* no one, and we passed through Orda [the Golden Horde]; and we went through Saraj. And we came into Buzan. Here three Tatars met us and gave us false reports...'

(45)   Идох же в тавѣ по морю мѣсяць, а **не видѣх** ничего. На другий же мѣсяць увидѣх горы Ефиопскыя... (16)

---

[24] Compare another example: *I kanun Spasova dni priěxal xozjajoči Maxmet xorosanec", i bil esmi emu čelom,* **čtoby sja** *o mně* **pečaloval**. This is translated into Modern Russian: *Nakanune Spasova dnja priexal kaznačej Muxammed, xorasanec, i ja bil emu čelom,* **čtoby on** *za menja* **xlopotal** 'On the eve of Savior's Day the treasurer Muhammed, a Xorosanite, arrived, and I petitioned him to *plead my cause'*. Here the Modern Russian takes the atelic end of the scale, choosing to represent Mohammed's intervention as a condition or process, rather than a single event.

'I sailed in the ship across the sea for a month, and *didn't see* anything. In the second month I caught sight of the Ethiopian mountains...'

However, some contextual differences can be found: first of all, the duration given in (44) is implicit, rather than explicit; there is no clear marker at either end of the act. In contrast, the period of time in (45) is set explicitly at a month. In (44), Nikitin tells how his ship made it as far as Buzan without encountering any pirates or robbers. The negated derived form emphasizes that the way was clear; they were not expecting anything or anyone in particular. In (45), however, Nikitin summarizes the fact that despite his searching, he saw nothing at sea for a whole month. Finally, he catches sight of the mountains; this inceptive meaning is rendered in Old Russian and Modern Russian with the (proto-) perfective.

Example (46) is a generalized context for the verb *viděti:* the Indians cover themselves while eating so as not to be seen.[25] No endpoints for the act are given

(46)   А едят, покрываются платомъ, **чтобы** никто **не видѣлъ** его. (10)
       'And when they eat, they cover themselves with a cloth, *so that* no one might
       see (*čtoby ne videl''*) them'

In (47), however, the act could be a momentary one: the ship is sighted by the emperor, as a result of which the Tatars shouted out to them.

(47)   Поѣхали есмя мимо Хазтарахан, а мѣсяць свѣтит, и царь нас
       видел и татарове к нам кликали: ... (6)
       'We sailed by Astraxan, and the moon was shining, and the king *saw (videl)*
       us, and the Tatars called out to us...'

This interpretation is quite likely, and the Modern Russian translation reflects it by using the perfective *uvidel* 'saw, glimpsed' instead. However, a less inceptive, more descriptive reading is also possible, juxtaposing three simultaneous elements: the shining moon, the visibility of the ship, and the Tatars' shouts. While such a reading is less intuitive, the non-past *měsjac' světit* 'the moon is shining' lends some weight to this descriptive interpretation. The verb form *videl* 'saw', however, gives no clue as to the duration or character of the act; it could stand for either. This situation recalls the aspectually indifferent nature of *viděti* in earlier texts, but it is the only form to do so.

The root {vid-} is more sparsely attested in this text than in other texts in this survey; of the six forms with this root, two are prefixed protoperfectives, and one is an unprefixed derived form *(vidali).*[26]

---

25   We have already stated that for the verb *pokryvati* 'cover' the context is at least weakly iterative.
26   This may be due to the fact that Nikitin often represents acts of perception as being volitional; the verbs *smotriti, posmotriti, prizrěti* 'look' appear another five times in the text. However, the presence of these other verbs does not explain the paucity of forms entirely.

(48)   А Келекот же есть пристанище Индѣйскаго моря всего. А проити его не дай бо(г)[27] никакову костяку: а кто его **не увидит**, тот поздорову не приидет морем. (11)
'And Kelekot is the port for all the Indian Sea. And God preserve any ship that passes by; and whoever *doesn't see (ne uvidit)* it will not make it across the sea'

Despite this low rate of attestation, the number of forms with *uvidĕti* represents a much higher proportion of the total than in other texts. In the Primary and Suzdal' Chronicles, only eight forms of *uvidĕti* were attested, as compared to 199 forms of *vidĕti*, and no forms of *uvidĕti* were attested in the *Tale of the Taking of Tsargrad*, compared to thirty-nine forms of *vidĕti*. In light of these numbers, we might have expected not to find any overtly perfective-like verbs from the root *vid-* in the *Journey*.

Moreover, both uses of *uvidĕti* in this text fall within the range of the modern perfective: they indicate the entrance of a place into one's field of vision. This new, inceptive form seen in (45) and (48) is evidently encroaching on the old anaspectual form, as represented in (47).

The *Journey* therefore represents a halfway point between the anaspectuality of these predicates in earlier texts and their aspectuality later on. While the lexically determined shape of the act can lend it a certain aspectual vagueness, an Aktionsart partner for the verb is clearly in place, allowing it to participate at times in the aspectual opposition.

It is worth returning for a moment to the unprefixed derived form *ne vidali* 'we did not see' in (44). Derived forms of this sort exist for all the predicates found in the punctual atelic category—*vidati* for *vidĕti* 'see', *slyxati* for the unattested *slyšati* 'hear', and *divovati sja* for the form **diviti sja* 'be surprised' (unattested in this text). They do not exist for stative predicates; however, they do exist marginally for atelic actions (see section 6.2).

These derived unprefixed forms are often claimed to be strictly iterative formations; if they are, that categorization belongs to a later period. In this text, they are more likely to convey emphatic negation. The iterative reading may reflect the fact that a negated punctual predicate can be read two ways: as a failure at a point, or as a failure at numerous points. In this particular sort of context (negated acts, especially in the past tense), a punctual act can seem more articulated than a stative act; likewise, an atelic action has more potential for being viewed as a series of repeated acts than a stative act does. A discourse distinction that arises in a particular lexical class (ordinary punctual vs. emphatic) may transform itself into a grammatical distinction (single act vs. iterative act) holding across all verbs of this class.

Interestingly enough, a large proportion of the unprefixed derived forms are found with punctual predicates, telic as well as atelic. Of the remaining unprefixed

---

[27] The reading *bog* 'God' is from the Troickij ms.; the Ètterov ms. has the less comprehensible *bo* 'for'.

derived forms, four represent abstract acts denoting a change in perceived rights or state *(lišati* 'deprive', *puskati* 'allow, permit', *srěčati* 'meet') and two represent semelfactive acts *(strěljati* 'shoot', *imati* 'seize'). Only two represent nonpunctual telic acts *(klanjati sja* 'bow', *ronjati* 'drop, shed'). In these verbs, however, the act yielded by the new form is less likely to be perceived purely as iterative; it may appear in a progressive, durative or generalized context instead. The difference here between the simplex and the derived form more closely approaches a purely aspectual one for these verbs, which again argues for grammatical aspect's origins in the telic predicate class, possibly as a way of distinguishing processes and repeated acts from the "closed" quality of telic acts. Its extension into atelic acts is evidently less successful at this stage; the differentiation between forms is not as advanced or clear.

6.7. CONCLUSIONS

The Journey across Three Seas occupies a medial place in the history of aspect compiled here. A short text, written largely with a conversational flavor, it is less useful for lexical studies than the lengthier literary texts used elsewhere in this work. However, it provides an important counterpoint to the more literary style of the *Tale of the Taking of Tsargrad,* a work written in the same period. Compared to the *Tale,* the *Journey* displays a less rigid approach to the tense systems, freely using non-past forms in past narration. This particular feature brings to mind the more colloquial passages in the Chronicles and foreshadows a usage common in Kurbskij's work (see chapter 8): it is innovative in character, as Maslov posited in his article on the Old Russian imperfect.

The present–future distinction is also less rigid than in the *Tale,* bringing to mind the situation in the Chronicles. In this case, literary usage (exemplified by the *Tale)* has apparently gone farther in the direction of codification than colloquial usage (exemplified by the *Journey).*

The *Journey* reflects an aspectual system in the process of formation. A clear difference exists between protoperfective and protoimperfective forms, although it is not certain whether this represents in every case an aspectual opposition. Simplex verbs, while generally obedient to aspectual rules, occasionally show signs of nonaspectual behavior. This is consonant with the fact that they are paired with prefixed verbs not only aspectually, but by virtue of an Aktionsart relationship. However, this stage—where unambiguously protoperfective counterparts to atelic acts are being formed by prefixation—shows progression toward a grammatical aspectual system. Formerly, verbs with atelic predicates had expressed a range of features without regard for these features' aspectuality, whereas in this text, inceptive and completive predicates are no longer expressed exclusively by the simplex. Instead, an inceptive–stative distinction has arisen that is morphologically equivalent to the increased telicization that prefixes bestowed on telic predicates. Many verbs with primarily atelic predicates, such as the ones discussed in section 6.6, retain the ability to express various Aktionsart meanings, but they do so with less frequency, giving up these meanings to specific prefixed forms. The caution employed in this chapter in labelling forms "protoperfective" and "protoimperfective" is therefore justified, inasmuch as the distinction between these two classes is not precisely what is meant by the corresponding Modern Russian categories.

An aspectual system still in formation correlates with other morphological evidence found in this text. If true aspectual pairing is created—for the most part—only by suffixation, and not by prefixation, then the lack of suffixed forms in many contexts indicates that many verbs in this text lack aspectual pairs in Old Russian, even if they have them in Modern Russian.

A consistent theme in the discussion has been the presence of suffixed forms that, contrary to expectations, do not qualify as a regular, protoimperfective pair to the protoperfective. This might be expected if the protoperfective had a wider range of meanings than the derived form, but in fact, the derived form appears to possess usages that are off limits to the protoperfective. We observed this phenomenon with certain pairs of verbs: *razbivati–razbiti* 'engage in piracy–break, rob' and *skazyvati–skazati* 'put forth as true–say, tell' in section 6.3, and *pobivati–pobiti* 'be victorious–murder, beat' in section 6.4. The relexicalization of differences between the prefixed form and the derived form is a consistent feature of this text, especially with the most ancient derived forms. It coincides neatly with the fact that aspectual "pairs" in this text are, as mentioned earlier, not always limited to expressing differences in perspective: they can also differ lexically. Notably, none of the "pairs" given above have survived into standard Modern Russian with the same meanings, indicating that this process of relexicalizing aspectual differences may have been a temporary phenomenon caused by a more complex and lexically-oriented aspectual distinction in Old Russian.

7. The Taking of Tsargrad

7.0. INTRODUCTION TO THE TEXT

The Tale of the Taking of Tsargrad in 1453 by the Turks is a late fifteenth-century work attributed to one Nestor Iskander. The text suggests that he was a prisoner of the Turks after the battle that resulted in the fall of Constantinople. His account seems to be that of an eyewitness, although the myths surrounding the founding of Constantinople are reported with equal authority.[1] The text is both entertaining and didactic; it provides a vivid account of battles and heroism while setting the scene for the final demise of the Greeks and the passing of Christianity's torch to the Russians. The style is more consistently literary and high-flown than that of the *Journey* or the Chronicles; I observed in chapter 6 that Nikitin's style is paratactic, with virtually no participles and few subordinating conjunctions, while the Chronicles contain a mix of paratactic and hypotactic styles. In contrast, Iskander shows a decided preference for hypotaxis, as seen in his long, complex sentences and generous use of participial forms.

This difference also indicates divergent narrative strategies. Where Nikitin recounts events in a strict chronological ordering and piles descriptive passages together without hierarchical constraints, Iskander employs two slightly more sophisticated approaches. In narrative passages, he situates the reader in the midst of the action, focusing on one thread of it, and then makes glancing references to events occurring around it. In descriptive passages, he picks a focal act or event and presents other acts as connected to it or working towards it. Iskander thus uses many forms showing simultaneous action (in progressive contexts, with imperfect tense forms and present participles), whereas Nikitin tends to present events in strings, either single-time or repeated (iteratives). Both factors—the inventory of verb forms and the narrative strategy—pose an interesting ontological problem: do verb and tense inventories influence narrative strategy or does narrative strategy determine the type and variety of verb forms used? Regardless of which viewpoint one subscribes to, the two factors are apparently linked in the set of devices used by fifteenth-century Russian writers.

Unlike the *Journey,* which is a largely colloquial and intimate account of a trip, and unlike the Chronicles, which have a range of styles, from highest to lowest, the *Taking of Tsargrad* represents a stylistic extreme in the secular literature of fifteenth-century Russia. Iskander is able to produce a text that adheres to the Russian Church Slavic norms of the time. His text has a complete past tense system, including imperfect, aorist and perfect tenses, and the full array of

---

[1] Furthermore, many aspects of these legends are patently false; they refer to the struggle between Christianity and Islam in the fourth century A.D., several centuries before Islam came into being.

participles and verbal adverbs. By and large, Iskander employs "correct" forms and uses them "correctly."[2] (A notable exception are the forms of the third person plural aorist and the third person singular imperfect, which are sometimes interchanged.) As is usual in Old Russian texts, participle forms occasionally appear where the modern reader expects finite tense forms. From examining the tense systems, then, we might expect this text to be linguistically more conservative than the *Journey,* but more progressive than the Chronicles.

7.1. TSARGRAD AND THE HISTORY OF ASPECT

The differences between the *Journey* and the *Taking of Tsargrad* underscore the variability of the Old Russian aspectual system across the varied styles of fifteenth-century secular prose. Numbers will tell part of the story, but not all of it.

A number of phenomena observed in the *Journey* appear, albeit more faintly, in this text, but the contrasts are striking. First, the variety of derived verbs in the *Taking of Tsargrad* is much higher. Nikitin had twenty-seven such verbs, while Iskander makes use of some seventy-seven. Second, the distribution of these verbs by derivational suffix is different. Nikitin has a clear split between prefixed derived verbs, which are formed with {-(i/y)vaj-}, and unprefixed derived verbs, which are formed with {-aj-}, {-jaj-}, etc. The numbers are roughly even, with fifteen in the first category and twelve in the second. In comparison to Nikitin's roughly equal number of {-(j)aj-} and {-(i/y)vaj-} verbs, Iskander has a clear preponderance of -{(j)aj-} verbs: forty-seven to fourteen (77 percent of all derived verbs). The ratio of unprefixed derived verbs to prefixed derived verbs is also much lower for all kinds of verbs. Nine out of forty-seven verbs forming derived verbs with the suffix {-(j)aj-} (19 percent) are unprefixed; two out of fourteen verbs with one of the {-v-} suffixes (14 percent) are unprefixed, both of those using the {-vaj-} suffix. There is, however, no clear morphological split between prefixed and unprefixed derived verbs.

Here we are faced with an apparent contradiction. Iskander's text should be the more conservative one, yet it has a larger number of derived verbs, and the number of instances where simplexes in the Old Russian correspond to derived verbs in the Modern Russian translation is nowhere near as striking as in Nikitin's text. The obvious conclusion is that the apparently more conservative text has the more developed aspectual system.

After looking at the particular verbs involved, however, I have rejected this conclusion. In fact, it is the variety of forms that testifies to the text's archaic character. Many of the derived verbs that appear in the *Taking of Tsargrad* are no

---

[2] By "correct" I mean "historically and linguistically correct" as opposed to "correct by the standards current at the time and place of writing." It is beyond the scope of this study (and not particularly useful for my purposes here) to define the latter in any meaningful way. Designating a form or set of forms as "correct" is of interest only inasmuch as it helps demonstrate the place of the text in the literary canon and suggests the author's relationship to previous and concurrently existing texts.

longer extant in Modern Russian and probably belong more to the Church Slavic literary tradition than to the living language of the time. The text also shows a noticeable preference for {-aj-} suffixes, some of which are archaic in Modern Russian (cf. Old Russian *ustrajati* 'match, fit, suit', which is replaced by Modern Russian *ustraivat'* 'suit'; Old Russian *nakazati (nakazaju)* 'preach, teach', which is replaced by Modern Russian *nakazyvat'* 'order, punish'; and Old Russian *ulovljati*, which is replaced by Modern Russian *ulavlivat'* 'catch').[3]

7.2. LEXICAL ASPECT

In chapters 4 and 5, I showed that lexical categories were the primary vehicle for determining aspectual behavior in the Old Russian of the Primary Chronicle and the Suzdal' Chronicles. To what extent is this claim still valid for aspect of the fifteenth century? This question is especially relevant for the *Taking of Tsargrad*, whose elaborate tense system (reminiscent of that of older texts, in contrast to that of the *Journey*) lends itself to such investigations.

In the following sections I will refer to the lexical aspectual categories outlined in section 2.7 and used in subsequent chapters. While certain features of the lexical aspectual system remain in this text, the indications of aspectual regularity are much stronger. Nonpunctual acts show almost total participation in the aspectual system, while punctual acts show increasing susceptibility to aspectualization based on their telicity. Behavior within the aspectual system, however, is still influenced by lexical class. The more innovative and interesting trends discussed in this chapter will rely on contextual interpretation of data, although the lexicon continues to play a role in assigning aspect and usage.

In the discussion of the Chronicles, I looked at the lexical data in two ways: certain diagnostic verbs represented each class in the first chapter, while in the next chapter, data from other verbs were examined. The smaller quantity of data available from the *Taking of Tsargrad* made it more practical to skip the diagnostic approach and proceed directly to analyses of all verbs in the text by lexical class.

7.3. ATELIC PREDICATE CLASSES

The atelic predicate classes are punctual atelic, stative, and atelic action. The punctual atelics—a small and relatively homogeneous group of predicates—retain much of their anaspectual quality, while the remaining atelic predicates no longer show signs of anaspectual behavior. The criteria I used to judge aspectuality are

---

[3] The Modern Russian equivalents given here are not found in this text; due to shifts in meaning or idiosyncratic changes in the translation, the Old Russian verbs are translated with verbs based on different roots. A good example is *ustrajati*, which here carries the meaning 'build, ready', better conveyed in Modern Russian by *stroit'*, *gotovit'*. The modern verb *ustraivat'–ustroit'* means 'suit, situate'—a related meaning, but not close enough to justify using it in the translation.

modality of the non-past tense; usage in the past tense; usage in the infinitive; function and behavior of prefixed forms.

7.3.1. Punctual atelic predicates

The punctual atelic predicates encompass mainly involuntary perceptions and reactive emotions. Although a number of punctual atelic predicates are attested in this text, only two of them appear in simplex form: *viděti* 'see' and *slyšati* 'hear'. (The others, *diviti sja* 'be surprised' and *mysliti* 'think', appear only in prefixed form and are thus less useful for this analysis.)

7.3.1.1. Past tense forms. Examples with *viděti* 'see' in the non-past tense are few and far between. I found two examples of the former, both in the meaning 'now we see' (present). There were no examples of *slyšati*. Much of my argument will thus rest on the interpretation of past tense forms, of which there is a great sufficiency. It is noteworthy that only aorist forms appear with these two verbs, although a variety of contexts are represented. The verbs are often used inceptively, as in (1)-(3).

(1) И яко взыдоша паки гражане на стѣну и **видѣша** во рвѣ множество туркъ, абие зажигааху бочкы съ смолою и пущааху на них, и погорѣша вси. (234-236)
'And when the city-dwellers went up again on the wall and *saw (videša)* the multitude of Turks in the ditch, they immediately lit the barrels with pitch and heaved them down on the Turks, and they all burned up.'

(2) Но дню уже преспѣвшу, егда **видѣша** туркы башту дѣлающих, вскорѣ пустиша на них изо многых пушек и не даша им дѣлати. (252)
'But once day had come, when the Turks *saw (videša)* the men building the tower, they quickly fired on them from many cannons, and did not let them build.'

(3) Магумет же окаанный, яко **видѣ** тму велию над градом, созва книжник и молнъ и вопроси их... (256)
'The cursed Magumet, when *he saw (vidě)* a great cloud over the city, called his learned men and mullahs, and asked them...'

However, they can also indicate an act of some duration, as in (4) and (5). In (4), for example, the people watch a flame shoot out of the upper windows of the church and surround the cupola; the miracle mentioned in (5) is chronicled in (4).

(4) Собравшим же ся людѣм мнозем, **видѣша** у великие церкви Премудрости божиа у вѣрха из вокон пламеню огнѣну велику изшедшу и окруживщу всю шею церковную на длъгъ час. (242)
'When many people had gathered [there], *they saw (videša)* a great tongue of flame leap out of the windows at the top of the great Church of Wisdom and surround the whole cupola of the church for a long time.'

(5)   И тако прѣдстави ему онѣх мужей, иже **видѣша** чюдо... (244)
      'And so he presented to him those men who *had seen (viděša)* the miracle...'

Sometimes, as in (6)-(8), the aorist of *viděti* and *slyšati* indicates an instantaneous act. In (6), the people hear the sound of bells (i.e., first hear their chime).

(6)   И яко **слышаша** люди звон церквѣй божьих, абие укрѣпишася и охрабришася вси и бьяхуся с туркы крѣпчае перваго... (230)
      'And as soon as the people *heard (slyšaša)* the bells of God's churches, immediately they all took heart and strengthened their resolve, and they fought with the Turks more fiercely than before...'

(7)   Цесарь же, яко **слыша** божие изволение, поидѣ в великую церковъ и паде на землю, прося милость божию и прощенье согрѣшением... (258)
      'The emperor, when *he heard (slyša)* God's will, went into the great church and fell to the ground, asking for God's mercy and forgiveness for his sins...'

(8)   И поидѣ в церковь, и **видѣ** мрьзость запустение в святилище божие и ста на мѣсте святѣм его. (262)
      'And he went into the church, and *saw (vidě)* the baseness of neglect in God's sanctuary, and stayed in that holy place.'

Some examples, such as (9)-(11), are ambiguous. In (10), they might be seeing all the corpses at once, or panning their eyes across the landscape slowly; there is no indication in the text.

(9)   От иных же паки **слышахом**, яко оставшеи от сущиих съ цесаремъ у Златых врат, украдоша его тоа нощи, и отнесоша его в Галату, и сохраниша его. (262)
      'From others, *we* then *heard (slyšaxom)* that those who remained of those who had been with the emperor at the Golden Gate had stolen it [his body] that night, and taken it off to Galatia, and preserved it.'

(10) И **видѣша** полны рвы трупиа, а ины в потоцѣх и на брѣзех... (226)
      'And *they saw (viděša)* the ditches full of corpses, and others in the rivers and on the banks...'

(11) **Видѣ** изшедших полно поле и во все улици идущих много, и удивися толику народу от одноа храмины изшедчим... (262)
      '*He saw (vidě)* the square full of those coming out [of the church] and people walking off into all the streets, and marveled at so many people coming out of a single building...'

The aorist is used as a general past tense; it tends to represent acts of negligible duration, but is not limited to them. The past tense of these verbs shows a distinct lack of aspectuality.

7.3.1.2. Infinitives. Although the infinitive forms show a similar division between generalized contexts, which usually incorporate some duration; inceptives; and instantaneous usages, the balance here is toward the first group.

Examples (12)-(14) present generalized contexts for the use of the infinitive, both negated and otherwise.

(12) И не бѣ тоя нощи **слышати ничтоже**, развѣе стонание и вопль сеченых людей... (232)
'And *there was nothing to hear (slyšati)* that night except the groaning and howling of wounded people...'

(13) И **бѣ** страшно **видѣти** обоих и дрьзости и крѣпости. (238)
'And *it was* frightful *to see (viděti)* the daring and strength on both sides.'

(14) Он же, безвѣрный, не тако помышляше, но в 2 день посла **видѣти** мертвыя своя, и яко сказаша ему много мертвых, вскорѣ посла мнози полкы взяти трупиа своя. (228)
'The infidel did not think so, and the next day sent *to see (viděti)* his dead, and since they told him of many dead, he soon sent many troops to collect his corpses.'

Examples where the infinitive shows inception, as in (15), are also found. Example (16) can also be read as inceptive, since the guards rushed to find out what had happened.

(15) и внезаапу взгрѣме земля, акы гром велий... и **бѣ слышати** трескот, и сътрение тур, и вопль и стонание людцкых страшно... (234)
'...and immediately the earth roared like a great thunderclap... and *there was heard (bě slyšati)* a frightful crash and the crumbling of the towers, and the people.'s wails and moans...'

(16) нощи убо против пятка освѣтися град всь, и видѣвше стражи тѣчаху **видѣти** бывшее, чааху бо — туркы зажгоша градъ... (242)
'on the night preceding Friday the whole city lit up, and having seen this, the guards sped *to see (viděti)* what had happened, for they expected that the Turks had set the city on fire...'[4]

Sometimes the act could be perceived as instantaneous, as in (17) and (18), but a sense of greater duration is more likely.

(17) Цесарь же, взем боляр, поидѣ по стенам града, хотяще **видѣти** ратных... (226)
'The tsar, taking his nobles, went along the city walls, wanting *to see (viděti)* the troops...'

---

[4]   Also appears as examples (31) and (44).

(18)   И повелѣ выслати вон, да поидут коиждо въ свои дом, хотяше бо
       видѣти уряд и сокровища церковнаа... (262)
       'And he ordered them sent out, and for everyone to go home, for he wanted *to
       see (viděti)* the church's decorations and its treasure store...'

With the infinitives, then, the weight is toward the other end of the spectrum: usage implying duration is the rule, not the exception. The infinitive usage in this text makes *viděti* and *slyšati* look like protoimperfective verbs, although evidence for anaspectuality is present.

7.3.1.3. Prefixed derivatives. The behavior of these verbs' prefixed derivatives provides some more evidence for a Modern-Russian-style aspectual system, although the evidence is not unanimous. Curiously enough, this text has no attestations of the prefixed form *uviděti* 'see, glimpse', although it is attested in other texts of the period and earlier. There are several examples of *uslyšati* 'hear'. Three of them are past participle forms, three are aorists, and one is an imperative. The aorists do not seem greatly different in usage from those of *slyšati*.

A similar situation exists for the stems *-čutiti, -diviti sja*, which do not have simplex forms attested in the text.[5] The prefixed forms *očutiti* 'sense, feel, see', *udiviti sja* 'be surprised' are found and are mainly perfective in behavior, as in (19)-(21).

(19)   Стратиги же и воины и вси людие, **очютивше** своего цесаря,
       охрабришася вси и скакаху на турки акы дивии звѣри. (250)
       'The commanders and soldiers and all the people, *having seen (očjutivše)* their
       emperor, took heart and jumped upon the Turks like wild animals.'

(20)   И тако наполниша град преславными и дивными вещми, ими же и
       блаженный Андрей Критцкий, **удивився**, рече... (222)
       'And so the city was filled with most wondrous and strange things, about
       which the blessed Andrej Kritckij, *awestruck (udivivsja)*, said...'

(21)   Видѣвша же съ стѣны три братеники пять мужей онѣх срачин,
       бьюще тако силнѣ гражан, скачиша съ стѣны, нападоша на них и
       сечахуся с ними лютѣ, яко **удивитися** турком и не дѣяти их,
       чающе убиеным быти от них. (252)
       'When the three brothers-in-arms saw five of the Saracen men from the wall
       fighting the city-dwellers so fiercely, they jumped from the wall, fell upon
       them and did fierce battle with them, so that the Turks *were shocked
       (udivitisja)*[6] and did nothing, expecting to be killed by them.'

---

5   It is doubtful whether a verb **čutiti* is attested in Old Russian. In Sreznevskij I find no attestation for **čutiti*, only one for *čuti [čuju]* that corresponds to the meaning of *očutiti*. In this text, *očutiti* may serve as a suppletive perfective for *viděti* 'see'.

6   The Old Russian *jako* 'so that' + infinitive, with a logical subject in the dative *(turkom* 'the Turks') here is rendered by a past tense in English; see also (22) and others.

The exception is (22), where people marvel while watching how long the drops of rain endure on the ground. (The Modern Russian translation bears out this observation, using the stylistically marked simplex *divilis'*.)

(22) воздуху убо на аере огустившуся, нависеся надъ градом плачевным образом, ниспущаше аки слѣзы капли велици...и терпяху на земли на долгъ час, яко **удивитися** всем людем и в тузе велицей и во ужасе быти. (254)
'for when the air had thickened higher up, it hung over the city in a mournful fashion, letting loose large drops, like tears...and they remained on the ground for a long time, so that all the people *were surprised (udivitisja)* and in great despair and terrified.'

This durative context is weakly echoed in (23). The observer marvels at how many people came out of the church (when they obviously must have spent quite some time getting out, and he must have spent a long time watching them).

(23) Видѣ изшедших полно поле и во все улици идущих много, и **удивися** толику народу от одноа храмины изшедчим... (262)
'He saw the square full of those coming out [of the church] and people walking off into all the streets, and *marveled (udivisja)* at so many people coming out of a single building...'

For the most part, then, the prefixed form of *diviti sja* seems perfective, although perhaps not consistently so.

7.3.1.4. Participles. Given the paucity of evidence it is worth considering a few other categories, namely participial forms. Here the scale swings back in the other direction. There are fifteen participial forms of *vidĕti* in this text and six of *slyšati*. Of these, only one—in (24)—is a present participle, indicating a prolonged viewing of his people's torment that co-occurs with his crying and sobbing.

(24) Цесарь же бѣ плача и рыдая не престааше, **видяще** падѣние своих людей, а помощи ниоткуду чающе... (232)
'The emperor was crying and sobbing unceasingly, *seeing (vidjašče)* his people fall, and expecting no help from any quarter...'

The remainder are past participles. They express varying degrees of past or completed action. Some represent an instantaneous act, as in (25).

(25) Он же, лукавый, се **слышав**, порадовася в сердци своем... (236)
'The cunning fellow, *having heard (slyšav)* this, rejoiced in his heart...'

Instantaneous perceptions can indicate news heard or people seen, as in (26) and (27), where translations have perfective *uslyšav* 'having heard', *uvidel* 'he saw'.

(26) Магмет же окаанный, **слышав** восточнаго бегиларбеа убийство, плакаше много... (256)

'The accursed Mohammed, *having heard (slyšav)* of the murder of the eastern bey, mourned him greatly...' [7]

(27) **Видѣв** же безбожный туркъ, яко не успѣ ничтоже, но паче свсих погуби, и повелѣ магистром вскорѣ прибавити пушки и пищали мнози на битье града... (228)
'The godless Turk, *having seen (viděv)* that he had not succeeded anywhere, but had rather put his own men to death, ordered his commanders to add many more cannons and harquebuses to fire at the city...'

Some acts, however, are more prolonged, as in (28).

(28) Туркы же, **слышав** рыдание и смятѣние людцкаго, абие възкличав, напустиша всеми полкы и потопташа гражан... (252)
'The Turks, *having heard (slyšav)* the sobbing and confusion among the people, immediately whooped, and they let loose with all their troops and trampled the city-dwellers...'

Past participles can also govern a clause with a present participle, indicating that the action seen or heard took place over a longer time.

(29) он же, **видѣв** Рахкавѣя лютѣ **секуща** турокъ, обнажив меч, нападѣ на нь, и сѣчахуся обои лютѣ. (238)
'*having seen (viděv)* Raxkavej fiercely *slashing (sekušča)* at the Turks, he bared his sword and fell upon him, and they both fought fiercely.'

(30) **Видѣв** же стратигы и вси гражанѣ болма **пребывающих** туркъ, начаша бѣжати... (254)
'*When* the commanders and all the city-dwellers *saw (viděv)* that the Turks *were* ever *increasing (prebyvajuščix)* [in number], they began to flee...'

On the balance, the participle forms suggest a protoperfective verb rather than a protoimperfective one; most of the remaining forms are of the type *se slyšav* 'having heard this', as seen in (25). Some past participle forms represent acts concurrent with the perception, indicating a perception of greater duration—one that could equally well be represented by a present participle, as it is in the Modern Russian translation of (31), which has *vidja* 'seeing¹'.

(31) нощи убо против пятка освѣтися град всь, и **видѣвше** стражи тѣчаху видѣти бывшее, чааху бо — туркы зажгоша градъ... (242)
'on the night preceding Friday the whole city lit up, and *having seen/seeing (viděvše)* this, the guards sped to see what had happened, for they expected that the Turks had set the city on fire...' [8]

---

[7] A bey is a feudal Turkish lord and commander of forces from his region. This sentence also appears in examples (46) and (244).

[8] Also appears as examples (16) and (44).

The conclusion to be drawn is that aspectuality in these two verbs oscillates between protoperfective (aorist and past participle) and protoimperfective (infinitive and non-past). Evidence from prefixed formations suggests protoimperfectivity. I would class these two verbs as anaspectual.

This anaspectuality explains why out of sixty-eight forms in the Modern Russian text that are perfective where an imperfective might be expected (to match the Old Russian form), thirty-three of them are forms of *viděti* 'see' and *slyšati* 'hear'. In some instances, the Modern Russian perfectives *uvidet'* 'see, glimpse', *uslyšat'* 'hear, catch wind of' indicate a feeling of inception or sequentiality that was adequately conveyed by the simplex form in Old Russian (see (1) through (3), (10), (17), (18) and (25) through (30)). In two instances, the Modern Russian uses a verb with volitional meaning *(posmotret'* 'look') to escape the punctuality imposed by *uvidet'* 'glimpse', as in (14) and (16); in three others it focuses on the component of acquiring knowledge, which is prevalent in the Old Russian verb (modern *poznat'* 'become acquainted', *uznat'* 'recognize', *dogadat'sja* 'deduce').

7.3.2. Stative acts

In examining stative predicates in the Chronicles, I showed that they frequently lacked criteria for clear aspectual marking, although they had a natural tendency toward imperfectivity. In the *Taking of Tsargrad*, such criteria are no longer lacking; stative predicates show all the signs of being protoimperfectives.

7.3.2.1. Non-past forms. A selection of non-past forms from the verbs *mněti, podobati, stojati, věděti, zvati sja* is reproduced below. (The verbs *žiti, bojati sja, deržati, čajati, ljubiti, ležati, molčati, sijati, vladeti, znati,* which were also included in the textual survey, had no non-past forms but will be considered in other parts of the analysis.) Predictably, there are few non-past forms; the text in general has them only rarely (most often in direct discourse, which occurs infrequently). Virtually all the forms of these verbs found in this text are contained within the scope of Modern Russian imperfective usage. The use of *mnju* 'I think, I believe' in (32), for instance, is parenthetical; it represents the narrator's present view of a situation.

(32) и абие возопиша всь клирик и весь народ сущий ту...рыданием и стонанием, яко мнѣтися церкви оной великой колѣбатися, и гласи их, **мню**, до небесъ достигаху. (258)
'and immediately all the priests and people who were there...let out a cry of sobbing and moaning, so it seemed as if that great church was swaying and their voices, I *believe (mnju),* reached the heavens.'[9]

Likewise, in (33), the non-past *podobaet'* 'it is fitting' is an impersonal way of expressing the general appropriateness of the act. There may be a hint of futurity in

---

[9] This passage also appears in examples (51), (183), and (232).

this predicate (i.e., that it will prove a fitting place once the city begins to be built), but if so, then it is a slight one.

(33) «Въ Византию **подобаеть** Костянтину-граду създатися.» (216)
' "It *is fitting (podobaet')* to build Constantine's city in Byzantium." '

The forms *stoit* 'he has been standing', *věst'* 'he knows' in (34) and (35) represent states that were present at the time other acts occurred.

(34) «Понеже он, зловѣрный, тако многа дни **стоит** безбранно, паки готовиться, но да пошлем к нему о миру» (236)
'"Since the infidel *has stood* for so many days without attacking, and further is making preparations [for a new assault], let us send to him proposing a cease-fire." '

(35) И посла еи къ патриарху, да обложет ю златом и сребром, и сохранит ю, якоже сам **вѣсть**. (262)
'And he sent it [the emperor's head] to the patriarch, so that he might bronze it in gold and silver and preserve it, as *he* himself *knew*.' '[10]

Example (36) does express futurity with the particle *da*, and refers to a state that is brought into being by the pronouncement.[11]

(36) И так устави, **да ся зовет** град той Цесарьградом. (220)
'And he proclaimed *that* the city *was to be called (da sja zovet)* Constantinople.'

In this text, then, the present vs. future dichotomy of the non-past form seems to have been resolved in favor of the present sense for this group of verbs.

7.3.2.2. Past tense forms. The number of past tense forms in this lexical group is much higher. (Again, this is not a property of the lexical group, but of the text.) While the examples are not copious, they allow us to draw certain conclusions. First, there is only one aorist in the entire class of predicates, which is (37); the remaining twelve are drawn from the imperfects that make up the remainder of the class. The aorist in (37) represents an act taken as a whole, a duration summed up in a single point ('he did not sleep that night' = 'all night long there was no sleep').

(37) Магумет же, видѣвъ толикое падѣние своих и слышав цесареву храбрость, тоя ночи **не спа**, но совѣтъ велий сотвори... (254)
'Mohammed, having seen so many of his men fall, and having heard of the emperor's courage, *did not sleep (ne spa)* that night, but held a great council...'

---

[10] Also appears as example (103).
[11] The presence of a present tense performative act invokes a future state ('Let this city be called Tsargrad' = 'from this moment, that is what it will hereby be called'), and thus naturally blurs the line between present and future.

The imperfects in (38)-(49), however, all represent actions in progress; they are explanatory, providing motive to an ongoing or incipient act. In (38) and (39), the form *bojaše sja* 'was afraid' provides background to the actions *povelě* 'ordered', *ustaviv* 'set up'.

(38) ...а на цесаря повелѣ навадити пушки и пищали, **бояше** бо **ся** его, да не изыдет из града со всеми людьми и нападет напрасно на нь. (256-258)
'...and he ordered them to train their cannons and harquebuses on the emperor, for *he was afraid* that he [the emperor] would come out of the city with all his people and attack him suddenly.'

(39) Магмет же окааный, паки вскорѣ урядив... и пушки и пищали уставив, **бояше** бо **ся** цесаря. (258)
'The cursed Mohammed then regrouped his troops... and distributed his cannons and harquebuses, for he *was afraid* of the emperor.'

In (40)-(42), the form *čajaxu* 'expected' gives motivation to the acts *poidě* 'went', *strěliša* 'shot', *povelě* 'ordered'.

(40) И тако поидѣ... в святую великую церковь молбы и благодарение вздаяти... **чаяху** бо уже отступити безбожному, толико падѣние видѣв своим. (226-228)
'And so he went... into the holy cathedral to make prayers and supplications... for they *expected* already to give in to the infidel, having seen so many of their own fallen.'

(41) И яко утрудиша стѣну, навадив, стрѣлиша из болшие пушки, уже **чаяху** разорити стѣну. (230)
'And when they had weakened the wall, having taken aim, they shot from the large cannons, for they already *expected* to bring down the wall.'

(42) паки безбожный повелѣ прикатити ону пушку велию, бѣ бо увязана обручи железными, **чаяху** укрѣпити ю. (234)
'then the infidel ordered to bring forth the great cannon, for it was encircled with iron hoops, [which] they *expected* to strengthen it.'

In (43), the imperfect is simultaneous with another act that is ongoing (*ponužajušče* 'exhorting').

(43) но огни безчислѣные безбожный сотворше, сам скакаше по всѣм мѣстом, крыча и вопиа, понужающе своих, **чааше** иже пожрети град. (250)
'but when the infidel had made countless fires, he himself jumped from place to place, shouting and crying out, urging on his own men; he *expected (čaaše)* that they would swallow the city.'

The verb *čajati* seems to have an inceptive sense on occasion; it appears in (44) and (45) in the imperfect, meaning 'be struck by the expectation, begin to expect'.

(44) ...и видѣвше стражи тѣчаху видѣти бывшее, **чааху** бо — туркы зажгоша градъ; и вскликаше велием гласом. (242)
'...and having seen this, the guards sped to see what had happened, for they *expected (čaaxu)* that the Turks had set the city on fire, and they cried out[12] in a great voice.'

(45) И тако неции сказаша яко и сам цесарь в серци своем вознесеся, но и отшествие поганых **чаяху**, не вѣдаху бо божие изволение. (254)
'And so some said that the emperor himself had fallen victim to his pride and they even *expected (čajaxu)* the pagans to retreat, for they did not know God's will.'

Example (46) juxtaposes the emotion *ljubjaše* 'he loved' (imperfect) with another ongoing act *(plakaše* 'he cried (imperfect)'), or alternately places Mohammed's love for his subordinate into an immediately prior time frame.

(46) Магмет же окаанный, слышав восточнаго бегилярбеа убийство, плакаше много: **любяше** бо его мужества ради его и разума... (256)
'The accursed Mohammed, having heard of the death of the eastern bey, mourned him greatly; for *he (had) loved* him for his courage and wisdom...'[13]

The verb *mněti* has two distinct senses captured here. In (47) and (48), the reflexive form means 'seem', whereas in (49) the nonreflexive form means 'think, be under the impression'. All three are in the imperfect tense.

(47) ...также и от плача и рыданиа градцкых людей и жон и дѣтей, **мняшеся** небу и земли совокупитися и обоим колѣбатися... (226)
'so that from the cries and sobbing of the men and women and children in the city *it seemed (mnjaašesja)* that the heaven and earth had come together and both were shaking...'

(48) Он же, безвѣрный, **мняшеся** поруган быти, и вскоре заповѣда туры прикатити къ граду всеми силами... (234)
'the infidel *thought (mnjašesja)* that he had been defeated, and quickly commanded [his men] to roll the gabions up to the city with all their might...'

(49) ...и таким суровством **мняше** бо внѣзаапу похитити град. (248)
'...for in this horrid racket *he intended (mnjaše)* suddenly to capture the city.'

---

12 Here I read 3. pl. aorist *vsklikaša* for 3. sg. imperfect *vsklikaše* (which has no antecedent and makes no sense in the context anyway). Parts of this passage appeared earlier as examples (16) and (31).

13 Parts of this passage appear in examples (26) and (244).

Both readings lend themselves to backgrounding, and in all instances the imperfect indicates that the act precedes or motivates another act.

7.3.2.3. Infinitives. There are five stative infinitives in this text, and all of them show a state whose context emphasizes its quality or conditions, as in (50)-(52), or a general truth, as in (53) and (54). Some longer duration or implicit repetition and habit are implied in each of the examples; these clear markers of imperfectivity compare to the more ambiguous message from the same verbs of an earlier period (see chapters 4 and 5). In (50) the phrase *dast' im žiti* indicates that the houses were given to them to live in.

(50) ...домы велиа создав, дасть им **жити** в градѣ со устроением великим и царскыми чины, яко и своя домы и отчьства им забыти. (220)

'...having built great homes, he gave them to them *to live (žiti)* in the city with grand accoutrements and imperial ranks, so that they might forget about their own houses and homelands.'

Of the five examples, this one is the only one even remotely likely to have an inceptive meaning ('begin to live, take up residence'). More typically, (51) offers the phrase *nepodvižno dr'žati,* indicating continuous adherence to their faith.

(51) Зустунѣя же не токмо свое мѣсто снабдяше, но и по стѣнам града обхожаше и укрѣпляше и наставляа люди, да не отпадуть надежда, и на бога упование неподвижно **дрьжати**, и не ослабляти в дѣлехъ, от всеа душа и от всего сердца братися съ невѣрными... (228)

'Zustuneja not only defended his own place, but walked around the walls of the city and encouraged and urged the people not to give up hope, and *to hold (dr'žati)* unflinchingly to their trust in God, and not to falter in their deeds, to fight with all their heart and soul against the infidel...'

In (52), the infinitive phrase *jako mnětisja* 'so as to seem' expresses durativity, referring to the period of time when they were shouting and crying.

(52) и абие возопиша всь клирик и весь народ сущий ту... рыданием и стонанием, яко **мнѣтися** церкви оной великой колѣбатися... (258)

'and immediately all the priests and people who were there... let out a cry of sobbing and moaning, so *it seemed (mnětisja)* as if that great church was swaying...'

The expression *ne možaxu stoati* in (53) implies duration or repetition; they could not remain on the wall (a period of standing is implied) or they repeatedly could not stand there (each time they tried) thanks to the attacks of the enemy.

(53) Гражане же от бесчисленнаго стреляния не можаху **стоати** на стѣнахъ, но, западше, ждаху приступу, а инии стрѣляху ис пушек, ис пищалей, елико можаху, и многы туркы убиша. (226)

'The city-dwellers could not *stand (stojati)* on the walls because of the incessant shooting, but, having fallen back, they waited for the assault, and others shot the cannons and harquebuses as much as they could, and they killed many Turks.'

In (54), the verb *vladěti* occurs in a list of things the citizens were empowered by law to do.

(54)   И к тому законы многы устави, яко идолская капища святителем Христовым и христьяном точию **владѣти** и рядити. В среду же и в пяток поститися страстѣй ради Христовых, а недѣлю праздновати въскресения ради Христова. (216)
'And in addition he set down many laws so that only prelates of Christ and Christians could *own (vladěti)* and manage idolatrous temples. On Wednesday and Friday [they were ordered] to fast for the sufferings of Christ, and on Sunday to celebrate, because of the resurrection of Christ.'

This form could be regarded as being in a degenerative iterative context; after all, the act is applied to many people, but given that it is a stative the difference between iteration and continuation is unclear. It is less complex to consider the context a generalized one.

7.3.2.4. Prefixed and suffixed forms. All the evidence presented so far makes stative predicates look like protoimperfectives. Prefixed forms of these verbs, however, continue to show variation in their aspectual assignment. Unlike in other lexical classes, nonaspectualizing spatial prefixes are still evident, but their number is balanced by those with little or no spatial meaning that seem purely aspectual. A third group is either deponent in this text, missing one or more crucial verb forms, or does not display a clear tendency toward one or another sort of prefixation.

First I will consider the stative predicates *znati* 'know', *bojati sja* 'fear', *molčati* 'be silent', *ljubiti* 'love', which have inceptive, perfectivizing prefixes. All six of the examples are inceptive counterparts to the statives on which they are formed: *ubojati sja* 'take fright', *vozljubiti* 'fall in love, take to someone', *umolčati* 'fall silent', *poznati* 'come to know'. They represent the three most common Old Russian inceptive prefixes. In general, this pattern is characteristic of Modern Russian verbs as well; statives are often "paired" in traditional aspectology with perfectives that express the beginning of that state, either through prefixation or suppletion.[14] Despite this general similarity, subtle differences in usage belie a range of meanings. For instance, (55) is strongly inceptive (becoming afraid entails a further state) whereas (56) is less clearly so; the present vs. future distinction

---

14   This is not to claim that such pairs ordinarily considered suppletive (such as *sěděti* 'sit', *sěsti* 'sit down') historically bear no relation to each other; a seemingly suppletive inceptive often bears a distant phonetic (and close genetic) relationship to the stative, although prehistoric Russian and Slavic phonetic alterations and the death of ablaut as a productive process made the shared root opaque even before the Old Russian period.

seems to drive the choice of prefixed form here, indicating that the non-past of the simplex form may have already lost its ability to imply future action.

(55)   Но подобает тобѣ, цесарю, изыти из града на подобное мѣсто, и услышавше людие твои и братия твоа к тебѣ приидут на помоч, но и арбанаша **убоявся** приидут к сим же... (234)
'But it is fitting for you, the emperor, to leave the city for an appropriate place, and having heard this, your people and brethren will come to help you, and even the Albanians, *having taken fright (ubojavsja)*, will come as well...'

(56)   з днешняго дне **да не убояться** гнѣва моего, ни убийства, ни пленения. (262)
'from this day forth *let them not fear (da ne ubojat'sja)* my wrath, nor murder, nor imprisonment.'

The function of the aorist form *vozljubiša* in (57) is unclear. It is evidently inceptive; however, the prefixed form may in fact serve more as an intensifier than to truly point out the inceptivity of the act. This leads to the (unsurprising) conclusion that pointing out the beginning of an act is more forceful than simply stating its existence, possibly because of the implicit contrast between "before" and "after."

(57)   и **возлюбиша** его вси людие и послушаху его во всѣм, иже сказывааше им. (228)
'and all the people *took a liking (vozljubiša)* to him, and they obeyed him in every matter which he put to them.'

A similar rationale could be argued for the use of *da poznajut'* 'let them realize' instead of **da znajut*' 'let them know' in (58).

(58)   ...да не рекут: «Гдѣ есть богъ их?», но **да познают**, яко ты еси богъ наш, господь... (248)
'...let them not say: "Where is their God?" but *let them realize (da poznajut)* that you are our God, Lord...'

Examples (59) and (60) indicate that the prefixed form retains more stativity from the simplex verb than do Modern Russian inceptives of this sort.[15] In (59), for instance, the desire to read the aorist *uml'ča* 'fell silent' as purely inceptive is balanced by the presence of a supposedly simultaneous event with the participial *ispuščaja slezy* 'shedding tears'. The modern translations indicate this duration with the forms *molčal* 'he was silent¹' in (59) and *molčali* 'they were silent¹' in (60).

(59)   Цесарь же на долгъ час **умльча**, испущая слезы, и тако рече им: ... (234)

---

[15] Alternately, they could have more durational value remaining from the simplex; this possibility is discussed in section 7.6.1.1.

'The emperor *fell silent/was silent (uml'ča)* for a long while as he shed tears, and then he said to them...'

(60) Кир Лука же и архидуксъ и Николай епархъ **умлъчаша** на долгъ час и тако рекоша... (240)
'Kir Luka and the archduke and Nikolaj the eparch *fell silent/were silent (uml'čaša)* for a long time and then said...'

There are four examples of protoimperfectives formed by prefixing a stative. These are formed on the roots *ležati, stojati*. The three prefixes represented in (61)-(64)—which are {raz-}, {pred-}, {pri-}—all have a spatial component to their meaning. The prefixes {pri-} and {pred-} contain this as their only contribution to the meaning and use of the verb; both their derivatives occur in imperfective-type contexts, and appear respectively in the imperfect tense and as a present participle.

(61) Он же болма **прилежааше** мыслию на Трояду, идеже и всемирная побѣда бысть греком на фряги. (216)
'He *inclined (priležaaše)* more in his thoughts toward Troy, where the Greeks had had a world-renowned victory over the Phrygians.'

(62) Но убо паки да придѣм къ **предлѣжащому**. (260)
'But let us come back to *what lay before (predlěžaščomu)*.'

The prefix {raz-}, however, has a secondary function; as well as expressing motion out from a point in all directions, it also has an inceptive component, which might explain its function as an aorist, expressing momentary action in (63) with the key word *abie* 'suddenly', and as an imperfect, expressing action concurrent with another state in (64), concurrent with *ne vědaaxu* 'they did not know').[16]

(63) В 2-й же день, егда услышаша людие отшествие святаго духа, абие **растаяшася** вси, и нападѣ на нихъ страх и трѣпет. (244)
'On the next day, when the people heard about the departure of the Holy Spirit, everyone suddenly *lost their composure (rastajašasja)*, and fear and trembling descended upon them.'

(64) Бояре же и вси людие и фряговѣ, иже бѣша с ним, **растааху** и не вѣдааху, что сотворити. (252)
'The nobles and all the leaders and the foreigners who were with him *felt lost (rastaaxu)* and did not know what to do.'

---

[16] Interestingly enough, the Modern Russian translations of (63) and (64) use the form *rasterjalis'*, from a perfective verb which when applied to multiple themes has a distributive meaning ('get lost or become disoriented one after the other'). This reading explains the use of the imperfect tense as a sort of iterative—although it does not seem as certain to me that the Old Russian form conveys this same distributivity.

In the Chronicles {raz-} was used both spatially, with stative predicates, and with an Aktionsart component in the telic group of predicates. In this text, Aktionsart prefixation has clearly spread to the statives. The presence of one verb fulfilling both forms suggests that this is an intermediate stage in a prefix's migration from purely spatial meaning to the class of Aktionsart prefixes.

A number of simplex verbs—*deržati* 'hold', *čajati* 'expect', *počiti* 'rest', *vladěti* 'master, rule'—have complex paradigms, with prefixed and derived forms. The most clear-cut of these verb families is the one formed with the root *-počiti*.[17] The simplex is unattested, but a derived unprefixed verb, *počivati*, is found in (65) in the imperfect tense. The context is durative; the Turks' lack of rest coincides with their battle against the Greeks.

(65)   Туркы же, якоже предирекохом, по вся дни брань творяще гражаном, **не почивааху**. (246)
       'The Turks, who, as we mentioned before, were making war all day against the city-dwellers, *did not rest (ne počivaaxu).*'

The verb *počivati* is unambiguously protoimperfective in its one attestation. A prefixed simplex *opočiti* is seen in (66) and (67), respectively in the infinitive and the aorist tense.

(66)   Турки же по вся места бьяхуся без опочиванья день и нощ, пременяющеся, не дающе нимала **опочити** градцкиим, но да ся утрудят, понеже уготовляхуся къ приступу; и так творяху отбои до 13 ден. (224)
       'The Turks fought without rest in all locations, day and night, relieving each other, not letting the city's residents *rest (opočiti)* in the least, so that they would exhaust themselves, for they [the Turks] were preparing their assault; and they did this until the thirteenth day.'

(67)   И даша ему мало брашна и питие, и тако **опочи** той нощи. (252)
       'And they gave him a little food and drink, and so he *rested (opoči)* that night.'

In both sentences the verb describes a holistic view of the action that is probably best labelled protoperfective, although protoimperfectivity cannot be ruled out. The derived verb, *opočivati*, presents a more articulated view of the action, stressing interruption of an act in progress, as in (68), where the present participle is used with an imperfect form of the copula: the reason no men went to church was that they were in the middle of recuperating from their ordeal. In the case of (69), the infinitive stresses an act that is repeated or intense in nature, with the intensity bringing a stative act closer to being an atelic action.

---

[17] Although this looks like a prefixed verb, Vasmer reconstructs a proto-Slavic form *počiti*, with {po-} as part of the root. This potential confusion may, however, explain the presence of two verbs apparently identical in meaning, *počivati* and *opočivati*.

(68) ...понеже вси людие **бяху** еще **опочивающе** от безмерныя и неприемныя истомы. (232)
'...since all the men *were resting (bjaxu opočivajušče)* due to their immeasurable and unbearable exhaustion.'

(69) турки бо отъидоша от града, а гражане же падаху **опочивати**, и не бѣ тоя нощи ничесоже. (254)
'for the Turks left the city, and the city-dwellers fell down *to rest* (opočivati), and nothing happened at all that night.'

A slightly different picture appears with verbs formed from *vladěti*. Although a simplex form is attested in the *Taking of Tsargrad* (see (54)), there is also an unprefixed derived verb *vladati*, a prefixed derived verb *obladati* and even a derived verb with two prefixes *(izoobladati)*. Once again the unprefixed derived form, which is found as a present participle in (70), is used for a more processual, articulated act than is the simplex ('to be currently ruling' vs. 'to rule').

(70) Магумет седѣ на престолѣ...и **изообладаше владающих** двѣма части вселѣнныя, и одолѣ одолевших гордаго Артаксерксиа... (264)
'Mohammed ascended the throne...and *took command (izobladaše) of those who ruled (vladajuščix)* the two parts of the universe, and overcame those who had overcome the proud Artaxerxes...'

The prefixed non-past form of *obladati (ob + vladati)* in (71) is similar if not identical in meaning to the unprefixed ones; it is most likely an original spatial prefix that has by and large lost that meaning.

(71) О, горѣ тобѣ, Седмохолмий, яко погании тобою **обладают**, ибо колико благодатѣй божиих на тебѣ восияша... (260)
'O woe is thee, o city of seven hills, for the pagans now *rule over (obladajut)* you, and how many divine graces illuminated you...'

The other verb in (70), *izoobladati*, could be further proof of this point. The fact that it occurs in the imperfect tense makes the interpretation found in the Modern Russian translation *(stal povelevat'* 'started to order, to issue directions') seem unlikely; given the nature of the tense and the root, we would expect it to indicate some sort of state, and the prefix {iz-} does not usually indicate inception. It could, however, be further proof that the prefix of *obladati* has lost its original spatial meaning: to an already nonspatial *obladati* is added the prefix {iz-} with a spatial meaning, indicating that from his throne (point of origin) he 'rules over the two parts of the eternal'. This spatial component is in turn rather weak, and the form *izoobladati* turns out to be rather similar in meaning and usage to *vladati*.

The prefixed forms of *deržati* reflect a similar tendency toward imperfective-like usage. In (72), for instance, the verb *soderžati* means 'contain' with a present, generalized sense attributed to the non-past, and in (73), the verb *uderžati* appears in the imperfect with a meaning 'restrain, hold back', indicating an activity of long duration in the past.

(72) Сия убо вся и ина многаа прорицания и знамения писания **съдрьжить** о тебѣ, градѣ божий... (266)
'For the writings *contain (s"dr'žit')* this and many other prophecies and signs about you, o divine city...'[18]

(73) Сия вся изрѣкшим, паки уготовляхуся на брань, кающеися о послании къ Могамѣту, зане тѣм **удрьжаху** его. (236)
'Having said all this, they began again to prepare themselves for battle, ruing their missive to Mohammed, for with it they *had held (udr'žaxu)* him [there].'

The latter, however, can also have a resultative sense, which is seen in the infinitive in (74).

(74) ...стретоша его стратиги на полом мѣсте, но не возмогоша **удержати** его... (258)
'...the commanders met him on an open place, but could not *contain (uderžati)* him...'

This aspectual variation in the meaning of *uderžati* may explain the creation of unambiguously protoimperfective forms like the imperfects from reflexive *uderžavati sja* in (75) and nonreflexive *uderževati* in (76), both of which make explicit a processual component to the verb's meaning.

(75) их же бо достигаше, разсѣкаше их надвое, а иных прѣсѣкая на полы, **не удрьжаваше** бо **ся** меч его ни о чем. (242)
'for as he reached them, he clove them in twain, and cutting others apart on the fields, his sword *showed no restraint (ne udr'žavaše sja)* in any way.'

(76) ...вниде въ ратных, бьяше ихъ мечемъ по плещу и по рѣбром; аще и по коню ударить — падаху подъ ними , и **не удрьжеваше** бо мечь его ни збруи, ни конская сила. (254)
'he went into the foot soldiers, beating them with his sword across the shoulders and ribs; if he struck against a horse, they fell beneath them, and neither armor nor horsemen *could restrain (ne udr'ževaše)* his sword.'

At first glance, then, the evidence from prefixed verbs seems to contradict the tendency for simplex statives to be unambiguously protoimperfective; the perfectivizing component of prefixation is a hallmark of participation in the aspectual system. Prefixed statives do not exhibit this trait regularly; they show a range of functions from protoperfective to protoimperfective, with a strong bias toward the latter.

---

[18] Here I read *pisanie* for the plural *pisania*, or assume that neuter plurals take a 3. sg. verb, under Greek influence.

However, this apparent contradiction with the remaining evidence from stative predicates fails to take into account a diachronic perspective on aspect. By the time of the *Taking of Tsargrad,* stative verbs have nearly completed their move from anaspectual to protoimperfective verbs, and one of the characteristics of a protoimperfective uncovered in chapters 4 and 5 was that their prefixed forms are protoperfectives. However, it is reasonable to expect that long-standing prefixed verbs built from simplex statives might not suddenly become protoperfectives just because the simplex has become protoimperfective. After all, the prefixed forms have a certain status as independent lexemes, and if those lexemes have stative properties, then, like other stative acts I have discussed in this chapter, these prefixed forms are now redefined as being protoimperfective. On the other hand, Aktionsart prefixes and other, more abstract prefixes (as compared to spatial prefixes) often cause action to be interpreted as protoperfective, and I have shown that these nonspatial prefixes are applied frequently to statives in this period. The tension between these two forces is evident in the aspectual ambiguity of verbs like *uderžati* 'withstand, restrain', *opočiti* 'rest', where the prefix is no longer clearly spatial and yet also lacks the limiting force of Aktionsart, letting much of the stative component of meaning come through. The existence of special progressive forms like *opočivati* 'rest', *uderžavati, uderževati* 'withstand' testifies to the ambiguity of their unsuffixed counterparts.

7.3.3. Atelic actions

Like statives, atelic actions are fully protoimperfective in the *Taking of Tsargrad.* In the Chronicles I adjudged atelic actions to be largely aspectual, if not yet completely so; thus I can require less strenuous proof of their protoimperfective status. Any differences between atelic actions and statives will be worthy of note.

7.3.3.1. Non-past tense forms. There are only a few non-past forms of atelic actions, most describing present acts. The small number of forms is partially a function of style and subject matter; very little of the text occurs in direct non-past narration, although present participle forms are quite common to indicate action contemporaneous with the finite past tense form.[19] The examples themselves show the fluid borders of this lexical category. In (77), for instance, the verb *dějati* occurs in the non-past, in the phrase *dějati bran'ju* 'hinder, impede'.

(77)　Цесарь же заповѣда, **да не дѣют** их никоторою **бранью**, яко да очистят рвы и потоци. (228)
　　'The emperor ordered them *not to hinder (da ne dějut... bran'ju)* them in any way until they cleared out the ditches and streams.'

---

[19] Present participle forms are very common with atelic actions, possibly because this grammatical form focuses heavily on the performance of action, regardless of telos, which is also a characteristic of atelic actions as a lexical class.

Here an atelic reading is the only one possible, but with other nouns it could easily have a telic usage. The remaining examples of *dějati* in the non-past from this text have the meaning 'touch, harm', putting them in a highly telic lexical class.

Another problem is presented by (78) and (79). While the non-past form in (78) is an atelic action, (79) shows the non-past of *moliti* indicating communication ('pray' here occurs in a secondary meaning, unconnected to the religious activity), making it a punctual telic act.

(78) ...припадаем и вслѣдуем, всем сердцемъ **молим** и ищем милость твою. (246)
'...we kneel before you and follow you, with all our hearts *we pray for (molim)* and seek your mercy.'

(79) **Молим** тя: изиди из града, да не вси вмѣсте погинем. Бога ради изиди! (254)
'*We beg (molim)* of you: leave the city, so that we will not all perish together. For the love of God, leave!'

Examples (80) and (81) show *biti sja* used atelically in the non-past to mean 'battle with someone, struggle with someone'.

(80) Сие же видѣв, цесарь повеле велможам и мегистаном... клаколы ратные на всѣх странах изъставити, да коиждо их вѣсть и хранит свою страну, и вся яже на бранную потребу устряеть, и **да бьет-ся** с турки съ стѣны, а из града не выежчати. (224)
'Having seen this, the emperor ordered the grandees and potentates[20]... to set up the war bells on all sides, so that each of them might know and protect his own side, and make everything needed ready for the defense, *so that* they *could fight (da b'etsja)* with the Turks from the walls, and not leave the city.'

(81) ...покрыло бяше град и войско все, яко не видѣти друг друга съ кѣм **ся бьет**... (226)
'...it had covered the city and all the troops, so that they could not see each other [or] with whom each *was fighting (sja b'et)* ...'

The distribution of tenses with *biti* and its reflexive form often predicts its meaning. Atelic meaning as defined above (Modern Russian *sražat'sja* 'do battle') occurs in the imperfect and non-past with a reflexive particle; a semelfactive meaning 'shoot at, bombard, strike' (Modern Russian *streljat'*, *obstrelivat'*, *udarjat'*) is linked with the nonreflexive infinitive *biti*. There are a few counterexamples (one out of twelve infinitives, three out of twenty-three imperfects) but it is only in the participial forms that there is a reasonably even divide between telic (including both semelfactive meaning and a usage corresponding to the more

---

[20] The difference between these two ranks of military leaders is not clear; the title *megistan* is defined in dictionaries of Old Russian (and in the notes to this book) as *vel'moža* 'grandee' and in Greek dictionaries μεγισταν is also 'grandee'.

highly telic Modern Russian *ubivat'* 'kill') and atelic predicates, which have respectively five and three attestations.

As to the temporal assignment of the non-past forms, the three forms with the exhortatory particle *da* in (77) and (80) are future, whereas those without it—(78) and (81), ignoring the red herring of (79)—describe a present act. Since futurity is implied only after *da,* we can view this as a kind of compound future or subjunctive. At any rate, the evidence is numerically for variation in the temporal function of the non-past, although the single conditioning environment for futurity and the small number of examples makes this claim suspect.

7.3.3.2. Past tense forms. Atelic actions in this text are attested in the imperfect tense, but never in the perfect or aorist tenses. These imperfect forms are usually found in progressive, durative and iterative contexts, suggesting that the verbs belong to the protoimperfective aspect. A significant percentage (thirty-nine out of forty-six, or 85%) of the examples come from the verbs *biti* (twenty-three attestations) and *seči* (sixteen attestations); only a few of them are given below.

With true atelic actions, pure iteration is the least commonly encountered of the imperfective-like categories; instead, since telicity is absent, imperfect tense forms are more likely to be found in progressive or durative contexts. Some actions, which are usually telic, are considered atelic by analogy (the example I have used before is *pisati* 'write'), and these will be more likely to have a fully or partially iterative reading. A progressive context appears in (82) with the imperfect tense.

(82) Сущие же людие в градѣ, грекы и фрягове, выеждая из града, **бья-хуся** с турки, не дающе им стѣнобьеныя хитрости нарежати, но убо силе велице и тяжце сущи, не возмогоша им никоея пакости сотворити, зане един **бьяшеся** с тысящею а два — с тмою. (222)
'The people in the city, Greeks and foreigners, riding out of the city, *did battle (b'jaxusja)* with the Turks, not allowing them to erect their wall-destroying machines, but because of their great strength and number, they could not do them any harm, because each one *was fighting (b'jašesja)* with a thousand, and two—with several thousand.'

The imperfect forms *ratovaxusja* 'were fighting' and *usilovaxut* 'were overpowering' in (83) and (84) are juxtaposed against other acts, to which they form a background.

(83) И братия его не успѣша, понеже распря велия бѣ межу ими, и с арбанаши **ратовахуся**. (228)
'And his brothers did not make it, because a great quarrel had arisen between them, and they *were fighting (ratovaxusja)* with the Albanians.'

(84) Феодор же тисячник, совокупився съ Зустунѣем, поскориша на помощ, и бысть сѣча велия, но убо туркы **усиловахут** ихъ. (240)
'Theodore the tysjačnik, having joined forces with Zustuneja, hurried to their aid, and there was a great battle, but the Turks *were overpowering (usilovaxut)* them.'

A durative context appears in the imperfect in (85).

(85) Убо в 6 день маиа мѣсяца паки безвѣрному повелевшу бити града в то же мѣсто, идѣже и прьвѣе **бьяхут** и изо многых пушек по три дни. (238)
'For on the sixth of May, the infidel again ordered to attack the city in the same place where they had earlier *attacked (b'jaxut)* it with a multitude of cannons for three days.'

Durative contexts can have an explicit time frame, as in the imperfect form in (86). In other instances, they can have an implicit time frame created by surrounding acts, as in (87), where the imperfect shows that the defense of the field was successful only while Zustuneja was there; once he left, the Greeks lost confidence and retreated.

(86) И так **сѣчахуся** имаяся за руки на всѣх стенах, дондеже нощная тьма их раздѣли... (226)
'And so they *fought (sěčaxusja)* hand to hand on all the walls until the dark of night divided them...'

(87) Се же бысть изволѣнием божиим на конѣчную погибѣль граду, понѣже полое оно мѣсто он **храняше** великою силою и мужеством... (252)
'This was God's will for the final destruction of the city, since he [Zustunea] *had been protecting (xranjaše)* that open place with great strength and courage...'

A distributive action (where one act is performed at various times by various people, creating the effect of a single ongoing performance without respect to completion) is found in the imperfect in (88).

(88) градцкие же люди такоже вопияху и **кричаху** на них, бьющеся с ними крѣпко. (226)
'the city-dwellers too cried out and *shouted (kričaxu)* at them, fighting them fiercely.'

One attested iterative context—(89)—is actually an imposter, since it shows a semelfactive use of the imperfect of *sěči* (its literal meaning of 'slice, cut' as opposed to *sěči sja* 'fight with someone').

(89) Он же, един имѣя мѣч в руцѣ, **сечаше** их и, на них же возвращашеся, бежаху от него и путь ему даяху. (242)
'But since he alone had a sword in his hand, *he sliced (sečaše)* at them, and the ones he attacked fled from him and cleared his way.'

Example (89) points out the interactive quality of lexical nature and contextual nurture; a context that is iterative for a semelfactive predicate may be progressive or durative for an atelic action. How we evaluate it depends on both the verb and the surrounding material.

The atelic actions attested in the imperfect tense run the gamut from more abstract notions that could involve the performance of any number or type of actions (*xraniti* 'protect', *usilovati* 'try', *biti sja* 'fight', *sěči sja* 'fight', *ratovati sja* 'do battle') to more specific acts with a single consistent feature (*kričati* 'shout', *moliti sja* 'pray', *plakati* 'cry'). The former are hardest to recognize as atelic acts and have much in common with statives. Notably, a large class of atelic actions are missing from both the non-past and imperfect corpora of this text: actions such as *pisati* 'write' that can also be accretive and telic. These do appear, but only as infinitives.

7.3.3.3. Infinitives. A number of atelic actions take the form of infinitives in this text. Six examples were attested with *brati sja* 'battle', two of which are reproduced below. All three examples of *zvoniti* 'ring' were virtually identical to the one in (96). Of numerous infinitives with *biti,* only two had atelic meaning. No signs of anaspectuality are present. Some infinitives come accompanied by indications of continuous action, like *bez opočivanija* 'without resting' in (90), or indications of specific duration, like *iny pjat' měsjac'* 'five more months' in (91).

(90)   И в седмый же день паки безверный повеле ити войску къ граду и тако **ся бити,** якоже и первие, без опочивания. (228)
'And on the seventh day, the infidel then ordered the troops *to* go to the city and *fight (sja biti)* as they had done before, without resting.'

(91)   «Се уже пять месяць прошли, отнелиже начахом **братися** с туркы, просяще милость божию, и аще будеть воля его, еще можем и ины пять месяць **братися** с ними.» (240)
' "Behold, five months have gone by since we started *to fight (bratisja)* with the Turks, asking for God's mercy, and if it be His will, we can *fight (bratisja)* with them for five more months." '

Other infinitives occur in contexts that act as triggers for the protoimperfective aspect, like the verb *načati,* found above in (91), and in (92) and (93).

(92)   В 14-й же день турки, откликнувше свою безбожную молитву, начаша сурны **играти** и в варганы и накры бити... (224)
'On the fourteenth day the Turks, having recited their godless prayer, began *to play (igrati)* the zurnas and the pipes, and to bang on the drums...'

(93)   Онем же зрящим, начаша **плакати** грько, впиюще: «Господи помилуй!» (242)
'When they saw this, they began *to cry (plakati)* bitterly, calling out: "Lord have mercy!" '

Still others represent recurrent actions to be performed on a regular basis, like the verbs *postitisja* 'fast' and *prazdnovati* 'celebrate' in (94), which are accompanied by their specified intervals *(v pjatok* 'on Friday', *(v) neděļju* 'on Sunday').

(94)   И к тому законы многы устави, яко идолская капища святителем Христовым и христьяном точию владѣти и рядити. В среду же и в пяток **поститися** страстѣй ради Христовых, а недѣлю **праздновати** въскресения ради Христова. (216)
'And in addition he set down many laws so that only prelates of Christ and Christians could own and manage idolatrous temples. On Wednesday and Friday [they were ordered] *to fast (postitisja)* for the sufferings of Christ, and on Sunday *to celebrate (praznovati),* because of the resurrection of Christ.'

Other verbs, while lacking a clear specification of duration, have adverbial complements that emphasize the character of the action, suggesting that its manner and processual nature are important. Such adverbial expressions occur above in (93): *plakati gr'ko, vpijušče* 'cry bitterly, calling out'; as well as in (95): *molitisja s rydaniem i stonaniem* 'pray with weeping and groaning'; and—marginally—(96): *zvoniti po vsemu gradu* 'call throughout the whole city'.

(95)   Градцкые же люди, вшед на стѣнах от мала и до велика, но и жены мнози противляхуся им и бьяхуся крѣпце, яко патриарху и святителем и всему священническому чину токмо остатися по церквам божьим и **молитися** с рыданием и стонанием. (230)
'Since the people of the city, large and small, had gone out on the walls, even many women were taking part and fighting fiercely, so that only the patriarch and the prelates and all those of priestly rank remained in God's churches and *prayed (molitisja)* with weeping and groaning.'

(96)   Цесарь же объежаше по всему граду, понужая люди свои, дающе им надѣжу божию, и повелѣ **звонити** по всему граду на созвание людем. (226)
'The emperor went around the whole city, encouraging his people, giving them divine hope, and ordered [his men] *to ring bells (zvoniti)* throughout the city to call the people together.'

While infinitives are thus found in different protoimperfective contexts—durative, progressive, generalized—as well as occurring in iterative contexts and after markers conditioning the protoimperfective aspect like *načati,* their range of usages does not extend to the "completed" or "momentary" end of the spectrum. The evidence from infinitives comes down resoundingly on the side of protoimperfectivity for atelic actions.

7.3.3.4. Prefixed and suffixed derivatives. Unlike the anomalous evidence from their counterparts in the stative category, prefixed and suffixed verbs formed from atelic actions have a pattern of development fully consonant with a Modern-Russian-like aspectual system. While some of the verbs dealt with earlier, like *biti* and *sěči,* have extensive verb families derived from them, I have chosen not to discuss those verbs here, since the prefixed and derived forms usually make reference to a semelfactive or highly telic meaning of the simplex, not to its atelic meaning. I observed in earlier portions of this discussion that atelic actions have a strong processual component, so the task here is to figure out what semantic and aspectual components prefixation and suffixation add to the simplex verb.

The simplest and most widely found type of prefixation is the addition of inceptivity, which is found in (97)-(100). Example (97) has the aorist tense; the verbs in (98) are in the non-past tense.

(97) Магумет же окаанный... заиграв въ всѣ игры и в тумбаны, и вопли великими **возшумѣша**, аки буря сильная... (248)
'When the accursed Mohammed... started all the instruments and the kettledrums, great howls *rang forth (vozšuměša)*, like a mighty storm...'

(98) И кто о сем **не восплачеться** или **не возрыдает**! (260)
'And who *would not burst out crying (ne vosplačet'sja)* or *sobbing (ne vozrydaet)* over this!'

The two examples (out of nine in the text) of *vskričati* 'cry out' deserve some mention. In (99) a typical aorist denotes a one-time inceptive act; (100) is an imperfect indicating actions performed by numerous individuals at different times, but always at the same point in a series of actions.

(99) Абие **вскрича** воинство все, приступиша къ граду всеми силами... (230)
'Suddenly all the soldiers *cried out (vskriča)*; they attacked the city with all their might...'

(100) Греки же, бьющеся с ними, побѣгааху от них, а турки **вскрычааху** на них и вскоре нападоше множество их, чающе уже одолѣвше. (238)
'The Greeks, fighting with them, would run away from them, and the Turks *would let out a yell (vskryčaaxu)* at them, and soon a multitude of them would attack, expecting that they had already won.' [21]

The use of the imperfect here with a protoperfective verb could imply iteration, especially of the distributive type (numerous individuals crying out, not all at once). I posited earlier in this chapter that inceptives formed from statives have more residual duration than other inceptives. This example supports extending the hypothesis to all forms derived from verbs with predominantly atelic predicates.

Prefixation and suffixation can also change the meaning of the verb slightly, making it more abstract, more telic, or more concretely processual. In this lexical class, where the simplexes have such a strong processual component, the predicate

---

[21] The Modern Russian translation uses perfectives here, implying that the actions occurred only once, which does not seem to fit the use of imperfects in the Old Russian.

can hardly become more processual, leaving the other two options available. The verb *xraniti* is represented by the prefixed form *soxraniti* and the derived prefixed *soxranjati*, both of which append a more abstract meaning to an already somewhat abstract verb ('preserve' vs. 'protect'). In addition to this heightened abstraction, the notion of preservation is slightly more telic; 'protect' focuses on action taken to ward off a threat, while 'preserve' focuses on a goal or future reason for the protection. The verbs *soxranjati–soxraniti* constitute an obvious aspectual pair; contrast, for instance, the use of the aorist in a realized telic meaning in (101)—'they preserved him', implying some final goal or time for which he was then kept—with the progressive sense in (102), where 'preserving' is given as a characteristic along with other participial forms.

(101)   От иных же паки слышахом, яко оставшеи от сущиих съ цесаремъ у Златых врат, украдоша его тоа нощи, и отнесоша его в Галату, и **сохраниша** его. (262)
'From others we then heard that those who had remained among the ones with the emperor at the Golden Gate had stolen him [i.e., his body] and taken it to Galatia, and *preserved (soxraniša)* it.'

(102)   К сим же и... мати Христа... во вся времена бяше цесарьствующий град **сохраняюще** и покрывающе, и от бѣд спасающе, и от неисцелных напастей премѣняюще. (222)
'And in addition... the mother of Christ... *preserved (soxranjajušče)* the reigning city at all times and sheltered it, and kept it from afflictions and delivered it from injurious attacks.'

The non-past form *soxranit* in (103) describes a future act, and the imperative *s"xrani* in (104) has the force of an immediate, locally applicable need.

(103)   И посла еи къ патриарху, **да** обложет ю златом и сребром, и **сохранит** ю, якоже сам вѣсть. (262)
'And he sent it [the emperor's head] to the patriarch, *so that* he might bronze it in gold and silver and *preserve (soxranit)* it, as he himself knew.'

(104)   «Ты убо... не остави град сей достоания твоего, но яко мати крестьянскому роду заступи и **съхрани** и помилуй его, наставляа и научая в вся времена...» (220)
'"Do not leave this city of your achievement, but as mother of the Christian nation intercede and *preserve (s"xrani)* and have mercy on it, educating and instructing at all times..."'

The paradigm of verbs from the simplex *braniti* 'battle, fight' is less clear from this text. The sole form of *obranjati* found here is the present participle in (105), apparently with a meaning close to Modern Russian *oboronjat'* 'defend, stave off'.

(105)   Тако, въскричав, нападоша на них множество туркъ, онѣм же, **обраняющеся** от них, уидоша в град. (252)

'So, when they had cried out, a multitude of Turks descended on them; and they, *defending themselves (obranjajuščesja)* from them [the Turks], retreated into the city.'

The prefixed derived form here is again more abstract and more telic than its simplex counterpart, although both are protoimperfectives. With the simplex, the battle is against a present threat; the focus is on the action. With the derived form, the subject staves off an attacker with a thought to how it will be after the attacker is defeated; the focus is on the goal or future state.

The prefix {po-} appears in (106) and (107), respectively in infinitive and past participial forms.

(106) И повелѣ патриархъ **позвонити** по всему граду, заповѣдая всѣм людем, иже не бяхуть на брани, и женам, и дѣтям, къиждо их, да поидуть к своему приходу... (232)
'And the patriarch ordered *to ring the bells (pozvoniti)* throughout the city, commanding all the people who were not fighting—the women and children, every one of them—to go to their parishes...'

(107) Цесарь же, паки **помолився** стратигом и всим мѣгистаном и вельможам, тако и народу, укрѣпи их... (256)
'The emperor, then, *having prayed (pomolivsja)* for the commanders and all the potentates and grandees, and also for the people, gave them strength...'

The use of *pozvoniti* in a context identical to that of *zvoniti* (see (96)) suggests that the difference is not contextually conditioned, but aspectual. While {po-} could be inceptive here, it could also be read to have a more direct, immediate, forceful impact than the unprefixed form. (It is notable that the Modern Russian translation renders both *zvoniti* and *pozvoniti* as *zvonit'* 'ring¹'.) The form of *pomoliti sja* in (107) is further proof of the multiple meanings of *moliti sja;* it is related to the telic meaning 'entreat' found in (79), rather than to the atelic meaning 'engage in prayer'.

The verb *nadějati sja* 'hope, place trust in' found as an imperfect form in (108) proves once more that prefixed verbs can become semantically and thus sometimes even aspectually independent of their simplex antecedents.

(108) Тако убо съвѣтующе, мнози на то укланяхуся, **надѣяху** бо **ся** на цесаря, зане вѣдяаху храбрости и силу его... (240)
'So he advised, and many were partial to this advice; for *they trusted (nadějaxu sja)* in the emperor, since they knew his bravery and strength...'

This verb's status as the only simple prefixed protoimperfective in the lot of atelic actions testifies to the possibility of such a complete split. It seems likely that the early date of this semantic divergence is responsible for the fact that both verbs ended up in the protoimperfective camp.

7.4. TELIC PREDICATE CLASSES

The format for this section differs from that of section 7.3. In that section, I demonstrated that with the exception of the smaller punctual atelic class, atelic predicates have aspectualized completely in this text. I used a four-part test for aspectuality also employed in chapters 4 and 5; my goal was to show the differing results between the Old Russian of this text and the Old Russian of the Chronicles.

Since my contention in chapters 4 and 5 was that nonpunctual telic predicates were by and large aspectual already by the time of the Chronicles, I will not devote the same emphasis to this proof in my discussion of these lexical classes. Instead, I will examine some features of telicity and issues that it raises in aspectual usage and assignment. For punctual telic acts, it would again be appropriate to invoke the four-part test; however, the dearth of simplex verbs in this category makes it difficult to do so. Instead, I will approach punctual telicity by examining several verb families that predominantly express punctual telic acts.

7.4.1. Overview of nonpunctual telic predicates

Nonpunctual telic predicates describe an act with two salient characteristics. First, the act heads toward a goal. Second, the act, when considered without the attainment of the goal, always implies a certain minimum amount of process.

The boundaries between the nonpunctual telic predicates and their adjacent categories are somewhat flexible, as was mentioned in section 7.3. Atelic actions often group a series of acts together to give a single, nondynamic picture; often these acts can be treated separately and found to be telic. Similarly, the point at which an act becomes capable of excluding telos but remaining instantaneous depends largely on whether we perceive it as an abstract, mental change or not, so many verbs hover on the border of punctuality and nonpunctuality.

Within the nonpunctual telic categories there is also a good deal of variation. There is certainly a range from most strongly telic—those predicates, like *umirati* 'die', where failure to reach telos negates the act, where process and goal are strongly juxtaposed—to a weaker telos, found in accretive predicates like Old Russian *stroiti dom"* 'build a house', where every application of process produces some measure of movement toward the goal. Many verbs cannot be reliably typed into one or another category. Instead, their usage varies across the range of nonpunctual telic meaning.

This variation is also revealed in the meanings of prefixed forms. Prefixation of simplex verbs can have a number of effects on predicate classes. It can make a predicate more strongly telic by highlighting process, as opposed to a more clearly defined goal. It can also make a predicate more punctual by giving it a less concrete, more abstract meaning. On chart 2.7.3.1, prefixation generally acts to move a verb down and/or leftward on the chart. It is no accident, then, that garden-variety perfectives make their home at the lower left corner of the chart.

In the following sections I will discuss several features that are typical of the Old Russian nonpunctual telic predicates, or that distinguish Old Russian nonpunctual telic predicates from their Modern Russian counterparts.

7.4.1.1. Telicity and aspectual singularities. *The Tale of the Taking of Tsargrad* has a number of aspectual oddities that can be attributed to the influence of telicity. The first oddity concerns highly telic acts. For example, the verbs *umereti, pomereti* 'die' have no suffixed counterparts **umirati,* *pomirati in this text. However, we do find multiple demises described with the verb *padati* 'fall'. It seems that at a certain high degree of telicity, "progressivity" as such does not exist, or exists only selectively. In its place are verbs describing repetition or distribution as a "process," and these verbs serve as aspectual counterparts. One can assume that it is the formation of a suffixed verb from the prefixed form that introduces the possibility of process into the act. (This possibility is sometimes realized, although not always.) A similar situation exists with the semelfactive *udariti* 'strike', whose protoimperfective representation is found in the verb *biti* 'hit, beat', not in the verb **udarjati,* which is not found in this text. The fact that this text lacks three quite common Old Russian verbs marks it as a relic of an older language situation.[22]

7.4.1.2. Telicity and meaning. In this section, I will explore the proposition that differing degrees of telicity have a substantial impact on meaning and usage. I will start with some observations about the verb *dĕlati* 'do, make, build' and then compare it to the verb *tvoriti* 'do, make, create'.

The verb *dĕlati* is attested eight times. One attestation is in the non-past tense, one is a participle, and the remainder are infinitives. The simplex expresses an act whose result accrues as the act proceeds. The context is most often progressive (this is especially clear with the verb *načati* 'begin'), but there is little emphasis on progress toward a goal. The least telic examples are the infinitive in (109) and the non-past in (110).

(109) Но дню уже преспѣвшу, егда видѣша турки башту **дѣлающих**, вскорѣ пустиша на них изо многых пушек и не даша им **дѣлати**. (252)
 'But once day had come, when the Turks saw the men *building (dĕlajuščix)* the tower, they quickly fired on them from many cannons, and did not allow them *to build (dĕlati).*'

(110) И паки: «Елико сътвориши, елико **дѣлаеши** — ненавидит сия душа моа». (246)
 'And further: "However much you achieve, however much you *do (dĕlaeši)*— my soul despises this." '[23]

The infinitive in (109) expresses no goal whatsoever; the Turks are prevented from doing any work whatsoever. Example (110) has higher telicity; there is no

---

22 That is not to say that the Old Russian of this period did not have these verbs, merely that the author may have preferred other, more archaic-sounding forms.
23 Discussed below as example (236).

clear object expressed, although the comparison with a protoperfective verb in the first part of the sentence ('however much you achieve^P, however much you do^I') does lend an air of greater completion to the act. Moving further up the telicity ladder, the infinitive in (111) has a goal, but it is far from clear what will constitute attainment of it ('build a city' is nebulous at best), and the goal of the infinitive in (112) is similarly hazy ('make strong').

(111) ...а магистры и градцкые дѣлатели раздѣли надвое, ибо единой странѣ повелѣ размерити градцкие стѣны и стрелници и начати град **дѣлати**, а другой странѣ повелѣ размерити улици и площади на римской обычай. (218)
'...and the magistrates and the city-builders he divided into two groups: one side he ordered to measure out the city walls and towers and begin *to build (dělati)* the city, and the other side he ordered to measure out the streets and squares according to Roman practice.'[24]

(112) ...а гражане начаша башту ширити и **дѣлати** крѣпко о всѣй прогалинѣ... (238)
'...and the city-dwellers began to widen the tower and *to make (dělati)* it strong along the breach...'

With concrete objects, such as *baštu* 'tower', *dvor carskij* 'emperor's court' in (113)-(115), the infinitive predicate is more strongly telic.

(113) И тако начаша **дѣлати** церкви божиа, и двор царский, и иные домы славны велможам и мегистаном и всем сановником и воды сладкие приводити. (218)
'And so they began *to build (dělati)* God's church, and the emperor's court, and other famous houses for the grandees and potentates and all the courtiers, and to bring in sweet water.'

(114) Епарху же паки повелѣ разрушеное мѣсто все заставити дрѣвом и башту **дѣлати**... (242)
'Then he ordered the eparch *to* shore up the destroyed place completely with logs and *build (dělati)* a tower...'

(115) Зустунѣя же пакы повелѣ сѣбя нести тамо и начат **дѣлати** башту с усердием великим. (252)
'Zustuneja again ordered them to take him there and begin *to build (dělati)* a tower with great zeal.'

This is supported by the appearance of a protoperfective verb indicating result in (114): *razrušenoe město vse zastaviti drěvom* 'shore up the destroyed place completely with logs' is juxtaposed with *dělati baštu* 'build a tower'. However, this variable telicity is evident in (113), where a specific, goal-oriented object *(dělati*

---

[24] Also discussed as examples (223), (234), and (254).

dvor carskij 'build the emperor's court') occurs with two less specific objects (*cerkvi božia... i inye domy slavny* 'God's churches... and other famous buildings'). Sometimes there is focus on both the goal and the process, as in (115): *dělati baštu s userdiem velikim* 'build a tower with great fervor'; and earlier in (109). In (115), the focus on process comes from the instrumental complement; in (109), the participle *dělajuščix* is progressive because the moment of perception (*viděša* 'they saw') interrupts it. The simplex, then, has a range of telicity from barely telic to highly telic, and a range of processuality from minimal to maximal.

Prefixed forms of this verb found in the text are *predělati, zadělati, zadělyvati*, and they share the semantic variability of *dělati*. In (116), the verb *predělati* 'redo, remake' has high telicity; the command is to recast the cannon to make it stronger, implying completion as a prerequisite to greater strength.

(116) ...а пушку ону велию паки повеле **предѣлати** того крѣпчае. (232)
 '...and the large cannon he then ordered them *to recast (predělati)* stronger.'

In (117), the derived infinitive *zadělyvati* occurs to show that even the very process of filling the gap was excluded.

(117) В другие удариша, и распадеся стѣны великое мѣсто, но уже вечеру наставшу, туркы начаша стрѣляти изо многых пушек в то же мѣсто, тако и чрез всю нощь, не дающе гражаном **задѣлывати** того мѣста. (238)
 'They struck the others, and a huge part of the wall collapsed, but since evening had already come, the Turks began to fire from many cannons into the same place, so that throughout the whole night they did not allow the city-dwellers *to repair (zadělyvati)* that place.'

Example (118), however, has an unexpected prefixed form with a present participle.

(118) Гражане же в день бьяхуся с туркы а ночи влазяаху в рвы, и пробиваху стѣны ровныя от поля, и изныряху землю по застенью в многые мѣста, **задѣлающе** многы съсуды зъ зелием с пушечным; такоже на стѣнах уготовляаху многые съсуды, наполняюще смолья и сѣры... (234)
 'The city-dwellers fought with the Turks by day, and by night they crawled into the trenches and undermined the trench walls on the field side, and dug up the earth beyond the wall in many places, *filling (zadělajušče)* many vessels with gunpowder; also on the walls they prepared many vessels, filling them with pitch and sulfur...'

In contrast to the process-oriented focus of the derived form in (117), example (118) places a greater emphasis on iterativity and distributivity. Evidently the more processual form *zadělyvati* is not acceptable for repeated, completed results. Instead, a compromise form appears: the prefixed form, with its greater telicity (and thus ability to imply repetition and completion), is used with a present participle to imply action concurrent with the previously used imperfects of derived verbs (*zadělajušče mnogy s"sudy* 'filling many vessels'). The effect is twofold. The telicity of *dělati* and its derived forms is called into question, as is the aspectual status of *zadělati*.[25]

This series of developments would be unlikely for a highly telic predicate. However, as I have shown, *dělati* at times verges on the atelic. A comparison with its near-synonym *tvoriti* will prove instructive. (All attestations of *tvoriti* in the text are given below.)

It is immediately evident that the verb *tvoriti* is used with abstract meanings more often than is *dělati*. Note infinitive usages such as *tvoriti žertvy* 'make sacrifices' in (119), *tvoriti bran'* 'defend' in (120) and the participial usage of *tvoriti bran'* in (121). (Further examples will be found with the protoperfective form *sotvoriti*.)

(119) Жидом же отинуд **жертвы не творити,** и на распятие не осуждати никогоже, нечестия ради креста Христова. (216)
'Jews from then on were *not to conduct sacrifices (žertvy ne tvoriti)*, nor to condemn anyone to crucifixion, so as not to dishonor Christ's cross.'

(120) повелѣ всему воинству приступити къ граду и **брань творити** по вся дни (232)
'he ordered all the soldiers to move upon the city and *do battle (bran' tvoriti)* all day'

(121) Туркы же, якоже предирекохом, по вся дни **брань творяще** гражаном, не почивааху. (246)
'The Turks, as we said earlier, *did battle (bran' tvorjašče)* with the city-dwellers all day without resting.'

Tvoriti can also be used to summarize a series of other acts in a way that *dělati* cannot, as in the imperfect in (122). It has in addition a more abstract and telic meaning, seen in the non-past in (123).

(122) Турки же по вся места бьяхуся без опочиванья день и нощ, пременяющеся, не дающе нимала опочити градцкиим, но да ся утрудят, понеже уготовляхуся к приступу; и так **творяху** до 13 ден. (224)
'The Turks fought without rest in all locations, day and night, relieving each other, not letting the city's residents rest in the least, so that they would exhaust themselves, for they [the Turks] were preparing their assault; and *they did (tvorjaxu)* this until the thirteenth day.'

---

[25] Protoperfectives in the imperfect tense are, as we have noted, not cause for questioning aspectual assignment. However, present active participles of such verbs are considerably rarer and thus worthy of note.

(123) О, колико зла **творит** преступление! (260)
'Oh, how much evil transgression *creates (tvorit)!*'

Despite its greater abstractness and higher telicity, *tvoriti* can still be used to represent a progressive context, as in (120) and (121), or a durative context, as in (123).

The verb *sotvoriti* is attested twenty-five times in the *Taking of Tsargrad;* and a representative sample of usages is given below. *Sotvoriti* has many functions that are parallel to that of *tvoriti*. Its ability to summarize a series of acts is amply attested, as in (124)-(126), which have respectively aorist, infinitive and non-past forms.

(124) и тако **сотвори**: послав из Рима и от иных стран, събрав достославных велмож и мегистан... с множеством людей ихъ ту приведе и, домы велиа создав, дасть им жити в градѣ... (218)
'and this is what he *did (sotvori):* having sent from Rome and other countries, he gathered renowned grandees and potentates... brought them here with a multitude of people, and, having built grand houses, gave them to them to live in in the city'

(125) Боляре же и вси людие и фряговѣ, иже бѣша с ним, растааху и не вѣдааху, что **сотворити**. (252)
'The nobles and all the people and the foreigners who had been with him became confused and did not know what *to do (sotvoriti).*'

(126) «И что **сотворим**, помощи ниоткуду чающе?» (234)
' "And what *shall we do (sotvorim),* since we expect no help from any quarter?" '

It is used in conjunction with abstractions to signify their creation or expression, as in (127), which has an aorist, and (128), which has the non-past.

(127) ...събрав всь священнический чин... **сътвориша** литию и молбы... (220)
'...having called together all the priestly caste... they *made (s"tvoriša)* supplications and prayers...'

(128) «...но да изыдеть цесарь изъ града въ Амморѣю...оставивше мнѣ град пустъ, и азъ мир вѣчный **сътворю**, да не вступлюся въ Амморѣю...» (236)
' "...but let the emperor leave the city for Morea...having left me the city empty, and I *will make (s"tvorju)* an everlasting truce that I shall not enter Morea..." '

Sotvoriti is also used with more visible or concrete objects, as in (129) and (130), both of which have irregular participial forms.

(129)   А ини турки, мнози мосты **сотворше**, на конях въѣжяху. (240)
        'And other Turks, *having built (sotvorše)* many bridges, rode in on horses.'

(130)   ...сѣча же не преста, но огни безчислѣные безбожный **сотворше**,
        сам скакаше по всѣм мѣстом... (250)
        '...and the battle did not stop, but the infidel, *having made (sotvorše)* countless
        fires, jumped about himself from place to place...'

Just as with *zadělati*, the protoperfective *sotvoriti* is easily used with multiple objects to express iteration, as in (127), (129) and (130), although in these instances the iteration is already finished.

In fact, there is no reason to suspect that *sotvoriti* is anything other than an aspectual partner of *tvoriti,* possibly with a slight resultative meaning that could easily be lexical in origin. This immediately raises two problems. First, it is common wisdom that prefixation as a form of aspectualization did not come into existence until the seventeenth century or thereabouts. Second, it is puzzling that *tvoriti* should have a paired prefixed protoperfective, while *dělati* lacks one.

To address the first point, there is as far as I can tell no justification to be found in these texts for believing that prefixation is incapable of creating a pure aspectual counterpart. Scholars who insist that prefixation is incapable of creating aspectual pairs say this because they believe that since suffixation creates purely aspectual differences, it must have been the only driving force behind the creation and regularization of the aspectual system. While this study confirms the preeminent role and function of suffixation, it cannot be ruled out that some prefixes were quickly emptied of their meanings and forced into service as aspectualizers. The number of verbs this pertains to is very small, but I see no compelling reason to distinguish the pairing of *tvoriti–sotvoriti* from that of *napadati–napasti* 'attack', for instance, in any meaningful fashion. As was mentioned in section 5.7.4, allowing some early prefixal pairs does not present as many theoretical obstacles as has heretofore been imagined.

A neat solution suggests itself as well to the problem of *tvoriti* vs. *dělati*. In previous chapters, I noted the strong tendency for abstract acts to be perceived as perfective. As a more abstract, more telic act, the former inclines naturally toward perfective-like functions. One of the verbs derived from *tvoriti* is thus quickly and completely co-opted for the expression of aspectual differences. With *dělati*, which is much more accretive in nature, prefixes retain their meanings more robustly.

In texts like the Chronicles which are in many places less self-consciously "literary" than this text, accretive telics like *pisati, dělati* tend to have a protoperfective formed by simple prefixation. It is notable that the *Taking of Tsargrad* entirely lacks the form *sdělati,* which is amply attested in earlier periods. This fact may testify to the more colloquial nature of this form; the form *napisati,* by contrast, does appear twice, once in the meaning 'paint a picture' and once in the sense 'write down', making it a fairly close aspectual partner to *pisati,* but perhaps not as close as it appears to be in the Chronicles. In the *Taking of Tsargrad,* this step backwards from the situation in the Chronicles can be seen as an example of linguistic conservativism in one particular work, rather than an indication of the general state of the language.

7.4.1.3. Iteration in nonpunctual telic predicates. It has already been remarked that iteration in Old Russian is not linked with the use of only one aspect. Instead, the perception of the act as it takes place determines whether a protoperfective or protoimperfective verb is used.

Evidence is given in section 7.6.1.3. that nonpunctual telic acts, with their tension between goal and process, are especially susceptible to using protoimperfective forms where Modern Russian expects a perfective. Old Russian's lack of a conative function for the protoimperfective makes this strategy less semantically ambiguous than it would be in Modern Russian.

7.4.2. An overview of punctual telic acts

Punctual telic acts are those whose telos can always follow momentarily upon its inception. It was established in chapters 4 and 5 that punctual telic predicates deserve to be treated differently from other telic predicates, because their plasticity of duration lends itself to anaspectuality in the Old Russian of the Chronicles. By the fifteenth century anaspectuality is no longer a question, but these predicates are still set apart from other telic predicates thanks to their highly elaborated suffixal morphology and quirky aspectual assignment.

Most of the verbs in the *Taking of Tsargrad* that fall into the punctual telic category are communicative; among them are *blagodariti* 'thank', *prizyvati* 'call on', *skazyvati* 'tell', *vozglašati* 'appeal', *vprašati* 'ask a question', *otvěščavati* 'answer', *proslavljati* 'praise'. Others represent telic acts so abstract that no duration need be assigned to them, like *blagosloviti* 'bless', *osuždati* 'condemn', *zabyvati* 'forget', *spasati* 'save', *kajati sja* 'repent'.

I would ordinarily begin with an examination of simplex verbs in this category. However, I found only three attested simplex verbs: *moliti* (in one restricted meaning 'entreat'), *rěči* 'say', and *spasti* 'save'. The remainder are prefixed. This pattern fits the lexical characteristics of these predicates. I remarked in chapter 4 that protoperfective simplexes are most likely to be found with highly telic predicates (see the discussion of *umirati–umereti, padati–pasti*). Moreover, in a previous section I observed that abstractness as a quality of the action can increase with prefixation. It should not be surprising, then, that highly telic, highly abstract verbs have a very low proportion of simplexes.

Instead of looking at simplex verbs, I will examine both simplex and prefixed verbs in the punctual telic category. The results will therefore not be exactly parallel to those found in section 7.3, but will point up interesting characteristics of predicates in this group. As before, I will begin with the non-past tense and proceed to the past tense, the infinitive, and on to general remarks about prefixed forms.

7.4.2.1. Non-past forms. There are very few non-past punctual telic predicates in this text. Since most express communication and most references to communication are to inform that something has already been said, the overwhelming majority are in a past tense. The behavior of prefixed forms is regular. If suffixed, they indicate present acts in the non-past, as in (131).

(131) ...и яко неистовы еже на нас милость божью и щедрот отвращаемся и на злодѣяния и бѣзакония **обращаемся**... яко же есть
писано: «Злодѣяниа и безакониа превратят престолы сильных»
(222)
'...and like the ignorant we turn away from God's grace ad generosity toward us, and *turn (obraščaemsja)* towards evil deeds and lawlessness... for as it is written: "Evildoing and lawlessness will overturn the thrones of the mighty." '

If unsuffixed, these forms indicate future acts in the non-past, as in (132).

(132) «Се место Седмохолмы **наречется** и **прославиться** и **возвели-
читься** в всѣй вселеннѣй паче иных градов...» (218)
' "This place *shall be called (narečetsja)* Seven Hills and *will be glorified (proslavit'sja)* and *exalted (vozveličit'sja)* throughout the universe more than all other cities..." '

Futurity can also be found with the non-past in (133) and (134), with the particle *da* having varying degrees of exhortatory strength.

(133) Всѣмогущая же и животворящая троица **да** мя **приобщить** пакы
стаду своему и овцам пажити своеа, яко **да** и азъ **препрославлю** и
возблагодарю великолѣпное и превысокое имя твое. (266)
'*Let* the almighty and life-giving Trinity *admit (da... priobščit')* me again to their flock and to the sheep of their pasture, *that* I too *might glorify (da... preproslavlju)* and *give thanks (da vozblagodarju)* to Your mighty and exalted name.'

(134) ...**да посрамяться** врази твои и **да постыдяться** от всякыя силы, и
крѣпость да сокрушиться... (246)
'...*may* your enemies *be disgraced (da posramjat'sja)* and let them *be shamed (da postydjat'sja)* by all Your might, and may their strength crumble...'

The behavior of unprefixed forms is less predictable, and because there are so few examples, it is difficult to generalize. In some instances the non-past has a future sense; this is typical for the verb *rěči* 'say', as in (135).

(135) Тогда Вовус возопиет, и Скеролаф восплачет, и Стафории
речет: ... (264)
'Then Vovus will cry out, and Skerolaph will burst into tears, and Staphorius *will say (rečet)*...'

In other cases, the unprefixed form has a present sense, being a speech act as in (136) or an earlier request still in force, as in (137).

(136) «**Молим** тя: изиди из града...» (254)
    ' *"We beg (molim) of you: leave the city..."* '

(137) «Понеже цесарь тако благо съвѣща и **просит** мир, и азъ се
    сотворю...» (236)
    ' *"Since the emperor has decided so wisely, and asks (prosit) for peace, I will
    do as follows..."* '

Although *rěči* has not come down into Modern Russian, both *prositi* and *moliti* express functions expected from their Modern Russian aspectual assignments.

Aspect seems here to correlate with lexical meaning, specifically with telos: the communicative verb *par excellence, rěči* 'say', supports this notion by indicating future acts, corresponding to the protoperfective aspect. Verbs like *moliti* 'entreat', *prositi* 'ask', which add more components of meaning, emphasize process and bend the act toward a processual reading (present, thus correlated with the protoimperfective aspect). But the paucity of non-past examples would admit any number of shakily supported conclusions. It is worth keeping the non-past data in mind while examining the complex question of past tense forms.

7.4.2.2. Past tense forms. The evidence from the aorist, perfect and imperfect tenses is more substantial and at the same time more problematic. While parts of the system function as expected, a general correlation of tense, morphology, and aspect remains elusive. Consider first the more orderly portion of the system, the unsuffixed verbs.[26] The single unprefixed verb *rěči* appears as a perfect indicating a single past act viewed as a completed unit, as in (138).

(138) Сам бо Владыка **реклъ есть**... (224)
    'For the Lord himself *has said (rekl" est')*...'

The remainder express past acts with an aorist tense; note especially (139), where the Modern Russian imperfective *sogrešali* translates the Old Russian *s"grěšixom* 'we have sinned'. Here the Old Russian aorist protoperfective serves to establish a fact *(konstatirovat' fakt),* a feature best conveyed in Modern Russian by the imperfective. The Modern Russian imperfective also implies that the period of sinning has come to an end (i.e., posits a durative context), and that the end of the sinning means the reversal or negation of its result; this discourse feature appears to be absent from the Old Russian aspectual choice, since it is not incompatible with the Old Russian protoperfective.

(139) Мы же... **съгрѣшихом** и бѣзаконовахом, господи, пред тобою...[27] и
    тмократне разгнѣвахом и озлобихом твоего божества, забывающи
    твоих великих дарований и препирающе твоих повелений... (224)

---

26 It is only "more orderly" if we ignore the text's imperfect forms of *skazati*, such as *skazaše* or *skazaaše* '(he) said', whose plural subjects make them likely scribal errors for the aorist *skazaša* '(they) said'.

27 There is a gap here in the Old Russian text.

'For... we *have sinned (s"grěšixom)* and broken laws, o Lord, in Your sight... and many times we have become angry and insulted Your divinity, forgetting your great gifts and defying Your commandments...'

The verb *skazati* appears in the aorist in the meaning 'recount, tell of' in (140), showing the event as a whole, as does the verb *izložiti* in (141) in the meaning 'lay out, explain.'

(140)   И бысть цесарь во ужасе велицем и, созвав книжники и мудреци, **сказа** им знамение. (218)
'And the emperor was greatly horrified, and, having called together his scholars and wise men, *told (skaza)* them of the sign.'

(141)   И пакы, егда попущением божиим внидохом въ град, врѣмянем испытах и собрах от достовѣрных и великих мужей вся творимая дѣяниа во градѣ противу безвѣрных и въкратце **изложих** и хри-стяномъ предах на въспоминание преужасному сему и предивному изволению божию. (266)
'And then, when with God's permission we went into the city, over time I asked about and gathered from reliable and great men all the things which came to pass in the city against the infidel, and briefly *laid* them *out (izložix)* and passed them on to Christians so they might remember this most awful and mysterious manifestation of God's will.'

The three verbs *voprositi, sprositi, isprositi* occur once each in the text, all in the aorist, with similar meanings ('asked').

(142)   И тако **испроси** у цесаря хужшее мѣсто града, идѣже болши приступают туркове. (228)
'And so *he asked (isprosi)* the emperor for the worst place in the city, where the most Turks were attacking.'

(143)   Онъ же возрадовася зѣло и вскоре позва боляр и стратиг и **спроси** их, да рекут ему истинну, аще то есть глава цесарева. (262)
'He was greatly overjoyed, and quickly summoned the nobles and commanders and *asked (sprosi)* them to tell him truthfully if it was the emperor's head.'

(144)   Магумет же окаанный, яко видѣ тму велию над градом, созва книжник и молнъ и **вопроси** их... (256)
'The cursed Mohammed, when he saw the great darkness over the city, called his learned men and mullahs together and *asked (voprosi)* them...'

Noncommunicative verbs in this class lend themselves to an aorist interpretation: the act, viewed as a whole, need not distinguish duration, as in (145)-(147).

(145) И **позва** боляр и стратиг... (260)
'And he *summoned (pozva)* the nobles and commanders...'

(146) «Пощади, господи, пощади их же **искупил еси** животворною кровию своею...» (246)
'"Spare them, o Lord, spare the ones *You redeemed (iskupil esi)* with Your own life-giving blood..."'

(147) ...и яко неистовы еже на нас милости и щедрот твоих отвратихомся и на злодѣяние и бѣзаконие **обратихомся**, ими же далече от тебѣ отступихом. (224)
'...and like ignorant men, we turned away from Your grace and generosity to us, and *turned toward (obratixomsja)* evil deeds and lawlessness, through which we distanced ourselves greatly from You.'

The one ambiguous verb is the Church Slavic form *blagodariti*, which appears in both the aorist as given in (148) and a compound past form given in (149).[28]

(148) И видѣвше ту сущие людие **благодариша** бога. (230)
'And having seen this, the people who were here *gave thanks (blagodariša)* to God.'

(149) Цесарь же с патриархом и всь священный клирик **бяху** по всѣм церквам молящеся и **благодаряше** бога, чающе уже конец бранемъ. (236)
'The emperor, with the patriarch, and all the clerics of the church *were* praying and *giving thanks (bjaxu... blagodarjaše)* to God in all the churches, expecting a quick end to the battle.'

This could easily be attributed to its status as a "marked" form in the lexicon whose discourse level and subject matter (highly religious in nature) exempt it from normal rules of aspectual behavior, as sometimes occurs in Modern Russian.

For unsuffixed verbs, then, the past tenses of choice are foremost the aorist and secondarily the perfect. Examples of the imperfect can be explained away by reference to external factors. Based on prior observation in the nonpunctual telic category, we might expect the suffixed verbs to appear in clear progressive and durative contexts, hopefully correlated with the imperfect tense. In some verbs, the imperfect tense is indeed found regularly, although its functions do not correlate with those of nonpunctual telic predicates. In every one of the examples below, the most plausible explanation for the imperfect tense and the derived suffix is not process, but iteration.

---

28 The form *bjaxu blagodarjaše* in (149) is an odd hybrid between a compound tense—usually formed with byti 'be' plus the participle *(bjaxu blagodarjašče)*—and the imperfect tense (*blagodarjaše*, or, in the plural, as expected here, *blagodarjaxu*). The form in the text is doubtless an authorial or scribal error for *blagodarjašče*.

(150) Онѣм же возвращающемся, **сказаваху** цесарю различныя мѣста преславная, а наипаче похвалиша ему Македонию и Визандию. (216)
'As they returned, *they told (skazavaxu)* the emperor about various wondrous places and especially praised Macedonia and Byzantium to him.'

(151) ...и возлюбиша его вси людие и послушаху его во всѣм, иже **сказывааше** им. (228)
'...and all the people came to love him, and they obeyed him in whatever *he told (skazyvaaše)* them.'

In (150), scouts returning at various times bring reports to the emperor. Example (151) takes the form of a "whenever A, then B" iteration. In (152), the imperfect forms *ob"eždaaše* 'travel around', *obraščašesja na molitvu* 'turn to prayer' with the adverb *počastu* 'frequently' show that the action was repeated in a sequence numerous times.

(152) Цесарь же объеждааше вкруг града почасту, укрепляя стратигъ и воин, такоже и всѣх людий, да не отпадут надѣжею, ни ослабляют съпротивлением на врагы... и пакы **обращашеся** на молитву. (224)
'The emperor *would* often ride around the city, encouraging the commanders and the soldiers, and all the other people as well, so that their morale would not fall, nor would they slacken in their resistance to the enemy... and *he would return (obraščašesja)* again to his prayers.'

(153) Ты же, яко неистовен, еже на тебѣ милость божию и щедрот отвращашеся и на злодѣяние и безаконие **обращашеся**. (260)
'You, like an ignoramus, turned away from the divine grace and generosity [given] you, and *turned (obraščašesja)* to evil deeds and lawlessness.'

The reference in (153) is similarly to Constantinople's unfortunate tendency to turn away from grace and toward evil-doing, hence the use of the imperfect tense. The only sentence of this sort that is not clearly iterative is (154), where the imperfect *skazovaaxu* could suggest durativity, although the use of *necii* 'certain people' suggests not a single group but various individuals at different times.

(154) Неции же в них, знающе град, **сказовааху** им величества града и пространства, и яко не коснѣться им смрад. (232)
'Certain people among them, knowing the city, *described (skazovaaxu)* the city's size and spaciousness to them, and how the stench would not touch them.'

The use of the imperfect to mark iterativity was comparatively rarer in the nonpunctual telic group; here it seems to be the norm. Once again, lexical groupings will explain this fact. I showed earlier that with nonpunctual telic acts, the simplex expresses the action summed up as a whole, whether the goal is completed or not. The morphological realization of iterativity depends on whether sequence or simultaneity is present; the former is expressed by simple prefixed verbs, the latter by suffixed ones. Suffixation provides greater articulation of the act, which most often expresses itself as explicit process. In punctual telic predicates, though, expressing process seems less natural. As seen in the nonsuffixed examples, punctual telics often fail to express implied duration, summing up the act with an aorist form of a simple prefixed verb. Furthermore, the possibilities of expressing iteration with the imperfect tense and a suffixed verb are greater. It seems likely that if progressivity and durativity as protoimperfective contexts are associated with the nonpunctual telics, then iterativity as an protoimperfective context could have an equally natural association with the punctual telics.

There are a large number of verbs formed from the roots -*věstiti* and -*větiti*, however, which show a completely different usage pattern. This pattern is similar to that found with derived forms of *prositi* in the Chronicles. All relevant examples appear below; neither the simplex verbs **věstiti*, **větiti* nor any prefixed forms of them occur in the *Taking of Tsargrad*. Instead, forms derived with the suffix {-jaj-} are found in the aorist and sometimes the imperfect as well. Double-suffixed forms add a second suffix (either {-vaj-} or {-ovaj-}) and do not appear in the aorist tense.

The complete disappearance of the simplexes **věstiti*, **větiti* is not a unique feature of this text; Dostál claims that they are unattested in Old Church Slavic, and Sreznevskij shows only one attestation for each. What is interesting is that the forms replacing them are not reliably imperfective or perfective. Example (155), for instance, has the aorist of *otvěščati* 'answer' used to indicate a single, closed event (the Modern Russian translation has the perfective *otvetil* 'he answered').

(155)   И тако **отвѣща** посланником... (236)
        'And he *answered (otvěšča)* the emissaries as follows...'

The double-suffixed forms *otvěščavati* and *otvěščevati* indicate iteration and duration. In (156), a scene is described in which many clerics are telling the emperor something, but he does not obey them. The imperfect is simultaneous with the two prior acts.

(156)   И не послушаше их, но **отвѣщаваше** им: «Воля господня да
        будетъ!» (256)
        'And he did not obey them, but *answered (otvěščavaše)* them: "Let the Lord's
        will be fulfilled!" '

Similarly, in (157), the emperor is telling his people that he will die with them, while a multitude of people respond, presumably each at a different time. The form of the verb is imperfect.

(157)   «Помните слово, еже рѣх вам и обѣт положих: не дѣйте менѣ да
        умру здѣ с вами». Они же **отвѣщаваху**: «Мы вси умрем за церкви
        божия и за тебя». (258)

' "Remember what I told you and what pledge I gave: do not hinder me from dying here with you." They *answered (otvěščavaxu):* "We will all die for God's church and for you." '

Example (158) has an imperfect tense form in a progressive context: the emperor does not acquiesce to those who want him to leave, but continues to answer that there is no way to hide from God's wrath.

(158) Патриархъ же паки начат крѣпко увѣщевати цесаря, да изыдет ис града, тако же и боляре всѣ, глаголюще ему: «Тебѣ, цесарю, изшедшу из града... мочно есть и граду помощи...» Он же не уклонися на то, но **отвѣщеваше** им: «Аще господь богъ нашь изволи тако, камо избѣгнѣм гнѣва его». (244)
'The patriarch then began to strongly urge the emperor to leave the city, and so did all the nobles, saying to him: "You, o emperor, by leaving the city... could help the city..." However, he did not acquiesce to this, but *answered (otvěščevaše)* them: "If the Lord our God has willed it so, where could we escape His wrath?" '

The verb *s"věščati* 'inform, impart' works somewhat differently from *otvěščati*. Examples (159) and (160) both use the aorist tense to express a unitary act with a definite result, and the Modern Russian translations are appropriately perfective.

(159) Цесарю убо во градѣ с патриархом тако и вси людие совет **съвѣщааша** не благ, глаголюще: ... (236)
'For in the city, all the people thus *gave* the emperor and the patriarch poor *advice (s"věščaaša),* saying...'

(160) «Понеже цесарь тако благо **съвѣща** и просит мир, и азъ се сотворю: ...» (236)
' "Since the emperor *has decided (s"věšča)* so wisely, and asks for peace, I will do as follows..." '

The Modern Russian translations reflect this in their use of perfectives: the translation of (159) has *dali^P ploxoj sovet* 'they gave^P poor advice', the translation of (160) has *raz cesar' rešil^P tak mudro* 'since the emperor has decided^P so wisely'). A similar sense is found with the aorist in (161).

(161) ...и еже **съвѣща** окаанный божиим попущением тако и сотвори: ... (242)
'...and what the cursed one *decided (s"věšča),* so, by God's leave, he did...'

Example (162), however, is slightly different. Although the aorist tense is used, the context indicates more duration: first we learn that the eparch assumes the infidel will retreat, following which we are told that the infidel has no intention of doing so; the contrast implies the simultaneity of these calculations.

(162)   Епарху же паки повелѣ разрушеное мѣсто все заставити дрѣвом и
        башту дѣлати, чающе има уже отступити, окааным. Безбожный же
        Магумет **не** тако **съвѣща**, но по три дни събрав баши свои и сан-
        чакбиев... (242)
        'Then he ordered the eparch to shore up the destroyed area completely with
        logs and to build a tower, expecting the accursed ones to retreat. The infidel
        Mohammed, however, *did not decide (ne...s"věšča)* this way, but after three
        days, having gathered his pashas and commanders...'[29]

(Modern Russian respects this simultaneity with the translation *bezbožnyj Mogomet ne tak dumal*[I] 'the infidel Mohammed did not think[I] so'.) The aorist is used in its typical summative sense here, but the context adds duration by analogy to the preceding clause.

If this were not confusing enough, (163) has *s"věščati* in the imperfect tense, where the sense of duration and simultaneity is bolstered by context.

(163)   Великий же доместик и с ним логофет и ини мнози велможи
        съвѣщааху, да изыдеть цесарь из града... (240)
        'The head domesticus and with him the logothete and many other grandees
        advised (s"věščaaxu) the emperor to leave the city...'[30]

Here two opposing opinions are presented: those who believe they should stand and make a fight, regardless of the cost, because it is God's will; and those who believe the first priority is to sneak the emperor out of the city. This form is translated appropriately by the Modern Russian imperfective *sovetovali* 'they advised'. The same verb thus expresses a range of acts, both perfective-like and imperfective-like.

There is also a double-suffixed form *s"věščevati* found in the imperfect tense.

(164)   ...сказаша окаанному турку, яко пуска она велия слияся добрѣ, и
        тако **съвѣщеваашe** еще поискусити ю... (236)
        '...they told the cursed Turk that the large cannon had been successfully recast,
        and so *he considered (s"věščevaaše)* testing it once again...'

The act *s"věščevaaše* represents a state of mind that continues over the passage, and yet is somehow conative, since the focus is on the decision, not the act itself. This meaning is conveyed in Modern Russian by the verb *porešili*[P] 'decided[P]', taking a decidedly different reading of the passage.[31]

---

[29] *Commander* translates the text's *sančaxbej*, which is a mid-level warlord in the Turkish army.

[30] *Domesticus* and *logothete* were two high-ranking civil positions in Constantinople.

[31] The Modern Russian translation apparently reads the form *s"věščevaaše* as a mistake for the aorist 3. pl. *s"věščevaša*. Such mistakes are not inconceivable—they occur elsewhere in the text, even with the doubled {-aa-} as here—but it does not seem justified in this instance. The singular reading works quite well, so the translator doubtless

The verb *uvěščati* 'persuade' is attested once in the imperfect, seen below in (165). Its context is nearly identical to that of the sole attestation for *uvěščevati*, making this an ideal place for comparisons. Both the suffixed form and the double-suffixed form express the conative function 'tried to convince'. However, the contrast between act and anullment of the expected result is strongest in the double-suffixed form found in (166), also using the imperfect tense.

(165) И взем, отвѣдоша его от народа и много **увѣщаху** его, да изыдеть из града, и, дав ему конечное целование, стоня и рыдая, возвратишяся вси на уреченное место. (258)
'And, having taken him, they led him away from the people and *tried* hard *to convince (uvěščaxu)* him to leave the city, and, having said their final farewells to him, moaning and sobbing, they all returned to their places.'

(166) Зустунѣя же паки, пришедше со инѣми боляры, много **увѣщевааху** цесаря со слезами и рыданием, да изыдеть из града. И не послуша их. (244)
'Zustuneja, then, having come with the other nobles, *tried* hard *to persuade (uvěščevaaxu)* the emperor with tears and sobbing, that he should leave the city. And he did not heed them.'

Example (165) situates the pleading in the surrounding events. It is not clear from the text, but the imperfect here with a protoperfective verb could represent numerous attempts, or one prolonged attempt. At any rate, the predicate indicates a bounded or summarized act, successful or not; the imperfect tense gives either duration or iteration. In contrast, (166), which has the double-suffixed form, places special emphasis on the tears and sobbing that accompanied the request to leave the city. The emperor's refusal to obey them is summed up immediately afterwards; their pleas are rendered irrelevant.

Several features thus distinguish the past tense forms of punctual telic acts from those of other acts, especially the aspectual ambiguity of some prefixed derived forms and an increased reliance on derivation to express iteration. The apparent tendency toward perfectivization observed with certain roots can be explained by lexical factors: high telicity, high abstraction and the ability to punctualize are consonant with interpreting acts as more perfective-like than imperfective-like. Examples like (162) and (165) serve as a caution to resist for the time being the labels 'perfective' and 'imperfective' for verbs of this group.

7.4.2.3. Infinitives. These forms allow us to bypass issues of simultaneity and sequence and concentrate on the question of pure aspectuality. Most of the infinitives of this class are prefixed; a majority are unsuffixed. A suffixed form, *osuždati* 'condemn' is used under negation in (167).

---

changed the reading to give added support, in the form of an aorist, for an inceptive (instead of conative) reading of the verb.

(167) Жидом же отинуд жертвы не творити и на распятие **не осуждати** никогоже, нечестия ради креста Христова. (216)
'Jews from then on were not to conduct sacrifices, and they *were not to condemn (ne osuždati)* anyone to crucifixion, so as not to dishonor Christ's cross.'

The double-suffixed forms in (176)-(178) below all appear after the verb *načati*, which is a progressive context. In all other instances, the protoperfective is used.

If these verbs were truly anaspectual, the same suffixed or simplex forms that express open-ended iteration, conativity, and process would be used to sum up an act. This distribution of forms would reflect the potential of this lexical class to express action from momentary to prolonged. Instead, however, verbs expressing momentary or summarized acts are different from those expressing repeated or open-ended acts. For example, the simplexes and prefixed verbs in (168)-(170) refer to multiple acts with numerous participants considered as a completed unit.

(168) ...и, домы велиа создав, дасть им жити в градѣ со устроением великим и царскыми чины, яко и своя домы и отчьства им **забыти**. (220)
'...having built great homes, he gave them to them to live in the city with grand accoutrements and imperial ranks, so that they might *forget (zabyti)* about their own houses and homelands.'

(169) «Егда бо,— рече,— прострете рукы ваша къ мнѣ — отовращу счи мои от вас, а и аще придѣте **явити** ми **ся** — отовращу лице свое от вас.» (246)
' "For if you stretch out you hands to Me," He said, "I will avert My eyes from you, and even if you come *to appear (javiti...sja)* before Me, I will turn My face away from you." '

(170) «...днесь приидѣ час **прославити** бога и пречистую его матерь и нашу вѣру христьянскую!» (230)
' "...today the time has come *to praise (proslaviti)* God and His immaculate mother and our Christian faith!" '

Others, like (171) and (172), need not necessarily refer to a single act and may refer to multiple acts or a longer process, but are still represented by the protoperfective infinitive.

(171) ...и ослаби нам в врѣмя се, в еже **обратитися** нам и **покаятися** твоему благоутробию. (224)
'...and take pity on us in this time, in which we are *to turn* (obratitisja) [to You] and *repent (pokajatisja)* in Your mercy.'

(172) И всѣд на фарис, поидѣ къ Златым вратам, чаяше бо **стрѣтити** безбожнаго. (258)
'And when he had mounted his steed, he went to the Golden Gates, for he expected *to meet (stretiti)* the godless one.'

The verbs *spasti (sja)* and *prizvati* in (173)-(175) also describe acts that occur in potentially iterative or progressive contexts, except the summative property of the verb evidently takes precedence.

(173) Не хощеши бо, владыко, создание твоих рук погубити... но хощеши всѣм **спастися** и в разум истинный приити. (246)
'For You do not want, o Lord, to destroy the creation of Your own hands... but You want everyone *to be saved (spastisja)* and to come into true understanding.'

(174) «Не приидох праведных **спасти**, но грѣшным на покояние, в еже **обратитися** им и живым быти.» (224)
' "I did not come *to save (spasti)* the righteous, but [to bring] the sinners to repentance, which they *can turn (obratitisja)* to and live [eternally]." '

(175) «Не приидох праведных **призвати**, но грѣшных на покаание». (246)
' "I did not come *to call upon (prizvati)* the righteous, but [to bring] the sinners to repentance." '

The double-suffixed infinitives in (176) and (177) have a strong conative bent.

(176) Сия же увѣдав велможи и Зустунѣя, собрався вкупѣ с патриархом, **начаша увѣщавати** цесаря, глаголюще... (234)
'Having learned this, the grandees and Zustuneja, having met together with the patriarch, *began to pressure (načaša uvěščavati)* the emperor, saying...'

(177) Патриархъ же... поиде к цесарю и **начаше увѣщавати** его, да изыдеть из града. И яко не послуша их цесарь, рече ему патриархъ... (244)
'The patriarch... went to the emperor and *was beginning to pressure (načaše uvěščavati)* him to leave the city. And since the emperor did not heed him, the patriarch said to him...'

Following the use of the double-suffixed verb *uvěščavati* 'convince' is an explicit negation of the result; the emperor refuses to listen. (The negation follows immediately in (177), somewhat later in the case of (176).) The infinitive in (178) is more oblique: the infidel begins to negotiate a peace settlement, but he apparently has no intention of truly ending his attack.

(178) Он же, лукавый, се слышав, порадовася в сердци своем, чающе, нужа некая прииде граду, и, отложше свое отступление, **нача съвѣщевати** о миру. (236)
'When the perfidious one heard this, he rejoiced in his heart, thinking that some trouble had come to the city, and, putting off his retreat, *he began to negotiate (nača s"věščevati)* for peace.'

The negotiations are bound to end in failure, and thus the double-suffixed infinitive takes on a conative function.

7.4.2.4. Conclusions. Punctual telic predicates do not seem as fully anaspectual as they did in the Chronicles. In fact, the only evidence of aspectual indifference is in the past tense system. In the non-past and infinitive, aspectuality governs the behavior of these predicates: whether they express present or future action, and whether they express a prolonged, repeated or summarized act.

Only in the past tense is there deviation from this scheme. First, there is evidence that tense can combine with the natural temporal plasticity of these predicates to overrule grammatical aspectual functions. Second, there is evidence that derived forms express iterativity as often or more often than duration.

Although lexical influence is on the wane in this group, its strong influence is shown in the morphology of these verbs. Few of them are simplexes; prefixed verbs dominate, with their derived forms occasionally being reinterpreted with perfective-like meaning. This trend illustrates the convergence of punctuality or summation with perfectivity.

Conativity and iterativity are featured traits of derived predicates in this group. This fact also follows from lexical features: the attainment of telos is not at issue, since for all these predicates telos can be attained instantly. Instead, what is brought into question when duration and iteration occur is the effectiveness of the act. In the *Taking of Tsargrad* and the earlier texts I examined, there is no consistent evidence for conativity as a protoimperfective trait in other lexical categories. Conativity may thus start in the punctual telic predicates as a feature of protoimperfectivity and thence work its way into other verbs later on as a marker of the imperfective aspect.

7.4.3. Semelfactive acts

If punctual telic acts are those where telos cannot be separated from duration, then semelfactives take this inclusiveness one step further: the act itself consists only of the instantaneous attainment of the goal. Process—insofar as these verbs can be said to express process—consists of blending repetitions into a continuing act. Typically these continuing acts are qualitatively different from other iteratives and processes; they are not purely processes, because the goal is reached over and over, and yet they are not purely iteratives, since the performance of the individual act is of such minimal significance. Some semelfactives are human acts, like *sěči* 'slice', *udariti* 'strike', *strěliti* 'shoot', *poxvatiti* 'seize'; others are natural phenomena, like *trjasti* 'shake', *kolebati sja* 'sway'.

7.4.3.1. Unanalyzable semelfactives. I will begin with semelfactives that are either simplexes or pseudosimplexes, verbs which are not readily analyzed into stem and prefix. (The only one falling into this latter category is *udariti*, which behaves like a simplex, rather than as a prefixed form of *dariti* 'bestow'.) Several types of semelfactive action are attested here. In (179), the simplex aorist describes a single shot from multiple cannons; this is a protoperfective, a single, durationless act.

(179) И яко утрудиша стѣну, навадив, **стрѣлиша** из болшие пушкы, уже чаяху разорити стѣну. (230)
'And when they had weakened the wall, having taken aim, *they shot (strěliša)* from the large cannons, for they already expected to bring down the wall.'

When the context is explicitly progressive, as in (180) after *načati*, the unprefixed derived form *streljati* appears. The derived infinitive in (180) indicates repetition expressed as duration; this can be considered a protoimperfective.

(180) ...но уже вечеру наставшу, турки начаша **стрѣляти** изо много пушек в то же мѣсто, тако и чрез всю нощь, не дающе гражаном задѣлывати того мѣста. (238)
'...but since evening had already come, the Turks began *to fire (strěljati)* from many cannons into the same place, so that throughout the whole night they did not allow the city-dwellers to repair that place.'

Half of this pattern is attested with the verb *skočiti (skačiti)* 'jump' as seen in (181); a single leap by numerous people is given by the simplex aorist, since all the leapers attain the same goal for the same purpose.

(181) Видѣвша же съ стѣны три братеники пять мужей онѣх срачин, бьюще тако силнѣ гражан, **скачиша** съ стѣны, нападоша на них и **сечахуся** с ними лютѣ, яко удивитися турком и не дѣяти их, чающе убиеным быти от них. (252)
'When the three brothers-in-arms saw from the wall five of the Saracen men fighting the city-dwellers so fiercely, *they jumped (skačiša)* from the wall, fell upon them and *did* fierce *battle (sečaxusja)* with them, so that the Turks were shocked and did nothing, expecting to be killed by them.'

Modern Russian uses different verbs in translating these semelfactive acts. In (181), *skačiša* is translated by *sbežali^P* 'ran down^P'; in (179), *strěliša* becomes *vystrelili^P* 'fire^P a shot'. Prefixation adds direction but also reduces the semelfactive character of the act. Once there is a trajectory, the indivisible act becomes divisible and, as a process, is subject to articulation.

Some of the verbs listed above are not derivationally related to true semelfactive verbs. The infinitive *kolěbati sja* in (182) and (183) expresses only the process of swaying back and forth; individual shivers are not attested.

(182) И яко **удариша** по тому месту, начат стена **колѣбатися**, а в другые удариша — и сбиша стены с вѣрху акы саженей пять... (230)
'And as *they struck (udariša)* that place, the wall began *to sway (kolěbatisja)*, and *they struck (udariša)* again, and brought down the wall from the top for about five sažens...'

(183) и абие возопиша всь клирик и весь народ сущий ту... рыданием и стонанием, яко мнѣтися церкви оной великой **колѣбатися**, и гласи ихъ, мню, до небесъ достигаху. (258)

'and immediately all the priests and people who were there let out a cry of sobbing and moaning, so it seemed as if that great church *was swaying (kolěbatisja)* and their voices, I believe, reached the heavens.'

In (184) and (185) the infinitive *biti* refers to a series of blows that blend together into a single action, whether performed with sword, cannon or drum. (In (184) Modern Russian has *obstrelivat'*^{I} 'fire^I, shell^I', related to the semelfactive *strelit'*^{P} 'fire^P'.)

(184) Он же, безвѣрен сый и лукавъ, посланникы отосла, а град повелѣ **бити** пушками и пищалми, а ины стѣнобьеные хитрости нарежати и приступы градцкые уготовляти. (222)
'That godless and crafty man sent the emissaries away, and ordered *to fire (biti)* on the city with cannons and harquebuses, and to assemble other machines for destroying the wall and to prepare for entrance to the city.'

(185) В 14-й же день турки, откликнувше свою безбожную молитву, начаша сурны играти и в варганы и накры **бити**... (224)
'On the fourteenth day the Turks, having recited their godless prayer, began to play the zurnas and the pipes, and *to bang (biti)* on the drums...'

Biti is linked semantically to the verb *udariti* 'strike', which focuses on the delivery of single blows, as seen in the aorists in (182) and the non-past form in (186).

(186) ...внидѣ в ратных, **бьяше** ихъ мечемъ по плещу и по рѣбром; аще и по коню **ударить**— падаху подъ ними, и не удрьжеваше бо мечь его ни збруи, ни конская сила. (254)
'he went into the footsoldiers, *and was striking (b'jaše)* them with his sword across the shoulders and ribs; if *he struck (udarit')* against a horse, they fell beneath them, and neither arms nor horsemen could restrain his sword.'

Similarly the imperfects of *sěči* found in (181), (187) and (188) expresses only repeated cuts; the focus is clearly on the pace and character of the actions, not on the results of any individual stroke, as the accompanying adverbs attest *(ljutě; surovo; tjažkim i zvěroobraznym rveniem* 'cruelly; severely; with a harsh, animal-like roar').

(187) ...Мустафа вскорѣ наидѣ на грѣкы со многою силою, и **сечааше** их сурово, и прогна их в градъ... (240)
'...Mustapha quickly fell upon the Greeks with many men, and severely *beat (sečaše)* at them, and chased them into the city...'

(188) ...и нападѣ на турки... и смѣшався с ними, **сечахуся** тяжким и звѣрообразным рвением, и прогнаша их к полому мѣсту. (256)
'...and he fell upon the Turks... and having gone into their midst, *they fought (sečaxusja)* with a harsh, animal-like roar, and they chased them as far as the open space.'

7.4.3.2. Prefixed semelfactive roots. Prefixed verbs from semelfactive roots need not remain true semelfactives. For contrast's sake, I will take a selection of prefixed forms from the same roots. Examples (189) and (190) show that we are no longer dealing with semelfactives.

(189) Цесарь же, подав ему щит, отвѣде ему копие и ударив его мечем въ главу, и **разсече** его до сѣдла. (256)
'The emperor, having parried with his shield, deflected his spear and hit him in the head with his sword, and *clove* him *apart (razseče)* down to the saddle.'

(190) их же бо достигаше, **разсѣкаше** их надвое, а иных **пресккая** на полы, не удрьжаваше бо ся меч его ни о чем. (242)
'for as he reached them, he *would cleave (razsěkaše)* them in twain, and *cutting* others *down (presěkaja)* on the fields, his sword showed no restraint in any way.'

In (189), the emperor cuts a Turk apart down to the saddle; the act is described in the aorist tense. If this were a semelfactive act, there would be no question of the extent of the act. A semelfactive act occurs and is indivisible; there are no differing degrees of completion. If there are, the act is admitted to have duration and progression toward its goal. Likewise, in (190), the action is iterative, but the iterativity is of a type foreign to iterative semelfactives. What we find in (190) is a series of acts subject to repetition only in a series: those whom he caught up with, he clove in twain. The cleaving occurs in each instance only after a chase. Iterative semelfactives, however, present repetition as an unbroken series of repetitions that gives the feeling of a single, ongoing act, and the use of the imperfect *razsekaše* here goes against that convention.

The remainder of the examples are attested only in unsuffixed form. Some indicate place, such as the destination of a leap in (191) and (192). Both are attested in the aorist.

(191) Наутрия же яко видѣша туркы стѣну не задѣлану, вскорѣ **наскачиша** и бьяхуся з грѣки. (238)
'The next day, when the Turks saw that the wall had not been patched, *they quickly jumped up there (naskačiša)* and and battled with the Greeks.'

(192) И яко уже учиниша мѣсто велико, абие вскрычав, множество людий **вскочиша** на то мѣсто, друг друга топчюще, тако же грѣкы из града, и сечахуся лицем к лицу, рыкающе, акы дивии звѣри. (238)
'And when they had already made a large hole [in the wall], then, with a cry, a multitude of people *jumped into (vskočiša)* that place, trampling each other, and the same [with] the Greeks [coming] out of the city, and they fought face to face, howling like wild animals.'

Other verbs indicate inception of an act, as do the aorist forms *vztrepětaša* 'trembled', *potrjasesja* 'shook' in (193), *poxvati* 'seized' in (194) and *zaxvati* 'picked off' in (195).

(193) «Господи, господи, страшное естьство и неисповедимая сила, юже древле горы, видѣвше, **втрепѣташа** и тварь **потрясеся**, солнце же и луна, ужасешеся, блистанием их погибѣ, и звѣзды небесныя спадоша.» (224)
' "O Lord, o Lord, your being is awesome and your strength incomprehensible, having seen which the mountains long ago *began to tremble (vztrepĕtaša)* and the world *shook (potrjasesja)*, the sun and the moon were terrified and their light went out, and the stars of heaven fell." '

(194) И се змии внезапу вышед из норы, потече по мѣсту, и абие свыше орел, спад, змия **похвати** и полетѣ на высоту, а змий начат укреплятися вкруг орла. (218)
'And this snake, having suddenly come out of its hole, slithered about the city, and immediately an eagle from on high, having swooped down, *seized (poxvati)* the snake and flew up into the skies, and the snake began to wind itself around the eagle.'

(195) И божиим велением поиде ядро выше стены, токмо семь зубов **захвати**. (230)
'And by God's will the cannonball went high of the wall; *it only picked off (zaxvati) seven spikes*.'

The Modern Russian translation in each case also provides a prefixed perfective, often but not always with the same prefix, but at least with one expressing an identical or similar meaning.

7.4.3.3. Conclusions about semelfactive acts. Semelfactives behave much the same in Old Russian as in Modern Russian, but their frequency of occurrence is higher in the *Taking of Tsargrad*. Modern Russian often uses highly telic predicates where Old Russian has a semelfactive, especially if that semelfactive seems to apply to multiple events construed as a single event. As in Modern Russian, adding a prefix to an Old Russian semelfactive predicate creates a highly telic, nonpunctual predicate.

7.4.4. Conclusions about telic predicates

Telic predicates encompass three large groups examined in this chapter. By far the largest and most heterogeneous is the nonpunctual telic group. Smaller groups of punctual telic and semelfactive predicates round out the system. While the nonpunctual telic predicates are plainly aspectual, as are the semelfactives, the punctual telics are still somewhat shaky in their adherence to developing aspectual norms and constraints. Aspectual considerations are easily overruled by tense considerations in the more elaborately developed past tense system.

The place and function of derived verbs differs across the telic group. In the nonpunctual telics, the function of a derived verb springs from its ability to express process more explicitly than a simple prefixed verb can. With punctual telic acts, the function of a derived verb springs from its ability to express repeated action. The semelfactive group reflects both possibilities, since its derived verbs represent iteration as process. This mixing of functions across the telic group provides an impetus for the introduction of iterativity as a function of protoimperfectivity, where previously it had been outside the aspectual system.

7.5. CONTEXTUAL ASPECT: CAUTIONARY TALES

The simplest way of studying changes in aspect is to compare the Old Russian text with a modern translation and note where divergences occur. In the *Taking of Tsargrad* I tracked the following five correspondences:

A. Modern secondary imperfective = Old Russian simplex
B. Modern simplex imperfective = Old Russian derived form
C. Modern form in {-vaj-} = Old Russian form in {-aj-}
D. Modern imperfective = Old Russian (proto-)perfective
E. Modern perfective = Old Russian (proto-)imperfective

These five comparisons generated lists useful for tracking differences between Modern Russian and Old Russian aspect.

7.5.1. Difficulties in comparing aspectual data

Used indiscriminately, such comparisons yield copious amounts of irrelevant and misleading information. For instance, it is useful to track morphological correspondences (like those in A, B, or C) only when they involve the same root. An example is the Old Russian form *pobivaxu,* which appears in the Modern Russian translation as *napadali* 'attack'. Morphologically, then, an Old Russian {-vaj-} form corresponds to a Modern Russian {-aj-} suffix. The comparison, however, is meaningless, since nowhere in either Old or Modern Russian are there derived forms of *biti* with an {-aj-} suffix or derived forms of *pasti* with a {-vaj-} suffix. An accident of semantic change or an act of literary license on the part of the Modern Russian translator could thus be misconstrued as a meaningful piece of data.

In the other two categories (D and E), I believe it is meaningful when an aspectual divergence appears between the two texts, regardless of whether the roots are identical. Such comparisons can help establish the overall place of aspect in the text. However, this data should also be treated with care. Simply counting all such instances and comparing will skew the portrait of the aspectual situation. For instance, the *Taking of Tsargrad* has forty situations where the presence of Old Russian protoperfective verbs suggests a perfective for the Modern Russian translation, but in fact the Modern Russian text has imperfectives instead. On the other hand, the Old Russian has sixty-eight situations where the use of a protoimperfective verb suggests a corresponding Modern Russian imperfective, but instead, the Modern Russian translation uses a perfective verb.

It thus appears—based on sheer numbers—that the domain of the Old Russian protoimperfective covered many slots assigned in Modern Russian to the perfective aspect, while the Old Russian protoperfective occupies correspondingly fewer of the slots called imperfective in Modern Russian. The clear and yet erroneous conclusion is that in general Old Russian protoimperfectives have a much wider range of functions than their Modern Russian counterparts. Extrapolating from this, we might even conclude—once again, in error—that the perfective's domain is in the process of expansion in Russian while the imperfective's domain has over time contracted.

If we examine which verbs are used, we will find that thirty-three situations out of the sixty-eight mentioned above are examples of *viděti* 'see' and *slyšati* 'hear' being rendered as *uvidet'* 'see^P', glimpse^P', *uslyšat'* 'hear^P', *uznat'* 'find out^P', come to know^P' or a related perfective verb. While this finding is interesting, it is clearly a lexical problem related to the properties of these extremely common verbs; figuring these numbers in with the rest of the data will have a disproportionate impact on any context-based conclusions.

The upshot is that Modern Russian translations of Old Russian texts are useful tools but pose substantial methodological hazards that often invalidate the "statistical" data they offer. Comparisons of aspect in an Old Russian text and its Modern Russian translation are significant only when the examples are considered first individually for their usefulness and appropriateness and possibly then in larger quantities to see if trends do appear.

To check certain aspectual choices in the Modern Russian translation, I asked two native speakers to choose aspectual forms in selected translated passages. The results of this small survey are noted where interesting and appropriate.

7.6. PERFECTIVITY AND IMPERFECTIVITY IN CONTEXT

The task here is to compare Old Russian protoperfectives that map in a Modern Russian translation to imperfectives and vice versa. Cautiously accepting the existence of a "protoperfective" and "protoimperfective" aspect for Old Russian allows us to propose three possible interpretations for these data. We could claim that the verbs in question are anaspectual in Old Russian and become aspectual later; alternatively, we could say that in Old Russian these verbs belong to one protoaspect and in Modern Russian to the other aspect; or as a third possibility, we could posit that in these situations, contextual factors dictated or allowed particular forms in Old Russian, but in the modern language the same factors dictate or allow different forms.

Certainly all three factors help to explain these aspectual or pseudoaspectual features in the Old Russian text. I will discuss the first possibility only briefly, since I have found anaspectuality to be by and large lexically determined, and thus it has been treated in greater depth in earlier sections of this chapter. The second possibility is of less concern, since shifts in aspect seem fairly random in Old

Russian and are unlikely to have a dramatic impact on the overall shape of the aspectual system. The third possibility is the most interesting, since it gives a clearer picture of how aspect and context interacted in Old Russian.

7.6.1. Old protoperfectives map to modern imperfectives

The situations in which an Old Russian protoperfective corresponds to a Modern Russian imperfective can be divided into five categories. They concern inceptive acts, acts with negation, iterative contexts, durative contexts, and acts of communication.

7.6.1.1. Inceptive acts. In eight verbs, an Old Russian protoperfective inceptive act has a different cast in the Modern Russian translation. Sometimes the Modern Russian uses a prefixed derived form; sometimes it uses a simplex imperfective. All of the examples below show the inception of a protoperfective act in Old Russian that appears as an imperfective in Modern Russian. In (196) and (197), Old Russian inceptive aorists *uml'ča, uml'čaša* 'he fell silent, they fell silent' are replaced in Modern Russian by the corresponding stative past tense forms *molčal, molčali* 'he was silent, they were silent' in (196a) and (197a).

(196) Цесарь же на долгъ час **умльча**, испущая слезы, и тако рече им... (234)
'The emperor *fell silent* for a long time, shedding tears, and then said to them...'

(196a) *tr:* Цесарь же долго **молчал**, обливаясь слезами, и так им ответил... (235)

In (196) the motivation is the concurrent act that follows *(ispuščaja slezy* 'shedding tears'); in Modern Russian, concurrent events have to be expressed with both verbs in the imperfective, as in (196a). Also at issue is the fact that this act is durative: it is limited in time by the fact that the emperor's silence is broken by his statement. In the Old Russian example, the inceptive form gives enough feeling of duration to serve that purpose, but in Modern Russian this durative context makes a stative imperfective more natural.

Compare (196) to the following example: *Kir Luka že i arxiduks" i Nikolaj eparx" uml'čaša na dolg" čas i tako rekoša...* 'Kir Luka and the archduke and Nikolaj the eparch *fell silent/were silent* for a long time and then said...'(240). Once again, the Modern Russian translation has an imperfective past tense for the Old Russian inceptive aorist: *Kir Luka arxiduka i eparx Nikolaj dolgo molčali i skazali tak...* (241); this is a fainter echo of the principle invoked for (196).[32]

---

[32] I do not make much of the distinction between Old Russian *na dolg" čas"* and Modern Russian *dolgo;* the former is used with both protoperfective and protoimperfective verbs and seems to translate into Modern Russian equally well as *dolgo* or *nadolgo*.

In (197), a similar tension exists; the Old Russian resolves it by focusing on the inception of the stative act, where the Modern Russian translation turns to an imperfective verb in (197a) to convey the notion that the darkening of the sky had a fixed duration that eventually passed, parallel to the imperfective *šla bitva* 'the battle proceeded'. Native speakers concurred with the translator's choice of aspect here.

(197) ...и бысть сѣча премрачна, зане стрелы их **помрачиша** свѣт. (250)
'...and the battle was in the deepest dark, for the arrows *darkened (pomračiša)* the world.'

(197a) *tr:* ...и шла битва в сумраке, ибо стрелы **затмевали** свет. (251)
'...and the battle proceeded in twilight, for the arrows *darkened (zatmevali)* the world.'

The remainder of the examples follow this pattern to a lesser degree. Other factors may interfere, however, as in (198), where inceptivity and futurity collide: the Turk flings his corpses over the city walls, so that they might decay and putrefy the city (*da* plus non-past in Old Russian).

(198) Безвѣрный же трупиа своих людей не восхотѣ взяти, помышляаше мѣтати их порокы в град, **да согниют и усмердят** град. (232)
'The infidel did not want to collect the dead bodies of his men; he planned to fling them into the city with catapults, *that they might putrefy and stink up (da sognijut i usmerdjat)* the city.'[33]

(198a) *tr:* Неверный же не хотел убирать трупы своих воинов, задумав метать их катапультами в город, **чтобы разлагались** там и **смердели**. (233)
'The infidel did not want to collect the bodies of his men, having planned to fling them into the city with catapults, *that they might putrefy there and stink (čtoby razlagalis' tam i smerdeli).*'

The Modern Russian translation in (198a) uses imperfectives in a purpose clause to imply the duration of the act, and native speakers affirmed the correctness of this choice. Inceptivity in Old Russian is obviously weaker, not so closely limited to the moment of inception as it is in Modern Russian. Instead the inceptives retain a close tie to the atelic predicates from which they are derived, and with it some flavor of duration and ability to function in what is basically a durative context. In the Modern Russian aspectual system, durativity is largely relegated to the preserve of the imperfective aspect, making imperfective forms more likely in these places.

There is some variation in the exact nature of the relationship between original and translated predicate, which lexical groups can explain. For instance, predicates that follow this pattern of behavior are sometimes atelic, as in (199) and (200).

---

[33] Also seen below as example (225).

(199)   ...и терпяху на земли на долгъ час, **яко удивитися** всем людем и в тузе велицей и во ужасе быти. (254)
'...and they remained on the ground for a long time, *so that* all the people *were amazed (jako udivitisja)* and were in deep distress and horror.'

(199a) *tr:* ...и оставались они на земле долгое время, **так что дивились** все люди и пришли в отчаяние великое и ужас. (255)
'...and they remained on the ground for a long time, *such that* all the people *were amazed (tak čto divilis')* and fell into deep distress and horror.'

(200)   И тако, **поувидѣв** смерть свою, идѣт въ Иерусалимъ, да предасть цесарство свое богу, и оттолѣ вцаряться четыре сыновѣ его... (264)
'And so, *having foreseen (pouviděv)* his own death, he will head to Jerusalem, to hand his kingdom over to God, and afterward four sons of his will come to the throne...'

(200a) *tr:* И затем, **предвидя** смерть свою, отправится в Иерусалим, чтобы предать царство свое богу, и с той поры воцарятся четыре сына его: ... (265)
'And so, *foreseeing (predvidja)* his own death, he heads off to Jerusalem, to hand his kingdom over to God, and afterwards four sons of his will come to the throne...'

In other instances, however, the predicates show acquisition of a quality, as in the aorists in (201), where the qualities acquired are inherently stative, but the process of acquisition is obviously not. The translation in (201a) evidently focuses on the fact that the strength and courage of the city-dwellers was temporary.[34]

(201)   И яко слышаша люди звон церквѣй божьих, абие **укрѣпишася** и **охрабришася** вси и бьяхуся с туркы крѣпчае перваго... (230)
'And as the people heard the ringing of God's churches, they instantly all *took heart (ukrěpišasja)* and *mustered their courage (oxrabrišasja)* and fought with the Turks more fiercely than before...'

(201a) *tr:* И когда слышали люди звон колоколов в церквах божьих, тотчас же все **укреплялись духом** и **наполнялись храбростью**, и бились с турками яростнее, чем прежде... (231)
'And as the people heard the bells ringing in God's churches, they instantly all *took heart (ukrepljalis' duxom)* and *were filled with courage (napolnjalis' xrabrost'ju)* and fought with the Turks more fiercely than before...'

---

[34] Native speakers said the passage in (201a), which was given to them in a somewhat more extensive context, but without further information about the text, was odd. They preferred perfectives: *totčas že vse ukrepilis' duxom i napolnilis' xrabrost'ju*. The reason given was that these represent *zakončennye dejstvija* 'completed actions'; however, in light of the citizens' eventual failure and surrender, the imperfectives found in the translation are understandable.

The inceptives in (201) are thus opposed to telic processes in (201a), which seem more palatable choices for the Modern Russian translator.

7.6.1.2. Negation. Modern Russian is said to prefer imperfective verbs in negated sentences. Whether this is strictly true or not, the Modern Russian translation of this text affirms that Modern Russian has a stronger preference for imperfectives in such sentences than does Old Russian. Negated verbs in Old Russian appear easily as both protoperfectives and protoimperfectives; in (202) and (203), for instance, the non-past with *otpasti* 'lose' is negated, where its Modern Russian equivalent *terjat'* in (202a) and (203a) is imperfective.[35]

(202) Цесарь же объеждааше вкруг града почасту, укрѣпляя стратигъ и воин, такоже и всѣх людий, **да не отпадут надѣжею, ни ослабляют съпротивлением** на врагы, но да уповають на господа вседрьжителя... (224)
'The emperor would often ride around the city, encouraging the commanders and the soldiers, and all the other people as well, *so that* their morale *would not fall, nor would they slacken in their resistance (da ne otpadut nadĕžeju, ni oslabljajut s"protivleniem)* to the enemy, but rather have faith in the Lord Almighty...'

(202a) *tr:* Цесарь же часто объезжал город вдоль стен, воодушевляя военачальников и воинов, а также и всех людей, **чтобы не теряли** они надежды, **не ослабляли** бы сопротивление врагам, а уповали бы на господа-вседержителя... (225)
'The emperor would often ride around the city along the walls, encouraging the commanders and the soldiers, and all the other people as well, *so that they would not lose hope, nor would they lessen their resistance (čtoby ne terjali oni naděždy, ne oslabljali by soprotivlenie)* to the enemy, but rather have faith in the Lord Almighty...'

(203) Цесарь же и велможи с ними скакааху по всему граду, плачуще и рыдающе, молящеся боляром... **да не отпадуть надѣжею ни да ослабѣют** дѣлом, но дьрзостию и вѣрою несумнено братися сь врагы... (248)
'The emperor and the grandees with him hastened about the city, crying and sobbing, pleading with the nobles...*that they not lose hope nor slacken in their deeds (da ne otpadut' naděžeju ni da oslaběiut dělom)*, but rather with bravery and faith fight implacably with their enemies...'

---

[35] Native speakers had problems with the translations in (202a) and (203a). In (203a) they admitted both *čtoby ne terjali*^{I} and *čtoby ne poterjali*^{P} *naděždy* 'so they might not lose$^{I/P}$ hope', although the speaker preferring the latter then amended the aspect of the following verb as well: *čtoby ne poterjali*^{P} *naděždy, ne poddalis'*^{P} *slabosti v dele svoem* 'that they might not lose^P hope, give in^P to weakness in their actions'. This is clearly a discourse question in Russian, with two discourse interpretations conditioning the appearance of one or another aspect, whereas the Old Russian mixture of aspects excludes this possibility.

(203a) *tr:* Цесарь же в окружении вельмож объезжал весь город, с плачем и рыданием моля вельмож... **чтобы не теряли надежды, не поддавались** слабости в деле своем, но с отвагой и непоколебимой верой боролись бы с врагами... (249)
'The emperor and the grandees with him hastened about the city, crying and sobbing, pleading with the nobles... *that they not lose hope, not succumb to weakness (čtoby ne terjali nadeždy, ne poddavalis' slabosti)* in their deeds, but rather with bravery and unshakable faith fight with their enemies...'

This pattern is repeated several times with this verb in similar but not identical constructions; it appears with the aorist of *prestati* 'stop' in (204).

(204) И уже солнцу зашедшу и ночи наставши, сѣча **не преста**, но огни безчислѣные безбожный сотворше... (250)
'But although the sun had gone down and night had fallen, the battle *did not stop (ne presta)*, for the infidel had made countless fires...'

(204a) *tr:* И даже когда зашло солнце и настала ночь, битва **не прекращалась**, так как приказал безбожный зажечь бесчисленные факелы... (251)[36]
'And even when the sun had gone down and night had fallen, the battle *did not stop (ne prekraščalas')*, for the infidel had made countless fires...'

Less telic acts, such as *oslabljati–oslaběti* 'weaken', show more variation in Old Russian; note that in (202), the derived non-past *oslabljajut* occurs, whereas in (203) the simple prefixed non-past *oslaběut* is found. Both are translated by Modern Russian imperfectives in (202a) and (203a). In (201) above, I noted that the Old Russian text tends toward protoperfectives for the acquisition of an ability or quality; the similar example of *oslabljati–oslaběti* 'weaken' show that accretive telic processes can be expressed by a protoimperfective in Old Russian, although the tendency toward protoperfectivity is still evident.

The driving factor in all these instances is most probably not the existence of negation, but the fact that the negative contexts indicated are all durative; that is, the negation of these acts occurs during a period of time specified by the acts in the main clause or the subordinate clause. As noted earlier, durativity in Old Russian is not a marker of imperfectivity in the way it is in Modern Russian.

7.6.1.3. Iterative acts. I posited earlier that expression of iterativity in Old Russian is not a feature of a single protoaspect. Instead, iterative acts are subject to aspectual interpretation in the same way as noniterative acts. Example (205) shows how Modern Russian and Old Russian have different aspectual reflections of iterative contexts.

---

[36] In this context, both native speakers finally decided on the imperfective *ne prekraščalas'*, since the description of the battle continues on, but one initially admitted a perfective *ne prekratilas'* until she read further.

(205) Мы же окаянныи, тая вся презрѣв, **съгрѣшихом** и бѣзаконовахом, господи, пред тобою (...) и тмократне **разгнѣвахом** и **озлобихом** твоего божества, забывающи твоих великих дарований и препирающе твоих повелений... (224)

'We, the accursed, having overlooked all of this, *have sinned (s"grěšixom)* and broken laws, o Lord, in your eyes (...) and many times *we have become angry (razgněvaxom)* and *insulted (ozlobixom)* Your divinity, forgetting Your great gifts and defying Your commandments...'

(205a) *tr:* Мы же, несчастные, всем этим пренебрегли, **согрешали** и беззаконничали, господи, перед тобой, и многократно **гневили** и **озлобляли** тебя, боже, забывая твои великие благодеяния и попирая твои заветы... 225)

'We, the misfortunate, having neglected all of this, *have sinned (sogrešali)* and broken laws, o Lord, in your eyes... and many times *we have become angry (gnevili)* and *insulted (ozlobljali)* You, o God, forgetting Your great and holy deeds and defying Your commandments...'

In Old Russian the presence of the adverb *tmokratne* 'numerous times' is sufficient to convey repetition; the remaining verbs can be aorist protoperfectives, to convey completion and punctuality *(s"grěšixom* 'we have sinned', *ozlobixom* 'we became embittered') or protoimperfectives *(razgněvaxom* 'we became angry') to imply simultaneity. In Modern Russian, however, the adverb *mnogokratno* 'many times' conditions the use of the imperfective aspect throughout, as seen in (205a).

Example (206) lacks a conditioning adverb, but the iterativity of the context is made clear by the plural subject *(mnogim,* found here in the dative with an infinitive construction: 'so that many of them would die').

(206) И паки от множества огнѣй и стрѣляниа пушек и пищалей обоих стран дымное курение згустився, покрыло бяше град и войско все, яко не видѣти друг друга съ кѣм ся бьет, и от зелейнаго духу многим **умрети**. (226)

'And then, from the numerous fires and firing of cannons and harquebuses on both sides, a foggy smoke had congealed and covered the city and all the troops, so that they could not see each other and with whom they were fighting and many *were to die (umreti)* from the poisonous stench.'

(206a) *tr:* И тогда от множества огней и пальбы с обеих сторон из пушек и пищалей клубы густого дыма покрыли весь город и все войско так, что не видели друг друга сражающиеся и многие **умирали** от порохового смрада. (227)

'And then, from the numerous fires and fusillades from both sides from cannons and harquebuses, clouds of thick smoke had covered the whole city and all the troops such that they could not see each other as they fought, and many *died/were dying (umirali)* from the stench of the powder.'

In Modern Russian, this conditions an imperfective reading as seen in (206a), which also fits with the progressive nature of the sentence.[37] The Old Russian protoperfective lets the dative subject convey iterativity, while focusing attention on the collective number of deaths and their place on the time line as the final point of a series of events.[38] A similar situation occurs in (207)-(209).

(207) И так сѣчахуся имаяся за руки на всѣх стенах, дондеже нощная тьма их раздѣли: туркы убо отидоша въ свои станы и мертвыа своя позабывше, а градцкие людие **падоша** от труда яко мертвы... (226)
'And so they fought hand to hand on all the walls, until the dark of night divided them: for the Turks went off to their camps, having forgotten their dead, and the city-dwellers *fell (padoša)* as if dead, exhausted by their work...'

(207a) *tr:* И так бились врукопашную на всех стенах, пока ночная темнота их не разъединила; турки отошли в свои станы, забыв даже об убитых своих, а горожане **попадали** от усталости, словно мертвые... (227) [39]
'And so they fought hand to hand on all the walls, until the dark of night divided them; the Turks went off to their camps, having even forgotten about their dead, and the city-dwellers *fell (popadali)* from exhaustion as if dead...'

(208) Но дню уже преспѣвшу, егда видѣша туркы башту дѣлающих, вскорѣ **пустиша** на них изо многых пушек и не даша им дѣлати. (252)
'But once day had come, when the Turks saw the men building the tower, *they quickly fired (pustiša)* on them from many cannons, and did not let them build.'

(208a) *tr:* Но уже настал день, и когда турки увидели возводящих башту, тут же **обстреляли** их из многих пушек и не дали им строить. (253)
'But day had already come, and when the Turks saw the men building the tower, straightaway *they fired (obstreljali)* on them from many cannons, and did not let them build.'

(209) ...вниде в ратных, бьяше ихъ мечемъ по плещу и по рѣбромъ; аще и по коню **ударить** — **падаху** подъ ними, и не удрьжеваше бо мечь его ни збруи, ни конская сила. (254)

---

[37] My Modern Russian speakers disagreed on this example; one preferred a perfective *umerli*, but the other liked the imperfective *umirali*, because she said it showed that the deaths happened slowly and one by one.

[38] In fact, the Old Russian of Iskander does not have any examples of *umirati*, which is well attested in the chronicles and other, older sources. Often the verb *padati* seems to serve in its place. See 7.4.1.1. for other examples of this suppletion.

[39] My informants did not like the form *popadali*, preferring the unprefixed imperfective *padali*.

'...he went into the foot soldiers, and was striking them with his sword across the shoulders and ribs; if he *struck (udarit')* against a horse, they *would fall (padaxu)* beneath them, and neither arms nor horsemen could restrain his sword.'

(209a) *tr:* ...ворвался в ряды врагов, нанося им удары по плечам и по груди; если же и коня **поражал** — **падал** тот перед ним, и не удерживали меч цесарев ни конские доспехи, ни сила конская. (255)[40]

'...he tore into the ranks of the enemy, striking blows against them across the shoulders and breast; if he *struck (poražal)* a horse, it *would fall (padal)* before him, and neither mounted arms nor horsemen could restrain the emperor's sword.'

Example (210) is more problematic. Here the protoperfective *odolějut* 'defeat' follows the protoimperfective *premogajut* 'overpower'.

(210) «...понеже о единем мѣсте токмо братися, о разрушимѣм, многыми людми невмѣстно, а малыми людми — премогают нас и тако **одолѣют** нас.» (242)
' "...for it is difficult for a large number of people to fight in one particular place, in a breach, and [if we go out] with a small number of people, they overwhelm us and so *will defeat (odolějut)* us." '

(210a) *tr:* «...ибо в одном-единственном месте—в проломе— трудно сражаться множеству людей, а если в небольшом числе выходим, то превосходят нас силой и **одолевают**.» (243)
' "...for in one particular place — in the breach — it is difficult for a large number of people to fight, and if we go out with a small number of people, they overwhelm us and so *defeat (odolevajut)* us." '

The difficulty lies in how the context is to be interpreted. The Modern Russian translation in (210a) clearly views this as an iterative situation, as witnessed by the use of *odolevajut¹*: 'whenever we go out [against them] in a small number, they overpower us and *defeat¹* us'. (An entirely progressive reading of the Modern Russian—'Since now we go out [against them] in a small number, they have the upper hand and *defeat* us'—is not justified.) Part of the difficulty can be seen in the Modern Russian omission of the Old Russian words *i tako* 'and thus', which suggest a sequence of actions. In the Old Russian, a protoperfective act follows a protoimperfective; iterativity is possible, but the most logical reading is that the

---

[40] This example caused some problems. One speaker preferred *poražal* followed by *upal;* the other initially chose a perfective *porazil*, but then immediately switched to *poražal* when she saw the imperfective *padal*, which she found preferable. The second speaker also vehemently discounted the grammaticality of the first speaker's choices. (Note that both interpretations reflect the singular forms found in the Modern Russian translation, not the mixture of singular and plural found in the Old Russian text.)

Greeks have the upper hand *(premogajut nas)* and thus will beat *(odolějut)* the Turks. "Perfectivity" here only indicates sequencing and distancing.

The Modern Russian translation in (210a) could be likened to an English translation that must convey a polysemantic Russian past tense form by choosing between English continuous, simple past, and perfect tenses. Greater precision forces a loss of plasticity; here, the translator's choice makes this clear.

7.6.1.4. Contexts with duration. I already noted that Old Russian inceptive protoperfectives can function in durative contexts; noninceptive protoperfectives can occasionally express duration as well. The Old Russian examples here focus on the act as a whole, viewing it as a complete action; the Modern Russian ones treat these acts as processes, emphasizing duration through use of the imperfective. Examples (211) and (212) show that the Old Russian protoperfective retains the ability to show duration. Modern Russian most often lacks this ability, and thus the imperfective appears, as seen in (211a) and (212a).

(211) ...тако же и сий царствующий град...тмочислеными бѣдами и различными напастьми много лѣта **пострада**. (222)
'...so did this reigning city...*suffer (postrada)* for many years through innumerable afflictions and various attacks.'

(211a) *tr:* ...так и этот царствующий город...в течение многих лет **страдал** от неисчислимых бед и различных напастей. (223)
'...so did this reigning city...in the course of many years *suffer (stradal)* from innumerable afflictions and various attacks.'

(212) Измлада взят быв и обрѣзан, много врѣмя **пострадах** в ратных хожениих, укрываяся семо и онамо, да не умру въ оканной сей вѣре. (266)
'Having been captured as a young man and circumcised, *I suffered (postradax)* a long time in military campaigns, protecting myself this way or that, that I might not die in this cursed faith.'

(212a) *tr:* Измлада пленен был и обрезан, долгое время **страдал** в ратных походах, спасаясь так или иначе, чтобы не умереть в окаянной этой вере. (267)
'Having been captured as a young man and circumcised, *I suffered (stradal)* a long time in military campaigns, saving myself this way or that, that I might not die in this cursed faith.'

In (213) and (214), the emphasis of the sentence changes slightly in the change from Old Russian to Modern Russian; the imperfectives in the translations (213a) and (214a) add a processual component that is not evident in the Old Russian, which emphasizes a single, unitary act.

(213) От вопля же и крычания людцкаго обоих... и от стуку оружиа и блистаниа мняшеся всему граду от основания **превратитися**. (230)

'From the cries and shouts of people on both sides... and from the thump of guns and the flashing it seemed that the whole city *would be overturned (prevratitisja)* at its foundations.'

(213a) tr: От воплей же и криков сражающихся людей... и от стука оружия и сверкания его казалось, что весь город **содрогается** до основания. (231)
'From the cries and shouts of people on both sides... and from the thump of guns and their flashing it seemed that the whole city *was being shaken (sodrogaetsja)* to its foundations.'

(214) Сия вся слышавше, цесарь и патриархъ и вси людие, абие встенавше от среды сердца и руце на небо **воздвигше**, глаголаху... (236)
'Having heard all this, the emperor and the patriarch and all the people immediately groaned from the bottom of their hearts, and *having raised (vozdvigše)* their arms to the heavens, said...'

(214a) tr: Услышав все это, цесарь и патриарх и все люди восстонали из глубины души и, **простирая** руки к небу, восклицали... (237)
'Having heard all this, the emperor and the patriarch and all the people groaned from the depths of their souls, and *raising (prostiraja)* their arms to the heavens, exclaimed...'

Example (215) has a different sense in Modern Russian than it does in Old Russian. In it, the Old Russian uses all protoperfectives, whereas Modern Russian in (215a) has two imperfectives *(razmerjat', načinat')* and one perfective *(nametit')*.

(215) ...а магистры и градцкые дѣлатели раздѣли надвое, ибо единой странѣ повелѣ **размерити** градцкие стѣны и стрѣлници и **начати** град дѣлати, а другой странѣ повелѣ **размерити** улици и площади на римской обычай. (218)
'...and the magistrates and the city builders he divided in twain: one side he ordered *to measure out (razmeriti)* the city walls and towers and *to begin (načati)* to build the fortifications, and the other side he ordered *to measure out (razmeriti)* the streets and squares according to Roman practice.'

(215a) tr: А магистров и градостроителей разделил на две группы: одним из них велел **размерять** место под городские стены и башни и **начинать** возводить укрепления, а другим **наметить** улицы и площади по римскому обычаю. (219)
'...and the magistrates and the city builders he divided into two groups: one of them he ordered *to measure out (razmerjat')* the area by the city walls and towers and *to begin (načinat')* to erect the reinforcements, and the others he ordered *to lay out (nametiit')* the streets and squares according to Roman practices.'

I propose that the Modern Russian imperfectives show simultaneity (one group is responsible for both measuring and beginning construction; the other group has only one task) where the Old Russian does not specify simultaneous action, suggesting in fact sequential action. Since groups of people are involved, of course, the Modern Russian interpretation cannot be excluded, but it once again imposes a stricter ordering than is evident from the original.[41]

7.6.1.5. Speech functions. Verbs of speech, which fall into a single lexical category (punctual telics), were discussed in section 7.4.2, and I will refer to some of the conclusions drawn therein. This text has six examples of Old Russian protoperfectives showing up as imperfectives in Modern Russian; these involve the Old Russian verbs *rěči* 'say', *skazati* 'recount, tell', *izrěči* 'say' and the Modern Russian verbs *govoriti* 'say, speak', *otvečati* 'answer'.

In all these instances, the Old Russian protoperfective is the neutral means of conveying that an act occurred; the Modern Russian imperfective also conveys the occurrence of an act, but adds a discourse-based, modal, or idiomatic function. Changes in aspect from the Old Russian text to the Modern Russian translation do not involve primarily changes in duration; rather, it is the expanded textual functions of the Modern Russian imperfective that make its use more likely. In (216) the choice of a Modern Russian imperfective *otvečali* 'they answered' to translate the Old Russian *rekoša* 'they said' implies a break in the flow of conversation, making the act of answering a background to the victor's proclamations.

(216)   Они же, страхом одержими, **рекоша** ему: «То есть сущаа глава цесарева». (262)
'Overcome by fear, they *said (rekoša)* to him: "This is truly the emperor's head." '

(216a) *tr:* Они же, охваченные страхом, **отвечали** ему: «Это действительно голова цесаря». (263)
'Overcome by fear, they *answered (otvečali)* him: "This is truly the emperor's head." '

This distinction is not made explicitly in the Old Russian text. In (217), however, it is easier to argue that the Modern Russian imperfective *govorili* 'they said' indicates durativity or iterativity, along with placing the act in the background of the narrative—while none of these functions is attributable to the Old Russian protoperfective *skazaša* 'they said'.[42]

---

[41] My native consultants confirmed that the Modern Russian translation imposes a particularly narrow view of these acts; both preferred perfectives *razmerili, načali, nametili* instead of the translation's imperfectives.

[42] Holden 1990 attributes discourse functions of foregrounding and backgrounding to Old Russian aspect, a position I do not agree entirely with, and I think examples like (217) and (218) prove this point. If Old Russian aspect did express discourse functions, we

(217)   И тако неции **сказаша** яко и сам цесарь в сердци своем вознесеся,
        но и отшествие поганых чаяху, не вѣдаху бо божие изволение.
        (254)
        'And so some *said (skazaša)* that the emperor himself had fallen victim to his
        pride and they even expected the pagans to retreat, for they did not know God's
        will.'

(217a) *tr:* И некоторые **говорили**, будто бы и сам цесарь в сердце своем
        возгордился, и даже понадеялись на отступление поганых, не
        ведая божественной воли. (255)
        'And so some *said (govorili)* that the emperor himself had fallen victim to his
        pride and they even began to expect the pagans to retreat, for they did not
        know God's will.'

Modern Russian can also use the imperfective conatively to imply that an act never reached fruition or had no effect, while Old Russian often retains a protoperfective here based on the objective fact that the act was completed. Examples (218a) and (219a) are in this vein.

(218)   Сия и ина многая **изрѣкше** цесарю и кърабли и катаргы даяхут
        ему Зустунѣевы. (234)
        '*Having said (izrekše)* these and many other things to the emperor, they tried to
        give him Zustuněja's ships and galleys.'

(218a) *tr:* Это и многое другое **говорили** цесарю и предлагали ему
        корабли и катарги Зустунеевы. (235)
        '*They said (govorili)* this and many other things to the emperor and offered
        him Zustuneja's ships and galleys.'

(219)   Оружия же, иже мѣтаху на нь, якоже прѣди **рѣкохомъ**, вся суетно
        падаху и мимо его лѣтающе... (254)
        'The weapons they hurled at him, as *we said (rěkoxom")* before, all fell wide
        and went flying by him...'

(219a) *tr:* Оружие же, которое метали в него, как мы уже **говорили**
        ранее, все падало всуе и мимо его пролетало... (255)
        'The weapons they hurled at him, as we have already *said (govorili)* before, all
        fell wide and went flying by him...'

In (218), his counsellors explain to the emperor why he should leave the city, but their pleas have no effect. In (219), we are reminded that an event was previously mentioned. By repeating the event to put it in context, the narrator consigns the previous telling to background lacking effect on the present

---

would expect protoimperfectives in both places. See my discussion of Holden 1990 in chapter 3.

narrative.[43] As seen earlier, (217) tells how men of little faith doubted the emperor's decisions; because these detractors are backgrounded and removed from the main course of the story, Modern Russian uses an imperfective. I noted elsewhere that conativity in Old Russian is most often found with punctual telic predicates, but these examples suggest that Modern Russian goes even farther in this direction.

In (217)-(219), Old Russian has a protoperfective, suggesting that the association between general factual contexts and the Modern Russian imperfective cannot necessarily be projected back onto Old Russian, or at least onto all Old Russian verbs. Given the perfectivizing propensities of the punctual telic predicate class and its variable duration, we can posit that protoperfectives in the aorist tense had the same scope as a comparable protoimperfective in another class.

Example (220) is a fixed use of the form *reče* to mean 'it is said'; the modern translation reflects this idiom with the form *govoritsja*.

(220)   ...злодѣяние бо, **рече**, и безаконие превратит престолы сильных. (260)
'...for evildoing, *it is said (reče)*, and lawlessness will overturn the thrones of the powerful.'

(220a) tr: ...злодеяния ведь, **говорится**, и беззакония низвергнут престолы могучих. (261)
'...for evildoing, *it is said (govoritsja)*, and lawlessness will overturn the thrones of the powerful.'

Elsewhere, as observed in section 7.4.2, actions that Modern Russian interprets as imperfective because they appear in durative contexts are conveyed in Old Russian by a protoperfective. This is the case in (221), which has Old Russian *reče* 'said^P' but Modern Russian *govoril* 'said^I', where the act of speaking is interpreted as prolonged or continuous with another act.

(221)   Стратиги же... отвѣдоша цесаря, да не всуе умреть. Он же, плача горько, **рече** им: «Помните слово еже рѣх вам и обѣт положих: не дѣйте менѣ, да умру здѣ с вами». (258)
'The commanders... led the emperor away, so he might not die in vain. He, crying bitterly, *said (reče)* to them: "Remember what I *told (rěx)* you and what pledge I gave: do not hinder me from dying here with you."'

(221a) tr: Стратиги же... увели цесаря, дабы не погиб он понапрасну. Он же, горько сетуя, **говорил** им: «Вспомните, что я сказал вам и какой зарок положил: не удерживайте меня, да умру здесь с вами.» (259)
'The commanders...led the emperor away, so he might not die in vain. He, agonizing bitterly, *said (govoril)* to them: "Remember what I *told (skazal)* you and what pledge I gave: do not hinder me from dying here with you."'

---

[43] Modern Russian speakers admitted only the imperfective *govorili* 'said' here.

Another possibility is that the difference here is purely stylistic: the translator may have chosen *govoril* to avoid using the form *skazal* '(I/he) said' twice in a row. (This problem does not arise in the Old Russian text, which has *reče* 'he said' and then *rěx* 'I said'.)

7.6.1.6. Background noise. Sometimes the Modern Russian translation reflects a different reading of priorities in the text, and cannot be said to point out particular differences between Modern Russian and Old Russian aspect.

(222) Онѣм же возвращающемся, **сказаваху** цесарю различныя мѣста преславная, а наипаче **похвалиша** ему Македонию и Византию. (216)

'As they returned, *they told (skazavaxu)* the emperor about various wondrous places and especially *praised (poxvališa)* Macedonia and Byzantium to him.'

(222a) *tr:* Вернувшись, **рассказали** они цесарю о различных местах преславных, а особенно **расхваливали** Македонию и Византию. (217)

'Having returned, they *told (rasskazali)* the emperor about various wondrous places and especially *praised (rasxvalivali)* Macedonia and Byzantium.'

In (222), the Old Russian text emphasizes the repetition and duration of the emissaries' reports with protoimperfective *skazavaxu* 'they told' and then summarizes them with the protoperfective *poxvališa* 'they praised'. The Modern Russian presents the emissaries' reports as a package, using perfective *rasskazali* 'they recounted', and revisits the accounts in greater detail with imperfective *rasxvalivali* 'they praised'. While not at all a misreading of the Old Russian text, the Modern Russian translation does change the text's emphasis slightly but noticeably.

7.6.2. Old protoimperfectives map to modern perfectives

On the whole, this group of verbs is less interesting from a contextual point of view than the group just discussed. A plurality of the verbs that appear unexpectedly as perfectives in Modern Russian are translations of Old Russian *viděti, slyšati* 'see, hear'. Four further examples represent verbs of communication, from the punctual telic lexical group. These have been dealt with under the appropriate lexical headings.

Two further verbs show a shift from historical present to perfective past, which is worth noting. The most substantial group remaining (with twenty attestations) replaces an Old Russian imperfect tense formed on a derived verb with a Modern Russian past perfective. A few isolated groups of lesser interest will be dealt with together at the end of this section.

7.6.2.1. Historical present tense forms. There are two examples of a derived non-past verb in the Old Russian appearing as a perfective past tense in the Modern Russian translation.

(223) И абие цесарь, възбудився от сна, вскорѣ **посылаеть** в Византию магыстров и градцкых дѣлателей готовити мѣсто. (216)
'And immediately the emperor, having awakened from his dream, swiftly *sends (posylaet')* magistrates and city-builders to Byzantium to prepare the location.'[44]

(223a) *tr:* И цесарь, воспрянув от сна, немедля **послал** в Византий магистров и градостроителей, чтобы они подготовили место. (217)
'And immediately the emperor, having awakened from his dream, swiftly *sent (poslal)* magistrates and city-builders to Byzantium, that they might prepare the location.'

(224) Сия убо вся увѣдев, тогда властвующей туркы безбожный Магумет, Амуратов сынъ... абие **збираеть** воя многа землею и морем, и пришед внезаапу град обступи со многою силою. (222)
'Having learned all this, the current ruler of the Turks, the infidel Mohammed, son of Amurat... immediately *gathers (zbiraet')* many troops on land and sea, and having arrived, quickly encircled the city with numerous forces.'

(224a) *tr:* Узнав обо всем этом, властвовавший тогда турками безбожный Магомет, Амуратов сын... поспешно **собрал** множество воинов на суше и на море и, неожиданно приступив к городу, окружил его большими силами. (223)
'Having learned all this, the current ruler of the Turks, the infidel Mohammed, son of Amurat... swiftly *gathered (sobral)* many troops on land and sea, and having approached the city unexpectedly, quickly encircled it with great forces.'

The significance of the change in aspect in the Modern Russian of (223a) and (224a) is minimal; it is the presence of historical present forms in Old Russian in (223) and (224) that argues for understanding aspect as a fully codified system in Russian by this time. At least for the verbs presented above, there is a regular correspondence between a protoperfective (past) form and a derived (protoimperfective present) form that can replace the protoperfective form without changing the meaning of the sentence.

7.6.2.2. Imperfect tense forms. In section 7.6.1, I proposed giving Old Russian protoperfectives a slightly wider semantic range than Modern Russian perfectives, encompassing some duration as well as inception and completion. Here I will advance a similar argument for granting Old Russian protoimperfectives a stronger inceptive and completive component than is usually held to exist for their Modern Russian counterparts. At the same time, I attribute to Modern Russian imperfectives—especially highly telic ones—a capacity for expressing frustration or eventual failure that is not evident in the Old Russian.

---

[44] Seen again below as examples (234) and (254).

Inceptive meaning of the imperfect form is most evident in (225) through (227), where the Modern Russian text resorts to a perfective with a marked inceptive prefix to convey the meaning of the Old Russian form. In (225), the Old Russian protoimperfective *pomyšljaaše* 'he thought about' implies this idea was new to him, hence the translation in (225a): *zadumav* 'he began to think, got an idea'.

(225) Безвѣрный же трупиа своих людей не восхотѣ взяти, **помышляаше** мѣтати их порокы в град, да согниют и усмердят град. (232)
'The infidel did not want to collect the dead bodies of his men; *he planned (pomyšljaaše)* to fling them into the city with catapults, that they might putrefy and stink up the city.'[45]

(225a) *tr:* Неверный же не хотел убирать трупы своих воинов, **задумав** метать их катапультами в город, чтобы разлагались там и смердели. (233)
'The infidel did not want to collect the dead bodies of his men, having decided *(zadumav)* to fling them into the city with catapults, that they might putrefy there and stink.'

The predicates here are usually stative in nature, as is *čajaxu* 'expect, hope' in (226); as has often been remarked, inceptivity is a frequent meaning found with Old Russian statives.

(226) И тако неции сказаша яко и сам цесарь в сердци своем **вознесеся**, но и отшествие поганых **чаяху, не вѣдаху** бо божие изволениє. (254)
'And so some said that the emperor himself *had fallen victim (voznesesja)* to his pride and *they* even *expected (čajaxu)* the pagans to retreat, for *they did not know (ne vědaxu)* God's will.'

(226a) *tr:* И некоторые говорили, будто бы и сам цесарь в сердце своем **возгордился** и даже **понадеялись** на отступление поганых, **не ведая** божественной воли. (255)
'And some said that the emperor himself *had fallen victim (vozgordilsja)* to his pride and *they* even *took hope (ponadejalis')* that the pagans would retreat, *not knowing (ne vedaja)* God's will.'

However, this is not always the case, as the form *sečaxusja* 'they fought' in (227) shows; this is an iterative semelfactive, which also conveys the meaning 'they began to fight', as found in (227a).

(227) Видѣвша же съ стѣны три братеники пять мужей онѣх срачин, бьюще тако силнѣ гражан, **скачиша** съ стѣны, **нападоша** на них и **сечахуся** с ними лютѣ, яко удивитися турком и не дѣяти их, чающе убиеным быти от них. (252)

---

[45] Earlier discussed as example (198).

'When the three brothers-in-arms saw five of the Saracen men from the wall fighting the city-dwellers so fiercely, *they jumped (skačiša)* from the wall, *fell upon (napadoša)* them and *did* fierce *battle (sečaxusja)* with them, so that the Turks were shocked and did nothing, expecting to be killed by them.'

(227a) *tr:* Тогда три воина-побратима, увидев со стены, что сарацины истребляют горожан, **сбежали** оттуда, **напали** на турок и яростно **схватились** с ними, а те, ошеломленные, не сопротивлялись им, страшась быть убитыми. (253)
'When the three brothers-in-arms saw from the wall that the Saracens were decimating the city-dwellers, *they ran down (sbežali)* from there, *fell upon (napali)* them and *fell into* fierce *battle (sxvatilis')* with them, and the Turks, ovecome, did not resist them, fearing to be killed.'

In (228)-(232), the Modern Russian perfective serves a different function: that of resolving a confusing ambiguity arising in the Modern Russian imperfective but evidently not in the Old Russian. One of the best-established and most prevalent modern functions of the imperfective aspect is the conative function, indicating a failed attempt. Maslov 1948 notes that conativity appears only with imperfectives of Modern Russian verbs that are highly telic; the classic conative sentence he cites is *umiral, no ne umer* 'he was dying, but did not die'.

In (228), the two prefixed derived verbs are replaced in Modern Russian by corresponding prefixed perfectives.

(228) Грѣки же, вышед из града, **побивааху** во рвѣх турки, кои еще живи бяху, и, собравше их въ многые кучи, **съжигаахут** их вкупѣ со оставшими турами. (236)
'The Greeks, having left the city, *killed (pobivaaxu)* the Turks that were still alive in the ditches, and, having gathered them into numerous piles, *burned* them *up (s"žigaaxut)* together with the remaining gabions.'

(228a) *tr:* Греки же, выйдя из города, **перебили** во рвах еще оставшихся в живых турок и, собрав их в несколько куч, **сожгли** вместе с уцелевшими турами. (237)
'The Greeks, having left the city, *killed (perebili)* the Turks that were still alive in the ditches, and, having gathered them into several piles, *burned* them *up (s"žigaaxut)* together with the remaining gabions.'

The tension here revolves (once again) around the concept of distribution of action over a limited set of objects. Old Russian derived verbs fulfill a distributive function easily; Modern Russian imperfective verbs do as well, but have more possible interpretations than just that one. In this instance, the imperfectives must have seemed too situational, not conclusive enough to the translator; by using perfectives, he conveys the sense of completion that the Old Russian derived forms give, and avoids an open-ended, progressive reading of the events. This is not directly related to conativity, but the connection is clear: Modern Russian imperfectives may imply failure or nullification of the act once the set of objects is seen as closed in number or effect.[46]

Example (229) tangles with the issue of conativity more directly. Here the Old Russian *vozvraščaxu* 'they returned' creates a problem following so many protoperfectives; conativity with protoimperfectives is much more likely with many perfectives around.

(229) Цесарю же погнавшу напрасно и всѣм велможам и стратигом, и, минувше цесаря и велмож, стратиги поскориша на помощь и срѣтоша народ мног бѣгающе, и бья, **возвращаху** их. (240)
'The emperor and all the grandees and commanders quickly gave chase, and, passing the emperor and the grandees, the commanders sped to their aid and met many people fleeing, and, giving battle, *turned* them *back (vozvraščaxu).*'

(229a) tr: Цесарь же и все вельможи и стратиги вскочили на коней, и, обогнав цесаря и вельмож, стратиги поспешили на помощь, и встретили множество бегущих людей, и с побоями **возвратили** их. (241)
'The emperor and all the grandees and commanders leapt onto their horses, and, passing the emperor and the grandees, the commanders sped to their aid and met many people fleeing, and with much fighting *turned* them *back (vozvratili).*'

The meaning of the sentence is, of course, altered by the choice of perfective in (229a), but the change is minor. A similar change occurs in (230), where the Old Russian imperfect *napadaxu* 'they attacked, were attacking', from the derived verb *napadati,* gives a sense of several acts that come together to evoke a perfective-like result; the Modern Russian in (230a) avoids the question of success or failure by compressing these multiple acts into one.[47]

(230) Стратигом же всѣм, сънѣмшимся съ Зустунѣем, **нападаху** на турки сурово и **взратиша** ихъ до стѣны. (240)
'All the commanders, having met up with Zustuněja, *attacked (napadaxu)* the Turks viciously, and *pushed* them *back (v"zvratiša)* to the wall.'

(230a) tr: Стратиги же все, объединившись с Зустунеей, **напали** яростно на турок и **оттеснили** их до стен. (241)

---

[46] Speakers confirmed that the imperfectives here sound odd; they preferred the perfectives *perebili* 'they killed', *sožgli* 'they set fire', although one of them briefly entertained the possibility of saying *سžigali* 'they set fire¹' before dismissing it.

[47] My informants had difficulty with this sentence. They inclined toward the imperfective *napadali,* based on the presence of the adverb *jarostno* 'fiercely', but admitted both *ottesnjali* and *ottesnili,* depending on context. Their answers confirm my suspicion that the Modern Russian translation renders only one of several possible meanings of the Old Russian text.

'All the commanders, having joined with Zustuneja, *attacked (napali)* the Turks viciously, and *pressed* them *back (ottesnili)* to the wall.'

The perfective *iznemogli* 'became exhausted' in (231a) serves a different function: it sidesteps the problem of simultaneity vs. sequence by suggesting that all the city-dwellers exhausted themselves at once and as a result then began to drop.

(231)   Турком убо множеством много суще, пременяхуся на брань, гражаном же всѣгда единым; отъ многаго труда **изнемогаху** и **падаху**, аки пияни. (256)
'Since there was a great multitude of Turks, they relieved each other in battle, but the city-dwellers were always the same ones; they *became exhausted (iznemogaxu)* and *fell (padaxu)*, as if drunk, from the difficulty of their labor.'

(231a) *tr:* Турок же было многое множество, а горожане — изо дня в день все те же — от великой усталости **изнемогли** и **падали**, словно пьяные. (257)
'There was a great multitude of Turks, but the city-dwellers — day in, day out the same ones — *became exhausted (iznemogli)* and *fell (padali)*, as if drunk, from great fatigue.'

This is essentially a pluperfect usage; their exhaustion occurred before the narrative's time frame. The imperfect derived *dostigaxu* 'they were reaching for, they reached' in (232) poses a similar problem for the Modern Russian translation in (232a).

(232)   ...и абие возопиша всь клирик и весь народ сущий ту... яко мнѣтися церкви оной великой колѣбатися, и гласи ихъ, мню, до небесъ **достигаху**. (258)
'...and immediately all the priests and people who were there let out a cry of sobbing and moaning... so it seemed as if that great church was swaying and their voices, I believe, *reached (dostigaxu)* the heavens.'

(232a) *tr:* ...и снова раздались вопли всего клира и находившегося тут народа... так что казалось, что эта огромная церковь зашаталась, и голоса их, думается мне, **достигли** до небес. (259)
'...and once again there resounded the cries of all the priests and people who were there... so it seemed as if that great church was swaying and their voices, it seems to me, *reached (dostigli)* the heavens.'

The use of an imperfective in Modern Russian could imply either impermanence of the result (it lasted for only a certain duration) or failure to attain it. While using the perfective *dostigli* 'reached' changes the meaning slightly, compressing all the actions into a single moment, it eliminates these possible confusions from the Modern Russian text.

Example (233) is the red herring of the lot; here the use of a perfective in Modern Russian seems gratuitous.

(233) И яко взыдоша паки гражане на стѣну и видѣша во рвѣ множество туркъ, абие **зажигааху** бочки съ смолою и пущааху на них, и погорѣша вси. (234-236)
'And when the city-dwellers went up again on the wall and saw the multitude of Turks in the ditch, they immediately *lit (zažigaaxu)* the barrels with pitch and heaved them down on the Turks, and they all burned up.'

(233a) *tr:* И когда взошли снова горожане на стену и увидели во рве множество турок, тотчас же **зажгли** бочки со смолой и побросали на них, и те все сгорели. (235-237)
'And when the city-dwellers went up again on the wall and saw the multitude of Turks in the ditch, they immediately *lit (zažgli)* the barrels with pitch and heaved them down on them, and they all burned up.'

The effect of the new perfective is to insinuate that all the pots were lit at once, then one by one thrown down. The Old Russian does not support this conclusion.

All of these predicates fall into the "highly telic" lexical category; this assignment influences their behavior in Old Russian, suggesting particular readings for Old Russian forms, and decides the fate of their Modern Russian counterparts. Furthermore, all the problems seen in this section involve contextual problems or, on an even larger level, textual issues of temporal, causal, and narrative connections between events. The examples show that Modern Russian has developed these textual features farther along aspectual lines than Old Russian had, but this development is not unidirectional; while the Modern Russian translation reminds us of the constant focus on result and termination of action in the modern language, the Old Russian has a sharper focus on initiation of action and a tendency to assume it where it is unmarked for both protoperfectives and protoimperfectives.

7.6.2.3. A grab bag of other forms. The remainder of the verbs in this group—Old Russian protoimperfectives that correspond to Modern Russian perfectives—are either present participles, infinitives or non-past forms. Examples (234) and (235) show the Old Russian simplex's greater capacity for expressing the action as a whole, as compared to the Modern Russian forms in (234a) and (235a).

(234) И абие цесарь, възбудився от сна, вскорѣ посылаеть в Византию магыстров и градцкых дѣлателей **готовити** мѣсто. (216)
'And instantly the emperor, having awakened from his dream, swiftly sends magistrates and city-builders to Byzantium *to prepare (gotoviti)* the location.'[48]

(234a) *tr:* И цесарь, воспрянув от сна, немедля послал в Византий магистров и градостроителей, **чтобы они подготовили** место. (217)
'And immediately the emperor, having awakened from his dream, swiftly sends magistrates and city-builders to Byzantium *that they might prepare (čtoby oni podgotovili)* the location.'

---

[48] Seen also as examples (223) and (254).

(235)   Епарху же паки повелѣ разрушеное мѣсто все заставити дрѣвом и башту **дѣлати**, чающе има уже отступити, окааным. (242)
'He ordered the eparch again to shore up the destroyed area completely with logs and *to build (dělati)* a tower, expecting the accursed ones to retreat.'

(235a) *tr:* Епарху же цесарь снова повелел заделать бревнами разрушенное место и **построить** башту, надеясь, что уже отступят они, окаянные. (243)
'The emperor ordered the eparch again to shore up the destroyed area completely with logs and *to build (postroit')* a tower, expecting the accursed ones to retreat.'

In both of them the simplex infinitives—*gotoviti* 'prepare' and *dělati* 'do, build'—refer to the entire process, start to finish; Modern Russian uses the perfective infinitives *podgotovit'* and *postroit'* to convey this overview of the action. This feature of the Old Russian simplex is consistent with the argument advanced in section 7.7.2., where I show that Modern Russian simplexes represent actions that in Old Russian require the articulated, process-oriented viewpoint of the derived form.

Examples (236) and (237) have Old Russian simplexes that require a Modern Russian prefixed form to convey future modality, as in (236a) *procarstvuet* 'he will reign'.

(236)   И въ возвращение его открыються сокровища земная, и всѣ обогатѣють, и никтоже нищ будеть, и земля дасть плод свой седмѣрицею, оружия ратная сътворят серпове. И **царствует** лѣт 32, и по нем въстанет ин от него. (264)
'And when he returns, the earthly treasure-houses will open, and everyone will become wealthy, and no one will be poor, and the earth will yield its fruit sevenfold, and they will beat their weapons into plowshares. And *he will reign (carstvuet)* for thirty-two years, and after him another of his family will arise.'

(236a) *tr:* И когда возвратится он, откроются людям сокровища земные, и все разбогатеют, и никто не будет нищим, и земля принесет плоды сам-семь, а из оружия воинского сделают серпы. И **процарствует** он тридцать два года и после него станет другой от рода его. (265)
'And when he returns, the earthly treasure-houses will open for the people, and everyone will become wealthy, and no one will be poor, and the earth will yield its fruit sevenfold, and they will beat their weapons into plowshares. And *he will reign (procarstvujet)* for thirty-two years, and after him another of his family will arise.'

While it is tempting to read these as proof of aspectual indifference, the number of such forms in the text is quite small, and these two examples illustrate some of the problems they present. The verb *carstvovati* 'reign' in (236), for instance, is a denominalization with an {-ovaj-} suffix, and as such is somewhat less reliable as an aspectual form; given its high style and sacred character, it instead fits the mold of a biaspectual verb similar to the class found in Modern Russian.

(237) И паки: «Елико **сътвориши**, елико **дѣлаеши** — ненавидит сия душа моа». (246)
'And further: "However much you *achieve (s"tvoriši)*, however much you *do (dĕlaeši)* — my soul despises this." '[49]

(237a) tr: И другое: «Что ни **сотворишь**, что ни **сделаешь** — все ненавистно душе моей.» (247)
'And further: "Whatever you *achieve (sotvoriš')*, whatever you *do (sdĕlaeš')* — all this is repugnant to my soul." '

Example (237) depends more closely on a fixed phrase; the Modern Russian expression *čto ni...* in (237a) is regularly followed by a perfective, and its sense is clearly related to that of the graphic-exemplary meaning *(nagljadno-primernoe značenie)* found with the perfective aspect. An action cited once in the perfective non-past becomes a precondition for the phenomenon that follows. The Old Russian conditioning environment *eliko* + non-past can be construed as a future act or a present one: 'However much you *shall achieve*, whatever you *do*...'[50]

Examples (238) and (239) show what appears to be an inceptive meaning in the forms *dajušče* 'giving, showing', *imĕjušče* 'having'; it cannot be ruled out, however, that the use of a Modern Russian perfective simply fits with Modern Russian phraseology better than a corresponding imperfective *(okazat'^{P} počesti* 'honor^P' instead of *okazyvat'^{I} počesti; obresti^P nadeždu* 'find hope' instead of *imet'^{I} nadeždu* or *obretat'^{I} nadeždu)*.

(238) Его же видѣв, цесарь обрадовася зѣло, **дающе** ему честь велию, понеже вѣдом бяше цесарю. (228)
'Having seen him, the emperor rejoiced greatly, *showing (dajušče)* him great honor, since he was known to the emperor.'

(238a) tr: Увидев его, очень обрадовался цесарь, **оказал** ему великие почести, ибо знал его и раньше. (229)
'Having seen him, the emperor rejoiced greatly; *he did (okazal)* him great honors, for he had known him even before.'

(239) «Тебѣ, цесарю, изшедшу из града съ елицыми всхощеши, паки, богу помогающу, мочно есть и граду помощи, и ины грады и вся земля надѣжу **имѣюще**, тако вскорѣ не предадутся безвѣрным.» (244)

---

[49] Discussed above as example (110).
[50] This example also suggests a fine but necessary lexical class distinction between the Old Russian verbs *tvoriti* and *dĕlati*: the former is very result-oriented (more highly telic) while the latter is more an activity or process (accretively telic). In Modern Russian this distinction has receded into the background thanks to semantic and stylistic shifts. (See section 7.4.1.2.)

' "You, o emperor, by leaving the city with as many people as you want, could then, God willing, help the city as well, and other cities and the whole land *would have (iměsušče)* hope, and would not give in so quickly to the infidel." '

(239a)   *tr:* «Ты, цесарь, когда уйдешь из города с теми, с кем захочешь, с божьей помощью сможешь и городу помочь, и другие города и вся земля **обретут** надежду и в скором времени не отдадутся неверным.» (245)

' "You, o emperor, if you leave the city with whomever you want, can, God willing, then help the city as well, and other cities and the whole land *will find (obretut)* hope, and will not give in so quickly to the infidel." '

Example (240) is trickier. One might expect the verb *razuměti* 'understand' to be protoperfective in Old Russian, although given its provenance (a prefixed form of a verb that is always stative) it could as well be protoimperfective. (This is especially likely because the Modern Russian equivalent, *razumet'*, is imperfective.) The presence of an exhortatory *da* adds a further element for consideration.

(240)   Но убо **да разумѣеши**, о окааннѣ, аще вся прежереченная Мѣфо-дием Патаромскым и Лвом Премудрым и знамения о градѣ сем съврьшишася... (264)
'But *you should understand (da razuměeši)*, o cursed one, if everything fore-told by Methodius Patarskij and Leo the Wise and the signs about this city come to pass...'

(240a)   *tr:* Но **да познай**, о несчастный, что если свершилось все, пред-вещанное Мефодием Патарским и Львом Премудрым и знамениями о городе этом... (265)
'But *realize (da poznaj)*, o cursed one, if everything foretold by Methodius Patarskij and Leo the Wise and by the signs about this city comes to pass...'

Here the imperative form acquires an inceptive reading in the Modern Russian translation from the form *poznaj* 'realize, recognize'. Thanks to the use of the imperative and the clear perfective form, this translation seems stronger than the original. I render the Old Russian as 'you should understand', where the translation has 'now be aware'. If an imperative form is to be used, then the perfective makes sense in Modern Russian; imperfective imperatives have different spheres of usage, connected with iteration, compulsion, general suggestions, and politeness conventions.

These examples, then, seem less useful than those discussed in earlier sections. For the most part they reflect idiosyncratic differences between Old Russian and Modern Russian that do not lead to any unified conclusions about Old Russian aspect. Some examples, however, do seem to support more general conclusions proposed in other sections of this chapter.

7.7. THE ROLE OF SECONDARY IMPERFECTIVIZATION

Discrepancies in the presence or absence of aspectual suffixes, and the types of suffixes used, are not exactly common in the *Taking of Tsargrad* and its Modern Russian translation, but there are a significant number of them. With thirteen examples, the most numerous are simplex verbs in the Old Russian text that correspond to derived verbs in the Modern Russian translation. There are seven cases of the reverse: an Old Russian derived verb that corresponds to a Modern Russian simplex. Finally (not exactly fitting this description, but along similar lines), there are four instances where an Old Russian derived verb in {-(j)aj-} corresponds to a Modern Russian verb in {-vaj-}.

All of the verbs discussed in this section are protoimperfective or protoimperfective in nature; as mentioned before, I have considered only discrepancies where the Old Russian and Modern Russian share a common root, due to the morphological nature of the problem.

7.7.1. Derived form found only in Modern Russian

The thirteen verbs in this class show two patterns of behavior. In the first, the Modern Russian derived form allows a greater degree of directionality or specificity than the Old Russian. In the second, the Modern Russian offers a more appropriate lexical alternative for Modern Russian, the simplex having been lost entirely or restricted in its function. In (241a) and (242a) the Modern Russian adds a directional component; the prefix {c-} indicates motion downwards, making this more specific than the Old Russian unprefixed derived forms in (241) and (242).

(241) Мужайтеся и крѣпитеся, и не ослабляйте в трудѣх, ни отпадайте надежею, **кладающе** главы своа за праваславную вѣру и за церкви божиа, яко да и нас прославит всещедрый богъ! (230)
'Be brave and strong, and do not slacken in your toils, nor give up hope, *laying [down] (kladajušče)* your heads for the Orthodox faith and for the church of God, so that the ever-generous God might celebrate us!'

(241a) *tr:* Мужайтесь и крепитесь и не поддавайтесь слабости в деле своем, не теряйте надежды, **слагая** головы свои за православную веру и за божьи церкви, и да прославит нас всещедрый бог! (231)
'Be brave and strong, and do not give in to weakness in your toil, nor give up hope, *laying down (slagaja)* your heads for the Orthodox faith and for the church of God, so that the ever-generous God might celebrate us!'

(242) падаху бо трупиа обоих стран, яко снопы, съ забрал, и кровь их **тѣчааше** яко рѣкы по стѣнам. (230)
'for corpses were falling on all sides—like sheaves—from the railings, and their blood *flowed (těčaaše)* like rivers down the walls.'

(242a) tr: ...ибо убитые с обеих сторон, словно снопы, падали с заборол, и кровь их ручьями **стекала** по стенам. (231)
'for the killed were falling on all sides—like sheaves—from the railings, and their blood *flowed (stekala)* in streams down the walls.'

The prefix {o-} is also found with this group; its directional meaning, while evident, is modified in two of the three examples. *Osmatrivat'* 'examine' in (243a), as opposed to *smotret'* 'look', implies a thorough examination.

(243) Зустунѣя же и вси велможи поидоша по стенам града, **смотряще** стен и трупия неврьных, и тако сказааше цесарю и патриарху до 35 000 убьеных. (232)
'Zustuněja and all the grandees went along the city walls, *surveying (smotrjašče)* the walls and the corpses of the infidel, and so they told[51] the emperor and the patriarch there were up to 35,000 dead.'

(243a) tr: Зустунея же и все вельможи прошли по городским стенам, **осматривая** их и считая трупы неверных, и назвали цесарю и патриарху число убитых — до тридцати пяти тысяч. (233)
'Zustuneja and all the grandees went along the city walls, *surveying (osmatrivaja)* them and the corpses of the infidel, and so they told the emperor and the patriarch the number of the dead — up to 35,000.'

Oplakivat' in (244a), as opposed to the simplex *plakat'* 'cry', has the more specific meaning 'to mourn (by crying)'.

(244) Магмет же окаанный, слышав восточнаго бегиларбеа убийство, **плакаше** много: любяше бо его мужества ради его и разума... (256)
'The accursed Mohammed, having heard of the death of the eastern bey, *mourned (plakaše)* him greatly; for he (had) loved him for his courage and wisdom...'[52]

(244a) tr: Магомет же окаянный, услышав, что убит бегиларбей восточный, долго его **оплакивал**, ибо любил его за мужества его и разум... (257)
'The accursed Mohammed, having heard the eastern bey was killed, *mourned (oplakival)* him at length; for he (had) loved him for his courage and wisdom...'

Only *očiščat'* 'clean, cleanse', in (245a), is nearly identical to the simplex *čistit'* in meaning, differing only by virtue of the degree of thoroughness it suggests.

---

51 Here I read *skazaša* 'they told [aorist]' for *skazaaše* 'he was telling [imperfect]', although the latter is also possible.
52 Seen earlier as examples (26) and (46).

(245) И се слышав, салтан возрадовася и посла град **чистити**, улици и поля. (262)
'And having heard this, the sultan rejoiced and sent *to cleanse (čistiti)* the city, its streets and squares.'

(245a) *tr:* И услышав об этом, обрадовался султан, и послал **очищать** город, улицы и площади. (263)
'And having heard this, the sultan rejoiced and sent *to cleanse (očiščat')* the city, its streets and squares.'

All three verbs with the prefix {o-}, however, add a component of increased processuality and motion toward a goal that is less evident in the Old Russian original.

Examples (246) and (247) still fall into the first group of verbs (those where the Modern Russian form is similar in meaning to the Old Russian form, although lexically more specific), although the semantic shift from Old Russian to Modern Russian is wider in (246) and (247) than it was in (241)-(245). In (246a), the Old Russian *pisati* 'write' from (246) is translated as Modern Russian *zapisyvat'*. The latter is more specific, meaning 'take notes, jot down'. The use of a derived imperfective in Modern Russian allows the translator to match in a word the regular, repeated quality of the action.

(246) Тако и нынѣ в сѣм великом и страшном дѣле ухитряяся овогда болѣзнию, овогда скрыванием, овогда же совѣщанием приятѣлей своих, уловляя врѣмя дозрением и испытанием великым, **писах** в каждый день творимая дѣяниа вне града от турков. (266)
'And so contriving even now in this great and fearful enterprise, sometimes feigning sickness, sometimes hiding, sometimes with the aid of my friends, seizing time for investigation and much questioning, *I have written (pisax)* every day of what has occurred outside the city among the Turks.'

(246a) *tr:* Так вот и ныне в этом великом и страшном деле ухитрялся я, когда под видом болезни, когда скрываясь, когда с помощью приятелей своих, изыскивать время все рассмотреть и обо всем разузнать, подробно **записывал** день за днем обо всем, что совершалось вне града у турок. (267)
'And so I contrive even now in this great and fearful enterprise, sometimes under pretense of sickness, sometimes hiding, sometimes with the aid of my friends, to seize time to look things over and find things out; *I have written (zapisyval)* day after day about everything that has occurred outside the city among the Turks.'

Example (247) could arguably belong to the next group; Modern Russian has two verbs, *veličat'* and *vozveličivat'*, the former with a more concrete meaning ('honor'), the latter with a more abstract one ('exalt'). There is also a slight telic difference; the latter predicate is less processual, more focused on the final goal rather than the process.

(247) О, горѣ тобѣ, Седмохолмий, яко погании тобою обладают, ибо колико благодатѣй божиих на тебѣ восияша, овогда прославляя и **величая** паче иных градов, овогда многообразне и многократнѣ наказая и наставляя благыми дѣлы и чюдесы преславными... (260)
'O, woe is thee, seven-hilled city, for the pagans now rule over you, and how many divine graces illuminated you, sometimes praising and *exalting (veličaja)* [you] above all other cities, sometimes in many ways and many times teaching and instructing through blessed acts and most glorious wonders...'

(247a) *tr:* О горе тебе, Седьмохолмый, что поганые тобой обладают, ибо сколько благодатей божьих в тебе просияло, порой прославляя тебя и **возвеличивая** более всех иных городов, иногда самым различным образом и многократно наказуя, и наставляя дивными деяниями и чудесами преславными... (261)
'O, woe is thee, seven-hilled city, that the pagans now rule over you, for how many divine graces were illuminated in you, at times praising and *exalting (vozveličivaja)* [you] above all other cities, sometimes in the most varied of ways and many times teaching and instructing through strange acts and most glorious wonders...'

Context does not suggest clearly which meaning the Old Russian intended; this example could thus represent either a semantic shift in the translation (the author could be somewhat arbitrarily reaching for a more abstract and more telic interpretation of the act) or a grammatically motivated change (reduction of the simplex's domain could force the choice of a secondary imperfective instead of a simplex).

The remainder of the verbs fall into the category of grammatically motivated changes. In these instances the Old Russian verb is inappropriate in Modern Russian; either it no longer exists or it is semantically more restricted in its usage. The functions of the Old Russian simplex are taken over by a Modern Russian derived form of the same verb. For instance, the verb *rjaditi* 'manage' in (248) does not correspond to a similar Modern Russian verb in (248a); the best equivalent is instead a derived double-prefixed imperfective *rasporjažat'sja* 'be in charge' from the same root.

(248) И к тому законы многы устави, яко идолская капища святителем Христовым и христьяном точию владѣти и **рядити**. (216)
'And in addition he set down many laws so that only prelates of Christ and Christians could own and *manage (rjaditi)* idolatrous temples.'

(248a) *tr:* К тому же не раз издавал он указы, что языческими храмами могут владеть и **распоряжаться** лишь святители Христовы и христиане. (217)
'And in addition he set down laws more than once so that only prelates of Christ and Christians could own and *manage (rasporjažat'sja)* idolatrous temples.'

Example (249) is similar; the verb *širiti* 'widen' has fallen out of use, replaced by a modern derived form, *rasširjat'*, which makes use of the prefix {raz-}, often used to suggest distribution or motion in several directions at once.

(249)   И турки убо начаша пакы стрѣляти из пушек на разрушенное мѣсто, гражане начаша башту **ширити** и дѣлати крѣпко о всѣй прогалинѣ... (238)
'And the Turks began again to fire their cannons at the shattered spot, and the city-dwellers began *to widen (širiti)* the tower and to make it strong along the breach....'

(249a)   *tr:* И турки начали снова стрелять из пушек по разрушенному месту, а горожане начали **расширять** башту и возводить ее по всей ширине пролома... (239)
'And the Turks began again to fire their cannons at the shattered spot, and the city-dwellers began *to widen (rasširjat')* the tower and to raise it along the whole width of the breach....'

This is also true to a certain extent of *stereči* 'guard' in (250); the Modern Russian verb *stereč'* is rarer than its derived forms (represented in (250a) by a past participle of *podsteregat'*).

(250)   Всехъ же воин собрашася с ним до трѣю тысящ, и обрѣте во вратѣх множество туркъ, **стрѣгущи** его... (258)
'They collected all the soldiers with him, to three thousand, and he found at the gates a multitude of Turks, *guarding (strĕgušči)* him [Mohammed]....'

(250a)   *tr:* Всех же воинов собралось с ним до трех тысяч, и увидел он в воротах множество турок, **подстерегавших** его... (259)
'All the soldiers were collected with him, to three thousand, and he saw at the gates a multitude of Turks *who were guarding (podsteregavšix)* him [Mohammed]....'

An Old Russian verb need not fall out of use entirely for replacement to be necessary. Sometimes the semantic range of the simplex contracts, with more specific prefixed derived forms taking over individual meanings. Example (251) shows that Old Russian *moliti* means both 'pray' and 'entreat', where the modern verb is restricted to the former meaning. A prefixed derived form, *umoljat'*, takes over the latter meaning.

(251)   Цесарь же паки объежааше по всѣму граду, плачуще и рыдающе, **моля** стратиг и всих людей, глаголюще... (230)
'The emperor again rode around the whole city, crying and sobbing, *imploring (molja)* the commanders and all the people, saying....'

(251a)   *tr:* Цесарь же, как и прежде, объезжал весь город, плача и рыдая, **умоляя** стратигов и всех людей, говоря им... (231)

'The emperor, as before, rode around the whole city, crying and sobbing, *imploring (umoljaja)* the commanders and all the people, saying....'

The Old Russian verb *biti* is widely attested in the meanings 'hit, strike, kill', where its Modern Russian counterpart is deponent: since the form *b'ja* is archaic, *bit'* does not have a verbal adverb, and the translator is thus forced either to modify the syntax of the sentence or to use a verbal adverb from a more specific, restricted form. In (252) and (253), the translator does the latter.

(252) Баши же, и воини и нарядчики их понужающе туркъ и **бьюще** их, въскликааху и вопиаху на них. (248)
'The pashas and the soldiers and their leaders, hounding the Turks and *striking/killing (b'jušče)* them, called out and shouted at them.'

(252a) *tr:* Баши же, и воини, и начальники их силою гнали турок, **избивая** их, призывая и угрожая. (249)
'The pashas and the soldiers and their leaders, drove the Turks forth with their strength, *wounding (izbivaja)* them, calling to them and threatening them.'

(253) Цесарь же, пригласив своих, со восклицанием многым внидоша во все полки их, и, **бья** их, прогнаша из града. (256)
'Once the emperor, had summoned his men, with much exclamation they went into the ranks, and, *striking/killing (b'ja)* them, chased them from the city.'

(253a) *tr:* Цесарь же, созвав своих, с кликами врезался в ряды врагов и, **избивая** их, прогнал из города. (257)
'The emperor, having summoned his men, with much exclamation sliced into the ranks of the enemy, and, *wounding (izbivaja)* them, chased them from the city.'

Old Russian *biti* is replaced in Modern Russian by *izbivat'* in (252a) and (253a), with the meaning 'wound, damage'. Here the simplex's utility has been restricted, and more precise, highly telic verbs have forms that perform the tasks formerly assigned to the simplex.

7.7.2. Derived form found only in Old Russian

Contrary to expectations, there are seven examples in this text of Old Russian prefixed derived forms that appear in Modern Russian as simplex or unprefixed derived forms. In this Old Russian text, prefixed derived imperfectives fulfill a specialized function: they appear in progressive and iterative contexts more regularly than a simplex form (sometimes exclusively so). Many of these distinctions, as we have seen, exist or are even further developed in Modern Russian. In some cases, however, Modern Russian fails to offer a particular distinction found in this text.

A good example is the trio *gotoviti~ugotoviti~ugotovljati* 'prepare, make ready', all of which are amply attested. The simplex verb *gotoviti* is preferred in contexts that hint at the entirety of the act, whereas the derived protoimperfective *ugotovljati* concentrates on expressing the action as process. This verb set is an excellent test case, because the simplex and the derived form are lexically nearly identical. Note that in Old Russian, *gotoviti* appears in contexts where the act as a whole is indicated, as in the infinitive in (254), whereas the Modern Russian translation has a perfective purpose clause *čtoby oni podgotovili* 'so that they might prepare' in (254a).

(254)   ... и абие цесарь, възбудився от сна, вскорѣ посылаеть в Визандию магыстров и градцкых дѣлателей **готовити** мѣсто. (216)
'...and immediately the emperor, having awakened from his dream, swiftly sends magistrates and city-builders to Byzantium *to prepare (gotoviti)* the location.'[53]

(254a)   *tr:* И цесарь, воспрянув от сна, немедля послал в Византий магистров и градостроителей, **чтобы они подготовили** место. (217)
'...and immediately the emperor, having awakened from his dream, swiftly sent magistrates and city-builders to Byzantium *so they might prepare (čtoby oni podgotovili)* the location.'

A similar holistic interpretation of *gotoviti* is found in (255), where the infinitive appears in sequence with a protoperfective infinitive, *pribaviti* 'add'.

(255)   ...и повелѣ магистром вскорѣ прибавити пушки и пищали мнози на битье града и ины стенобитныя козни **готовити**. (228)
'...and he ordered the magistrates to quickly add more cannons and harquebuses to shell the city, and *to ready (gotoviti)* the other wall-destroying machines.'

(255a)   *tr:* ...и повелел воеводам немедля увеличить число пушек и пищалей для обстрела города и **готовить** другие стенобитные машины. (229)
'...and he ordered the magistrates to quickly increase the number of cannons and harquebuses for shelling the city, and *to ready (gotovit')* the other wall-destroying machines.'

In (256), however, the simplex non-past (found in both original and translation) represents an ongoing action, showing that such an interpretation is not restricted to suffixed verbs.

(256)   «Видим, цесарю, яко сей бѣзвѣрный не ослабѣет дѣлом, но паче **готовиться** на болшее дѣло.» (234)

---

53   Seen earlier as examples (223) and (234).

' "We see, o emperor, that this infidel will not slacken in his work, but rather *is making plans (gotovit'sja)* for a bigger attack." '

(256a) *tr:* «Видим, о цесарь, что этот безверный не откажется от своего замысла, но снова **готовится** к большему приступу.» (235)
' "We see, o emperor, that this infidel will not renounce his plan, but *is making* further *plans (gotovitsja)* for a bigger attack." '

In the remainder of the examples, the derived form *ugotovljati* focuses attention exclusively on articulation of the process. In (257), *ugotovljati* appears in sequence with *biti* and *narežati* 'set up', which also indicate ongoing processes.

(257) Он же, безвѣрен сый и лукавъ, посланникы отосла, а град повелѣ бити пушками и пищалми, а ины стѣнобьеные хитрости нарежати и приступы градцкые **уготовляти**. (222)
'That godless and crafty man sent the emissaries away, and ordered to fire on the city with cannons and harquebuses, and to assemble other machines for destroying the wall and *to prepare (ugotovljati)* for an assault on the city.'

(257a) *tr:* Он же, коварный иноверец, послов не принял, а город повелел обстреливать из пушек и пищалей, и собирать различные стенобитные орудия, и **готовиться** к приступу. (223)
'That godless and crafty man did not receive the emissaries, and ordered to fire on the city with cannons and harquebuses, and to assemble other machines for destroying the wall and *to prepare (ugotovljati)* for an assault [on the city].'

Example (258), with a suffixed imperfect *ugotovljaxusja* 'they were preparing themselves' catches the action in the midst of occurrence, as does a similar form in (259), which focuses on the ongoing preparation of the vessels filled with pitch and brimstone and the repetition of this action.

(258) Турки же по вся места бьяхуся без опочиванья день и нощь, пременяющеся, не дающе нимала опочити градцкиим, но да ся утрудят, понеже **уготовляхуся** к приступу; и так творяху до 13 ден. (224)
'The Turks fought without rest in all locations, day and night, relieving each other, not letting the city's residents rest in the least, so that they would exhaust themselves, for *they [the Turks] were preparing (ugotovljaxusja)* themselves for the assault; and they did this until the thirteenth day.'

(258a) *tr:* Турки же нападали на город со всех сторон непрерывно, день и ночь, сменяя друг друга, не давая нисколько отдохнуть горожанам, чтобы те изнемогли, так как **готовились** к приступу; и так вели бои в течение тринадцати дней. (225)
'The Turks attacked the city uninterruptedly from all sides, day and night, relieving each other, not letting the city-dwellers rest in the least, so they would exhaust themselves, for *they [the Turks] were preparing* themselves *(ugotovljaxusja)* for the assault; and they waged war this way for thirteen days.'

(259) Гражане же в день бьяхуся с туркы, а ночи влазяаху в рвы, и пробиваху стѣны ровныя от поля, и изныряху землю по застѣнью в многые мѣста, задѣлающе многы съсуды зъ зелием с пушечным; такоже на стѣнах **уготовляаху** многые съсуды, наполняюще смолья и сѣры... (234)
'The city-dwellers fought with the Turks by day, and by night they crawled into the trenches and undermined the trench walls on the field side, and dug up the earth beyond the wall in many places, filling many vessels with gunpowder; also on the walls they *prepared (ugotovljaaxu)* many vessels, filling them with pitch and sulfur...'

(259a) *tr:* Горожане же днем бились с турками, а ночью спускались во рвы и делали подкопы в откосах рва в сторону поля, и прокопали землю за стенами во многих местах, закапывая множество сосудов с пушечным порохом; также и на стенах **приготовляли** множество сосудов, наполняя их смолой, и серой... (235)
'The city-dwellers fought with the Turks by day, and by night they crawled into the trenches and undermined the trench walls on the field side, and dug up the earth beyond the wall in many places, filling many vessels with gunpowder; also on the walls they *prepared (prigotovljali)* many vessels, filling them with pitch and sulfur...'

The Modern Russian translations in (258a) and (259a) reflect the iterativity of the context more exclusively, as is clear from the use of *prigotovljat'*, which implies completion of the act(s) in question. Example (260) is the least processual form of *ugotovljati*, but even here this infinitive is sequenced with another process *(bratisja* 'do battle').

(260) туры убо и лѣсници и ины козни многы приступые повелѣ **уготовляти**, а воином паки повелѣ братися съ гражаны. (242)
'he ordered them *to prepare (ugotovljati)* the gabions and ladders and other siege weaponry, and ordered the troops to do battle again with the city-dwellers.'

(260a) *tr:* ...приказал **готовить** туры и лестницы и другие осадные орудия, а воинам приказал снова биться с горожанами. (243)
'he ordered them *to prepare (gotovit')* the gabions and ladders and other siege weaponry, and ordered the troops to do battle again with the city-dwellers.'

Not all verbs follow this clear a format; there are numerous verbs attested in the text where the lexical difference between the simplex and its prefixed forms is substantial enough to make the choice of one over the other obligatory. (Prefixed forms of *biti* 'hit, attack' and their derivatives like *razbivati–razbiti* 'break' or *ubivati–ubiti* 'kill' are good examples of this, as are the various compounds of *žeči* 'burn', which never occurs in simplex form in this text: things only burn up, through, into, etc.) Still, even here the choice is not always clear. Occasionally in this text a protoperfective verb is used with imperfect or present participle endings, indicating that if, in a pinch, the secondary imperfective still does not have the lexical spread or clout to be authoritatively used in context, the protoperfective can stand in for it. Once again, this is evidence of the flexible nature of aspect and the predominance of lexical features over grammatical ones at this stage of the language.

The remaining four forms where a Modern Russian unprefixed form replaces an Old Russian prefixed derived one either fit into the pattern *gotoviti~ugotovljati* (such as *xraniti~soxranjati* 'protect–preserve') or represent semantic alterations (such as *menjati~premenjati* 'change–exchange').

7.7.3. Old and modern derivational suffixes are different

In four instances the Old Russian verb is built on the suffix {-aj-} or {-jaj-}, where the Modern Russian verb is built on a {-vaj-} suffix. Examples (261) and (262) have the Old Russian verb *otvraščati sja* 'turn away', which is derived from *otvratiti sja*.

(261)   Но убо понеже естьство наше тяжкосердно и нерадиво, и яко неистовы еже на нас милость божью и щедрот **отвращаемся** и на злодѣяния и безакония обращаемся...якоже есть писано: «Злодѣяниа и безакониа превратят престолы силных»... (222)
'But since our nature is coarse of heart and negligent, and like the ignorant *we turn away (otvraščaemsja)* from God's grace and generosity toward us, and turn towards evil deeds and lawlessness...for as it is written: "Evildoing and lawlessness will overturn the thrones of the mighty"...'

(261a) *tr:* Но так как по природе своей мы грубы сердцем и нерадивы, и, словно безумные, **отворачиваемся** от милости бога и щедрот его к нам, и обращаемся на злодеяния и беззакония... как писано: «Злодеяния и беззакония разрушат престолы могучих»... (223)
'But since by our nature we are coarse of heart and negligent, and like the ignorant we *turn away (otvoračivaemsja)* from God's grace and generosity toward us, and turn towards evil deeds and lawlessness... for as it is written: "Evildoing and lawlessness will overturn the thrones of the mighty"...'

(262)   Ты же, яко неистовен, еже на тебѣ милость божию и щедрот **отвращашеся** и на злодѣяние и безаконие обращашеся. (260)
'You, like an ignoramus, *turned away (otvraščašesja)* from God's grace and generosity toward you, and turned to evil deeds and lawlessness.'

(262a) *tr:* Ты же, словно безумный, **отворачивался** от божественной милости к тебе и щедрот и тянулся к злодеяниям и беззаконию. (261)
'You, like an ignoramus, *turned away (otvoračivalsja)* from God's grace and generosity toward you, and were drawn to evil deeds and lawlessness.'

Modern Russian *otvoračivat'sja* in (261a) and (262a) is normally paired with a different verb, *otvorotit'sja*, but given the Old Russian literary tendency—strongly expressed in this text—to avoid pleophonic forms, it is not surprising that literary Old Russian does not make the same semantic distinction as Modern Russian. (Modern Russian uses the nonpleophonic verb *otvraščat'sja* in a more abstract meaning—'avoid'—and the pleophonic verb *otvoračivat'sja* in a more concrete meaning—'turn away'.)[54]

The correspondence in (263) and (263a) between Old Russian *zakalati* 'strike, stab' and Modern Russian *zakalyvat'* is more straightforward; here the {-aj-} suffix is replaced by {-yvaj-} in Modern Russian.

(263)   И тако прогнаша турковъ к полому мѣсту, и сгустившимся ту множеству народу, побиша их гражане безчислено, **закалаху** бо их аки свиней, дондеже проидоша полое мѣсто... (254)
'And so they chased the Turks as far as the breach, and, when a multitude of people had amassed there, the city-dwellers killed countless of them, for *they stabbed (zakalaxu)* them like pigs, until they passed through the breach...'

(263a) tr: И так отогнали турок от разрушенного места и столпилось там множество врагов, и без числа перебили их горожане, **закалывая**, точно свиней, пока они проталкивались через пролом... (255)
'And so they chased the Turks from the destroyed area, and a multitude of the enemy amassed there, and the city-dwellers killed countless of them, *stabbing* them like pigs, until they passed through the breach...'

Example (264)-(264a), where the modern translation replaces Old Russian *nakazaja* 'instructing' with *nakazuja*, is more complex.

(264)   О, горѣ тобѣ, Седмохолмий, яко погании тобою обладают, ибо колико благодатѣй божиих на тебѣ восияша, овогда прославляя и величая паче иных градов, овогда многообразне и многократнѣ **наказая** и наставляя благыми дѣлы и чюдесы преславными... (260)
'O, woe is thee, seven-hilled city, for the pagans now rule you, and how many divine graces illuminated you, sometimes praising and exalting [you] above all other cities, sometimes in many ways and many times *teaching (nakazaja)* and instructing through blessed acts and most glorious wonders...'

(264a) tr: О горе тебе, Седьмохолмый, что поганые тобой обладают, ибо сколько благодатей божьих в тебе просияло, порой прославляя тебя и возвеличивая более всех иных городов, иногда самым различным образом и многократно **наказуя** и наставляя дивными деяниями и чудесами преславными... (261)

---

54 Definitions and aspectual pairings are from the *Slovar' russkogo jazyka v četyrex tomax* published by the USSR Academy of Sciences (1981-1984 edition).

'O, woe is thee, seven-hilled city, that the pagans now rule you, for how many divine graces were illuminated in you, at times praising and exalting [you] over all other cities, sometimes in most varied fashion and many times *teaching (nakazuja)* and instructing through wondrous acts and most glorious wonders...'

I find no Modern Russian verb **nakazovat'* in contemporary dictionaries, although participles from it survive in legal language (e.g. *nakazuemyj* 'punishable'). The more usual Modern Russian form would be *nakazyvaja,* but this has the modern meaning 'punish'. The form *nakazuja* could be part back-formation from these participial adjectives, part denominalization from *nakaz* 'order'. At any rate, the form **nakazaja* is unacceptable in Modern Russian; some other replacement is necessary.

Although the data from this last group of verbs are not particularly interesting as individual examples, their existence as a definable class and the absence of counter-examples (Old Russian verbs with {-vaj-} suffixes corresponding to Modern Russian verbs with {-(j)aj-} suffixes) testify to the general slide toward {-vaj-} suffixes.

7.8. CONCLUSIONS

In this chapter I have examined the role of aspect as it interacts with lexical groups and contexts in the *Taking of Tsargrad,* a Russian text of the late fifteenth century. In the system posited for earlier centuries, lexical groups play a major role in determining aspectual applicability and function. The role of lexical groups is substantially reduced in this text; predicates in most groups seem to participate in an aspectual system similar in many respects to that of Modern Russian. Statives and atelic actions have moved from the anaspectual to the aspectual category, with their verbs falling into the protoimperfective group. Nonpunctual telics continue the consolidation of aspectuality. Evidence for anaspectuality is strongest on the punctualizing side of the spectrum—and at that most strongly in the atelic class, and in the past tense domain of the telic class. The ability to punctualize an act is therefore highly conducive to keeping verbs outside the aspectual system, while atelicity, although also functioning in this fashion, provides less of a pull toward anaspectuality. Chart 7.8.1 indicates these features.

The net result of the lexical analysis is to show that anaspectuality is confined to a smaller corner of the verbal system in this text. Only punctual atelics and several isolated categories in other lexical classes are still anaspectual. The verbal system is clearly an aspectual one dominated by the opposition of protoperfective vs. protoimperfective.

The most significant differences between the aspectual system found in this text and that of Modern Russian occurs in the realm of context, not the lexicon. As sections 7.5 through 7.7 show, the Old Russian aspectual opposition differs substantially from the Modern Russian opposition in several respects.

Chart 7.8.1. Aspectuality by lexical groups in The Taking of Tsargrad

Punctual, non-telic − TELIC	*Non-punctual, non-telic*
ANASPECTUAL	MOSTLY ASPECTUAL
(IV)	(II)
(−, −)	(+, −)
+PUNCTUAL	−PUNCTUAL
PARTIALLY ASPECTUAL	FULLY ASPECTUAL
(III)	(I)
(−, +)	(+, +)
Punctual, telic + TELIC	*Non-punctual, telic*

Note: Coordinates show the presence (+) or absence (−) of two features (punctuality, telicity) in that order; Roman numerals (I-IV) rank aspectuality from most to least aspectual.

First, duration is not entirely restricted to the imperfective aspect as it is in Modern Russian. Protoperfective verbs in Old Russian, especially inceptives, have a restricted capacity to indicate duration. Second, iterativity is moving into the protoimperfective fold of functions and usages, although sequentiality vs. simultaneity plays a considerable role in aspectual choice to an extent not possible in Modern Russian. Third, the Old Russian protoimperfective lacks a consistent conative function. The differences are perhaps minor, but they all point in the same direction. Aspect in Old Russian, despite its widespread character, has nowhere near the pervasiveness or range of idiosyncratic meanings and functions it does in Modern Russian.

8. The Grand Prince of Muscovy

8.0. THE TEXT

Unlike the authors of other works in this study, who toiled anonymously (such as the authors of the Russian chronicles) or are known only by name (such as Afanasij Nikitin and Nestor Iskander), Prince Andrej Mixajlovič Kurbskij was a well-known figure on the sixteenth-century Russian political landscape. An initial ally and later opponent of Ivan IV, he authored the monograph *Istorija o velikom knjaze moskovskom (A History of the Grand Prince of Muscovy)*, an account of Ivan's rise to power and descent into despotism at the hands of corrupt and wicked advisors, and a substantial body of correspondence with the tsar is attributed to him as well (although its authenticity is the subject of some debate).

Kurbskij's monograph is a different sort of history from that written in the chronicles or travelogues of an earlier era. As opposed to the strict historical sequencing used by earlier authors, Kurbskij chooses and orders the presentation of events to support a thesis: specifically, that although the early part of Ivan's reign was marked by substantial military and bureaucratic achievements, Ivan later became a cruel and arbitrary ruler under the influence of a group of self-serving advisors, who played on Ivan's natural suspiciousness and paranoia. While the narrative is more or less subordinate to this overarching plan, the work is not uniform in style; some parts are philosophical and analytic, while other parts present more or less straightforward descriptions of battles.[1] The tone varies from neutral to ironic to righteously indignant, depending on the event narrated. In comparison to the other works discussed here, the *History of the Grand Prince of Muscovy* is most similar in style to the *Taking of Tsargrad,* although Kurbskij's descriptions of foreign customs recall more closely Nikitin's close attention to everyday details.

The language of Kurbskij's *History* is generally conservative, with many Church Slavic forms and words. It does, however, contain a large number of Polonisms. Russian with a heavy admixture of Polish was a common written code in certain spheres—the West Russian chancellery language of the Grand Duchy of Lithuania is a case in point—but rarely was such a mixture used for non-business (i.e. literary-didactic) discourse. Not until the following century, with the large-scale territorial gains in the west, did Russian begin to absorb Polish words into its everyday vocabulary at such a large rate (Vlasto 1986: 363). Kurbskij's language probably contained many items that, although common enough in western Russia, were unfamiliar to the average educated Muscovite; for this reason, the text has

---

[1] The battle accounts are somewhat longer and more detailed than they need to be to advance the narrative line; Kurbskij uses them to establish his own credentials by boasting about some of his early victories and to show the devotion of the troops to their tsar, who repays them with indifference and capriciousness.

frequent notes giving Russian equivalents for Kurbskij's original choice of words. It is not known whether any of these notes are Kurbskij's own; at least some were added by scribes later on (*Pamjatniki literatury drevnej Rusi, XVI. vek:* 606).[2]

The Polonisms in the text have only a minimal impact on this study. First, they are less frequent in the verbal morphology and lexicon than in the nominal sphere. Second, such insertion of lexical items undoubtedly reflects the fact that Kurbskij spent much of his life in western Russia; many of his campaigns were conducted there (including some described in the *History),* and he later defected to Poland, where his History may have been written. In any event, in this study obvious West Slavic items in the verbal lexicon (***trvala*** *bitva mala ne na dvě godiny* 'the battle *lasted* for almost two hours') were not collected, and once actual Polish lexical items are discounted, the features discussed here as different from Modern Russian could not conceivably (with one exception) come from Polish interference.[3]

I collected data from the first fifty pages of the History, as printed in the edition *Pamjatniki literatury drevnej Rusi;* the complete text in this edition is ninety-one pages long. While an accounting of the entire text would undoubtedly have brought to light more verb forms, using only the first half had a number of advantages. Foremost, the corpus was reduced to a more manageable size. This meant that I was able to include a more complete inventory of verb roots than was possible for the Primary and Suzdal' Chronicles, and I had room to include more context with my examples, making it easier to extract contextual information from the data.

This approach is especially appropriate for the later period of Old Russian, where contextual factors do play more of a role in determining what form the aspectual distinction took. While the number of verbs and verb forms covered would undoubtedly rise were the entire text canvassed (because of individual lexical items appearing only once or twice in the entire work), it is unlikely that the proportions of forms would change significantly, or that my overall conclusions about large groups of verbs would differ. To be safe, though, I will avoid inferring too much from the absence of particular forms or verbs when the verb root as a whole is only sporadically attested.

8.1. THE STATE OF THE VERBAL SYSTEM

New research into the state of the verbal system in Old Russian has shed considerable light on the troublesome perfect–aorist opposition. As opposed to older,

---

[2] It is not hard to imagine that Kurbskij himself was responsible for some of the translation notes; he was no stranger to the use of such textual notes, and made use of them frequently in the *History* to add tangential facts and references.

[3] While Polish aspect differs from Russian in numerous ways, most concern explicitly modal forms that I did not examine here in depth. Potentially significant for this study was the Polish use of perfective verbs in explicitly iterative situations. However, since this is also a well-established feature of Old Russian (and one still present to an extent in Modern Russian), there is no reason specifically to ascribe this feature to Polish influence. (See Brooks 1975, Netteberg 1953, Holvoet 1989, Lenga 1976.)

ahistorical approaches, which treated all of Old Russian as a single corpus, newer studies have taken an explicitly diachronic look at the data (Klenin 1993) or have explored the opposition in single, lengthy texts (Timberlake 1995). Both these studies support the view that an older resultative–nonresultative opposition gradually gives way to a more textually-based or discourse-oriented opposition. Klenin notes that the classic resultative perfect, which appears in both Old Church Slavic and Old Russian, is maintained throughout the Primary and Suzdal' Chronicles, but that an increase in the frequency of the perfect in the course of the text corresponds to a rise in nonresultative uses of the perfect, which she ties to specific discourse considerations and presumptions. Timberlake argues that the aorist is used in the *Life of the Archpriest Avvakum* to mark narrative features: the beginnings and ends of episodes and certain significant events, as opposed to the perfect, which is the ordinary tense of narration.

The predominance of these extragrammatical considerations in determining tense points to another fact: that *temporal* distinctions between the perfect and aorist tenses were practically nonexistent by the time of Kurbskij's text. Aorists and imperfects are, however, still maintained alongside the perfect; Kurbskij's language has a deliberately archaic style that is reflected in the verbal forms he uses. Despite his frequent use of aorist and imperfect forms, these tenses are clearly not part of Kurbskij's native spoken language. First, he frequently confuses aorist and imperfect forms; aorist 3. pl. forms in *-aša* are often substituted for imperfect 3. sg. forms in *-aše*, and vice versa. Second, and more interestingly, a spoken Russian "substrate" can be detected in Kurbskij's verbal paradigms for these tenses. For instance, Kurbskij writes, *Vy, o tom" ne trudivšus', ni protorov mnogix" nalagajušče, vnidoša v nix" (306)* 'You, without making any great effort or suffering any losses, *went into* them (our cities)'. Here, the verb form *vnidoša*, originally a 3. pl. form, is used in place of the 2. pl. *vnidoste*. I see in this the analogy of the perfect tense, which has the same participle, *vošli*, for all forms of the plural, with an optional copula (see chart 8.1.1 and example (86)). The reason for the 3. pl. form's predominance could be its high frequency in literary texts, as against the relatively low frequency of the 2. pl. form.

Chart 8.1.1. Analogical levelling in the plural of the aorist tense

Person	Innovative form (perfect)		Kurbskij's aorist		"Correct" aorist
1.	my (esmi) vošli		my vnidoxom		my vnidoxom"
2.	vy (este) vošli	<—>	*vy vnidoša*	≠	vy vnidoste
3.	oni ((sut')) vošli	<—>	oni vnidoša	=	oni vnidoša
Format	1. pl. = 2. pl. = 3. pl.		1. pl.; 2. pl. = 3. pl.		1. pl.; 2. pl.; 3. pl.

Overt reductions in the verbal paradigm are few, however; for the most part, Kurbskij retains the trappings of the Old Russian tense system, even if he does not consistently distinguish between the various forms and their functions. For instance, participles come in a variety of forms that seem more dependent on whim than on any particular agreement pattern (in particular, participles in -šču,-šči, and -šče are used interchangeably, and the final type is frequently confused with imperfect forms in -še).

Another example of multiple forms for a single function is the partial disappearance of semantic differences between the aorist and perfect tense; Kurbskij uses both aorists and perfects for ordinary sequential narration, and it is common for both aorist and perfect forms of a verb to occur in virtually identical contexts, making it clear that there is a large area of semantic overlap. While episodes tend to have a predominating tense—either aorist or perfect—the competing tense is often found within the episode as well, to no particular semantic effect. Some verbs seem more likely to occur in the aorist, probably because they are well-known from the Old Russian lexicon; other verbs are rarely found in the aorist, possibly for the opposite reason. For Kurbskij, the aorist was probably an alternative set of past tense forms to the perfect; aorist forms were preferred where possible, no doubt because of their status in the literary language as the "correct" tense for normal narration of a story line.

If the aorist is no longer fully a tense (in the sense that it no longer has a function autonomous from that of the perfect), we should examine the possibility that, by this time, aorist usage has come to be a secondary marker of protoperfective aspect. There is substantially more basis for such a claim in this text than there was for earlier texts. After all, if the aorist tense clearly no longer existed in the spoken language of the time, it is reasonable to expect that the newly arisen categories of perfectivity and imperfectivity might determine the usage of these older forms. However, the distribution of aorist and imperfect forms in Kurbskij's *History* belies this explanation. Several protoimperfective verbs appear frequently with aorist forms (e.g., *viděx* 'I saw', *bišasja* 'they fought' *deržaša* 'they held'). Considering these verbs to be biaspectual does not help, as the aorist still occurs with typically imperfective contexts. The aorist, when its forms can be clearly separated from the imperfect, is still reserved for events limited in time, whether internally (by the structure of the event) or externally (by time constraints made explicit or implicit in the context).[4] The use of the aorist in Kurbskij is thus at least partially consistent with its use in older texts, whether for semantic reasons or merely by imitation of the forms seen in those texts.

It seems likely that Kurbskij used the aorist as a set of forms similar in function to the perfect but more restricted in scope. The restrictions on aorist use were both lexical (it was found most frequently with certain verbs) and semantic (it could be used only for events limited in time). This hypothesis makes sense from the point of view of the language learner. If he used only forms he had read in literary texts,

---

4   As follows from the previous discussion, Kurbskij also uses the perfect in these situations to identical effect.

he would in effect be formulating lexical restrictions on the use of the aorist, while the semantic restriction is a single rule he could easily deduce from reading or be taught. These two types of restrictions would reinforce each other and contribute to the maintenance of the aorist as a viable set of forms (even if it was more or less used as a stylistic subset of the perfect tense).

This approach obviates the need to explain how a category like aspect, which was undoubtedly pervasive in the spoken language by this point but unrecognized as a formal element of written Russian grammar, could have somehow found reflection in a tense opposition that was codified in the grammar but almost certainly extinct in the spoken language. On the face of it, the two categories have complementary features (the protoperfective–protoimperfective opposition is [+spoken], [-codified], while the aorist–imperfect opposition is [-spoken], [+codified]), making it tempting to propose that some combination of them created a reflection of the spoken language in the codified one. Given the situation described above, however, it is difficult to imagine a mechanism that could directly cause, say, protoperfective verbs to be consistently realized as aorists.

What, then, is the state of aspectual relations in Kurbskij's text? Many features of the aspectual opposition we see in Modern Russian are already present in the *History*. The few apparent examples of anaspectual behavior are easily traced to other sources. However, there are a number of consistent discrepancies between Modern Russian and Kurbskij's Russian that are worth examining. First, simplex verbs in the *History* often correspond to derived forms in the modern translation, suggesting that simplexes have a more restricted range of meaning in the modern language than they did in the sixteenth century. Second, the protoperfective aspect as it appears in this text places less emphasis on result. Third, discourse features receive a different treatment in Kurbskij's text than they do in a modern translation of it.

8.2. FROZEN ANASPECTUAL FORMS

In earlier chapters, I cited evidence that large portions of the Old Russian verbal system resisted classification into one or another grammatical aspect. By the sixteenth century, it becomes considerably more difficult to make this assertion; most verbs' behavior marks them as belonging to one or another aspect.[5] Since this was shown conclusively for aspect of the fifteenth century, it will not be necessary to repeat the process here. However, it is interesting to note that some of the original anaspectual forms do survive into this period. They are used instead as fixed expressions in particular forms; their lack of aspectuality does not extend to other forms.

A good example is the verb *viděti* 'see', which, along with other types of involuntary perception, showed the weakest aspectual affiliation in all its possible predicates in the Chronicles. In the *History*, however, its affiliation with the

---

[5] It is not necessarily the case that these aspects correspond exactly to "aspect" as we understand it in Modern Russian; this point will be taken up in the following section.

protoimperfective aspect is clearer. Of six aorists attested in the *History*, all express an action of unspecified duration; only one could represent an inceptive. Examples (1) and (2) are representative of the aorists found in the *History*.

(1)   ...хоругви християнские... поидоша ко граду сопостатов. Град же **видехом** аки пустъ стоящ, иже а ни человѣкъ, а ни глас человѣчь ни единъ отнуд слышашеся в нем... (236)
'...the Christian ensigns... went to the enemy's stronghold.[6] And we *saw (vidĕxom)* the stronghold standing as if empty, for not a man was there, nor was a single human voice to be heard from anywhere within...'

(2)   Сие воистину дивное сам очима своима **видѣх** не во едином от градов, но и во других некоторыхъ. (296)
'And this wondrous thing I truly *did see (vidĕxom)* with my own eyes, not just in one of these strongholds, but in several others as well.'

In (1), the event is explicitly durative; the aorist marks a temporary perception, a false relief that will soon be dashed. Example (2) is an affirmation of a fact: Kurbskij backs up his generalizations about the cowardly behavior of German rulers by claiming that he observed it in numerous places. The event is not clearly punctual in nature, and the implicit repetition of the act lends more credibility to a protoimperfective reading.

Example (3) has the only aorist with a possible inceptive reading.

(3)   Очхнув же ся уже потом, аки по малѣ годинѣ, **видѣхъ**, аки над мертвецом, плачющимъ и рыдающим двема слугам моимъ, надо мною стоящимъ, и другимъ двема воином царскимъ. Азъ же **видѣхъ** себя обноженна лежаща, многими ранама учащенна... (258)
'I came to later, after a short while, and *saw (vidĕx")* my two servants crying and sobbing, standing over me, as if over a dead man, and two other soldiers of the tsar's as well. I *saw (vidĕx")* myself lying naked, covered with numerous wounds...'[7]

(3a)   *tr:* Очнулся я, видимо, скоро и **увидел** над собою двух слуг своих и двух каких-то воинов царских: стоят и плачут и рыдают, как над мертвецом. Сам же я, **вижу**, лежу повержен, покрыт многими ранами... (259)
'I apparently came to quickly and *saw (uvidel)* over me my two servants and two of the tsar's servants: they stood and cried and sobbed as if over a dead man. I myself see *(vižu)* that I lie prone, covered with numerous wounds.'

---

[6] I follow the Modern Russian translator in reading *grad* as 'fortress, stronghold' and *město* as 'city' for this text. Fennell sometimes translates *grad* as 'citadel' and other times as 'city', at times in reference to the same place (1965: 34).

[7] In previous chapters I translated *cesar'* as 'emperor'; here I have translated it variously as 'tsar' (referring to the Russian monarch) or 'king' (referring to the ruler of Kazan' or other countries).

Kurbskij says that after he awakened, he soon saw people crying over him. The inceptivity of the act is balanced by the duration implied in the acts he witnessed (the implications of this will be discussed in the next section); the Modern Russian translation in (3a) has *uvidel* 'glimpsed, saw', which incorporates momentariness and a certain accidental, involuntary quality into the act and necessitates that the durative acts of crying and sobbing be shunted into a separate clause. The mismatch between Old and Modern Russian forms, then, is not as significant here as it might seem; the change of aspect is accompanied by a change in the domain of the predicate, which no longer directly encompasses the perception of states (*plačjuščim" i rydajuščim* 'crying and sobbing'). The second time *vidĕx"* is repeated in the following sentence, the translation uses the historical present *vižu* 'I see' to indicate perception of a state.[8]

A similar situation holds for infinitives with *vidĕti*. I found two in the text. Example (4) shows impossibility expressed with an infinitive; this general factual use of the protoimperfective infinitive is common.

(4) Тогда стрѣл густость такая, яко частость дожда, тогда камения множество безчисленное, **яко** и воздуха **не видѣти**! (250)
'Then the arrows flew so thickly, as often as rain, then an innumerable multitude of stones, *so that* even the air *[was] not visible (jako ne vidĕti)!*'

Examples (5) and (5a), however, contains another aspectual mismatch similar to the one found above.

(5) Во единомъ же градѣ случилося намъ таково **видѣти**: идѣже была пятерица великородных з дворы ихъ, кътому два ротмистра с полки своими, и ту жь под самым мѣстом яко нѣкоторых воинов, такъ человѣков всѣнародных биющихся немало с мимошедшым полком татарскимъ... (296)
'In one fortress we happened *to see (vidĕti)* the following: that there were five nobles with their retinues, and in addition two commanders with their troops and here, right outside the city itself, several soldiers and many ordinary people were fighting with the Tatar regiment that was passing through...'

(5a) Вот что пришлось нам **увидеть** в одной из крепостей: было там пятеро благородных со своими свитами и, кроме того, два командира со своими отрядами, а у города тут же несколько воинов и множество простых людей бились с проходящим татарским полком... (297)
'Here is what it fell to us *to see (uvidet')* in one of the fortresses: there were five nobles with their retinues and in addition two commanders with their troops, and here, right by the city, several soldiers and a multitude of common people were fighting with the Tatar regiment passing through...'

---

8   The historical present probably appears thanks at least in part to the historical present used in the previous clause. It also, however, frees the translator of the obligation to make another awkward aspectual choice.

The Modern Russian perfective infinitive *uvidet'* in (5a) shows the accidental quality of the encounter, as suggested by the finite form *slučilosja* 'it happened' in the original Old Russian text (Modern Russian *prišlos'* 'it fell to someone'. A proform *takovo* 'such a thing, the following' (Modern Russian *vot čto* 'this thing, the following') is a placeholder in the first clause for the rest of the sentence; it indicates what they saw. The remainder of the Old Russian sentence has been set off with a colon, although the syntax suggests a more direct connection: the next clause starts with the subordinating conjunction *idĕže* 'where'.[9]

The net effect is that no drastic rewriting is necessary to make the Modern Russian perfective acceptable, although the translation does opt for a colon to separate the clauses and leaves off the conjunction, breaking the connection between the verb and the object of seeing. The Modern Russian *vot čto nam prišlos' uvidet'* 'here is what it fell to us to see' is thus syntactically one step removed from what was actually seen: an ongoing process. The Old Russian uses a protoimperfective to match the duration of what was observed and is consequently more closely connected to the process sighted.

Neither aorists nor infinitives of *vidĕti*, then, show the same sort of anaspectual behavior they exhibited in early Old Russian. Instead, they consistently represent acts of indefinite or prolonged duration. Modern Russian perfectives in the translation indicate not that the acts are of brief duration, but rather that the act is involuntary or accidental, and they necessitate rewriting the sentence to avoid making it seem as if the act is indeed fleeting.

The situation is quite different if we turn to past active participles, which constitute the bulk of the examples for this verb (eighteen out of twenty-seven attested forms of *vidĕti*). Here thirteen out of eighteen forms are translated by a perfective verb, and virtually all of them represent an act whose most salient feature is that it indicates a change in previous perception, which gives rise to a reaction. These acts all entail a result stemming from the sight (actual or metaphorical) of an object. Metaphorical sightings—or, more accurately, perceptions—are found in (6) and (7), where the Modern Russian has a perfective verb from a different root (respectively *ubedivšis'* 'having convinced himself'; *zametiv* 'having noticed'). In (6), the 'when' clause (which lists all the reasons for the Christians' exhaustion and is omitted below) is summed up later by the perfective *urazumĕl* 'he grasped/understood'.

(6) **Видѣв** же царь казанский, яко уже изнемогло было зѣло войско християнское... егда же, яко рѣх, **уразумѣл** сие яко царь ихъ, такъ и вне града бусурманские воеводове утружение войска нашего, тогда тѣм силнѣе и частѣйше отовнѣе наѣзжали и из града исходили. (242)
'*When* the king of Kazan' *saw (vidĕv)* that the Christian soldiers were already very exhausted... when, as I have said, both their king and the Muslim generals

---

[9] Fennell's edition uses the same punctuation (1965: 130).

(7) А той Селиверстръ-пресвитеръ, еже преже даже не изгнанъ былъ, **видѣв** его, иже уже не по бозе всякие вещи начинает, противъ ему и наказуя много... (316)
'And this Silvester-presbyter, when he still had not yet been banished, *having seen (vidĕv)* that he [the tsar] was already starting to do all sorts of things contrary to God's will, [would] also lecture him frequently...'

The remainder of the examples all concern things which could be physically sighted by the subject. They have different reflections in the Modern Russian translation; in (8)-(10), the translation has a present verbal adverb or a prepositional phrase, interpreting the result as beginning while the object is still in sight.

(8) **Видѣвше** же сие *(при виде этого)*, абие совѣтоваше цареви послати по древо спасенное до Москвы... (248)
'*Having seen (OR vidĕvše/MoR pri vidĕ ètogo)*[10] this, they immediately advised[11] the tsar to send to Moscow for the Holy Wood...'

(9) Егда же **видѣв** *(видя)*, яко не возможе уже помощи собѣ, тогда на едину сторону отобраша женъ и детей своихъ... (254)
'When he *saw (OR vidĕv/MoR vidja^I)* that he could no longer help himself, then he cleared his women and children off to one side...'

(10) ...они же, не послушав, **видевше** *(видя)* явственный божий гнѣвъ, на них пущенный, а нашимъ подающе помощь. (284)
'...and they, having disobeyed, *saw (OR videvše/MoR vidja^I)* the manifest wrath of God released on them and helping our troops.'[12]

In other instances, the Modern Russian translation uses a past verbal adverb or a perfective past tense form to mark the moment of perception or understanding as occurring only after the sighting has concluded, as in (11) and (12).

(11) **Видѣвше** же *(увидев)*, бусурманы и ради бы назад к лѣсу... (244)
'*Having seen (OR vidĕvše/MoR uvidev^P)* [this], the Muslims would gladly [have gone] back to the forest...'

---

[10] The form marked OR renders the Old Russian verb; the one marked MoR gives the Modern Russian equivalent, marked with a superscript for aspect, from the parentheses following the form in the Old Russian text.

[11] Here I read *sovětovaša* 'they advised [aorist]' for *sovětovaše* 'he was advising [imperfect]'.

[12] Fennell reads it as a pluperfect: "for they *had seen* the manifest wrath of God which had been visited upon the people of Narva" (1965: 113). This is a plausible reading, but not a necessary one.

(12) Народи же руские, **видевше** (увидело), иже стѣны меские пусты, абие устремишася чрез реку... (284)
'The Russian people, *having seen (OR videvše/MoR uvidelo^P)* that the city walls were deserted, immediately headed across the river...'

On the face of it, then, the verb *viděti* presents evidence for anaspectuality only in the past participle, where it draws no regular distinction between acts with duration and those without. I propose that the past participle of the simplex *viděti* effectively serves as the participle for the prefixed verb *uviděti* as well, which is found only in the non-past and perfect tenses here. In effect, the past participle of *viděti* is a "frozen form," possibly thanks to its widespread usage in Old Russian and the innovative, not entirely literary feel of the prefixed *uviděti*. Another contributing factor is that in virtually all meanings, 'see' is lexically punctual, implying a range of possible durations, from an instantaneous completion of a perception to a prolonged state.

The verb *slyšati* 'hear' provides an instructive contrast. It is attested eight times, with three of those attestations being past active participles. However, the prefixed form *poslyšati* is attested twice, and the form *uslyšati* six times, meaning that the prefixed form is used as frequently as the simplex, which was not the case with *viděti* (where the simplex appeared twenty-seven times, versus only three appearances of the prefixed form). With *uslyšati*, the past active participle appears twice, and its usage is indistinguishable from that of the unprefixed verb. If there are contextual or pragmatic differences between the use of *slyšav* in (13) and *uslyšavše* in (14), then those distinctions are quite fine.

(13) И тѣ слова **слышав** (услышав) от святаго, исповѣдахом ему по ряду. (264)
'And *having heard (OR slyšav/MoR uslyšav^P)* these words from the holy man, we relayed them to him in turn.'

(14) **Услышавше** же сие, Силиверстъ и Алексѣй начаша молити... (310)
'*When they heard (uslyšavše)* this, Silvester and Alexej began to pray...'

A similar case can be made for the past participles *slyšavše* 'having heard' in (15) and *uslyšavše* 'having heard' in (16). Each represents a completed event that causes another event to occur at a later point in time.

(15) Клеветницы же, **слышавше** (узнав), иже и тамо в чести имѣют оныя мниси его, сего ради завистию разсѣдаеми, ово завидяще мужу славы, ово боящися... и оттуды похватиша его и завезоша на Соловки... (316)
'The slanderers, *having heard/learned (OR slyšavše/MoR uznav^P)* that there his monks held [him] in honor, were beside themselves with jealousy, some envying the man his fame, others fearing... and from there they seized him and carried him off to Solovki...'

(16) Егда же о смерти его **услышавше**, клеветницы возопиша цареви: «Се твой изменикъ самъ себе здалъ ядь смертоносный и умре.» (314-6)

'*Having heard (uslyšavše)* about his death, the slanderers cried out to the tsar, "Behold, your traitor has now himself taken a deadly poison and died." '

Example (17), in contrast, uses the past participle to express an act that simply occurred in the past, without reference to subsequent events.

(17) «Первие, нежели отдани суть епистоли наши, мню, благочестие твое **слышавше** *(слышало)*, яковъ здѣ мятеж творити дерзнула неправда». (316)

' "Your honor already *heard (OR slyšavše/MoR slyšalo¹)*, I believe, before our epistles were sent off, what sort of disturbance untruths have managed to cause here.' "

All of the forms above, with the exception of (17), are replaced by perfectives in the Modern Russian translation. If (14) and (16) indicate a more immediate connection, both temporally and syntactically, between the act of hearing and the result, then in (13) and (15), a sequence of events clearly exists, but the verb form serves to summarize and mark the end of a previous speech rather than to advance the narrative.

The point of this exercise is that while forms like *viděv* 'having seen', *slyšav* 'having heard' continue to have anaspectual functions, in the latter verb the protoperfective functions are fulfilled by participles of protoperfective forms. In other verbs, like *voevati* 'make war', they have virtually disappeared altogether (there are no occurrences of *voevav* 'having made war' in this text, although the present participle *vojujušče* 'making war' is found five times). In the latter category we can also find verbs like *stojati* 'stand' (one past active participle vs. nine present active participles, out of a total of forty-four attestations) and *ležati* 'lie' (no past participles vs. ten present participles out of a total of twenty-eight attestations). While many atelic predicates have aorist forms, I have already shown that aorist usage does not correspond to perfectivity in a binary aspectual system. Forms like *viděvše* 'having seen' and the occasional attestations of *slyšavše* 'having heard' are best thought of as fossilized forms, mandatory in the case of *viděti* 'see' and optional in the case of *slyšati* 'hear', that recall a former aspectual indifference but do not express it themselves. Where an opposition between prefixed and simplex participles has come into being, as with *slyšav–uslyšav* 'having heard', the variation may develop a distribution based on textual or discourse principles that at least partially mirrors changes occurring in the aspectual system at large.[13]

---

[12] It is interesting to note that the past active participle form *videv* 'having seen' is still at least marginally acceptable in Modern Russian, since it does show up once in the translation.

8.3. TESTS FOR ASPECTUALITY

Although I have established the existence of a more or less grammatical system of aspect for fifteenth-century texts, I did this almost entirely on a semantic basis. I will now put the *History* through some of the formal Modern Russian aspect tests—both grammatical and contextual—to see how Kurbskij's Russian matches up to later and earlier models of aspect. Some of the tests that will be relevant are the existence of a compound future tense restricted to certain (i.e. imperfective) verbs; the appearance of a historical present tense formed from protoimperfective verbs, as opposed to the protoperfective verbs used in normal preterite discourse; and the strict conformity of verbs to one or another aspect, as opposed to an ambivalence that comes from competing lexical factors.

8.3.1. The compound future with *budu* + infinitive

The presence or absence of this form is considered the aspectual test *par excellence* in Modern Russian. All imperfective verbs have it, if only marginally; no perfective verbs do, and the test is a purely morphological one. None of the earlier texts showed clear signs of this form being used as a future tense.[14] My sample from the *History,* however, has two clear examples of this future tense and three questionable examples. Example (18) has two forms of the verb *iměti* 'have' with future reference in a progressive context.[15]

(18)   «И аще хощеши самодержець быти, не держи собѣ совѣтника ни единаго мудрѣйшаго собя, понеже самъ еси всѣхъ лутчши. Тако будеши твердъ на царстве и всѣхъ **имѣти будеши** в рукахъ своихъ. И аще **будеши имѣть**[16] мудрѣйшихъ близу собя, по нужде будеши послушенъ имъ.» (266)
   ' "And if you wish to be an absolute monarch, do not retain even a single advisor who is wiser than you, for you yourself are the best of all. In this way you will sit firmly on your throne and *you will have (iměti budeši)* everyone in your hands. But if *you (will) have (budeši iměť)* wiser men near you, out of necessity you will be obedient to them." '

The forms in (19) could be interpreted as compound futures, but alternate readings are possible.

---

[14] There are examples in the Chronicles of *budu, budeši* etc. with the perfect participle (the "l-participle"), but usually this occurs with protoperfective verbs; it is clearly closer to a future perfect.

[15] The absence of an overt future form in the translation is a peculiarity of the English conditional and does not imply anything about the Russian, which is clearly future in sense.

[16] Fennell gives a variant reading *budeši imel,* on the model of the Polish future (forms of *budu* + the perfect participle) (1965: 82).

(19) А чего же ради сие творяху? Того ради воистину, да не будетъ обличенна злость ихъ и **да невозбранно будетъ имъ** всеми нами **владѣти** и, суд превращающе, посулы **грабити** и другие злости **плодити** скверные, пожитки свои умножающе. (310)
'But why were they doing this? Truthfully, for this reason: so that their evil would not be discovered, and *so that there would be no impediment for them to rule (da nevozbranno budet" im" vladěti)* over us all, and, perverting justice, *to extract (grabiti)* bribes and *hatch (ploditi)* other disgraceful evils, multiplying their own property.'[17]

(19a) *tr:* Но ради чего делали они это? Ради того, поистине говоря, чтобы злоба их не была обличена и **чтобы могли** они беспрепятственно **господствовать** над нами и, извращая суды, **вымогать** посулы, **плодить** другие скверные преступления и **умножать** свою собственность. (311)
'But why were they doing this? Truthfully, for this reason: so that their evil would not be discovered, and *so that they could without impediment rule (čtoby mogli oni besprepjatstvenno gospodstvovat')* over us, and, perverting justice, *to extract (vymogat')* bribes and *hatch (plodit')* other disgraceful crimes and multiply their own property.'

The Modern Russian translation in (19a) neither supports nor denies a compound future reading for the sentence; on the one hand, it seems to imply a compound future reading by shunting the Old Russian dative subject into the nominative and reading the adverb *nevozbranno* 'unimpededly' as modifying the verb *vladěti* 'rule' instead of as an independent predicate, but on the other hand it hedges by injecting the notion of possibility (*čtoby oni mogli* 'so that they would be able') instead of futurity. The Old Russian permits a different interpretation: the infinitives are not part of a compound future but rather are the complements of the predicate *nevozbranno budet"* 'it will be unimpeded'.

Still, (19) raises interesting questions. It may be that (18) and (19) represent different stages in the formation of the compound future tense. Example (19)—which is an older usage, well-attested in Old Russian texts—shows a potential situation that, given a bit of syntactic reinterpretation, yields a greater focus on the infinitive rather than the adverb as predicate. Example (18) shows this combination of *budu* with infinitive already morphologized as a form of the verb. It suggests that the creation of the compound future tense may be a type of univerbation, where elements originally syntactically subordinated to other sorts of predicates become syntactically subordinate to the verb instead.

---

17 The *Monuments* edition reads: *i drugie zlosti ploditi, skvernye požitki svoi umnožajušče* 'to hatch other evils, multiplying their own disgraceful property.' However, its translation (in 19a) follows the more logical punctuation above given in Fennell (1965: 152).

8.3.2. The historical present

One of the tests cited both by Maslov and Forsyth as proof of the existence of aspectual pairing is the ability to convert an account of a past act into the present tense using different verbs. This differentiates the Russian historical present from the English, which utilizes the same verbs in both.

Past: "He *stood* up, *went* over to the window, and *looked* out."

Hist. Present: "He *stands* up, *goes* over to the window, and *looks* out."

According to Forsyth, the verbs in the new utterance are imperfective partners of any protoperfective verbs in the original utterance. Maslov uses this test to different effect. He notes that the result is more or less an aspectual pair, but he objects that for many verbs, there may be more than one possible imperfective partner, casting doubt on the sacred notion of the "pair" as a complementary whole and suggesting that many commonly accepted "pairs" may be related by lexical aspect as well as by grammatical aspect.

We can, however, accept Forsyth's point that the historical present test is the most ironclad proof of pairedness that can reasonably be expected, keeping in mind that grammatical aspect may in many respects be subordinate to lexical aspectual considerations in Modern Russian as well. Instead of using the historical present test as an absolute indicator of grammatical pairing, I will use it in this section to determine how close the Old Russian system of this text is to the Modern Russian system.

The historical present occurs frequently in Kurbskij's writing. Several extended samples of it are given below. In all the examples, as might be expected, prefixed derived verbs (secondary imperfectives) are prominent. Sometimes they represent a sequence of acts, as in (20) and (21), where a series of past events are linked causally and temporally.

(20) Что же по сем царь нашъ **начинает**? Егда же уже оборнился божиею помощию, храбрыми своими ото окрѣсных враговъ его, тогда **воздаетъ** имъ: тогда **платитъ** презлыми за предобрѣшие, прелютыми за превозлюбленнѣйшеѣ, лукавствы и хитролествы за простые и верные ихъ службы. А яко же сие **начинаетъ**? Сице: первие **отгоняетъ** дву мужей оныхъ от себя предреченных... (310)
'What does our tsar *begin to do (načinaet)* after this? When he has already defended himself—with God's help—with his bravest men against his nearby enemies, then *he returns the favor (vozdaet")*: then *he pays them back (platit")* for their kindest of deeds with the most evil of deeds, for the most loving of deeds with the cruelest of deeds, for their simple and true service with perfidy and cunning. And how *does he begin (načinaet")* this? Here is how: first, *he banishes (otgonjaet")* from his court the two men mentioned earlier...'

(21) И что же еще ктому первие **начинаетъ** и **дѣлает**? **Собираетъ** соборище — не токмо весь сенатъ свой мирский, но и духовныхъ всехъ... **призываетъ**, и ктому **присовокупляетъ** прелукавыхъ некоторыхъ мнихов... И **посаждаетъ** ихъ близу себя, благодарнѣ послушающе ихъ... Что же на том соборище **производятъ**? Чтут, пописавши, вины оныхъ мужей заочне. (314)

'And what else *does* he then *embark upon (načinaet")* and *do (dĕlaet)* first of all? He *convenes (sobiraet")* a council: he *summons (prizyvaet)* not only his whole civic senate, but all the priests as well... and then *adds* several most treacherous monks... And he *seats (posaždaet")* them near himself, and gratefully obeys them... So what *do they make happen (proizvodjat)* at this council? Having written them down, they *read off (čtut)* the crimes of these men in their absence.'

Sometimes events in the historical present are connected logically but not necessarily temporally, as in (22) and (23). Here the acts probably do not follow one another; one may praise people and request oaths of them at the same time one is loving them, as in (22); and making war, invading a country, and capturing prisoners are all part of the same campaign and do not happen in any particular relative order, as in (23).

(22) Царь же, напився от окоянныхъ со сладостнымъ ласканиемъ смешанного смертоносного яду и самъ лукавства, паче же глупости, наполнився, **похваляетъ** совѣтъ и **любитъ** и **усвояетъ** ихъ в дружбу и присягами себѣ и ихъ **обязуетъ**... (312)

'The tsar, having drunk of the deadly poison mixed with sweet flattery from those cursed ones, and having filled himself with treachery, or more nearly stupidity, *praises (poxvaljaet)* the[ir] council and *loves (ljubit")* and *accepts (usvojaet")* them as his friends and *binds (objazuet")* them to himself with oaths...'

(23) Паки **ополчаются** противъ его оставшие князи казанские... и **воюютъ** зелнѣ, не токмо на градъ на Казанский приходяще с великих лѣсовъ, но и на землю Муромскую и Новаграда Нижняго **наѣзжаютъ** и **пленятъ**. (272)

'Again the remaining princes of Kazan' *take up arms (opolčajutsja)* against him... and they *fight (vojujut")* bitterly, marching not only against the fortress of Kazan' from the great forests, but they also *ride against (naĕzžajut")* and *take captives in (plenjat")* the land[s] of Murom and Nižnij Novgorod.'

If the forms in (20)-(23) are true historical presents in the modern sense of the word, they should have the same meaning and function as the forms in (24)-(34), which are all past tenses formed from the same verbs or related protoperfective verbs.[18] Comparing the forms in (24)-(34) with the forms in (20)-(23) does in fact

---

[18] If no corresponding form is given in (24)-(34) for a verb found in (20)-(23), then no such form appeared in the data collected.

yield approximately the same results as would be found in Modern Russian: a certain number of the verbs display no discernable shift in meaning or shape of the act from past to historical present, while others display a more evident shift in meaning, which in Modern Russian indicates that the pairing is lexical in nature rather than aspectual.

Examples (20) and (24) contain the verbs *otgonjati–otognati*, both in the meaning 'banish, drive away'.

(24) А князя Семена ото очей своихъ **отогналъ** даже до смерти его. (220)
'And Prince Simeon *he banished (otognal")* from his sight even unto his death.'

In both instances, the predicate is telic and is performed on a small number of persons (one person in the perfect in (24), two people in the non-past in (20)). The non-past *načinaet"* also appears in (20) in the meaning 'starts out'; a lexically identical usage appears in (25) with the aorist *načaša* 'started out'.

(25) И **начаша** иноко, совѣтоваша ему, сирѣчь, да идешь паки за Оку, а оттуды к Москвѣ... (278)[19]
'And *they took a* different *tack (načaša)*; they advised him, saying: you should cross the Oka again, and go from there to Moscow.'

Neither has an object, and both indicate a punctual (instantaneous) beginning of a series of acts. A similar analysis applies to the pair *opolčati sja–opolčiti sja* 'arm oneself' in (23) and (26), and the pair *usvojati–usvoiti* 'win over' in (22) and (27). In (26) and (27) the aorist is used, as opposed to the earlier non-past forms.

(26) Егда же разсмотриша и увѣдаша о насъ, **ополчишася** противу насъ. (232)
'When they had looked around and realized we were there, *they took up arms (opolčiša)* against us.'

(27) Егда же **усвоиша** тую землю ко христову наречению, тогда обещашася возложение господеви и похвалу имяни пречистые его богоматере. (306)[20]
'When *they won* this land *over (usvoiša)* to the name of Christ, then they promised its rendering unto the Lord and praise in the name of His immaculate Mother.'

---

[19] Fennell reads from a different ms.: *i načaša inoko sovetovati emu* 'and they began to advise him differently'.

[20] Fennell reads from a different ms.: *togda obeščašasja v vozloženie Gospodevi, i na poxvalu imjani prečistye Ego Bogomatere* 'they pledged themselves to the service of the Lord and to the praise of the name of His most pure Mother' (1965: 144-5).

A similar analysis applies to *proizvoditi–proizvesti* 'produce' in (21) and (28) and *poxvaliti–poxvaljati* 'praise' in (22) and (29).

(28) Царь же нашъ со всѣми сигклиты и стратилаты вниде в совѣт о семъ и совѣт в конецъ добръ, благодати ради божии, **произведе**: ... (242)
'Our tsar, with all his senators and commanders, entered into council about this, and by the grace of God he *produced (proizvede)* in the end a good decision: ...'

(29) ...и не токмо, рече, богъ совѣтъ Рагуила, тестя его, **похвалил**, но и в законъ написалъ, яко пространнѣе в предреченныхъ его словесах зрится. (268)
'...and, it is said, not only did God *praise (poxvalil)* the advice of Raguel, his [Moses'] father-in-law, but wrote it into the law, as is more throroughly seen in his aforementioned words.'

In all of these cases, the meaning of the derived protoimperfective used in the historical present is virtually indistinguishable from that of the protoperfective verb used in a past tense (the aorist in (28); the perfect in (29)).

The situation with *ljubiti* 'love', *voevati* 'fight, make war', *pleniti* 'capture' and the past tense forms found in (30)-(34) is slightly different. For instance, the non-past *ljubit"* 'he loves' in (22) does not describe the same sort of action as the past participle *vozljubivša* 'having fallen for' in (30).

(30) Внегда же путь господень оставили и вѣру церковную отринули, многаго ради преизлишняго покоя, и **возлюбивша** же и ринушася во пространный и широкий путь... тогда от того имъ приключишася. (294)[21]
'When they left the Lord's path and rejected the church's faith for a great and most excessive tranquillity, *they* both *took a liking (vozljubivša)* to and hurled themselves down the wide and easy path... then for this reason these things happened to them.'

The historical present *ljubit"* 'he loves' gives no indication that the act has a beginning or end; rather, it suggests that the tsar's love for them was an ongoing state. As such, it is best matched with a past tense form *of the same verb,* as found in the perfect *ljubil"* in (31).

(31) Се таков нашъ царь былъ, поки **любилъ** окола себя добрых и правду совѣтующих... (278)

---

[21] Fennell reads from a different ms.: *mnogago radi preizlišnjago pokoja i vozljubivša že rinušasja vo sprostrannyj i širokij put'*... 'because they *loved* excessive tranquillity, they rushed on to the broad wide way...', but calls the variant in his text "obscure" (1965: 128-129). More accurate might be: '*having taken a liking* to excessive tranquillity...'

'Such was our tsar, so long as *he loved (ljubil")* the men around him who were good and counselled the truth...'

A similar case should be made for the historical present form *vojujut"* 'they fight/make war' in (23); it does not express the same meaning as the protoperfective perfect *povoeval* 'started a war' in (32), but rather is closer to the aorist/imperfect form of the same verb, *voevax"* 'I waged/ was waging war' in (33).

(32) Он же **не повоевал** *(не начав военных действий)*, оттуды возвратился к Ордѣ со всѣми силами своими... (288)
'He *did not start a war (OR ne povoeval/MoR ne načav^P voennyx dejstvij)*, but instead returned to the Horde with all his forces.'

(33) И **воевахъ** потомъ тыждень цѣлый и возвратихомся съ великими богатствы и корыстьми. (302)
'And *I waged war (voevax")* then for a whole week and we returned with great riches and booty.'

A more subtle difference occurs between non-past *plenjat* 'they take captives' in (23) and the protoperfective aorist *popleniša* 'they took captives' in (34).

(34) ...яко самых побиша, такоже женъ и детей ихъ немало **поплениша**, и христианских людей от работы свободили немало и возвратишася восвояси здравы. (292)²²
'...they both killed those very ones [the Tatars] and *captured (popleniša)* no few of their women and children, and freed many Christian people from slavery and returned home in good health.'

The form *plenjat* is treated as an atelic act; prisoners are taken, but nothing is said about them. The act's importance is in the behavior of the men who took prisoners. In (34), however, the fact that many people were actually imprisoned is emphasized; the act is telic and thus not to be equated with the act in (23).

A familiar pattern is taking shape here. Telic predicates perform as expected in an aspectual test, where atelic predicates fail to show pairing. However, atelic predicates do participate in the past–historical present opposition; in other words, they are aspectual, even if they are not paired. This situation mimics the modern one described in Maslov 1948, indicating that grammaticality is present in Old Russian aspect, at least to the extent we wish to admit it for Modern Russian.

8.3.3. Monoaspectuality, biaspectuality, and anaspectuality

In chapter 4, I established a number of criteria for finding a verb to be anaspectual. Among them were semantic criteria: the ability to express with the

---

22 Fennell reads from a different ms.: *pleniša* 'took many of their wives and children prisoner'. This is closer in meaning to the historical present *plenjat* from the same verb.

same verb different lexical aspects in both perfective-type and imperfective-type contexts (a verb might have both inceptive and stative meanings, for instance) and the expression of a range of meanings that are not immediately classifiable as one or another aspect. Another criterion was morphological: the failure of prefixation to effect a change in aspect.

A biaspectual verb, by contrast, would have a single lexical shape (not varying Aktionsarten) and be used in two types of situations: those that can be clearly identified as perfective and those that can clearly be identified as imperfective. The criteria therefore distinguish three degrees of aspectuality: monoaspectuality (in which each verb has only one aspectual assignment, as is the norm in Modern Russian), biaspectuality and anaspectuality.

Using these criteria, I identified a number of verbs in the Old Russian of the Chronicles that had anaspectual predicates and made predictions about which verbs were likely to have anaspectual traits based on the lexical shape of their predicates. However, in the Old Russian of the sixteenth-century *History*, there is no further basis for claiming that predicates of these verbs are anaspectual. A quick examination of several of these verbs gives evidence of consistent aspectual behavior, with examples to the contrary being few and far between.

The verb *stojati* 'stand', for example, has only one example (out of forty-four) that could reasonably represent a perfective-type act, and it is with a past active participle, which we have already identified as a type of contextual idiom. The remainder of the forms all describe an ongoing state, whether open-ended or limited in time by a specific phrase of duration. There are no clearly aorist forms: some of the imperfects are ambiguous and could be interpreted as aorists, although none of them express an Aktionsart characteristic of anaspectuality, such as inception, resultativity, or exhaustion. There are only two prefixed forms of the verb found in this text: *predstojati* 'serve' and *ustojati* 'remain, endure'. The former retains its protoimperfective character, possibly because its religious overtones mark it as a Church Slavic item not subject to the standard rules of the aspectual system. The latter appears twice, both times with a perfective sense. Compare this to the infinitive and pluperfect forms of *ustojati* from the Chronicles reprinted respectively in (35) and (36).

(35)   аще ли вы будет(е) кр(е)стъ цѣловати к братьи или г кому. а ли оуправивъше сердце свое. на немже можете **оустояти**. тоже цѣлуите. и цѣловавше блюдѣте. (Primary Chronicle, 245)
'if you will swear oaths to your brothers or anyone else, then, having tested your heart as to whether you can *depend (oustojati)* on it, swear the oaths and having done so, be on your guard.'[23]

(36)   и стояша днии много. ни король поступи к Галичю. ни Олговичи. король же омиривъ Ляхы. поиде за горы. Олговичи же поидоша назадъ. **бяху** бо **ся** обои **оустояли**. (Suzdal Chronicle, 427)

---

[23] This sentence appeared as example (86) in chapter 4.

'and they stood for many days; neither did the King proceed to Galicia, nor did Oleg's men. When the king had subdued the Poles, he went across the mountains. Oleg's men went back, for *they had* both *held up (bjaxu sja oustojali)* against each other.'

In (35), the reading could be durative or inceptive; the context does not specify, and this sort of ambiguity is typical of anaspectual forms. The form in (36) expresses duration in a more straightforward fashion. The evidence from the Chronicles, then, suggests a hesitation in aspectual assignment. Sreznevskij confirms this lack of aspectual commitment: the definitions for *ustojati* are *ostat'sja^P stojat'*, *ne dvinut'sja^P*, *ustojat'^{P}*, *prevozmoč'^{P}*, *podčinjat'^{I} svoej vlasti* 'remain^P standing, not move^P, hold up^P, overcome^P, have^I under one's power'.

The numbers of examples are not large enough here to be convincing by themselves, but this development is not limited to the verb *stojati*. Similar developments occur with the verbs *ležati* 'lie', *ljubiti* 'love', *stereči* 'guard', *mniti* 'think, deem', *iměti* 'have', and so forth.

In chapter 5, I examined a type of "biaspectuality" that turned out to be a refutation of the "one verb, one aspect" rule that, by and large, holds in Modern Russian. The "biaspectuality" of verbs like *vniti* 'go into', *vtešči* 'flow into' in Old Russian was seen to result from the confluence of two differently-shaped predicates, one telic and one atelic, in a single verb. Looking in the *History* for geographic descriptions—where atelic usage of these verbs was reasonably frequent in the Chronicles—we find a different aspectual picture. In every instance, Kurbskij admits only two possibilities. First, a simplex verb may appear. If motion is expressed, then it is determinate, as in the non-past forms in (37).

(37) ...поѣхал первие в монастырь Троицы живоначалные... яже **лежитъ** от Москвы двадесять миль на великой дорозе, которая **идет** к Студеному морю. (262)
'...first he went to the monastery of the life-giving Trinity... which *lies (ležit")* twenty miles from Moscow on the great road which *leads (idet)* to the Arctic Sea.'

Second, a prefixed derived verb may appear, as in the non-past forms in (38) and (39).

(38) И на третей же день двигнушася в путь, и преидохомъ четыре мили аки за 3 дни, бо тамо немало рѣкъ, еже **впадаютъ** в Волгу... (234)
'And on the third day they set off, and we covered four miles in about three days, for there are many rivers which *fall into (vpadajut")* the Volga...'

(39) ...тѣ живут башкирцы вверхъ великие рѣки Камы в лѣсах, яже в Волгу **впадает** ниже Казани дванадесят миль. (260)
'...these Baškirians live in the forests up the great river Kama, which *falls (vpadaet)* into the Volga twelve miles below Kazan'.'

Prefixed derived forms and simplex forms can, of course, be mixed in a single sentence, as happens with the non-past forms in (40).[24]

(40) Под самое мѣсто **течетъ** и **впадаетъ** под уголную вежу в Казан-реку. А **течетъ** *(вытекает)* изъ ѣзера, Кабана глаголемаго, немалого, которое езеро **кончится** аки полверсты от мѣста. (236)
'It *flows (tečet")* outside the city proper and *falls (vpadaet")* into the River Kazan' below the corner tower. And it *flows (OR tečet"/MoR vytekael¹)* out of the lake called Kaban, a decent-sized one, a lake which *ends (končitsja)* about a half-verst from the city.'

There are two important points that come forth from these examples. First, the ability of the simple prefixed form to express both telic and atelic meanings has been reduced; now the simplex form or the derived form conveys the atelic meaning. Hence, the organization of aspect is no longer conducted on a sublexical level, governed by the lexical character of predicates. This leads to the second point. To express a stative act or an atelic action, a verb must fit into a particular grammatical and morphological category; these two lexical categories have become features of imperfectivity, such that atelic acts are no longer exempt from aspectual assignment. The evidence from geographic descriptions shows that Kurbskij's aspectual system in many basic ways resembles the one in Modern Russian.

8.4. THE RANGE OF THE OLD RUSSIAN SIMPLEX

In chapters 6 and 7 I showed that the spread of prefixed derived forms is one of the predominant developments in later Old Russian aspect. Verbs whose "aspectual" opposition was actually a lexical aspectual opposition, contrasting a simplex verb with a prefixed form whose denotative meaning was different, continued the process of creating verbs by suffixation of the prefixed form. These new suffixed forms hewed more closely to the meaning of the prefixed form and eventually supplanted the simplex form in certain (or all) meanings. Morphologically speaking, then, the history of aspect demonstrates the expansion of the derived forms' spheres of usage at the expense of the simplexes they were formed from. However, the new forms did not immediately supplant the simplexes in all contexts and meanings.

Kurbskij's text, like the other texts examined in this study, has a relatively large number of simplex forms replaced by derived forms in the translation and relatively few derived forms that are replaced by simplex forms in the translation. There are fifty-three simplexes in the Old Russian text that correspond to a Modern Russian derived form (twenty-three with a {-vaj-} suffix, thirty with an {-aj-} suffix), and

---

24 The verb *končiti* is not attested in other texts of this survey, nor does Sreznevskij recognize its existence. The prevailing East Slavic forms appear to be *skončavati* or *končati* as protoimperfective and *skončati* for protoperfective. The use of *končiti* as a protoimperfective is probably a Polonism (as in Modern Polish *kończyć*, Modern Czech *končit*, which are both imperfectives).

only seven derived forms in the Old Russian text that correspond to a Modern Russian simplex. In addition, there are seven forms where an Old Russian {-aj-} suffix corresponds to a Modern Russian {-vaj-} suffix, and one Old Russian verb with a {-vaj-} suffix corresponding to a Modern Russian verb with an {-aj-} suffix. The general direction of change is evident from these examples.

As in previous discussions, I will approach the question of the spread of derived protoimperfectives from two viewpoints. I will examine the distribution of forms in Kurbskij's text, as well as comparing discrepancies between the Old Russian text and its modern translation. The caveats mentioned in section 7.5 will hold for this discussion as well.

8.4.1. The greater specificity of prefixes

Prefixed verbs usually offer a more specific meaning than the simplexes they are derived from. Often this greater specificity comes from the addition of a directional component to the act or a limit on the temporal contour of the act. The act conveyed by such a prefixed verb can sometimes also be subsumed in the meaning of the simplex, but many simplexes in fact eventually restrict their usage to exclude those areas covered by their common prefixed derivatives.

Many of the prefixal pairs are already well established in Kurbskij's text and have already assumed a range of meanings and usages similar to what they have in Modern Russian; examples are *sobirati–sobrati* 'collect', *načinati–načati* 'begin', *razrušati–razrušiti* 'destroy'. These particular prefixal formations have a long history. With other prefixal pairs, however, an Aktionsart relationship between derived, prefixed and simplex form is still evident. For instance, the simplex verb *terpěti* 'suffer' is attested twice in this sample. In (41), it indicates a process expressed in the non-past: on the day Christ was crucified, all Christians suffer along with him.

(41) И на самый день, в онже господь нашъ Иисусъ Христос за человѣческий род плотию пострадалъ, и в той день, ему по силе своей кождый християнинъ подобяся, страстемъ его **терпитъ**, в посте и в воздержанию пребывающе... (282)
'And on the very day on which our Lord Jesus Christ suffered in the flesh for the race of man, on that day, every Christian, in emulating him according to his ability, *suffers (terpit")* his passions, fasting and abstaining...'

It can also be used to sum up a state, as in (42), where the Germans send an emissary to the Livonian magistrate for help, saying that they cannot withstand the Muscovite assault. (The Modern Russian translation here is perfective for both the finite verb and the infinitive: *ne smožem*[P] *ustojat'*[P] 'we will not be able[P] to withstand[P]'.)

(42) «Аще, рече, не дадите помощи, мы от такой великие стрелбы не можемъ **терпѣти**, подадимъ град и мѣсто». (282)

' "If—he said—you do not give us help, *we cannot (ne možem")* withstand *(terpěti)* such a great assault; we will surrender the fortress and the city." '

The prefixed form *preterpěti* means 'withstand, suffer through'; the alteration to the lexical meaning is an alteration in the temporal structure of the act. The tribulations suffered by the subject are reanalyzed as having a finite range whose limits are reached and exceeded, ending the suffering. In (43), the monk Maksim is said to have survived many years of bondage and imprisonment; the prefixed perfect *preterpěl* indicates that his sufferings are now over, as is made explicit several sentences later.

(43) Много бо **претерпѣл** от отца его многолѣтных и тяжкихъ оков и многолѣтнаго заточения в прегорчайшихъ темницах, и других родов мученей искусил неповинне по зависти Даниила митрополита... (262)
'For at the hands of his father,[25] *he suffered through (preterpěl)* long years of harsh bondage and lengthy imprisonment in the very worst of prisons, and in his innocence experienced other types of tortures as a result of the Metropolitan Daniel's envy...'

Example (44) has a protoperfective verbal adverb under negation: a Muscovite, tortured by the Crimean khan, does not make it through the experience without revealing what he knows of the tsar's plans.

(44) Послѣди же, по несчастию, наиде дву, един же ему вся по ряду исповѣда, муки **не претерпѣвъ**, еже написали мудрые наши писари. (276)
'Finally, unfortunately, he found two, one of whom—*having failed to withstand (ne preterpěv")* the torture—told him everything in detail that our wise scribes had written down.'

The negated protoperfective indicates that the unnamed Muscovite did undergo torture; it is his failure to remain silent all the way through that is at issue. In (45), however, the prefixed derived present participle *preterpěvajušču* 'who withstands/ withstood' indicates that numerous sufferings were overcome; the context is iterative, and the act is assumed to have followed a pattern of repetition in which one hurdle after another is overcome.

(45) Много кратъ ото многихъ свѣтлыхъ мужей вопрошаемъ быхъ с великимъ стужанием, откуды сия приключишася такъ прежде доброму и нарочитому царю, многожды за отечество и о здравии своемъ не радящу, и в военныхъ вещахъ сопротивъ враговъ креста христова труды тяжкие и бѣды, и безчисленные поты **претерпѣва-ющу**, и прежде от всѣхъ добрую славу имущему. (218)

---

[25] Fennell notes that "his" father refers to Ivan the Terrible's father, Tsar Vasilij III (1965: 77).

'Many times I have been asked with great insistence by many illustrious men: how did all this come to pass to such a formerly good and well-respected tsar, who so many times for his kingdom's sake paid no mind to his own health, and *who* in military matters against the enemies of Christ's cross *withstood (preterpěvajušču)* innumerable trials and difficult labors and misfortunes, and who formerly enjoyed good repute with all?'

This is a prototypical pattern for a prefixed derived verb: as opposed to the relatively broad meaning of the simplex, the prefixed derived form conveys one specific interpretation of the possible temporal paths of the act, and as opposed to the prefixed form that is unsuffixed, the prefixed derived form is found in ongoing or repeated contexts.[26] This example is also prototypical in that the context is iterative; in both Old and Modern Russian, not all prefixed verbs that have an Aktionsart relationship to their simplex can actually form derived verbs, and those that can tend to appear in iterative or progressive contexts, not in generalized contexts.

In (41)-(45), the Old Russian simplex has an existing prefixed derived form, and this is the case for many such roots. In fact, in a great number of them, no simplex is attested in the sample, only a derived form. (Such is the case, for instance, with the causatives *utešati* 'comfort', *rasširjati* 'expand, widen', *ozdravljati* 'get better', *vozbuždati* 'incite, prompt', *ugotovljati sja* 'make ready', *ugoždati* 'satisfy, indulge, gratify', *uklonjati sja* 'avoid, give way', *ukrašati* 'adorn', *ukrepljati* 'support', among others.)

However, in a number of instances, no derived form is present in the Old Russian; instead, only a simplex and a prefixed form are found. One particularly good example of this phenomenon is the Old Russian verb *biti* 'strike, hit, kill'. In Kurbskij's text, it is attested with the prefixed forms *izbiti* 'slaughter, inflict a wound', *ubiti*, *pobiti* 'kill' but with no corresponding derived forms for these verbs. Instead, the simplex acts as a partial aspectual "pair" to the prefixed form, while the Modern Russian translation uses a prefixed derived form with greater lexical or temporal specificity. There are three different lexical meanings expressed here with present participles of *biti*. One describes fighting, as seen in (46); a second is striking something, as in 'striking the air' in (47). Both meanings are expressed in Old and Modern Russian with the simplex verb; the Old Russian forms are present participles.

(46)   Того бусурманы зѣло возбраняше, ово **биюще** со града, ово, вытекающе, вручь секошася. (238)[27]

---

[26] Of course, protoperfectives can be found in iterative contexts, but at this point in history, the prefixed derived form expresses repetition without the help of contextual features.

[27] Fennell reads from a different ms.: *togo busurmany zelo vozbraniša* 'this was fiercely contested by the Mussulmans' (1965: 40-41). This form (aorist, protoperfective) is aspectually atypical from a modern point of view, since it represents a temporally

'The Muslims did their best to fight this off; either *shooting (bijušče)* from the fastness, or, making sorties, they engaged in hand-to-hand combat.'

(47) Такоже и властели земли тоя... с печенеги вкупѣ высоко скачюще и воздухъ **биюще**, и так прехвалне и прегордѣ другъ друга пьяни восхваляюще... (294)
'Thus the rulers of this land... together with their lackeys *would* jump on high and *strike (bijušče)* the air, praising each other so lavishly and proudly when drunk...'

Two other meanings, 'wound' and 'kill', are expressed by the simplex *biti* in Old Russian, but in the Modern Russian translation occur with the prefixed derived verbal adverbs *izbivaja* 'wounding, slaughtering', *ubivaja* 'killing', as in (48)-(50). The Modern Russian translation 'kill' is warranted by other contextual information in (48) and (49), whereas (50) has a range of possible meanings.

(48) Потом поспѣшишася другия стратилаты с пѣшими нашими ручничными стрелцы и сопроша бусурмановъ яко конныхъ, такъ и пѣших, и гониша ихъ, **биюще** *(избивая)*, аже до самых врат грацких, и несколко живыхъ поимаша. (236-8)
'Then other generals hastened with our foot-musketeers and fell upon the Muslims, both cavalry and infantry, and they chased them, *slaughtering (OR bijušče/MoR izbivaja^I)* them, as far as the very gates of the stronghold, and captured several of them alive.'

(49) Христианское же воинство гониша за ними, **биюще** *(избивая)* ихъ, и яко на пол-2 мили трупия бусурманского множество лежаше, и ктому аки тысечю живыхъ поимаше. (244)
'The Christian troops chased after them, *slaughtering (OR bijušče/MoR izbivaja^I)* them, and for a mile and a half there were a multitude of Muslim corpses lying [there], and in addition they captured about a thousand alive.'

(50) Наше же войско великое з горы оные да потиснуша ихъ зѣло, паче же задний конецъ татарского полку, секуще и **бьюще** *(убивая)*. (254)
'Our great army was pressing them sorely down from that mountain, especially the rear section of the Tatar regiment, hacking at them and *wounding/ slaughtering (OR bijušče/MoR ubivaja^I)* them.'

The derived forms in the translation indicate the more grammatical nature of aspectual relations in Modern Russian; apparently, even at the end of the sixteenth century, Old Russian "aspectual" oppositions were often lexical aspectual oppositions instead.

---

limited, failed act with a perfective (however, see section 8.5), but it does at least have a 3. pl. form.

Further examples of this phenomenon can be found with other simplexes. Although the prefixed derived verb *otděljati* 'divide, separate from' is found in (51), it is used in the historical present in recounting how the tsar's new advisors helped him by separating him from his old advisors.

(51) Паче же и согласных его на зло прежде бывшихъ овых **отделяют** от него (яж быша зѣло люты), овых же уздают и воздержатъ страхом бога живаго. (226)
'Furthermore, of those who had formerly been in agreement with him in evil, they *separate (otděljajut)* some from him (those who had been especially cruel), and others they restrain and hold back with fear of the living God.'

In the static, geographical description found in (52)—which is a footnote to the main text—the simplex still prevails in the Old Russian version but not in the Modern Russian translation, where it is replaced by the prefixed derived form *otdeljaet^I* 'separates off^I'. Both original and translation use the non-past tense.

(52) **Танаис по-римски, а по-роску Дон, яже Еуропу **дѣлит** *(отделяет)* со Асиею, яко космографии описуют в землемерителной книзѣ... (228)
'**The Tanais in Latin, and in Russian the Don, which *divides (OR dělit/MoR otdeljaet^I)* Europe from Asia, as the cosmographers describe in their book of geography...'

Temporal lexical modifications in the Modern Russian forms are seen in (53) and (54).

(53) Егда же уже обронился божиею помощию, храбрыми своими ото окрѣсных враговъ его, тогда воздаетъ имъ: тогда **платитъ** *(отплачивает)* презлыми за предобрешие... (310)
'When he has already defended himself—with God's help—with his bravest men against his nearby enemies, then he returns the favor: then he *pays them back (OR platit"/MoR otplačivaet^I)* for their kindest of deeds with the most evil deeds...'[28]

(54) Тогда, глаголю, царь всюду прославляем был и земля руская доброю славою **цвѣла** *(расцветала)*, и грады предтвердыя аламанския разбивахуся... (298)
'At that time, I tell you, the tsar was celebrated everywhere, and the Russian land *blossomed (OR cvěla/MoR rascvetala^I)* with good renown, and the mightiest German citadels were laid low...'

In (53), the Old Russian uses the non-past of the simplex *platiti* 'pay', where the Modern Russian has the non-past of the more telic *otplačivat'^{I}* 'pay off^I'. In (54), the Old Russian uses the perfect of the simplex *cvesti* 'flower', where the Modern

---

[28] This passage was discussed in full as example (20).

Russian has the past tense of the more lexically specific *rascvetat'* 'be in full bloom¹'. Neither root is attested with any prefixed forms in Kurbskij's text.

Other similarly behaving verbs in this text are *liti* 'pour', *tvoriti* 'do, make', *rězati* 'slice', *uzdati* 'rein', *šeptati* 'whisper'.

8.4.2. Concrete vs. abstract meaning

Another way in which prefixed verbs can differ from simplex verbs is in the abstractness of the new verbs they create. While the final result may be a verb with a different temporal contour, the main effect of prefixation is a far-reaching semantic alteration of the verb. In this and following discussions, we will be concerned mainly with protoimperfective forms—that is, with simplex forms and derived prefixed forms—and we will leave aside simple prefixed forms, which are protoperfective. A good testing ground for the issues is Kurbskij's use of the simplex verb *pisati* 'write' and its derivative *opisovati* 'describe'. The simplex verb can refer to the existence of a text, as in the non-past form in (55).

(55) Яко и Златоусты **пишет** во епистоли своей ко Инокентию... (316)
 'As Chrysostom *writes (pišet)* in his letter to Innocent...'

Writing is most often mentioned as a process, usually a telic one, as opposed to a profession. Kurbskij several times makes reference to how long it would take him to write down everything he knows or has seen, as in (56) and (57); variations on this refrain are used to change topics or excuse glossing over a point.

(56) А естли **бы писал** по ряду, яко тамо под градом на кождый день дѣялося, того бы цѣлая книга была. (246)
 'And if *I wrote (by pisal)* about it in detail, what happened every day beneath the fortress, there would be a whole book of it.'

(57) «Аще бы из начала и по ряду рѣхъ, много бы о том **писати**, яко в предобрый рускихъ князей род всѣял диявол злые нравы...» (218)
 ' "If I began at the beginning and in detail, there would be much *to write (pisati)* about: how the devil sowed evil mores in the most excellent line of Russian princes..." '

Similar meanings are found in (60) and (61). The simplex also appears in (62) in a progressive context: the holy teachers were horrified when they wrote down the tortures performed on the saints, and the horror and writing are understood to be simultaneous.

The derived verb *opisovati* 'describe' is used only in a generalized context: it refers to facts that are already written down, similar to the context seen in (55).[29]

---

[29] There is no sharp distinction between the competing derived forms *opisovati, opisyvati*, and *opisavati* in Old Russian; although *opisyvat'* is the one that survives, the presence

Kurbskij mentions a description in an atlas—(58)—and the description of the Volhynians' bravery—(59). Both forms (respectively *opisujut, opisujetsja*) are non-past.

(58)   **Танаисъ по-римски, а по-роску Донъ, яже Еуропу дѣлитъ со Асиею, яко космографии **описуютъ** в землемерителной книзѣ... (228)
'**The Tanais in Latin, and in Russian the Don, which divides Europe from Asia, as the cosmographers *describe (opisujut)* in their book of geography...'[30]

(59)   А о тѣхъ волынцахъ не токмо въ крайникахъ мужество ихъ **описуется**, но и новыми повѣстьми храбрость ихъ свидѣтел-ствуется... (296)
'And about these Volhynians: their bravery *is described (opisujetsja)* not only in the chronicles, but their courage is also attested in recent stories...'

The Old Russian distinction between *pisati* 'write' and *opisovati* 'describe' is lexical, but it also falls into a larger category of concrete vs. abstract acts. It is notable that in Modern Russian the derived verb *opisyvat'*[I] 'describe[I]' has far more potential for describing progressive acts and acts that have a physical representation than the Old Russian form of this verb; the infinitives in (60)-(61) and the present participle in (62) are all translated by corresponding Modern Russian forms of *opisyvat'*[I].

(60)   Князь великий Василий Московский ко многимъ злымъ и сопротивъ закона божия дѣломъ своим и сие приложил. Иже и **писати** *(описывать)*, и исчитати, краткости ради книжицы сея, невмѣстно... (218)
'The Grand Prince of Moscow, Vasilij, added this to his many evil deeds and acts against God's laws. Which it is not fitting *to describe (OR pisati/MoR opisyvat'*[I]*)* and enumerate here, in the hopes of keeping this book short...'

(61)   ...сие премину и оставлю по ряду **писати** *(описывать)*, сокращения ради истории... (308)
'...this I will pass over and leave off *writing/describing (OR pisati/MoR opisyvat'*[I]*)* details, in order to condense the story...'

(62)   И аще святые великие учители ужасалися, **пишуще** *(описывая)*, от мучителей на святыхъ дерзаемые, колми паче намъ, грѣшнымъ, подобаетъ ужасатися, таковую трагедию возвѣщати! (220-222)
'And if the great holy teachers were appalled, *describing/writing (OR pišušče/ MoR opisyvaja*[I]*)* what was inflicted on the saints by their torturers, how much more appropriate it is for us sinners to be appalled, recounting such a tragedy!'

---

of adjectives like *neopisuemyj* 'indescribable' testifies to the existence of the *-ovati* form as well in an earlier stage of the language.

[30] Seen earlier as example (52).

It is possible that the act of writing as an act of description remained associated in Kurbskij's language with the physical act (*pisati*), whereas in the modern language the derived verb (*opisyvat'*) expresses both the physical and the abstract meaning with ease. The relationship between these two verbs shows how the Old Russian forms, even if both of them did in fact exist, may have a different relationship to each other and different spheres of usage than the same Modern Russian verbs.

Another case involves the simplex verb *braniti* 'defend' and the derived form *obranjati*, with an almost identical lexical meaning. The simplex *braniti* is used to describe physical defense in battle; it is often found in this text with the adverb *krěpce* 'fiercely', as seen in (63)-(65). The forms are respectively in the aorist tense, the imperfect tense, and the infinitive.

(63) ...и крепце **бронихомся**, яко и со гетманом его Даниломъ сведохом колко битвъ и две одержахомъ. (306)
'...and *we defended ourselves (bronixomsja)* fiercely, and we engaged in several battles with his hetman Daniil, and won two [of them].'

(64) Егда же приидоша во град внезапу такъ много воинства свежего, в пресветлые зброи оболченнаго, абие царь казанский со всѣмъ воинством начаша уступовати назад, обаче **браняшеся** *(оборонялись)* крѣпце. (254)
'When so many fresh troops clad in most brilliant armor suddenly came into the fortress, immediately the king of Kazan' with all his troops began to fall back, although *he defended himself (OR branjašesja/MoR oboronjalis'[1])* fiercely.'[31]

(65) Царь же со всѣми остатними затворился в дворе своемъ, нача **бронитися** *(обороняться)* крѣпце, аки еще на полторы годины биющеся. (254)[32]
'The king with all his remaining men locked himself in his courtyard; he began *to defend himself (OR bronitisja//MoR oboronjat'sja[1])* fighting on for about an hour and a half.'

The reflexive form is used to indicate defense of oneself, as opposed to the nonreflexive form, which indicates fighting on someone's behalf.

(65) Онъ же, мняще малый люд, выѣхалъ самъ **бронити** со всѣми людми, яже бѣ во градѣ. (302)
'Thinking there were few people, he himself rode out *to defend (broniti)* [the town] with all the people he had in the stronghold.'

---

[31] The Modern Russian plural reading *oboronjalis'[1]* is not supported grammatically by the Old Russian text, although it is logical enough, given the previous plural form *načaša*. Fennell follows the singular reading as well: 'strongly defending himself' (1965: 63).

[32] Fennell reads *branitisja*, with Church Slavic phonology, instead of the Polish *bronitisja*. For more on this, see the discussion of example (70).

While a majority of attestations of the simplex verb involve physical defense, it also on occasion implies protection of an ideal. This can be connected to a physical defense, but need not be, as in the present participial form in (67).

(67)   Заисте, того ради: егда бѣша о вѣрѣ христианской и въ церковныхъ догмѣтехъ утверженны и в дѣлехъ житейских мернѣ и воздержнѣ хранящеся, тогда яко едины человѣцы наилепшие во всѣхъ пребывающе, себя и отечество **броняще**. (294)
'In truth, for this reason: when they stayed firm in their Christian faith and the dogmas of the church and remained moderate and modest in their daily deeds, then to the last they continued to be the best men in every way, *defending (bronjašče)* themselves and their homeland.'

The derived form *obranjati* does not mark a simple physical response; instead, it represents metaphorical defense or protection. In (68), a non-past form appears with *da* as a subjunctive; the Cheremisians are scolding their recently decapitated king for failing to successfully defend his people, but they are referring not only to his lack of prowess in battle but also to his failure overall as a shepherd of his flock.

(68)   «Мы было взяли тебя того ради на царство з дворомъ твоимъ, **да обороняеши** нас; а ты и сущие с тобою не сотворилъ намъ помощи столько, сколько воловъ и коровъ наших поѣлъ. А нынѣ глава твоя да царствует на высокомъ колѣ!» (280)
' "We had chosen you and your retinue for our kingdom, *that you might defend (da oboronjaeši)* us; but you and those with you have not given us help equal to the number of oxen and cows you have eaten. So now let your head rule on a tall pike!" '

In (69) and (70), when reference is made to defending one's kingdom or homeland, it is divorced from an actual reference to fighting or physical defense. The forms are respectively infinitival and present participial.

(69)   Тогда время было над бусурманы християнскимъ царемъ мститися за многолѣтную кровь християнскую, безпрестанне проливаему от них, и успокоитися собя и отечества свое вѣчне ибо ничего ради другаго, но точию того ради и помазаны бываютъ, еже прямо судити и царства, врученные имъ от бога, **обороняти** от нахождения варваров. (292)
'Then it was time for the Christian kings to avenge themselves on the Muslims for the many years of Christian blood that they had shed, and bring peace to themselves and their homeland eternally; they were anointed for no other reason but this one: to judge truthfully and *to defend (obronjati)* from barbarian invasions the kingdoms entrusted to them by God.'

(70)   ...яко славний и похвалний в дѣлехъ ратныхъ явишася, отечество свое **обороняюще**, ни единова, ни дважды, но многажды показашеся нарочиты. (298)

'...for they showed themselves [to be] glorious and praiseworthy in their military deeds, *defending (obronjajušče)* their homeland; not once, nor twice, but many times they proved their worth.'[33]

The simplex, then, has a wider range of meanings than the derived form, which is restricted to metaphorical uses of the word 'defend'.

Kurbskij uses the Church Slavic reflexes (*branjašesja, branitisja, obronjajušče*), the Russian pleophonic reflexes (*oboronil esi, oboronjaeši*), and the Polish reflexes (*bronitisja, bronjašesja, obroniša, obronjati*) of this verb root interchangeably, although the Polish forms are most common. This causes a problem when we attempt to compare the Modern Russian forms to the Old Russian ones. The modern verb *branit'*^{I} is defined as *rugat'*^{I} 'curse^I, denigrate^I'; the reflexive *branit'sja*^{I} means *ssorit'sja*^{I} 'quarrel^I'. The pleophonic simplex *boronit'*^{I} means 'harrow^I (a field)'; however, the prefixed pair *oboronit'–oboronjat'*^{I} is defined as 'protect^I by repulsing an attacker, defend^I from something'. The *Slovar' russkogo jazyka v četyrex tomax* (1981-1984) records no prefixed form **obranjat'*.

Sreznevskij defines *braniti* as *mešat'*^{I}, *prepjatstvovat'*^{I}, *vozbranjat'*^{I} 'hinder^I, impede^I, forbid^I', and *braniti sja* as *tjagat'sja*^{I} 'vie^I with, match^I swords against'; *boroniti* he defines the same way, with the added definition *zaščiščat'*^{I} 'defend^I', and *boroniti sja* is defined as *zaščiščat'sja*^{I} 'defend^I oneself'. All of these entries are cross-referenced to the corresponding pleophonic or nonpleophonic definition, indicating that the breakdown of forms may be less rigid than appears at first.

Despite the welter of forms, the general direction of change is clear. We would not expect the simplex in Modern Russian to retain the meaning 'defend, protect', and in fact it does not; the Old Russian simplex is consistently translated by the Modern Russian forms *zaščiščat'(sja)*^{I} 'defend^I (oneself)' and *oboronjat'(sja)*^{I} 'protect^I (oneself)'. The latter form, which is most interesting for our purposes, appears in (64) and (65) above.

To summarize the situation in Old Russian and Modern Russian: in Kurbskij's text, the simplex expresses a range of submeanings within the general meaning 'defend'; the prefixed derived form expresses only the more abstract meaning 'protect'. Other meanings ('quarrel', 'harrow') are not attested in this sample. By the Modern Russian period, the simplex no longer expresses the meaning 'defend'; it appears only with these other meanings. The prefixed derived form is used for both abstract and concrete realizations of the concept 'defend'. An abstract–concrete differentiation between simplex and derived form has given way to a clear lexical split; the simplex's sphere of usage has retreated in face of the expanded usage of the derived form.

While these two roots—*braniti* 'defend' and *pisati* 'write'—are the best attested in this text, there are numerous other examples of concrete vs. abstract distinctions between simplexes and prefixed forms, and several places where I found semantic shifts favoring expansion of the prefixed form in Modern Russian. Among these

---

[33] Here I read *pokazašasja* 'they proved [aorist]' instead of *pokazašesja* 'he proved [imperfect]'. Fennell also reads *pokazašasja* (1965: 132).

roots are *žeči* 'burn', *ždati* 'wait', *mysliti* 'think', *pitati* 'feed, raise', *praviti* 'lead, direct', *staviti* 'place', *xraniti* 'preserve', *suditi* 'judge'.

8.4.3. Contextual distinctions in usage

There is a third pattern of differentiation between simplexes and their prefixed derived forms. Often, the text shows us some evidence of competition between the simplex and the prefixed derived form, and this competition delineates contexts for each form's use. These distinctions in usage can reflect an alteration in the temporal shape of the event that is far slighter than the one observed above with *terpěti* and *preterpěvati* 'endure'. Compared to *terpěti* and *preterpěvati*, the verbs *mstiti*, *otomščati* 'avenge' are related by a relatively subtle form of Aktionsart prefixation. The prefixed form *otomstiti*, unattested in my sample, means 'take revenge', and has a resultative meaning. The suffixed form *otomščati* is hard to differentiate from the simplex *mstiti* on purely semantic grounds; it is easier to define contexts in which the two verbs occur and then try to disambiguate them. (All attestations of the two verbs are given below.) The simplex *mstiti* occurs in three different contexts. In (71), the infinitive form *mstiti* 'revenge' is presented as a process, parallel to *poduščati* 'urge on'.

(71) Егда прииде к седмомунадесять лѣту, тогда тѣ же прегордые сингклитове начаша подущати его и **мстити** имъ свои недружбы, единъ против другаго. (222)
'When he reached his seventeenth year, then those same prideful counsellors began to urge him on and *to avenge (mstiti)* their own hatreds through him, one against the other.'

No particular beginnings or ends are hinted at; the important point is the tsar's role in the politics of the court. (The Modern Russian translation captures this nicely: *senatory odni vpered drugogo stali^P naus'kivat'^{I} ego i ispol'zovat'^{I} ego dlja mesti v svoej vražde* 'the senators one by one began^P to urge^I him on and *use^I him for revenge* in their enmity'.) In (72), the verb appears in the simplex infinitive; possibly because this act is punctual in character, it bears comparison to a completed telic infinitive (*uspokoitisja sobja i otečestva* 'satisfy oneself and one's homeland') later on in the sentence.

(72) Тогда время было над бусурманы християнскимъ царемъ **мстити- ся** *(отмстить)* за многолѣтную кров християнскую, безпрестанне проливаему от них, и успокоитися собя и отечества свое вѣчне... (292)
'Then it was time for the Christian kings *to avenge themselves (OR mstitisja/ MoR otomstit'^{P})* on the Muslims for the many years of Christian blood that they had shed, and to bring peace to themselves and their homeland eternally...'

Modern Russian translates this verb with a perfective infinitive *otmstit'*,[34] possibly to keep the aspects parallel and suggest closure in both cases; however, the Old Russian is more open-ended. The statement 'it was time to avenge himself' does not necessarily imply a goal or result; it could easily highlight the fact that it was time to begin an undertaking.[35] In this case a Modern Russian penchant for aspectual consistency takes precedence over a subtle distinction in meaning in the Old Russian text.

Example (73) also provides a context devoid of clues about the goal of the act; Satan's revenge against the Christians is simply presented as an ongoing process (a progressive context with a present participle).

(73) Приявши же сатана человѣческий скверный языкъ яко орудие сице похвалился губити роды християнские со своимъ стаиникомъ, аки бы **мстяще** *(отмщая)* християнскому войску... (260)
'When Satan had taken up the foul human tongue as his weapon, he even boasted that he would destroy the race of Christians with his minion, as if *he were taking revenge (OR mstjašče/MoR otmščaja[1])* on the Christian soldiery...'

Here the translator chose the derived verb *otmščat'*, emphasizing the telic nature of the process of revenge, instead of stressing the process at the cost of the eventual goal. Example (74) is the sample's only attestation of the derived form *otomščati*, used here as a present participle.

(74) Понеже не токмо богъ разумъ и даръ духа храбрости тогда подавал, но явления нѣкоторыя достойным и чистыя совести мужем в нощных видѣниях изъявилъ о взятию града бусурманского, к сему подвижуще воинство, яко мню, **отомщающе** бесчисленное и многолѣтное разлияния крови християнские, а оставльшихся еще тамо живых избавляюще от многолѣтныя работы. (248)
'Since God at that time dispensed not only reason and the gift of courageous spirit, but also manifested by night to men of merit and of clear conscience several visions of the taking of the Muslim town, in addition encouraging his troops, as I see it, *seeking revenge (otomščajušče)* for the innumerable and interminable pouring of Christian blood, and freeing those who still remained alive there from their interminable servitude.'

Here, taking the Moslem fortress is equated with revenge against the infidel and the freeing of the remaining Christian captives. Possibly influenced by the strong telic nature of the act *vzjatie grada* 'the taking of the fortress', which this passage

---

[34] This Modern Russian translation uses the forms *otmstit'*[P], *otmščat'*[I], without the fleeting [o] from the original prefix {otъ-}, while the Old Russian text has forms with the fleeting [o]. While the forms *otomstit'* and *otomščat'* are used as well in Modern Russian, for consistency's sake I will use the forms found in the translation when referring to Modern Russian.

[35] Compare to the Modern Russian construction *pora* + imperfective verb 'it is time to do x/to be doing x'.

elaborates on, Kurbskij chose a verb that reflected a strong drive toward a single goal.

In light of (74), we can revisit the discrepancy between original and translation in (73). Once again, the Modern Russian derived form seems to have a wider scope than the Old Russian form, and this wider scope includes use in generalized contexts. Although this root appears in only four examples in this sample, the pattern coincides with that seen earlier for other roots.

In some cases, the meanings of the simplex and the prefixed derived form are so close that it is difficult to discern with surety differences in meaning or usage between them. This is the case with the verbs *xvaliti*, *poxvaljati*, and *vosxvaljati*, all of which mean 'praise'. The simplex *xvaliti* is found twice in the data. In (75), Kurbskij criticizes the tsar's advisors for praising the tsar despite his actions; the context is weakly iterative, with a present participle in the Old Russian and an imperfective past tense in the translation. In (76), Kurbskij interrupts his narration to add that he does not intend to praise himself in telling his story; the context is progressive, with a present participle in Old Russian, and an imperfective non-past in the translation.

(75) Егда же начал приходити в возрастъ, аки лѣт в дванадесятъ... начал первие безсловесных крови проливати, с стремнинъ высокихъ мечюще ихъ... а пѣстуномъ ласкающим, попущающе сие и **хваляще** *(расхваливали)*, на свое горшѣе отрока учаще. (222)
'When he began to come of age, at around twelve years of age... he began first to pour the blood of dumb creatures, flinging them from high precipices... and his fawning tutors, in allowing this and *praising (OR xvaljašče/MoR rasxvalivali^l)* him, taught him to their own detriment.'

(76) Молюся, да не возмнитъ мя хто безумна, сам себя **хваляща** *(хвалю)* ! (256)
'I pray that no one might think me irrational for *praising (OR xvaljašča/MoR xvalju^l)* myself!'

Examples with the prefixed derived form *poxvaljati* do not differ in meaning from those with *xvaliti*. The contexts they appear in, however, differ slightly, emphasizing what was praised or how it was praised. In (77), we are told that the wicked monks around the tsar praised his wisdom in resolving to journey to St. Cyril's monastery, saying it was a decision pleasing to God. The verb is a present participle in Old Russian and an imperfective past tense in the translation.

(77) Ктому ласкающе его и поджигающе миролюбцом и любоименным мнихом и **похваляюще** *(расхваливали)* умиление царево, аки богоугодное обѣщание. (264)
'In addition, monks who were worldly and who loved earthly things [were] fawning on him and encouraging and *praising (OR poxvaljajušče/MoR rasxvalivali^l)* the tsar's intention as a pledge pleasing to God.'

In (78), similarly, we are given an example of how Chrysostom praises St. Paul. The verb is non-past in both the Old Russian text and the translation.

(78) Подобно ленился еси прочести... во другомъ слове, в последней похвалѣ о святомъ Павле, сирѣчь во 9, емуже начало: «Обличили насъ друзи нѣкоторые», яко он **похваляет** *(хвалит)*, нарицающе даръ духа совѣтъ от бога данный. (268)
'You were similarly too lazy to read... in another homily, that is in number 9, which begins: "Some of our friends have accused us," how he *gives praise (OR poxvaljaet/MoR xvalit¹)*, calling the gift of the spirit advice given by God.'

Example (79) has the reflexive present participle *poxvaljajuščisja* 'boasting'; despite the different meaning of the reflexive, this form, like the other uses of the prefixed derived form, has an explicit complement. Kurbskij is describing how the evil advisors rejoiced at the monk Silvester's exile, falsely bragging that Silvester had been fairly judged.

(79) ...и оттуды похватиша его и завезоша на Соловки... идѣже бы и слухъ ево не обрелся, **похваляющися** *(хвастаясь)*, аки бы то соборне осудиша его, мужа нарочитого и готаваго отвещати на клеветы. (316)
'...and from there they seized him and carted him off to Solovki... where nothing could be heard of him, *boasting (OR poxvaljajuščisja/MoR xvastajas'¹)*, as if the whole council had condemned him, an upright man ready to answer any slanders.'

Example (80)—which appeared earlier in this chapter as (22)—does not fit into the above schema; however, because it appears in the historical present, it may follow the aforementioned tendency in the historical present to use a derived form instead of a simplex.

(80) Царь же, напився от окоянныхъ со сладостным ласканиемъ смешанного смертоносного яду и самъ лукавства, паче же глупости, наполнився, **похваляет** *(расхваливает)* совѣтъ и любитъ и усвояетъ ихъ в дружбу и присягами себѣ и ихъ обязуетъ... (312)
'The tsar, having drunk of the deadly poison mixed with sweet flattery from those cursed ones, and having filled himself with treachery, or more nearly stupidity, *praises (OR poxvaljajet/MoR rasxvalivaet¹)* the[ir] council and loves and accepts them as his friends and binds them to himself with oaths...'

The two examples of the prefixed derived form *vosxvaljati* in the sample follow the same pattern as the forms of *poxvaljati*: they are followed by a direct quotation of their praise, as in (81), or by an indirect quotation of it, as in (82). Both forms are present participles.

(81) И воистину, дѣла разбойнические самые творяше и иные злые исполняше... ласкателем же всѣм таковое на свою бѣду

восхваляющим *(расхваливали)*: «О, храбръ, — глаголюще, — будет сей царь и мужественъ!» (222)

'And truly, he did simply criminal things and committed other evil crimes... while all the fawners, to their own discredit, *praised (OR vosxvaljajuščim/MoR rasxvalivali^I)* this: "O," they would say, "what a brave and courageous tsar this one will be!"'

(82) Такоже и властели земли тоя... с печенеги вкупѣ высоко скачюще и воздухъ биюще, и так прехвалне и прегордѣ другъ друга пьяни **восхваляюще** *(похвалялись)*, иже не токмо Москву або Константинопол, но аще бы и на небѣ былъ турокъ, совлещи его со другими неприятелми своими обѣщающе. (294)[36]

'Thus the rulers of this land... together with their lackeys, would jump on high and strike the air, *praising (OR vosxvaljajusče/MoR poxvaljalis'^{I})* each other so lavishly and proudly when drunk, promising that if there were to be a Turk not only in Moscow or Constantinople but even in heaven, they would drag him out with their other enemies.'

It is tricky to translate these forms into Modern Russian. The modern language has a simplex *xvalit'* 'praise', with a reflexive *xvalit'sja* 'brag, boast'. Both have prefixed forms *poxvalit', poxvalit'sja, vosxvalit', vosxvalit'sja*, which are perfective and correspond to the reflexive and nonreflexive meanings of the simplex. Modern Russian recognizes a secondary imperfective *poxvaljat'sja* 'boast, brag' as a nonliterary form *(prostorečie)* and the form *poxvalivat'* 'praise', with the same nonliterary feel. (These forms appear to be fixed with or without the reflexive; the forms **poxvalivat'sja* and **poxvaljat'* are not recognized.) Modern Russian also has a form *rasxvalivat'^{I}* 'lavish^I praise on, praise excessively', which appears in the Modern Russian translation but is not attested in this sample or indeed at all in Old Russian, according to Sreznevskij. There is also a perfective *rasxvalit'* in Modern Russian with the same meaning.[37]

In the Modern Russian translation, the distinction found in the Old Russian text is not evident. Instead, the Modern Russian forms distinguish primarily legitimate praise, rendered by forms of *xvalit'^{I}* in (76) and (78), from excessive or fulsome praise, rendered by *rasxvalivat'^{I}* in (75), (77), (80) and (81). In (82), the nonliterary Modern Russian form *poxvaljalis'^{I}* appears for Old Russian *vosxvaljajušče*; here the translator may be striving to convey the vulgarity of the drunken infidels' claims. The single Old Russian reflexive, *poxvaljajuščisja* in (79), is rendered with the synonym *xvastat'sja^I* 'brag^I' in the Modern Russian translation.

---

[36] Fennell reads *vosxvaljašči*, a present participle from a protoperfective verb *vosxvaliti*.

[37] The reflexive *rasxvalit'sja^P* 'start^P to praise more and more' is not a direct relative of these forms; rather, it is an Aktionsart modification of *xvalit'^{I}* formed by adding the affixes {raz-} and {-sja} directly to the simplex and parallel to other formations like *razgovorit'sja^P* 'warm^P to a topic', *razbolet'sja^P* 'fall^P seriously ill'. Verbs of this type do not have derived imperfectives with the same meaning; the verb *rasxvalivat'sja^I* 'heap^I praise upon oneself' is defined simply as the "passive form of *rasxvalivat'^{I}*."

To summarize these developments, a fine distinction in the original text between a simplex expressing the act as a whole and a prefixed derived verb expressing a more fully explicated—and thus more processual—view of the act did not seem to develop into a full-fledged distinction between event and process of the sort seen in (71)-(74) with *mstiti* and *otomščati*. Instead, the prefixed derived forms that were developing were relegated to nonliterary status, and another type of semantic distinction—that of simple praise vs. inappropriate praise—arose with the prefix {raz-}. At least for the translator of this text, it is the distinction between "good" praise and "bad" praise that motivates the choice of simplex vs. prefixed derived form, not the difference between process and event.

Another troublesome change occurs when a prefixed derived form in the Modern Russian translation replaces a simplex in the Old Russian text (or sporadically vice versa), and the small number of examples catalogued means there is little to no information about the state of the opposition in Old Russian or how it came into existence. An example of this change is the replacement of Old Russian *diviti sja* 'be surprised' with Modern Russian *udivljat'sja*. The Old Russian verb *diviti sja* is replaced in the Modern Russian translation in all three instances—found in (83)-(85)—by a form of *udivljat'sja*. (In the modern language, *divit'*, *divit'sja* is a colloquial form, while the standard literary language has *udivljat'*, *udivljat'sja*.)

(83) ...и в сицевую высоту онаго, прежде бывшаго окаянного, возводятъ, яко и многимъ окрестным языком **дивитися** *(удивляться)* обращению его и благочестию. (226)
'...and they lead him, the formerly cursed one, up to such a height that many nations around *marvel (OR divitisja/MoR udivljat'sja^1)* at the change in him and at his good honor.'

(84) И иные словеса отрыгающе хулные съ яростию многою, яко и всѣм нам **дивитися** *(удивлялись)*, зрѣще. (244)
'And they spewed forth other profanities with great savagery, so that all of us who were watching *were shocked (OR divitisja/MoR udivljalis'^{1}).'*

(85) Всѣм же со града зрящим и **дивящимся** *(удивлялись)*, которые же не вѣдяще о цареве отданию, мняще царя Казанского между ихъ ѣздяща. (258)
'Everyone watched from the fortress and *marveled (OR divjaščimsja/MoR udivljalis'^{1})*; those who did not know of the king's capitulation thought that the king of Kazan' was riding out among them.'

The most curious point in this set of examples is the Modern Russian translation of (86), in which the colloquial past tense *divilis'^{1}* appears for the Old Russian protoperfective aorist *udivišasja* '[we] were astonished'.[38]

---

[38] See section 8.1 on the use of the 3. pl. form here.

(86)   Мы же **удивишася** *(дивились)* разуму мужа и словеству, и держа-
       хом в почести его за стражею. (308)
       'We *marveled (OR udivišasja/MoR divilis'¹)* at the knowledge and erudition of
       this man, and held him in esteem while he was our captive.'

This appears to be an arbitrary shift in perspective; the Old Russian indicates an inception or a momentary surprise, which in the Modern Russian text is reworked to show that as the German captive spoke, the Muscovites continually revelled in his eloquence. The preference for the nonstandard *divit'sja* must be construed as a stylistic choice on the part of the translator.

Other examples of sparsely attested change from simplex to derived forms occur with the verbs *šeptati* 'whisper', *gotovati* 'prepare', *končiti* 'finish', *kryti* 'cover, hide', *zvati* 'call', and *groziti* 'threaten'.

8.5. RESULTATIVITY, CONATIVITY AND ASPECT

Despite the aspectual similarities between Kurbskij's text and Modern Russian, there are numerous indications that Kurbskij's aspectual system was not identical to the aspectual system of the modern language. Following the constraints laid out in previous chapters (see especially the discussion in chapter 7), I checked places in the text where apparent aspectual mismatches occurred between the original text and a Modern Russian translation (an Old Russian protoperfective corresponding to a Modern Russian imperfective, or vice versa). Certain lexical peculiarities then had to be weeded out. For instance, the use of *viděv"* 'having seen' to represent perfective-like acts, as discussed earlier, is not of much interest in this case; further, problems that seem at this stage to be purely morphological rather than semantic in nature—such as the assignment of aspect to *otvěščati* 'answer', *veleti* 'order', and *oběščati* 'promise'—were also ignored. Other extraneous mismatches I judged to be the result of syntactic changes (such as the use of the historical present in either the text or the translation, but not in both), and these were discarded as well. Still, there remains a fairly large number of pairs for which the apparent aspect of the Old Russian verb does not match that of the Modern Russian one.

8.5.1. Problems with resultativity

One extensive type of mismatch occurs when the act, while rendered as whole and complete, need not imply result or consequence in the discourse. In these cases, an Old Russian protoperfective corresponds to a Modern Russian imperfective. The examples show two differences between Old and Modern Russian aspectual usage. Examples (87) and (88) demonstrate a familiar pattern: repeated acts in the past are adequately conveyed in Old Russian by a protoperfective past tense form (here, respectively, a perfect and an aorist) and an adverb like *mnogoždy* 'many times'.

(87)   И не хотяше покою наслажатися... но **подвигся** многожды самъ,
       не щадечи здравия своего, на сопротивнаго и горшаго своего
       супостата — царя казанского. (230)

(87a) *tr:* Он уже не хотел наслаждаться покоем... но сам **поднимался** не раз, не щадя своего здоровья, на враждебного и злейшего своего противника — казанского царя. (231)
'And he no longer wanted to content himself in peace... but numerous times *went forth (podnimalsja¹)*, not sparing his own health, against his bitter and most evil opponent: the king of Kazan'.'

(88) И многожды **умолчахъ** со воздыханиемъ и слезами, не восхотѣхъ отвѣщати. (218)
'And many a time *I fell silent (umolčax'')* with sighs and tears; I did not want to answer.'

(88a) *tr:* И каждый раз со вздохами и слезами я **отмалчивался** и не хотел отвечать. (219)³⁹
'And each time with sighs and tears I *fell silent (otmalčivalsja¹)* and did not want to answer.'

Of these two sentences, (87) is the more clear-cut; (88) has an added conative feature, which will be discussed shortly. A further example of this sort is (89); the Old Russian protoperfective perfect focuses on the threefold occurrence of the act, while the Modern Russian imperfective past in (89a) focuses on its repetition.⁴⁰

(89) И всѣхъ первие вразихся во весь полкъ он бусурманский и памятую то, иже, секущеся, три разы в нихъ конь мой **оперся** и в четвертый разъ зѣло раненъ повалился в срединѣ ихъ со мною. (256)
'And I was the first of us to cut into the Muslim regiment at all, and I remember that, as I slashed, three times among them my horse *plunged into (opersja)* them, and the fourth time, deeply wounded, collapsed in their midst with me.'

(89a) *tr:* Впереди всех врезался я в басурманский тот полк и помню, что трижды во время сечи **упирался** во врагов мой конь, а в четвертый раз, тяжко раненный, повалился вместе со мною посреди них. (257)

---

39 Both native speakers I consulted chose the imperfective *otmalčivalsja* with no hesitation whatsoever.

40 Another possibility is to read this as a conative act: the horse did run up against the enemy, and it is only that the first three engagements did not succeed in causing a result. This extended conative sense may support the Modern Russian use of an imperfective, but it hardly seems necessary. See (93) below, which is also both iterative and conative in the extended definition proposed in 8.5.2. However, the two native speakers I consulted both agreed that iterativity was the reason for the imperfective here; they could admit the perfective *upersja* only if the act occurred once, they said.

'I was the first of all to slice into the Muslim regiment, and I remember that thrice during the battle my horse plunged *(upiralsja^I)* into the enemy ranks, and on the fourth time, badly wounded, it fell, with me astride it, among them.'

The second type of usage is exemplified by the protoperfectives *rěx" by* 'I would tell (aorist)' and *ostal bě* 'had remained (pluperfect)' in (90) and (91).

(90) И отвѣщахъ имъ: «Аще **бы** из начала и по ряду **рѣхъ**, много бы о том писати...» (218)
'And I answered them: "If I *would tell (by rěx")* [the story] from the beginning and in detail, there would be much to write about..." '

(90a) *tr:* И я отвечал им: «Если **бы рассказывал** я с самого начала и все подробно, много бы пришлось писать о том...» (219)
'And I answered them: "If I *would tell the story (by rasskazyval^I)* from the very beginning and in full detail, there would be much to write about..." '

(91) Еще бо **бѣ** ихъ **остал** полкъ, аки шесть тысещей абo мало мнѣйше. (256)
'For there still *remained (bě ostal)* of their regiment about six thousand or a little less.'

(91a) *tr:* **Оставалось** их еще в полку тысяч шесть или немного меньше. (257)
'There *remained (ostavalos'^{I})* of them in the regiment about sx thousand or a little less.'

In (90a) and (91a), the Modern Russian imperfective form is not so much an indication of duration as it is a statement of neutrality with regard to the act's effects. A perfective *rasskazal by* in (90a) would imply sequencing of the acts; a perfective *ostalos'* in (91a) would focus attention on how few soldiers remained in the opposing army, instead of implying that this is background information Kurbskij took into account in planning his attack. I propose that the Old Russian protoperfective was not necessarily opposed to the protoimperfective by a discourse feature of resultativity, as it is in Modern Russian; in other words, the aspectual opposition did not have the same consistent "foregrounding" and "backgrounding" features that it does in Modern Russian. In these examples, the Old Russian protoperfective simply serves as a summary of the act, much as the Modern Russian imperfective does. In using imperfectives in (90a) and (91a), the Modern Russian translation is subtly adjusting the value of the given information for the discourse at large, an evaluation that the Old Russian text does not make through its aspectual choices in (90) and (91).[41]

---

[41] Two native speakers both preferred the perfective *rasskazal by* in (90), while allowing the imperfective form; this lends support to my hypothesis that the Modern Russian imperfective expresses only some of the possibilities available here.

8.5.2. Aspect and conativity in Old Russian

It was mentioned above that conativity could also be read into the Modern Russian usage in (88a). Kurbskij states that on many occasions he held his tongue when asked to tell his story; however, the following sentence informs us that, despite his previous silences, he was prevailed upon to say something about his experiences. On the level of the sentence, then, his silence is iterative; on the level of the larger context, it is durative, ending in failure—a conative context. Kurbskij's text has several other such examples, where an Old Russian protoperfective conveying failure to reach a goal is translated into Modern Russian by an imperfective.

(92) И **умыслиша** оттуду, аки из града единаго выѣзжаючи, паки ударяти на войско християнское. (244)
'And they *intended (umysliša)* from there to strike again at the Christian troops, riding out from one of the fortresses.'

(92a) *tr:* Они **намеревались** делать оттуда вылазки как из крепости и снова нападать на христианское войско. (245)[42]
'They intended *(namerevalis'¹)* to make sorties from there as from a fortress and fall again on the Christian troops.'

(93) (над нихже, яко многожды **рѣхом**, ни единъ прыщъ смертны во царствие поветренѣйши быти... может) (310)
'(as we *have said (rěxom)* many a time, not a single deadly pestilence could be a greater plague in the kingdom than could they)'

(93a) *tr:* (я уже не раз **говорил**, что ни от одной смертоносной язвы не может быть большего мора в царстве, чем от них) (311)
'(I have said *(govoril¹)* more than once that there could be no greater plague in the kingdom from a single deadly pestilence than from them)'

In (92) and (93), the context makes clear that the act, whatever its intention, failed to be realized or have an effect. In (92), the Moslems plot their counterattack; their plan is foiled, however, as the Christians eventually drive them back. In (93), Kurbskij expresses his frustration at the fact that his words are so often ignored; the Modern Russian imperfective in (93a) does not necessarily mean that he was prevented from giving his advice, so much as it implies his advice was not heeded.[43] Old Russian aspect apparently does not recognize either of these situations as requiring a protoimperfective form; neither the failure of an act to reach its logical conclusion nor the failure of a completed act to have an effect compels the use of a protoimperfective. This situation is diagrammed in chart 8.5.2.1.

---

42 Two native speakers also chose the imperfective *namerevalis'* in this sentence.
43 My native speaker consultants both agreed that the imperfective *govoril* was the only acceptable choice here.

446   *Context and the Lexicon*

Chart 8.5.2.1. Conativity in Old and Modern Russian

Language	Successful act	No result = failure (extended conativity)	Incompleteness = failure (canonical conativity)
Old Russian	pf./impf.?	pf./impf.?	pf./impf.
Modern Russian	pf./impf.	impf.	impf.

This lack of a conative–nonconative distinction in Old Russian aspect is also found in places where an Old Russian protoimperfective corresponds to a Modern Russian perfective.[44] The evidence is indirect: a modern perfective is used to avoid giving a conative reading where it is not appropriate, meaning that the Old Russian protoimperfective form apparently does not convey conativity. Example (94) has an Old Russian simplex verb in the infinitive corresponding to a Modern Russian prefixed perfective infinitive in (94a). Sreznevskij defines *cěliti* as *lěčit'*[I], *vračevat'*[I], *iscěljat'*[I] 'treat[I], doctor[I], heal[I]'.

(94)   Сице, мню, блаженный малую присовокупляетъ благокознению, еюже великое зло **целити** умыслил. (224)
        'In this way, I think, this blessed man added a bit of well-intentioned intriguing, through which he thought *to cure (celiti)* a great evil.'

(94a)   *tr:* Так и блаженный, я полагаю, прибавил немного благих козней, которыми задумал **исцелить** большое зло. (225)
        'In this way, I propose, the blessed man added a bit of well-intentioned intriguing, through which he thought *to cure (iscelit'*[P]*)* a great evil.'

A Modern Russian imperfective *isceljat'* 'treat, cure' in (94a) would have two functions: it would describe the process of curing someone, but in this context, it could also indicate a failure to cure someone during a course of treatment. Old Russian lacks this second meaning, and thus it retains a simplex to describe the process, while Modern Russian opts for a prefixed form, to avoid confusion.

Similarly, in (95), the protoimperfective present participle *ukrěpljajušču* 'supporting' describes God's support for the tsar through the medium of his advisors; this support results in the tsar's decision not to retreat, paving the way for his future victory.

(95)   Единова в лютую зиму, аще и не взял мѣста оного главнаго, сиирѣчь Казани града, и со тщетою немалою атойде, но всяко не сокрушилося ему сердце и воинство его храброе, **укрепляющу** богу оными совѣтники его. (230)
        'And if once in that cruel winter he did not take their capital city—that is, the fortress of Kazan'—and retreated with great losses, neither his will nor his

---

44 This same phenomenon was discussed in chapter 7.

military braveness were crushed, since God *was supporting (ukrepljajušču)* him through his advisors.'

(95a)   *tr:* И хоть не взял он в одну суровую зиму этого столичного города, то есть крепости Казани, и отступил без всякого успеха, вовсе не впали в уныние душа его и храбрая его воинственность, притом что бог **поддержал** его через советников. (231)
'And though in that cruel winter he did not take the capital city—that is, the fortress of Kazan'—and retreated with no success, his soul and military braveness were not at all laid low, as God *was supporting (podderžival¹)* him through his advisors.'

Using a Modern Russian perfective in (95a) avoids suggesting that this support was ineffective or temporary. Compare this situation to that of (96), where the participle *ukrěpljajušče* 'encouraging' simply indicates that this urging was simultaneous with opposing advice, without giving a hint as to who eventually prevails.

(96)   И начаша инако, совѣтоваша ему, сирѣчь, да идешъ паки за Оку, а оттуды к Москвѣ; нѣцыи мужественнѣйшии **укрепляюще** его и глаголюще, да не дастъ хрепта врагу своему и да не посрамитъ прежние славы своея добрые... (278)
'And they started and advised him differently, saying: cross the Oka again and go from there to Moscow. Some braver men *encouraged (ukrepljajušče)* him and said that he should not turn tail to his enemy nor cast shame on his previous glorious repute...'

(96a)   *tr:* Начали все заново и советовали ему, чтобы он шел, дескать, за Оку, а потом к Москве, притом что кое-кто из самых мужестеенных **вселял** в царя твердость, говоря, чтобы не обращался к врагу тылом, чтобы не позорил прежнюю добрую славу свою... (279)
'They began again and advised him to go across the Oka and from there to Moscow, while a few of the bravest *tried to instill (vseljal¹)* resolve in the tsar, saying that he should not turn tail to his enemy nor cast shame on his previous good repute...'

Here the Modern Russian in (96a) uses an imperfective past tense, *vseljal tverdost'* 'was/were instilling¹ resolve', but adds the conjunction *pritom čto* '(mean)while' first, making it clear that temporal limitation, not frustration of intent, is implied by the imperfective form.

In (97), Kurbskij accuses the tsar of having been reluctant or too lazy to read John Chrysostom's words; the Old Russian perfect is protoimperfective, while the Modern Russian translation in (97a) chooses a perfective rendering.

(97)   Подобно **ленился еси** прочести златыми усты вещающаго о семъ во словѣ о духу святом... (268)

"Similarly, *you were too lazy (lenilsja esi)* to read what Chrysostom says about this in his missive about the Holy Spirit...'

(97a)   *tr:* Точно так же **поленился** ты прочесть того, кто златыми устами говорит об этом в слове о святом Духе... (269)
'Just in this way you *were too lazy (polenilsja^P)* to read what he of the golden mouth [i.e. Chrysostom] says about this in his missive about the Holy Spirit...

An imperfective in the Modern Russian leaves open the option that at some later point the tsar's stalling abated, and he did in fact get around to reading Chrysostom. Instead, the perfective *polenilsja*, when used with the infinitive as is done here, has the meaning *ne sdelat'^{P} čego-libo iz-za leni* 'fail to do^P something as a result of laziness'. Compare this to the simplex *lenit'sja* in Modern Russian: *ispytivat'^{I} len'*, *lenivo otnosit'sja^I k čemu-libo* 'experience^I laziness, have^I a lazy attitude toward something'. The Modern Russian in (97a) avoids a conative reading by using the perfective form.

Example (98) is the apparent counterexample of the group; in it, the verbal adverb phrase *beruči sebě na razmyšlenie* 'taking under consideration' is translated by the Modern Russian *želaja^I vzjat'^{P} sebe na razmyšlenie* 'desiring^I to take^P under consideration'.

(98)   ...они же... абие начаша просити премирья аки на 4 недѣли, **беручи** себѣ на размышление о поданию мѣста и града. (282)
'...they... immediately began to ask for a cease-fire for about four weeks, *taking (beruči)* under consideration the surrender of the city and fortress.'

(98a)   *tr:* ...немцы тотчас... стали просить перемирия, **желая взять** себе на размышление о сдаче города и крепости недели четыре. (283)
'...the Germans immediately... began to ask for a cease-fire, *desiring to take (želaja^I vzjat'^{P})* under consideration the surrender of the city and the fortress for four weeks.'

Although a conative reading is possible for the form in (98), the Modern Russian in (98a) is probably angling at the futurity of the clause: the Germans, after all, are not yet being allowed to consider their possibilities; they are merely asking for permission to do so, which has yet to be granted by the Muscovites.

In all of the above examples, it is possible to find as well an undercurrent of temporal difference between the Old and Modern Russian forms. One could potentially analyze these data by appealing to a different use of time and duration in Old Russian, as has often been done: the Old Russian protoimperfective would have a more Aktionsart quality to it, imparting duration, while the Old Russian protoperfective would be unmarked for duration. This theory harks back to Potebnja's belief that the Old Russian verbal system was organized around *stepeni dlitel'nosti* 'degrees of duration'. There may be some advantages to this approach, but it only accounts for (94)-(97); it will not account for the Old Russian protoperfectives that appear in Modern Russian as imperfectives in (92) and (93), nor will it account for the ones that will appear in the following section.

It is more fruitful to claim that the central role of conativity in these Modern Russian contexts is linked to the fact that conativity usually co-occurs with explicit duration: by definition, a progressive or durative context shows only a portion of an event, excluding its endpoints. In this sense, conative contexts constitute a subset of the progressive and durative contexts, in which excluding the goal of the act may or may not imply its failure. Another suggestion as to the source of conativity in the imperfective will be considered in the following section.

8.6. RESULT AND DURATION UNDER NEGATION

In Modern Russian, a negated perfective (*on ne vzjal^P ètu knigu* 'he didn't take^P that book') implies that the subject intended to, attempted to, wanted to, or was expected to do something—possibly on account of prior behavior—but in the end did not do it, or had not yet done it at the time of the narrative. Negation is thus oriented toward the result of the act or lack thereof, a clear discourse consideration. Negating the perfective categorically rules out fulfillment of the act, but does so by negating only the attainment of the goal while presuming that the attempt or intent did exist. A negated imperfective, by contrast, does not rule out fulfillment of the act at some later point—in this sense it is less categorical than the negated perfective—but does so by applying over a wider scope than the negated perfective: it negates any implied intention, volition, or attempt as well. Thus, *on ne bral^I ètu knigu* 'he didn't take^I that book' implies that the subject never intended or tried to take the book. Chart 8.6.1 describes this pattern.[45]

As Chaput 1984 notes, the relationships between aspectual usage in the affirmative and aspectual usage under negation is best explained by discourse considerations—presuppositions of the speaker and addressee—in Modern Russian. In Old Russian, by contrast, this presupposition- and result-oriented bias, which gives the addressee three types of information (about the discourse, the status of the result, and only occasionally about the duration of the act), is absent; instead, a different aspectual distinction can prevail under negation in Old Russian that parallels the usage of aspect outside negation. This type of negation is found especially with verbs that indicate ability or volition. With the verbs *moči–vozmoči* 'be able', *xotěti–vosxotěti* 'want', *davati–dati* (only in the sense of 'permit, allow') the Old Russian negated protoperfective does not emphasize a failure contrary to expectations; instead, it simply shows lack of an act over a specified period of time. For example, uses of *vozmoči* 'be able' like (99) are common in the *History*. Kurbskij uses a protoperfective perfect to show a temporal limitation on the soldiers' abilities to get in or out of the city.

---

[45] This discussion of aspect in negated sentences is based on Chaput 1984. Chart 8.6.1, however, is not solely from Chaput 1984, but represents a summary of this and other sources on discourse implications of aspectual choice.

Chart 8.6.1. Scope of aspectual negation and result in Modern Russian

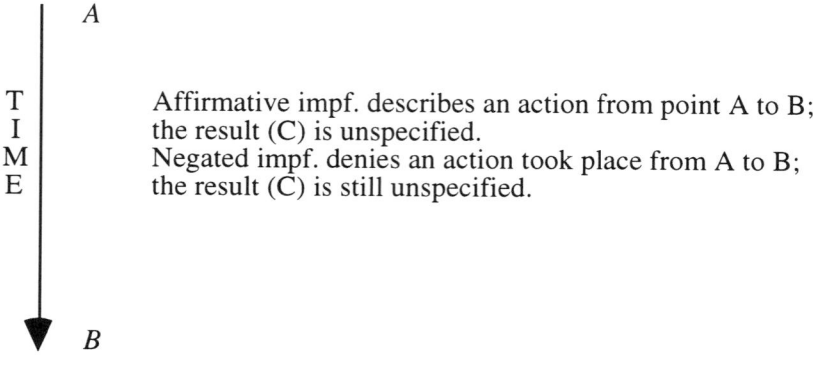

(99) И абие в той день обступихом мѣсто и град бусурманский полки християнскими и отняхом ото всѣхъ странъ пути и проѣзды ко граду: **не возмогли** они никакоже ни из града, ни во град **преходити**. (238)
'And suddenly that day we surrounded the Muslim city and stronghold with Christian regiments and blocked the routes and approaches to the stronghold; they *could not (ne vozmogli) cross out (prexoditi)* of the stronghold, nor into it at all.'

(99a) *tr:* И как раз в тот день обступили мы христианскими полками басурманский город и крепость и перекрыли со всех сторон пути и подходы к крепости: казанцы никак **не могли передвигаться** ни из крепости, ни в крепость. (239)
'And on the very day we surrounded the Muslim city and fortress and blocked the routes from all sides and approaches to the fortress: the men of Kazan' *could not (ne mogli^I) move about (peredvigat'sja^P)*, neither out from the fortress nor into it.'

The infinitive complement is protoimperfective. In (99a), however, it is the negated Modern Russian imperfective that shows the time limitation; a negated perfective would have implied a failure to follow through that ran counter to expectations. This use of the protoperfective contrasts with the protoimperfective aorist *ne mogoša* in (100), where the enemy's inability to enter or leave the city has undefined endpoints.

(100) И стояли есмо подъ темъ великимъ мѣстомъ и градомъ двѣ недели, пришанцовався и заточа дѣла и все мѣсто тое облечши, от негоже **не могоша** уже **ни изходити, ни вгодити** в него. (286)
'And we stood outside that great city and fortress for two weeks, having dug trenches and placed cannons, and surrounded the whole city, from which *they could neither exit, nor enter (ne mogoša ni izxoditi, ni vgoditi)* it.'

(100a) *tr:* Стояли мы под этим большим городом и крепостью две недели, выкопав шанцы, разместив пушки и обложив весь город, так что **нельзя было ни выйти, ни войти** в него. (287)
'We stood under that great city and fortress for two weeks, having dug trenches and placed cannons, and surrounded the whole city so that *it was impossible to either exit or enter (nel'zja bylo^I ni vyjti^P, ni vojti^P)* it.'

The Old Russian protoperfective under negation, then, occurs in durative contexts, while the protoimperfective under negation appears in progressive contexts. Consequently, the Old Russian protoperfective seems largely restricted to temporal negation; it tends not to negate expectation the way the Modern Russian perfective does under negation in (100a). A similar contrast occurs between (101) and (102).

(101) И воистинну, на всякий день аки три недѣли тое бѣды было, яко и брашна намъ оного зѣло нужнаго **не дали приимати** многожды. (240-2)
'And truly, each day for three weeks this misfortune continued, for many times *they did not let (ne dali)* us *take (priimati)* our very meager rations.'

(101a) *tr:* И действительно, ежедневно в течение трех недель происходило это несчастье, так что зачастую **не давали** нам **употребить** крайне скудное наше питание. (241-3)
'And truly, this misfortune occurred daily for three weeks, so that often *they did not let (ne davali)* us *partake (upotrebit')* of our quite meager foodstuffs.'

(102) Так худые люди и ничемуже годные чаровницы тебя... держали пред темъ аки во оковахъ, повелѣвающе тебѣ в мѣру ясти и пити и со царицею жити, **не дающе** тебе ни в чесомже своей воли а ни в малѣ, а не в великомъ, а ни людей своихъ миловати, а ни царствомъ твоимъ владѣти. (312)
'Thus did bad people, and good-for-nothing sorcerers... hold you then as if in fetters, ordering you to eat and drink with moderation, and to live with the tsaritsa, *not allowing (ne dajušče)* you your own will in anything—not in the slightest or greatest measure, nor to take mercy upon your own people, nor to reign in your own kingdom.'

(102a) *tr:* Столь скверные люди и бесполезные колдуны тебя... как в оковах содержали до сих пор, приказывая тебе есть и пить в меру, жить с царицей, ни в чем **не давая** тебе свободы — ни в малом, ни в великом, ни милости людям своим даровать, ни царством своим управлять. (313)

'Such base people and good-for-nothing sorcerers... held you as if in fetters up till then, ordering you to eat and drink with moderation, live with the tsaritsa, not allowing *(ne davaja^I)* you any freedom—in matters neither small nor great, nor to grant your people mercy, nor to run your own kingdom.'

The protoperfective past *ne dali* 'they did not let' in (101) holds over a specified period of time (three weeks), whereas the protoimperfective *ne dajušče* 'not allowing' in (102) is presented as an act of unspecified duration that co-occurs with other acts ('ordering', 'holding'). The limitation of time in (103) is more contextual in nature but is nonetheless unequivocal: Kurbskij says he did not want to talk about the tsar for a long time but eventually broke down under the weight of constant questioning.

(103) И многожды умолчахъ со воздыханиемъ и слезами, **не восхотѣхъ** отвѣщати. Последи же, частыхъ ради вопрошений, принужденъ былъ нѣчто рещи отчасти о случаехъ приключшихся таковыхъ. (218)
'And many a time I fell silent with sighs and tears; *I did not want (ne vosxotěx")* to answer. Later, though, because of the frequent requests, I was compelled to say something in part about these events that have occurred.'

(103a) *tr:* И каждый раз со вздохами и слезами я отмалчивался и **не хотел** отвечать. В конце концов постоянные расспросы принудили меня кое-что рассказать о том, что же все-таки произошло. (219)
'And each time, with sighs and tears, I fell silent and *did not want (ne xotel^I)* to answer. In the end, constant requests compelled me to say something about what did in fact happen.'

The context is therefore durative, as compared to (104), where the aorist *ne xotěša* says nothing about duration, but simply expresses the captors' attitude toward their prisoner.

(104) И держаша его жива аки два лѣта и потом убиша его: **не хотѣша** его а ни на откуп, о ни на отмѣну своихъ дати. (272)
'And they held him alive for about two years, and then killed him; *they did not want (ne xotěša)* to take a ransom for him, nor to trade him for their own men.'

(104a) *tr:* Держали его живым года два, а потом убили его: **не хотели** ни выкуп за него взять, ни в обмен за своих отдать. (273)
'They held him alive for about two years, and then killed him; *they did not want (ne xoteli^I)* to take a ransom for him, nor to trade him for their own men.'

A more troubling problem involves the infinitive complement of a negated verb. In the Old Russian examples (99) and (100), the negative modifies a protoperfective verb, while the following infinitive is protoimperfective.[46] In (99a) and (100a), however, the negative modifies a Modern Russian imperfective verb, while the infinitive complement is perfective. This picture is not consistent for all infinitive complements of negated verbs, but it does pose a problem when it occurs: what governs the choice of aspectual forms in the two texts?

There are two ways to answer this question. In general, the Modern Russian choice of a perfective infinitive can indicate lack of result: the scope of the negation applies to the infinitive as well as to the finite verb, and the importance of negating the first act is in its effect on the second. A negated imperfective infinitive implies that the important factor is the absence of ability or state; a negated perfective infinitive focuses on the lack of result.[47] In places where a negated finite form suggests a denial of ability or permission, a perfective infinitive complement is more natural: the negated perfective aspectually implies a contradiction of volition or expectation, just as the negated finite form implies it lexically.

Old Russian does not assign protoaspects on the basis of possible results or expectations of the act; instead, aspect indicates the endpoints of the act in a more or less consistent fashion, and does not indicate discourse features. The protoimperfective infinitive in these circumstances indicates the lack of any action during the period in question. In Old Russian, then, negation extended over a period of time suggests a protoimperfective complement to a negated protoperfective form; volition and expectation are indicated by the presence or absence of lexical elements, not by the aspect of the finite form or the infinitive.

If volition and expectation can be marked lexically by auxiliary verbs, they can also be marked by certain prefixes, such as {do-} 'as far as, up to'. Example (105) presents an explicit parallel between infinitives after negated verbs and lexical volition or expectation under negation.

(105)   И **не доѣзжаючи** монастыря Кирилова, еще Шексною-рѣкою
         плывучи, сынъ ему, по пророчеству святаго, умре. (272)
         'And *without reaching (ne doězžajuči)* St. Cyril's Monastery, while they were still sailing on the River Šeksna, his son died, as the holy one had foretold.'

---

[46] Despite other aspectual fluctuations in this verb family, *priimati* 'take' in (101) is not protoperfective. The protoperfective *prijati* is well-attested in this text; there are no derived forms other than *priimati*. Contrast this to *poimati* 'seize', which is amply attested in perfective contexts. Only one example of *pojati* is attested, while a double-derived form *poimovati* is also attested. The differing assignments of *priimati* and *poimati* are confirmed by Sreznevskij.

[47] The fact that infinitive assignment resembles assignment of the finite form is made explicit by comparing these similar Modern Russian sentences: *my ne vyšli^P* 'we didn't go outside^P' vs. *my ne mogli^I vyjti^P* 'we couldn't go outside^P'. Despite the presence of the auxiliary *moč'^{I}* 'be able^I' in the second sentence, the two sentences often have the same meaning, although the first sentence has a broader range of potential meanings than the second ('we tried to go out but couldn't'; 'we intended to go out but didn't'; 'we were expected to go out but didn't').

(105a) *tr:* Но **не доехали** они до Кириллова монастыря, а плыли еще по Шексне-реке, когда, по пророчеству святого, умер его сын. (273)
'But *they did not reach (ne doexali^P)* St. Cyril's Monastery, and were still sailing on the River Šeksna when, as the holy one had foretold, his son died.'

The Old Russian participial form *ne doězžajuči* 'without reaching' implies a progressive context; the tsar's son dies during their journey, before they reach the monastery. The Modern Russian in (105a) uses the perfective past *ne doexali* 'they did not reach/had not reached' instead; the resort to a finite form reveals a problem inherent in the translation. The negating of lexical volition implied in the prefix {do-}, requires a perfective verb; the sense of progressivity is then lost, as there is no grammatical way to show progressivity with a perfective verb. However, by resorting to finite forms, the stronger sense of sequencing implied by a perfective verbal adverb is avoided. The combination of conativity and progressivity is suggested by the perfective past tense *ne doexali* 'they did not reach' and the imperfective past tense *plyli ešče po Šeksne-reke* 'they were still sailing along the Šeksna river'; the word *ešče* 'still' is needed to accurately depict the situation.

The Modern Russian *ne doexali^P* in (105a), however, is at least mildly ambiguous, indicating either an interrupted act ('they had not yet reached the monastery when...') or a failed act ('they did not reach the monastery'). A few sentences later, it is mentioned that the party did finish their journey to the monastery after the child's death, and this conclusively establishes the first reading as the correct one. This ambiguity results from the fact that negation in Modern Russian centers around the existence of a result, whereas negation in Old Russian focuses on the duration of the act. The Old Russian form *ne doezžajuči* thus expresses interruption of a process while admitting that the process took place, whereas neither Modern Russian form can convey this same meaning unambiguously.

In (106), a similar negation of lexical volition shows the aspectualization of volition in Modern Russian but not in Old Russian. The example differs from (105) in that the heathen king's failure to reach the other side is absolute; the enemy never does get there.

(106) И **не доходя**, от нас сталъ аки за пять миль, за великими крѣпостьми блатъ и за рекою единою. К нам же **дале не пошелъ**, подобно боялся... (286)
'And *without reaching (ne doxodja)* us, he stopped about five miles short, beyond great barriers of swamps and one river. He *came no further (dale ne pošel")* toward us; he was probably afraid...'

(106a) *tr:* Но, **не дойдя** до нас, стал он в милях пяти за рекой и большими непроходимыми болотами. А **дальше** на нас **не пошел**, вероятно, боялся... (287)
'But, *not having reached (ne dojdja^P)* us, he stopped about five miles short, beyond the river and great, impassable swamps. And he *came no further (dal'še ne pošel^P)* toward us; he was probably afraid...'

The second boldfaced predicate in (106) bears witness to the fact that an Old Russian negated protoperfective (*dale ne pošel*" 'he did not go any further') can correspond to a Modern Russian negated perfective, as in (106a), expressing frustration of expectation or intention. However, cases like these may indicate aspectual concord by coincidence rather than by similarity of meaning. The Old Russian *pošel* often had an inceptive meaning 'set out', and thus the negated protoperfective in (106) may simply indicate that no such inception occurred. The Modern Russian in (106a), on the other hand, has a clear contrary-to-expectation reading (the enemy was expected to advance further but did not). It is worth examining a few more protoperfectives under negation to determine if this potential discourse function was present or not in Old Russian.

In the sorts of contexts that immediately interest us here—past tense forms under negation—protoimperfectives heavily outnumber protoperfectives in Kurbskij's text. The negated past tense protoperfectives do not in fact show regular signs of negating volition, although there is some evidence that they negate expectations. Example (107), which parallels the usage found in (95)—*serdcem" ne sokrušili* 'they did not break their will'—could indicate a fact contrary to expectations: despite the awful odds, the enemy did not succeed in bringing them to despair, although the implication is that they tried.

(107) Корыстовники же оные предреченные... в таковое абие бѣгствс вдашеся, яко и во врата многие не попали, но множайшие и с корыстми чрез стѣну металися, а иные и корысти повергоша, толко вопиюще: «Секут! Секут!» Но за благодатию божиею храбрыхъ сердцемъ **не сокрушили.** (252)
'These aforementioned plunderers... immediately set off running such that many did not even get through the gates, but a great number with their plunder hurled themselves over the wall, and others abandoned their plunder, merely crying: "They're attacking! They're attacking!" But through the grace of God they *did not break (ne sokrušili)* the will of the brave.'

However, it could also sum up the Muscovite opposition during this attack—another use of the negated protoperfective in a durative context. In (108)—seen earlier as (68)—the Cheremisians address their ruler.

(108) «Мы было взяли тебя того ради на царство з дворомъ твоимъ, да обороняеши нас; а ты и сущие с тобою **не сотворилъ** намъ помощи столько, сколько воловъ и коров наших поѣлъ. А нынѣ глава твоя да царствует на высокомъ колѣ!» (280)
' "We had chosen you and your retinue for our kingdom, that you might defend us; but you and those with you *have not given (ne sotvoril")* us help equal to the number of oxen and cows you have eaten. So now let your head rule on a tall pike!" '

In this passage, they conclude that their chosen ruler and his retinue have failed to deliver the help they expected, despite the ruler's prodigious consumption of

Cheremisian beef. Once again, it is the expectations that are countered with the negated protoperfective; no sense of volition is intended.

Example (109) shows that discourse functions did not apply to all negated protoperfectives. Here the negated protoperfective perfect *ne polučil* 'did not receive' simply indicates a lack that predated the advice: there are gifts that the tsar did not receive from God, but this hardly indicates volition or expectation.

(109)   Царь, аще и почтенъ царствомъ, а даровании, которыхъ от бога **не получил**, должен искати добраго и полезнаго совѣта не токмо у совѣтниковъ, но у всеродныхъ человѣкъ... (268)
'A tsar, even if honored by his kingdom, and by gifts which *he did not receive (ne polučil)* from God, must seek good and useful advice not only from his advisors, but also from all sorts of people...'

In Old Russian, as in Modern Russian, many negated protoperfectives simply indicate negation of the act—without specifically indicating a result or a process. Sometimes, then, the Old Russian protoperfective matches the function of the Modern Russian perfective, either by showing a reversal of expectation or by simply noting the lack of result. In other places, though, the Modern Russian may imply expectations and a failure to fulfill them that are lacking in the Old Russian text.

The negated Old Russian protoperfective focuses more on explicitly limited duration than its Modern Russian counterpart does, and this difference is symptomatic of the Old Russian aspectual system in general. Old Russian does not invoke the same pragmatic and discourse-oriented concerns about results that we find in Modern Russian. Instead, it delineates duration and clear endpoints of an act in a more systematic fashion. Occasionally, with negated protoperfectives, it is possible to see the beginnings of a system concerned with expectations of speaker and addressee, but for the most part, extragrammatical concerns such as volition and ability are not expressed through aspectual forms, as is seen from the usage patterns of negated modal verbs and negated verbs with the prefix {do-}.

The lack of systematic representation of discourse features through aspect recalls the failure to represent conativity in Old Russian aspect, which was discussed in section 8.5.2. Conativity is also a function of discourse (when not lexicalized, as with *iskati* 'search') and the speaker's imposition of volition and expectation on the performer of the act.

8.7. CONCLUSIONS

Kurbskij's text yields several important clues about the development of aspect in Old Russian. First, it testifies to the increasing regularity of the aspectual system in Old Russian. More and more, verbs can be used in only one out of two possible sets of meanings and contexts, and to the extent possible, each verb is paired with a form expressing the complementary set of meanings. This is shown by the use of three tests: the compound future test; the historical present test; and the sublexical aspect test. In all three cases, Kurbskij's aspectual system shows more signs of regular, grammatical aspect than do the earlier texts in this survey. Isolated signs of anaspectuality, such as certain tenses and forms of verbs of perception, no longer fit into a larger pattern of anaspectuality in the verbal system and are best seen as relics of an older organization of the verbal system.

The status of conativity, volition, and other discourse features in the aspectual system illustrates one major difference between the Old Russian and Modern Russian verbal systems. In the Modern Russian verbal system, imperfective verbs often express conative acts, and negated perfective verbs often express frustration of intent, expectation, or volition. Infinitive complements of verbs indicating various forms of possibility fall into the latter category when the auxiliary verb is negated. Furthermore, conativity in Modern Russian is extended not only to situations where an act fails to take place or fails to be completed, but also to situations where a completed act fails to have the desired result. This means that punctual acts, which are difficult to conceive of as "incomplete," can also be conative; for example, if an utterance fails to have an effect on the hearer, it can have a conative reading in Modern Russian. Modern Russian thus has a means of extending conativity to lexical classes not covered in a narrow definition of conativity. Old Russian has such forms (see chapter 7), but they tend to be specialized double-suffixed verbs.

Although discourse features play a pervasive role in the Modern Russian aspectual opposition, in Old Russian their role is smaller. Protoimperfective forms rarely convey conativity; instead, contextual information in the sentence conveys conativity. Protoperfective forms under negation can have these discourse functions, but most often these functions are expressed through other explicit features in the context or in the lexical item (here, the prefix or the modal verb).

Adding discourse features to an aspectual system has a complex effect on the nature of the aspectual system. On the one hand, it is an expansion of the scope of aspect. In Old Russian, discourse features do not have a measurable impact on aspect, whereas in Modern Russian they condition the appearance of one aspect or the other. Chart 8.7.1 maps out what the expanded Modern Russian imperfective–perfective opposition now expresses.

This expansion of the use of the aspectual opposition comes at a price: in adding to the number of functions aspect encompasses, it dilutes the ability of the aspectual opposition to express some of its central functions economically, without extra contextual markers. The Old Russian aspectual system of this text, while less versatile, provides clearer markers of duration because it does not attempt to convey discourse features in a systematic fashion.

Another difference between the Old and Modern Russian aspectual systems found here is the wider prevalence of derived imperfectives in Modern Russian. This text has numerous Old Russian protoimperfective simplexes that are translated consistently in the Modern Russian version by derived imperfectives. In other places, the Old Russian makes a semantic distinction or a usage distinction between a simplex verb and its derived counterpart, while the Modern Russian translation shows the absence of this distinction, or a shift in the distinction favoring wider usage of the derived verb.

Chart 8.7.1. Some Modern Russian realizations of the aspectual opposition

Affirmative sentences

I:		**P:**
no mention of result	vs.	presence of result
frustrated attempt (conativity)		success or completion of an act
volition		
expectation		

Negative sentences

I:		**P:**
temporary absence of result	vs.	permanent negation of a result
lack of attempt		frustrated attempt (conativity)
lack of volition		negation of expectation or desire
lack of expectation		lack of success

The shift from simplexes to derived forms is considered a crucial process in the history of Russian, because it shows that lexical aspectual markers, like prefixation, give way to "purely aspectual" markers, like suffixation. A corollary assumption is that the aspectual system is "simplified" or "regularized" in the course of this development. The first claim is probable, if we leave aside for a moment the question of whether Modern Russian suffixed verbs are all equal—that is, whether suffixation always transforms perfectivity into imperfectivity in exactly the same way. The second claim is not supported by either Old Russian or Modern Russian data, which indicate that the Old Russian simplex–prefixed opposition is not realized purely as a "prefixed derived–prefixed nonderived" opposition in Modern Russian. The slight semantic differentiations found in the Old Russian text, which indicate a system in the process of change, often correspond to a similarly complex system of simplexes and prefixed forms, both suffixed and nonsuffixed, in Modern Russian. The data presented suggest that the creation of derived forms, while a strong ongoing tendency, was highly individualized, with varied influences and results in each case.

The creation and increased use of suffixed forms thus by no means simplifies the idiosyncratic state of affairs seen in Old Russian aspect; rather, the Modern Russian picture is equally as complex as the Old Russian one but differs from it in two respects. First, the increased number of suffixed forms in Modern Russian means that the match in meaning between perfective and imperfective verbs is closer, making the pair more purely aspectual. Second, the lexical and valence distinctions characteristic of the Old Russian situation are likely in Modern Russian to be replaced by textual, stylistic, discourse, or pragmatic distinctions. In other words, a competition between simplex and derived form whose spheres of usage are defined by valence or by lexical meaning is typical of Old Russian. In Modern Russian, a competition between simplex and derived form is more likely to involve stylistic levels or emotional content of words; the choice of forms suggests a discourse strategy.

9. Russian Aspect and Language Change

9.0. STRUCTURE OF THE CHAPTER

This concluding chapter gives a thumbnail sketch of some recent theories of language change and puts the development of Russian aspect into a cross-linguistic perspective by gathering together some language-specific trends discussed throughout this study and checking how they fit into, expand, or modify the analysis of language change. While this work primarily treats the development of a particular language, the overall picture of aspectual development plotted here has ramifications for how we understand the processes of grammaticalization of morphemes and other types of language change.

With the prosperity of grammaticalization in recent years as a topic of diachronic linguistic study, a number of the traditional assumptions about the processes it includes and invokes have been widely debated, and connections have been drawn between grammaticalization and other fields of linguistic investigation, such as cognitive science. Some overall trends are sketched in section 9.1. Of particular relevance to this study are the necessity of proceeding from meaningful word to non-word (section 9.2); the relationships between grammaticalization, metaphors and metonyms in language (section 9.3); the connection between grammaticalization and semantic abstractness (section 9.4); and the role of telicity in assigning a future function to one aspect (section 9.5). Concluding remarks appear in section 9.6, and an epilogue is found on the final page.

The analysis in sections 9.1 through 9.5 of this chapter is programmatic and serves more as an outline for future investigation than as a thorough discussion of the ideas in question.

9.1. GRAMMATICALIZATION AND LANGUAGE CHANGE

The observation that the pieces of language we recognize as grammar-marking morphemes change from time to time dates from the nineteenth century. This phenomenon was described early on as "semantic bleaching" or "weakening": a word that originally had a clear lexical function can gradually be co-opted for use as an obligatory, semantically empty marker with a function defined in the grammar. Classic examples from Meillet (1966: 169-170) are negative particles: French *ne... pas* 'not', originally from *ne* 'not' and *pas* 'step'. The latter slowly came to be required as part of the negative verb marker and lost its original semantic load in these contexts. The development of the perfect tense in French is another well-attested process: an independent verb allied with a participle changed into an auxiliary verb with a participle that expresses a result of a past act enduring into the present, and from there evolves into a generalized marker of the past tense with no specifically "perfect" meaning (Benveniste 1968: 89-92). Meillet notes that grammaticalization leaves the form in question with an expanded range of meanings and usages from strongly lexical (*je suis celui qui suis* 'I am the one who is') to purely grammatical and nonlexical (*je suis parti* 'I left'), with intermediate stages displaying varying degrees of semantic strength (*je suis chez moi* 'I am at home', *je suis malade* 'I am sick').[1]

In the 1970s and 1980s, the notion of grammaticalization was revisited, reworked and incorporated into more general theories of linguistic change and morphological development, including those of Givón and Bybee.[2] It has also been applied in historical reconstructions of languages with no written traditions; most notable in this vein are works by Heine and Reh (1984) and Heine, Claudi, and Hünnemeyer (1991a and b). Most recently, Traugott has set forth an expanded view of grammaticalization, which proposes that a straight path from "more meaning" to "less meaning" is not the only possible route for the semantic development of morphemes. Traugott instead posits several types of change that involve lexical, grammatical, and discourse levels of language.

The history of Russian aspect provides an interesting perspective on these questions. From a linguistic standpoint, Russian is well described and has a long recorded history; in addition, it is an inflected language that has remained so throughout its history, unlike the Germanic or Romance languages. Its morphological markers have been relatively stable, and all the markers attested in aspectual use are extant in some sort of aspectual role from the time of the earliest writings. From a typological standpoint, the aspectual opposition is the predominant feature of the Modern Russian verbal system; many prominent studies of grammaticalization, by contrast, have concentrated on the development of single words into temporal markers or the creation of single tenses within an established tense system. A study of Russian aspect covers numerous semantic changes and morphological markers that—to a certain extent—eventually come to reflect a single aspectual opposition. Therefore, examining Russian aspect will provide a counterbalance to some trends seen in the development of Western European languages and will offer a look at how grammaticalization interacts with other competing (and sometimes countergrammaticalizing) processes that also act to shape the Russian aspectual system.

9.2. THE PATH(S) OF GRAMMATICALIZATION

As mentioned above, the canonical view of grammaticalization in the early twentieth century was that a word begins with a strong lexical meaning, which through repeated use gradually loses its distinctness, both semantically and

---

[1] Cited in Hopper and Traugott (1993: 21). German and the North Slavic languages exhibit analogous developments in the perfect tense.

[2] Some scholars prefer the terms "grammaticization" or "grammatization." There are various arguments for and against all the terms; I follow Traugott's reasoning in using "grammaticalization," since it has the longest pedigree historically and the arguments against it are not particularly weighty.

phonetically; in addition to its original meaning, it takes on meanings that are more abstract or more grammatical in nature. The two forces that were said to drive this process were the need for ease of speech and clarity of expression. Ease of speech meant that phonetic reductions were constantly taking place, "wearing away" the existing words and morphemes and morphemes in the language; clarity of expression meant that speakers constantly had to recruit new words and items to shore up the meanings and categories represented by the abraded forms. The examples of grammaticalization given in section 9.1 are in fact explained adequately (if minimally) by the simple laws depicted in chart 9.2.1.

Chart 9.2.1. The basics of grammaticalization

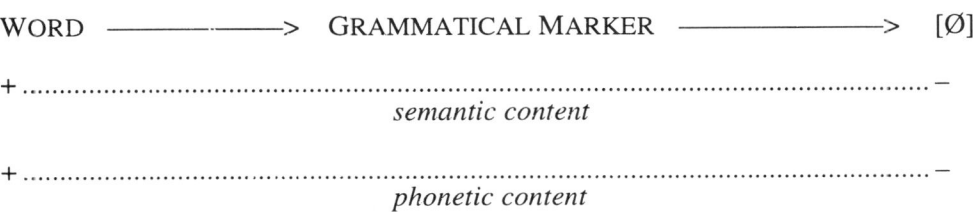

As the scope of investigation into these processes widened in the 1970s, it became evident that grammaticalization was in fact a feature of language change that was widely applicable across languages and across linguistic phenomena, from word order (English and Hebrew) to tense formation (French, Spanish) to adverbs (Old English). However, for this new, expanded definition of grammaticalization, the path of development proposed by Meillet and later by Benveniste was not adequate. It neither described the particulars of the process of change in enough detail nor gave an accurate picture of the final results of the process.

In a series of articles from 1982 to 1991, Traugott described the possible paths a word or marker could take in the course of grammaticalization. In her original formulation (1982: 257), lexical items are reinterpreted into grammatical proposition markers, grammatical text markers, or grammatical expressive markers. Within each of these categories, there is a sliding scale between more and less personal features. The main path of transformation is from the propositional (referential) to the textual and the expressive, but from any of these three categories, a marker may be transformed into a "dummy marker" and thence disappear altogether (although this need not necessarily happen).

In later articles (Traugott 1990, Traugott and König 1991) she simplified this plan, extending it to all semantic change (1990: 497-498) and stating that semantic change yields a shift "from meanings grounded in more or less objectively identifiable extralinguistic situations to meanings grounded in text-making (for example connectives, anaphoric markers, etc." (Traugott and König 1991: 189). This statement can be expanded into three tendencies: that meanings "based in the external described situation" give way to meanings "based in the internal situation," which is "evaluative, perceptual or cognitive"; that "meanings based in the described situation" give way to "meanings based in the metalinguistic situation;" and that "meanings tend to become increasingly based in the speaker's subjective belief, state or attitude toward the situation" (Traugott 1990: 499-500).

Nichols and Timberlake (1991) provide a counterbalance to Traugott's generalization of semantic change and grammaticalization. Using historical data on the Russian predicate instrumental, they argue that too much attention is given to the endpoints of the process of grammaticalization and not enough to the language-internal processes that shape the changes taking place (1991: 144). The Russian predicate instrumental was a particularly apt choice for this study precisely because it is an example of change in a language's grammar that does not introduce new morphemes, the loss of old ones, or the simplification of a system. Instead, it involves the gradual extension of the predicate instrumental—through textual analogy—from a very limited set of contexts to a much wider (but not exclusive) set. Nichols and Timberlake propose "retextualization" as a less teleological cover term for the processes that cause this sort of change.

The history of Russian aspect confirms portions of both these lines of thought. One tenet of grammaticalization is that it begins from a reinterpretation in one corner of a system and gradually spreads to the remainder of the system.[3] In the case of Russian aspect, this reinterpretation happens when a certain kind of telicity begins to be linked explicitly first with temporal and then with aspectual limitations, which up to that point had been conveyed contextually. A protoaspectual opposition based on prefixation and suffixation as aspectualizers develops for nonpunctual telic acts and gradually spreads to the remainder of the verbal system. This change is represented in chart 9.2.2.

The Old Russian aspectual system reconstructed for the Chronicles catches this change in process in two respects. First, it shows regular usages of both grammaticalized prefixes in the telic class (a newer prefixal function) and nongrammaticalized prefixes in the atelic class (the original spatial function of prefixes). The expansion of telicizing prefixes into the atelic class is also attested. Second, Old Russian derivational suffixes start out having a clear aspectualizing function (explicit process vs. nonexplicit process) only in the nonpunctual telic class of predicates; for punctual telic predicates they tend to add iterativity or other nonaspectual functions, and the consistent ability to express explicit process as opposed to result comes only later.

As for the direction of change, the system does clearly move from the propositional domain (lexical aspect, which is based in objectively observable features of acts) to the textual or expressive domain (quasi-grammatical, context-oriented, and later discourse-oriented aspect, which establish the effects an act has on its immediate and more remote contexts and on understandings of the relationship and attitudes that exist between speaker and addressee)—but this generalization holds only if one emphasizes the discourse-based nature of Modern

---

[3] I am grateful to Gary Holland for suggesting this interpretation.

Russian aspect and downplays the objective qualities of the quasi-grammatical aspectual opposition. (Evidence for the recent provenance of discourse-based aspectual meaning in Russian was given in sections 8.6 and 8.7.)

Chart 9.2.2. The spread of aspect in Old Russian

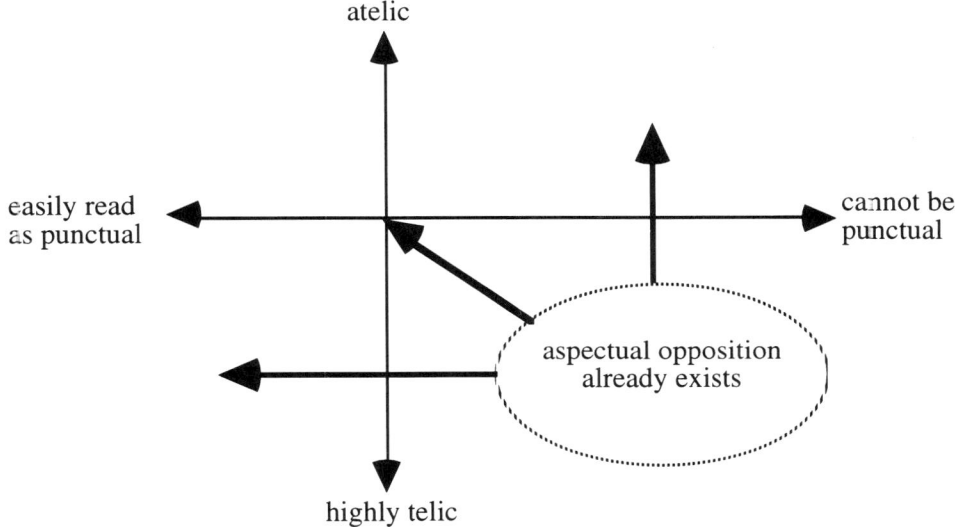

Earlier in this analysis, I examined relations between the simplexes, simple prefixed verbs, and suffixed verbs that form aspectual networks in Russian. This examination confirms that aspectual markers are moving from the propositional to the expressive component; as was seen in chapter 8, the Old Russian distribution of derived forms vs. simplexes is primarily lexical (differing meanings) or contextual (different valences and modifiers), whereas the difference between the same simplex and its derived form in Modern Russian often has an expressive character, indicating different emotional evaluations of the act or different styles of speech and writing.

However, the outlines of this development also support Nichols and Timberlake's conclusions that diachronic changes in the grammar need not apply only to discrete lexical entities and need not inevitably push the markers involved toward a final grammatical resting place or toward phonological reduction. The development of aspect, after all, involves prefixation and suffixation, as well as a host of related textual developments, and does not lead to the enshrining of any one item as a "grammatical" marker of aspect. Rather, after a thousand years, the morphemes involved in determining Russian aspect are still the same; only their distribution and their relations have changed.

The specific features of Old Russian aspect related to grammaticalization will be discussed in the following three sections.

9.3. METAPHORS, METONYMS, AND ASPECT

It has often been suggested that the human capacity for metaphoric or metonymic representation (or both of them) plays a crucial role in grammaticalization. A meaning or function associated with one form spreads to another form in the same realm or to nearby elements in the sentence (metonymy) or is inferred from a "similar" form in a different realm (metaphor), thus extending and changing the meaning of the target form. In practice, as Heine, Claudi and Hünnemeyer note (1991a: 64), the boundary between them is fuzzy. Two recent monographs on grammaticalization (Heine, Claudi and Hünnemeyer 1991a and Hopper and Traugott 1993) agree that use of metaphor and metonymy need not be mutually exclusive, and that both are involved in grammaticalization.

As an example of this interaction of metaphor and metonymy, Hopper and Traugott cite the development of an English future tense *be going to*. Originally a verb of direction plus a purpose clause, a syntactic reanalysis redefines it as a tense marker plus an action. By analogy, this usage is extended to all possible verbs, not only those where motion is necessary to reach the goal (1993: 88). In this approach, then, metonymy precedes metaphor and lays the groundwork for it (see chart 9.3.1).

Chart 9.3.1. Hopper and Traugott (1993: 61) on metonymy and metaphor.

Syntagmatic axis: mechanism is reanalysis

Stage I	be PROG	going V_{dir}	to visit Bill Purpose clause	
Stage II	be going to TENSE		visit Bill V_{act}	*Paradigmatic axis: mechanism is analogy*
	(by syntactic reanalysis/metonymy)			
Stage III	be going to TENSE		like Bill V	
	(by analogy/metaphor)			

(In *Grammaticalization*, © Cambridge University Press, 1993. Reprinted with the permission of Cambridge University Press.)

This approach assumes greatly expanded definitions of "metonymy" and "metaphor." In Hopper and Traugott's analysis, metonymy takes place not only between contiguous concepts but also between contiguous syntactic items, making reanalysis the syntactic result of metonymy. Metaphor is said to include all kinds of analogical replacement as well, and analogy is defined as the mechanism for realizing metaphor (1993: 87-89). However, this example is probably too clean-cut; the mechanisms of reanalysis and analogy need not be neatly slotted into two opposite overarching principles of language change labelled respectively "metonymy" and "metaphor."

Heine, Claudi, and Hünnemeyer take a less binary view of these processes. They refer to the type of metonymy used above as "context-induced reinterpretation" and see it as a gradual precursor to an inevitable metaphoric leap of reinterpretation. Whereas the contexts for the former are manifold, metaphoric shifts move along certain favored channels, the most general of which is PERSON > OBJECT > ACTIVITY > SPACE > TIME > QUALITY (1991a: 65). The direction of the arrows indicates the extension of meaning from one category to the next; items applicable to persons are later extended to objects, then to activities, and so forth.[4] The items themselves then develop branching structures representing their extensions into different meanings.

The data from Russian aspect can be of use here on several counts. As Brinton (1988) showed for English, aspectual development is a particularly thorny area for this sort of investigation, because of the breadth of its application across the verbal system, its numerous morphologically unrelated components, and the difficulties of establishing endpoints for the process. This complexity makes it difficult to justify attaching one metaphor to one word or morpheme. Brinton's solution (1988: 106, 114, 236) was to define metonymy and metaphor as distinct but parallel and competing processes: in her reckoning, the development of aspectualizers in English is purely metonymic, not metaphoric, because the shifts in meaning are gradual, concern closely related notions, and preserve meaning rather than bleaching it.[5] The data from the history of Russian aspect support Brinton's suspicion of invoking sudden, early metaphoric shifts prefiguring the final attested stage and will show more support for gradual change—although, paradoxically, some of these early minor changes in Russian seem more metaphoric than metonymic in character. In addition, the development of Russian aspect includes numerous simultaneous processes (prefixation, suffixation, abstraction, etc.) and presents some interesting counterexamples to the general notion of metaphoric and metonymic extension.

This complexity is not immediately evident in examining the history of Russian aspect. At first, the process of creating a grammatical aspectual system in Russian

---

[4] Heine Claudi, and Hünnemeyer say that these shifts move from less to more abstract; this usage of the word "abstract" is somewhat different than ordinary usage. See section 9.4.

[5] One difficulty with Brinton's account is her reliance on a clear divide between metonymic and metaphoric relations, when a cline might be a more appropriate model; another is her assumption that metaphoric change inevitably involves semantic bleaching, which, as Brinton correctly points out, does not take place in the evolution of aspectualizers.

appears to be a straightforward case of grammaticalization: the extension of originally spatial lexical markers to the entire verbal system with aspectual (abstract) meaning. Furthermore, at a certain point, prefixes and derivational suffixes do obtain grammatical functions, respectively those of perfectivizers and imperfectivizers. This much is old news.

This study has focused on the later, historically attested processes that constitute this change, and that consequently present a more complex and gradual picture of aspectualization. In the aspectual system of the Chronicles, prefixed forms and the process of prefixation have an ambiguous status. The numerous purely spatial, nonaspectual uses of prefixes in Old Russian suggest that in the prehistoric era, prefixes had a spatial meaning, which applied both to stationary situations and acts that presumed some sort of motion. Several reinterpretations must take place to account for both the situation in the Chronicles and developments seen in later texts.

First, states that do not explicitly involve location and actions that do not strictly involve travel become equated with states of location and acts of motion. Since some actions *(rěka teče* 'the river flows') apparently end up being perceived as more similar to states than to motions, this remapping must take account of action contours, establishing a system of lexical aspect for the Prehistoric Slavic verb. As a consequence, spatial prefixes acquire the more general ability to attach to verbal forms of nonspatial predicates. This first phase must have occurred quite early—in Prehistoric Slavic, at any rate—because prefixation is attested with all types of acts from the very earliest Russian texts. Without attestation, it is difficult to pin a label on the process; it clearly represents a change (whether metaphoric leap or metonymic creep) that says that 'space' is not just for indicators of location and motion, because all acts occur in a location and all changes are a type of movement.

A corollary to this process is that once nondirectional acts accept prefixes to show "direction," large numbers of prefixed forms crop up in the telic class, prompting a reinterpretation of spatial prefixes. In this reinterpretation, spatial prefixes indicate various kinds of goals (i.e. not strictly destinations) for the act. This process must start later or last longer than the first reinterpretation mentioned above, because it is still running its course in the Old Russian period.

Once the addition of a prefix clearly indicates that an act becomes "goal-oriented," or possibly "more goal-oriented," a reanalysis of the type "labelling the goal means attaining the goal" takes place. If these verbs ever did express process or generalized action, at this point they lose that ability and become limited to expressing goal attainment, with all the corresponding limitations on their tense and contextual usage it implies.

There is now a standard against which to judge the simplexes expressing telic acts. Those simplexes that do not explicitly label the goal with a separate morpheme are sorted out into the more and less telic; the latter begin to be perceived as indicators of action.[6] While they do not lose their ability to hint at the *presence*

---

[6] Maslov 1961 makes a similar case for the separation of simplexes by telicity, letting the more highly telic of them *(pasti* 'fall', *lišiti* 'deprive') become perfectives, while the rest become imperfectives *(pisati* 'write', *stroiti* 'build').

of a goal, they do lose their ability to mark its attainment. This process of loss begins first with the telic, nonpunctual acts (and will not overtake all the simplexes involved, such as the highly telic *pasti* 'fall', although it will affect a majority of them, such as *pisati* 'write'); it is retarded in the punctual telic class (*suditi* 'judge') thanks to the fact that duration is not an obligatory component of these acts. This is the beginning of a grammatical aspectual distinction in the telic, nonpunctual class, and it is at this stage that we first encounter Old Russian in the Chronicles.

Later in the process, these aspectual distinctions spread to atelic acts and punctual telic acts. Two further changes take place in the course of Old Russian. At the outset, in the Chronicles, lexical class distinctions—and thus aspectual distinctions—revolved around the predicate as a whole; at some point a syntactic reanalysis puts the aspectual burden on the verb form. This change is metonymic (in the syntactic sense in which Hopper and Traugott use the word). Second, "aspect" as a potential part of the grammar evolves from being primarily lexical in character—distinguishing a type of realized telicity—to distinguishing wholeness or completion in general, from whence it develops into its modern form, where wholeness and completeness are judged against other acts in the context and in the situation at large. This change is essentially metaphoric. However, this study has shown that the implementation of this metaphoric shift is not instantaneous and furthermore provides no indication that the metaphor "took hold" at one particular moment early in the aspectualization process. Rather, the metaphor appears to have taken hold piecemeal, or perhaps only as the change was nearly complete.

I mentioned earlier that the distinction between metaphor and metonymy might not be as clear as Brinton 1988 and Hopper and Traugott 1993 make it out to be. The path of aspectualization I proposed above for Russian illustrates this point. Incremental metonymic change is supposed to precede metaphoric change, and yet many of the early changes I proposed, while having only incremental results in usage, depend on quantum changes in the meaning of the forms. Furthermore, the final metaphoric change proposed is realized over a long period of time, and it is difficult to know where in the process to place the metaphoric reinterpretation. The final change could easily be metonymic, not metaphorical, since in some ways it merely works out the results of earlier metaphoric changes and extends them to the remainder of the verbal system. A more satisfactory result is achieved if metaphor and metonymy are accepted as poles on a continuum, with some changes containing elements of each.

9.3.1. Metaphoric and anti-metaphoric processes

A complicating factor touched on in this study is that aspectualization is in some respects an *antimetaphoric* process in that it limits the possible meanings of a lexeme, making them more specific and directed; it does not expand the possible meanings of a form. In the Chronicles, a simplex like *stojati* 'stand', *pisati* 'write', *suditi* 'judge' had a range of possible meanings defined and limited only by lexical and contextual features, but as aspect develops as a quasi-grammatical distinction, the simplex loses a number of those possibilities: it is restricted to use in certain tenses and certain contexts, and those functions it loses are given over to another verb, its prefixed "aspectual partner." A quasi-grammatical distinction thus expands its scope metaphorically as the semantic scope of individual lexemes is reduced.

Suffixation, the other primary morphological process of aspectualization, also plays a dual role. The suffixes used for aspectual derivation are clearly prehistoric in origin and are linked with the formants of the imperfect tense, but their path toward aspectualizers is complex. An imperfective verb in Modern Russian normally appears in a range of contexts (iterative, generalized, progressive, durative) that are not basic to the original suffixed verbs of Old Russian. In this study, it was observed that suffixed verbs representing nonpunctual telic acts were likely to appear in progressive contexts, whereas suffixed verbs expressing telic punctual acts were more likely to appear in iterative contexts. This distribution indicates that the use of suffixed forms in both meanings was originally lexically determined and did not simply spread from one lexical class to another (what Hopper and Traugott (1993) call metaphoric extension), but rather merged two converging uses of the suffixed form.

In a way, the development of suffixed forms also constitutes an antimetaphoric process: instead of a simplex form adding meanings, the creation of suffixed forms "spins off" a simplex's existing metaphoric meanings, reducing its sphere of usage to a subset of its old meanings, usually the most basic of them. Listed here are a few examples found in this study:

(1) *zvati~nazyvati* 'call, name', where the Old Russian simplex refers to people, animals or places, and the Modern Russian simplex refers only to people, with the latter two categories expressed (most neutrally) by the derived form (see chapter 6);

(2) *biti~izbivati* 'strike, kill, wound', where the Old Russian simplex has all forms and meanings, while the Modern Russian simplex yields to a derived form in some meanings and contexts; likewise *cvesti~rascvetati* 'flower, blossom', *platiti~otplačivati* 'pay, pay off', *pisati~zapisyvati* 'write, write down' (see section 8.4).[7]

In addition, the introduction of suffixed forms also reduces the contexts in which simple prefixed verbs appear; witness their use in the Chronicles to describe states (*rěka vteče* 'the river flows into') as compared with the use of suffixed verbs for this purpose in Kurbskij (*rěki vpadajut"* 'the rivers fall into'). A fuller explanation of this phenomenon is found in section 8.3.3.

I observed at various points in this study that the development of derived forms is not characterized by a tidy movement in the direction of any one particular feature; rather, there are several directions of change—and a generous amount of Brownian motion—in the semantic and contextual differentiation of derived forms from their original simplexes. This is not the sort of pattern associated with the great intuitive leaps of metaphoric change; rather, it suggests a welter of timid applications of analogy or metonymy.

---

[7] Hopper and Traugott (1993: 104-105) do note that generalization of meaning in one sphere often results in contraction of meaning in other spheres, but they do not expand on this point.

This is not to suggest that metaphoric processes do not occur; it simply suggests that metaphor played only a limited role in the development of Russian aspect. At any rate, an anti-metaphoric process like secondary imperfectivization in some respects assumes a metaphoric expansion of the simplexes in the preceding era. At a point in prehistory, the Russian simplex obtained a great flexibility in its ability to express meanings tangentially related to the verb's central meaning; the process driving this semantic expansion was probably metaphoric. The stages of Russian I have examined in this study portray the divestiture of these acquired meanings, presumably so that the process of metaphoric growth can begin once again.

9.4. ASPECTUALIZATION AND ABSTRACTNESS

From the earliest descriptions of grammaticalization, it was implicitly or explicitly linked to the process of *abstraction,* defined as the addition or suppletion of more abstract meanings to what began as a concrete meaning of an item.[8] More recent works on grammaticalization have preferred to view abstraction as a separate process that sometimes coincides with grammaticalization and sometimes does not. For instance, Heine, Claudi and Hünnemeyer claim that a shift in potential agreement or reference such as PERSON > OBJECT is metaphoric and leads in the direction of grammaticalization, but it seems unlikely that it also represents a greater degree of abstractness; after all, people and things are both equally concrete. Not all types of grammaticalization are abstractions, by their definition, and not all types of abstraction are grammaticalization. Their subsets of abstraction include generalizing abstraction, which is the process of creating larger and more general categories around one central feature in a taxonomic structure (in this sense, 'tree' is more "abstract" than 'oak'); isolating abstraction, which segments off a single, noncentral feature of an item; and metaphorical abstraction, which covers all other types. It is metaphorical abstraction that most often participates in the early stages of grammaticalization (1991a: 41-45).

The evidence from Old Russian aspect shows that abstraction does have an effect on the development of aspect, but it is unclear that this effect uniformly speeds up or slows down the development of grammatical aspect. If we limit our definition of abstraction to the type Heine, Claudi and Hünnemeyer label "metaphorical abstraction" (on the principle that this type is basic, and other types are extensions of it), then abstraction, when used with respect to verbs, is connected foremost to the process of prefixation (but not to all examples of prefixation) and the new "abstract" event is most likely to be one in which human perception plays a large role. In chart 2.7, abstraction moves events leftward (increasing punctuality) and downward (increasing telicity); nonabstract prefixation moves events

---

[8] I will use "abstractness" to mean "the property of being abstract" and "abstraction" to mean "the process of becoming abstract." This distinction is not found in everyday English, but it seems necessary for this discussion. Heine, Claudi, and Hünnemeyer also find such a distinction useful; they appeal to an "intuitive" difference in meaning between the two words (1991a: 41).

downward only (increasing telicity) if at all. In the history of Russian, increasing telicity leads to increased ease of aspectualization, while increasing punctuality blurs aspectual distinctions. Making an act more abstract through prefixation creates a form that will eventually be perfective, but simplexes that undergo abstraction without prefixation do not undergo aspectual assignment (e.g., *moliti sja* 'pray, say prayers' > 'beg, entreat' is anaspectual in both meanings in early Old Russian).

Scholars have noted that greater abstractness does not inevitably imply greater generality of meaning (as Heine, Claudi, and Hünnemeyer implicitly acknowledge by distinguishing generalizing abstraction from the other sorts). In Russian, at least, the process of prefixation usually creates a more lexically specific form, with a more limited range of possible valences. Examples from the Chronicles are *bljusti* 'guard, stand watch' vs. *sobljusti* 'protect'; *pasti* 'fall, fall down, prostrate oneself, die' vs. *napasti* 'attack'; *pisati* 'write' vs. *opisati* 'describe'; *praviti* 'lead, direct, do' vs. *ispraviti, upraviti* 'correct'. Suffixation likewise can, in certain cases, cause a change in meaning that is more abstract; witness Nikitin's *razbiti* 'break up' vs. *razbivati* 'be a pirate, be engaged in piracy'.

Furthermore, if we consider the prefix, which would be the actual "abstracting" morpheme, it is doubtful whether or not we can assign a coherent grammatical meaning to it that has any kind of predictive value. In virtually all of the examples above, it is impossible to assign a lexical or grammatical meaning to the prefix (or suffix) that connects it with the meaning of the simplex.

Abstraction thus has a limited predictive value for Russian aspectualization in the early historical period. The creation of an aspectual system cannot adequately be described as a shift from "concrete" to "abstract" meaning; neither does abstraction render predictable the changes in lexical items caused by prefixation. Abstraction has thus been confined in this study to occasional lexical shifts; however, it may not be a necessary part of the description even at this low level.

As noted earlier, one distinction that partially overlaps with the abstract–concrete opposition is the punctual vs. nonpunctual opposition, which is connected with the distinction between physically perceptible events and events that depend on a mental evaluation or response in order to be perceived. The latter are punctual; the former, nonpunctual. This correspondence is not exact, because semelfactive events are punctual and yet physically perceptible, but it is close. Labelling events "mental vs. physical" provides one advantage over the "abstract vs. concrete" definition: it shows that changing the latter into the former implies transferrence between one realm and another. Implicit in the notion of abstraction is the prejudice that more abstract concepts are a step up on the same hierarchy, offering a greater degree of universality, when in fact just the opposite may be true.

9.5. TELICITY, ASPECT AND FUTURITY

Studies by Bybee with Pagliuca and Perkins (1991), Dahl (1989), and Pagliuca (1985, 1987) have been aimed, in whole or in part, at developing a typology of future constructions and at reconstructing probable paths of development for them. Typologically, Bybee et al. find that futures most commonly develop from modal constructions and motion verbs; aspectual paths to futurity are rarer, and when they do develop, Bybee et al. find that imperfective forms are far more likely to obtain future meaning than perfectives (Bybee, Pagliuca and Perkins 1991: 20-22).

Bybee et al. do not devote much time to discussing aspectual sources for futurity. The studies concentrate on modal and motion constructions; the analysis of aspectual sources of futurity are limited to stating that "aspectual grams that have a future use are semantically very old, having gone through a long development before reaching the stage of signalling imperfective or present" (Bybee, Pagliuca and Perkins 1991: 45). The evidence for this statement is that aspectual future grammatical markers are morphologically closely bound to the verb stem and tend to convey futurity only in certain contexts; the age of this type of usage is defined explicitly by comparison with other, more closely studied patterns.

Bybee and Dahl do discuss the unusual place of Slavic languages in the general aspectual–temporal typology. They find that most perfective–imperfective oppositions apply only in the preterite; the future and the present (i.e. the non-past) are usually the province of the imperfective aspect alone. Slavic languages, and Russian in particular, constitute prominent counterexamples to this aspect–tense correlation because "morphologically the opposition between perfective and imperfective aspect is almost wholly independent of the category of tense in Russian; verbs of both aspects have both past and non-past (present) forms" (Bybee and Dahl 1989: 87). They ascribe this difference to the Slavic languages' generalization of telic, bounding prefixes to a much wider class of verbs and to their subsequent creation of new, imperfective forms through suffixation.

Later studies by Bybee et al. on the future employ statistics from their GRAMCAT database, which contains data from seventy-five genetically diverse languages. Slavic is not represented in the database, either because of, or despite, the anomalous character of Slavic aspect.

The present study, however, yields more precise historical information about the connection between telicity, futurity and perfectivity in Slavic.[9] In the Old Russian of the Chronicles, highly telic acts tend strongly to use the non-past form for futurity. As mentioned earlier, prefixation is largely correlated with high telicity, although this correlation is not entirely reliable at this early date; there are telic forms with this future sense that are unprefixed and atelic forms with prefixes that do not have a future sense. (Some inceptives formed from statives, like *postojati* 'begin standing', do regularly express futurity.)

However, there are other ways to show futurity in Old Russian. Periphrastic expressions with *xotěti* 'want', *jati* 'seize', *načati* 'begin' are all frequent. Furthermore, a large number of non-past forms representing punctual acts or atelic acts show fluctuation between present and future meaning. In these cases, it is contextual information that determines the assignment of the form.

---

[9] I will confine my remarks to the historical period of Slavic, since other studies have provided reasonable explanations of the prehistoric genesis of the perfective future; see chapter 3.

Furthermore, non-past forms of telic acts do not always indicate futurity, even at this stage. As was seen in section 5.2.4, numerous modal interpretations of the non-past are allowed that indicate possibility, permission, likelihood and so forth. As Fleischman (1982) points out, these modal interpretations of the future are quite common even in languages with unambiguously marked future tenses; if such usages are a sign of a category's great age, as Bybee and Dahl propose, then it is curious that such uses appear even at the beginnings of grammatical aspect in Russian and that they do not seem to have increased inordinately in quantity as history marched on. Instead, the original picture in Slavic could well resemble that found with punctual predicates in Old Russian, where a tendency to express futurity or presentness depends on the character of the act and where the interpretation of any given form depends on the presence (or absence) of contextual indicators. Old Russian takes the route of interpreting high telicity—and later, perfectivity—in the non-past as having mainly future reference (while leaving room for certain other modal interpretations), whereas some other Slavic languages (like Czech) place more emphasis on modal interpretations of the highly telic perfective non-past forms and less emphasis on futurity.

This sort of analysis complicates the grammaticalization process. Futurity, then, does not develop according to the rules of grammaticalization nor yield the ideal development shown in chart 9.5.1.

Chart 9.5.1. An idealized development of futurity in Old Russian

LEXICAL FORM
(original meanings of the aspectual markers) —>

GRAMMATICAL FORM
(markers of futurity) —>

EXPRESSIVE OR DISCOURSE FORM
(modal markers of belief, permission, etc.)

Instead, it has a more complex and ambiguous provenance. Futurity is clearly connected from early on with whatever lexically limited form of perfectivity can be reconstructed for Prehistoric Slavic and Old Russian. But this limited perfectivity can also indicate other possible interpretations of the act, which are modal and/or contextually bound. These other features may predominate in other Slavic languages, and are equally durable. Taking these caveats into account, a revised and expanded timeline of futurity in Russian would look more like chart 9.5.2.

This complex and wordy state of affairs can be reduced to a chart (9.5.3) diagramming the uses of non-past forms from Old Russian to Modern Russian (in which time runs from left to right). This schema needs to be refined and tested more closely against Old Russian data, and therefore constitutes grounds for future research.

Chart 9.5.2. Hypothesized development of futurity in Russian.

Stage I. Prehistoric Russian
- Futurity comes to be the norm for the non-past of highly telic acts.
- Contextually-defined non-past temporal reference is the norm for other acts.
- Non-past forms have a number of other modal uses.

Stage II. Early Old Russian
- The protoperfective member of the opposition (which applies only in telic acts) is a regular indicator of futurity in non-past actions.
- Non-pasts that are perceived as non-protoperfective can still have either future or present reference, although the tendency runs to present reference
- This tendency to present reference is strongest for nonpunctual telic acts that are closely related to protoperfectives (i.e. *staviti* with respect to *postaviti*).
- This tendency to present reference is weaker for telic acts that are also punctual (i.e. *prositi, kazati, grěšiti*). For these acts, context is still the determining factor for present or future reference.
- Modal uses of the non-past mean there are other uses for the non-past of protoperfectives, i.e. in gnomic statements, certain conditional sentence types, types of iterative sentences.

Stage III. Late Old Russian.
- Imperfectivity coalesces as a more coherent class as aspectual oppositions are extended to all verbs, and most opportunities for future reference in the protoimperfective are lost. (Those that remain are modal.)
- The lack of regular aspectual pairing for all verbs means that lexical features can still predominate in assigning present vs. future or bound vs. unbound meaning, especially in conditional and iterative sentences.
- This problem begins to disappear as more derived imperfectives appear and their uses become more universal.
- A compound future tense begins to develop from a reanalysis of impersonal future constructions.
- Modal functions are still found.

Stage IV. Modern Russian.
- Perfectivity and future reference of the non-past are closely linked.
- Modal functions of the perfective non-past are still common, although their meanings are more strictly defined with respect to imperfective forms.

Chart 9.5.3. The non-past tense and telicity through time

HIGH TELICITY ————————> PERFECTIVITY

Lexical features indicate tense of form	Nonfuture modal uses	Nonfuture modal uses
(Future is contextual or periphrastic)	Future use normal (except punctuals!)	Future use normal

NONHIGH TELICITY —————> IMPERFECTIVITY

Lexical features indicate tense of form	Modal future Contextual future	Modal future —
(Future is contextual or periphrastic)	Periphrastic futures	One periphrastic future
(Present is contextual or rarely periphrastic)	Present use is normal esp. for telics (unless also punctuals!)	Present use is normal

LEXICAL ASPECT ———————> QUASI-GRAMMATICAL ASPECT

9.6. CONCLUSIONS

This study has attempted to answer a number of questions about the development of Russian aspect using data from five Old Russian texts. In places, the texts have pointed to a relatively clear path of development; in others, they have indicated a diversity of potential directions.

The direction of change in Old Russian is clear. At the beginning of written history, the aspectual system is still in its infancy. Nonpunctual telic predicates distinguish aspect regularly, while other predicates do not. Tense usage and tense function are subordinate to lexical classifications, not to aspect; if aspect can be seen as a grammatical distinction at this early date, then it holds a status similar to that of motion verbs in Modern Russian, where a clear distinction between determinate and indeterminate is made for one lexically defined class of words and considered superfluous for the rest of the lexicon.

Predicates that are not both telic and punctual show a growing tendency through the Old Russian period to take on functions characteristic of only one aspect. In the Chronicles, forms that express atelic acts are also used for more momentary events, such as the inception of that atelic act. Prefixes attached to such forms are likely to lack the temporally limiting properties they have with telic acts. Lexical distinctions in this early stage of Old Russian thus determine whether a form plays by aspectual rules or does not.

However, by later in the Old Russian period these lexically based differences have by and large disappeared or are found only residually with certain forms of punctual atelic acts. At that point, aspectual limitations apply to virtually every form in the verbal system. As for punctual atelic acts, despite the high frequency of the remaining nonaspectual forms (such as past participles), and the centrality of these items in the lexicon (e.g. 'see', 'hear', 'be surprised'), by this point they represent a vastly reduced number of forms and can thus easily stand apart as exceptions to the system as a whole.

The most fundamental change in the aspectual system is this reorganization of a lexical system into a quasi-grammatical one; this change applies first and foremost to simplex verbs and to simple prefixed verbs. A second stage in aspectualization that runs concurrently with it concerns the creation of suffixed forms and the standardization of their meanings. This process is important if the so-called grammatical aspectual system is to be divorced from its lexical beginnings. An opposition between *pisati* 'write' and *vpisati* 'write in' is both aspectual and lexical; the limitation on time that causes us to perceive the prefixed form as highly telic is inextricably entwined with a lexical difference in meaning. For a long time, then, while aspectual distinctions between forms existed, the relationships between forms did not regularly look like what we would call "aspectual pairs": two verbs with identical lexical meaning and complementary distribution and usage of forms. In later Old Russian texts, I have tracked the usages of derived forms and noted how they differ from their Modern Russian counterparts.

The first noticeable tendency with suffixed forms is that the contexts they are found in depends on their lexical group: with punctual telic acts, suffixed forms are found mostly in iterative contexts, whereas with nonpunctual telic acts, they are mainly found in progressive contexts. Later in Old Russian, this tendency disappears and is replaced by finer distinctions involving the degree of progressivity, the type of object and so forth. Whether the suffixed form ever becomes an exact imperfective match to its prefixed perfective form seems to be a random matter that is not wholly resolved in the Old Russian period. Even by the end of the Old Russian period, lexical aspectual matches of the sort *pisati–vpisati* 'write–write down' are more common than they are in Modern Russian, whether a derived form exists for the given verb or not.

Russian also undergoes a number of changes in its use of contextual features to determine aspect. In Modern Russian, four basic environments condition the use of the imperfective aspect: generalized contexts, progressive contexts, durative contexts, and iterative contexts. The only ones that regularly require a protoimperfective (or anaspectual) form from the very earliest date are the generalized context and the progressive context. The others show a high degree of variability. Durative contexts often have protoperfective forms in Old Russian, as do iterative contexts. In most cases, an evaluation of the characteristics of the act and its situation in the flow of events provide the rationale for choosing one aspect or another. The closing off of these options in Modern Russian indicates a fundamental difference in the way these situations are perceived: whereas in Old

Russian, the focus is on the characteristics of the individual act and its relation to the surrounding acts, in Modern Russian aspect plays a governing role, determining how events relate to each other, imposing a degree of aspectual uniformity on a sentence. In a sense, iterative acts in Modern Russian operate in either an "imperfective template" or a "perfective template" that is applied to the entire string of events, determining whether the string is perceived as occasional and vivid or regular and habitual; these templates are absent from Old Russian.

Conativity is a regular feature of Modern Russian aspect that plays a much smaller role in Old Russian aspect. In Modern Russian the use of an imperfective form often includes the implication that an effort was made to perform an act, but the attempt failed; this function is evidently absent from the Old Russian protoimperfective, even as recently as the sixteenth century. Some sources for imperfective conativity are evident, but their adoption into the grammar must occur at a later date.

In sum, the history of Russian aspect is the retreat of a lexically based aspectual system in favor of a more grammatically and contextually based one. Remnants of the lexical aspectual system are numerous, persistent, and unavoidable, and it is the interaction of lexical and contextual features that creates the environment for the partial grammaticalization of aspect in Russian.

9.7. EPILOGUE, FROM THE FINAL PAGE OF THE LAURENTIAN MS.

Радуется купець прикупъ створивъ. и кормьчии въ отишье приставъ и странник въ о(те)чьство свое пришед. також радуется и книжныи списатель. дошед конца книгам. також и азъ худыи недостоиныи и многогрѣшныи рабъ Б(о)жии Лаврентеи мних... И нынѣ г(о)с(по)да о(т)ци и брат(ь)я. оже ся гдѣ буду описалъ или переписалъ или не дописалъ. чтите исправливая Б(ог)а дѣля. а не клените. занеже книги ветшаны. а оумъ молодъ. не дошелъ. (487-488)

§

'The merchant rejoices when he has made a good bargain, as does the sailor come to harbor and the traveller come to his native land; so rejoices the scribe, having reached the end of his books. And thus do I, the poor unworthy and sinful servant of God, the monk Laurentius.... And now, sirs, fathers and brothers, wherever I will have poorly scribed, or twice transcribed, or failed to inscribe, read it and correct it, for the sake of God, and do not malign me, for as these books are ancient, and my reason young, it has not fully grasped them.'

Bibliography

SCIENTIFIC LITERATURE AND DICTIONARIES

Apresjan, Ju. D. 1967. *Èksperimental'noe issledovanie semantiki russkogo glagola (Experimental research on the semantics of the Russian verb).* Moscow: Nauka.

Benveniste, Émile. 1968. Mutations of linguistic categories. Tr. Yakov Malkiel and Marilyn May Vihman. In *Directions for historical linguistics,* ed. W.P. Lehmann and Yakov Malkiel, 85-94. Austin: University of Texas Press.

Borkovskij, V.I. and P.S. Kuznecov. 1965. *Istoričeskaja grammatika russkogo jazyka. Izdanie vtoroe, dopolnennoe. (A historical grammar of Russia. Second edition, expanded.)* Moscow: Nauka.

Borodič, V. V. 1953. K voprosu o formirovanii soveršennogo i nesoveršennogo vida v slavjanskix jazykax. (On the question of the formation of the perfective and imperfective aspect in Slavic languages.) *Voprosy jazykoznanija* (no. 2): 68-86.

—. 1954. K voprosu o vidovyx otnošenijax staroslavjanskogo glagola. (On the question of aspectual relations in the Old Church Slavic verb.) *Učenye zapiski Instituta slavjanovedenija AN SSSR* 9: 50-138.

Brooks, Maria Zagorska. 1975. *A Reference Grammar of Polish.* The Hague: Mouton.

Brinton, Laurel J. 1988. *The development of English aspectual systems.* Cambridge: Cambridge University Press.

Budich, Wulf. 1969. *Aspekt und verbale Zeitlichkeit in der I. Novgoroder Chronik.* Graz, Austria: Akademische Druck- u. Verlagsanstalt.

Bybee, Joan L., and William Pagliuca. 1985. Cross-linguistic comparison and the development of grammatical meaning. In *Historical semantics, historical word formation,* ed. Jacek Fisiak, 59-84. Berlin, New York and Amsterdam: Mouton.

—. 1987. The evolution of future meaning. In *Papers from the seventh international conference on historical linguistics,* ed. A.G. Ramat et al., 109-122. Amsterdam: John Benjamins.

Bybee, Joan L., and Östen Dahl. 1989. The creation of tense and aspect systems in the languages of the world. *Studies in Language* 13 (no. 1): 51-103.

Bybee, Joan L., William Pagliuca, and Revere D. Perkins. 1991. Back to the future. In *Approaches to grammaticalization.* Vol. 2, *Focus on types of grammatical markers,* ed. Elizabeth Closs Traugott and Bernd Heine, 17-58. Amsterdam and Philadelphia: John Benjamins.

Chaput, Patricia R. 1984. On the question of aspectual selection in denials. In *The scope of Slavic aspect,* ed. Michael S. Flier and Alan Timberlake, 224-233. Columbus, Ohio: Slavica.

Chung, Sandra and Alan Timberlake. 1985. Tense, aspect and mood. In *Language typology and syntactic description,* ed. Timothy Shopen, 202-258. Cambridge: Cambridge University Press.

Chvany, Catherine V. 1984. Backgrounded perfectives and plot-line imperfectives: Towards a theory of grounding in text. In *The scope of Slavic aspect,* ed. Michael S. Flier and Alan Timberlake, 247-273. Columbus, Ohio: Slavica.

—. 1990. Verbal aspect, discourse saliency, and the so-called "perfect of result" in modern Russian. In *Verbal aspect in discourse: Contributions to the semantics of time and temporal perspective in Slavic and non-Slavic languages,* ed. Nils Thelin, 213-235. Amsterdam and Philadelphia: John Benjamins.

Comrie, Bernard. 1976. *Aspect.* Cambridge: Cambridge University Press.

Dahl, Östen. 1981. On the definition of the telic–atelic (bounded–nonbounded) distinction. In *Tense and aspect,* ed. Philip J. Tedeschi and Annie Zaenan, 79-90. Syntax and Semantics 14. New York: Academic Press.

—. 1985. *Tense and aspect systems.* Oxford: Basil Blackwell.

Delbrück, B. 1897. Vergleichende Syntax der indogermanischen Sprachen. Strassburg.

Dostál, Antonín. 1954. *Studie o vidovém systému v staroslověnštině. (Studies on the aspectual system of Old Church Slavic.)* Prague: Státní pedagogické nakladatelství.

Durst-Andersen, Per. 1992. *Mental grammar: Russian aspect and related issues.* Columbus, Ohio: Slavica.

Eckert, Eva. 1984. Aspect in repetitive contexts in Russian and Czech. In *The scope of Slavic aspect,* ed. Michael S. Flier and Alan Timberlake, 169-180. Columbus, Ohio: Slavica.

Fielder, Grace. 1990. Narrative context and Russian aspect. In *Verbal aspect in discourse: Contributions to the semantics of time and temporal perspective in Slavic and non-Slavic languages,* ed. Nils Thelin, 263-284. Amsterdam and Philadelphia: John Benjamins.

Fleischman, Suzanne. 1982. *The future in thought and language: Diachronic evidence from Romance.* Cambridge: Cambridge University Press.

Forsyth, James. 1970. *A grammar of aspect: Usage and meaning in the Russian verb.* Cambridge: Cambridge University Press.

—. 1972. The nature and development of the aspectual opposition in the Russian verb. *Slavonic and East European Review* 50 (no. 121): 493-506.

Galton, Herbert. 1976. *The main functions of the Slavic verbal aspect.* Skopje: Macedonian Academy of Sciences and Arts.

Gasparov, Boris. 1990. Notes on the "metaphysics" of Russian aspect. In *Verbal aspect in discourse: Contributions to the semantics of time and temporal perspective in Slavic and non-Slavic languages,* ed. Nils Thelin, 191-212. Amsterdam and Philadelphia: John Benjamins.

Givón, Talmy. 1971. Historical syntax and synchronic morphology: an archaeologist's field trip. *Chicago Linguistic Society* 7: 394-415.

Heine, Bernd, Ulrike Claudi, and Friederike Hünnemeyer. 1991a. *Grammaticalization: A conceptual framework.* Chicago: University of Chicago Press.

Heine, Bernd, Ulrike Claudi, and Friederike Hünnemeyer. 1991b. From cognition to grammar: Evidence from African languages. In *Approaches to grammaticalization.* Vol. 1, *Focus on theoretical and methodological issues,* ed. Elizabeth Closs Traugott and Bernd Heine, 149-188. Amsterdam: John Benjamins.

Heine, Bernd, and Mechthild Reh. 1984. *Grammaticalization and reanalysis in African languages.* Hamburg: Helmut Buske Verlag.

Holden, Kyril T. 1990. The functional evolution of aspect in Russian. In *Verbal aspect in discourse: Contributions to the semantics of time and temporal perspective in Slavic and non-Slavic languages,* ed. Nils Thelin, 131-158. Amsterdam and Philadelphia: John Benjamins.

Holvoet, Axel. 1989. *Aspekt a modalność w języku polskim na tle ogólnosłowiańskim.* (Aspect and modality in Polish on the basis of Common Slavic.) Prace Slawistyczne 77. Wrocław: Wydawnictwo Polskiej Akademii Nauk.

Hopper, Paul. 1982. Aspect between discourse and grammar. In *Tense–aspect: Between semantics and pragmatics,* ed. Paul J. Hopper, 3-18. Amsterdam and Philadelphia: John Benjamins.

—. 1991. On some principles of grammaticization. In *Approaches to grammaticalization.* Vol. 1, *Focus on theoretical and methodological issues,* ed. Elizabeth Closs Traugott and Bernd Heine, 17-36. Amsterdam: John Benjamins.

Hopper, Paul J., and Sandra A. Thompson. 1980. Transitivity in grammar and discourse. *Language* 56 (no. 2): 251-299.

Hopper, Paul J., and Elizabeth Closs Traugott. 1993. *Grammaticalization.* Cambridge: Cambridge University Press.

Institut russkogo jazyka AN SSSR. 1981-1984. *Slovar' russkogo jazyka. (Dictionary of Russian.)* 4 vols. Moscow: Izdatel'stvo Russkij Jazyk.

Isačenko, A.V. 1960. *Grammatičeskij stroj russkogo jazyka v sopostavlenii so slovackim. (The grammatical structure of Russian in comparison with Slovak.)* Vol. 2, *Morfologija.* Bratislava: Slovenská akadémia vied.

Jakobson, Roman. 1927 (1971). Zur Struktur des russischen Verbums. Reprinted in *Selected writings.* Vol. 2, *Word and language,* 3-15. The Hague and Paris: Mouton.

Janda, Laura A. 1994. "The spread of athematic 1sg -*m* in the major West Slavic languages." *Slavic and East European Journal* 38 (no. 1): 90-119.

Klenin, Emily. 1993. The perfect tense in the Laurentian manuscript of 1377. In *American contributions to the eleventh international congress of Slavists,* ed. Robert A. Maguire and Alan Timberlake, 330-343. Columbus, Ohio: Slavica.

Kölln, Hermann. 1957. *Vidové problémy v staroslověnštině. (Aspectual problems in Old Church Slavic.) Universitatis Carolina, Philologica* 3 (no. 1): 67-100.

Košelev, A.K. 1958. K voprosu o sozdanii tipov pervonačalnoj parnosti po vidu v drevnerusskom jazyke. (On the question of the formation of initial aspectual pairs in Old Russian.) *Vestnik Moskovskogo universiteta. Istoriko-filologičeskaja serija* 2: 3-39.

Kučera, Henry. 1983. A semantic model of verbal aspect. In *American contributions to the ninth international congress of Slavists, Kiev, September 1983.* Vol. 1, *Linguistics*, ed. Michael S. Flier, 171-184. Columbus, Ohio: Slavica.

—. 1984. Aspect in negative imperatives. In *The scope of Slavic aspect*, ed. Michael S. Flier and Alan Timberlake, 118-128. Columbus, Ohio: Slavica.

Kukuškina, O.V. 1978. Iz istorii vida russkogo glagola. (From the history of Russian verbal aspect.) In *Vestnik Moskovskogo universiteta, serija filologija* (no. 1): 51-61.

Kuryłowicz, Jerzy. 1929. La genèse d'aspects verbaux slaves. *Prace filologiczne* 14: 644-657.

Kuznecov, P.S. 1953. K voprosu o genezise vido-vremennýx otnošenij drevnerusskogo jazyka. (On the question of the genesis of aspectual-temporal relations in Old Russian.) *Trudy instituta jazykoznanija AN SSSR* 2: 220-253.

—. 1959. *Očerki istoričeskoj morfologii russkogo jazyka (An outline of Russian historical morphology).* Moskva: Izdatel'stvo AN SSSR.

Lenga, Gerd. 1976. *Zur Kontextdeterminierung des Verbalaspekts im modernen Polnisch.* München: Verlag Otto Sagner.

Lyons, John. 1977. *Semantics.* Vol. 2. Cambridge: Cambridge University Press.

Maslov, Ju. S. 1948. Vid i leksičeskoe značenie glagola v sovremennom russkom literaturnom jazyke. (Aspect and verbal lexical meaning in Contemporary Standard Russian.) *Izvestija Akademii nauk SSSR, otdelenie literatury i jazyka* 7 (no. 4): 304-316.

—. 1954. Imperfekt glagolov soveršennogo vida v slavjanskix jazykax. (The imperfect of perfective verbs in Slavic languages.) *Voprosy slavjanskogo jazykoznanija* (no. 1): 68-138. Moscow: Izdatel'stvo AN SSSR.

—. 1959. Voprosy proisxoždenija glagol'nogo vida na IV. meždunarodnom s"ezde slavistov. (Issues around the origin of verbal aspect at the Fourth international congress of Slavists.) *Voprosy jazykoznanija* (no. 2): 151-157.

—. 1961. Rol' tak nazyvaemoj perfektivacii i imperfektivacii v processe vozniknovenija slavjanskogo glagol'nogo vida. (The role of so-called perfectivization and imperfectivization during the rise of Slavic verbal aspect.) *Issledovanija po slavjanskomu jazykoznaniju*, 165-195. Moscow: Izdatel'stvo AN SSSR.

—. 1973. Universal'nye semantičeskie komponenty v soderžanii grammatičeskoj kategorii soveršennogo/nesoveršennogo vida. (Universal semantic components in the content of the grammatical category 'perfective/imperfective aspect'.) *Sovetskoe slavjanovedenie* (no. 4): 73-83.

Matthews, David. 1995. Preterites in direct discourse in three Old East Slavic chronicles. *Russian Linguistics* 19 (no. 3): 299-317.

Mayo, Peter J. 1984. *The morphology of aspect in seventeenth-century Russian (Based on texts of the* Smutnoe Vremja). Columbus, OH: Slavica.

Meillet, Antoine. 1915-1916 (1966). Le Renouvellement des conjonctions. *Annuaire de l'École pratique des Hautes Études, section historique et philologique.* Reprinted in *Linguistique historique et linguistique générale.* Champion: Paris.

Miller, J. 1985. *Semantics and syntax.* Cambridge: Cambridge University Press.

Mourelatos, Alexander P.D. 1981. Events, processes and states. In *Tense and aspect,* ed. Philip J. Tedeschi and Annie Zaenen, 191-212. Syntax and Semantics, vol. 14. New York: Academic Press.

Němec, Igor. 1956. Kategorie determinovanosti a indeterminovanosti jako základ slovanské kategorie vidu. (The category of determinacy and indeterminacy as the basis for the Slavic category of aspect.) *Slavia* 25 (no. 4) 496-534

——. 1958. *Genese slovanského systému vidového.* (The genesis of the Slavic aspectual system.) Rozpravy ČSAV, Řada společenských věd, vol. 68, no. 7. Prague: Czechoslovak Academy of Sciences.

Netteberg, Kristine. 1953. *Études sur le verbe polonais.* Copenhagen: Rosenkilde og Bagger.

Nichols, Johanna, and Alan Timberlake. 1991. Grammaticalization as retextualization. In *Approaches to grammaticalization.* Vol. 1, *Focus on theoretical and methodological issues,* ed. Elizabeth Closs Traugott and Bernd Heine, 129-146. Amsterdam and Philadelphia: John Benjamins.

Nikoforov, S.D. 1952. *Glagol: ego kategorii i formy v russkoj pis'mennosti vtoroj poloviny XVI. veka. (The verb: its categories and forms in Russian written texts of the second half of the sixteenth century.)* Moscow: Izdatel'stvo AN SSSR.

Potebnja, A. A. 1977. *Iz zapisok po russkoj grammatike. (From notes on Russian grammar.)* Vol. 2, no. 2: *Glagol.* 2d. ed. Moscow: Prosveščenie.

Rassudova, O. P. 1982. *Upotreblenie vidov glagola v sovremennom russkom jazyke.* Moscow: Russkij Jazyk. Tr. Gregory M. Eramian, under the title *Aspectual usage in modern Russian.* Moscow: Russky Yazyk, 1984.

Ružicka, Rudolf. 1957. *Der Verbalaspekt in der altrussischen Nestorchronik.* Berlin: Akademie-Verlag.

Šeljakin, Mikhail. 1984. On the essence of the category of aspectuality and its lexical-semantic level in Russian. In *Aspect Bound,* ed. Casper de Groot and Hannu Tommola, 39-52. Dordrecht: Foris.

Silina, V. B. 1982. Istorija kategorii glagol'nogo vida. (The history of the category of verbal aspect.) In *Istoričeskaja grammatika russkogo jazyka. Morfologija: glagol (A historical grammar of Russian: morphology: the verb),* ed. R. I. Avanesov and V. V. Ivanov, 158-279. Moscow: Izdatel'stvo Nauka.

Sreznevskij, I. I. 1890-1912 (1989). *Materialy dlja slovarja drevne-russkago jazyka po pis'mennym" pamjatnikam".* (Materials for a dictionary of Old Russian according to literary monuments.) St. Petersburg: Imperatorskaja akademija nauk". Reprinted as *Slovar' drevnerusskogo jazyka,* 6 vols. Moscow: Izdatel'stvo Kniga.

Szemerényi, Oswald. 1970. *Einführung in die vergleichende Sprachwissenschaft.* Darmstadt: Wissenschaftliche Buchgesellschaft.

Timberlake, Alan. 1982. Invariance and the syntax of Russian aspect. In *Tense—aspect: Between semantics and pragmatics,* ed. Paul J. Hopper, 305-331. Amsterdam and Philadelphia: John Benjamins.

—. 1984a. The temporal schemata of Russian predicates. In *Russian morphosyntax,* ed. Michael S. Flier and Richard D. Brecht, 35-57. Columbus, OH: Slavica.

—. 1984b. Reichenbach and Russian aspect. In *The Scope of Slavic aspect,* ed. Michael S. Flier and Alan Timberlake, 153-168. Columbus, Ohio: Slavica.

—. 1995. Avvakum's aorists. *Russian Linguistics* 19 (no. 1): 25-43.

Townsend, Charles. 1980 (1975). *Russian word-formation.* Corrected reprint. Columbus, Ohio: Slavica.

Traugott, Elizabeth Closs. 1982. From propositional to textual and expressive meanings: Some semantic-pragmatic aspects of grammaticalization. In *Perspectives on historical linguistics,* ed. W. P. Lehmann and Y. Malkiel, 245-271. Amsterdam and Philadelphia: John Benjamins.

—. 1990. The unidirectionality of semantic change. In *Papers from the fifth international conference on English historical linguistics,* ed. Sylvia Adamson et al., 497-518. Amsterdam Studies in the Theory and History of Linguistic Science no. 65. Amsterdam and Philadelphia: John Benjamins

Traugott, Elizabeth Closs and Ekkehard König. 1991. The Semantics-Pragmatics of Grammaticalization Revisited. In *Approaches to Grammaticalization.* Vol. 1, *Focus on Theoretical and Methodological Issues,* ed. Elizabeth Closs Traugott and Bernd Heine, 189-218. Amsterdam: John Benjamins.

Ul'janov, G. K. 1890-1895. *Značenija glagol'nyx osnov v litovsko-slavjanskom jazyke (The meaning of verbal stems in Balto-Slavic).* Warsaw.

van Schooneveld, C. H. 1959. *A semantic analysis of the Old Russian finite preterite system.* The Hague: Mouton.

van Wijk, N. 1927. Die sogenannten Verba iterativa in Altkirschenslavisch. *Indogermanische Forschungen* 45: 93-104.

—. 1929. Sur l'origine des aspects du verb slave. *Revue des études slaves* 9: 237-252.

Vaillant, André. 1939. L'Aspect verbal du slave commun: sa morphologisation. *Revue des études slaves* 19: 289-314.

—. 1946. La dépréverbation. *Revue des études slaves* 22: 5-45.

Vlasto, A. P. 1986. *A linguistic history of Russia to the end of the eighteenth century.* Oxford: Clarendon Press.

Vendler, Zeno. 1967. Verbs and times. In *Linguistics in philosophy,* 97-121. Ithaca, NY: Cornell University Press.

Yokoyama, Olga T. 1986. *Discourse and word order.* Pragmatics and beyond no. 6. Amsterdam and Philadelphia: John Benjamins.

TEXTS, TRANSLATIONS AND COMMENTARY

Cross, Samuel Hazzard and Olgerd P. Sherbowitz-Wetzor, eds. 1953. *The Russian Primary Chronicle: Laurentian text.* Cambridge, Mass.: The Medieval Academy of America.

Fennell, J.L.I., ed. 1965. *Prince A.M. Kurbsky's History of Ivan IV, edited with a translation and notes.* Cambridge: Cambridge University Press.

Lavrent'evskaja letopis'. 1926 (1977). *Polnoe sobranie russkix letopisej, t. 1. (Complete collection of Russian chronicles, vol. 1.)* Leningrad: Postojannaja istoriko-arxeografičeskaja komissija Akademii nauk SSSR. Reprinted as: *Die Nestorchronik.* Forum Slavicum 48. Munich: Wilhelm Fink Verlag.

Contains the complete text of the Laurentian ms., as well as comparisons to and interpolations from the Radzivil and Academy mss. of this text. Old Russian citations from here.

Nikitin, Afanasij. Xoženie za tri morja. (The journey across three seas.) 1986. In ed. Lur'e, Ja. S., and L.S. Semenov. 1986. *Xoženie za tri morja Afanasija Nikitina. (Afanasij Nikitin's Journey across three seas.)* Leningrad: Izdatel'stvo Nauka.

Nikitin, Afanasij. Xoženie za tri morja. (The journey across three seas.) 1984. In ed., trans. N. I. Prokof'ev, *Kniga xoženij: zapiski russkix putešestvennikov XI-XV vekov.* Moscow: Sokroviščà drevnerusskoj literatury.

Povest' vremennyx let: tekst i perevod. (The Russian Primary Chronicle: text and translation.) 1950. ed. D. C. Lixačev and B.A. Romanov. Moscow and Leningrad: Izdatel'stvo Akademii Nauk SSSR.

Pamjatniki literatury drevnej Rusi. (Monuments of Old Russian literature.) 1978-1989. Moscow: Xudožestvennaja literatura.

The texts *Xoženie za tri morja* and *Povest' o vzjatii Car' grada turkami v 1453 godu* are from the volume *II. polovina XV. veka* (1982). The text *Istorija o velikom knjaze moskovskom* is from the volume *II. polovina XVI. veka* (1986). Translations into Modern Russian are on facing pages. Citations from these three texts and translations into Modern Russian are from this edition.

Šaxmatov, A. A. 1908 (1967). *Razyskanija o drevněǰsix" russkix" lětopisnyx" svodax". (Investigations of the oldest Russian chronicle redactions.)* Saint Petersburg: Imperatorskaja arxeografičeskaja kommissija. Reprinted in *Russian Reprint Series.* The Hague: Europe Printing.

—. 1938. *Obozrenie russkix letopisnyx svodov XIV-XVI vv. (Overview of Russian chronicle redactions of the fourteenth through sixteenth centuries.)* Moscow: Izdatel'stvo AN SSSR.